What's Wrong With the U.S. Economy?

A POPULAR GUIDE FOR THE REST OF US

WHAT'S WRONG WITH THE U.S. ECONOMY?

SORRY
NOT HIRING

A POPULAR GUIDE FOR THE REST OF US

By the Institute for Labor Education and Research

South End Press
Boston

Copyright © 1982 by The Institute for Labor Education and Research
Library of Congress Number: 82-80690
ISBN: 0-89608-010-2 (paper)
        0-89608-011-0 (cloth)

Art direction and illustration by Howard Saunders.
Design by Howard Saunders with David M. Gordon.
Production by Kathryn Geiger, Lydia Sargent, and the South End Collective.
Production of charts, graphs and tables by Vanalyne Green and Val Dubasky.
Illustrations by Howard Saunders with the following exceptions: pp. 8, 75, and 80 by Luis Arvello; pp. 44, 45, 78(part), and 176 by Josh Brown.
Photographs by Earl Dotter and Robert Gumpert of Image Network.

Photo Credits:

Earl Dotter: cover, pp. 18, 47, 51, 55, 59, 89, 100, 101, 163, 175, 182, 192, 195, 211, 212, 214, 220 (both), 223, 227 (man), 228, 229, 231, 235, 250, 251, 253, 265, 266, 274, 276, 282, 283, 300, 301, 309, 315, 325, 367, 371, 379.

Robert Gumpert: pp. xxiv, 49, 53, 65, 133, 155, 169, 187, 191, 205, 217, 224 (both), 227 (woman), 237, 239, 241, 245, 277, 279, 281, 308, 368, 369.

Other photographs: p. 30, Library of Congress; p. 31, Margaret Bourke-White, Time-Life; p. 50, Museum of the City of New York; p. 74, Archives of Labor History and Urban Affairs, Wayne State University, Detroit; p. 116, National Archives; p. 117, Library of Congress; p. 233, American Iron and Steel Institute; p. 268, Library of Congress; p. 285, Rare Book Division, N.Y. Public Library and Library of Congress; p. 291, Archives of Labor History and Urban Affairs, Wayne State University; p. 293, Library of Congress; p. 306, Univ. of Washington Library, Seattle.

Permission to reprint material from Studs Terkel, *American Dreams Lost and Found,* © 1980, by Studs Terkel, granted by Pantheon Books, a Division of Random House, Inc.

CONTENTS

1773

"The die is now cast; the colonies must now submit or triumph. We must either master them or totally leave them to themselves and treat them as aliens."

—King George III of England, 1773[1]

1776

"O! ye that love mankind! Ye that dare oppose not only the tyranny but the tyrant, stand forth! ...Freedom hath been hunted round the Globe.... O! receive the fugitive, and prepare in time an asylum for mankind.... 'Tis not in numbers but in unity that our great strength lies...."

—Tom Paine, *Common Sense*, 1776[2]

1786

"I hold that a little rebellion now and then is a good thing.... It is a medicine necessary for the sound health of government...."

—Thomas Jefferson, 1786[3]

1974

"Some people will obviously have to do with less.... Yet it will be a hard pill for many Americans to swallow—the idea of doing with less so that big business can have more."

—Business Week magazine, 1974[4]

1980

"My pa was a mill hand and a self-educated man. He brought me up to believe in the American system. I believe in the words of Jefferson and Tom Paine: the American Dream that people have a right to say what they wanta say, do what they wanta do, and fashion a world into something that can be great for everyone. Not to have someone fuck you over."

—Ed Sadlowski, local steelworkers union official, 1980[5]

Why Do We Need This Book?

The need for a popular guide to what's wrong with the U.S. economy is obvious. It must address two critical and immediate concerns:

■ First, the U.S. economy seems completely out of control. Our current economic problems have become our most severe social headache. In the most recent polls available to us before publication, conducted in November 1981, 77% of U.S. adults agreed that the U.S. economy is "seriously off on the wrong track." Asked to name the most important problems we face as a nation and as individuals, 72% cited economic problems while only 26% mentioned other problems like foreign affairs or crime.[1]

■Second, almost all of us are being asked to make major sacrifices to solve these economic problems. Nearly half of all U.S. adults agree that our economic problems have affected them "a great deal."[2] As if we weren't already in bad enough shape, most of us have recently faced demands for major wage concessions, cutbacks in unemployment benefits, huge reductions or even the elimination of major social programs—all the while accepting major tax relief for the wealthy and huge increases in military expenditures. Is this the only way to get out of our current mess?

We must obviously understand our economic problems before we can begin to solve them. *What's wrong with the U.S. economy?* **This book aims to provide much of the economic information and understanding we need.**

But who are we? Who is "the rest of us"?

Although the economic crisis affects nearly everyone, this book has *not* been written for everyone in the United States.

A very small group of people controls the giant corporations which run the economy. While the rest of us fuel the engine, they steer the machine; we do the work while they make the most important decisions. This book is not for them because they already have their own books and their own economics.

This book is for the rest of us. Despite the many differences among us—in income, jobs, tastes, and culture, there is one overwhelming similarity: *we depend on our own labor for our economic survival.* The box on the next page highlights the differences among three groups of U.S. households—*working* households, *affluent* households, and *wealthy* households.[3] This book is for the 90%. **We are working people. We are ordinary citizens—the real majority.** This book is for us.

Why now?

It appears to many that we need a book like this for aid and comfort against the "new right" and the economic onslaught of the Reagan administration.

In fact, we have needed something like this book for years. We now feel and hear about the conservative assault on working people every day. But the groundwork for these attacks was prepared several years ago by the giant corporations who run our economy. We may blame the recent conservative gains, but *many of our problems flow from a self-conscious corporate effort to protect and advance business interests.*

Corporations have always been snake peddlers. But large corporations in the U.S. became especially frightened in the mid-1970s when opinion polls revealed that many working people were beginning to blame the largest corporations for most of our troubles. One poll showed that half of all U.S. residents agreed that "big business is the source of most of what's wrong in this country today." A series of Harris polls found that those expressing a "great deal of confidence" in the heads of large corporations had fallen from 55% in 1966 to only 15% in 1975.[4] The corporate confidence rating had nearly fallen off the charts in less than a decade.

These results stunned many corporate leaders. "I find these figures impossible to accept," a former president of the U.S. Chamber of Commerce responded.[5] "Those figures leave me incredulous," an ITT executive replied.[6] "How did we let the educational system fail the free enterprise system?" another executive asked. "Where did we go wrong?"[7]

Some business leaders thought they knew why their ratings had slipped. "We have been successful in selling products," one executive lamented at a corporate leadership conference, "but not ourselves."[8] At the same conference another executive concluded that "we have been negligent in educating our own [employees].... They don't seem to understand that their success is directly linked to the success of management."[9] Phillips Petroleum appealed to business in one of its ads: "Too many of us have chosen to keep a low profile through the growing storm of disapproval....It's time American industry took a stand for Free Enterprise."[10]

U.S. industry answered the call. Corporations began to "look out," as one business leader put it, "for the welfare of the free enterprise system."[11] As another executive admitted in an interview, corporations began to advocate "the necessity for capitalism and the superiority of our system and the need for the profit motive."[12] Particularly in their approach toward the media, one business journalist recently observed, "companies have decided to take the offensive."[13]

And they're backing their "offensive" with ready money. "Don't quote me," one corporate official admitted about the business campaign on economic issues, "but we're propagandizing, we're selling."[14] Hundreds of companies have climbed aboard the sales bandwagon, according to *Fortune* magazine, and they're spending "tens of millions in the process."[15] The examples on pages xii and xiii provide only a few concrete illustrations of this widespread propaganda campaign.[16]

Source: See note #3

Who Are the Rest of Us? The 1980 Story

There are roughly 80 million households in the U.S.

* A small group of *wealthy households* controls most of the wealth— In 1980, roughly 400,000 households, or 0.5% of all U.S. households, earned above $125,000. They earned, on average, $96,000 a year in unearned capital income.

* *Affluent households* need to work but nonetheless live very well. In 1980, 9.5% of households, or 7.6 million households, earned between $36,000 and $125,000. Because they averaged close to $9,000 a year in unearned income, they had a nice cushion of discretionary income for their rainy days.

* The rest of us are *working households*. The remaining 90% of U.S. households—roughly 72 million in all—depend on wage-and-salary earnings plus pensions for our survival. (Nearly 95% of our total earnings come from these two sources.) We have no cushions. The box summarizes these differences for U.S. households in 1980:

	Number of Households	% of Households	Income Range	Ave. Earned Income	Ave. Unearned Income
Working Households	72,300,000	90.0%	$0–36,000	$ 14,200	$ 888
Affluent Households	7,400,000	9.5	36,000–125,000	48,700	8,900
Wealthy Households	400,000	0.5	More than 125,000	127,000	97,000

Don't quote me, but...

The Business Roundtable

The Business Roundtable is a national organization of corporate executives. Formed in 1972, its 190 corporate members represent at least 63 of the 100 largest industrial companies in the U.S. (We know this much only because a Congressional investigation forced the Roundtable to divulge its membership list. It's "the most powerful lobby in Washington," one reporter noted, "and it is practically a secret society.")[24] It launched its public campaign by spending $1.5 million in 1975 for a series of ads in *Reader's Digest* which defended the corporate economy with gusto. "There was a strong feeling," as one Roundtable observer put it, that, "dammit all, we gotta do *something*."[25] Having launched its public activities with ads, it now fuels them with vigorous lobbying. It spends at least $2 million a year to coordinate direct political contacts in Washington. "A Congressman is impressed by the head of a corporation coming in to see him," a Roundtable organizer explained recently. "Before, it was below a businessman's dignity to do that."[26]

"Dear Employee"

Many companies have turned increasingly to "economics education" campaigns for their employees. The main purpose of these campaigns, as a report on a major survey of such corporate programs concluded, is that employees "have to be 'sold' on the virtues of the free enterprise system."[32] It is nearly impossible to estimate how much money corporations devote to this propaganda campaign. Based on the sample returns of this recent survey, it is reasonable to conclude that the largest 1,000 corporations spent roughly $50 million in 1981 on economics education programs for their workers.[33] Companies are paying growing attention to the role of supervisors in the campaign. "It is obvious," as the report on these corporate programs concluded, "that if the supervisor doesn't know much about the business and the economy in which it operates, he or she can't communicate this vital information to the people under supervision." What is "this vital information" being communicated? The majority of companies with employee education campaigns have focused on traditional concerns—in the report's words, on "the survival of the free enterprise system, the danger of 'creeping socialism...'."

The Ad Council Campaign

The Advertising Council has been waging a huge "economics education" campaign to spread the corporate word about the economic system. It began with $2.5 million to develop and publicize a cute little pamphlet, complete with "Peanuts" cartoons, called *The American Economic System...and your part in it*. (The ads were plastered on buses, subways, billboards, TV, and radio.) For their work on behalf of the business system, the Ad Council received a $239,000 subsidy from the U.S. government. By early 1978, there were 3.6 million copies of their booklet in print. Their ads had been carried ("at no cost for time and space") by over 400 television stations, 1,000 radio stations, and 3,000 daily and weekly newspapers. The "second phase" of the Ad Council's campaign began in late 1977—featuring quizzes on "How High Is Your E.Q.?

(Economic Quotient)." The Ad Council has received cooperation from the American Library Association and its 6,800 member library branches, as well as support from the three major television networks, which agreed to "run public service messages encouraging viewers to visit their local libraries" to study Ad Council materials about the economy.[17] They recently released a third product—another cute booklet on inflation called *Dollars and Sense*.[18] Does the Ad Council campaign reflect a burning desire to serve the "public interest"? One Ad Council supporter explained his enthusiasm for the project: "It seems unbelievable that [our] system...should in fact be in jeopardy. But...we business men and women better realize the situation before it becomes too late."[19]

we're propagandizing, we're selling." —corporate executive

It's time American Industry took a stand for Free Enterprise.

Here's Why. Foc... oline prices. Car p... digit inflation.

The Amer... feel like they ha... punched in th... Repeatedly.

They d... care, about... regulations... ...have...

Phillips Funds a Film

Phillips Petroleum spent $800,000 producing five films on "American Enterprise." "It's gone past the point where an isolated business has come under attack," as Phillips explained in an ad. "The system itself is in danger. And if we don't stand up for it, who will?"[20] By January 1982, the distributor reported that more than 40 million students had seen the series in the United States and that it had received more than a million showings in secondary schools in the country. As the sponsors proudly reported in 1979, "The five *American Enterprise* films have become the most widely seen educational series ever."[21]

Moving Into the Schools

Many corporations focus directly on the schools. At the college level, the business community is investing heavily in contests, internships, company-designed courses, and—perhaps most frequently—faculty "chairs" and professorships. By early 1978, corporations had financed at least twenty professorships in "private enterprise" and another twenty or more were in the works. The purpose of these corporate bequests has been clear. As the sponsor of a professorship at Ohio State University explained, "I felt a real need for someone to teach about American free enterprise."[27]

Corporations are focusing at least as much attention on elementary and secondary schools. Many schools are now teaching more about economics. A *New York Times* survey recently concluded: "Part of the push is coming from industry, from oil companies, from chambers of commerce and a wide range of businesses. They see economics courses as one way to achieve a greater understanding of business."[28] The author of a detailed study of corporate educational programs argues that most of the corporate-supported programs are not what they claim to be. "None of it is economic education, it is publicity about free enterprise," she says. Schools want new programs. "What happens," she suggests, "is that the corporations step in and pick up the tab."[29]

Most of the corporations share the same long-range ambitions. As one corporate consultant promised hopefully, "what is being taught in the universities today will be the generally accepted concept ten years from now."[30]

Mobil Socks It to 'Em

If we tell you oil companies don't make enough profit, you'll have a fit.
Oil companies don't make enough profit. Sorry.

It has been more than five years si...
...der this head...

Capitalism: moving target

...wrong with business ...dless. Nearly ...right

Ford changed course and bounced back with the Mustang, which quickly showed its tailpipe to the competition by breaking all sales records for a new ...car.) ...oved so closely to the ...onsive to it. ...most

In 1978, Mobil Oil was already spending $21 million a year on a public affairs department which engages in what it calls "advocacy advertising." By now it probably spends nearly $5 million a year on ad space alone, entertaining readers of *Parade, Family Weekly*, the *New York Times*, and other outlets with its militant support of the corporate interest. "People know that if they take a swipe at us," a Mobil executive reported when their campaign began, "we will fight back."[22] An ad executive recently purred with admiration at the Mobil campaign: "Imagine what would happen if all the Fortune 500 companies did that. The atmosphere would change overnight!"[23]

Few of these corporations feel satisfied with the results of their campaigns. Their reaction, in general, has been that they need to escalate their propaganda warfare. The report on employee "economics education" summarizes many executives' views:

> ....it would appear that nothing short of a massive effort will alter the current decline in status of business today in the eyes of virtually every public constituency whose support it must have to maintain its economic and political health. In this context, the words of Theodore Roosevelt are as valid today as they were... when he uttered them: 'American public opinion is a vast ocean. It cannot be stirred with a teaspoon!'[34]

Although the corporate campaign sometimes seems like overkill, it grows more serious all the time. Most corporations have already decided that they need to go beyond relatively toothless "economics education" and focus their energies on political lobbying.

More than 500 corporations and 1,500 trade associations maintain lobbying offices in Washington; now business knows, as one lobbyist put it, "if you want to have a say, you've got to get in the pit."[35] The U.S. Chamber of Commerce has formed 1,200 Congressional Action Committees—with about 100,000 local business members—to pressure individual senators and representatives; its publications can immediately reach seven million readers.[36] A group of business trade associations has begun to coordinate "action conferences for business leadership" around the country to encourage companies to form corporate "political action committees" (PAC's). At least partly through these efforts, the number of corporate PAC's increased from 89 in 1974 to nearly 1,000 by 1980; by contrast, labor unions support only about 225 PAC's.[37] In one particularly concentrated campaign, a coalition of about five hundred corporations and trade associations, spending several hundred thousand dollars, coordinated the business campaign against the 1978 Congressional legislation for labor law reform. "Labor and the White House thought they could get the bill through...," one business lobbyist explained. "They simply didn't realize how strongly business would react."[38]

As most political observers now agree, the effects of this business campaign have been sweeping. The 1981 session of Congress told the story with dramatic clarity. The Reagan administration was proposing huge cuts in social programs. Out of modest concern for fairness, its initial proposals included some cuts in appropriations for the Export-Import Bank, which largely benefits multinational corporations. The minute the multinationals heard about the cuts, they went to work on Congress. The cuts were quickly erased. The corporate lobbyists "came out of the woodwork," the Reagan budget director reports, "and we weren't prepared to deal with it."[39]

And so it went with the legislation proposing tax cuts. As one journalist reports: "The tax lobbyists of Washington, when they saw the outlines of the Reagan tax bill, mobilized the business community, the influential economic sectors from oil to real estate. In a matter of days, they created the political environment in which they flourish best—a bidding war between the two parties." They got what they wanted. "The final tax legislation would yield, in total, an astounding revenue loss for the federal government of $750 billion over the next five years."[40]

This corporate offensive is not going to disappear overnight. Corporate leaders have finally realized, as *Fortune* magazine concludes, that "to defend business effectively, a coherent political position must be advanced."[41] Criticizing an earlier generation of business advocates, a corporate lobbyist regretted that they never wanted "to play hard ball."[42] Business now means business. "We should cease to be patsies," a corporate executive urged at a management conference, "and start to raise hell."[43]

It will not be easy to resist this corporate propaganda campaign. At the least, we could usefully follow some of their example. They have been defining their interests, studying the economy, promoting their preferred policies, and spreading the corporate word. We need to do for ourselves what they've already begun to do on their own behalf: we need to define our own interests, study how the economy affects those interests, develop policies which serve our needs, and spread a "popular message" which explains and advocates our own point of view.

This book has been written to support that effort. It is only a beginning. We cannot successfully counter corporate ideas with a single book. We need a massive and continuing effort to define, interpret, and articulate our needs and interests.

Douglas Fraser, president of the United Auto Workers, wrote in July 1978: "I believe leaders of the business community, with few exceptions, have chosen to wage a *one-sided class war* in this country—a war against working people, the unemployed, the poor, the minorities, the very young and the very old, and even many in the middle class in our society."[44]

The evidence suggests that Fraser is right. It is time to retaliate—to make it a *two-sided* battle. **We have no other choice.**

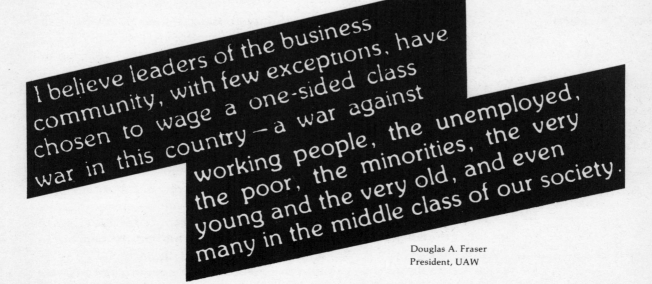

I believe leaders of the business community, with few exceptions, have chosen to wage a one-sided class war in this country — a war against working people, the unemployed, the poor, the minorities, the very young and the very old, and even many in the middle class of our society.

Douglas A. Fraser
President, UAW

How To Use This Book

This is not your typical economics text. Many books discuss current economic problems, but this one takes a fairly unique approach to those issues. *What's Wrong With the U.S. Economy?* differs from other books about the economy in five important ways.

1. Most books make "economics" seem very mysterious. "The economy" is something outside us with its own laws and magic. This treatment often contributes to a feeling that we cannot control the economy; instead, the economy seems to control us.

We begin with a different perspective. We assume that *we are the economy*, that *our* activities make *it* happen. Working with this assumption, our initial question, "what's wrong with the U.S. economy?," translates directly into a different and more relevant question: "How can *we* make the economy work better for *us*?"

2. Most books about the economy pretend that there is only one legitimate approach to economics and that everyone in our society has the same economic interests. "We're all in it together!" We don't share that illusion. We begin with a strong suspicion that the interests of large corporations conflict with the interests of almost all the rest of us. In that sense, this book begins and ends with a clear objective—to articulate and advance our interests *against* theirs.

Some readers may worry that an "advocacy" book cannot be "objective," that our purposes will somehow "bias" our analysis. We do not agree. With this as with any other analysis, the proof is in the results: Does our analysis make sense? Is it consistent with the available facts and evidence? Does it make more sense than other analyses? Does it lead in directions which seem both promising and possible?

We take these standards seriously. We presume that neither we, the authors, nor you, the readers, yet know all the answers. We must pursue those answers as carefully and coherently as we can. The roughly 1,200 footnotes at the end of this book suggest some of the care we have taken for our part in that pursuit.

3. Roughly 1,200 footnotes? Help! Another boring textbook!

Most books about the economy are boring indeed. We think this usually stems from authors' lack of concern for their readers, leading typically to both dry and difficult presentations.

Because we are eager to begin a dialogue with readers about our current economic problems, we pursue a different level and tone. We have tried to make this book as accessible and lively as possible. We have written a book which we think everyone with at least some high school education can understand. And we have tried to find ways to make the discussion as interesting and—is it even imaginable in an economics book?!—as amusing as we could.

At the same time, we have not confused lively and accessible with condescending and easy. This is both a serious and a demanding book. We believe that both the immediacy of the current economic crisis and the seriousness with which we have prepared this book will encourage everyone to read it with a comparable kind of commitment.

4. With all these ambitious objectives, we knew from the beginning that our book could never be pure text or one-dimensional

HOW TO READ A GRAPH

There are a number of graphs in this book, especially in Chapters 18 and 19. There are no tricks in them. They're easy to read, especially because they present simple trends.

Fig. 0.1

This One Goes Up . . .

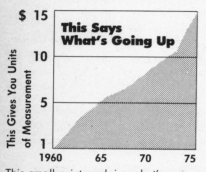

This small print explains what's going up—for instance, that the number of dollars disappearing into Swiss bank accounts (measured in constant dollars, in 1972 prices) has more than doubled since 1960.

Source: This tells you how to check up on us.

Fig. 0.2

. . . And This One Goes Down (There Are Lots of These)

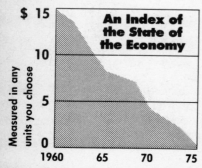

Many of the graphs make important points; be sure to read the small text below. Or do you need us to tell you that nearly everything that matters is going down?

Our American Economic System is ☐ good ☐ bad.
(check one)

Most Americans (about 80%) believe that our economic system —with its individual freedom—is the best in the world, yet some changes are needed. To help give you a clearer picture of our system on which to base decisions, a special booklet has been prepared. For a free copy, write: "Economics," Pueblo, Colorado 81009.

The American Economic System.

A public service of The Advertising Council & U.S. Department of Commerce

The American Economic System... and your part in it.

I KNOW SOME PEOPLE WHO OUGHTTA SEE THIS.

monologue. We've used two (somewhat playful) "gimmicks" to enhance and enliven the book.

a) *The Rest of Us Meet the DUPE.* The first aims to clarify and highlight the corporate perspective on the economy. Business ideas dominate almost all economic discussion in this country, but many of us often take those ideas for granted because corporate ideas flow so subtly through the media. Sometimes we need to squint to see their message clearly.

In order to sharpen people's focus on these corporate ideas, we have consolidated the business viewpoint and given it a name. We call it the Dominant (Unofficial) Perspective on the Economy. Or DUPE for short. We refer throughout the book to the DUPE (meaning their analysis); we talk also about DUPEsters, DUPE pushers, DUPE ads, and DUPE addicts. We've used four pieces as standard reference sources for the DUPE analysis:

■ *The American Economic System—and your part in it*, first published by the Advertising Council as part of the bicentennial events of 1976.[1] We call it *the DUPE booklet.*

■ The film series, *American Enterprise*, funded by Phillips Petroleum and widely distributed in the schools since 1977.[2] We call it *the*

DUPE film and quote frequently from the teachers' guide for the film series.

■ A special supplement prepared by *U.S. News and World Report* in 1978 called the "ABC's of How Our Economy Works."[3] We call it *the DUPE primer.*

■ The recent book and TV series by Milton and Rose Friedman, *Free to Choose*, which has brought the DUPE to the best-seller list and public television.[4] We call it *The Gospel According to DUPE.*

We quote from these sources frequently in order to avoid citation without representation. We have tried to summarize the DUPE as coherently as possible...and to have a little fun in the process.

b) *The Curious World of Dupe Dagain*. A comic strip? In a book on economics? Dupe and his friends work mostly at Short Circuit Electric. Most of them are members of local 1207 of FIERCE—the Federation of International Electrical, Radio, and Communication Employees. They're stuck together, struggling together, and in their own way growing together. They share the common experience of facing the 1980s with

Name: Arthur 'Dupe' Dagain
Born: 11/1/22
　　　　　Allentown, Pa.
Status: Married to Beatrice Lloyd,
　　　　　Housewife,
　　　　　3 children, all married
　　　　　5 grandchildren
Job: Skilled trades, maintenance

wonder and trepidation. Will they make it? Will we?

5. Most authors who write about economics build from a largely academic experience. This book grows out of a very different kind of background.

We at the ILER have been conducting courses with working people for the past eight years. We hope that this book captures some of the spirited dialogue we've enjoyed with our course participants since 1974.

We also hope that this book continues that dialogue. While books can't be tailored precisely to each reader's needs, we've tried to structure this book so that readers could use it in a variety of ways. Some may want to thumb through the book quickly to get a sense of its general direction before beginning to read it closely. Some may also want to pay special attention to the opening and closing sections of each chapter, since the connections among the chapters are especially important and help guide the direction of the book's analysis.

Name: Elizabeth R. Ames
Born: 8/25/48
Fresno, Ca.
Status: Divorced,
2 children
Job: Secretary

We also hope that many of you will read this book together—in your own courses and study groups. Because the book grows out of that kind of collective discussion, we think it will be most effective if people use it in the same kind of environment. Pass the book around. Show it to your friends. Start your own courses and groups. We are eager to provide suggestions for different ways of developing these collective uses.

We hope, finally, that many of you will communicate with us directly. We plan future editions of this book. Send us your criticisms and suggestions, your Bronx cheers and applause. How would you like the book to be different? What other kind of help would you like? And let us know how you're using the book so that we can make similar suggestions to other people and groups.

In the end, more and more of us must get involved in this kind of education. We need to communicate with each other. We need to take apart the DUPE and construct an analysis of our own. We hope that this book can help serve as a useful beginning.

Name: Norman W. (No-Way) Wray
Born: 5/4/44
Dothan, Alabama
Status: Married to Willow Poole,
Customer service rep,
First Federal Savings
Job: Paintsprayer

Institute For

LABOR
EDUCATION and RESEARCH

The Institute for Labor Education and Research (ILER) is a non-profit organization based in New York City. We do research, teach courses, and provide educational materials for "the rest of us."

The Institute began eight years ago when the Oil, Chemical, and Atomic Workers asked us to develop a course about the economy for rank-and-file union members in New Jersey. That first course took place during the worst recession in postwar history; course participants were eager to understand why the economy was creating such severe problems for working people.

The economy has hardly improved in recent years and we have been organizing workshops and courses for working people ever since. More than 50 local unions in the northeastern United States have sponsored these programs. We have also taught courses and workshops for other non-union groups of working people both in the northeast and as far away from our home base as Butte, Montana. This book has emerged from and reflects the lessons we have learned from our teaching experience.

Almost all of our courses and workshops have taken place in local union halls under the official sponsorship of the local union leadership. Our courses are not part of any credit-bearing or degree-granting educational program. Neither we nor the local unions have been trying to provide a ticket of admission to higher occupational stations. We have sought, rather, to equip stewards, activists, and rank-and-filers with the information, skills, and strategies they need to begin tackling their problems on and off the job. How do we deal with management on the shop or office floor, at grievance hearings, at the bargaining table...? Why the sudden rash of management demands for givebacks and concessions? Who's ripping us off in the market place? Can we link up with other groups to begin solving our problems and serving our own needs?

Name: Rosie Rivera
Born: 7/6/58
Chicago, Ill.
Status: Single
Job: Assembler

We have always encouraged working people in our programs to define their own educational needs and agendas. As a result, this *Popular Guide for the Rest of Us* has been an unusually cooperative project. There are many suggestions in this book—about how the economy works, what's wrong with it, and what we can do to fix it. These suggestions have grown out of thousands of discussions with workers and activists in our workshops and courses. None of those participants bears final responsibility for what we have written here, of course, but we think that many will hear their own voices in much of what follows.

Name: Gus Wojnamski (Ski-bo)
Born: 9/20/45
        Hamtramck, Mich.
Status: Married to Jeannie Szymanski,
        Nurses aide,
        1 child, 'Booger', age 10
Job: Stockman

Our own contributions to the book also reflect a cooperative and collective process—involving the time and commitment of many both inside and outside our Institute.

David M. Gordon, director of the ILER, originally conceived the idea for this kind of guide for working people. He is the principal author of the text—having written both an earlier, more primitive draft and the final manuscript of the text in its current form—and supplied much of the energy ensuring the book's final appearance.

Howard Saunders is responsible for the art direction and design of the book. He also created the cartoon world of Dupe Dagain—the receptacle of *all* the myths of our economic culture—and the other captives at Short Circuit Electric. Saunders was aided, abetted, and sometimes thwarted by David Gordon, who provided a conceptual structure for the comic strip, contributed the "symmetry of his logic" as editor and frequent critic, and even managed a funny line here and there along the way.

Mike Merrill wrote the first draft of most of the text in its present form before taking a two year leave from the ILER in 1977 for family reasons. When he returned in 1979, Merrill served within the ILER as the principal editor of the final draft.

Other ILER staff also played important roles in shaping the book. John Evansohn, Les Leopold, and Cydney Pullman helped, through their teaching and editorial comments, to shape the content of Part II. Judy Hilkey joined these three in contributing to the analysis of

Reaganomics in Part V—particularly through preparations for a major rank-and-file conference we hosted in the spring of 1981. June Sager provided especially useful help with some of the most tedious data-gathering chores and David Howell, Rick McGahey, Mark Maier, and Sharon Szymanski provided some important research help in early stages of the work.

The entire former and present staff of the ILER deserves credit as well, helping keep the Institute alive, helping make our teaching and contacts possible. In addition to those already mentioned, we express our thanks to Ron Blackwell, Mary Feldblum, Franca Freedman, Jane Hammond, Mike Hooper, and Sally Silvers.

Several outside readers made important editorial contributions, reading drafts as they episodically appeared, helping correct our substantive transgressions and deviations. We thank Ron Blackwell, Karen Durbin, Dick Logan, Ros Petchesky, Rayna Rapp, Juliet Schor, and Bill Tabb. David Gordon's contributions to this book have also benefited enormously from joint research and writing on related issues with Sam Bowles and Tom Weisskopf.

Name: Francis X. (Cushy) Beale
Born: 2/4/20
Walpole, Mass.
Status: Divorced
Job: Local President, Federation of International Electrical, Radio and Communications Employees

We owe perhaps our greatest gratitude to the members of the South End Press collective—not to mention our abject apologies. They have remained committed to this book despite our many delays, broken promises, and shattered schedules. It is testimony to their personal patience, hard work, and political dedication that this book has finally appeared.

We dedicate this book to the working people and trade unionists with whom we have worked during the past few years. They bear no responsibility for the views presented here. But they constantly sustained us with their belief in and commitment to the labor movement as a home for critical discussion and a force for social change. Their spirit and activism is living evidence that a decent and humane future is possible in the United States.

—The Staff of the Institute for Labor Education and Research
853 Broadway, Room 2014, N.Y., N.Y. 10003

Short Circuit Electric, Heartland, Ohio.
Built June 1938. A Division of Amalgamated Industry.

PART I: ECONOMIC NIGHTMARES

1.
What's Happened to the American Dream?

"The United States is the only country in the world where you can do anything you want as long as you don't bother anybody. You wanna be rich? You can be rich. You wanna work? You can work....You can do anything."

—cabdriver in Boston[1]

"I don't remember dreams when I was a child. Our dream was to get through the week until payday. That the food would last from one week to the next....No one gave us any reason to dream. The grownups had no dreams, so they couldn't pass anything on to their children that they didn't have themselves."

—grandmother, former waitress, community organizer[2]

For millions of people in the United States, the "American Dream" has turned into a nightmare. At the plant, in the office, at home, in the bars, on the streets...the same insistent question keeps running through our conversations like a nagging reminder from the bill collector: *What's Wrong With the U.S. Economy?*

When we conduct workshops on the economy, we ask participants to list the economic problems which they think are most urgent. The specific lists vary from time to time and place to place, of course, but their main outlines are almost always the same. Three principal problems appear in every discussion:

■ *the growing difficulty in making ends meet*—as a result of both unemployment and inflation;

■ *deteriorating work conditions*—as a result of both hazards on the job and supervisory harassment; and

■ *declining quality of life in our homes and communities*—as a result of both health hazards and economic insecurity.

This list contains no surprises. But what sometimes surprises people in our workshops is the scope and depth of these problems. Many of us are encouraged to regard these kinds of economic difficulties as our own personal concerns, the products of our own individual failures and laziness. When we look at the numbers,

Good Thing We Still Have the Secret Ballot

however, this sense of individual blame fades before the breadth and intensity of popular distress.

In order to focus as much as possible on the common plight of the rest of us, we begin this book with a brief review of available data on our three main economic problems. The cold, hard facts tell a depressing story. We, as a nation, are in deep economic trouble. The DUPEsters prefer to ignore many of these facts because they're intent on promising a magical mystery tour to renewed prosperity. We can't escape the facts because we live with them everyday.

HEY BUDDY, CAN YOU SPARE A ~~DIME~~ *Buck*?

1. Making Ends Meet

"I keep getting a raise, but everything else goes up. It don't do you any good."

—steelworker in Alabama[3]

"I'm working and I'm trying to give my children a little better...but I'm not getting any place. I'm in the hole each month. We're not starving, but my kids get a little tired of eating eggs and franks."

—clerical worker, mother of four[4]

Millions of households in the United States must constantly worry about paying the bills. Inflation won't leave us alone. Despite the trillions of dollars of U.S. wealth, economic survival is a real and persistent problem for more of us than anyone dares to count.

We can start with the average working household in the United States. How have our standards of living fared in recent years?

Prices have more than doubled in just ten years: it cost roughly $2.25 in 1981 to buy what cost only $1.00 in 1971. The average worker also paid about $2.50 in taxes in 1981 for every tax dollar paid in 1971. Interest rates have also soared, hitting hard at those who must borrow to stay afloat.

Workers' take-home pay has not kept pace. We can trace the assault on our standards of living by looking at numbers on *real spendable earnings*—the amount we have left to spend from our wage-and-salary incomes after inflation and taxes have taken their bites. The graph on this page shows, for the years from 1960 through 1980, the weekly real spendable earnings of the average U.S. worker with three dependents. Between 1972—when it reached its postwar peak—and 1981, *the purchasing power of the average worker's earnings declined by 16%.* Over the past 25 years, we have been racing on a treadmill. The country's gross national product (GNP) more than doubled during the 1970s, but *the standard of living provided by the average worker's earnings was lower in 1981 than it was in 1956.*[5] And some call it progress.

What has been true for the average worker has also been true for almost all U.S. households. Between 1973 and 1979, prices rose by 63%. Only *wealthy* and *affluent* households—the top 10% of the income distribution—were able to keep up with inflation. The median incomes

---

The average worker's earnings bought less in 1981 than they did in 1956

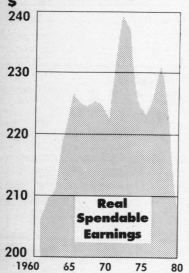

Fig. 1.1
Back to the 1950s— The Real Purchasing Power of The Average Worker's Weekly Earnings (in $1980)

The graph measures the purchasing power of the average worker's weekly earnings, controlling for inflation and taxes. (To control for inflation, the earnings are expressed in 1980 dollars. To control for taxes, it is assumed that the average worker had three dependents.)

Source: See note #5

of every group of *working* households *all* grew more slowly over those recent years than the level of prices.[6]

Confronted with these facts, some may shrug and dismiss their urgency. Aren't all these data like "real spendable earnings" just a bag of economists' tricks? What really counts, many would probably argue, is that people live very well in this country—whether at 1956 levels or at 1981 levels. What's wrong with what we had in 1956 anyway?

This kind of argument comes from watching too many TV commercials—many of which are aimed, in any case, at affluent and wealthy households. The deeper and less pleasant truth is that millions of U.S. households can barely afford basic necessities.

Let's look at the numbers more closely.

In 1980, the average U.S. family earned about $22,500 a year. The U.S. Bureau of Labor Statistics has calculated what an average family of four living in a city could afford in 1980 with about that much total income.[7] The box on this page details the items which this average family could afford.

By the time the family finished paying taxes, it had only $18,000 left for everything else. After covering basic household necessities, it had $957 to cover "other items" including children's allowances, legal expenses, lessons, bank charges, and all lodging away from home (including hotels and motels). The budget provided for *no* savings for a rainy or any other day. Some apologists might call this affluence, but most of us would call it barely getting by.

How many households in the U.S. enjoy this kind of luxury? *Half of all working households must live on less each year than this spare family budget—adjusted for family size—provides. Roughly one-half of all working households in the U.S. were unable to save anything at all.*[8] Affluence is still reserved for the few.

Many households in the U.S. do even worse, living perilously close to starvation. "Millions of Americans are hungry at least part of their lives," according to the *New York Times*, and "many suffer from malnutrition."[9] A study funded by the Carnegie Foundation concluded in the mid-1970s that "a quarter to a third of all American children are born into families with financial strains so great that their children will suffer basic deprivations."[10]

The Average Working Household's Standard of Living

Fig. 1.2

Total household income	**$23,134**
Total household consumption	**17,926**
Food	5,571
Housing	5,106
Transportation	2,116
Clothing	1,292
Personal care	471
Medical care	1,303
Other necessities	1,109
All extra consumption	957
Total household taxes	**5,208**
Personal income tax	3,781
Social security & disability	1,427

This is a typical budget for a family of four with a working household head, one other adult, and two children, aged 13 and 8. Does this kind of budget afford luxuries?

The budget provides for....

* 1 toaster every 33 years;
* 1 family meal out every five weeks;
* 1 man's suit every 4 years;
* 5 record albums a year;
* 5 movies per adult per year; and
* 1 6-pack of beer every 2 weeks.

Source: See note #7

Fig. 1.3

Government officials have defined a "poverty standard" necessary for survival. In 1979, an urban family of four needed at least $7,400 to reach this poverty standard. During that year, 25.2 million people, or 11.6% of the total U.S. population, lived in a household which earned less than this poverty income (adjusted for family size).[11]

The government's own studies admit that households cannot possibly stay at this poverty level for long without suffering serious health problems: the diet provided by this budget, according to the government, is designed only for "temporary or emergency use...." More than one-ninth of the U.S. population is forced to live on incomes which, by the government's own figures, are adequate only for "short-term use when funds are extremely low."[12] Others have used a more plausible measure of poverty, referring to polls reporting what "Americans...consider the smallest amount of money a family...needs to get along...." Roughly one-fifth of the population lives in households earning less than this more reasonable standard.[13]

"Over the years," the DUPE booklet boasts, "our GNP has increased astonishingly."[14] It still does. But who gets to taste the fruits? For millions of us, there aren't enough apples to go around.

Finding and Keeping a Job. One of the reasons that working households have so much trouble making ends meet is that so many of us have problems finding and keeping a job. The shadows of unemployment grow longer every year:

"It was the worst blow I ever had. I've been divorced. My father died a few months before I got fired....I was persuaded that I must be...as bad as the company must have thought I was to fire me, but much worse than that....It doesn't simply take away your self-confidence. It destroys you. Utterly."

—professional in publishing after layoff[15]

"A lot of people say blacks just want welfare—they don't want to work. That is stuff. It's a matter of pride to have a job. But I have no job, no future."

—middle-aged unemployed black woman[16]

"So I just came home and told my wife, 'That's it....' I am getting old, and when one mechanical engineering job pops up here or there they have wholesale applicants. They get forty or fifty resumes on one opening."

—middle-aged unemployed engineer[17]

"I was one of those dumb kids that stayed on line all night to get one of those summer jobs that pay next to nothing. But there were too many of us and too few jobs."

—unemployed black teenager[18]

Job insecurity affects U.S. workers in many different ways. In February 1982, 9.6 millon were out of work, roughly 9% of the labor force. Even government representatives admit that these official statistics understate the seriousness of the real problems of joblessness. We can look at complete data available for 1980 to see why:

■ Millions look for work and cannot find it. These are the people the government tracks with its monthly figures, counting workers as "unemployed" if they do not have a job *and* have looked for work during the past four weeks. At any one time in 1980, on the average, more than 7.4 million workers did not have a job and were looking for work.[19] That was equivalent to the entire population of Chicago, Los Angeles, and Philadelphia combined.

■ Those figures count the number of jobless workers at any one time. During an entire year, many more workers are unemployed *at one time or another*. During 1980, 22.4 million workers—or roughly one in five—experienced at least one period of unemployment during the year.[20] Unemployment is not a rare tropical disease; it is more like the economic equivalent of a common cold.

■ There are also millions who want but cannot find regular full-time work who are not even *counted* by the government as "unemployed."

One group of workers is not counted because, although they want a job, they have grown discouraged and are no longer actively looking. (They believe, often accurately, that their continual searching would meet continual frustration.) During 1980, at any one time, there were 2.1 million potential workers who were not actively looking for work—and therefore not counted as unemployed—"for economic reasons."[21] These "discouraged workers" need jobs too.

Another group of people wants full-time work but, because they cannot find it, are working part-time "involuntarily." In 1980, there were 4.2 million workers in this dilemma, people who were eager to work full-time but could not find full-time work.[22]

In fact, regular work was so difficult to find that only about 70% of full-time workers were able to stay at work the full year round.[23]

These numbers all help dramatize how serious the unemployment problem has become. In 1980, as Figure 1.3 helps show, *13.8 million workers were "unemployed," in the fullest sense, at any one time. At some time or another during the year, at least 32 million workers—more than one-quarter of the labor force—suffered one or another problem finding or keeping a job.*[24] How many people must have trouble with unemployment before we begin to regard it as more than an isolated problem?

Inequalities. The problems of making ends meet have become more and more widespread, but they also continue to afflict some people much more than others.

■ The typical female worker in 1979 earned less than half as much per year as the typical male worker. The typical black family earned only 57% as much as the typical white family, while the median hispanic family managed only 70% of the median white family earnings.[25] Even among white males, inequalities persist: white men who come from the most affluent families (in the top 10% of the income distribution) are more than *ten times* more likely to wind up in the top fifth of the income distribution than white men from the poorest families (in the bottom 10% of the income distribution).[26]

■ Unemployment rates among women workers in 1980 were only 8% higher than those among men workers. But differences by race and age were much more striking. Black unemployment rates were more than twice white unemployment rates, while hispanic unemployment rates were 1.6 times higher. Unemployment rates among all teens had climbed close to 20%, while black teenage unemployment had climbed to nearly 40%.[27]

All these problems add up. Those closest to their impact are running scared. "There is fear throughout the plant," as one auto-worker in New Jersey remarked in 1980. "People are afraid they're going to lose their homes and cars."[28]

Deteriorating Working Conditions

"I'm very surprised more accidents don't happen....I go through a shirt every two weeks....My coveralls catch on fire....[Indicates arms] See them little holes? That's what sparks do. I've got burns across here from last night....A job should be a job, not a death sentence."

—auto assembly line worker[29]

"You're there just to filter people and filter telephone calls. You're there just to handle the equipment. You're treated like a piece of equipment, like the telephone."

—office receptionist[30]

"Some men work eight hours a day. There are mothers that work eleven, twelve hours a day. We get up at night, a baby vomits, you have to be calling the doctor, you have to be changing the baby. When do you get a break, really? You don't. This is an all-around job, day and night."

—part-time social worker, full-time mother[31]

When we work for someone else, it means that our bosses make critical decisions affecting our lives at work. In making those decisions, they mind their own interests, not ours. And we often pay the price.

The price tag is most evident when we suffer physical harm. One of the major causes of injury and illness in the United States is work. Government figures indicate that over 14,000 U.S. workers are killed in work accidents each year, as many U.S. citizens as were killed in the

Another Poor Slob on the Line

WHERE'S BOOGER?

HE'S GOT THE MEAN-MAMA BLUES.

WHAT ABOUT?

ASK 'IM YOURSELF SUGARDADDY!

Vietnam War during the worst year of casualties. Roughly 200,000 people are estimated to die each year from illness caused by their work. Over 2.2 million more are either permanently or temporarily disabled from work accidents and occupational diseases *each year*. And all these numbers are gross underestimates because of under-reporting. A recent government study estimates that "at least 25 *million* serious [occupational] injuries and deaths go uncounted each year...."[32] U.S. workers are an army of walking wounded.

And these workplace hazards appear to be growing more and more severe. It is possible to compare health-and-safety risks on the job over a number of years—by looking at trends in the industrial accident rate. (This is expressed as the relative number of workdays lost as a result of industrial accidents in each year.) The industrial accident rate *nearly doubled* between the early 1960s and the late 1970s. By 1979, it was 10% higher than during the worst year of high-speed production in World War II.[33]

Corporations ignore these health hazards as much as possible. A recent government survey found that "one out of four American workers is exposed on the job to some substance thought to be capable of causing death or disease." The survey found that most corporations refuse to consider that workers even "have a right to know about workplace hazards." Another survey found in 1977 that 78% of all U.S. workers reported that they were exposed to one or more health and safety hazards on their jobs; nearly one-sixth—the equivalent of roughly fifteen million workers today—reported they had suffered

"work related illness or injury during the last three years."[34]

There are less obvious physical hazards on the job.

■ Millions work at boring and repetitive jobs. The chances of physical disability are twice as high for someone with a repetitive job as for someone with a more varied job;[35] if you fall asleep at the lathe, you're liable to end up with beveled fingers.

■ Many other workers have jobs which are full of stress and pressure. The chances of physical disability are three times as high for those with stressful jobs as for those with more tranquil routines;[36] if the pace never lets up or the supervisor is constantly on your case, you're much more likely to suffer fatigue and anxiety. "Things have got so bad," one phone worker recently reported, "that they had to install a self-tester [for blood pressure] in the cafeteria."[37] Many studies have found close connection between job problems and anxiety, tension, and even psychiatric hospitalization.[38]

More and more workers in the United States have begun to feel the toll. We're either pushed to the limit or bored to death. A 1977 survey found that job satisfaction among production and nonsupervisory workers had reached the lowest point since the surveys began in 1950.[39] Another survey found that declining job satisfaction in the 1970s was "pervasive, affecting virtually all the demographic and occupational subclasses examined."[40]

Working people tell the story better than the survey data. "I don't understand how come more guys don't flip," as one auto worker put it. "I bet there's men who have lived and died out there, never seen the end of that line. And they never will—because it's endless. It's like a serpent. It's just all body, no tail. It can do things to you...."[41]

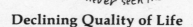

"I bet there's men who've never seen the end of the line. It's like a serpent. It can do things to you."

Declining Quality of Life

"The biggest polluter is the thing we produce, the automobile. The livelihood that puts bread on your table....What the hell good is my livelihood if the air's gonna kill me anyway. There are so many priorities that have to be straightened out."

—auto worker in Ohio[42]

"If I had the power in this country, first thing I'd do in nursing homes...[would be] free care for everybody. Those hospitals that charge too much money and you don't have insurance and they don't accept you....Things [are] so bad for old people today....It makes you sad, because if you live long enough, you figure you will be the same."

—aide in a nursing home[43]

"Until I know who to blame [for my son's leukemia], I'm not going to blame anyone.... But if I find it's any one factory..., then I'll go over there and I'll tear it down, brick by brick."

—mother of disabled boy in New Jersey[44]

Our lives off the job aren't so hot either. Disasters like Three Mile Island and Love Canal have become household words. It feels as if the fabric of our lives is beginning to unravel.

We might not mind higher prices if the quality of basic necessities were improving. But the opposite often seems the case: with many of the basic necessities in our lives, it appears that we're both paying more *and* enjoying it less. The quality of many foods has suffered dramatically: tomatoes in the supermarket taste like cardboard, and many kinds of fresh fish and meat have been laced with mercury, additives, and other toxics. Take the common potato—"the more a potato gets processed," recent studies reveal, "the more its price goes up and its nutritional value goes down...."[45] The quality of health care is probably an even more obvious example: even for those who can afford to go to the doctor, potentially dangerous surgery is frequently prescribed when it is unnecessary; young women are often exposed to sterilization abuse; and we're fed drugs more often than is healthy or warranted.[46] For many of us, we're never quite sure whether we'll find a doctor or get treatment or receive health insurance reimbursement. Sometimes it seems safer to put up with our illnesses than to go for medical help.

Just plain living involves pervasive physical hazards. The list of food and drugs which "may be dangerous to your health" grows longer and longer. Our kids' toys are liable to burn them, shock them, or irritate their skins. Evidence is mounting that several widely-used building materials such as foam insulation release toxic fumes. The air we breathe is only slightly healthier than cigarette smoke. Our streets are so clogged and our cars so unsafe that more than 50,000 people still die from auto accidents every year.[47]

And communities are becoming more and more aware of the most frightening risks of all—contamination from industrial and nuclear wastes, sudden explosions or clouds from chemical and nuclear dumps,...even the risk of nuclear melt-down in neighboring reactors. "We almost lost Detroit," a nuclear engineer sighed after a near disaster at the Enrico Fermi plant in 1966.[48] How many more Three Mile Islands will we face in the 1980s?

Some of the worst problems are the most intangible. For many of us, life in our communities seems askew. Old neighborhoods change and our streets seem unsafe. Old friends and relatives move away in search of work. At times it seems as if the foundations of our daily lives are crumbling. As they crumble, we feel less and less control. "These are the uniform complaints of jobholders, home buyers—" a *U.S News and World Report* survey concluded in 1978; "people...feel that something is badly out of kilter...." "I get the feeling that tough times are around the corner...," as one worker in the survey put it. "I feel powerless."[49]

THE DUPE: SPEAKING WITH A FORKED TONGUE?

"The economy is basically healthy: the problems we have now are less economic than emotional."
                    —chief economist, Bank of America, 1977[50]

"The standard of living of the average American has to decline. I don't think you can escape that."
—chairman, Federal Reserve Board, 1979[51]

"It's like the old saying, 'Don't ever have a political philosophy that can't fit on a bumper sticker.' "
—politician on economy, 1980[52]

Our economic problems aren't going away. More and more of us recognize their urgency. More and more of us realize that we must act to solve our current crisis...both quickly and decisively.

Some of this has come as a surprise to many of us. During the 1960s, we became accustomed to expectations that prosperity would last forever. Those kinds of old habits, like old soldiers, rarely die.

But there was another reason that we adjusted so slowly to changing circumstances. As stagflation began to spread during the 1970s, DUPE representatives kept assuring us that everything was just fine:

■ In 1969 and 1970, the economy slumped and unemployment rose. In the middle of the recession, (then) Congressman Gerald Ford held our hands and promised that "the problem of inflation has been defeated.... the danger of any recession is nil."[53]

■ By 1973 and 1974, prices were spiralling upward, unemployment was beginning to rise, and workers were getting angrier. Should we be worried? Not yet. *Fortune* magazine happily predicted in July 1974 that, "by comparison with the past eighteen months, the next eighteen will seem almost sunny...."[54]

■ From early 1974 through the middle of 1975, despite *Fortune's* predictions, the economy plunged through the worst economic slide since the Great Depression of the 1930s. Had we finally reached the point where we should take matters into our own hands? Not yet. In their forecasts for the year 1976, economists said that the economy's recovery was "normal," "well-balanced," and "careful, deliberate." "This year promises to be a better year than the previous two," one leading economist explained to the *New York Times*.[55] We were supposed to take heart.

■ By 1977 we were getting used to hard times. All of the problems reviewed in the previous sections had taken deep root. Somebody up there must have noticed. But still, they kept repeating the same assurances. As the chairman of the Federal Reserve Board put it in January 1978, "Things are going much better in the economy than most people realize. It's our attitude that is doing poorly. We need a new sense of confidence in ourselves...."[56] They talked as if we needed nothing more than a nasal decongestant.

While the DUPE pushers were rubbing our backs with one hand, they were setting us up for a sucker punch with the other. As early as 1973-74, many corporate executives had begun to conclude that people must accept *less* so that corporations could have *more*. "Profits are vital to the primary engine of the U.S. economy," *Business Week* magazine explained in 1974. **"Yet it will be a hard pill for many Americans to swallow—the idea of doing with less so that big business can have more."**[57]

"We have to convince the have nots that they can become the haves . . . by supporting us."
—corporate executive

Their solution, as we saw in "Why We Need This Book," was a propaganda campaign. "Tighten your belt," Warner and Swasey Co. urged in a 1975 ad, "not your noose."[58] "We have to convince the have nots," as one executive put it at a corporate conference, "that the way they can become the haves is not by tearing down our system but by supporting us."[59] They recognized that many people wouldn't like the message, but they vowed to push it nonetheless.

And what they couldn't win with their message, they began to grab with their hands and their power. Aiming at working people's basic tools of resistance and control, corporations began going after labor unions with a vengeance. Union-busting management consultant firms were giving them a big boost. Union busting became a big industry. (See Chapters 12 and 19)

Corporate planners also began attacking basic government services. By 1974-75, particularly in New York City, bankers and bond holders began to demand layoffs of municipal workers and cutbacks in social spending. We had to accept the sacrifices, they told us, or they wouldn't lend us any more money. Their demands quickly became an offer we couldn't refuse.

These corporate assaults began to pay off almost immediately. While they were asking us to make sacrifices, they were beginning to laugh all the way to the bank. Between 1976 and 1979, while the average worker's real spendable earnings were declining by 2.1%, the total profits of the largest 500 industrial corporations were increasing by 24% (controlling for inflation). The profit rate of those top 500 corporations climbed from 13.5% to 15.9%—an increase of nearly one-fifth.[60] The salaries of top corporate executives were also beginning to soar. The average total compensation of a sample of roughly 500 top executives from leading corporations increased by 18% between 1976 and 1979 (controlling for inflation), featuring "the highest increases" in the 1970s. As the box on this page shows, the 20 best-paid corporate executives in 1980 earned from a "low" of $1.5 million a year to a high of $3.3 million.[61] The only pills they had been swallowing were filled with gold.

Less Democracy and More "Government"?

Corporate leaders also began to recognize that they might have to pursue drastic political steps in order to persuade the "have-nots" to accept their proper medicine. One international business group which began to talk about this possibility in the mid-1970s is the Trilateral Commission. (It was launched by David Rockefeller and includes leading corporate executives, with a smattering of politicians and union leaders, from the U.S., Europe, and Japan.)[62]

Some Trilateral Commission working papers posed the choices very starkly: either people will have to accept less or corporations will have to accept less. Corporations obviously want more. The problem is that people are also demanding more, not less, especially from their governments.

This has made it much more difficult for the corporations to shape public policy to their own ends. After World War II, as one working paper puts it, "[President] Truman had been able to govern the country

Fig. 1.4

Could You Make Ends Meet on These Salaries?

In 1980, a magazine surveyed 508 top executives in 252 of the largest U.S. companies.

Their average total compensation per year was only **$983,676.**

Here are the top 20, listed by company and total compensation (in $ millions).

Company	Total Compensation (in millions)
Cabot	$3.330
NL Industries	3.225
Exxon	3.060
Union Pacific	3.054
Union Oil of Calif.	3.026
General Dynamics	3.012
Union Pacific	2.798
Standard Oil (Ind.)	2.587
MCA (Universal Picts.)	2.467
NL Industries	2.369
Union Pacific	2.061
Rockwell International	2.029
Esmark	1.961
Standard Oil (Ind.)	1.889
Hughes Tool	1.870
AMAX	1.701
Shell Oil	1.700
Time	1.682
Atlantic Richfield	1.613
Cabot	1.551

Total compensation includes salary, bonus, and long-term income.

Source: See note #61

with the cooperation of a relatively small number of Wall Street lawyers and bankers." By the end of the 1960s, the paper despaired, "this was no longer possible." There was "too much democracy." That has meant, from the corporate point of view, too little "governability." The government must find a way, the report concludes, to exercise more control. And that will undoubtedly have to involve curtailing the democratic rights of "major economic groups."[63]

This wavering commitment to democracy reappears whenever business leaders talk among themselves. At one series of corporate leadership conferences in 1974-75, business executives were remarkably candid about their political views. A sampling of quotations captures their concerns: "I think we are long overdue for a serious examination and major overhaul of our system of government." "A representative democracy has never worked in the history of the world and we are seeing that here." "Dolts have taken over the power structure and the capacity of the nation in the U.S...." "Can we still afford one man, one vote?" "We are in serious trouble. We need to question the system itself: one man, one vote."[64]

Sony . . . the One and Only

Two journalists covering the conferences later summarized the prevailing mood. "A number of executives spoke vaguely of the need for 'war-time discipline,' and 'a more controlled society.' " They wrote: "While the critics of business worry about the atrophy of American democracy, the concern in the nation's boardrooms is precisely the opposite. For an executive, democracy in America is working too well— *that is the problem.*"[65]

ARE WE IN A REAL ECONOMIC CRISIS?

"What are we going to do? Put all our kids to work at Burger King? Or take in each other's washing?"
> —chief official, AFL-CIO, 1980[66]

"It's funny money. I feel uneasy. It brings to mind the things that happened in this country in the 1920s and the upheavals that occurred in other countries."
> —housewife in New York, 1980[67]

It's obvious that corporate leaders have been speaking from both sides of their mouths. One side flatters while the other condemns. One side promises prosperity while the other insists that working people bear the burden of sacrifice. One side brags about freedom in the United States while the other side privately considers dismantling our democratic rights.

Many of us listen to the corporate double talk and conclude that corporations are nothing but rip-off artists. They're obviously speaking with forked tongues so they can grab a bigger share of the pie.

They clearly want a bigger share of the pie. But they've always been greedy. Why did they move to the attack with such renewed force in the mid-1970s?

There is an available answer which many people in the U.S. are taking more and more seriously. It may be that there is a major *economic crisis* underway which has been threatening everyone's interests—including the corporations. If this were true, then corporations would be tryng to protect themselves against further erosions in their own positions.

What is an "economic crisis"? And how do we know if we're in one?

In more stable periods, the economy goes up and down as if it were riding a small roller coaster. These ups and downs are usually called "business cycles." The ups are called "booms" and the downs are called "recessions." One of the main characteristics of these short business cycles is that our lives don't change very much *before* and *after* the cycle. Most of us get our jobs back. We live in the same places. We get our food from the same stores. The same collective bargaining rules apply. The government uses the same laws and pursues the same kinds of policies.

In other times, periods of what we call "crisis," the economy goes through a different kind of process. Everything seems like it's disintegrating. Social relationships begin to dissolve. When and if the economy recovers, it looks very different than it did before the crisis. Those of us who are old enough to remember can compare the American economy after the Great Depression and World War II with the way it looked and felt during the 1920s. It was substantially different. Hardly any major institutions worked in the same way as before. (One of the most important changes, of course, was the formation of the major industrial unions, like the autoworkers' and steelworkers' unions. Collective bargaining would never be the same.)

If that is what makes an "economic crisis," then there are many hints that we're in the middle of a crisis...because there are important changes in our basic economic, social, and political relationships going on all around us. Some have already begun to touch our lives.

■ Unions have been forced to make major bargaining concessions for the first time since they consolidated their power after World War II. "Everybody voted for it," as one local member explained a recent giveback. "It's just a matter of survival."[68]

■ Entire communities have experienced the earthquake tremors of plant shutdown and relocation—forcing many to abandon their homes and neighborhoods in search of work. The earth seems to be shifting beneath us.

■ Many have found that college is no longer the yellow brick road to fame and fortune. College costs have soared. College graduates have had more and more trouble finding work. The yellow brick road goes

nowhere. It's being replaced, as one citizen commission observed in 1980, by a "way of life that worships wealth and power and makes economic profit the arbiter of all human values."[69]

■ We have long prided ourselves on our democratic system. But some of that has changed as well. In 1974-75, for example, a private group of bankers determined that New York City finances should be controlled by a special committee called the Emergency Financial Control Board (EFCB). Were the board members elected? No. Did they represent the people? All three "public" representatives on the board had business backgrounds.[70]

Explaining widespread concessions to business in another context, a member of the Detroit City Council concluded: "I think we are so desperate for jobs we will do anything. We are trapped. The multi-national corporations are doing the economic planning for the world."[71]

There are many more examples like these. They all tell the same kind of story. Big changes are taking place. The stakes are high. Many of the changes directly threaten our interests.

Corporations reached these conclusions ahead of most of the rest of us. They've been pushing hard for more control because they've been struggling to protect their own interests during what they perceive as a time of economic crisis. "The American capitalist system is confronting its darkest hour," as one executive put it recently.[72] "We are tumbling on the brink," another said.[73] "In the dictionary sense," the chairman of General Motors said recently, "a crisis means a moment for decision....I think the business community—at least in America—has come to such a moment."[74]

Most of the rest of us have finally joined them. In a recent poll of U.S. adults conducted in November 1981, 61% agreed that "the economy is in a real crisis." Only one-fourth thought that the crisis would be over within the next two years. And more than 60% concluded that our current economic problems have "fundamental" roots.[75]

PEOPLE ARE RESISTING, BUT....

"It would be necessary to go back to the 1930s and the Great Depression to find a peacetime issue that has had the country so concerned and so distraught."
—leading public opinion pollster, 1979[76]

Working people feel more and more desperate. Despite their despair, many have also been involved in struggles to resist corporate pressure and protect our own working and living conditions.

61% agree that "the economy is in real crisis"

■ Despite threats of plant shutdown and high unemployment rates, hundreds of thousands of workers have gone out on strike to demand higher wages and protect themselves against spiralling inflation.

■ Hundreds of thousands of workers have also waged wildcat strikes to protect working conditions, walking out over shaky mine walls and excessive heat in the plant.

■ Thousands of women office workers have begun to join in both unions and informal organizations to protest abuse of clerical workers and discrimination against women in hiring and promotion.

■ Scores of thousands of urban residents, particularly minority groups, have been fighting against cutbacks in public hospitals, social services, and special educational programs.

■ Older people have begun to challenge widespread age discrimination—pushing at the same time to protect social security benefits—while thousands of the handicapped have mobilized against barriers to their equal social participation on and off the job.

■ Tenant groups have been fighting rent increases and deteriorating housing conditions throughout the country, aiming to protect themselves against higher prices.

■ Both black and hispanic movements have continued to fight for affirmative action and equal opportunity in hiring and public services.

■ Coalitions of gays have organized to push for laws barring discrimination on grounds of sexual preference and to protect themselves against scapegoating in a period of crisis.

■ Community groups almost everywhere have been organizing against rip-off utility rates and the hazards of both nuclear plants and chemical wastes.

■ Many rural communities have become more and more active, fighting corporate land grabs, rampant speculation, and land abuse.

Many of these protests culminated in a huge demonstration in Washington, D.C. in September, 1981. It was called Solidarity Day. More than 400,000 came to march for unity among working people and strong actions to protect our working and living conditions against corporate and conservative assaults. The rally was sponsored by a broad coalition of labor, community, women's, and minority groups.

All of these protests and demonstrations have been fueled by rising anger. They have been spreading as the anger itself has spread. The struggles have produced many victories. But the problems persist and the real force of our numbers has not yet been harnessed.

One important limitation is that different groups have been isolated from each other. Oil workers in Texas often don't know about mineworkers' parallel struggles over health and safety conditions. Tenants' groups in California can't easily learn from the experiences of Coop City residents in New York City.

There is another, equally important explanation. It comes from the way we *think* about our problems. Our analysis tends to keep us isolated and divided. There are several important ways in which that happens.

One way is that we tend to blame *ourselves as individuals* for our own problems. Maybe my family would be better off if we managed our budget better and pinched pennies? Maybe I could get ahead if I were smarter? Or worked harder? The problem with that view is that it isolates each of us from everyone else, putting us in competition with each other. So that we can never take advantage of each other or our combined collective strength.

Another way is that we tend to blame *each other* for our problems. Consumers sometimes blame inflation on workers' wages. Native workers sometimes blame layoffs or job competition on illegal immigrant workers. Industrial workers tend to blame some of their job problems on ecologists' demands for environmental protection, while environmentalists tend to blame resistance to their demands on "short-sighted" trade unionists. Taxpayers blame rising taxes on "welfare chiselers" and municipal workers trying to protect their own working and living conditions. White men blame job problems on women and minority workers struggling for affirmative action.

The problem with this view is that we all end up fighting each other. *Every single one of us belongs to a group which someone else is blaming for its problems.* So we tend to blame back. We tend to blame everyone but the corporations and the economy.

And we can thank the corporations, in part, for these divisions.

As we saw earlier in the section on "Why We Need This Book," corporations are spending millions of dollars to create sympathy for their problems. In doing that, they direct our attention away from them and on to ourselves or others. They're the ones who tell us to do with less. ("Tighten the belt," as Warner-Swasey put it, "not the noose.") They're the ones who blame inflation on labor unions. They're the ones who say that welfare has to be cut.

Unless we begin to throw off that perspective, we shall remain isolated and divided. Our own protests will work at cross purposes with other group protests. Our individual protests will not add up.

How do we begin escaping from this rut? The DUPE perspective builds from a view of the economy. They tell us that we have no other choices because the structure of the economy permits no other choices. If we want to counter the DUPE perspective, we need to develop a common understanding of the economy—of how it works and what's wrong with it. We need to base that understanding on our own experiences as working people. We need to build from that understanding toward some common strategies for solving our problems. That old saying told it straight: United we stand and divided we fall. *If we want to lift the corporate yoke from our shoulders, we need to free our minds from the corporate perspective on the economy.* The DUPE perspective serves their interests. We need an understanding which will serve our own.

The next section of this book begins to lay a foundation for that understanding.

PART II: HOW DOES THE ECONOMY WORK?

"I don't know much about economics [but] I do know we're in serious trouble."

—former U.S. Senator[1]

"When I was a kid in Ohio, one of my favorite spots was the land along the B&O tracks, a lone spot outside the city about ten miles....These men came from every spot in the U.S. and these men had been in every spot of the U.S. Represented every type of life in the U.S.: some men college graduates, some from factories, some workers in transit, unemployed, the regular migrant worker that goes from harvest to harvest...It was amazing how much these men knew about life, because they had lived it."

—retired union organizer[4]

"People have to be educated. Poor people and working people are taught, at least by this society, that they're made to be just shit workers. You run the factories, you make our cars, while we get fat....Something is wrong."

—27-year-old community organizer[2]

"We're told that some issues are too complex for ordinary people. Bullshit. It's the best argument to delude the people....If we're gonna have democracy in this country, by God, we're gonna have to start telling people the facts."

—33-year-old environmentalist[3]

The U.S. economy is the richest and most powerful in the world. But somehow, despite all that wealth and power, most of us face crippling economic problems. Many of us work harder and harder just to stay in place. It feels as if our tires are spinning on ice.

How can we deal with our economic problems more successfully? How can we effectively improve our working and living conditions?

The next seven chapters take the first necessary steps toward answering those questions by reviewing *how the economy works.* If we learn more about its operations, we can improve our chances of making it work for us.

Chapter 2 on **"What is Capitalism?"** begins with a brief look at the basic features of our economy. One of the problems with the Dominant (Unofficial) Perspective on the Economy—what we're calling the DUPE for short—is that it presents a superficial portrait of the economy, sketching it selectively, ignoring much of what matters most. When we are careful to study every aspect of our economic structure, we find a much more complicated picture than the DUPE pushers portray. Where do we turn next? We saw in Chapter 1 that working people in the United States face three main economic problems—*making ends meet, deteriorating working conditions* and *declining quality of life.* Chapters 3, 4 and 5 explore the sources of each of these problems in further detail:

■ Working people have more and more problems making ends meet. But every time we demand more, we're told that profits deserve higher priority. We keep bumping into the importance of corporate wealth and profits. Chapter 3 pursues a simple question: **"Where Do Profits Come From?"**

■ We also face hazard and harrassment on the job. When we protest, we confront corporate influence through their control over production. We work for them and they tell us what to do. Although we often resist, their control gives them great advantages. Chapter 4 on **"Bosses vs. Workers"** asks a second simple question: how and why do corporations control working people on the job?

■ We experience a third problem— declining quality of life. Prices soar and we face the constant threat of damage and disease from chemicals, radioactivity, and a hundred other dangers. This insecurity is brought to us by its prime sponsor, the *market.* Chapter 5 on **"The Money Go-Round"** asks a third set of important questions. How does the market work? Why does it promote insecurity? Can we tame it?

The economy doesn't stand still, waiting idly for us to solve these three critical problems. It changes constantly. How do those changes affect our ability to solve our problems? Will they make it easier to begin improving our own working and living conditions? Chapter 6 on **"Bigger, Bigger,...and Better?"** traces the paths along which the economy changes. It asks whether the economy will reduce our problems as it changes—or compound them.

At that point, we'll finally be ready to mark our score cards. The economy isn't performing well now. Can we make it work better as it is...or do we have to make some basic changes in its operations? The final two chapters of this section pursue those questions: Chapter 7 asks, **"Will the Economy Solve Our Problems?"** Chapter 8 on **"Can't the Government Fix It?"** looks at whether or not the government can improve the economy, making it serve our interests more effectively.

2.

What is Capitalism?

The U.S. economy is a vast and complicated system. There are millions of households and millions of business enterprises. People work in all kinds of different jobs and live in all kinds of different communities. Products pass through thousands of hands on their marathon journey from seller to buyer to seller to buyer....

How do we make sense out of this complex network of economic activity? Where do we begin learning how the economy works?

Who makes our American Economic System work?

Business? Labor? Government? Investors? Consumers? Most people don't know.

The shocking fact is that less than 3% of people quizzed in a recent study could define the roles of all these groups in our American Economic System.

Even most businessmen, educators and thought leaders lacked basic understanding. Why the concern?

In the months and years ahead, we're all going to be called upon to make great decisions as our system adjusts to new conditions everywhere, both home and abroad.

And, if we don't understand the basic functions of our system, how can we decide what to keep, what to change?

That's why we're offering a new booklet that explains the American Economic System. It is easy to read, interesting—and free.

Every American ought to know what it says.

The American Economic System.
It's one of your basic freedoms.

"Economics" Pueblo, Colorado 81009
Please send me a free copy of the booklet about our economic system.

Name
Address
City
State   Zip

AMERICAN ECONOMIC SYSTEM CAMPAIGN
MAGAZINE AD NO. AES-2845-76 — 7" x 10" (110 Screen)
Volunteer Agency: Compton Advertising, Inc. Volunteer Coordinator: William A. Bartel, Vice President, Celanese Corp.

WORK HARDER AND QUIT COMPLAINING?

The DUPE tells us not to bother with such complicated questions. If we don't like our economic lives, the DUPE pushers suggest, we can take care of business ourselves. And if we can solve our problems on our own, they conclude, why should we worry about the economic maze surrounding us?

Got Money Problems?

"Look, I know it's nobody's fault but mine that I got stuck where I am. I mean...if I'd applied myself, I know I got it in me to be different, can't say anyone did it to me."

—sanitation worker in Boston[1]

"This was the American Dream. This is what my father was always pounding into my head...the big office, the big car, the big house....[So now I feel] I'm a flop because of what I've come to....'You're a bum'—this is the picture I have of myself."

—30-year-old former salesworker[2]

The DUPE provides us with a simple manual for solving our problems. It suggests two basic guidelines.

First, we should quit complaining and take responsibility for our own lives. "I think people, individuals, should look at themselves," a corporate executive suggested in a recent interview.[3] How does one succeed in our economy? "Through hard work, ingenuity, thrift, and luck," replies the Gospel according to DUPE.[4] *Ask not what our country can do for us*, the DUPE implores, *but ask what we can do for ourselves*. Until we have exhausted our own remedies, we have no right to expect help from others.

Second, we can improve our working and living conditions simply by studying and working harder. Need more money? "The worker who steadily learns more," as Warner and Swasey Co. puts it in a recent ad, "will always earn more." Want a higher standard of living? "It's only too true that many people do not have...luxuries," Warner and Swasey replies. "That's what education and ambition are for—to help earn them."[5] In short, we should become more productive. Got an economic problem? Get a better job. Can't get a better job? So it goes.

Work harder and quit complaining? The conclusion seems harsh. But we hear the message repeated so many times, its logic begins to seem inescapable. According to one poll in the 1970s, more than 80% of people in the U.S. agreed that "whenever I fail, I have no one to blame but myself."[6]

Either we make it or we don't. Since we earn what we deserve, we deserve what we earn. These conclusions reverberate throughout our daily lives.

> **"You didn't get this just through a friend. You got it through hard work and that's the only way you're gonna get it."**
>
> —48-year-old construction worker[7]

> **"If only I had what it takes, things would have been different."**
>
> —young shoe salesworker[8]

Working Harder Isn't Enough

The problem with the DUPE advice is not so much that it's harsh but that it's much too simplistic. The DUPE is misleading because it leaves out nearly as much about our economy as it includes.

The DUPE booklet summarizes the analysis underlying this formula for self-improvement: "We earn income by applying our skills, efforts, and resources to some productive purpose and being paid for it... We produce goods and services for others—and income for ourselves."[9] In a nutshell, the DUPE suggests that we earn more if we work harder or move into more productive jobs.

One strand of the analysis is obviously correct: some U.S. workers earn more than others because they have jobs which pay more. But that obvious fact is only part of the picture. For many people in the United States, income is *not* directly proportional to the work we do. Three important examples help illustrate the incompleteness of the DUPE analysis:

1. *Many people do almost exactly the same kind of work but receive different incomes from their jobs*—not because they apply themselves to more or less "productive purposes" but simply because they are different people. These differences exist throughout the economy. They are sketched in Figure 2.1 on this page. It compares the median earnings of different groups of workers by race and by sex who worked full-time during 1969 throughout the year, were the same age, had the same level of education, and *worked at the same kind of job*. As nearly as we can tell from the data, they were applying themselves to the same "productive purposes." The differences in their incomes were striking:

Among computer specialists, women earned only $9,403 in 1969

Fig. 2.1

Equal Pay for Equal Work? (The 1970 Story)

The salary figures compare earnings for workers (by race or by sex) who worked full-time during 1969 throughout the same year, were the same age, had the same level of education, and worked at the same kind of job.

Source: See note #10

while men earned $12,613. Female factory operatives had median earnings only 54% of male earnings in that occupation. Black men working as retail salesmen and sales clerks earned less than three-quarters of what white men earned doing the same work. Hispanic printing craftsmen received only seven-eighths of what white men in the same occupation received. Black women working as sales workers earned 13% less than white women sales-workers.[10]

Why do diffferent people get different wages for the same work? Can women and minority workers count on improving their incomes simply by working harder?

2. *There are millions of workers who have steady jobs but never receive any income for their work.* Housewives, in particular, spend at least 40 to 50 hours a week working around the house.[11] They earn no money for their labor. The work is difficult and "productive." But still no income. And the non-payment isn't because women "love" to do extra work around the house for nothing. Many women hate housework and many men and children also make important "productive contri-butions" in the home. Still no pay.

This work is obviously significant. If houseworkers were actually paid for the jobs they perform at wage levels for comparable work, economists estimate that they would have earned at least $350 billion in 1980.[12] Why are so many workers paid nothing for such valuable labor? How much good will it do housewives if they work harder and quit complaining?

3. *Some people get loads of money even though they don't do any work for it at all.* Almost 22% of all personal income received by U.S.households each year is "property income." It goes to people who own stocks or their own businesses, rent their real estate, or receive interest on loans they've made. In 1980, this property income amounted to almost $475 billion.[13] The wealthiest households in the country earn so much of this property income that they don't have to "hold down a job" at all. (Internal Revenue Service data for 1978 show that millionaires earned only 15% of their total incomes from wages and salaries.[14]) Most of these wealthy households receive money whether they spend time "working" for it or not. What explains their easy times? What "productive service" do they contribute? Why do they earn so much while doing so little?

These examples show that the DUPE rule about jobs and income is much too simple. 1) Some people do the same job and earn different incomes for their work. 2) Others work very hard and earn nothing for those tasks. 3) A smaller group—they happen to be the wealthiest people in the country—earn most of their income whether or not they put in any hours working.

And these exceptions are obviously not trivial. Women and minority workers now receive nearly a third of all wage-and-salary income. Unpaid household work and property income combined were equiva-lent in 1980 to about $750 billion. Taken together, these three cases accounted for almost exactly *half* of all personal income received in the United States in 1980.[15]

A general rule which works no more than half the time is clearly

Beats the Hell Outta Working

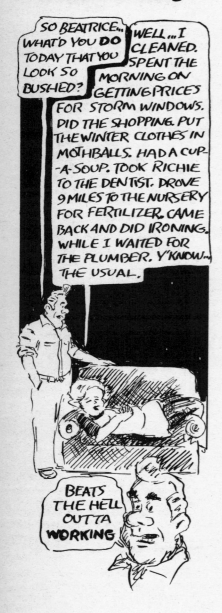

SO BEATRICE... WHAT'D YOU DO TODAY THAT YOU LOOK SO BUSHED?

WELL...I CLEANED. SPENT THE MORNING ON GETTING PRICES FOR STORM WINDOWS. DID THE SHOPPING. PUT THE WINTER CLOTHES IN MOTHBALLS. HAD A CUP--A-SOUP. TOOK RICHIE TO THE DENTIST. DROVE 9 MILES TO THE NURSERY FOR FERTILIZER. CAME BACK AND DID IRONING. WHILE I WAITED FOR THE PLUMBER. Y'KNOW... THE USUAL.

BEATS THE HELL OUTTA WORKING

incomplete. The DUPE prescription about jobs and income distorts too many important situations for us to trust in its simple suggestion that we should work harder and quit complaining.

This means that we have a tough job ahead. If we can't rely on the DUPE manual, we will have to create one of our own. We will need to develop a much more complete picture of our economy than the DUPE pushers provide.

WHAT IS AN ECONOMY?

The DUPE definition of our economic system can be summarized in a single sentence: "Capitalism refers to a market economy," as the DUPE booklet puts it, "with resources owned primarily by private individuals and groups."[16] Nothing more. Nothing less.

The problem with this definition is that it does not directly answer a number of economic questions which we have already seen to be very important. Who does the basic work in the economy? How is work divided among various groups of people? Who reaps the fruits of that labor? How do we satisfy our needs in the home? Does everyone benefit equally from our work? We need to develop a much richer analysis of the economy in order to address these basic concerns.

What Tasks Does an Economy Perform?

Most of us work for someone else—for a wage or salary—or else live in a household which depends on wage and salary income. Most of us also work in our own households, doing tasks without pay. One kind of work involves us in a *wage economy* at the factory or office. The other involves us in a *household economy* at home. The two kinds of economies operate in very different ways, but both fulfill certain basic economic needs.

In order to survive from day to day and year to year, we must all find ways of producing the basic things we need. We must all eat, and we all need clothes and shelter. These kinds of necessities are called the *means of physical subsistence.*

People also typically decide that some things are "necessary" even though they aren't strictly required for physical survival. We in the United States seem to need a television set even though we could

---

A general rule which works no more than half the time is clearly incomplete.

---

probably "survive" without one. The Nambikwara Indians of the Amazon must paint their bodies even though they could live if they didn't. These kinds of necessities can be called the *means of cultural subsistence.* They provide us with a way of identifying ourselves and lending meaning to our lives.

People live together in families, tribes, clans, villages, cities, nations—in some kind of *society.* Societies assume the basic burdens of subsistence. A society must find a way of *producing* the means of physical and cultural subsistence. It must also find a way of *distributing* these means of subsistence among its members so that everyone will be able to survive.

A society achieves these tasks of production and distribution through its *economy.* An economy is a way of producing and distributing the goods and services people need to survive. This suggests that we need to explore three basic questions if we want to understand how an economy works:

1) How does an economy distribute the means of producing these goods and services among its members?

2) How does it divide up the work that needs to be done?

3) How does it distribute the products of that labor?

We review these questions in the following paragraphs and then summarize our answers on page 29 with an "Economic Checklist" for studying how different economies work—especially our own.

The Means of Cultural Subsistence

1. Wealth and the Means of Production

Throughout history people have always used some of the things they produce to help make more things later on. We've used some of our labor to make plows to help with future corn production. Or looms to help with future shirt production. Or trucks to aid in future car distribution. Those things which are not consumed from day to day and have obvious social value are called *wealth.* Some of the wealth in an economy, such as tools and machines, has value because it helps produce the means of physical subsistence. Other wealth—gold crowns, body paint and television studios—has value because it helps produce the means of cultural subsistence. The wealth which is used to produce goods and sevices is called the *means of production.*

Who has control over the wealth a society produces? What determines which people get to use the land and tools and trucks and factories and offices?

a) *Control of Wealth.* Throughout history, societies have regulated access to the means of production in two very different ways.

In many societies, people have controlled the wealth together. These economies have used a system of **common-wealth** or **common**

property. *No one in the society could be excluded from the use of social wealth or from access to it.* In the Middle Ages, for instance, villagers held much of the land in common. Everyone was entitled to farm some strips of that land. In the early U.S. colonies, many villages had "common greens" or "commons" on which every village family had the right to graze its cows. Even in the United States today, some social wealth is enjoyed in common. No one can be excluded from most of our highways, for example, and everyone in our households is entitled to use the household tools for cleaning and cooking. (Many women only wish that men and children would put that household wealth to work a little more often.)

Other societies have used a system of **private property** to distribute social wealth. Some individuals or groups have had *exclusive* control over at least some of the total wealth of their societies. When they have "owned" land or tools or parks, they have had the right to prevent everyone else from using them. In slave societies, for example, plantation owners privately controlled their slaves; neither other plantation owners nor the slaves themselves could use this "social wealth" to produce for their own consumption.

b) *How Equally is Wealth Shared?* When economies have private property, it makes a great difference how that wealth is distributed. Some economies with private property have shared the wealth quite **equally.** In colonial New England, for example, four-fifths of the households owned at least some land and seven-eighths owned at least some tools for production.[17] This meant that almost everyone could produce much of what she or he needed and didn't have to depend too much on others. At the other extreme, many economies with private property have shared the wealth very **unequally.** In slave economies, for instance, the largest group of people—the slaves themselves— owned almost nothing; the masters owned nearly everything and therefore controlled access to the means of production.

2. The Division of Labor

No society can last more than a few days unless at least some people spend time in production. Even if food grows wild, someone has to pick it. But who does the work? And how are decisions about work made?

a) *Within Worksites.* The first place to look is at the "point of production"—the location where the work actually takes place. Almost every economy has a characteristic worksite—a peasant household, a factory, a slave plantation. The basic rules of production apply at this level.

In some economies, people have **shared** work at the worksite. Everyone contributed at least some of her or his time and energy to the basic tasks of production. In some primitive economies, everyone helped produce food, shelter, and clothing together. In early U.S. farming households, men, women, and children all shared in the chores around the farm; no one escaped work unless he or she were somehow unable to work because of age or disability.

In many other economies, people have not shared labor within worksites. Instead, some have **controlled** the labor of others. Many

people have toiled while others—their bosses—have not worked. Slaves worked under the control of plantation owners; the masters never lifted a hoe. Feudal serfs often worked a couple of days a week on their lords' land; the lords plotted and intrigued against each other while the serfs did the work that supported them all.

Why have workers been willing to continue under that kind of control? Usually the bosses have rooted their power in some kind of control over *the means of production*. Plantation masters owned their slaves as well as their land, for example, and could legally order the workers to do whatever they wanted. If the workers refused, the master could starve them, whip them, or jail them.

Bosses have also usually developed highly-structured *systems of labor management* to help control—by carrot or by stick—their recalcitrant workers. Even on slave plantations, for example, masters relied on elaborate methods for prodding their slaves in the fields.[18]

b) *Among Worksites*. In many economies, people don't produce everything they need within a single worksite. Auto makers in the U.S. economy get steel from one set of factories, for instance, and tires from another. How is work divided among different worksites?

Many people throughout history have made **cooperative** production decisions. Different worksites have directly planned the division of labor among themselves. In the United States in the early nineteenth century, one household farm might raise pigs. Another farm might raise corn. They would exchange products—the first farm's pigs eating the second farm's corn and the second farm getting some of the pork later on. *This division of tasks was planned in advance.* Each worksite relied on the other and knew more or less how much product it would get. They cooperated consciously in allocating their labor.

Many other economies have made **disconnected** decisions among units of production. Each factory or household or farm makes whatever and however much it wants to at the time. Its decisions are largely independent of other units' decisions. Auto companies in the U.S. don't know for sure that steel and tire companies will make what they need, and the suppliers have no guarantee that the car manufacturers will buy everything they produce. Each unit relies on an impersonal exchange through a market to buy or sell what it needs. *There is no conscious advance planning among units of production.* Instead of getting together to make cooperative decisions, the various units of production don't get together at all.

3. The Distribution of Products

No matter how many products people in a society make, they won't be able to survive for more than a few days if they can't get hold of the basic goods and services they need. How do economies divide their products among their members?

In some economies, distribution is fairly simple. In hunting and gathering societies, for example, each family can do the same kind of work and make the same kinds of things. Each can be largely self-sufficient if it chooses.

Even in these societies, some trade takes place anyway. Some people—such as infants, or the aged, or the infirm—will always be unable to help themselves completely. Everyone else will have to pitch in to help support them. *This kind of distribution requires some rules.*

Almost every society also involves at least some specialization of labor among worksites. Some people make more of one product than they need and trade some of their surplus for other products they need. They may make their deals directly, at bazaars, in stores, through computers...however they can. *These exchanges also require rules for distribution.*

When societies make these rules for distribution, they must address three main questions: a) Who gets at least a share of what is produced? b) How much of the social product do individual households receive? c) What means of exchange will people use when they make trades?

a) *Who Gets a Share?* There have been two main methods throughout history for establishing who gets at least a share of what is produced.

Many economies have distributed their product through **mutuality.** The exchange is mutual because everyone who gets some of the product *also* contributes in some way to producing it. Those who don't produce don't get. These mutual systems still exist in many parts of the world. And they also operate in many of our own homes in the United States. Although most U.S. households don't own many means of production, there is still a kind of mutual economy in which household members work and share wages. Some household members, especially adult women, do a great deal of unpaid work in the home. Some work for money outside the home. Some people don't work now or work much less. Everyone eats (more or less) together. Eventually, those who don't work now may help support the others later on and share in household work more fully. The circle of mutuality will be closed.

Many other economies have relied on methods for distribution involving **exploitation.** Some members get a share of the products *even though they have not contributed to basic production and even though those who* *make the products have not freely agreed to share them.* Through this exploitative relationship, those who make the products must ultimately surrender a share to those who haven't worked.

How does this kind of exploitation happen? Sometimes the non-workers take products by force. (Pirates have always operated this way.) More typically, non-workers have taken a share of the products *because they have controlled the means of production.* In Europe during the Middle Ages, a peasant usually spent half of his or her time working for the local lord.[19] The peasant did all the work, but the lord got at least as much of the product as the peasant. The lords maintained this privileged position because they controlled most of the land. They were able to use this power to force the peasants to turn over a large portion of the food they raised themselves.

b) *How Much Do Households Receive?* To each according to his or her needs? Economies have also differed in determining how much product individual households receive. What rules apply?

Some economies have based the division of their products at least partly on **need.** Some households get more food than others because they have more mouths to feed. In many European countries, for example, families get a special allowance from the government for each child they have, allowing larger families to claim a larger share of total social product than smaller families.

Other economies pay little or no attention to family need in distributing products. These economies distribute products according to **power over resources.** Each household's share of products depends on *how much income or wealth it controls,* not on how much it needs to get by. Feudal lords' families got lots of food in the Middle Ages because they controlled the land, not because they had lots of children. Peasant families with many children never got special treatment when the lords' agents came around to pick up the feudal rent. Need didn't matter.

c) *Means of Exchange.* When people secure products through some kind of market, they usually have to "pay" for the products with something. What do they use as a means of exchange?

People have sometimes relied on direct **barter.** They have directly traded goods, with each party giving up a useful good or service in exchange for something it wants for its own consumption. Cows for lumber. Corn for cloth. Comic books for baseball trading cards.

Many societies have also used a standard currency of exchange, called **money,** as means of payment. People have used beads and gold coins and paper bills and credit cards and many other forms of money. Economies which rely principally on money as a means of exchange are often called *market* economies. What matters is that some standard currency be widely accepted so that people can agree on prices for different products in terms of those money units. When people have secured *most* of what they need for subsistence through the market, we say that those economies have relied on **commodity exchange.** What matters is that people end up acquiring the largest part of what they need through impersonal relations in the market—coated with a veneer of dollar signs—rather than through direct social relationships.

An "Economic Checklist"

This review provides us with the ingredients we need for studying the U.S. and other economies. We now know where to focus our attention and what to look for. Figure 2.2 on this page provides a summary checklist which we can apply to any economy in order to inspect (and reject?) its basic characteristics.

Fig. 2.2

An Economic Checklist... Or, What the DUPE Ignores

Economic Issues	Possible Ways of Organizing an Economy	
1. Wealth & the Means of Production?		
a) Who Controls Them?	*Common Wealth*	*or Private Property*
b) How Equally?	*Equally*	*or Unequally*
2. The Division of Labor?		
a) Control Within Worksites?	*Shared Work*	*or Controlled Work*
b) Decisions among Worksites?	*Coordinated*	*or Disconnected*
3. Distribution of Products?		
a) Who Gets a Share?	*Mutuality*	*or Exploitation*
b) How Much of a Share?	*By Need*	*or By Power over Resources*
c) With What Means of Exchange?	*Barter/Social Relations*	*or Market Exchange/ Commodity Exchange*

The list may seem somewhat long, but every item on the checklist is crucial. We saw earlier that the DUPE analysis ignores some basic questions about our economy. We can now see why. The DUPE definition of capitalism, presented on page 23, concentrates on only two of the six dimensions on the checklist—on distribution with money as the means of payment and on private property ownership. This preoccupation with market exchange and private property misses more than half the boat.

WHAT IS U.S. CAPITALISM?

How is the U.S. economy organized? Is there one economy, or many? How do we weigh the importance of big businesses and small, of private and public sectors, of households, factories, and offices? Once again, where do we begin?

One easy way of sharpening our focus is to glance quickly at our economic history. The U.S. economy has not always worked the way it does now. When we look back at its development since the American Revolution, we find that one kind of economy—what we'll call capitalism—has steadily expanded its influence. Tracing the historical emergence of capitalism in the United States helps highlight its most important features. (It will also begin to give us some practice in applying our economic checklist.)

The Early United States Economy

Around 1800, there were three main economic systems in the U.S. One belonged to the Native Americans. A second was the slave economy in the south. The third was the family farm economy mostly located in New England and the mid-Atlantic states.[20]

The Native American economy was eventually destroyed by frontierspeople and the U.S. Army. The slave and family economies provided the soil from which our present economy grew.

Southern Slavery. In 1800, when the "new nation" was still young, there were more than four million people in the United States. Almost 900,000 were slaves.[21] They lived on plantations and smaller farms throughout the south. Their masters were entitled to use (and abuse) the slaves in any way they chose. Most plantations grew cotton or tobacco and also produced most of the other products they needed, including food. Our checklist helps outline the structure of this slave economy.[22]

1. Control over social wealth was based on private property, since masters could exclude others from use of their slaves. And that wealth was obviously distributed unequally, since the slaves owned virtually nothing, poor whites owned a little, and plantation owners controlled everything else.

2. Work was hardly shared; the masters' foremen hovered over the slaves constantly, occasionally resorting to the biting crack of their whips. And since plantations were largely self-sufficient, there was little division of labor among worksites. Cotton and tobacco planting was not coordinated, so this aspect of the slave economy involved disconnected production.

3. How were products divided? Within the plantations, masters gained their shares of social product through exploitation of their slaves. The distribution of products between masters and slaves depended on power over resources, but the distribution of goods *among* the slaves depended partly on need—on the size of slaves' families or the individual slaves' physical needs for calories and clothing.

Within the plantations, people rarely used money in the exchange and distribution of products. But the plantations were also involved in trade with the outside world. Their size and power depended on the external demand for tobacco and cotton. These products were sold through commodity exchange in the market. Most of the ports in the south were piled high, as a contemporary observed in 1814, "with mountains of Cotton, and all your stores, ships, steam and canal boats [were] crammed with and groaning under the weight of Cotton...."[23] The masters' dependence on the cotton trade tied their fates to external markets almost as tightly as their slaves were bound to them.

Family Farming. There was another kind of economy throughout most of the rest of the eastern United States which consisted of family farms in the southern, mid-Atlantic and New England states. These farms produced by themselves almost everything they needed for physical subsistence. They had their own rules for regulating their economic production and distribution.[24]

1. In the family farms of 1800, social wealth was controlled through a system of private property. But, in contrast to the plantation economy, as we have already noted, wealth was distributed fairly equally. Most farms were roughly the same size. Most farmers owned their own tools and storage facilities. And there was even some

property which people owned jointly—holding it in common—such as tools and barns or common mills for processing grain.

2. The division of labor was based on a "family labor" system. Work was mostly shared. Everyone in the family participated in necessary tasks. Children began working by the time they were old enough to haul a pail and pull a hoe. Older people continued tending animals until they could scarcely walk. There were few bosses.

One way in which the labor was controlled, not shared, was that men had ultimate authority within the families. To both women and children, they acted at least partly as "bosses," using their authority to avoid some of the more menial tasks and to spend less time at work than most adult women.

The division of labor among units of production was usually organized on a cooperative basis. "When there was a job beyond the family's capacity—the raising of a house or a barn—", as one economic historian writes, "the neighbors turned to and made it a community enterprise."[25] This cooperation was planned in advance so that farmers could set aside several days for the collective project. When emergencies struck, such as lightning hitting a barn, everyone pulled together as quickly and cooperatively as possible.

3. Within the families, the distribution of products was based primarily on mutuality, since everyone shared in the work. The division of product largely reflected need. Growing children got more milk than others. Larger people ate more. Those who wore out their clothes most quickly in their work had first claim on new clothing.

Within the family, finally, people used little money. Among families, people sometimes used money as a means of payment and sometimes relied on barter. Even when money was the means of payment, it did not dominate the relationships of exchange; these were not yet families dependent on commodity exchange.

Capitalism Emerges

These two kinds of economies now appear remote. Early battles over slavery, leading up to the Civil War, seem like ancient history. And self-sufficient family farms have been disappearing constantly ever since; there are now fewer than two million left in the economy.[26]

Between 1800 and the Civil War, a new kind of economy began gradually to replace these two older systems. Three critical changes began to transform the economic terrain.

Private Property, Unequally Distributed. Both on the family farms and on the plantations, private property was the major form of control over wealth. Capitalism arose first in the north, growing out of the family farm system. As it emerged, *the distribution of that (privately-owned) wealth became substantially more unequal.*

At the time of the American Revolution, as we have seen, most people owned their own property; they were mostly independent of others. Figure 2.3 on the next page shows that the vast majority of people—the least affluent 90% of families in New England and the middle colonies—owned well over *half* of all personal wealth.[27]

By 1870, the emergence of capitalism had eroded much of that independence. Many fewer people controlled their own wealth. The

Fig. 2.3
More Pie for the Rich

1774 — Top 10% **45%** — Other 90% **55%**

1870 — Top 10% **66%** — Other 90% **34%**

1962 — Top 10% **67%** — Other 90% **33%**

The pies show the percentage of total personal wealth controlled by the wealthiest 10% of households and the remaining 90% of households in the U.S.

Source: See note #27

Fig. 2.4
So Long to the Self-Employed

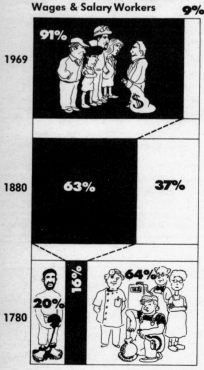

Wages & Salary Workers

1969 — **91%** — 9%

1880 — **63%** — 37%

1780 — Slaves **20%** — 16% — Self-Employed **64%**

Slaves   Self-Employed

The percentages show the share of the U.S. labor force in each of the three main labor force categories.

Source: See note #28.

least affluent 90% of families now controlled only *one third* of all personal wealth. The wealthiest 10% of families had seen their share rise from 45% to *two thirds*.

A century later, that inequality in personal wealth persisted. In 1962, the wealthiest 10% still controlled about *two thirds* of all personal wealth while the least affluent 90%—the working people of the United States—still owned only a *third*.

Wage Labor and Production for Profit. The consequences of increasing inequality were dramatic. Many people lost control of their own tools and buildings. Many immigrants came to this country and were never able to achieve their dreams of economic independence. *More and more people were forced to work for somebody else—mostly for employers involved in production for profit.* Figure 2.4 on this page shows the percentage of U.S. workers who have been self-employed and the percentage who have worked for a wage or salary.[28] In 1780, only 16% of the economically active population worked for a wage or salary. By 1880, after the emergence of capitalism had altered the economic landscape, 63% had to work for wages or salaries. Less than a century later, in 1970, 91% were wage-and-salary employees and only 9% were self-employed.

Commodity Exchange. The third major trend followed directly from the second. *Growing numbers of people were no longer able to produce for themselves. This meant that they had to buy their means of subsistence in the market instead of producing them on their own.* Commodity exchange continually expanded along with the growing number of workers who depended on it.

Figure 2.5 traces this development.[29] It shows the proportions of goods manufactured *within* the household. In 1810, before the market had undercut household production, households accounted for a minimum of 36% of all manufactured goods in the United States. By 1860, as the market had expanded, household production had virtually disappeared; the best available data suggest that only 1% of all manufactured goods were produced in the household. By 1970, so few goods were produced in the home that the government had stopped keeping separate track of them.

As all the charts show, the capitalist economy was mostly in place by the end of the Civil War. It had replaced family labor and slave labor with wage labor. It had replaced two primarily self-sufficient economic systems with the wider and wider spread of commodity exchange. And these changes were both caused and accompanied by a more unequal distribution of private wealth than had prevailed on the early family farms.

What Is U.S. Capitalism Today?

A kind of family economy still survives in the United States. We all live in one kind of household or another and these households all perform important economic functions.

Our household economies also still resemble the nineteenth-century family farms in several important respects. (See the checklist on page 36 for a summary.) There is one monstrous difference, however: almost all working households own almost no significant means of production. (That's what makes us working people.) The means of production are largely controlled by profit-making corporations. This means that we must work for employers outside our households and that we are dependent upon the capitalist economy which furnishes that wage-and-salary income. Because we control so little wealth on our own, few of us can escape this dependence. For this basic reason, we reach the simple historical conclusion that *the capitalist economy now dominates our lives in the United States.*

We have seen that the emergence of this increasingly dominant capitalist economy involved more unequally distributed private property, wage labor with production for profit, and commodity exchange with money. These observations help guide our final application of the "economic checklist" to U.S. capitalism today.

1. Control of social wealth and the means of production in the United States is now based almost entirely on *private property.* Owners of wealth can exclude others from use or access; none of us has the right to wander into a Budweiser factory on weekends and brew ourselves a couple of six-packs. *Private individuals or groups control 78% of the total social wealth in the United States.*[30]

And this privately-owned wealth is divided very *unequally. Less than 1% of U.S. households—the wealthiest 400,000 households—own more than one quarter of total personal wealth. Working households—the least affluent 73 million households—own only about one third of total personal wealth.*[31]

The wealthy own even greater shares of the means of pro-

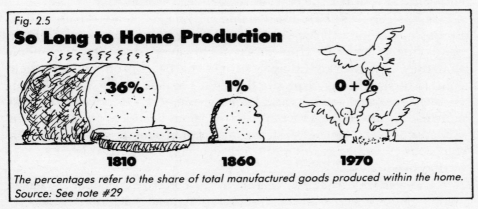

Fig. 2.5

So Long to Home Production

36% 1% 0+%

1810   1860   1970

The percentages refer to the share of total manufactured goods produced within the home.
Source: See note #29

What Is Capitalism?

duction—that part of the social wealth which is used to produce our means of subsistence. *The same 400,000 households control almost exactly half of all corporate stock in this country.* [32] Through that stock control, they monopolize the means of production.

2. This means that most of us don't own enough to produce what we need ourselves. *All we have is our ability to work.* So we must go to work for someone else. Our bosses are usually capitalists, people who are interested in producing goods in order to earn profits. When we hire out to the boss, the boss gains control over our activities inside the plant and office.

In this system, work at the point of production is *controlled*, not shared. The owners of General Motors do not share in the work of assembling autos. Instead, they control the work of their employees, however indirectly, and are able to use that control to avoid work themselves.

We can also see that work is divided among units of production on the basis of *disconnected* production decisions, not cooperative ones. Businesses don't directly coordinate their decisions with each other. Instead, they rely on the market to provide the supplies they need,

hoping that "demand" for products will bring forth enough "supply." Consumers are in the same position. (When we try to coordinate our production and distribution through food cooperatives or buying clubs, we discover how many obstacles stand in our way.) We have to sit back and wait for the market to "deliver the goods."

3. Basic shares of product depend on *exploitation*, not on mutuality. Bosses command a large share of social product because they have control over the production process. However hard they may moan that they have worked, they get their shares of product from their control of the means of production, not because they have rolled up their sleeves and joined the assembly line. (This is a controversial conclusion, of course; we pursue this issue in much more detail in Chapter 3.) Because they own the means of production, they also own the products which result and therefore gain access to at least a share of that product.

It is also clear that people's claims to a share of product are based mainly on *power over resources*, not on family need. Each household gets what it can buy in the market. The amount it can afford is limited by the amount of money it has to spend. No cash, no crops. We know that the government provides some help according to need—through welfare and food stamps, for instance. But it is equally obvious—and increasingly obvious with recent developments in government policy—that the main system of distribution disregards family need almost entirely.

We use *money* as a principal means of exchange. Both consumers and businesses depend on this system of *commodity exchange*. As consumers, we spend our incomes for products like food and cars. Businesses buy much of what they need for production through the markets. They buy steel and fuel...and workers. Barter has gone the way of the five-cent cigar.

Our checklist is complete. Figure 2.6 on the next page summarizes this review of the U.S. economy and compares it with the other economies which have played an important role in our economic history. We're now ready to sort carefully through this complex maze of economic relationships in succeeding chapters. And we can now evaluate how much difference it makes if we work with a more

complete understanding of the structure of U.S. capitalism than the narrow DUPE definition provides.

What U.S. Capitalism Isn't—A Reminder

Before proceeding further, however, we should note two important reminders.

First, capitalism is not the same thing as democracy and we must keep that distinction clear throughout our study. Capitalism is one way of organizing the *economy*. Democracy is one way of organizing the *political system*. An economy produces and distributes the means of subsistence and means of production, while a political system frames the way in which ultimate *social control*—including the means of violence centered in armies, police, and militias—is produced and distributed. It is possible to have different kinds of economic systems and political systems in combination at the same time. For example, capitalist economic systems have existed alongside fairly democratic political systems—as in the United States—and alongside repressive

Fig. 2.6
What Is
U.S. Capitalism?

Which Economy?		1. Wealth?		2. Labor?		3. Distribution?		
		a) Who Controls?	b) How Equal?	a) Within Worksites?	b) Among Worksites?	a) Who Gets Share?	b) How Much?	c) By What Means?
Early U.S.	Slave Economy	Private property	Very unequal	Controlled	Self-sufficient Some disconnected	Exploitation	By Power & Need	Market
	Family Economy	Mostly private Some common	Fairly equal	Shared with some (male control)	Self-sufficient Some coordinated	Mutuality (under male control)	By Need	Some barter Some market
U.S. Today	Household Economy	Mostly private Some common	Equal within Unequal among	Mostly shared	Disconnected	Mutuality (under male control)	By Need	Some barter Some market
	Capitalist Economy	Private property	Very unequal	Controlled	Disconnected	Exploitation	By Power	Commodity exchange

totalitarian regimes—as in Nazi Germany and Fascist Japan. As we examine our economic system, therefore, we must remember that we are not yet studying our political system. When we turn to an investigation of the relationships between capitalism and democracy in Chapter 12, we will finally consider the organization of politics as well.

Second, when we study capitalism we are studying more than just the "American way of life." Though we shall focus primarily on how the U.S. economy works, we must constantly remember that capitalism is an *international* system, not confined to this country alone. Its relationships extend around the world, linking people in the United States with people in many different countries. We can't solve our problems by studying them in one country. We need to scan the entire globe.

CAPITALISM—FOR BETTER OR WORSE?

Now that we've got capitalism, can we live with it for better or worse? Can we make that system serve our needs?

Different groups of people are beginning to have different responses to those questions. As we saw in "Why We Need This Book", many working people are beginning to blame big business for our problems while large corporations are spending millions to convince us that capitalism can promise salvation. How do we begin evaluating these different responses to U.S. capitalism?

It turns out that both groups agree about where we should start. Everyone seems to feel that *profits* are the major issue.

On our side, working people want more of social wealth to help meet our urgent household needs. And that leads us to question the amounts which corporations earn in profits. Recent polls suggest that people think big business rips us off. One survey found that a "majority of Americans want the government to put a ceiling on corporate profits."[32] Another series of surveys found that the percentage of U.S.

people who think that "business strikes a fair balance between profits and the public interest" plummeted from 70% in 1968 to only 20% in 1974.[33]

Meanwhile, corporations are insisting that profits aren't high enough. "If the public continues to believe that American industry is making a killing," one corporation has argued in a full-page ad, "that belief will lead inevitably to bad legislation which will stifle free enterprise....Without profit everybody loses."[34] Mobil Oil echoed these arguments in a recent corporate pamphlet: "The belief that business has prospered in recent years while individuals have suffered simply is not true....What a lot of people find difficult to swallow is that corporate earnings have to rise substantially above those of recent years if our country is not to get into even deeper trouble."[35]

Which view of profits is right? We need to understand where profits come from and why our views of the economy revolve so tightly around them.

Where do Profits Come From?

"There are too many billionaires."

—22-year-old worker[1]

"I would go to the store. I would see plenty of food, I would see clothes. Still I'd see the people that they didn't have it. I wondered why it was. I didn't know, nobody ever told me. The miners had to do all the work, but they didn't get the money for it. Somebody got the money while they done the work. They made ever'thing, but they didn't get it."

—long-time Appalachian resident[2]

"When we were kids we thought the steel mill was it....We just couldn't wait to get in there. When we finally did get in, we were sorry. (Chuckles).... I don't know where they got the idea that we make so much...it's the big bosses who are makin' all the big money and the little guys are makin' the little money....I got nothin' to show for it....After forty years of workin' at the steel mill, I am just a number."

—56-year-old inspector at U.S. Steel[3]

Working people and the corporations agree: profits are the key.

Corporations argue that we can't improve our working and living conditions unless corporations can invest more. And that requires higher profits. "Cutting back on profits business needs...," an Allied Chemical ad insists, "would be like squeezing the breath out of America's future."[4]

Many working people wonder about this argument. Corporate profits have been soaring for several years, as we saw in Chapter 1, while working people have been struggling to stay afloat. How can we be so sure that improving profitability will improve our working and living conditions? Only 20% of U.S. adults think that profits "mainly create prosperity" while 75% think, instead, that profits "mainly benefit stockholders."[5]

The conflict seems clear:

Most working people think that our own problems demand immediate solution. *If improving working and living conditions cuts into profits, so much the worse for profits!* Corporations argue that our economy can't solve anybody's problems unless profits get absolutely top priority. *If that requires reductions in our present living standards, so much the worse for our living standards!*

Who's right? Why do profits play such a central role in our economy? And why should our working and living conditions be so closely tied to something which "mainly benefits stockholders?"

We can't answer these questions unless we locate the origins of profits in our economy. We need to begin with a very simple question: *Where do profits come from?*

DO PROFITS COME FROM CORPORATE RIP-OFFS?

"You go to work for someone and they rip you off all day. Then you drive a car some other company ripped you off for, go shopping and get ripped off at the store and go home and get ripped off by the power company, the gas company and the landlord. It seems like the only thing you can do without getting ripped off by them is sit in the park and shiver."

—young worker in Massachusetts[6]

Many working people feel that corporations earn profits because of their monopoly power, because they are able to charge prices far above their costs. We have to pay those exorbitant prices because we can't buy from anyone else. Surveyed in 1975, more than three-fifths of U.S. adults agreed that "there is a conspiracy among big corporations to set prices as high as possible." In another poll, only 11% gave business a "high" rating in "providing value for the money."[7] The problem, many people believe, is that corporations are ripoff artists.

How do we make this idea more concrete? We can take the giant auto companies as an example. They make cars in order to make profits. In making the cars, they put out money for raw materials and machines and workers. These are their *costs of production*. We give them money for the cars we buy. These are their *sales revenues*. Profits equal the difference between total revenues and total costs. When the auto companies complain that they only make 4 cents on every dollar, they mean 96 cents out of every dollar in revenues must go to cover their costs.

By these definitions, the view that the giant monopolies are

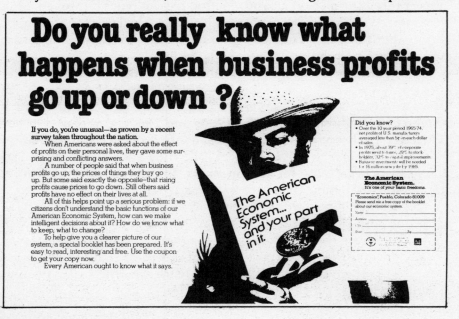

The problem, many people believe, is that corporations are ripoff artists . . .

ripping us off boils down to the simple argument that their costs don't warrant the prices they charge, that the basic source of corporate profits is their power to keep prices higher than they "should be." Does this rip-off analysis make sense?

It makes a lot of sense on the surface. Prices seem very high. We know that many corporations within a single industry, like steel or auto, charge roughly the same prices for comparable products, scrupulously avoiding price wars among themselves. Prices never seem to come down; they just keep rising.

When we probe beneath the surface, however, the rip-off perspective provides us surprisingly little help. It has two main flaws.

1. One problem is that it exaggerates the power of large corporations to determine the price at which they sell their products. Just because there are only a few giant firms making a product doesn't mean that they are totally exempt from competition. Corporations may try to fix prices high enough to permit huge profit margins, but that doesn't mean that they will always succeed. Competition casts its shadows on even the largest corporations.

For example, competition may increase corporate *costs*. Take the airlines. They're huge companies. During the 1960s and early 1970s, their prices were fixed by the government and they were largely protected from new competitors by route regulation. But they still competed frantically with each other. They devoted huge budgets to advertising. They showed movies, played music, served wine, dressed up their meals, and fiddled with their service. Every time one airline got an edge, the others raced to copy it. Despite the fact that their prices were fixed (and very high), competition continually eroded their profits by forcing them to increase their costs.

Competition among the largest corporations may also occasionally force them to lower their *prices*. Take color televisions and pocket calculators. When those products were first introduced (by huge corporations), their prices were very high. As other (large) corporations entered the market and production technologies improved, prices plummeted. The price of a comparable pocket calculator fell from about $80 to about $20 in a couple of years. The fact that only a few firms made the product did not prevent the decline.

Competition also comes from abroad. As auto and steel workers know only too well by now, both the Big Three in auto and the Big Eight in steel, despite their enormous size, have been hit hard by foreign competition. During the 1950s and 1960s, companies in both industries had been raising their prices continually in order to maintain their mark-up margins over costs. While they got fat and a little lazy, competitors began to steal their markets. Try to convince the workers at Chrysler that giant firms are immune to competition!

2. Another important problem weakens the rip-off analysis: it fails to look at both sides of the market—at the *buyers* as well as the *sellers*. We can illustrate this problem with a sequence of logical steps:

a) Consider the 500 largest corporations in the United States as a group. Together they constitute the core of the U.S. economy, accounting for 63% of all purchases and sales.[8] Suppose these corporate giants tried to charge prices far above their costs. What would happen?

b) The large corporations could earn sustained profits by charging far more than their costs justify *only* if their customers could continuously *afford* to buy the core economy's products. Small businesses, workers and people in other countries are the corporate sector's customers. Their income is derived from revenues from products they sell to the corporate sector and from wages that they earn from the corporate sector.

c) In other words, the corporate sector's customers can only earn enough to afford ripoff prices for corporate goods if the corporations are willing to pay high enough prices for the products they buy from small businesses and high enough wages to their workers. But, the more the corporations pay out to the rest of us, the higher their costs. And the higher their costs, the less their prices seem like ripoffs.

d) Thus, if the corporations refused to pay us anything but bargain basement prices and poverty wages, and then turned around and tried to charge ripoff prices, we wouldn't have enough money to afford what they wanted to sell to us. No customers, no profits. Nobody—not even the largest and most powerful corporations in the world—can make a profit if they can't find buyers for their merchandise.

As one oil worker recently explained about his own company, "The whole point is that Union Carbide is getting it, but it's got to come from somewhere else. Union Carbide may sell it, but it's got to come from somewhere."[9]

These arguments aren't intended to justify high corporate prices. Or to suggest that corporations never make relatively higher profits—for a while at least—because they are able to limit competition and keep their prices relatively far above their costs. The rip-off analysis certainly provides a partial insight. But since even the largest corporations are never entirely free from competition, rip-off profits are never entirely secure. And since monopoly profits create losses for others, rip-off profits can't go on forever. No matter how powerful the sellers in market economies, they can't completely escape from competition or the need for buyers.

The numbers support this suspicion. The best available evidence suggests that, *at most, barely more than 10% of total corporate profits can be attributed to the special monopoly pricing power of the giant corporations.*[10] That's much too small a share for us to feel satisfied with the rip-off explanation of profits.

If the rip-off analysis is inadequate, where do we turn for a better understanding of the origin of profits?

A Refresher: What Is Profit?

We can get one clue from a glance at different definitions of profits. The DUPE pushers keep talking about profits on sales: Mobil Oil took this tack in one of its recent pamphlets, for example, arguing that "most Americans have a greatly inflated conception of how much the average business earns from *each dollar it takes in.*"[11] But corporate investors actually pay little attention to that definition. Investors

. . . but barely more than 10% of corporate profits come from the monopoly pricing power of the giant corporations.

**First we work
for ourselves...**

measure the profitability of their investments by the profits they earn *on the capital they invest*, not on the sales revenues the corporation receives. (When we choose among savings banks, we measure interest on the net amount of money we deposit, not on the total flow of funds in and out of our accounts.) If a corporation "finds the return on [its] investment very low," as the DUPE primer puts it, this means that it "should think of going into some other line of work."[12]

Since Mobil Oil says we have an "inflated conception" of profits, let's take Mobil as an example. In 1980, Mobil received $59.5 billion in sales revenues on a net stock investment of $13.1 billion. Its net after-tax profits were $3.3 billion. Measured against sales, its rate of profit was "only" 5.5%. Measured against stock equity investment, however, its rate of return was a snappy 25.0%—or more than 4½ times greater than profits on sales.[13] That's something like the difference between chicken feed and filet mignon.

If investors care most about returns on their capital investments, then we should probably shift our focus. The bulk of capital investment goes into the means of production—into building and machines. That suggests that we need to study what affects the profitability of capital investments in the means of production. Let's leave the market behind for a moment and wander into the factories and offices of our economy.

DO PROFITS COME FROM WORKERS' LABOR?

"It's like assembly work....[For] about three months....I did piecework at Western Electric....[They] expected you to put out a production report and they expected your rates to be very high....

"Well, on this job we process bills. [We're] expected to do so many a day and put out so much money. So we have to total up and make out production reports daily, and in the last six months they've been putting a lot more pressure on us...I have trouble with that....My production report goes up and down. It depends on how I feel....But they must think I'm worth something, because I'm still there!"

—28-year-old clerk, former factory worker[14]

"I'm habitually late to work. I'm late almost every day because I personally, I resent punching a time clock. I don't want to be a number....There's no feeling to it....I think that's my way of getting back at them and I've told my boss that if I didn't punch a time clock, I positively would be in there every day on time."

—chemical worker in New Jersey[15]

The rip-off analysis comes from our experience as consumers in the market. What happens during the time we spend as workers in production? Are we ripped off at work? Instead of coming out of our wallets, do profits come out of the labor we perform as workers?

As we saw in Chapter 2, production in a capitalist economy

depends on wage-labor. Most people don't own enough tools and machines to work as independent producers. A few people own most of the means of production. Those of us who can't produce what we need on our own *must* work for those who control the necessary buildings and equipment.

When we're hired by employers, we sell control over our *labor power*—our power to labor or ability to work—for specific periods of time. This sale of labor power takes place in the market. The capitalist pays us a *wage or salary* in return for control over our labor. We agree to submit to the capitalist's supervision in return for that payment. This exchange seems fair enough, since each party gets something out of the deal. Don't we put in a "fair day's work" and get a "fair day's wage" in return?

Let's take a closer look at what happens on the job. Suppose our workers have just clocked in at the toaster plant of the Short Circuit Electric Corporation. Short Circuit owns the buildings and machines. It has already bought the necessary parts and supplies. It has hired its workers for the day.

Let's assume that the workers are earning $24 a day. Let's also assume that the company spends $12 per toaster to cover the necessary cost of parts and supplies. Suppose that each worker turns out two toasters during a four-hour day. Assume the toasters sell for $24 apiece. Each worker therefore produces, on average, $48 worth of toasters per day. Those revenues exactly cover the worker's wages and the other costs of the toasters he or she makes. [Expenses per worker = $24 in wages + (2 toasters × $12 costs per toaster) = $48 per day.]

There's no surplus left for the capitalist. The corporate owners look at their accounts and begin to moan. "We didn't go into this business to make toasters," they wail. "We're in this to make profits. Where are our profits?"

The capitalists realize that their ownership of the means of production gives them some extra clout. "Who says you bozos only have to work four hours a day?" they announce. "No more lolly-gagging about. Buncha lazy goldbrickers! From now on, if you want to work for me, you're working eight hours a day."

The capitalist is the boss. If the workers want to keep their jobs, they must put in the eight hours. Now they produce four toasters during the working day. The owners earn $96 on the daily output of each worker. They still pay $24 per worker in wages and now need $48 to cover the other costs of the toasters each worker makes—for a total of $72 per worker. That leaves a profit of $24 per worker. If 1,000 workers enter the Short Circuit gates every day, the company earns a cool $24,000 profit every day of the working year.

This example suggests one possible way of thinking about the origins of profits: *the ultimate source of profits in a capitalist economy is the extra time that workers spend on the job* **after** *they've produced enough goods to cover their own wages.* A different angle on the same example helps make this clearer. Each worker can make $12 per toaster—or $6.00 per hour. That means that workers can "earn" a net of $6.00 per hour toward their own wages. Since their daily wages are $24, they can produce

Then we work for them .

enough toasters to cover their wages during the first four hours of the working day. If they have to work more than four hours, they're working to produce extra products which, when they're sold, provide pure gravy for the boss.

These examples are hypothetical. But they are played out every day in our economy. Figure 3.1 provides data for General Motors for 1979. As the chart shows, GM workers worked 3 hours and 41 minutes each day to cover their own wages and the other 4 hours and 19 minutes for the bosses and owners. No wonder GM could afford to pay out $1.5 billion in dividends to its stockholders, who earned their

Fig. 3.1

THE 8-HOUR WORKING DAY AT GM, 1979

Workers needed only 3 hours, 41 minutes to cover their own earnings.

How to Divide GM's Revenues:

Once you take out what GM pays to its suppliers, what's left is often called *value-added*.

In 1979, GM's value-added was **$31.6 billion.**

Of that total, only **$14.6 billion** went to production workers.

income through the strenuous exercise of endorsing their dividend checks.[16]

We need a few definitions to develop this idea for further discussion. The time workers spend making enough products to cover their wages can be called *necessary labor time*. (It's the number of working hours which is "necessary" to cover the costs of "producing" that critical resource—workers' labor power—without which production could not take place.) The rest of the working day can be called *surplus labor time*. (It's "surplus" because workers' wages, the necessary costs of production, could be covered even if these additional, or surplus, goods were not produced.) The goods produced during surplus labor time have a value, since they'll fetch a price in the market. This can be called *surplus value.* It is equivalent to the amount of money which could be earned by selling these extra goods in the market.

Using these definitions, our discussion thus far suggests that **the**

foundation for corporate profits in U.S. capitalism is the surplus value which workers produce. We know that capitalists wouldn't earn a profit if workers spent *only* necessary labor time in the factory or office—only enough hours to produce sufficient goods to cover the necessary costs of production. And we know that production wouldn't take place if there weren't any profit—because the bosses wouldn't have any incentive to open their factory gates and office doors. But we know that production does take place. And that corporations earn profits. So we can conclude that workers put in extra hours—beyond necessary labor time—producing surplus value for their bosses. No

THE 8-HOUR WORKING DAY (Continued)

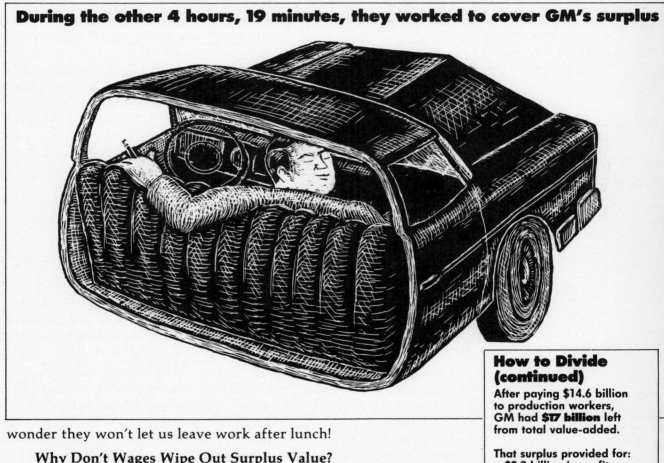

During the other 4 hours, 19 minutes, they worked to cover GM's surplus

How to Divide (continued)

After paying $14.6 billion to production workers, GM had **$17 billion** left from total value-added.

That surplus provided for:
$2.9 billion in profits
4.2 billion in management salaries

and 5.4 billion for investment and tools
4.5 billion in taxes

Source: Based on GM Annual Report; see note #16

wonder they won't let us leave work after lunch!

Why Don't Wages Wipe Out Surplus Value?

Not so fast, the DUPEsters reply. Don't workers' earnings depend on what they produce? How can they *not* get paid for this "surplus labor time?" "We know that as the value of efforts grows," as the DUPE film guide puts it, "our compensation grows along with it. People are paid for the value of their economic contribution."[17]

In order to respond to this DUPE argument, we need to study wages more carefully. We began the Short Circuit example simply by assuming that workers earned $24 a day. Why won't their wages keep increasing the longer they work?

We saw earlier that labor power is exchanged in the labor market. In this respect, it is a "commodity" like apples and oranges and toothpaste. There are buyers and sellers, prices and quantities, a deal and a purchase. For most commodities, as we learned in the previous section on "rip-off," prices are likely to stay very close to the costs of producing those products. If they drop too low, the sellers won't be able to provide the product. If they rise too high, competition will push prices back toward their costs or the buyers won't be able to afford them. Does the price of our labor power—our wages and salaries— follow similar rules?

The first part of the rule seems to apply quite directly: if the price—our wages—falls too low, we won't be able to continue providing the product—our labor power—for long. Why? We can't expend work effort unless we eat adequately. We can't show up for the job unless we can afford to get to work. We can't be productive if we can't stay healthy. We'll have trouble cooperating with others if we can't afford minimal necessary cultural means of subsistence—things like television, movies, and books which give some definition to our lives and help us understand the attitudes and perspectives of others with whom we work.

All this costs money. If our wages aren't high enough to cover those costs, we won't be able to work effectively for long. Employers will soon be forced to find other workers—and probably to pay them enough to sustain their labor power—*or* begin to pay enough to keep us going.

One way or another, employers will eventually have to pay wages high enough to cover the basic costs of workers' physical and cultural subsistence. They'll run out of workers if they don't.

But couldn't wages keep rising above the costs of producing labor power, eventually eroding the foundations for corporate profits?

Many of us can answer that question from our own working and bargaining experiences. Sometimes when we push for higher wages, corporations simply fire us and hire other workers who feel that they have no other choice than to work at the going wage. Or employers occasionally decide that the enterprise is no longer worth their while, shutting the gates and leaving us to pound the pavement for another job. Or corporations may pack their bags and move elsewhere, finding workers in another state or country willing to work for less. Back on the streets again.

In the end, the success of all these corporate strategies depends on two connected features of economic control in capitalist economies. 1) As long as there are plenty of available workers with no alternatives to wage-labor...and 2) as long as employers are able to decide unilaterally how and when to deploy their means of production, then the scales of power are tilted steeply in the bosses' direction.

Corporate bargaining leverage hinges, in short, on both the existence of a *reserve pool of wage-laborers* and on continuing *private and centralized ownership of the means of production*. When these conditions are fulfilled, employers are likely to be able to keep pushing wages back toward the costs of workers' subsistence. For us, too often, it's a choice between those wages or the unemployment line.

Some conclusions about wages are now at hand. Our paychecks

can't fall much below the costs of subsistence (or employers begin losing employees), and capitalists' power advantages tend to keep wages from rising much above that same level. In general, as a result, workers' wages will *depend primarily on the costs of producing labor power*, not on the "contribution" which workers make to production. Our earlier ideas about profits remain intact: it is very likely that capitalists can keep workers' wages from rising as high as workers' output, preserving the possibility that bosses can hold on to their precious surplus value. And the key to this possibility is the uneven balance of power between those who control the means of production and those who don't.

So where do profits come from? They obviously don't come from accidents or magic tricks. We've also seen that they don't come reliably or completely from rip-offs in the market. Rather, it appears that corporations make money off our backs in production because they control the means of production. Profits come from corporate power over workers, not from the stork. They are rooted in the basic structure of the economy. The DUPEsters try to disguise these conclusions however and whenever they can. But our own daily experiences as working people continually remind us that *we're* the source of *their* profits and wealth.

DON'T PROFITS ALSO COME FROM MACHINES AND RISKS?

"The founders of our Republic believed in the fundamental importance of an individual's being able to profit from his labors....They believed that enterprise was the key to a happy prosperous society. And they believed that the rewards of enterprise were a good thing, enriching people's lives and encouraging more enterprise."
—Textron Corporation pamphlet[18]

The DUPE argues that profits come from *risks* (which entrepreneurs take) and from *machines* (which corporations own). Aren't corporations just as entitled to their profits as workers to their wages? How can workers lay claim to either the badges of entrepreneurial courage or the fruits of corporate property?

In order to compare this argument with our own discussion of profits and surplus value, we need to look at the DUPE assertions about risks and machines very carefully.

1. The DUPE on *risks* is straightforward. According to the DUPE booklet, "Investors and entrepreneurs take on the risks of financing and owning on-going businesses and starting new ones."[19] Why do they take these risks? "If successful," the DUPE film teachers' guide suggests, "the enterpriser earns a profit. The risk is that there may not be a profit."

Why are they entitled to these rewards? "It's a fact," the DUPE film guide concludes, "that we would not enjoy the freedoms and benefits we do if it were not for the 'movers and shakers' who made

America happen."[20] The least we can do to show our gratitude is to grant them their just rewards.

Their are two main problems with this argument.

The first is becoming more and more familiar. Corporations argue that they deserve profits because they take risks. In fact we're almost always the ones who bear the costs of failure. When business slackens, we get laid off, not them. When one region declines, they pack up their stock certificates and move somewhere else; we're left behind to sift through the ruins. When their businesses approach bankruptcy,—as Penn Central, Lockheed, and Chrysler (among others) have in recent years—they scream for government bail-out and often get it. When we fall into debt, our creditors are rarely so considerate. "As a boardroom philosopher once remarked," according to *Forbes* magazine, "Socialize the losses and keep the profits private!"[21]

The second problem is even more important. Entrepreneurs need money in order to "take risks." Where does the money come from? It comes either from workers' savings or from profits. If it comes from savings, why shouldn't the savers get the *full* benefits of its application? If it comes from profits, why shouldn't the workers whose labor made those profits possible get full benefit from their use? We can think of it as a kind of insurance; insurance systems are supposed to

They don't earn profits because they built the machines or bought the hardware.

work so that people are protected against unpredictable disasters and recoup their premiums if the accidents don't occur. Why couldn't risk-taking in the economy operate as a sort of social insurance scheme. If our labor and savings make investments possible, why shouldn't we all both share the risks and enjoy the benefits which such investments create?

The answer, in the end, is that capitalists own the means of production and can therefore exclude the rest of us from both their use and their benefits. They don't have any more "courage" than any of the rest of us. Their privileged control of social wealth simply allows them to grab as much of social surplus product as they can.

2. The DUPE on *machines* builds on three assertions.

DUPE pushers argue that machinery increases output. "The use of machinery improves the productive process and encourages mass production. It also contributes to lower costs, lower prices, and more jobs."

They argue that corporate investment makes machinery possible. "Without these savings, there would be no capital goods."

Finally, they argue that corporations wouldn't make such productive use of their profits if they didn't get something out of it. "The basic incentive for businesses and individuals to invest in new capital goods is the hope of additional future income."[22] Corporations therefore have a right to the profits which result from their investments. "It is through human and capital investment that inventions are made available," the DUPE film teachers' guide concludes, "so, the economic rewards that result are justifiable."[23]

Viewed from our perspective, there are several serious problems with this argument.

■ Someone has to build the machinery. If machines help improve our standards of living, why shouldn't the workers who build them have a claim on the social benefits which those machines make possible?

■ Machines cost money. Where does a corporation get the profits to pay for capital goods? Suppose it begins without machinery and wants to buy some. According to the argument of the previous section, the money comes from the surplus value produced by the company's employees. If those workers didn't put in extra hours, the company wouldn't have the "savings" it needs to buy the machines. So why shouldn't workers whose labor makes the purchase possible have claim on the benefits they provide?

■ Someone has to start, operate, monitor, and maintain the machines. Suppose the installation of new machines at Short Circuit allows the workers in our previous example to produce one toaster every hour instead of one toaster every two. Why shouldn't the workers be able to take advantage of the machines *by working fewer hours or slowing down the pace of their work*—since they don't need to work as long or hard to produce enough goods to cover their wages? Why should capitalists enjoy the fruits of machines instead of workers whose labor makes those benefits possible? If the bosses want a claim on the machines' output, why don't they come down on the factory or office floor and help us run them?

Now the DUPE arguments about machines begin to crumble. They make three points:

1) They say that machinery increases productivity. Fine, we say. Let the workers who build and operate those machines enjoy the benefits of that productivity.

2) They say that corporate profits make machine investment possible. Fine, we say. Let the people whose labor provided those profits decide how much to invest and how the dividends from those investments should be distributed.

3) Stripped of the first two arguments, they have only their third assertion left. It amounts to blackmail. If you don't give us our profits, they threaten, we won't invest and you won't have any jobs or income. That threat rests on nothing more than their monopoly ownership of the means of production.

They don't earn profits because they built the machines, in the end, or because their own savings bought them. They earn profits because *the structure of our economy permits them exclusive control of the social wealth which everyone—except them!—has helped construct.*

WHAT MAKES PROFITS HIGHER OR LOWER?

We have one more question to answer. Any analysis of the origins of profits should also help explain what makes profits higher or lower. Can we use our analysis of surplus value to answer that question as well?

How Much Do They Pay Us?

The first factor which influences profits is obvious from the previous discussion. The higher our wages, other things being equal, the lower their profits.

The toaster example shows this obvious effect. When we left them, the workers were earning $24 a day and the bosses were earning a profit of $24 per worker. Suppose the workers finally manage to form a union and, after a long strike, boost their earnings to $30 a day. Assume that the bosses are not able to push the workers any harder on the line. Daily output stays at four toasters per worker. Total revenues per worker therefore remain the same, and so do other costs per toaster. This means that the $6 increase in daily earnings comes straight out of the bosses' pockets. Where once they banked $24 per worker per day, their profits have now dropped to $18 per worker. Pull out the crying towels again!

This conflict between wages and profits has continually threaded the fabric of relationships between employers and employees in the history of capitalism. When workers have tried to push their earnings above subsistence level, employers have looked for new sources of labor—often importing low-wage strikebreakers. And the quest continues as capitalism has spread into many corners of the world. Like major league scouts checking out ballplayers in the sandlots, corporations scour the globe for less expensive workers. One U.S. corporate executive recently explained the advantages of cheap labor in Singapore: "You could hire a girl for $20 U.S. a month, forty-eight hours a week..They don't mind sitting down and doing very tedious jobs on a continuing basis.."   If and when those workers protest, they

Unionists demonstrate for shorter hours, Union Square, N.Y., 1887.

face continuing blackmail threats. As one Mexican worker reported on their own mobilization: "We have 1,000 women sitting in here. The company said it will move to another country if we keep up our demands."[24]

How Long Is the Working Day?

Another factor has an equally simple effect on profits. The longer the working day, other things being equal, the higher the profits.

Our toaster example shows this effect very simply. Workers were earning $24 a day. When they worked eight hours a day, the capitalist earned a profit of $24 a worker. If workers stayed an extra two hours and their wages did not rise, profits would jump to $36 per worker. In this case, profits depend on the power of workers and bosses to determine the length of the working day. If bosses can force workers to put in more hours, profits will rise. If workers can shorten the working day, profits will fall. This contest over working hours has played an important role throughout the history of capitalist economies.

When owners first organized factories in England, for instance, they often tried to regulate the length of the working day by keeping the track of time to themselves. As one English worker complained at the beginning of the nineteenth century:

> There we worked as long as we could see in summer time, and I could not say at what hour it was that we stopped. There was nobody but the master and the master's son who had a watch, and we did not know the time. There was one man who had a watch....It was taken from him and given into the master's custody because he had told the men the time of day....[25]

In the United States, artisans had been used to six or eight-hour days when they controlled their own work. Once they entered the factories, their bosses insisted that they stay as long as possible. In 1839 in Massachusetts textile mills, the hours of work varied from a minimum of 11 hours and 24 minutes a day in winter—without a breakfast break—to a maximum of 14 hours 31 minutes a day in April—counting a half hour each for breakfast and dinner.[25] When the steel industry was reorganized in the late nineteenth century and craftworkers' power was broken, the same thing happened. In 1880 the average skilled steelworker worked 12.8 hours a day. By 1910, the average working day for a skilled worker had stretched to 14 hours a day.[26]

Workers in capitalist factories have always struggled to shorten the working day. The ten-hour-day movement began in the United States in the late 1840s. By the 1870s, many workers had started demanding the eight-hour day. After World War I, many began demanding a five-day week. And now, demands for the 30-hour week are just beginning to surface. The purpose of the movement has always been clear: the shorter the working day, the less time we spend in the service of our bosses' profits.

How Hard Do We Work?

Corporate profits also depend on how hard we work. The more energy we expend, other things being equal, the more surplus value they're likely to get.

We can extend the previous example to show this effect. Let's assume that workers are still earning $24 a day. When they worked eight hours a day, Short Circuit earned a daily profit of $24 per worker. Workers were making one toaster every two hours. Suppose the boss finds a way of forcing his workers to pick up the pace—by turning up the speed on the assembly line or by threatening to fire slower workers. Say the workers now finish one toaster every hour and 40 minutes. If they still work eight hours, they'll produce an average of five toasters a day. Other necessary costs total $60 and wages are still $24. Total costs now come to $84, the five toasters are worth $120, so the capitalist has increased his daily profit from $24 to $36 per worker, an increase depending entirely on the workers' greater exertion.

Capitalists have used speed-up to increase their profits throughout the history of our economy. When profits first began to fall in the early textile mills in the 1830s, for instance, bosses responded by increasing the workers' load from two spindles to three or four.[27] Later in the nineteenth century, as the ten-hour movement gained momentum, employers answered by brutal speed-up in sweatshops. As the pace of work raced ahead, accidents became more and more frequent. Historians estimate that industrial accident rates were higher between 1900 and 1910 than ever before.[28]

Workers have never accepted speed-up willingly. The young women working in the early textile plants "turned out" on marches to protest their deteriorating working conditions in the 1840s. At the turn of the century, workers organized strikes to protest their aching muscles and the risk of injury. By the 1920s, workers inside and outside unions had nearly perfected the art of resisting speed-up. As one study

Fred Wright

found during the 1920s, workers' deliberate "restriction" of output was a "widespread institution, deeply entrenched in the working habits of American laboring people."[29]

And, as every worker knows, the struggle over speed-up and stretch-out continues. One recent eruption in that struggle gained great notoriety. In 1971, General Motors gave its General Motors Assembly Division (GMAD) managerial control over its Lordstown Vega plant. As *Business Week* reported, "The need for GMAD's belt-tightening role was underscored during the late 1960s when GM's profit margin dropped from 10% to 7%."[30] GMAD resorted to crude force. They increased the speed of the assembly line from 60 cars an hour to over 100. At the former pace, workers had about a minute to complete their tasks on the line. Now they had to finish in 36 seconds or less. The company's incentive was obvious: they hoped to save $20 million a year from the speed-up alone.[31] And the workers' response was predictable. "People refused to do extra work," the local union president reported. "The more the company pressured them, the less work they turned out. Cars went down the line without repairs."[32]

How Productive Are We?

Profit levels also depend on the general level of workers' productivity.

We've already seen that capitalists can increase their profits by forcing employees to work faster or harder. Suppose that capitalists can double workers' output by redistributing jobs or making the division of labor more "efficient." A worker's average daily output increases to eight toasters but wages stay at $24. Costs rise to $120, revenues increase to $192, and profits increase to $72. All that's needed is some effective reorganization.

These kinds of productivity increases can come from either new machines or new methods for organizing the production process. Either way, what matters is a) that workers need less time to produce a given amount of output than before (without exerting more effort); and b) that the new machines or methods cost *less* than the value of the additional output they make possible.

The advantages for capitalists of such increases in productivity are obvious. Necessary labor time is reduced because it takes workers less time to produce enough goods to cover their wages. If capitalists can keep hours and work pace at the same levels and prevent wages from rising as fast as worker productivity, then the share going to the capitalist will increase. Surplus value will rise.

Added productivity also permits great flexibility for employers. On one side, they can lay off workers. If one worker can produce twice as much because of a new machine or work process, then the capitalist can get away with employing half as many workers in order to produce the same quantity of goods.

Or, the company can take advantage of increased productivity by expanding output. As long as they can keep finding new markets, they can produce as many more products as their more productive workers can churn out of the factory. Workers' wages will be covered early in the day and all the rest of the products will go into surplus.

Workers have usually been suspicious of capitalist innovations designed to "increase productivity."

■ They've learned from long experience that those wonderful innovations have often resulted in layoffs. As the American Federation of Labor (AFL) Executive Council resolved in 1936, "organized labor is determined to make sure that technological unemployment is not dealt with blindly in the years to come."[33]

■ Or that their working conditions get worse. A 1914 study of the causes of industrial accidents found that "by far the most significant" was the introduction of power machinery.[34]

■ Or that wages don't rise anywhere nearly as fast as their output. As one corporate observer noted with apparent surprise in 1931, "workers have an idea that they are worth more than management is willing to pay them. When they are not receiving the wage they think fair, they adjust their production to the pay received."[35]

Is this suspicion still justified? We will study closely in Chapter 7 the effects of productivity increases in the U.S. during the years of prosperity after World War II. For the moment, a much more general conclusion is apparent. As with increases in our working *hours* and our working *effort*, capitalists seek increases in our *productivity* in order to bolster their profits, not to express their gratitude for our continued and loyal service. Their success in reaping those productivity dividends—like surplus value itself—will depend on the strength of their basic control over the means of production.

ARE PROFITS GOOD FOR US?

"We at General Motors know there is no conflict between corporate profits and social progress. We know that each is necessary for the other."

—former chairman of GM[36]

"The boss is there for one damn purpose alone, and that is to make money, not to make steel, and it's going to come out of the workers' back."

—steelworkers local union official[37]

The DUPE analysis tells us that profits are good for workers and other living things—that corporate profits, as the GM executive puts it, are "necessary...for social progress." Like motherhood and apple pie, profits are the key to the good life. We're now ready to evaluate this position.

Corporate profits depend, first of all, on corporate control over labor in production and on their power to make us do what they tell us to do. Who is prepared to argue that the more control *they* have over *us* the better off we become?

Corporate profits also depend on low wages. We're told that future growth in the economy depends on our moderating our wage demands. But future growth seems to benefit them, not us. Workers' real spendable earnings, as we saw in Chapter 1, were no higher in early 1981 than they were in 1956. So we're supposed to put up with lower wages while we wait...for what? (We return to this question in

more detail in Chapter 7.)

The level of profits also depends, finally, on relations between workers and capitalists in the factory and the office.

■ Profits will increase if workers put in longer hours. Who wants to work longer hours for nothing?

■ Profits will increase if we work harder. Who wants to work harder for nothing?

■ Profits can also increase if workers become more productive. Isn't that at least good for us? It would be if we got to work shorter hours because of our increasing productivity. But our working hours have stayed basically the same for 30 years.

Or if shorter hours permitted others to get jobs. But unemployment hasn't dropped either.

Or if productivity increases were passed on to us through lower prices. But prices have been rising.

Or if our added productivity permitted our wages to rise. But wages have been stagnant for a while and many people are still poor.

It's no wonder that, in a recent poll, almost three-quarters of working people agreed that "company management and stockholders are the people who benefit most from increased productivity."[38]

Couldn't It Be Different?

It seems fairly obvious that corporate profits come out of our hides. Perhaps we could convince the corporations to have a little more "soul" and to pay more attention to our needs? Maybe some more sympathetic managers could take over the corporate giants?

A vain hope. Whoever runs the corporations in capitalist economies, unfortunately, they can't behave in any other way. No matter how soulful corporate managers might like to be, they have to chase after their profits anyway. They're locked in a two-front war and they can't escape from battle.

The first front involves the constant fights between capitalists—the continuing competition among firms. Throughout our discussion, we will call this *capitalist competition.* Suppose two capitalists start out from the same position. One of them listens to his workers' complaints and takes pity, aiming to improve their job satisfaction and rewards. The other pushes his workers as hard as before. The soft-hearted employer's profits will decrease. Suppose the cold-hearted boss uses his extra profits to invest in new equipment, lowering his costs of production. He could lower his prices, driving the soft-hearted boss out of business. Or if he doesn't want to start a price war, he could use his profit advantage to advertise everywhere, urging customers to buy the "real thing." If the soft-hearted boss maintains his "soulful" behavior, he's bound to lose his markets and face even more drastic losses. One way or the other, the soft-hearted employer will eventually have to abandon either his sympathies or his business.

The second front involves the fight between bosses and workers in production—the constant struggle for relative power and control in the factory and office. Throughout our discussion, we will refer to this as the *class struggle.* Just as corporate profits depend on their control over workers, it turns out that their *control over workers depends on their profits.* If new machines will help divide workers or help companies outlast a strike, they need profits to be able to invest in new machines. If a slight wage increase will help cool off workers for a while, they need extra profits to be able to grant the bonuses. If they need supervisors to keep track of their workers, then they need extra profits to pay the supervisors' salaries.

The oppositions between workers and capitalists run deep. Corporate control over workers doesn't come cheaply. Higher profits are necessary for corporations to maintain an edge in their battles with workers. And so, the struggles between workers and bosses force corporations to race after profits ever more frantically.

At last we're ready for some final conclusions about profits. We have argued that profits depend fundamentally on surplus in production—and not on either rip-offs in the market or bosses' risk-taking and entrepreneurial initiatives. We've also seen that the possibility of surplus value—and therefore of profits—hinges both on capitalists' control of the means of production and on the availability of a reserve pool of workers with nowhere else to go. And given this relative ceiling on wages, the level of surplus value will then depend on three factors: 1) whether or not corporations can lengthen the working day; and/or 2) whether or not they can force their employees to work harder; and/or 3) whether or not they can make their employees more productive and consequently reduce the part of the working day in which workers are making the goods and services necessary to cover their own wages.

What about the conflicting attitudes toward profits which we highlighted at the beginning of the chapter?

We have seen that profits are increased at a greater cost to working people of either lower wages, longer hours, harder work, or fewer jobs. From the workers' perspective, it is therefore difficult to imagine how profits can directly serve our interests.

From the corporate perspective, such a change would be a disaster: it would undermine corporate control over the means of production and their ability to organize work in a way that serves their interests above all else. For corporations, therefore, profits must come first: they need profits if they are to stay ahead of their competitors and maintain control over their workers.

There seems to be no way that the two sides could agree. Our voyage to the core of the economy makes it clear that this conflict of interest stems from capitalists' control of the *means of production—and through that control, of the process* of production. How did they get it? And what have working people tried to do about it?

4.

"He's the owner, the boss. He's down in Florida now. When he's here he just walks around with the other big bosses saying 'Why aren't you working?' Then he goes back to his plush office and sits. And we stay down in the dirt. It's a terrible greasy dirty place!"

—worker in small factory[1]

"They use time, stopwatches. They say, it takes so many seconds or hundreds of seconds to walk from here to there. We know it takes so many seconds to shoot a screw. We know the gun turns so fast, the screw's so long, the hole's so deep. Our argument has always been: that's mechanical; that's not human.

"The workers said, we perspire, we sweat, we have hang-overs, we have upset stomachs, we have feelings and emotions, and we're not about to be placed in a category of a machine....

"They got all the technological improvements....But one thing went wrong. (Chuckles.) They didn't have the human factor. We've been telling them since we've been here: we have a say in how hard we're going to work. They didn't believe us."

—local union president at Chevrolet plant[2]

Bosses vs. Workers

In our economy, according to the arguments of Chapter 3, profits depend primarily on the surplus labor of workers. Those arguments suggest that we can't solve our economic problems simply by taxing away corporate wealth, since taxation of wealth would not affect the bosses' control at the point of production. How did they get that basic control? How do they maintain it? What would we have to do to get it back?

ARE BOSSES NECESSARY?

"It's a sad story that employees who learn by trial and error or from fellow workers and shop stewards are rarely trained to do the job efficiently."

—corporate manual for supervisors[3]

"The managing staff has been away for two weeks, and everything is going fine. We can carry on production without them."

—French worker after plant occupation[4]

One reason we have bosses is obvious. They own the factories and equipment. They get the revenues from what we make. Their ownership of the means of production gives them the *right* to try to push us around as much as they want. The Bill of Rights doesn't apply once we step through the factory gate or the office door.

If that were the only reason for bosses' central role in production, it wouldn't be very difficult to figure out what to do. We could simply take the means of production away from them, laying claim to what we

have, in fact, made with our own sweat, skill, and energy. When a bully is beating on us with a stick, the simplest (though difficult!) solution is to gang up on him, take away his stick, and thus remove the most important source of his power.

But that may not be the *only* reason we have bosses.

Do Bosses Make a "Productive Contribution"?

The DUPE analysis suggests another reason. They say that "managers are producers," not bosses. "They 'produce' when they coordinate, plan, and organize the actual production of goods and services."[5] The DUPE film guide repeats this argument. "[Organizers] saw the potential in this country...," it says. "The ingredients were there. But someone was needed to pull it all together. And that was their role...and their achievement."[6]

This argument clearly touches on our own experiences. We all know that the work we do with others needs to be coordinated. If one worker slacks off on the assembly line, others have to double up. If the messenger doesn't arrive with yesterday's routing slips, today's accounts can't be settled. When two people are lugging a refrigerator down the stairs, it's a little treacherous if one of them suddenly decides to take a break.

Coming from the DUPE chorus, this anthem about "productive" bosses has two main verses.

The first verse says that production would grind to a halt if someone didn't weave together all its different threads. Without bosses, we would end up with tangled clumps of yarn instead of finished fabric. As the head of a division of General Motors has put it, "it is not the repetition but the chaos of the assembly process that is most discouraging [to workers]...."[7] Please save us, bosses, from our own chaos!

The second verse sings of laziness. People are so lazy, we hear, that we won't work unless we're supervised. "The vast majority of men want to stay put," Henry Ford argued. "They want to be led. They want to have everything done for them and to have no responsibility."[8] They "grow...lazy or careless," he insisted on another occasion.[9] Turn your back for a second, the DUPE chorus sings, and the goof-offs will be playing gin rummy. Without bosses, we'd have a lot of card sharks but nothing to eat or wear.

We hear these arguments all the time. But are they really accurate? One way of examining them is to think about other situations where we have worked without bosses.

Almost all of us have had experiences in organizing the "production" of something we wanted. When we were children, we organized our own club houses. In school, we often organized school dances, concerts, assemblies, or plays. We usually run our own bowling and softball leagues. We sometimes plan church or social raffles, bazaars, or benefits. We help neighbors put up home additions, repair their cars, or make their clothes. We usually run our own labor unions. Even common tasks around the house, like cooking and cleaning, are sometimes shared, and therefore "coordinated."

We do especially critical coordinating work on our own when disaster strikes or crises develop. We help direct traffic during blackouts. We evacuate people from their homes during natural disasters. We manage strikes when contract negotiations break down. During sit-downs, workers have run entire factories by themselves.

Sometimes the jobs involved in these projects are so small that we never formally discuss the division of tasks. Sometimes the jobs are bigger and require more formal coordination. So we select organizing committees or coordinators. They divide up the jobs and schedule tasks so they'll get done when they're needed.

But there are big differences between organizers and bosses. Bosses control our work and tell us to do things whether we want to do them or not. Organizers usually don't order us around; instead, they try to find ways for people to cooperate. (Though we sometimes need to be cajoled, we participate, in the end, because we care about the

A Helpful Tip for Management

BY NOW IT MUST BE OBVIOUS THAT **THE MOST CRITICAL FACTOR IN** THE RECENT DECLINE IN WORKERS PRODUCTIVITY IS THE WORKERS **LAZINESS!**

WHERE DOES THIS LAZINESS ORIGINATE? IN THE **WOMB** I BELIEVE.

DOES THE CHILD EMERGE PICKING UP AFTER HIMSELF? *NO!*

DOES HE RESPOND TO GENTLE PRESSURE TO **STOP** MAKING A MESS? *NO!*

project.) If we wind up with organizers we don't like—who're getting a little too big for their coordinators' britches—we can usually get together with others to replace the organizers and pick some people with a little more respect.

Unless, of course, those organizers have skills which none of the rest of us have. Then we have problems. We may have formal control over the project, but the organizer may be the only one who knows how to bring it off. Have you ever tried to show a film when you suddenly discover that the projectionist isn't going to show?

This helps highlight two different sources of bosses' control over our working lives. They have control because they own things; we didn't elect them and we aren't given the option of replacing them. They also have control because they are often the only ones who know how the whole thing "works."

Those sources of control help explain the verses of the DUPE anthem.

The first sings about chaos. **We wouldn't need bosses to prevent chaos if we shared the necessary information and skills ourselves.** We could coordinate ourselves.

The second verse sings about laziness and motivation. All of us have streaks of laziness in us. Sometimes working is the last thing we want to do. No matter how sluggish we may feel, however, we could motivate ourselves a whole lot more easily if *we* were in charge. **We wouldn't need bosses to kick us in the rear if we were working for ourselves and cared about our own projects.** We could motivate ourselves.

The question, then is why we don't have the kind of control and skills we would need to do it ourselves. Bosses are only necessary because they have made themselves necessary. How?

BOSSES HAVEN'T ALWAYS CONTROLLED OUR WORK

"Don't be foolish," scold the DUPE pushers. There have always been bosses. Some people are natural leaders and others are natural

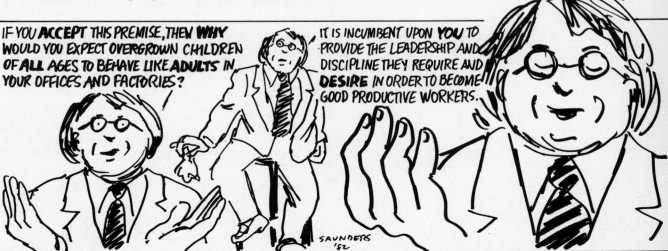

followers. It's human nature. Not every Indian can be a chief....

It's certainly true that there have been bosses during much of human history. Slavery has been very common, for instance. Slaves always understood who was boss, to be sure, particularly if the "massa's" whip had recently "motivated" them to work a little harder. Or in Europe in the Middle Ages, serfs could tell who were the bosses by the height of their castle towers.

But there have also been many places and times when there haven't been bosses. In many African societies, for example, people within a tribe allocated most land collectively. When they worked the common land, they organized their work on their own. And in the Middle Ages in Europe, many peasants also controlled their own land— a fact which most history books conveniently ignore. And those serfs who didn't own their land were free to organize their own work when they didn't have to toil on the lords' fields.

There were also many craftworkers in the Middle Ages who worked free of the bosses' lashes—particularly during the later years of feudalism. Artisans owned their own tools and their own shops; the lords rarely interfered. This was true even for very big projects involving many workers.

Shipbuilding is an interesting example. Large numbers of skilled workers were necessary to complete even relatively small ocean-faring vessels. Craftworkers organized their own work. In Venice, for example, the Governing Council sometimes tried to gain control of the yards, but they usually failed because they didn't know enough to organize it themselves. One merchant has left us with a regretful description of the production process at the shipbuilding arsenal: "When they have entered the Arsenal...[the workers] go wandering around...so that chiefs do not have certain workers assigned to them, nor do the workers know who are their chiefs."[10] And yet, somehow, the ships were built. The craft was so mysterious to the merchants that "the technique of production escaped regulation by the governing council and remained in the hands of the individual craftsmen."[11]

There is also a rich history in the United States of production without bosses. During most of the nineteenth century, as we saw in Chapter 2, people in the family economy shared their labor.

Especially in rural areas, these "bossless" workers were well organized. They managed huge projects, like the harvest, without any sharp city managers telling them how to do it. The fact that work was organized cooperatively often meant that work and play were combined. "The harvest scene was a time of great enjoyment," as one U.S. historian records it. "...Ten, fifteen and sometimes as many as a hundred reapers, both men and women, worked in one field as a gay, lively company."[12] Many other activities besides the harvest were organized in this cooperative way. Spinning parties were only one of many examples: "The women of the entire neighborhood, to the number of dozens, would assemble in a spinning and weaving party. They would spin and chatter the entire day; by evening there were woolen and linen cloths from which to make garments for summer and winter."[13] At dusk the men arrived. Everyone danced or shared in some

> **"In the Venetian shipyards, production escaped regulation by the governing council and remained in the hands of the individual craftsmen."**

other kind of entertainment. These work-and-pleasure occasions were repeated often—whenever hogs and cattle were butchered, sheep were sheared and their wool combed, homes were built, roads were repaired, or barnyards were cleaned.[14]

These examples suggest how people were able to get along without bosses. They owned their tools and equipment, so that others could not threaten them with dismissal. They knew how to do their own work, so that others could not take advantage of a skill monopoly. Working for themselves, they relied on themselves. Bosses weren't necessary, it turns out, because they had not yet sunk their claws into the flesh and bones of the production process itself.

THE BOSSES' STRUGGLE FOR CONTROL OF PRODUCTION

"[Dogs would make better workers than people.] They never go on strike for higher wages, have no labor unions, never get intoxicated and disorderly, never absent themselves from work without good cause, obey orders without growling, and are very reliable."

—factory owner, 1876[15]

"If the human machine could be controlled by the set rules that govern machine tool operation, the world would be a much different place."

—industrial engineer, 1910[16]

"They'd count how many minutes you sat in the goddamn can. The work was so rough, guys got old before their time. If you were workin' at forty-five, you were lucky, 'cause when you slowed down the production line, out you went. You'd go to the toilet, not to take a shit, but just to rest. There was no door, no privacy. I've seen guys go in the damn toilet and get five minutes sleep. The way they did it, they'd take a newspaper and learned how to tap their feet while they were sleepin'."

—former auto organizer[17]

Capitalists' efforts to gain control over production passed through two stages.

Seizing Control of the Means of Production
The first stage unfolded with the emergence of capitalism itself. In England, the first wage-labor force emerged during the eighteenth and early nineteenth centuries. Most people in England had supported themselves on their own farms, controlling their own land. During the eighteenth century, rich landlords threw many farm households off their land through a process called "enclosures." The landlords wanted to use the land for grazing sheep—since the demand for woolen textiles was increasing rapidly—and they didn't care about the needs of farming households. Landlords pushed legislation through Parliament which empowered them to "enclose" many fields, fencing them in for grazing land and keeping farmers off the fields. The farmers could no

"Sometimes as many as a hundred reapers worked in one field as a gay, lively company."

longer support themselves since they no longer controlled their own means of production. They wandered throughout the countryside, sometimes begging, sometimes reluctantly entering the new factories springing up in cities and rural areas. Most of them didn't like factory life, but where else could they go? As one British employer reminded some obstreperous miners in 1831:

> Be Not Too Rash! Pause before you further commit your-selves....If you do not work there are no wages and how are your Families to be provided for? Have you seriously thought of this?...Your places can and will be supplied by others who will be thankful to receive the Wages you now do. You and your Families will then be plunged into the greatest distress.[18]

During the eighteenth and nineteenth centuries in the United States, most people worked on their own farms and controlled their own land in the United States, as people had earlier in England. For a variety of reasons, U.S. farmers were more successful in holding onto their land than earlier generations of English farmers.

This success created a dilemma for the U.S. industrial capitalists, however: who was going to work in their factories? Who would work for a boss when they could easily set themselves up on a farm of their own?

The continuing crisis in Europe provided U.S. capitalists with a solution to their problems. Just as English landlords had evicted English farmers in the eighteenth century, Irish, German, Italian and Slavic landlords evicted farmers in those countries in the nineteenth century. Sometimes these evictions were accomplished in one blow and hastened by social disaster, such as the Great Potato Famine in Ireland and Southern Germany in the 1840s. At other times, the eviction was accomplished more slowly and less visibly, one family at a time.

The result in each case was the same. Many people who were once independent and worked without a boss had now lost control of their own means of production and needed to work for someone else. Many of these newly dispossessed people used what little resources they had left to immigrate to the United States.

Many of these propertyless immigrants, once they arrived, played the role for U.S. capitalists that U.S. farmers could not be forced to play: they went to work in the new factories. At the time of the Civil War, U.S. capitalists stepped up their efforts to attract new immigrants, flooding Europe with information about how to immigrate to the United States—"making hurried efforts," as one historian concludes, "to attract new immigrants—new workers to restore the labor surplus."[19] By 1890, the situation had reversed itself. As one observer noted, "the individual no longer works as independently as formerly, but as a private in the ranks, obeying orders, keeping step, as it were, to the tap of the drum, and having nothing to say as to the plan of his work, of its final completion, or of its ultimate use and distribution."[20]

The Drive to Capture Skills and Knowledge

The second stage in the bosses' struggle for control was just as important as robbing workers of their means of production. Employers

"Be Not Too Rash! If you do not work there are no wages and how are your families to be provided for?"

discovered that they could not maintain control over workers if skilled workers knew more about production than the bosses. Employers began to look for ways to free themselves from their reliance on the workers' knowledge and coordinating skills. They had to change the production process so there weren't any more skilled tasks for workers to perform. *Since they couldn't take the skills out of the workers, they tried to take the skills out of the work itself.*

The Use of Machinery. The separation of skilled workers from their skills was first pursued through the introduction of machinery. Before bosses could seize control of the planning of production, they had to find machines which mechanically performed most of the operations once performed by skilled workers. These kinds of machines helped the corporate "planners" tell machine operators how they were supposed to do their jobs. The bosses could learn quickly how the machine worked, particularly if they had bought it or invented it themselves. But they could never learn how skilled workers performed their craft except by becoming workers themselves. Machinery saved them the effort.

At the McCormick factory in Chicago in the 1870s and 1880s, for example, craft workers were essential at several important stages in the manufacture of reapers and other farm machinery. They regularly used their power to regulate the flow of production and to strike for higher wages. Cyrus McCormick was being driven to distraction. We must take "proper steps," he wrote during this period, "to weed out the bad element among the men."[21] In 1885 the company invested $500,000 in some new pneumatic molding machinery designed to displace all the skilled molders. The new machines divided jobs into separate, simple tasks which required few skills. Unskilled workers were hired to operate the machines. "Of the ninety-one Molders who had signed the petition requesting a wage restoration in March 1885," an economic historian writes, "not one was on the payroll for the beginning of the 1886 season."[22] By 1887, the skilled workers' union was wiped out. (McCormick's only remaining problem was that the machines, though they helped bust the union, were terrible. They had never been tested and kept breaking down. Production was stalled so repeatedly that profits dropped after the new machines were introduced. "The company later sued the manufacturer in an attempt to recover its investment. However, the machines did turn out enough castings to serve their purpose of smashing the union."[23])

The Turn Toward "Scientific Management." By the end of the nineteenth century, employers were discovering that new machines weren't enough to solve their problems. Machinery made it possible to get rid of skilled workers, they found, but it didn't guarantee effective control over workers' labor. They found, increasingly, that they needed to design new job tasks around the new machines in order to improve their control over the pace and rhythm of work. How could the bosses really "coordinate" production if the workers planned the way they spent their time on the job?

This drive for further control was called "scientific management"—also known as "time-and-motion" study. The father of scien-

tific management was a man named Frederick Taylor. The son of an affluent Philadelphia lawyer, Taylor rebelled against his family and apprenticed himself to a skilled machinist. He spent years in machine shops and metal factories learning how workers made their jobs easier. Wherever he worked, he discovered that "the workmen had carefully planned just how fast each job should be done, and they set the pace for each machine throughout the shop...."[24] Taylor eventually became a foreman. Every time he tried to nudge the workers to turn out a little more product, he discovered that the workers could always outfox him. Even though he had worked in the shop, he found that "the combined knowledge and skill of the workmen who were under him was certainly ten times as great as his own."[25] The workers' knowledge allowed them to retain control despite all the new machinery.

The problem for the bosses, Taylor observed, was that the "workmen...possess this mass of traditional knowledge, a large part of which is not in the possession of management."[26] The solution, he concluded, was to take the knowledge away from the workers by redesigning work. He thought this could be done in four ways.

■ First, work had to be broken into many simple tasks and divided among different workers. No individual worker should know too much. As work was subdivided, management should know how it fit together, not the workers.

■ Second, the *design* of work should be separated from its actual *execution*. There should be separate planning departments. The planners should determine how each job was to be done—down to the second—and nothing should be left to the imagination of the workers.

■ The third idea was critical. Once the planners had designed each task, workers should be given their instructions only one task at a time. If the workers knew what they were to do too far in advance, Taylor feared, then they would be able to do their own planning. Task assignment would be the most difficult to implement, since "the workmen have been accustomed for years to do the details of the work to suit themselves, and many of them...believe they know quite as much about their business as...the bosses."[27]

■ Fourth, Taylor urged that employers always find the right workers for the right jobs. These other schemes would never work, he argued, if workers in detailed tasks were too big for their britches.

Taylor eventually embarked on a crusade, after 1900, marching his principles around like holy gospel, parading the banner of scientific management. By the 1920s, many employers were experimenting with different ways of applying the principles. By the 1930s, workers throughout the country were getting used to the time-and-motion engineers, clipboards and stopwatches in hand, pacing through the shop snooping for ways to redesign the tasks of production. All those efforts shared the same underlying objective. Corporations were aiming, as Henry Ford explained the purpose of his famous assembly line, at "the reduction of the necessity for thought on the part of the worker and the reduction of his movements to a minimum."[28]

Easier Planned than Achieved

As the gospel of scientific management spread, however, corporations discovered that solutions to one problem often created new ones.

Skilled workers had often enjoyed their work, in part, because they performed many tasks and controlled their working time. When the bosses subdivided tasks, workers had less knowledge about the process of production and therefore, as it turned out, less motivation. Factories with scientific management techniques often had the most trouble recruiting workers.[29] Even when they succeeded, absenteeism was common and turnover among employees was very high. Especially if unemployment was low and jobs were plentiful, workers avoided the houses of scientific management like the plague.

Employers also discovered another problem with scientific management techniques as originally applied. The new job structures, like the machines before them, reduced divisions among workers. Skilled workers had originally controlled their own jobs *and* those of their unskilled assistants. Now all the workers were in the same boat. There was a firmer basis for workers' unifying against the bosses. The new techniques stimulated "sabotage, syndicalism, passive resistance," a machinists' union official concluded. "We did not hear of any of these things until we heard of scientific management and new methods of production."[30]

So bosses had to continue their struggles for control.

One method involved new-fangled *piece-rate* systems. Piece rates tie workers' wages directly to the amount they produce. The more you produce, the higher your wage—at least in theory. But it turned out that capitalists lowered the piece rate the minute that output reached a certain level. Taylor even suggested two different piece rates, one for the "average" worker and one for the "first-class" worker. "When employers...pay all of each class the same wages, and offer none of them inducements to work harder or do better than the average," Taylor wrote, "the only remedy for the men comes in combination; and frequently...is a strike."[31]

Bosses also tried to motivate workers by creating truckloads of new *job titles*, tying wages to rungs on the job ladder. If you wanted a higher wage, you had to work your way up the ladder. If you wanted to

"These divisions are imposed . . . that workers may be spurred . . . to greater exertion . . . ."—*IWW*

climb a rung, you had to please the boss. The ladders created competition and divisions among workers at different levels in the job hierarchy. These divisions broke down some of the unity which the subdivision of tasks had initially created. This effect was apparent to some workers as early as the turn of the century. The initial manifesto for the Industrial Workers of the World (IWW) noted in 1905, "These divisions, far from representing differences in skill or interests among the laborers, are imposed by the employers that workers may be pitted against one another and spurred to greater exertion in the shop...."[32]

The bosses also played upon *racial* and *ethnic* differences in order to create friction among workers. Workers from different groups were offered different jobs. Black and Eastern European workers were given the lowest jobs. A pay sheet of the Ford Motor Company after World War I shows, for instance, that the company paid workers different wages depending on their race and nationality.[33] And when skilled steelworkers began to strike in 1919, the local Chamber of Commerce distributed leaflets urging native-born workers to break the strike. The "foreigners want your jobs," the pamphlets warned, and should be kept in their places.[34]

Employers played on some of the same kinds of differences between *men* and *women* to achieve further control over the workforce. When corporations began hiring large numbers of office workers during the 1920s, for instance, they were able to find workers willing to accept menial clerical jobs by playing upon the lower expectations of women. One corporate office manual explained the logic of this strategy in 1925:

As a rule,...a woman is to be preferred for the secretarial position, for she is not averse to doing minor tasks...which would irk and irritate ambitious young men, who usually feel that the work they are doing is of no importance if it can be performed by some person with a lower salary....Women,...while by no means unambitious, are temperamentally more reconciled to such detail work, and do not seem to judge it from a similar standpoint.[35]

The Bosses' Struggle for Control Continues....

"Our company does the same thing. We don't have to think. I'm supposed to be a mechanic and I can't make a decision. [My friend]'s an operator. He has his job to do and he can't think. It's written down for him. You do this in such and such a time. This is industry's way of indoctrinating people so that they *don't* think....They fight them off every inch of the way, take the plants down south where they can have more control."

—oil worker, 1975[36]

Many of these stories are decades old. What about today?

In Chapter 18 we will review the principal changes in the organization of work since the 1930s. As we will see from that discussion, bosses' recent struggle to maintain and improve their control over production has not affected the basic story line. The bosses have had no recent change of heart. Continually pushing for more control over actual decisions about how work is done, they have recently moved toward ever more sophisticated machine and management systems.

1. *Machines.* Automation continues at a frantic pace. All too often, it has furthered the bosses' struggle for control by separating workers from skilled production and reducing their numbers. More and more, workers stand by while the machine does the work. Even more important, workers know less and less about the design of the production process as a whole. How can we deny the bosses' importance, in modern times, when they're the only ones who know how production works?

One important recent example of this kind of automation is "numerical control." In the machine tool industry, machinists traditionally controlled their machines. With numerical control, the machines receive instructions from coded messages and their operation is automatically regulated by monitoring devices. The engineers almost always design the control devices so that less-skilled workers can operate them. (After all, less-skilled workers know less and are less expensive.) Eventually, the skilled worker becomes superfluous. "Most of the functions of the skilled machinist," an article in the *Monthly Labor Review* recently observed, "have been shifted to the parts programmer."[37] The less the workers on the shop floor know about the design of production, the better for the bosses. Throughout manufacturing, *Fortune* magazine admits, modern machines typically "take over the more skilled jobs, such as machining or welding, leaving the menial tasks for humans."[38]

The same thing happens on the office floor as automation has invaded clerical work. Skilled secretaries and accountants often knew too much. Machines wouldn't cause so much trouble. So here they come. "Total word processing" technology is reducing secretarial work to the kind of monitoring which machinists now do. Perhaps most dramatically, computer programming has been broken down into routine, finely-specialized, increasingly unskilled tasks. Computer programmers initially knew something about virtually all aspects of computer operation. Now their work has been reduced to the most mindless kind of routine. As one computer manager described the work of his Operations Department: "Work gets turned over to Operations when it is documented and fully tested. After that, [workers are] expected to process it like [they] were processing shirts in the laundry. Top management has set standards so that they think [workers] can push a button and out pops the report."[39]

With this new routine, office machines have begun to exert much more control over work. "The computer may be to middle management," as one General Motors psychologist observed, "what the assembly line is to the hourly worker."[40] "This job is no different from a factory job," an operator in a large office agreed, "except that I don't get paid as much."[41]

2. *Management.* Corporations have devoted at least as much attention to new methods of organizing work—perfecting job ladders, reducing our initiative at every turn. As before, bosses have aimed these management systems directly at workers' power on the job.

What has changed has been their care and vigor, not their intent. Early efforts at scientific management were often superficial. One industrial relations expert observed after World War I, "employers so far have not fully appreciated as a means of combatting unionism the tremendous possibilities of...organizing the work in their plants into minutely subdivided jobs...[with] systematic lines of promotion...."[42]

It didn't take them long to absorb the lessons. After World War II, corporations devoted more and more attention to new methods of organizing work inside the factory and office. One historian writes about this period: "Labor and employee relations received increasing attention at higher levels of management. The staffs and programs of

Another Wildcat?

industrial relations departments absorbed a growing proportion of company budgets and labor costs....Supervisory selection, training, and practices...improved. In addition, managements...gained a much better understanding of unions, and, consequently, are in a position to anticipate union actions and reactions."[43]

A huge new apparatus of control emerged—an instrument of *bureaucratic control* with its own systems and rules, kings and barons, restrictions and loopholes, velvet gloves and iron fists. And there are millions of people charged with the responsibility of running this bureaucratic apparatus. We know them well because we see them every day on the job. By 1980, there was roughly one manager or foreman or supervisor for every ten production workers in the private sector.[44] They keep needing to enlarge the executive washrooms.

Every worker has had his or her own experiences with the people from "Labor Relations." In many of the classes we have taught, we have asked participants to make a list of things that management personnel and foremen have done to make it more difficult for them to get organized in order to solve their problems at work. Here is a sample of some of the items from those growing lists:

- *They play favorites.* One guy comes in late all the time but he's management's friend and never disciplined. Another guy, a strong union man, comes in 5 minutes late and they try to walk him out.
- *They undercut the grievance procedure.* They stall grievances so the members get mad at us. They push everything up to arbitration so we have to go broke just trying to get some justice.
- *They've got their plums for those who cooperate.* More than half of our former union officials have ended up in management. One guy got a $50,000-a-year job as a corporate president's chauffeur.
- *They're constantly trying to strikeproof the plant.* They hire more and more technicians who are management to do work that was done by production workers. So in case of a strike, they can run the plant without us.
- *They transfer our group leaders.* We had a good group growing in our office. We were protesting the unfair suspension of a six-months pregnant woman who was ten minutes late. All of a

sudden, the key person in the action got shipped off to another office.

....New machines, new management systems, same old story. If we as workers know too much, we might control production. If the bosses know it all, we'll have a harder time figuring out how to cut into their control and, ultimately, their profits. Two workers, one in a small plant, another in a huge one, tell parallel stories:

> When a job came open they called me and I took it. I was a skilled worker, one of about forty people who worked there. Of course, it was like any factory: they wanted to break me in on one job and keep me there. They tried to make sure I didn't learn about the whole process....Finally, one guy who worked there, who had frustrated ambitions to become a foreman, caught me making sketches of the way certain keys were made. He turned me in to the boss, and it was made pretty clear to me that I'd better not get caught doing it again.
>
> —worker at musical instrument plant in Oregon[45]

The old-timers agree that the work has gotten worse. It's speeded up by introducing new machinery, increasing the number of jobs per person and cutting crews....The provisions in the union contract give no protection. The company has a free hand in introducing new machinery, setting crew sizes and scheduling.

> —worker in modern steel factory[46]

WORKERS FIGHT BACK

"So with a prospect of working an indefinite length of time at these prices and under an overbearing and profane foreman, we struck and will stay out until the battle is fairly won."

> **—worker at Pullman plant, 1894[47]**

"Some of the machines have written on them 'Treat Me with Respect and I will give you Top Quality Work with Less Effort,'...I said we should have that printed on sweatshirts, and wear them to work...but we wouldn't be able to keep them on for five minutes, we'd be sent home for disrespect. We should have a whole lot made, and all wear them together....They couldn't send the whole shop home."

> **—worker at auto plant, 1972[48]**

Workers in the factory and office have never accepted the bosses' assaults lying down. We have always tried to conserve our energies and protect our wages. Every time the bosses have looked for a new way to wrest control from the workers or make us work harder, working people have looked for new ways to resist.

Early Union Struggles

Bosses originally tried to seize control by imposing factory discipline on workers. Skilled workers resisted this imposition by pooling their numbers and forming trade unions. By organizing themselves, they increased their strength. A boss could easily fire one worker standing alone. But if all the workers resisted together, the odds shifted dramatically.

Early trade unions focused directly on basic questions of control. An early union of construction workers complained, for instance, about the "tyranny" of employers who were "butchers and tinkers who never learned the trade, usurping the place of legitimate mechanics...." All the bosses were doing, the tradesmen wrote, was "driving men like slaves that they may enrich themselves from the blood and sweat of those whose necessity knows no law...."[49]

Throughout the United States from the 1840s through the 1870s, trade unions waged strikes to try to reclaim their control over working conditions. Many proposed cooperative societies, as the shoemakers put it, "to emancipate themselves from the system of wage slavery and become their own masters."[50] Their objections were clear and focused. They wanted to work and they wanted to be their own masters. The shoemakers voiced these protests for thousands of workers in their newspaper in 1845:

> Here we see a moneyed aristocracy hanging over us like a mighty avalanche...we find ourselves crippled and destroyed by human competition, and last, though not least, we see machinery introduced that will not only lessen but annihilate the last surviving hope of the honest mechanic.[51]

Trade unions were so successful that employers escalated the conflict. They moved quickly to introduce machines which would eliminate skilled workers. Workers continued to resist. The U.S. steel industry at the end of the nineteenth century was the scene of one of the most dramatic of these battles.

After the Civil War, steel companies were building larger and larger factories. They looked like large factories in other industries. But working relations inside were different. When the factories were first built, the skilled men ran the mills and the foremen had little authority. A company historian, writing in 1908, described the workers' power during this period with great resentment:

> ...every detail of working the great plant was subject to the interference of some busybody representing the Amalgamated Association. Some of this meddling was specified under the agreement that had been signed by the Carnegies, but much of it was not; it was only in line with the general policy of the union.[52]

The owners of the company realized that they could not readily increase their profits in those conditions. And their competition was knocking at the door. Carnegie concluded, as his partner wrote, that "the Amalgamated had to go."[53] The company embarked on a full-scale union-busting course. They built a huge fence around the plant. They erected barracks inside it. They hired a force of armed Pinkerton guards to keep the plant gates open. As soon as these preparations had been completed, the company announced that after July 4, 1892, no union man would be hired at the Homestead mills or any other Carnegie plant.

The steel workers quickly realized the seriousness of the challenge. They refused to quit either the union or the mills. The company locked them out. The workers mobilized. Only 750 of the plant's 3800 employees belonged to the skilled workers' union, but support for the strike was widespread. The union put a fleet of boats on the river, headed by the steam launch "Edna," to patrol for strikebreakers coming by water. When Pinkerton guards tried to land a flotilla of strikebreakers near the plant, workers moved to the shore to block their paths. Shots were exchanged.

The fighting spread. Workers in other plants joined in sympathy. "It is not our battle we are fighting," one worker from another Carnegie plant explained, "but for organized labor. They signed our scale, but we knew we would be the next victim."[54] The Governor of Pennsylvania appointed an experienced military commander to shepherd the strikebreakers into the plant. He could not believe the audacity of the workers. How could they be so bold, the Governor asked; "they believe the works are their's quite as much as Carnegie's!"[55]

When simple military maneuvers did not succeed, the company escalated again. They brought charges of treason, murder and riot against the strikers. The courts promptly issued indictments against many workers. Many were jailed and others fined. In the end, the company won. But the workers had made their purposes clear. They wanted control and they didn't want the company to mess around with what they had. "The firmness with which these strikers held on," Carnegie's main adviser admitted, "is surprising."[56]

The Battles Widen

Encouraged by Carnegie's success, many employers tried to break their unions. The battle for control over work grew more and more intense. After 1900, workers struck more frequently. Many of their strikes focused on issues of control. Textile workers in Lawrence, Mass. and Paterson, N.J. protested stretch-outs and new incentive pay plans introduced by the managers. Machinists at weapons factories fought to reduce the number of wage classifications and job titles in order to reduce divisions among workers. In the winter of 1917-1918, there were five city-wide general strikes in which workers in many industries fought together—often over the issue of control. The largest strike took place in Seattle in 1919. The leaders made clear their determination:

> Labor will REOPEN, under the management of the appropriate trades, such activities as are needed to preserve public health and public peace. If the strike continues Labor may feel led to avoid public suffering by reopening more and more activities UNDER ITS OWN MANAGEMENT.[57]

The point of the workers' struggle had become so clear, in at least some of the strikes, that corporations knew exactly how high the stakes had grown. As the U.S. Steel chief warned other steel owners during the

Union organizers, 1937.

1919 steelworkers strike, their primary objective was "retaining the control and management of your affairs, keeping the whole thing in your own hands."[58]

The 1920s, in contrast, were a lean period for labor unions. Many union leaders and radicals had been arrested during and after World War I. Large corporations had been enriched by war-time production and they used their new wealth to wage new battles against the labor movement. But workers fought back even without union support. The 1920s were years of "informal" workers' struggles against bosses' control. Workers organized themselves through their working groups and work teams. When the bosses tried to impose new production quotas at a Western Electric plant in the 1920s, for example, informal work groups organized to adjust the amounts reported in their daily production reports. Unorganized restriction of output was so widespread during the 1920s, one study concluded, largely because of workers' feelings "that they must hide from their employers their real capacity for work." And when the engineers appeared with their stop watches, the same study concluded, "they further stimulate deliberate efforts on the part of employees to hold back production."[59]

Informal work groups rely on guerrilla tactics. But workers have usually found that, sooner or later, these guerrilla platoons need to join forces in organized armies. When we form large unions, we are matching the strength of our organized numbers against the force of capitalists' wealth and control. There have been many dramatic moments in U.S. history when workers have moved to organize in this way.

Sitting Down to Victory in the 1930s

Perhaps the most dramatic took place during the 1930s. Workers developed new tactics and forms of struggle to forge large industrial unions.

The sit-down strike was the most powerful discovery. Strikes had become less effective because skilled workers had been cut out of the factory and it was always easier for the bosses to find unskilled strikebreakers. When striking workers began to sit down by their machines, however, bosses thought twice about trying to break the strike. They faced the problem not only of finding other workers but also of getting the workers out of the plant. The machines could have been damaged. And public opinion might have turned against the corporations if they had to evict the workers by force. Damage to machines and their public image were both bad for business.

Rubber workers in Akron, Ohio were the first to use sit-downs regularly. They apparently discovered the idea at a baseball game. Two factory teams were playing. They wanted a union umpire. When the non-union umpire declined to leave the field, the players sat down at their bases and fielding positions, refusing to continue until their demand was met. They won. When a dispute between employees and their supervisor later developed at one of the factories, the employees remembered the baseball game and sat down at their machines. They refused to work until their supervisor was transferred. They won that one too.[60]

Sit-downs began to spread as their effectiveness became known. The greatest sit-down strike took place in 1936 at the Fisher Body Plant No. 1 in Flint, Michigan. Despite the assaults of company goons and local police, the sit-downers held out for one and a half months, receiving food and supplies from their families and community. One historian has described some of the organization and activities within the plant:

> A committee of seventeen was in charge and reported daily to membership meetings. The sit-downers, organized into squads of fifteen under a captain, lived together in these groups in sections of the plant. Strike duty was six hours a day...consisting of picketing at the gates, patrolling, health and sanitary inspection, K.P.....Safety received priority. The ventilator in the paint department was kept running to carry off fumes; the union got GM to remove 1000 acetylene torches as a precaution; guards kept an eye out for live cigarette butts....[61]

General Motors tried every possible tactic to break the sit-down and the union. But strikers were too strong and too well-organized. After six weeks of battle and counter-battle, the company recognized the union.[62]

But union recognition was only part of the war. Profits were low during the Depression and the companies tried to boost them any way they could. The new unions had to struggle constantly to prevent speed-up, manipulation of the piece-rate system, and arbitrary supervisory abuses, to protest unsafe working conditions, and to establish seniority systems. Throughout the late 1930s, the sit-down strike became a weapon for all seasons. Between 1936 and 1938 alone, more than half a million workers participated in sit-down strikes.[63] One popular song told the story:

> "When they tie the can to a union man,
>   Sit down! Sit down!
> When they give him the sack they'll take him back,
>   Sit down! Sit down!
> When the speed-up comes, just twiddle your thumbs,
>   Sit down! Sit down!
> When the boss won't talk, don't take a walk,
>   Sit down! Sit down!"[64]

Where Would They Go without Us?

THE BATTLES CONTINUE

The union victories during the 1930s were great landmarks in the history of the workers' movement in this country. But they did not allow workers to sit back and count their paychecks. Employers have responded, as we saw above, with new machine and management systems.

So the struggles continue. Mine workers are protesting hazardous safety conditions. Auto workers are resisting automation. Computer workers are undercutting new task organizations. Doctors and nurses are walking out over increasing workloads in hospitals. The lists could fill newspapers—if the newspapers reported such things. The DUPE-sters say they don't understand why workers seem so troublesome and unhappy. It should be obvious. As a Chicago steelworker puts it:

> It's hard to take pride in a bridge you're never gonna cross, in a door you're never gonna open. You're mass-producing things and you never see the end result of it. I worked for a trucker one time. And I got this tiny satisfaction when I loaded a truck. At least I could see the truck depart loaded. In a steel mill, forget it. You don't see where nothing goes.[65]

Despite all the bosses' advantages, we often win our struggles in the factory or the office. But then we often bump up against another problem. We may make inroads on capitalist's control at the worksite, but that may expose us to more and more *insecurity* in our lives on and off the job. More and more, companies have been responding to workers' victories at one plant by expanding production at some other factory in some other location. They can do this because the market links all their plants—and our jobs!—together. And we are vulnerable because, in market economies, there are no cushions to soften the blow when we lose our jobs—and with them, our only means of support.

The DUPEsters tell us that the market is wonderful, boasting of its conveniences and the efficiency it ensures. But the market also seems to expose us to continuing risks and uncertainty. Which view is correct? It's time to follow the toasters out the loading docks of Short Circuit Electric and to track their journey through the marketplace of buyers and sellers, prices and quantities, bargains and ripoffs. Gaining more control over production won't be enough for us. How does the market work?

5.

The Money Go-Round

"I'll give it to the company: they're great with the public relations bit. G.E. puts out 2, 3 bulletins a week, and they're always telling [the workers].... that if they don't work harder, if they don't stop taking off days off, and quit taking so much time on their coffee break, and so forth, that they're gonna have to take the plant and move it to Singapore...They've scared people with it. This company, like a lot of companies, runs the thing by fear."
—control inspector at a General Electric plant[1]

"The more I earn the farther behind I seem to be. Money's something that's just out of my hands to control, you know?"

—a typesetter with a family[2]

We have already seen in Chapter 1 that millions of American households face continuing insecurity.

Workers face this insecurity from the threat of plant shutdowns or relocation. Corporations play on our fears of foreign competition and distant workers. Don't push too hard, they tell us, or we'll lose our jobs.

Consumers face insecurity from the continuing instability of prices and quantities in the market. Beef prices spurt. Oil prices soar. Interest rates keep climbing. Shortages sometimes develop. Our favorite stores close their doors.

Both sources of insecurity involve *the market*—the millions of exchanges between buyers and sellers. Factory relocations are possible because of the market links established among suppliers. Prices bob up and down because of the disconnected characteristics of market exchange. Insecurity and market exchange are inseparable.

Are markets necessary? Must they always be so insecure? Why have markets spread? Aren't they the key, as DUPEsters often insist, to efficiency and free choice?

The answers to these questions resonate through the title of this chapter: people in our economy are connected through the market exchange of commodities. And money makes the goods go round.

ARE MARKETS NECESSARY?

"You don't need statistics to know what is happening in the economy. If you can't afford to buy enough food, you will feel it in your stomach. If you can't afford fuel and clothing, you will know what is going on in the economy because you will be cold."

—senior tool-and-die maker[3]

We usually take it for granted. But if we think for a moment, it's not hard to see how much we depend on the exchange of commodities.

Take our lives as consumers: when we get hungry, most of us have to go to the supermarket to buy food. When we drive to work, we feel the gas money evaporating with every passing mile....We pay money for almost all the goods and services we consume.

Or suppose we're like the workers in Short Circuit Electric. Their jobs depend in part on whether the firm makes relatively inexpensive toasters. Which depends partly on the costs of metal for the body and coil, wire for the cord, chrome for the coating, rubber for the insulation...not to mention the cost of the factory and the assembly line and the machine tools and the machine parts....

Office workers share the same kinds of connections: clerical workers can't function without typewriters purchased from some other company...or without adding machines, paper, paper clips, desks, and filing cabinets...nor can we forget the elevator and air conditioning.

This dependence on commodities is built into the structure of the U.S. economy. Neither working people nor corporations have much choice.

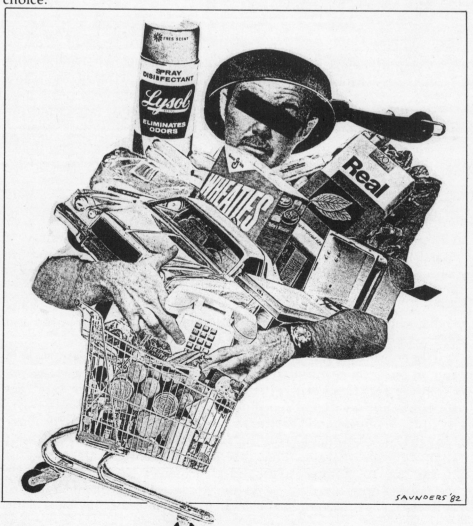

Fig. 5.1

Where Does a Hershey Bar Come From?

Cocoa beans from Ghana

↓

Sold by Ghana Market Bd.

↓

Milk from local dairy farms

↓

Wholesaled by cooperative distributor

↓

Sugar from Brazil, Mexico or U.S.

↓

Processed by Amstar Refining

↓

Almonds from Calif.

Wrapper paper from Maine or Northwest

Manufactured in Pennsylvania

↓

Marketed by wholesalers

↓

Sold by retailers

These connections are also global. Supplies from all around the world go into most of the products we buy. Take an auto assembled in Michigan. It includes, among other products, aluminum (for the engine and transmission) from Haiti, Surinam, or Jamaica; chrome (for alloys and trim) from Turkey or South Africa; copper (for wiring) from Rhodesia, Canada, or Zaire; and rubber (for the tires) from Malaysia or Indonesia. The auto parts themselves come, increasingly from all around the U.S., Europe, Latin America, and the Far East.[4]

Even the simplest products come to us through an extended commodity flow. Take the Hershey candy bar (with almonds). It's a little piece of candy in a plain brown wrapper. As Figure 5.1 on this page shows, the ingredients of the candy bar come from three states in the U.S. and three different countries abroad. From beginning to end, the production cycle of the candy bar may last a year. Before we buy it, the candy has already passed through at least ten different market exchanges on its journey from initial suppliers through the factory and wholesale distributor.[5] It's an experienced world traveler by the time it finally reaches the candy store counter.

What Do Markets Do?

The DUPE analysis of markets presents a simple view of their role. The DUPE booklet provides a clear summary:

> Using money is a most convenient way to exchange goods and services....Money makes buying and selling easy. The marketplace is wherever these transactions occur, where buyers and sellers come together to agree on the exchange of goods and services for money. Money markets are essential to the American economy. They permit buyers and sellers to influence each other and thereby largely determine what our economy produces and who produces it.[6]

This view suggests that one of the market's main functions is to coordinate production decisions. This coordination takes place through market prices. If prices for a product increase, suppliers will get a "signal" to produce more. The market sends these signals around the globe. As the Gospel according to DUPE explains this effect, "ripples spread out over ever widening circles, transmitting the information to people all over the world that there is a greater demand for...some product they are engaged in producing, for reasons they may not and need not know."[7]

There is little question that the market does serve this function in capitalist economies. But that does not mean that the market is the *only* way these functions can be performed. Even in our own capitalist economy, this function of coordination is fulfilled in a variety of ways.

One example involves the largest corporations. They produce many of their own supplies for their own factories and offices without relying on the market. They use their own internal sources of information to monitor costs and plan deliveries. They base their internal decisions on complex systems of data gathering and analysis. Products are manufactured and circulated for months and miles along these internal channels before ever seeing the light of the external market itself.

Corporations use these internal mechanisms instead of the market for many reasons. One of the most important is that they can monitor and control their exchanges more carefully than in the market. Inside the corporation, they can establish the temperature and conditions affecting production and distribution. Outside in the market, unexpected winds may often blow—upsetting the best laid corporate plans.

A second example is becoming increasingly important in our economy. Many people have tired of the unpredictability of the market and have been forming consumers' cooperatives and buying clubs to establish their own links with producers and suppliers. These efforts involve careful coordination. Consumers often establish independent contact with farmers, for example, to find out how much they can supply over what period of time. And buying clubs set up their own internal mechanisms for finding out what and how much their members want to buy.

Buying clubs side-step the market for many of the same reasons as with large corporations. Consumers often move away from market exchange in order to gain protection from the hills and dales of market price fluctuations.

There are different ways of coordinating production decisions, in short, and *the market is not the only way*. As a result, we need to look carefully at whether the market is a *desirable* mechanism for performing this critical function.

The DUPE insists that it's the best ever, of course. They argue that it performs virtual wonders for all of us who participate in market exchange. Once we look at markets more closely, however, they begin to lose some of their glitter. Studied critically, the wonders of the market take on a very different color.

CONVENIENCE? YES.
SECURITY AND INDEPENDENCE? NO.

"We owe all good things in America to the free market."
—corporate executive at business conference[8]

Most of us commonly enjoy the convenience of money and markets. We can shop for a wide variety of goods and services. With money in our wallets, we know we'll be able to pay for what we buy at the supermarket.

Modern markets do indeed provide plentiful, attractive, and frequently convenient choices. But we're studying markets and money in *capitalist* economies. Given the features of capitalist economies we first encountered in our "economic checklist" in Chapter 2, our enforced dependence on markets creates some serious problems.

Smooth Rides over Rocky Roads?

"The people come with nets to fish for potatoes in the river, and the guards hold them back; they come in rattling cars to

get the dumped oranges, but the kerosene is sprayed [on the fruit]. And they stand still and watch the potatoes float by, listen to the screaming pigs being killed in a ditch and covered with quicklime, watch the mountains of oranges slop down to a putrefying ooze; and in the eyes of the people there is a failure; in the eyes of the hungry there is a growing wrath."

—John Steinbeck, *The Grapes of Wrath*, 1939[9]

Markets in capitalist economies can be fair-weather friends. The structure of capitalist production and distribution makes them unpredictable and unreliable.

Disconnected production decisions create one kind of unpredictability. One producer never knows how much other firms will supply. Or how much consumer demand the economy will generate. Production quantities and prices aren't coordinated. Waste and shortages can often result.

In 1973 and 1974, for instance, the prices of fuel and grains suddenly spiralled. Chicken farmers were caught in a squeeze. They destroyed hundreds of thousands of chickens because it cost too much to raise them to maturity. According to the *Wall Street Journal*, one company in Arkansas alone "drowned 300,000 chicks and destroyed 800,000 eggs that would have hatched broilers."[10] Meanwhile, meat prices were climbing and people were cutting back on food consumption.

This kind of waste is very likely when production decisions are so disconnected. There is no way for money to smooth over all the bumps. We've recently experienced gas lines, fuel shortages, and housing scarcity. Markets may "permit buyers and sellers to influence each other," as the DUPE booklet puts it, but they never completely eliminate market friction, bottlenecks, or serious waste.

The *wage-labor system* also creates insecurities for working people in the market. We can't buy anything unless we have money. Our claims on money under capitalism are determined by our control over

Speaking of Choices . . .

ELIZABETH... WHAT'RE YOU UP TO LATER?

ACTUALLY... I'M FREE TONIGHT. MY EX HAS THE KIDS.

HOW ABOUT A LITTLE SHOPPING AND DINNER?

WHAT DO YOU HAVE IN MIND?

I WAS THINKING ABOUT FASHION VALLEY ON ROUTE 9.

WHAT ABOUT SERENDIPITY MALL ON THE INTERSTATE?

HMMM... THERE'S A CINEMA 8 AT CONSUMERO-UNO AND A SHAKEY'S.

resources, not by our needs. We can't get enough money to meet our needs unless we have an adequate job. Many people don't, so they go hungry or suffer malnutrition. All of us face the threat of sudden interruptions in our claims on the market if we suddenly lose our jobs. We may work for a company which decides to move its plant. Tough luck. We may work in an industry with rapid automation or declining demand—and a rash of layoffs. Tough luck. **Under capitalism, the market doesn't provide free passes for people who can't afford the price of admission.**

They say that "capitalism delivers the goods." The problem is that *sometimes the goods are late, sometimes they're not there when we need them, and sometimes they never come.* How long must we wait?

Consumers in the Driver's Seat?

"It seems like all there is to life is to go down there and work, collect your paycheck, pay your bills, and get further in debt. It doesn't seem like the circle ever ends. Every day it's the same thing; every week it's the same thing; every month it's the same thing."

—**29-year-old warehouseman in California**[11]

The brands parade on the supermarket shelves like bands and floats on the the 4th of July. So many colors and attractions. Where to look? How to choose?

In that particular sense, the market provides us with many choices. But our dependence on the market also places clear limits on our choices and alternatives. The market is an enforcer. It has little respect for individual differences. It only pays attention to the bottom line. If your life doesn't balance in the black, little else matters. All the different brands on the supermarket shelves don't help.

Sellers beware. We can try to sell our labor power for what we think we're worth as individuals, but if cheaper workers are available, forget it. Companies may try to maintain decent working conditions, but if

other firms drive their workers harder, forget it. People can try to start consumers' cooperatives, but if we can't scrape together enough cash for shelves and storage space, forget it.

Buyers beware. Suppose we get sick. If we don't have the money necessary to buy treatment or pay the doctor, we may sit for hours in crowded and understaffed clinics. Suppose we have lots of family and friends in a community. If corporations decide to shut down their plants and "run away," our "free choice" to stay where we live may suddenly evaporate. Suppose we've saved for years to buy a camper for trips. If we have to work overtime to make ends meet, we don't even have time to climb in the driver's seat, much less take it for a ride. As one worker in California complained:

> We bought the camper because we thought it would be a cheap way to get away on weekends. There's nothing I like more than going up to Clear Lake with the family—fishing, swimming. But Christ, I've been working every Saturday for the last sixteen months, so there's no chance to use the thing.[12]

As the market spreads, these problems of dependence grow more severe. Corporations have more options to pack up and move because there are more potential plant locations integrated into the market distribution system. Firms can find plenty of new customers if their old ones can't pay the price. We begin to float in a vast ocean of market connections. Our own personal needs matter less and less. We're reduced to the numbers on our credit cards and uncollected bills.

People and Dollar Signs

"When I was a kid, if I needed a loaf of bread and I didn't have a loaf of bread, and my neighbor had two loaves of bread, I would give him a basket of potatoes and I'd get a loaf of bread. You help me and I'll help you. If you had a job to be done in your house and I was over there busting my whatsis to help you get your job done; if I'd had a problem you would help me. Not today. [Several other workers agree.] Why? Because of the almighty dollar. Because a person won't help you today unless he gets a buck for it."
—a chemical worker in a classroom discussion[13]

These problems of market insecurity and dependence combine to create a final dilemma. The spread of the market in capitalism tends to split us apart, like individual atoms, severing our social relations with each other. Instead of sharing our problems and cooperating to solve them, the market encourages and often forces us to compete against friends, neighbors, and fellow workers. Catch-as-catch-can.

Market insecurities create competition among workers, for example—each of us clinging to our jobs, each of us grabbing for enough income to support our families. Suppose unemployment is high. That's a time when it might make sense for all of us to pool our efforts to generate jobs for everyone who needs one. But the market doesn't recognize us as groups. When we go out looking for a job, we walk alone. Faced with high unemployment, we are forced by the market to watch out for ourselves, protecting our own jobs, trying to keep others—like undocumented workers or new groups of minority workers—away. The worse our job problems, the harder the market makes it for us to join together to solve them.

With these kinds of effects, the market creates increasingly impersonal relations throughout our daily lives. Our connections with other working people are real. But those connections are disguised and hidden, cloaked in the packaging of products and the ring of cash registers. More and more, our contacts with each other are measured out in dollars and cents rather then through personal relations. Stripped of other kinds of social connections, we're left to float by ourselves.

This creates a conflict in our lives between individual and social loyalties. We know that we have won much of what we now have through the unions, associations, and social groups we have built for ourselves. But it is often difficult for us to maintain those social connections. Shifting job location makes our personal ties less and less reliable. Unemployment and inflation make our future jobs and incomes relatively insecure. Firms bombard us with ads. All this tempts us to define our status and self-esteem through the things we buy rather than through our relationships with the people we know . We maintain our decent social relationships *in spite of the market rather than because of it.* **The dollar sign casts a lengthening shadow over our lives.** That shadow clouds many working people's views about current conditions:

> **"The country is spending more money than it had and is forcing others to do the same....Everyone's wanting to get ahead. That's why we have some of the problems I was talking about. People push and shove and spend money because everyone around them seems to be doing the same thing."**
>
> —50-year-old working man[14]

> **"Everybody's out competing with everybody else...The competition's increased...The people were more content [twenty-five years ago]. They accepted each other not on how much income they had. Now, I don't know...We live faster and are trying to have more prestige. It reflects itself with the neighbors..."**
>
> —29-year-old working woman[15]

> **"Sure, life has changed...Everyone wants what everyone else has and usually they can't get it...And the only reason is so there will be more of the green stuff."**
>
> —54-year-old working man[16]

SO WHY DOES THE MARKET ALWAYS SPREAD?

We have seen that markets in capitalist economies pose critical problems for working people: they create insecurity and dependence, fracturing our personal relations. So why have money and markets spread so widely through the history of capitalist economies despite all these problems? Have people voted for markets because they valued the convenience more than they minded the dependence and insecurity? Or have markets been foisted on working people through a much more complicated process of choice and coercion?

The Initial Spread of Money and Markets

There have always been money and markets. People have used money for centuries—placing the badge of currency, as we've seen, on such varied goods as beads, cows, and playing cards. And there have always been some kinds of markets and trading—with Mesopotamian merchants and Marco Polos carrying luxuries across the globe.

What is much more recent is such *extended* market exchange and *dependence* on commodities. This arose with the emergence of capitalism.

In Europe, as late as the seventeenth century, market exchange in basic necessities was still very limited. Export trade in corn accounted for only about 3% of total corn consumption, for example; the rest was grown by localities for their own use.[17] Gradually, as people were thrown off their land and forced to follow the factories to the cities, more and more of them had to buy their food on the market. "Large-scale systems of purchase, warehousing and distribution," says one economic historian,"...did not appear until the eighteenth century, if then."[18]

In the early nineteenth century in the United States, similarly, most free families made most of their own products. The early farm, as one economic historian put it, was "a little world of its own."[19] A New England farmer described his family's self-sufficiency in a diary: "My farm gave me and my whole family a good living on the produce of it....I never spent more than ten dollars a year, which was for salt, nails and the like. Nothing to eat, drink or wear was bought, as my farm produced it all."[20] When families did need something on the market, they usually got it from friends in the village rather than buying it from unfamiliar sellers.

Household self-sufficiency eventually eroded. More and more people worked in factories in large cities. Fewer and fewer could grow their own food. As the nineteenth century progressed, families had to rely more and more on the market. The experience of shoemakers in Lynn, Massachusetts was typical:

> In 1830 nearly all the shoemakers of Lynn had owned their homes with some land about them. Even those who rented usually had large gardens where they were able to raise sufficient vegetables for their winter supply. Almost every family kept a pig and many had their own cow....[21]

The panic of 1937 was "less distressing" to the shoemakers than later depressions would be because they could support themselves on their own. "With a garden, a pig, and some fishing tackle the shoemaker could 'bid defiance to financial tempests.' "[22]

After the 1850s, most shoemakers lost control of their own businesses, abandoning their "little shops to work in the factories."[23] Since they no longer owned their own property, their vulnerability to unemployment and depression intensified dramatically. As the *New York Tribune* reported as early as 1845, "There are hundreds of them in the city constantly wandering from shop to shop in search of work, while many of them have families in a state of absolute want."[24]

This increasing dependence on wage labor and commodity exchange was bound to spread the use of money (rather than barter) for exchange. In Europe, "barter remained the general rule over enormous areas between the fifteenth and the eighteenth centuries."[25] In the United States, barter was still common through the early 1800s. When households needed something from someone else, they often traded

"Let the bloodhounds of money beware."

—populist orator, 1890s

for it in kind. A newspaper ad in New York in 1796 reported, for instance, that "all kinds of grain, viz., wheat, rye, flax-seed, etc., etc., will be received in payment."[26]

As people moved into the cities and trade took place over longer distances, barter became increasingly difficult. Money became more and more essential as a substitute. And that meant that people could only get along if they had enough. By the late nineteenth century, popular protest focused directly on the supply of money and bank control. If too little money was available, people felt the pinch. "To delegate to private and selfish interests the supreme sovereign function of issuing...money," an AFL resolution stated in 1898, "is to place in their hands the weal and woe of the people."[27] A farmers' spokesman was even more graphic: "The amount of circulating medium [must be] speedily increased...The people are at bay; let the bloodhounds of money who have dogged us this far beware."[28]

The Continuing Spread of Money and Markets

It wasn't only the needs of working people that prompted the spread of money and markets. Since the initial emergence of capitalism, corporations have also encouraged the spread of money and markets in their perpetual pursuit of profits. We saw in Chapters 3 and 4 that capitalists continuously search for less expensive and more pliant workers. They search along other dimensions as well.

Finding New Supplies. Capitalists are always looking for ways to lower their costs and expand production. This leads them to search continually for new sources not only of labor but also of natural resources which permit lower costs or expanding supply. If and when they find them, they must at least partly integrate the resource-rich areas into the world market. Extractive equipment must be installed.

Workers must be fed and clothed. Transportation must be arranged. All that requires money—which begins to spread outward like ripples from a stone plopping into a pond.

The quest for raw materials began to intensify toward the end of the nineteenth century. Corporations from the United States and Europe scoured the globe, looking for new lodes of raw materials.

Where they could, corporations from one country cornered supplies in others, capturing colonies to fuel the metropolis. European capitalists carved up Northern Africa. The British fought the Boers in South Africa and dug for gold and diamonds. In Latin America, different countries grabbed for different colonies. The British won the race for Chilean saltpeter and copper, for instance, and British private investment in Chile's mines immediately soared.[29] As in other colonies around the world, British capital dominated not only the mines but "the whole of the public life of the province in question...: railways, waterworks, and banks."[30]

The search for raw materials continues. The market has invaded Northern Alaska along the Alaskan pipeline. It has gone fishing for offshore oil along coasts around the world. The fate of entire governments now hangs on their decisions about how to market their resources. Increasingly, the market is virtually dictating the lives of people in nearly every corner of the globe.

Finding New Customers. Capitalists must sell the goods they produce. Their urgent quest for consumers also leads to the market's continuing expansion.

The corporations began their intensive search for new customers in the beginning of the twentieth century. They began to plan, as one business writer put it, to change working people from "wheelhorse" to "worker" and from "worker" to "consumer."[31] "Consumptionism is the name given to the new doctrine...," another business theorist wrote in 1926; "the idea that workmen and masses be looked upon not simply as workers and producers, but as *consumers*...Pay them more, sell them more, prosper more is the equation."[32] Hundreds of new products were introduced on the market: milk, citrus fruits, canned juice, mechanical refrigerators, washing machines, automobiles, readymade clothing.... The dependence on commodities deepened. As one sociologist observed in 1925:

> Factory products supplant home-made commodities, factory labor competes with and displaces household labor, and the family income...must now take the form of money to pay for the ready-made article...The less [the family] can produce at home, the more it must spend.[33]

The process continues throughout the economy. The auto industry provides a classic example. The car companies have constantly prodded us to buy new cars—to keep up with our neighbors, to acquire the "elegance" of a truly fine car," to burst from zero to sixty mph a split second more rapidly. Their marketing strategy was consciously designed to lure us toward new and more expensive models. *Fortune* magazine announced the strategy in 1953: "In the postwar sellers' market, [the auto industry] has found itself selling more car per car—more accessories, luxuries, improvements, and innovations. Now it has to plan it that way..."[34] Between 1956 and 1960, according to two economists, the companies' annual model changes cost a minimum of $5 billion *a year* over and above the basic costs of regular production.[35] In 1973, for instance, GM carefully substituted more expensive models for the simpler models of earlier years. "In effect," one Wall Street analyst noted, "we have the consumer being forced to upgrade his purchases."[36] And now we're all paying the price.

No Wonder People Have Always Protested

Both in the early years of capitalism and more recently, corporations and the wealthy have pushed markets on us to further their own pursuit of wealth and profits. Markets could be pushed on us because we lost the power to refuse when we lost control over the means of production. We've never been asked how we might want to reorganize them to preserve the convenience while reducing the dependence and insecurity. Given the continuing lack of alternatives, we obviously make the best use of markets we can.

But they haven't always worked for us. And people have always fought back. The best evidence of the depth and persistence of the problems with markets and money *in capitalist economies* lies in the record of people's continuing protests against them. We've mobilized against high prices, sudden shortages, tight money, and greedy merchants. All the choices in the world couldn't cool people's anger.

BUT WHAT ABOUT PRICES AND EFFICIENCY?

"The price system works so well, so efficiently, that we are not aware of it most of the time."
—the Gospel According to DUPE[37]

By now the DUPEsters are furious. How could we have been so misguided? We've missed the basic point, they'll insist, because markets and money allow an "invisible hand" to weave a web of economic magic.

Where are the laws of "supply and demand"? Where are the links between prices and efficiency? What are you people even talking about?

The DUPE argument about prices and efficiency is straightforward. We need the market, they argue, because market prices make everyone better off. If prices are too "high," consumers will shift their demand to some other products. If prices are too "low," consumers will form long lines in front of those counters, pushing prices back up to their "normal" levels. The prices which result, they suggest, are the best measure of the economic worth of goods and services.

Prices are set, in short, by the "law of supply and demand"—reaching their proper levels, as the DUPE primer puts it, through a "continuous tug of war between consumer and producer over price."[38]

If we interfere with market prices, we'll wind up in an economic pickle.

The problem with this DUPE argument is that it exaggerates the importance of the market in determining prices. Let's take one last look at how the market does and doesn't work.

Production and Prices

When people traded goods through barter, they pegged the terms of trade to the amount of labor they put into the products being exchanged. We have records of a trade in 1812, for instance, between two farmers in New York State. James Dunagin made ten pairs of shoes for Cornelius Brink and his family. In return, Dunagin received from Brink "one hundred herring, one bushel of potatoes, two bushels of rye" and also drew "one load of wood."[39] Brink and Dunagin did not settle on those terms arbitrarily. Both knew roughly how much time and effort Dunagin needed to make ten pairs of shoes. Dunagin's reward—"one hundred herring, one bushel of potatoes, two bushels of

What's in a Price?

rye...and one load of wood"—seemed fair compensation. Why? Because Brink and his family apparently needed an equivalent amount of time and effort to produce all those different goods in return.

We now use money to facilitate exchange. Instead of paying for shoes with bushels and pecks, we buy them with a standard currency. Prices are expressed in a common denominator. Does this change the way the terms of trade among commodities are set?

Not fundamentally. The amount of labor time and effort required to make a commodity will still have a decisive impact on its price. Lemonade is easy to make, so it's difficult to charge very much for it on the stand. Much more time and effort pour into the production of newspapers—both indirectly in cutting the trees for paper or building the presses; and directly, in writing the stories or setting the type. It takes even more time and effort to build an individual automobile. And still more time to build a large tanker. The prices of these products will obviously have to bear some relationship to the differences in the amount of labor which goes indirectly into their production.

How tight is this relationship between price and labor time? We've previewed most of this discussion in Chapter 3. Prices can't fall much below the total labor costs of any product—measured from the beginning to the end of the whole production cycle—because producers couldn't afford to continue production without suffering losses. And prices can't rise substantially above these labor costs for long. If they do, someone else will be able to make them more inexpensively. Or, in the long run, people won't be able to afford the goods because they aren't getting enough compensation in return for the labor they're putting into earning their own incomes. The amount of work required to produce a commodity, in this sense, acts as a kind of center of gravity for its price.

Within this context, the effects of changes in demand are likely to be short-lived. Suppose, for example, that everyone suddenly decides to "demand" some new product, like video tape decks, and its price initially jumps in response to the new demand. There is nonetheless likely to be enough competition among producers to keep nudging the price back down toward (direct and indirect) labor costs. In the end, those basic costs of production are likely to play a much more important role in establishing the relative price of those tape decks than people's sudden shift in preferences. Those costs are simply too important to be ignored.

The numbers confirm these suspicions. One study recently found that about *90% of the differences in prices among different products in the U.S. economy could be attributed to the different amounts of (direct and indirect) labor time involved in their production.*[40] That doesn't leave much room for differences in "demand."

What explains the small leftover differences between labor time and prices? What explains the remaining 10%?

Some of this difference represents temporary changes in people's preferences—in what the DUPEsters call "demand." But some represents just plain *noise*—static interference of little economic importance or use: cartels operating on the world market, interruptions in

transportation systems, sudden fluctuations in interest rates.

When static interferes with the radio signal, we can re-tune the dial. But when economic noises interfere with prices in a market economy, there is no dial we can turn. We must simply sit on our thumbs and hope that the interference will go away.

What About Money?

So where does money fit in? We don't carry labor-time stop-watches around in our pockets. It's very difficult to compare the labor content of a chair and a car. We talk dollars and cents, not hours and seconds.

Because labor time comparisons are so difficult, money has become increasingly common as commodity exchange has become more and more widespread. This has involved setting aside some standard commodity—which we call *money*—to serve as a common unit of value against which all the different products of labor can be measured.

People have used many different currencies throughout history—beads, jewels, cattle, whiskey and tobacco...almost anything fairly easy to make and carry around. (In Canada in the early eighteenth century, they even used playing cards. "In a 1711 issue," one economist reports, "spades and clubs were the currency of highest denomination; hearts and diamonds only half their value."[41]) For the last couple of centuries many countries in the capitalist world have relied heavily on paper money or gold as the *standard currency of last resort*, as the common unit of value to which their money and prices are ultimately pegged.

(Why gold? It can be easily standardized and weighed. It takes a lot of labor time to produce it, so that small units of gold can represent large units of other products. Since it doesn't dissolve or erode, it lasts for a long time. It's also a soft metal, which means that it doesn't have very many other productive uses and isn't "wasted" by serving this special purpose.)

Does this recent use of standard forms of money change our basic conclusions?

A recent example can help us answer this question. During the 1960s, as we shall see in detail in Chapter 18, the U.S. economy was pouring too many dollars into the hands of other businesses and governments abroad. The social (or labor-time) value of goods "made in the USA" hadn't increased as rapidly. So foreigners ended up holding more dollars than they needed or wanted. The dollar began to lose relative value, since there were so many floating around. It therefore took more dollars to buy an ounce of gold or a German mark or a Japanese yen. The dollar wasn't "worth" as much anymore.

What caused this price adjustment? The market wasn't operating by itself. The price changes—and the fluctuations in the value of different currencies—came about because of changes in *the relative costs of producing goods and services in different countries*. The "made in USA" label had lost value. This insight will prove decisive when we look more closely in Chapters 18 and 19 at the causes of recent inflation.

In the meantime, we have reason to doubt the DUPE argument

about prices and efficiency. The DUPE says that we need the market because prices in the market reflect a "tug of war" between buyers and sellers. But we have seen that the *costs* of producing goods and services have the most important effect on prices, even in market economies. And we saw earlier that there are a variety of ways of coordinating production decisions. There is nothing either magical or inevitable about markets and prices. If we don't like them, why should we keep them?

CAN'T WE CURE THE MARKET'S PROBLEMS?

Markets provide many conveniences, but markets in capitalist economies also create dependence and insecurity. Can we have the good without the bad? Can we retain the advantages and eliminate the disadvantages? Can we have market exhange without dependence and insecurity?

One possible solution would be some kind of economic *planning*. Instead of allowing decisions to be so disconnected, we could try to connect them through coordinated plans for supply and output. We could try to ensure that there was enough food in the stores and enough heating fuel to last the winter. What happens then?

Suppose our planners order capitalist corporations to produce greater supplies of goods on which they aren't making "enough" profit. There are three possible outcomes. (1) We might have to force workers in those industries to work harder in order to boost profits for the reluctant corporations. Most workers are already working hard enough. Do we want to put ourselves in the position of bossing

workers from outside the plant? This suggests that corporate profits should bear the burden of planning, not the workers. (2) But corporations may simply thumb their noses at our noble plans. "We're investing in some different industries where profits are higher," they'll tell us, "and we don't want to maintain the railroads any more." Their

freedom to invest where they please might scuttle our plans to moderate the anarchy of disconnected production. What would we do then? (3) We could enforce our plans and not accept corporate profits as an absolutely determining priority. We could place security of income and supply over the security of corporate profits. But then we would be doing much more than just regulating the market. We would be tampering with the basic foundations of the economic system. So the problem of planning is obviously more complicated than it sounds. (We'll return to it in later chapters for more detailed discussion.)

The basic problem is that we keep bumping up against the "bottom line" rules of markets in capitalist economies. Whatever changes we may want, we are supposed to satisfy capitalists' insistence on the highest possible profits. No matter where we turn, we keep confronting the same uncompromising demand.

All this means that we must accept the market's discipline unless we develop enough power to stand above it, withstanding its insistent bottom-line calculations. If we want higher wages, for instance, we have to develop alternatives to wage employment in case our employers decide to move the plant elsewhere. That would require controlling our means of production. Which would require gaining control of enough supplies, plant, and equipment to be able to produce

what we need. Which would require changing the way our entire economic system operates.

We've come full circle in our analysis of the U.S. economy. We've seen from earlier chapters that workers in individual factories and offices might want to gain control over those workplaces in order to control profits and working conditions. But we have seen in this chapter that our ability to control our own workplaces *and* to change our working conditions is limited by our dependence on market exchange. And we've also seen that efforts to reduce market dependence and insecurity would immediately raise issues about how the entire economy is organized. We can't fiddle with just one part of the system, it turns out, without raising questions about "the whole thing." If we want to eliminate problems in one part of the system, we have to consider changing nearly everything.

This seems like a tough order. Is there any hope that future changes in the economy might make it less burdensome and easier to change? Can we anticipate any rabbits out of some magician's hat in coming years? If we don't try to change it now, will the economy work any better in a decade or two? Our strategies for tackling our current economic problems obviously depend on these basic questions....And that is where we turn next.

6.

Bigger, Bigger, and ...Better?

"Automation? Depends how it's applied. It frightens me if it puts me out on the street. It doesn't frighten me if it shortens my work week. You read that little thing: what are you going to do when this computer replaces you? Blow up computers....(Laughs.) Really. Blow up computers. I'll be goddamned if a computer is gonna eat before I do! I want milk for my kids and beer for me. Machines can either liberate man or enslave 'im....It's man who has the bias to put the thing one place or another."

—Chicago steelworker[1]

We have seen that our problems have deep roots in the basic operations of the U.S. economy. Piecemeal change seems difficult.

Meanwhile, the economy is itself changing rapidly. As the economy changes, will it solve our problems by itself? Or will it make them worse?

Where is the economy heading? Where does change come from? What are the consequences?

WHAT'S UNDER THE HOOD?

"The American Dream is to be better off than you are...There's never enough of anything....Growth—better—faster....I feel a very heavy sense of compulsion, a sense of urgency. When I get in a car, I also feel it. I drive much too fast."

—corporate executive[2]

We have seen that capitalists can never rest. If they take a break, their competitors may sneak by them just as the tortoise passed the hare. If they relax on the job, workers may find new ways to resist exploitation. To stay in business, capitalist corporations must keep on the move. They must try to stay ahead of their competitors by lowering their costs and/or by stealing markets through introduction of new or better products. They must try to stay on top of their workers by developing new machines and job structures which increase output, keep workers divided, and reduce our ability to struggle at work. All of that requires investment—in machines, labor management, product design, advertising, and marketing. *And investment requires profits.*

This leads to a simple but fundamental conclusion: *capitalists must relentlessly race after profits.* Their cars must stay at full throttle. They can never fall asleep at the wheel.

We can refer to this race as the process of *capital accumulation*. In order to make profits, corporations need to invest. In order to invest, they need *capital*—both cash and access to the means of production. But in order to have that capital available, they need to have earned some profits. And in order to continue earning profits, they must continually have access to capital. So the dash for profits involves a broader quest for capital. The one can't be divorced from the other.

Corporate decisions, as we've also seen, have a profound impact on the entire economy. Since corporations control the means of production, they largely determine what gets produced and how. As they race after their profits, their policies and practices will shape the way we work, what we earn, and how we live. This suggests a simple preliminary conclusion: **the engine under the hood of our economy is the capitalist pursuit of profits.**

So far so easy. As corporations go in their chase after profits and capital, to a large degree, so goes the economy. But we now need to look much more closely at this race for profits— which we have called the process of capital accumulation. How does the continual corporate quest for more and more capital—in order to earn higher and higher profits—affect the way our economy grows and changes?

What kinds of steps must corporations take for successful accumulation of capital and higher profit returns? And what kinds of difficulties or pitfalls must they overcome at each step in order to achieve their desired goals?

These questions are particularly important if we want to understand what the economy will look like in the future. If profit-seeking has little impact on the economic environment, then we can assume that our growing economy will remain essentially the way it is today. (And the tasks of this chapter will be easy.) But if the corporate chase after profits tends to change the economy, then we'll have to study the character of these changes very carefully before we can reach clear conclusions about the future paths of U.S. capitalism.

Once Around the Track

The process of capital accumulation is a little like a race track, littered with various obstacles, screeching with the wheels of competing drivers, the checkered flag a distant and difficult goal. The reward for those companies who successfully complete one whole circuit of this course of capital accumulation is profit; only those who complete the whole circuit can earn a profit. The others must either coast back to the starting line and begin again—or drop out of the race altogether.

In order to study the process of capital accumulation, we can follow capitalists around this race course and watch the impact of their fine-tuning and acceleration. Watching their moves carefully, we can begin to judge what kind of mark they leave on the economy as they thunder along.

It turns out that there are four main parts to the course, each with its own obstacles and opportunities: 1) finding workers and supplies; 2) extracting surplus value in production; 3) finding buyers for final products; and 4) turning sales revenues into final profits.

1. *Finding Cheaper Workers and Supplies.* First, corporations can't produce any goods unless they have something to produce them with. So corporations begin the race for profits by using their cash to buy what's necessary for production. They hire workers, purchase raw materials, and secure machines. Where does this lead?

It should be reasonably obvious that corporations can potentially earn higher profits *if* they buy their factors of production at lower prices. They will constantly scour the market for cheaper raw materials and machines, or maybe even produce what they need themselves. They will also constantly search for cheaper sources of labor supply and, as we saw in Chapter 4, will try to keep their workers as disorganized and divided as possible. These efforts will have uncertain effects, however.

If and when corporations succeed, for example, their doing may also prove their undoing. As more and more corporations discover a new treasure of cheap supply, like natural gas, the growing demand may push supply prices as high as before. Or wages may suddenly

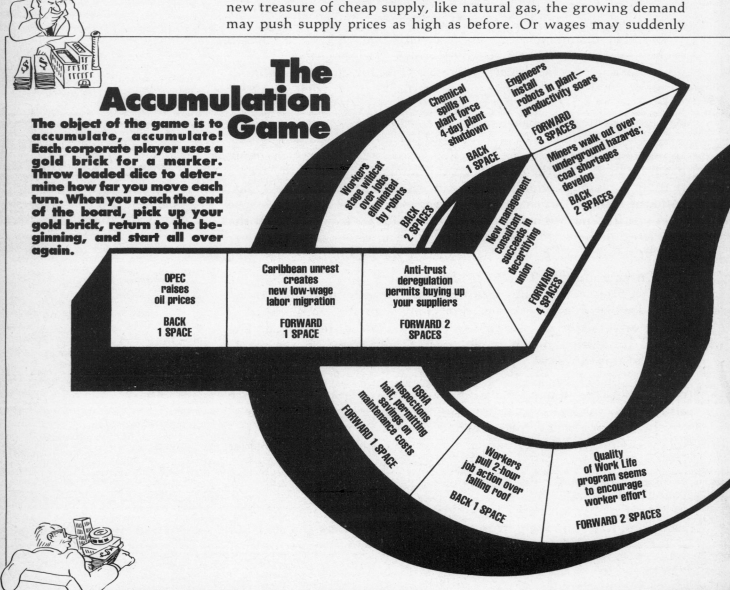

The Accumulation Game

The object of the game is to accumulate, accumulate! Each corporate player uses a gold brick for a marker. Throw loaded dice to determine how far you move each turn. When you reach the end of the board, pick up your gold brick, return to the beginning, and start all over again.

Chemical spills in plant force 4-day plant shutdown
BACK 1 SPACE

Engineers install robots in plant—productivity soars
FORWARD 3 SPACES

Miners walk out over underground hazards; coal shortages develop
BACK 2 SPACES

Workers stage wildcat over jobs eliminated by robots
BACK 2 SPACES

New management consultant succeeds in decentralizing union
FORWARD 4 SPACES

OPEC raises oil prices
BACK 1 SPACE

Caribbean unrest creates new low-wage labor migration
FORWARD 1 SPACE

Anti-trust deregulation permits buying up your suppliers
FORWARD 2 SPACES

OSHA inspections halt, permitting savings on maintenance costs
FORWARD 1 SPACE

Workers pull 2-hour job action over falling roof
BACK 1 SPACE

Quality of Work Life program seems to encourage worker effort
FORWARD 2 SPACES

begin to rise if corporations all flock after the same sources of cheap labor. And as these new workers are thrown together into factories and offices, they may recognize their common problems and organize strong unions. Through collective bargaining or militant action, they may be able to raise their wages far above what corporations "expected" to pay. *Corporations may discover occasional bargains, but they may not enjoy their savings forever.* Competition and/or class struggle are likely to erode those windfalls before long.

This continuing corporate quest for cheap supply will also create continuing uncertainty for workers. Corporate freedom to fire their workers and move their plants means that workers can never rest on past laurels, comfortably enjoying wage gains from previous years. Whenever corporations find some other workers available at lower wages, they'd rather switch than fight. Corporate loyalty to employees is only skin-deep. Which means that *workers must constantly worry that higher wages in the present may threaten job security in the future.* As long as corporations control investment and there are potentially less costly workers anywhere around the world, workers will continue to twist on

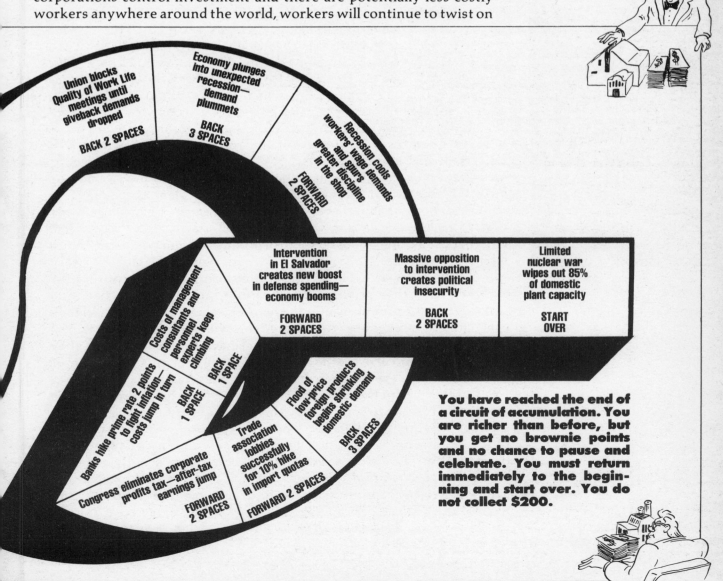

Union blocks Quality of Work Life meetings until giveback demands dropped

BACK 2 SPACES

Economy plunges into unexpected recession— demand plummets

BACK 3 SPACES

Recession cools workers' wage demands and spurs greater discipline in the shop

FORWARD 2 SPACES

Intervention in El Salvador creates new boost in defense spending— economy booms

FORWARD 2 SPACES

Massive opposition to intervention creates political insecurity

BACK 2 SPACES

Limited nuclear war wipes out 85% of domestic plant capacity

START OVER

Costs of management consultants and personnel experts keep climbing

BACK 1 SPACE

Banks hike prime rate 2 points to fight inflation— costs jump in turn

BACK 1 SPACE

Congress eliminates corporate profits tax—after-tax earnings jump

FORWARD 2 SPACES

Trade association lobbies successfully for 10% hike in import quotas

FORWARD 2 SPACES

Flood of low-price foreign products begins shrinking domestic demand

BACK 3 SPACES

You have reached the end of a circuit of accumulation. You are richer than before, but you get no brownie points and no chance to pause and celebrate. You must return immediately to the beginning and start over. You do not collect $200.

the horns of that dilemma.

2. *Increasing Surplus Value in Production.* Capitalists can only begin the second part of the course after they have completed the first. Having obtained factors of production at the lowest possible price, corporations must still succeed in combining them in the most productive ways in order to turn a profit on their investments. They must be able to push their workers hard enough to ensure surplus value. Unless they can count on that foundation for profits, they may never open the factory gates or the office doors.

Once again, corporate successes may pave the way for corporate failures. If corporations drive their workers too hard, the workers may either wear out or fight back. If the corporate quest for higher surplus value prompts the introduction of machines, the bosses may be more vulnerable to worker strikes (because of the size of their investment). Or the machines may link the workers in ways which help demonstrate their collective strength. Or the technology may pose such health risks that workers begin to demand more control over the production process. One factory owner in the late nineteenth century observed, "strikes are the bane of the factory owner's existence. With a plant worth perhaps a million dollars brought to a standstill,...a strike coming at an awkward time of year means tremendous loss."[3] *Since there are such sharp conflicts between the interests of workers and bosses at the workplace, corporations can never count on any strategy working for long.* Their struggle for greater workplace control goes on year after year.

And this quest also creates continuing difficulties for workers. If we resist the bosses' strategies for control, the bosses may switch to other, more disciplined workers. If we successfully tame one hazardous machine, employers may introduce an even greater menace to our health and safety. Or corporations may close the plant and move. This haunting choice shadows every working day: *our struggle to improve our working conditions now may jeopardize our job security in the future.* The risks persist as long as bosses control production and potentially more disciplined workers are available anywhere around the globe.

3. *Selling Products.* Third, corporations can't make a profit if they can't sell what they produce. Corporations must push the goods and services they've produced onto the market, selling them as fast as they can. The gross revenues from these sales will build up a mountain of money. Since the corporations wouldn't have begun the race if they didn't expect to earn profits, it's a good bet that this mountain of revenues will be even higher than the pile they had at the start.

But this part of the race is particularly likely to have unpredictable results. The less corporations pay their workers, for example, the less money the workers will have to spend on corporate products later on. Or the minute one corporation discovers a new and successful product or marketing device, other firms may copy it so adeptly that the pioneering corporation's profits dissolve and it's left paying the additional costs of product research, development, advertising, and promotional sales. *Corporate revenues can be just as unstable as their customers' incomes and manipulated tastes.*

Workers share some of these problems too. There will be more money for wages in any individual industry, like auto, if supply costs are low *and* product demand is high. But if supply costs are low, the wages of workers in other industries are likely to be low. Which means that the incomes of potential consumers will also be low. As incomes go, so goes product demand. Auto workers will be better off, in this example, if other workers are both *worse off* and *better off* at the same time. A neat trick! Corporate control over planning, disconnected production, and market uncertainties combine to *create an impossible balancing act for workers—between higher current wages and higher future product demand.* The risks continue as long as workers can't all get together to plan stable growth in both income and employment.

4. *Turning Revenues into Investments.* Capitalists must steer through a final obstacle if they are to complete the race successfully. They must be ready at the end of the course to make some new investments, since their future profits will depend on their continuing pursuit of capital after this first circuit has been completed.

But the capitalists can't plow all their revenues back into further investments. They'll keep some of it for their own consumption, paying out dividends and salaries for their houses and diamonds and long sleek cars. They'll use some more to cover the costs of sales, circulation, and overhead—paying the salespeople, accountants, lawyers, and advertising agents who help sell and monitor the flow of goods. If they borrowed money to put together their initial wad, they'll also have to pay interest to the capitalists who own the bank. And they'll pay taxes to the government. The less they have to pay to their clerks, the banks, and the Feds, the more they'll be able to keep for new investment (and themselves).

And then their problems may really begin. Suppose they pay lower wages to their clerks. Who will buy their products? Suppose they try to reduce their interest costs by borrowing less. That means they'll have to raise the extra cash out of their own budgets, cutting back in other areas and creating new dislocations. Suppose their moaning convinces the government to cut back on corporate taxes. If that leads to higher taxes on workers, who will buy their products? *It's often easy to sketch cost-savings schemes on ledger paper, but acting on those plans may create a hornet's nest of additional problems in the future.*

And options on this leg don't get any easier for workers either. Administrative workers face the same difficult choices between higher wages and future job security as production workers. Workers' wages could be higher if the company didn't spend so much on interest payments. But if the company has to raise its own capital instead of borrowing from the bank, how can we be sure that the money won't come out of our own wages and salaries? And if workers push the tax burden back on the corporations, what will happen to investment and, in the future, to our jobs? *The choices are tough as long as workers have so little control over the means of production and the allocation of total surplus.*

We have now completed one full circuit of the course. The corporations can't even pause to count their change. The money they have left after the fourth leg is called *retained earnings.* But they must speed immediately on to the next lap, plowing all these retained earnings back into production for another round of accumulation. Driven by fear of their competitors and by struggle with their workers, they will race on and on. Each time they successfully complete a lap, they keep alive their hopes of continuing accumulation. If they run a bad lap, they may be forced to pull off the track, dropping out of the competition.

But let's take a pit stop while they race ahead. What have we learned from our brief tour of the track?

It was easy to trace *where* the corporations drove in their pursuit of profits. But it turned out to be surprisingly difficult to gauge their impact. Wherever they turn, corporations apparently face continuing uncertainty—even the persistent possibility that their strategies will backfire. Meanwhile we as working people are constantly confronted with difficult choices between current gains and potential losses in the future. We know neither what's going to happen nor where to turn.

It turns out, then, that the tasks of this chapter are not easy at all. It seems clear that the process of capital accumulation is unlikely to leave the economy exactly as it is. Deciding what kinds of changes it will generate obviously requires much more careful investigation.

BIGGER, BIGGER....

"Everyone's afraid Big Daddy's going to abandon them.... Most of these women still want to believe Daddy's looking after them....He keeps throwing out the same tired line about costs being too high to give higher raises and they keep falling. Christ, I don't know. At least that's the way it was when I was there. Maybe it's changing now. Maybe with those departments being transferred they're finally realizing the company's been looking out for its own interests all these years, not theirs."

—former filing clerk for large insurance firm[4]

The process of capital accumulation seems confusing from the middle of the track. If we step back and take a more distant view, however, that process begins to acquire a more definite shape. However blurry it seems when we're in the middle of it, economic growth has several clear consequences *as long as capitalist priorities remain dominant in the economy.* Five effects seem most important: 1) "profitability" increasingly limits the choices available to us; 2) the scale of production becomes larger and larger; 3) corporations themselves grow bigger and bigger; 4) the economy experiences repeated instability; and 5) capitalism spreads around the globe.

1. Color It Capitalist
In the first decades of capitalist domination in any society, many people can live as before. Even though some workers march through the factory gates, most families still produce many things for them-

selves and enjoy traditional relationships with their families and friends.

As capitalist economies grow, these islands of tradition begin to shrink. *Capitalist relationships and priorities color more and more of economic and social life.* Mature capitalist accumulation begins to influence the tint and shading of every detail in our daily lives. How does this happen?

One important process affects people's lives as *producers.* As we have seen throughout the earlier chapters, the growth of capitalist economies forces more and more people to give up working for themselves and to begin working for capitalist employers. Farmers can no longer support themselves so they move to the cities. Craft workers find it harder to compete with mass-production firms; most wind up in the plant. Even professional people find it increasingly difficult to work on their own; more and more end up in large organizations. (The days of the independent lawyer hanging out a shingle have practically disappeared, as most lawyers now work for large firms.) Nearly everyone comes to share the common experience of reporting to work for someone else and coping with employers' domination of the working day.

Another important process affects our lives as *consumers.* As firms grow bigger and markets grow wider, more and more of the products we consume are shaped by the profit motive.

■   Food is one important example. Huge food processing corporations and supermarket chains prefer to haul and store food in large trucks and warehouses for wide markets. This means that they don't want foods which have irregular shapes, spoil quickly, or appeal to tiny segments of the consuming population. Fresh vegetables like tomatoes are hardened so machines can pick them and they'll last longer—even during the summer. Breads are baked with treated flours for long distance travel, so it gets more and more difficult to find unusual loaves with untreated flours. Increasingly throughout the United States, chickens are fed chemicals and fattened with artificial stimulants to help them survive the trip to distant markets. More and more, as we wheel our carts through the supermarket, we all face the same products with the same labels and the same ingredients—no matter where we live or what our tastes.

■ Music provides another example. A few giant record companies now dominate the popular music business. Their promotion departments heavily influence what's played on "Top-40" radio stations. Special regional music tastes don't appeal to record companies because the companies are geared for distribution to national markets. So special regional or ethnic music doesn't get recorded by the big companies. Groups with particular appeal find it harder to make a living. And music begins to sound more and more alike. If the popular music you like is "different," as a recent article on the popular music business concluded, "it probably isn't being recorded—and you have to go honky-tonkin' if you want to hear it."[5]

Eventually, capitalist priorities creep into every corner of our lives. Corporations grow larger and their operations cover expanding portions of the country and the globe. They can shut down plants in one place and expand production in another. Or they can transfer administrative and executive personnel from office to office. As a result, our preferences about where we live matter less and less. Ties to our neighbors and communities pale in importance. For more and more people, corporate profit criteria come to dominate "choices" about where we live. We grow accustomed to the moving van as a regular part of our lives.

The results of these forces are clear. In many important respects, our lives become more and more alike. Capitalist growth doesn't respect individual differences or regional tastes. Personal preferences are most submerged when they're shared by few others. There may be many different jobs and products to choose from, but there are also many kinds of jobs and products which *aren't* on the menu because they aren't profitable. It's a little like Henry Ford's quip about the Model T car in the 1920s. "You can get it in any color you want," he said, "as long as it's black."[6] These days we can lead any kind of life we want...*as long as corporations can profit from it.*

2. Up Against the Machines and Supervisors

Corporations are constantly driven, as we have already seen, to search for ways to lower their costs and control their workers.

The most immediate consequence of their scramble for profits is that they tend to *increase the scale of production.* More and more tasks in the factory and office are performed by machines. And more and more bosses and supervisors look over our shoulders.

a) *Machines.* There are two main reasons why capitalists tend to use more and more machines. The first is that certain kinds of large-scale production processes have clear cost advantages over smaller ones. We can see this most clearly by looking at three examples of how production has been organized historically.

The oldest system is *craft,* or *small batch production.* When only a few products are being made at a time or when goods are made to order, it is often difficult to organize production in ways which make the best use of workers' skills or the potential advantages of technology. (Luxury jewelry production is one of many current examples of this kind of production.)

Mass production systems become possible when large numbers of identical products are being made. Work can be broken down into many simple tasks and, typically, large numbers of goods can be made at small unit cost. (The auto assembly line is the classic example of this kind of system.)

Continuous flow production involves the largest scale investment in machines because it practically eliminates workers from the production process. It can be applied only if the market for a product is broad enough to support the investment involved. In addition to breaking production down into many small tasks, continuous flow processes also rely on machines to perform most of those tasks. (Oil refineries are one of the oldest examples of continuous flow production.) Where continuous flow production is possible, it usually results in very low unit costs.

From Corporate productivity ad

Over the long history of capitalist development, the movement from craft production through mass production to continuous flow processes has both lowered costs and dramatically increased the scale of the production process itself, involving more and more investment in machines. This does not mean that only huge corporations can make use of the most efficient machines. Or that our jobs must always be so boring in order to take advantage of advanced technology. (We discuss these questions in detail in Chapters 10 and 11.) It means much more simply that advanced technology can often reduce the costs of production and that capitalists have always raced to take advantage of these opportunities.

Which leads us to the second reason for a continuing increase in the mass of machines: *machine investment helps capitalists control workers.* Several factors contribute to this general effect.

■ Machines are obviously much easier to control than workers. They don't fight back and they don't go out on strike. (Machines break down but machine repair is more predictable than workers' strikes.)

■ Machines often help control workers by regulating what we do and controlling the speed at which we work. The more continuous the flow the less the chance that we will be able to re-design our work or resist the machines' work pace.

■ Machine production often makes it possible to get rid of craft workers who have their own ideas about production. Two efficiency experts, writing in 1914, concluded that this helped explain the success of Henry Ford's new assembly line: "The Ford Company has no use for experience, in the working ranks, anyway. It desires and prefers machine-tool operators who have nothing to unlearn....and will simply do what they are told to do, over and over again from bell time to bell time."[7]

■ Machine investment also tends to displace workers, widening the pools of reserve labor and thus curbing workers' ability to resist

their bosses. The move to continuous flow process has the greatest displacing effects, reducing the need for production workers to the barest minimum. (We examine the net effects of automation on employment in some detail in Chapter 7.) Workers in manufacturing have known the intimidating fear of losing jobs through automation for years. Now more and more office workers are facing the same threat.

b) *Supervisors*. Corporations rely on more and more bosses and supervisors for similar reasons.

The first grows directly out of the bosses' continuing drive for control over production *and* their continuing investment in machines reducing craft skills. When bosses strip us of our knowledge and control on the job, they create a vacuum in the production process: our different tasks need to be coordinated. Someone needs to join our separate efforts, forging a unified whole. As we saw in Chapter 4, capitalists have continuously sought this reduction in workers' power. This has created a continuous need for new mechanisms of coordination. Corporations have raced to fill the void. They began recognizing the seriousness of the problem in the U.S. after their major successes in reducing craft workers' strength around 1900. The pace of production seemed to be slowing, not increasing. Where were the dividends of their increased power? "Behind the confusion of fluctuating labor...," one corporate personnel expert concluded, "there is a greater chaos of inefficient management of...production and personnel."[8] Corporations have created the need for supervision, in this sense, by robbing employees of their own capacity to coordinate work. Less power to us *requires* more power to them.

The second reason for more supervision follows from the first. Workers have resisted these corporate efforts, creating unions to unify their collective force in opposition. This has, in turn, further spurred the growth of the bosses' supervisory machine. If we're getting together to plan resistance, they need someone to watch over us. If we're figuring out how to win a grievance, they need to beat us to the punch. They could not rely, as one corporate consultant concluded, "on the old-time haphazard methods of hiring labor."[9] As workers have strengthened their bonds through unions, corporations have hired more and more supervisors to act as a kind of dissolving agent, seeking repeatedly to *erode* these sources of workers' resistance and control.

In the end, these tendencies toward more machines and more supervisors reinforce each other. Machines reduce our skills and our ability to coordinate production. Which requires supervisors as a substitute. Which prompts worker reaction against the supervisors. Which requires even more supervision to outflank workers' resistance. And more machines to replace the most skilled or most militant workers. And therefore more supervisors to coordinate the machines.... The spiral continues as long as capitalists continue chasing their profits and control.

3. The Growth of Large Corporations
Corporations become ever bigger. Why?

The push toward more machines and supervisors is one of the most important sources of larger and larger corporations. Large corporations can better afford the investments necessary for advanced technologies. They can spread the costs of machines and supervisors over a much higher volume of business. Large firms are also more likely to be able to finance the research and development costs involved in the search for the most efficient machines and management systems.

But these are not the only reasons that capitalist firms tend to grow bigger and bigger. Even beyond this push from the organization of production, there are other important forces which reinforce the tendencies of corporations to grow. Suppose a smaller and a larger firm have already adopted the same kind of technology and are equally efficient in cranking out the goods. There are still some important reasons why *the larger firm will probably finish first in the race for profit.*

■ When business slackens, the large corporation may be able to weather the storm better than its smaller competitor. Even if their rates of profit are the same, the large corporation's asset reserves are likely to be much bigger and its staying power much longer. Just as those who have the biggest store of goods in their larders are always likeliest to survive a famine, so are large corporations in the best position to survive recessions and depressions.

■ Large corporations are often able to get better deals from their suppliers and buyers because they can promise a bigger set of orders or a larger volume of goods. This factor has had a big effect on U.S. farming, where food corporations such as Del Monte have contracted with relatively larger farmers—even though they haven't been any more "efficient" than the smaller ones—simply because they can produce in large volume and can save the corporations distribution and administrative costs.[10]

■ Large companies can also swing their weight more aggressively in pursuit of financial or political favors. A big company can make a bank quiver if it threatens to take its deposits elsewhere; a small firm can't even make the bankers sneeze. A big company can get all kinds of government favors and subsidies if it threatens to move its plant; a small firm can't even get its calls through to the bureaucrats.

■ Large companies are always in a better position to outbid small companies in merger bids or to carry out stock raids on prospering firms (because they have asset reserves to plunge into the stock market). Smaller companies are likely to be bought, not to buy.

All these advantages combine to grease a steady slide toward bigger and bigger corporations—even beyond the sources of growth in production. And this centralization of corporate power also reinforces the other general tendencies of capital accumulation—indirectly helping corporations find new workers and wider markets. The larger a corporation becomes, the more widely it can plan the allocation of its investments. If workers in one area get too powerful, large corporations can afford to move elsewhere. If some governments regulate prices in one place, corporations can move their sales to more hospitable terrain. Larger corporations can act more flexibly than smaller ones. They can more effectively manipulate their economic environments—reducing workers' strength and exposing widening circles of customers to the market. All capitalists try to find cheaper supplies, more docile workers, and ever-widening markets. The largest corporations usually go to the head of the class.

4. Riding the Economic Roller Coaster

Capitalist economies grow, but they never grow steadily. *Living in capitalist economies is like riding a roller coaster.* The economy goes up and down, up and down, alternately expanding and contracting. Corporations and the government keep trying to inflate the economy, but it springs more leaks than a garden hose.

There are four important reasons why capitalist economies are so susceptible to recession and depression:

a) *Too Much Chaos.* Because a capitalist economy involves production decisions made by many *disconnected* economic units, it is very vulnerable to sudden economic seizures. Suppose the price of oil suddenly climbs. Gas costs more. People will buy fewer cars. The auto

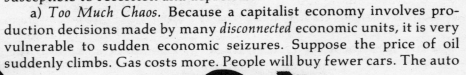

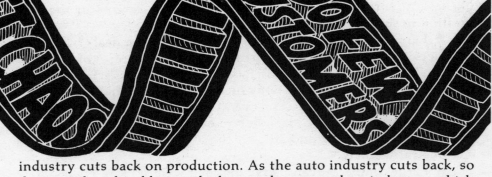

industry cuts back on production. As the auto industry cuts back, so does steel and rubber and glass and every other industry which supplies car manufacturers. Pretty soon the whole economy is quivering.

These kinds of disruptions are particularly likely as a result of the way investments are made in capitalist economies. When the economy expands, new buildings and machines are necessary for the consumer goods industries. When enough of them are built to support expanded production, the demand for machines and buildings dries up. With no new orders coming in, capital goods industries must then reduce their volume. As they lay off workers, consumer demand begins to shrink. And then the consumer goods industries must lay off workers too. Before we know it, the normal process of growth has produced a "normal" contraction.

These examples underscore the lessons of Chapter 5: *capitalist economies are vulnerable to sudden fits of instability because economic decisions are disconnected.* If something happens which reduces demand or profits anywhere in the system, everyone can suffer. Because the chaos of the market makes preventive medicine so difficult, an epidemic can spread before we can even sneeze for help.

b) *Demand Too Low.* Given the pressures of competition, capitalists are liable to kill the goose that lays their golden eggs. Capitalists search desperately for ways to control workers' wages. (They'll hire unorganized workers, blackmail unions, move their plants...; the bag of tricks is nearly bottomless.) As more and more capitalists slow the growth of wages, however, they may find that *the demand for their products is shrinking.* (When workers' incomes are declining, who's going to buy all those cars and toothbrushes?) As demand shrinks, so do profits. As profits begin to fall, some firms begin cutting back on production and laying off workers. Which reduces demand even further. The slow-down begins to spread.

c) *Wages Too High.* As the economy grows, more and more workers are hired. Unless new supplies of labor are continually uncovered at exactly the same rate, the reserve pools of workers begin to dry up. Competition in the labor market declines. Workers' bargaining power increases. Our ability to demand higher wages and to work less intensively also increases. Our growing bargaining power begins to cut into profits. As profits decline, capitalists cut back on production.

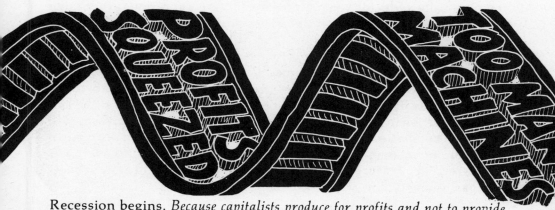

Recession begins. *Because capitalists produce for profits and not to provide employment, our own efforts to improve our working and living conditions may eventually lead to assaults on both.* We don't have enough power over how the means of production are used to lift us out of the trap.

d) *Too Much Investment.* Even increasing machine production creates potential barriers to continued growth. Machines themselves don't directly produce profits; as we saw in Chapter 3, surplus value depends on extra labor time. If workers did not stay for extra hours, there would be no reliable foundation for corporate profits. So when capitalists replace workers with machines, they *narrow* the foundations upon which their surplus value is based. As companies automate, they rapidly reduce the ranks of their production workers. Their profits will probably increase for a while, but they run the risk of going too far, laying off too many workers and reducing the exploitable labor time under their command.

In general, if workers are displaced too rapidly, the number of workers from whom surplus labor can be extracted may diminish so quickly—negating the increased worker productivity which new machines may permit—that corporate profits may *shrink* rather than *expand.* And as their profits shrink, some capitalists may cut back on production. If the cutbacks are sharp enough, we may start down the economic roller coaster again.

But why would capitalists ever be so stupid that they chose projects which lowered their rate of profit? The answer is that they may not have any other choice. *The insistent pressure of competition and class struggle may force capitalists to invest in machines which ultimately reduce their profits—despite their best intentions—because they are forced to "keep ahead."* Racing drivers frequently burn out their engines in the heat of the competition, even though they hope to complete the race, and capitalists may be pushed to mechanize too rapidly. There is some damage which even pit crews can't repair.

When all these potential sources of contraction are piled on top of each other, recession and depression seem more or less inevitable. Contraction isn't something which disrupts the economy by chance, a sudden bolt of lightning unpredictably blazing across the skies. The economy itself generates the forces causing recession and depression. Some firms may race ahead of others, creating bottlenecks and sudden seizures. Some corporations may suppress wages too rapidly or energetically, reducing consumer demand. As corporations grow, labor markets may become tight and workers' power may increase enough to erode profits. Some corporations may automate too rapidly, reducing the base for their potential profits. Any or all of these sources of disruption could strike at any time.

There are so many potential sources of contraction, indeed, that it should hardly be surprising when the economy falters. Given the lack of coordination in capitalist economies and the continuing pressures of capitalist competition and class struggle, it would be *more* surprising if the economy managed to grow steadily all the time. Booms and busts are as regular a feature of capitalist economies as sunlight and darkness are part of every day.

5. A System for All Nations

The global spread of capitalism does not end with its initial conquest of different societies. *The world-widening of capitalism continues throughout its history*—and with increasingly important impact.

In the early stages of capitalist development, distant colonies played limited economic roles. Some provided essential raw materials— like gold from the Americas and rubber from Malaya. Others provided essential supplies of new workers: the Irish moved to England and then to the United States, Europeans from all over moved to the United States, Koreans moved to Japan....to do the dirty work in capitalist factories.

As capitalism has continued to develop, more and more of its activities have spread everywhere. Raw materials and workers come from both advanced and less-developed countries. Capitalist factory production now takes place both in the advanced countries and in former colonies all around the globe—Hong Kong, Taiwan, and Korea in the Far East; Brazil and Mexico in Latin America; Nigeria and Zaire in Africa. Most products—even including food—are sold in markets all around the world. (Third World countries used to grow all of their own food; now, increasingly, they must buy much of it on the international market.) Many administrative services are also being transferred overseas. U.S. banks have been opening branches nearly everywhere, for instance, to help service the international growth of industry.

Why does capitalism keep spreading more widely across the globe? We have already studied the ingredients of an answer; we simply need to blend those ingredients together.

We have seen that capitalist firms can never stand still. As we saw in Chapter 3, capitalist competition and the class struggle constantly push corporations to seek higher and higher profits. This creates, as we've seen, continuing efforts both to find cheaper and more docile workers and to extend markets as widely as possible.

In the early stages of capitalist development, corporations were usually too small to organize this entire effort on their own. At most, they could afford to send labor recruiters and geologists overseas to search for cheaper workers and raw materials. They usually couldn't afford to establish production abroad or to organize the distribution and administration networks necessary to coordinate production on a world-wide scale.

As small firms have grown into multinational giants, corporations have acquired much more flexibility in their search for workers and markets. They can bring workers and products to the advanced countries, if it suits their purposes, or they can take both their capital and their distributive and administrative networks to where workers are. They will pick the sites which keep their costs as low as possible

Capitalism spreads like an inkspot as corporations pursue cheaper and more docile workers.

and insulate them from worker resistance as much as possible. Gazing out from the tops of their corporate towers, they can choose nearly any location they want.

This inkspot spread across the globe has created serious political problems for people trying to protect themselves through their governments.

Traditionally, most corporations have centered almost all of their activities within a single country. If people wanted to curb corporate excess, they could try to use their national governments to regulate business activity. Workers could pressure the government to guarantee workers' rights to unionize, to limit the working day, or to regulate health and safety conditions. Though corporations often used their influence with government officials to block that kind of legislation, working people could often use their numbers to tip the scales. Once laws were passed, corporations were officially obliged to obey them.

Now, multinational corporations have gained much more leverage over national governments. If working people threaten corporations with government legislation, corporations can threaten back with runaways. They can point to countries all around the globe where such legislation does not exist. "If you get rough on us," they can warn, "we'll move to where we get more sympathy." It amounts to an effort to reduce workers' wages and control *to the lowest common denominator*.

Not that workers in the less-developed countries have any more leverage than we do. As long as multinational corporations can choose among many different production sites, people at any particular location are vulnerable to corporate whimsy and multinational domination. Executives of giant corporations make many of the decisions which matter, *not* the people in countries where those companies happen to locate their plants and offices. "How can a national government make an economic plan with any confidence," a Wall Street investor recently asked, "if a board of directors meeting 5,000 miles away can by altering its pattern of purchasing and production affect in a major way the country's economic life?"[11]

None of this means that working people are helpless. It simply means that *we need to think of our economy in global terms*. We need to study the interests of everyone around the world, to understand the connections among people throughout the capitalist economy, and to develop solutions to our problems which build upon and take into account those kinds of links. Multinational corporations now plan on a world scale. We used to challenge them on our own block. Now, if we want to protect ourselves against their power, we'll have to beat them on all their turfs throughout the world.

...AND BETTER?

"Well, after about five more years things will have to go back as they were or else we'll be in a great big huge depression. If it does go back to where a person can make a living without choking to death, there won't be as much tension."

— young male worker[12]

We began this chapter by asking whether the economy would help us solve our problems or make them worse. After all this analysis, are we prepared to reach a conclusion?

We began by seeing that accumulation is driven by the corporate pursuit of profits. No matter how quickly capitalists race around the track, they're likely to push for less expensive factors of production, more surplus value in production, wider sales, and less drain on net revenues. The immediate effects of their race around the track are not always evident—firms and workers respond in such varied and complicated ways. We cannot always see the consequences of growth for the cloud of dust created by the race. And yet, over the years, through all that competition and struggle, that tumult and turmoil, as long as capital accumulation proceeds according to its own rules, we've learned that accumulation is likely to have several clear effects:

■ Our individual traditions and preferences are colored more and more by the wash of profitability. We get choices, but our choices are limited to those alternatives which provide profits to capitalist firms.

■ Corporations continually increase the scale of production, both replacing workers with machines and adding more and more supervisors. We're likely to lose both our jobs and our control over production in the process.

■ The race for profits creates constantly growing firms, with each corporate giant controlling a larger and larger share of the means of production. As it grows, each firm gains more and more leverage over our economic lives.

■ The race for profits in capitalist economies moves us up and down the economic roller coaster, subjecting us to alternate bursts of prosperity and stagnation. Stable growth remains beyond our grasp.

■ The system spreads around the world. As large corporations come to dominate this process, they acquire more and more flexible influence in their efforts to control working people. When direct control begins to erode in one place, they can outflank us by moving somewhere else.

That's not a promising beginning. There seem to be many areas in which the economy makes it *more* and *more* difficult for us to solve the critical problems we face. Our range of choices is narrowed. Our jobs and job control are undermined. Large corporations gain more and more leverage over our lives. The roller coaster ride continues to unsettle our working and living conditions. With multinationals operating on an increasingly world scale, our ability to solve our problems seems to diminish. *If we sit back and wait for the economy to solve our problems, we may die first.*

But the DUPE pushers insist that capitalist economic growth makes us better off. "The American free enterprise system is not perfect," as one corporate executive put it recently, "yet it has produced more benefits than any other system in history."[13]

So the next question for our investigation is clear. The detailed analysis in this chapter suggests that capitalist accumulation compounds many of our problems, continually reducing our ability to solve our own problems. The DUPE perspective argues that economic growth is the key to successful solution of those problems. Which analysis is correct?

Will the Economy Solve Our Problems?

"All my life, I had to work, never a day without work, worked all the overtime I could get and still could not survive financially. I began to say there's somethin' wrong with this country. I worked my butt off and just never seemed to break even."

—union organizer, former service station operator[1]

"If you want a long but pleasant evening's pastime, make a list of all the convenient things you have that your father did not have. And put opposite each what you think it is worth to you.

"Want to give them up—and go back?

"Or, take a map of the world and find the country (if you can!) where people like you have even half your luxuries and freedoms.

"And while you're at it, give a thought to the fact these luxuries and conveniences were developed by manufacturers in search of a profit..."

—corporate magazine ad in 1974[2]

We saw in the previous chapter that continuing capital accumulation is quite likely to undermine our ability to solve our major economic problems. If we want to improve our working and living conditions, apparently, we can hardly depend on the good grace of the capitalist system.

The DUPEsters do not agree. Future solutions to our problems will require, they argue, that we strengthen our economic system, not change it. The DUPE booklet makes the point clearly:

> For 200 years, America has prospered, defended individual freedoms, offered hope and opportunity to people from many lands and of many beliefs, and met challenges with confidence and determination. Our economic system has been a major element in this tradition. This system must continue to be a vital source of strength and achievement if we are to maintain our progress in the years to come.[3]

"Our economic system must continue as a vital source of strength."
—the DUPE booklet

We've already learned to treat the DUPE analysis with suspicion. Why should we believe them about the future course of our economy? It's time to mark our own score card.

When capitalist economies spread and grow, what impact do they have on our lives? How do working people fare at the capitalist dinner table? It seems important to study the pluses and minuses very carefully.

FIRST ENCOUNTERS OF THE ENJOYABLE KIND?

"Some of them stepped onto America's shores from the Mayflower. Others came by way of Ellis Island. And, of course, there were the native-born. But one thing is certain...in coming together, their courage, foresight, optimism—and sheer bluster—fused them into a remarkable entity...the American people....Wealthy or poverty-stricken, middle class or indentured servant, convict laborer or slave—America made room for them all."

—Teachers' Guide for DUPE film[4]

We begin with the first moments of people's exposure to capitalist accumulation—with the rites of passage through which people move as capitalism comes to dominate their lives.

What kind of welcome mat do people find on the capitalist doorstep? What happens to their working and living conditions? Does capitalism "make room for them all"?

Capitalists' continuing search for workers, raw materials, and markets has frequently disrupted other societies and economic systems. The spread of capitalism has featured a history of capital movement into the countryside and people's movement from the country to the city. These movements have often involved widespread dislocation, destruction, upheaval, and violence. A few moments in this history help tell the story.

Paving the Way for British Capitalism

Early in the emergence of capitalism, the British (and other European powers) began growing and mining their own sugar, tobacco, and metals in distant plantations and mines. Few Europeans were available for work in the colonies, so merchants and pirates began capturing slaves in West Africa and hauling them to work in the Americas. The slaves and their African societies—once prosperous civilizations—were devastated. Between the 1680s and the 1840s, at least four million slaves were shipped from West Africa by French, British, Portugese, and Dutch merchants.[5] Packed like sardines into impossibly crowded quarters, hundreds of thousands died en route.[6] Many others died before the journey began: "The Africans, taken in their sleep, were dragged into captivity unless they resisted," as one historian writes, "in which event they were slaughtered alongside the aged and infirm."[7]

And the native societies suffered far more than the loss of many able-bodied citizens. As the slave trade developed, African tribes were drawn into warfare with the slave traders and with each other. The "warfare exacted a price in deaths that was inevitably several times the number of captives enslaved and shipped to the coast."[8] This initiation to capitalist trade was a cruel rite; African societies and African slaves paid the price while European merchants and pirates reaped the profits.

A second group of people experienced the capitalist transition in England. These were the first factory workers pushed into the

What kind of welcome mat do people find on the capitalist doorstep?

expanding British textile industry. At best, their standard of living stagnated while the economy boomed; "the 'average' working man remained very close to subsistence level....His own share of the 'benefits of economic progress' consisted of more potatoes, a few articles of cotton clothing for his family, soap and candles, and some tea and sugar."[9] Housing conditions in the industrial cities created unprecedented problems of sanitation and squalor.[10] Althought the life expectancy of the middle and upper classes rose after the Industrial Revolution, the working classses suffered from spreading disease and industrial accident. One observer described the workers in the cotton mills in 1832. "I saw...a degenerate race—human beings stunted, enfeebled, and depraved—men and women that were not to be aged—children that were never to be healthy adults."[11]

A third group of people was rudely introduced to capitalism far away from England. The British textile industry needed new markets for its products. They looked, among other places, to India. There, a thriving independent textile industry flourished in which producers and consumers supported each other locally. British armies invaded India and destroyed the Indian textile industry. Even members of the English Parliament regretted, as one leading Lord put it, "the hand that in India has torn the cloth from the loom or wrested the scanty portion of rice and salt from the peasant of Bengal."[12] "Indian masses...perished in large numbers," an economic historian concludes, "because the Indian village community had been demolished."[13]

None of these three groups welcomed their original initiation to capitalist economic life with cheers and marching bands. African tribes fought the traders' invasion; slaves often rebelled or escaped in transit; and, once in the Americas, slave rebellions persisted throughout the plantation areas of the Americas.[14] (The recent novel and TV series "Roots" illustrated many of these struggles.) Workers in the English textile factories also fought the factories' invasion; the early years of the nineteenth century, as the historian E.P. Thompson puts it, were "aflame with agitations."[15] The peasants and workers of India also resisted the incursions of British textiles; rebellions erupted and sputtered throughout the late eighteenth and most of the nineteenth centuries.[16] For all these participants in early British accumulation, the emergence of capitalism was more a punishment than a picnic.

Providing Labor for U.S. Capitalism

The great migrations of people to U.S. capitalist factories in the nineteenth and twentieth centuries provide us with records of some other initial encounters.

The Flight from Europe. The first wave of migration lasted for about 100 years, from the 1820s through the 1920s. About 60 million immigrants came from Europe to the United States, hoping against hope to improve their lives.[17] Their migrations were far from easy.

The first great influx of Irish immigrants was sparked by potato crop failures in the mid-1840s. One and a half million poor farmers fled Ireland. In many cases, landlords and county officials had paid the farmers' passage, packing them off to somewhere, anywhere—simply

European immigrants arriving at Ellis Island, N.Y., late 1800s.

because this helped clear the land so that sheep and cattle would have wider fields for pasture.[18] We now remember this migration as a hopeful and heroic journey by many of our ancestors. But for the Irish during those years, the picture was blemished with tragedy. Some of the migrants found a better way of life, but many others died en route: Shipload after shipload arrived in America with half the passengers dead from cholera and the other half infected.[19] Another million who stayed behind died from starvation.[20] The landlords turning to commercial agriculture in Ireland never lifted a finger.

Many other migrants later left Europe because they were driven off the land by a process similar to "enclosures" in England. (See pp. 63-64.) For many, their interest in the U.S. was stimulated by the swarms of labor recruiters sent to Europe by thirsty American industrialists. The recruiters were called "Crimps" in England and "Newlanders" on the continent.[21] They literally marched through European fairs with fife and drum, advertising the glories of the "golden land."[22] For those who came, the ships were nearly as crowded as the boats bringing slaves; "the mortality rate could run in excess of fifty percent for a typical voyage."[23]

By the time the survivors arrived in the United States, it was growing more and more difficult for them to fulfill their dreams of economic independence. Earlier in the century, for example, a creditor could seize only part of a farmer's land as payment on a debt; farmers could continue earning money off the remaining land for future repayment. During the second half of the century, however, mortgage laws were changed in most states so that all of a person's land could be seized. Land had become more valuable and rich creditors now wanted the land more than they wanted the money.[24]

Many farmers were left with nothing but the clothes on their backs. Half as many returned to Europe as remained in the United States. Most of those who remained moved into the factories. The work was intense. Factory employees usually worked so hard, one newspaper columnist observed in the 1880s, that they had "to stop, now and then,...take off their boots, and pour the perspiration out of them."[25] The "golden land," for many, paid in fool's gold.

The Flight from the South. A second great wave of migration took place during the twentieth century as changing economic conditions drew many southerners, both black and white, to the industrial north.

■ When the U.S. entered World War I in 1917, northern capitalists needed workers to replace those who had gone off to war. Black newspapers in the midwest urged southern blacks to come north.[26] Several million people left their subsistence share-cropping behind.

■ The 1930s Depression ruined many farmers. Some of them, described by John Steinbeck in *The Grapes of Wrath*, moved to California. Others moved to northern cities. The economic crisis left them little choice.

■ After World War II, cotton-picking machines replaced farm workers throughout the south. The workers lost their livelihood on the land. One tenant farmer remembers: "They didn't need the labor no more. Bosses just tol' 'em to move."[27] Early migrants filled slums in the northeast and midwest. Many white farmers found nothing better than migrant labor work during the Depression. Blacks migrating north during the 1950s and 1960s found it more and more difficult to land decent jobs. The first generation had fled the south with hope and often discovered unexpected racial discrimination. The second generation found the transition even more difficult. As Claude Brown, a black writer from Harlem, wrote in the 1960s, "The children of these disillusioned colored pioneers inherited the total lot of their parents—the disappointments, the anger. To add to their misery, they had little hope of deliverance. For where does one run to when he's already in the promised land."[28]

First Encounters Continuing

These transformations are not simply relics of the past. The spread of capitalism continues. People are being introduced to it every day.

In the United States, although several million self-employed farmers and merchants remain, many find it more and more difficult to stay in business. In late 1980, close to 1,000 businesses were failing every month.[29] We continually join the ranks of wage laborers—few of us by choice.

Markets are also constantly extending. Partly as a result, patterns of housework are changing rapidly. Many households now purchase goods and services which they used to produce in their homes. As a result, we're beginning to encounter capitalism in areas of our lives where we didn't meet it before. The strain of adjustment has become a steady diet for nuclear family life in the U.S.

Around the world the process is in an earlier stage of development than in the U.S. Every year in the less developed countries, masses of peasants are losing control of their land and being thrown into the labor market. In Mexico, Brazil, the Caribbean, Nigeria, Pakistan, and India—to pick only a few examples—poor peasants are crowding into the slums of teeming cities. Few find work. Many beg or starve. Many die from disease or malnutrition. Their initial exposure to capitalism is like a lottery. A few lucky winners may find decent wages in the factories. The remaining participants pay the price.

Just as capitalism continues to spread, so have people's protests about its effects. In the U.S., farmers continue to fight against the growing difficulty of maintaining independent agricultural production. (In early 1978, for example, thousands of farmers "went on strike," rolling their tractors down the highways and into government capitals to demand higher and more stable price supports.) Small businesses have been clamoring for more tariff protection, lower minimum wages...and anything else that might help protect their endangered species. Spreading tension over changing family relationships has helped spark and enflame intense controversy over a number of critical social issues, including abortion rights, the Equal Rights Amendment, and affirmative action.

Overseas, people have resisted capitalist penetration at every turn. Peasant struggles have peppered the twentieth century with a continuing history of resistance and rebellion. When these moments of struggle have "gotten out of hand," capitalists have never hesitated to call in the police or the army. Figure 7.1 traces U.S. military intervention in Third World countries during the past 80 years.[30] It provides only a partial record of people's continuing determination to avoid or escape capitalist domination.

How do we sum up this historical record?

On one side of the ledger, the spread of capitalism has usually encouraged rapid economic growth, stimulating both production and consumption. Some people have been able to grab the golden ring—improving their standards of living, expanding their opportunities, gazing across new horizons.

On the other side, the spread of capitalism has directly caused

virulent death and destruction. Millions have died. Millions more have lost control of their lives. For more than 200 years, around the world, people have been cast adrift in the sea of capitalist expansion. And many have drowned.

With hindsight, it seems clear that the net balance *could* have been positive. Some of the benefits of growth could have provided for the less "lucky." Some of the rough edges might have been smoothed. Increasing productivity might have served people's needs rather than capitalists' hunger for profits. But it didn't happen that way. Capitalism doesn't look back. It doesn't worry about people's welfare. The system plows ahead like a bulldozer, crushing societies which block its way, leaving many victims in the rubble. As capitalism spreads, capital matters more than the lives of people.

WHAT'S THE SCORE NOW?

"We are the healthiest, wealthiest, best educated, most generous nation in the history of the world."
                    —U.S. executive at business conference[31]

The transition to life under capitalism may be like a painful adolescence. What about adulthood in capitalist economies? As we saw in detail in Chapter 1, most working people in the United States currently face serious economic problems. Does economic growth help reduce those problems once we've survived our first encounters?

The U.S. Military Meets the 3rd World

This is a *partial* list of occasions since 1900 when and where U.S. troops were used in 3rd World countries.

1900
China
1902
Panama
1903
Dominican Republic
1903
Syria
1903
Panama
1904
Korea
1906
Cuba
1907
Honduras
1910
Nicaragua
1911
China
1912
Turkey
1912
Nicaragua
1913
Mexico
1914
Haiti
1914
Mexico
1915
Haiti
1918
Cuba
1919
Soviet Union
1920
Guatemala
1922
Turkey
1925
Panama
1926
Nicaragua
1927
China
1933
Cuba
1950
Korea
1957
Lebanon
1962
Cuba
1964
Vietnam
1965
Dominican Republic

Source: See note #30

Fig. 7.1

Fig. 7.2

Does Growth Produce Jobs?

Between 1948 and 1966, the economy grew rapidly. Did the private sector produce enough jobs?

The adult population increased from 104.5 million to 131.2 million—by *26.7 million*, or *30%*.

Employment generated by the private sector increased from 50 million to 51.5 million—by only *1.5 million* jobs, or only *3%*.

As a result, the percentage of adults holding jobs generated by the private sector fell by 20%.

Source: See note #34

The DUPE pushers are confident. The DUPE booklet writes of "the economic wonder of the world." It promises that the economic system makes our lives better and better, scoring on every count. Struggling to subsist? "Over the years our GNP has increased astonishingly." Unemployment problems? "The American economy has shown an impressive ability to create new jobs." Too little control over our working and living conditions? "Americans still exercise many freedoms of economic choice." Inequalities got us fighting with our neighbors? "Our country goes where we—all of us together—decide we want to take it."[32]

The DUPE boasts sound a little silly these days; for many, the current crisis proves that their promises are hollow. But the DUPE would counsel patience. Our current problems are temporary. Economic growth, just around the corner, will make everything right once again. After all, they sneer, we didn't hear any complaints during the fifties and sixties! Such short memories!

Why not give them the benefit of the doubt? If U.S. capitalism ever had a chance to strut its stuff, that was the time. We can tally our score cards for those decades when the economy was growing rapidly. (When numbers prove helpful, we can study changes from 1948 to 1966, years at the beginning and end of this period during which unemployment rates were exactly equal and very low. Choosing these years for comparison helps ensure that we don't stack the deck against the DUPE or confuse the effects of growth with the effects of business-cycle expansion or recession.)

It's time to survey the evidence. When U.S. capitalism achieves peak growth, does it solve our economic problems? Any bets?

Employment and Unemployment

"We had 400 men who were supposed to be doing refining. Now, since the [new equipment] came in, they've lost more than half the work force they had. Now, when the truck comes in, I don't even have to be there to load up....I could be laid off any time. It would be a ghost town. They wouldn't miss me."

—45-year-old oil worker in New Jersey[33]

It's easiest to begin with the issue of jobs because everyone agrees how to measure them. The DUPE booklet boasts that "the American economy has shown an impressive ability to create new jobs." Has it?

We have already seen that corporations try to increase their profits, not to create jobs. Driven by this quest for profits, corporations continually automate, eliminating many jobs. They also import new workers or move their plants abroad, creating labor market competition and threatening many current jobs. Not a promising beginning. Where are all the new jobs supposed to come from?

The DUPEsters would answer, of course, that capitalists boost workers' productivity, permitting new growth in the economy, and that this growth dividend finances new employment. Did this happen during the 1950s and 1960s?

They're right on the first count: in manufacturing industries, the average worker produced almost twice as much per hour in 1966 as he or she did in 1948. But did this generate new jobs?

In 1948, there were 104.5 million people over 16 years old in the "non-institutional" U.S. population. By 1966, the adult non-institutional population had grown to 131.2 million, an increase of almost 30%. Did the private economy create plenty of jobs for all those additional (potential) workers?

In 1948, an average of 50 million workers were able to find employment in jobs generated by the private sector.

By 1966, employment generated by the private sector had scarcely grown at all. On average during that year, only 51.5 million workers held jobs created by the private sector.[34]

The adult population had grown by 30 million over those 20 years of prosperity, but the private sector only provided an additional 2 million jobs. The percentage of adults holding jobs generated by the private sector had *fallen* by 20%. (See Figure 7.2 for a summary.)

Wait a minute, many might reasonably insist. You're leaving out the government. The public sector provided lots of jobs over those years. Why don't you count those? You're loading the dice.

The answer is that we're taking questions one at a time. In this chapter we're asking whether the capitalist economy can or will solve our problems *on its own.* For the moment, there is little evidence that the private sector—even when it is growing very rapidly—creates many new jobs. The population grew from 1948 to 1966 but private-sector employment stagnated. We'll consider in the next chapter whether the government can make up for this weakness in the private sector.

In the meantime, it's little surprise that so many people face such serious job problems. We saw in Chapter 1 that at least 22 million workers experienced unemployment at one time or another during 1980. And many others didn't bother to look for work at all—because they'd given up hope—or settled for part-time work because they couldn't find full-time jobs. More and more worry about finding decent jobs.

Not fair, the DUPE responds, not fair! These are abnormally bad times. We'll straighten things out soon enough and then fewer people will be unemployed.

But is a slump "abnormal" in capitalist economies? As we saw in the previous chapter, the economy races up and down on a roller coaster of its own design and construction. Even the most secure employment is often threatened by capitalist recession and depression. Our analysis tells us that bad times are just as likely in capitalist economies as good ones.

The history of the U.S. economy supports this conclusion. More than a century has elapsed in the U.S. since capitalism finally took permanent hold at the end of the Civil War. Between 1865 and 1978, there were 17 separate business cycles in the United States, 17 trips over the booms and busts of capitalist growth. The U.S. economy experienced recessions and depressions for 57 of the 113 years during

that span—50.4% of the time.[35] Bad times have been at least as normal as years of expansion. Prosperity is only a half-time event.

In summary, we have strong reasons for doubting the DUPE claims about job creation. *Even when our economy has grown very rapidly, the private sector has created almost no additional jobs. And the economy prospers only about half the time.* What kind of odds would you need to bet that the private capitalist economy is going to provide steady employment for the millions of working people who need it?

Freedom and Necessity

"I'll tell you what it's like. It's like the Army. They even use the same words, like *direct order*. Supposedly you have a contract so there's some things they just can't make you do. Except, if the foreman gives you a direct order, you do it, or you're out."

—young auto worker in Ohio[36]

"The American Dream. (Laughs.)...Over the years I realized that every man, every human is a commodity to be exploited. The problem isn't the work itself...The question gets down to who the hell pays for it...Say you're a bookkeeper. Are you counting something of human value or are you counting for the Syndicate or the Pentagon? Are you a bookkeeper counting dead bodies or children at school?...I wanted to be at the drawing board, creative, doing something I believed in. But I became a pimp."

—50-year-old industrial designer[37]

The DUPE perspective boasts of the economic freedoms which capitalist economies create and maintain. As the DUPE booklet puts it, "Americans still exercise many freedoms of economic choice." What does economic growth do to those freedoms?

The most obvious effect of capitalist economic growth is that more and more of us become wage-laborers, losing whatever economic independence is provided by owning our own means of production. During these two decades of rapid growth the trend was clear: the number of "self-employed" in the U.S. economy fell from 18% of the labor force in 1950 to 9% in 1970.[38]

A second important consequence of capitalist economic growth, as we saw in Chapter 6, is that machine domination of the production process constantly increases. Even in office work, machines increasingly regulate the flow of workers' tasks. We have less and less control over what we do on the job. It's difficult to measure these effects in numbers, but the spread of machines undoubt-edly contributed to a steady decline in production workers' job satisfaction after the mid-1960s.[39] As the economy grows, more and more of us become dependent not only on the *owners* who pay our wages but also on the *machines* which direct and fragment our work.

And also on the bosses and supervisors who watch over us. The numbers tell us this story clearly. In 1948, there were only 13 supervisory workers for every 100 production workers in the private U.S. economy. By 1966, the ratio had increased by nearly 75%—rising steadily to 23 supervisory workers for every 100 production workers.[40] The minute we relaxed on the job, the supervisor was there to give us a shove.

A third important effect of accumulation, as we also saw in Chapter 6, is that *the largest corporations control more and more of economic life.* In 1948, the 200 largest industrial corporations controlled 48.2% of all manufacturing assets. By 1966, after two decades of prosperity, the largest 200 corporations had expanded their share to 60.2%.[41] (See Figure 7.3 on this page.) This expand-ing corporate power has had several other impor-tant effects:

■ The larger the enterprise, the more intensive the bosses' supervision of our work. In 1972, the ratio of non-production to production workers was 35% higher in establishments with 2,500 or more employees than in establishments below that threshold.[42]

■ The larger the corporation, the more easily it can undercut worker organization by shifting its factories around. Workers nor-mally have the greatest collective strength when the economy is growing rapidly; as unemployment falls, employees can usually organ-ize more effectively. But in the decades of prosperity after World War II, corporations were able to use their increasing flexibility to counter this traditional source of worker strength. Partly as a result, the percentage of workers who belonged to unions fell steadily during the 1950s and 1960s, dropping from 36% in 1950 to 28% of the (non-agricultural) labor force by 1966.[43]

■ Larger corporations can also set up operations overseas much more easily than smaller corporations. In 1967-68, for instance, 561 U.S. corporations were responsible for 90% of all U.S. foreign investment.[44]

■ As corporations grow larger, finally, they rely more and more on advertising and product manipulation—rather than price cuts—to stimulate consumption. Between 1948 and 1966, for instance, adver-tising expenditures quadrupled, increasing from $4.3 billion to $16.9 billion.[45] "Love it or hate it," as the DUPE primer argues, "advertising shows every sign of continuing as a key part of the economic system."[46]

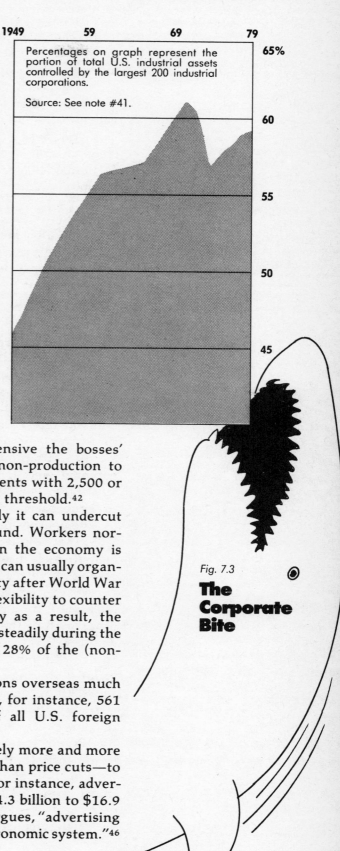

Percentages on graph represent the portion of total U.S. industrial assets controlled by the largest 200 industrial corporations.

Source: See note #41.

Fig. 7.3
The Corporate Bite

All of these changes seem to point in the same direction. More and more people became dependent wage-laborers. Machines assumed greater and greater control over our lives on the job. Bosses devoted more and more attention to supervising us on the job. Large corporations gained greater control over production and distribution. Through runaway shops and consumer manipulation, corporations gained more and more leverage over both workers and consumers.

And these changes cast serious doubt on the DUPE claims about freedom and necessity. We may "still exercise many freedoms of economic choice," as the DUPE booklet brags, but economic growth has hardly helped.

Equality and Inequality

"Equality means everyone having their fair share, their cut of the pie, so to speak. The U.S. falls short? Well yes, I suppose it does. There is a lot of poverty, a lot of unemployment and we still spent billions of dollars to send people to the moon."

—middle-aged woman in working class family[47]

Does the growth of capitalist economies reduce the divisions among us, providing working people with an increasingly equal voice and share in our society? The DUPE booklet argues that "our country goes where we—all of us together—decide we want to take it." But we saw in Chapter 1 that there are many divisions among people in the United States. Does a growing economy heal those divisions or rub them raw?

In 1949, the wealthiest 0.5% of U.S. families owned 19.3 % of all personal wealth in the country. Twenty years later in 1969, this wealthy group's share had slightly increased to 19.9%.[48] It seems hard to argue, based on those numbers, that economic growth was reducing the inequalities between the wealthiest few and all the rest of us.

What about divisions among working people? Did economic growth at least reduce some of the inequalities which keep us fighting among ourselves?

We can start with unemployment. We saw in Chapter 1 that joblessness is much higher among some groups of working people than others. All of these problems grew relatively worse during the two decades of rapid growth: compared to unemployment rates among adult white men, unemployment increased for *all* disadvantaged groups—among white women, black men, black women, and teenagers. One index of the divisions shows that *inequality in unemployment more than doubled during the 1950s and 1960s.*[49] When they passed out the pink slips, they were going to the weakest workers more than ever.

Trends in income inequality show the same pattern:

■ In 1948, the total income received by the most affluent 25% of working households was 6.7 times greater than the income received by the poorest 25% of working households. By 1966, this inequality had increased slightly—to a difference of 6.9 times.[50]

■ Between 1950 and 1970, professional workers increased their relative earnings over operatives. Male workers increased their earnings advantages over female workers.[51] Only along racial lines did inequality decrease: in large part as a result of the Civil Rights movement, black men slightly increased their earnings compared to white men, and black women dramatically reduced the gap between their incomes and those of white women.[52]

Those data suggest that inequalities in unemployment and earnings did not decrease while the economy grew rapidly—with the single exception of black earnings. But what about the fairness of the system? Didn't it become easier for people who worked harder to get ahead? Maybe the shape of inequality didn't change, but didn't those who ended up at the bottom "deserve" it? Didn't the ladders to success become easier to climb for those who really wanted to take advantage of them?

It's possible to test this widespread impression. We can look at the influence of family background on the earnings of white men—in order to keep separate the additional influence of race and sex—for workers who were reaching their career peaks around the beginning and end of this period of prosperity. If the argument about increasing mobility

Did You Ever Notice?

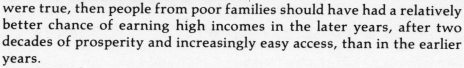

were true, then people from poor families should have had a relatively better chance of earning high incomes in the later years, after two decades of prosperity and increasingly easy access, than in the earlier years.

Once again, the DUPE claims about spreading equality are *not* supported by the numbers. For white men hitting their career peaks in the late 1940s, someone from the wealthiest 10% of households was more than *ten times* as likely to "make it"—ending up in the top 20% of the income distribution—as someone from the poorest 10% of households. After twenty years of prosperity, for white men hitting their career peaks in the late 1960s, the prospects of those from the poorest households had not improved. If anything, in fact, the odds against those from the poorest households had grown slightly steeper.[53] The economy had expanded and people were staying in school longer, but *the wealthy had at least as great a head start on the poor as before.*

The numbers seem relentless. No matter how we add them up, economic inequalities were apparently just as wide and deep at the end of 20 years' prosperity as at the beginning. If rapid economic growth is supposed to reduce economic divisions, where's the evidence?

Wealth and Subsistence

"People are better off now. There are more jobs, more money, longer vacations, shorter hours. And the conveniences are better, too."

—48-year-old working man[54]

"Things really don't seem to have changed very much to me. We don't really have much more."

—59-year-old working woman[55]

"So many people have double jobs to support their families....I don't think the big executives should get that much. Use it to feed the little people....They should cut down on the profits—anyone who has ever worked for [our company] knows [that]."

—51-year-old working woman[56]

Last but not least, we come to wealth and subsistence. The U.S. economy may not be good for much else, but doesn't its growth improve our standards of living? "Over the years," the DUPE booklet argues, "the GNP has grown astonishingly." Have our living standards continually benefited from that growth? Does a prosperous economy create such comfortable cushions that we can weather a few lean years?

There is no doubt that household incomes rose dramatically during the two decades of prosperity after World War II. Between 1948 and 1966, the annual income of the typical U.S. household increased by 125%—growing at a rate of nearly 7% a year.[57]

Prices also rose substantially over the same period. If we adjust household incomes in 1966 for the higher prices people faced after 18 years of growth, we still find that the typical household income had increased by 67% over 1948 levels.[58] Taxes also increased. Did incomes increase enough to cover not only inflation but also the deepening bite of the taxman? The share of households' income going to the government nearly doubled between 1948 and 1966, but controlling for both inflation and rising taxes, the typical household's income still increased by 34%.[59]

In short, *money incomes* had increased by 125%, *real incomes* (controlling for inflation) by 67%, and *real spendable incomes* (controlling for both rising prices and rising taxes) by 34%. Much of the rapid growth in household income was eaten by inflation and the government. But a 34% growth in real spendable incomes is nothing to be sneezed at. Had standards of living improved by as much?

We know from our own experience that the cost of living rose during those years not only because of inflation but *also* because we had to buy some things we didn't formerly need. As jobs and workers began moving around more rapidly, families began splitting apart; this meant that many people who used to live together now had to pay for more than one home. Cars became more and more necessary both for work and for shopping....Several studies clearly show the effects of these kinds of rising costs:

■ Budget experts have studied what an average U.S. household needed to live in "minimum comfort" during these decades of prosperity after World War II. Between 1947 and 1967, according to these studies, the cost of a working household's minimum basic budget *increased by 48%* (controlling for inflation)—largely because so many goods and services were required to maintain constant levels of "minimum comfort."[60] The average household's spendable earnings increased by only 34%. *Spendable earnings were not keeping pace with the rising costs of subsistence.*

■ Surveys over this period repeatedly asked people "what is the smallest amount of money a family of four needs to get along in this community?" Between 1947 and 1967, households' assessment of these minimum needs, controlling for inflation, *increased by 61%*.[61] Real spendable earnings, as we've seen, increased by only 34%. Although incomes were rising, according to surveys, *working households felt that our spendable earnings were not rising quickly enough to keep up with widening needs.*

These problems in covering new expenses show up in one very simple measure of people's living standards—basic nutrition. From 1948 to 1966, protein consumption per capita did not rise, calories consumed per capita declined by 2%, and vitamin A value consumed per capita decreased by 15%.[62] We may have been earning more bread, but those extra dollars weren't allowing us to afford more nutritious diets.

Between 1947 and 1967, what we earned was not keeping pace with the costs of subsistence.

DUPEsters typically answer these kinds of complaints with a simple reply. "We must realize," as the DUPE booklet puts it, "that our...standard of living is tied to productivity growth. As productivity increases, our standard of living increases."[63] If we're complaining about stagnant standards of living, they imply, we're really complaining about stagnant productivity. We didn't work hard enough. Or our wages and salaries rose so rapidly that corporations couldn't invest in machines which would have increased our productivity even faster. If we're not satisfied, we should blame ourselves, not the economy.

Is it true that slow growth in productivity imposed a ceiling on our standards of living? Should we have been satisfied with what we got?

We can examine this argument by looking at the relationship between our output and our incomes during those nearly 20 years of rapid growth between 1948 and 1966.[64] (Throughout the following discussion, we will control for the distorting effects of inflation by expressing data for 1948 in terms of the price levels which prevailed in 1966.) The summaries in Figures 7.3 and 7.4 in the page margins will help you follow the numbers.

In 1948, each production worker in the U.S. economy produced a net output (in 1966 prices) worth $4.52 per hour of work. By 1966, productivity had grown so rapidly that each production worker was now producing $7.20 an hour in net output. Controlling for inflation, each worker's hourly productivity had grown by $2.68. Did we get as much of this productivity dividend as possible, reaping the full returns in our standards of living?

In 1948, non-supervisory employees received an average (in 1966 prices) of $2.11 per hour in wages, salaries, and fringe benefits (after taxes)—what we've been calling real spendable earnings. By 1966, non-supervisory workers' hourly spendable earnings had increased to $2.97. Over those eighteen years, workers' hourly spendable earnings had increased by $0.86 an hour—or just 40%. This was not enough of an increase, as we've seen, to keep pace with what either budget experts or surveyed households thought were the rising costs of living.

Hourly spendable earnings up by $0.86, but hourly productivity up by $2.68? What happened to the other $1.82 an hour in higher net output? If we had been able to keep a decent share of that extra productivity dividend, our real standards of living might have improved. Where did it go?

Some of it obviously had to cover the rising costs of maintaining old machines and buying new ones. (After all, the DUPEsters keep reminding us, this investment helped create the productivity dividend in the first place.) But these costs account for only 35¢ of the missing $1.82.

Some of it also went to the government in rising taxes—out of both workers' income and business revenues. But this only accounts for $0.61 of the missing money. That still leaves $0.86 in the corporate kitty.

It turns out that corporations kept this missing $0.86 per hour of *our* net output for *their* own purposes—keeping 24¢ in rising property income and 62¢ for the steadily increasing costs of the bosses and supervisors who watched over our labor and their earnings.

Chapter 3 argued that workers could legitimately claim property income for ourselves—since it depends on the productive work we perform. Chapter 4 suggested that we could also coordinate our own work—getting rid of bosses and their control of workers. Suppose we had claimed this additional output which went into owners' income and rising expenses on bosses and supervisors? If those extra 86¢ an hour had gone to us instead of to them, our standards of living would have been 29% higher in 1966 than they were.

So it turns out that the DUPE argument is misleading. Our spendable earnings could have grown much more rapidly if we had more control over the allocation of surplus. While corporations were telling us to work harder and moderate our wage demands, they were spending more and more on themselves and on their control workers. They say that our "standard of living is tied to productivity growth." It is also tied to the struggle between corporations and workers over the

Fig. 7.4

Where Did All That Output Go?

Between 1948 and 1966, the average production worker's hourly output increased by **$2.68** an hour.

But...
the average production worker's spendable hourly wage increased by only **86¢** an hour.

Where did the remaining **$1.82** an hour go?

Of that $1.82,

* only **35¢** covered machine costs

* another **61¢** went to the government

* while **86¢** flowed into corporate coffers, paying for higher dividends and more supervisory personnel.

distribution of surplus. If we could have kept for ourselves what they diverted to property income and control workers, our wages could have been almost one third higher in 1966 than they were. **The more they keep for themselves, the less we get.**

All this discussion has not even touched on another critical issue. Even if our incomes had increased more than they did during a period of rapid economic growth, it still wouldn't help us cope with the quality of what we were getting for our money. During those years of rapid economic growth corporations were lacing foods with deadly chemicals...builders were using shoddy and dangerous materials in our housing...the auto industry was building cars to fall apart in a few years and the public transit system was deteriorating...cancer-causing chemicals were spreading throughout our work and community environments...hospitals were spending more time carving us up than curing our diseases...much of our rising tax burden was going into wasteful and probably unnecessary defense spending. The list goes on. We'll focus in detail on the quality of our working and living conditions in Chapter 11. For the time being, we should simply remember that the *quality* of those goods and services we buy also has a big impact on our health and happiness. The DUPEsters boast about the many fruits of capitalist economic growth. They forget to mention that many of those fruits are rotten.

Our discussion of wealth and subsistence has travelled a long and somewhat winding road. But the journey has obviously muddied the DUPEsters' glowing promises about prosperity. Our incomes did grow during this period of rapid economic growth. But so did prices and taxes. Real spendable incomes did not grow as fast as the real costs of maintaining our standards of living. The rapid growth of our productivity *might* have permitted substantial improvements in our standards of living, but capitalists were able to maintain enough control over surplus to prevent those potential improvements. If rapid economic growth is supposed to usher us down easy street, it's a well-kept secret.

AND NOW, THE GOOD NEWS?

So far in our examination, the capitalist economy has scored badly. Many people suffer tragically from their first encounters with capitalist economies. Those of us living in a mature capitalist economy such as the United States don't seem to fare well either. Must we search for a better way to organize our economic system?

There's one more question we need to explore before we jump to final conclusions. Isn't it possible that we can tame the economy, using the government to smooth its rough edges, saving some of its better features while eliminating its worst? Don't we want to avoid throwing out the baby with the bathwater?

The next chapter pursues those questions directly, exploring the relationship between the government and the economy. Can the government fix things up so that we can use the economy to solve our problems more effectively? Or does the economy exert such a powerful influence that our drive to tame it will crash into brick walls?

Fig. 7.5

Could We Have Been Better Off?

Of the **$2.68** increase in the average production worker's hourly output between 1948 and 1966,

only **86¢** went into higher production worker's spendable hourly wages.

Another **86¢** went into higher dividends and expenditures on supervisory salaries.

If we had claimed those extra 86¢ instead of the corporations and the wealthy, our spendable hourly wages would have climbed to **$3.83** in 1966, instead of $2.97.

If we had kept for ourselves what corporations diverted into property income and control workers' salaries, in short, our spendable wages would have been almost **one third** higher in 1966 than they were.

8.

Can't the Government Fix It?

"[Government regulators] have enormous power and influence in America today...They choose almost invariably to intervene—an intervention that endangers the good life which the capitalist revolution has done so much to produce...To reverse the damage already done, Americans must begin to cut back on the excessive regulation that has become such a hindrance to its economic vigor and progress."
—Mobil Oil newspaper ad[1]

"Q: Some people say that public officials in Washington tend to dominate and determine the actions of America's major corporations. Other people say that America's major corporations tend to dominate and determine the actions of our public officials in Washington. Which view do you feel is the more correct?
A: Washington controls the corporations...30% agree.
A: Corporations control Washington... 70% agree."
—1975 survey of sample of U.S. adults[2]

Working people in the United States face critical economic problems. The economy seems more likely to exacerbate our problems than to solve them. Has the time finally come to trade in the economy for a newer model?

Most of us have a stake in the current economic system—we have our jobs, maybe a few investments...trading in the economy would obviously involve sharp dislocations in our daily lives. Can't we avoid such a drastic step? Can't we use our government to shape the economy to our own needs and interests?

ONE STEP FORWARD, HOW MANY BACK?

"The social responsiblity of business is to make profits."
—business executive at management conference[3]

One response to those questions flows immediately from our own experience. Working people have won many victories by pushing for government intervention in the economy. For many of us, those victories have helped bring about significant improvements in our working and living conditions.

Some of our greatest triumphs came during the 1930s. After long and sometimes bloody struggles, working people won federal guarantees of the right to organize labor unions. Widespread popular demands for pension security helped create the social security system in 1935. Toward the end of the Depression, successful union organizing helped pave the way for minimum wage legislation.

More recently, working people have helped secure many benefits and significant protection on the job and in our communities. The black movement in the south prompted both the Civil Rights Act and the Voting Rights Act in the 1960s. Medicare and Medicaid legislation helped bring soaring medical costs within reach of many older and poorer households. The Occupational Health and Safety Administration (OSHA) has been an important tool for trying to improve our working conditions.

These concrete victories have touched all our lives. They have helped sustain at least a little faith in our political system and many working people continue to seek redress from the government.

At the same time, as we now recognize more clearly than ever, these victories are never secure. Attacks on many government programs have intensified dramatically in the past couple of years, but it isn't such a new experience. Nearly every time working people have made significant progress through government action, economic forces and corporate counter-attacks have threatened to push us back. A few examples tell the story:

■ After the great union organizing triumphs and the union protection legislation of the 1930s, business forces rallied. They pushed the Taft-Hartley Act through Congress in 1947, severely limiting unions' ability to organize. Much of the act was actually drafted by the National Association of Manufacturing.[4] During the 1950s and 1960s, at least partly as a result, labor union membership as a percentage of the labor force declined. Companies were able to move into areas where unions were weak. Many companies, like J.P. Stevens, openly flouted the labor law. The organized labor movement finally moved in 1978 to push for some important reforms in the labor law, hoping to overcome some of its weaknesses in unorganized industries and areas. Business interests mounted a vigorous counter-assault. Despite workers' early victories, the government has still not been able to provide *effective* guarantees of our right to organize.

■ Minimum-wage legislation has been under attack for years. Companies charge that they lose money if they hire unskilled labor at the minimum wage. They have urged exceptions to and ceilings on the minimum wage. Unions and working people have resisted these business demands, but support for the minimum wage has never been that secure. Pressure for a lower minimum wage for teenagers, now mounting with every month, grows out of a long history.

■ Occupational health and safety protection has faced a corporate siege throughout its history. Businesses have fought to limit funding for OSHA and to curb inspectors' rights to enter factories and offices. When working people have organized to demand effective health and safety protection, relying on the law for leverage, corporations have

Does America need more government regulation? Or less?

Your informed opinion is important. That's why we're offering a free booklet that explains the American Economic System. It is interesting and easy to read. Every American ought to know what it says. For a free copy, write: "Economics," Pueblo, Colorado 81009.

threatened to shut down their plants and move away, escaping the reach of the law. The battle has only begun.

Why are our victories so unstable and unreliable? Doesn't the government run the country? Don't we run the government?

Sometimes we blame the government's ineffectiveness on corrupt and ineffective politicians. If only we could elect honest and courageous leaders, then we could really get some action! The Watergate revelations seemed to confirm these suspicions. Polls show that faith in politicians continues to fall.

But that kind of explanation barely scratches the surface. There seem to be much deeper forces affecting the possibilities for government intervention. We have only won important gains when we've fought for them, sitting down in the factories during the 1930s and marching for civil rights during the 1960s. Business has won important victories—the Taft-Hartley Act of 1947, for example—when it has organized its own forces or caught working people napping. Even strong and apparently effective leaders with substantial support from working people, like Presidents Roosevelt, Kennedy, and Johnson, have beat hasty retreats when economic forces and corporate lobbying pushed them back. Could better politicians have made a dramatic difference?

We shall pursue this question in later chapters. But we can't answer it fully until we determine what kinds of economic forces limit what even the best politicians can accomplish. And that concern leads to another possible explanation for the shakiness of our victories gained through government action. We saw in Chapter 2 that our economic system has certain features which define it and distinguish it from other ways of running the economy. Capitalism is an economic system based on *private property, wage labor with production for profit, and commodity exchange.* It is certainly possible that these features of our economic system impose stubborn and uncompromising limits on the range of government options available to us. It often feels as if our political system provides us great leverage over the economy. In fact, the character of the economy may leave us politically straight-jacketed. It may be that we can wiggle our fingers but never really flex our political muscles.

The Economic Limits to Political Reform

Those are strong suggestions. Since they carry such sweeping implications, they warrant very careful examination. How would the character of the economic system "straight-jacket" the government?

Rights of *private property* present the first possible barrier to effective government reform. As we saw in Chapter 2, a system of private property means that those who control the means of production can exclude others from their use. If owners of factories and machines want to use them for their own purposes, our economic system protects their right to do so. The government can always encourage or even "require" owners to use their resources differently. In the end, however, the owners can always walk away, leaving their resources idle, taking their capital and investing it somewhere else.

Their drive for profits keeps them on the move.

For example, workers in Ohio petitioned Youngstown Sheet and Tube Co. through every possible mechanism, pleading with the company not to phase out the Youngstown works. More than 5,000 jobs were at stake. But the company decided it wanted to produce elsewhere. The workers could do nothing about it because the company's private property rights prevented workers' using the factory and equipment. The government could have seized the plant or bought it from the company, of course, but then it would have been crossing some critical economic boundaries—not simply smoothing rough economic edges but actually undercutting the private property foundations of the system.

Because of this basic economic power, private property rights also ensure that the government is always a couple of steps *behind* business. In many plants and offices where unions are not yet organized, for instance, companies can fire individual workers whenever they want. Workers can file suit with the government, of course, charging unfair labor practices or discrimination. But the suits move through the courts like turtles. In the meantime, the fired workers cope with unemployment and companies find replacements for them. As long as owners retain the basic rights to hire and fire, the government can do nothing more than dress workers' wounds. The only possible preventive medicine would be workers' or government control over hiring and firing. That, too, would cross some critical boundaries, changing some of the basic economic rules of the game.

This discussion points toward the importance of the second defining characteristic of our economy, its dependence on a system of *wage labor*. Because we own so little ourselves, we have to go to work for those who do control productive resources. That basic condition of economic dependence leaves us so vulnerable to corporate threats that we're always reluctant to push government reform very far.

For example, many of us learned about the critical importance of health-and-safety and environmental protection. We've pushed the government to intensify its regulation and inspection. But we continue to discover, through painful experience with runaway shops, that companies can move overseas, walking off with our jobs. We're vulnerable to their threats precisely because we have no other basis for economic security. When corporations tell us that government regulation has reached its limits—that they'll shut down if we take it any further—our dependence on the labor market makes it extremely difficult for us to call the companies' bluff. If we lose the game of chicken, we're out on the streets.

The system of *commodity exchange* places similar limits on the possibilities for government reform. Many of us have trouble buying what we need. Many products are shoddy or dangerous. Since we don't control the means of production, however, we can't produce what we want or need. The government can try to prohibit the production of some products, but companies can simply turn around and develop new products which may turn out to be just as dangerous. The government can weave a thicket of regulations, but companies can always ignore them or find new ways of evading them.

A system of commodity exchange, as we saw in Chapter 2, involves dependence on the *market* and *money* for the goods and services we need, with no other viable alternatives for securing them. In a system of commodity exchange, those who control the means of production ultimately determine what gets produced. The only way the government could fundamentally control the quantity and quality of the goods and services we buy would be to make them itself. As before, that would cross some critical economic boundaries.

In the end, all these arguments suggest that private corporations which control the means of production and produce for profit can continually keep ahead of the government. Their basic productive control provides them enormous leverage. *Every time the going with the government gets tough, the tough corporations get going*—hiking the bargaining stakes, threatening to shut their factories and offices, vowing to take their money elsewhere, manipulating our dependence on them for jobs and products. As long as corporations have so much control over the means of production, the government remains a political weakling, tears smudging its cheeks, begging the bullies on the block to "be nice."

CAN'T THE GOVERNMENT FIX IT ANYWAY?

"We have to tell a state considering additional restrictions on business: 'The next plant doesn't go up here if that bill passes.' "

—corporate executive at business conference[5]

"I'd like to see an America where so much power was not in the hands of the few. Where everybody'd get a fair shake. The establishment wants uneven odds. It's marking the cards....[They] mark the cards to make sure [they] don't lose."

—former U.S. Senator[6]

Those arguments seem powerful but the case isn't yet closed. All we've seen so far is that private corporate control, rooted in the basic features of our economy, makes it extremely difficult for the government *ultimately* to control corporate behavior.

But maybe the government doesn't need "ultimate control." Maybe our problems could be solved if the government could just nudge the corporations a little bit, pushing them barely enough to make a significant difference in our working and living conditions.

In order to explore that possibility, we need to review the major problems we currently face—the problems of *employment* and *control* and *inequality* and *subsistence* which we studied in the previous chapter. There's little evidence, as we concluded in Chapter 7, that the economy will solve those problems on its own. Our arguments in this chapter so far make it clear that the government can't change the world overnight. Can it make just enough difference to improve our working and living conditions?

Employment and Unemployment

Can the government push the economy toward full employment, significantly reducing prevailing levels of unemployment? We saw in Chapter 7 that the private sector, as it grows, tends to provide fewer and fewer jobs for each million dollars of total output. And that the economy has always travelled up and down the unemployment roller coaster, alternating periods of boom and contraction. Can the government make a basic difference in those historic patterns?

Corporations often suggest that the government provide tax incentives to business to encourage more and more investment and, they promise, more jobs with it. But government tax incentives to corporations simply permit companies to invest the additional funds however they choose. Both competition with other firms and conflicts with their workers tend to push corporations, as we've seen in earlier chapters, to replace workers with machines. Government tax incentives make it easier for corporations to pursue that kind of automation, helping them scrape together the funds necessary for machine investment.

And where does the tax incentive money come from? It represents lost revenues for the government, giving the public less money to work with on its own projects. If the government were to spend that same money directly instead of giving it to the corporations, it would create more jobs than the large corporations do with their subsidized investment. So providing tax incentives to business (instead of spending it on government projects) runs the risk of job loss, not job gain.[7] Not much hope for government relief through that strategy!

Can't the government spend money to create jobs directly? Between 1948 and 1966, during the years of rapid economic growth, government expenditures were responsible for creating roughly 15 million new jobs. Why can't the government just keep creating more and more jobs?

The government can finance job-creating expenditures in either of two ways.

First, it can raise additional revenues through additional taxes. Someone has to pay those taxes.

■ If workers bear the burden of the additional taxes, it means that working people as a whole are paying the price for the failure of the private economy to create jobs. And if workers are forced to reduce consumption as a result of the larger tax bite, the economy may not expand after all.

■ The government could try to impose the taxes on corporate profits and the wealthy. We've learned by now that corporations pull out their crying towels at the slightest hint of higher business taxes. If the government ignores their tears, companies begin to pack their bags. The only way the government can make the taxes stick—using part of undistributed corporate surplus to create new public jobs—is by restricting corporate freedom to move their capital around whenever they choose. That would involve changing the basic economic rules of the game. Short of those changes, it's extremely difficult for the government to create jobs while keeping a balanced budget.

Can't the government push the economy toward full employment?

Sam (as in uncle) and Dave (as in Rockefeller)

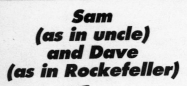

What about creating jobs by running a deficit? Many economists have suggested that the government *spend* more than it receives from current taxes—borrowing against the future. If the government seriously pursued full employment policies through deficit spending, it would also have to do something about inflation. In the end, that would require real price-and-profit controls, limiting corporate freedom to raise their prices whenever they wanted. And it would have to involve basic government planning of production levels in order to reduce the bottlenecks and shortages which would be likely to emerge. Our experiences during World War II suggest that the government can actually perform those tasks fairly well. But movement in those directions, once again, would alter the basic rules of the game, pushing the economy rapidly toward *coordinated* rather than *disconnected* production decisions.

Perhaps the government can't create jobs without upsetting the structure of the economy. But can't it at least smooth the business cycle, reducing the ups and downs of the economic roller coaster? Can't it provide us with a little more economic security?

Such a policy effort would require continuing government stimulus to prevent recessions. Economists promised us during the 1960s that the government could achieve that kind of economic management and that we could enjoy steady growth forever and ever.[8]

When we look back at those efforts, however, we can see how *the basic relationships of capitalist economies make full employment essentially impossible within the framework of capitalist control.*

As the economy continued to grow during the 1960s, labor markets got tight and unemployment dropped. Workers gained greater bargaining power because competition in the labor market was declining. We used that bargaining power to increase our wages and resist speed-up on the line. Business felt the strain and, as we could have predicted on the basis of our analysis in Chapters 3 and 4, companies began to experience declining profits. (The stronger workers get, the less surplus corporations are able to extract.) Business had only one recourse. Since workers' growing strength was based on tight labor markets, business needed loose labor markets. That meant higher unemployment. And that required a recession. By the end of the 1960s, many business and government leaders were calling for a

recession simply to discipline workers. "Many manufacturers...openly complained...," the *Wall Street Journal* reported in 1972, "that too much control had passed from management to labor."[9] A British banker echoed similar sentiments around the same time. "We've got to get some discipline back into this country's work force, and the only way to do it is to make the blokes damn grateful to have any sort of job at all."[10] Recession was the only possible salvation.

The lesson of this historical experience now seems clear. In order to maintain control over their workers, capitalists apparently require occasional doses of unemployment to reinforce labor discipline. From the capitalists' perspective, sustained full employment gives workers too much strength. If the government were to ignore capitalists and promote continuing full employment anyway, it would end up changing the basic rules of the game. Capitalists would lose much of their effective control of the means of production. Which is why they don't want anything to do with full employment. Several leading business executives made these preferences clear at a series of management conferences in 1974-75. One executive: "This recession will bring about the healthy respect for economic values that the Depression did." A second: "We need a sharp recession." A third: "People need to recognize that a job is the most important thing they can have. We should use this recession to get the public to better understand how our economic system works."[11]

We could conceivably have full employment. *But we can't have capitalist control and full employment at the same time.* One or the other has to give.

Freedom and Necessity

Can the government protect us from our growing economic dependence? Economic growth, we've learned, tends to force more and more of us to work as wage-laborers. It also promotes the growing power of the largest corporations. Can the government issue some security blankets to provide us a little economic warmth?

There are two different ways the governent could help provide people with more economic independence.

■ The first would involve supporting workers' cooperatives and companies on a major scale so that nearly everyone could consider that kind of alternative to dependence on wage-labor for large corporations. If we all had access to that kind of alternative, however, the corporations would lose their power—watching their employees switch over to alternative workers' enterprises or being forced to cave in to workers' demands in order to retain their employees. That would certainly change the rules of the game.

■ The second would involve providing effective income support to people whether they worked or not—a guaranteed minimum income. If we could choose between a decent income and the kind of work which capitalists impose on us, many would choose the income over oppressive work. Then where would the corporations find a labor force?

Either way, government protection against wage-laborers' economic dependence would assault the wage-labor system itself, one of the basic pillars of capitalist control. Which is why corporations and their government allies oppose effective income support programs. As one government official explained his opposition to higher income guarantees several years ago, "We are not remaking the American labor market in this bill and [we] fully realize that people are going to have to do the work that is available in our economy."[12]

What about growing corporate power? Can the government protect us from that kind of economic domination?

Large corporations achieve their power and money, as we have seen throughout the previous chapters, through the basic operations of the economic system. In order to control their power, we would have to control the conditions from which that power arises. That would involve controlling competition, limiting corporate profits, and regulating corporate behavior. The economic rules of the game say that the government can't move in those directions. Without such steps, the corporations can race ahead unchecked.

Once again, we're apparently faced with a choice between capitalist control or effective government intervention. The history of "anti-trust regulation" provides a clear case in point. Government anti-trust efforts, seeking to limit some of the excess power of the largest corporations, have never challenged the basic economic process of capital accumulation. As a result of that failure of will (or nerve), those anti-trust efforts have been doomed to irrelevance. After 80 years of government anti-trust activity, large corporations have more power than ever. *The government must either pose fundamental challenges to that power or resign itself to the inevitability of corporate domination. There is nothing in between.* Multinational corporations are too large to be bothered by mosquito bites.

Equality and Inequality

Can the government help reduce some of the divisions among working people, helping those in less affluent families to achieve a decent standard of living? Capitalists often seek to increase the divisions among us. Economic growth, at best, tends to reproduce them. Can the government help bring us closer together?

We are used to thinking that the government can make some dents in economic inequality through either of two kinds of efforts.

First, the government can try to legislate more equal hiring and promotion practices in industry, encouraging companies to end their discrimination against groups of disadvantaged workers. But there are three important barriers to these efforts. (1) Companies can claim that hiring and promotion remain their privileged domain (since they own the means of production). Without fundamental challenges to those prerogatives, government action requires legal suits shuffling interminably through the courts. (2) Even while the government is working on problems created by old inequalities, the process of capitalist growth continually creates new ones. As large corporations grow, for instance, they require more and more administrative personnel. Since the corporations are organized hierarchically—with centralized power at the top—the administrative bureaucracies are laced with inequalities. As these bureaucracies grow, so do the inequalities. Government programs to combat inequality must race simply to stay in place. (3) Capitalists' control over their employees, we saw in Chapter 4, depends to some degree on significant divisions among their workers. (A unified work force can bid up wages and resist exploitation on the job.) If the government pushes hard against inequality, capitalists will pull out their final trump cards—threatening to move away, to bring in new and different groups of unskilled workers, to evade the equalizing efforts however they can. If the government persisted, it would be forced, once again, to assault the basic economic foundations on which capitalist control of the means of production rests.

The government can also try to pursue a second path toward greater equality—by pushing income support programs. These involve efforts to compensate for the inequalities created in the labor market. As we saw in the previous section, however, these programs cost money and undercut labor market discipline. If pursued very far, they threaten the basic premises of capitalist control and wage-labor market operations.

Through either kind of effort, the government can push only so far before it bumps up against the basic characteristics of the economy. Inequality has deep roots. Pulling them out requires our digging very deep. *The government can try to dig up the roots of inequality, but we can't expect the garden to look the same afterwards.*

Recent government programs to combat inequality have encountered some of these difficulties. Between the mid-60s and the early 70s, government assistance to the poor increased dramatically through expanding public welfare and social security. While those programs were expanding, however, the growth of the economy itself was creating more and more inequality. Economic growth ended up washing out the effects of government assistance. After all those expenditures aimed at reducing inequality, we were back where we started. According to a major study of these government programs, "cash assistance made no overall progress" toward reducing relative inequality over those years.[13]

Wealth and Subsistence

Can the government improve our basic standards of living? Economic growth both increases the wealth and power of large corporations, as we've seen, and severely limits our ability to improve our own welfare. Can't the government unlock the door to health and happiness?

We begin to retrace our steps. Capitalist economic growth, we saw in Chapters 3 through 6, tends periodically to create unemployment and to extend labor markets around the world. This continually exposes us to competition from other groups of workers. That competition creates downward pressures on our incomes, pushing them back toward basic levels of subsistence. When we struggle to increase our bargaining position and our standards of living, we bump up against the limits imposed by labor market competition and

> **The government can try to dig up the roots of inequality, but we can't expect the garden to look the same after it tries.**

divisions. Every time we threaten profits, capitalists threaten our jobs. The government could help us unify, of course, by making it easier for workers to organize the unorganized throughout the economy. But union organizing depends critically on *limits* to corporate freedom to move their capital around from place to place. When we talk about government efforts to improve our standards of living in this way, we lead quickly to discussion about government challenges to the basic structure of the economy. We've returned to this conclusion repeatedly throughout this and earlier chapters. No matter where we enter the maze of our economic system, we end up at its basic foundations. Capital accumulation drives our economy forward. We can't seem to make significant inroads on our basic economic problems unless we challenge the structure on which capital accumulation proceeds. In the end, the government can only "fix" our problems if it "fixes" the way our economy is organized. *If you want a machine to behave completely differently, you can't transform it by greasing its gears and tinkering with a few parts. You have to rebuild it from scratch.*

DIDN'T THEY ALWAYS TELL US CAPITALISM WAS WONDERFUL?

"You never change your socks
And little streams of alcohol
Come trickling down the rocks....
There's a lake of stew,
And of honey, too—
In the Big Rock Candy Mountain."

—popular song[14]

We've come to the end of a long examination of how our economy works. Our conclusions are controversial. We've seen that our major problems have deep roots in the basic structure of our economy. We've seen that the process of capital accumulation makes it more and more difficult for us to solve them. The evidence suggests that the economy

A $200,000 Steak Dinner?

by itself solves none of our problems and makes some of them worse. We've seen that the government can't fix our problems without challenging the basic economic structures of capitalism. The picture looks grim.

This doesn't mean that we shouldn't pursue political solutions to our problems. It simply means that we should never underestimate the kinds of changes in the economic structure which our political efforts might require. Unless we are willing to contemplate those kinds of changes, the dynamics of the economy and the power of the largest corporations will place stringent limits on the potential for government reform, straight-jacketing our political efforts to solve our economic problems.

These conclusions will seem shattering to many of us. We've grown up hearing a continuing chorus of praise for capitalism. We've voted consistently for politicians who promise defense of the free enterprise system. We've been taught that capitalism is wonderful for us, for our children, and for other living things.

How can our past impressions and our present conclusions about the economy conflict so dramatically? Many of us have believed in capitalism. We now seem prepared to conclude that we can't solve our problems without somehow transforming the economic system. Why such a sharp discrepancy? Is there something wrong with the bill of goods they've sold us for decades? Or is there a critical flaw in our own analysis—hiding somewhere in the previous pages of this book—which compromises the conclusions toward which we've been moving?

One way to pursue these questions is to study Part II of this book all over again—poking its arguments, searching its evidence, probing for some hidden flaws. We invite you to pull out your magnifying glasses and launch that kind of even-more-skeptical inquiry.

There's also obviously another way to explore our puzzlement. What about all the arguments on behalf of capitalism which the DUPE pushers have fed us for so many years? In the next part of this book, we turn to a careful review of the main arguments which the DUPE makes in defense of capitalism. Are they for real?

PART III: THE "ECONOMIC WONDER OF THE WORLD"?

"Why must a supervisor be expected to know about economics? Mainly because this very important subject is so *misunderstood* by your employees....Scratch hard enough and you'll find that an employee's underlying lack of faith in the capitalistic system is at the root of much of your difficulty with his output and quality....To correct these vague misconceptions about business economics, it's up to you to know some of the basic truths about the way American capitalism works."

—a management text for supervisors[1]

"I learned all the whitewash things. I didn't learn about America in school. I learned what they wanted me to learn....In school, everything was just great: We never did anything wrong. Everything was justified. Up until I was thirteen, I believed that. After that, I turned myself off, and from then on it was my own opinion."

—student in Chicago technical high school[2]

The conclusions of the last seven chapters probably seem surprising to many of us. We keep hearing, as the DUPE booklet puts it, that the U.S. economy is the "economic wonder of the world."[3] But closer inspection reveals many flaws in its design. Capitalism provides plenty of profits for the few, but it creates and compounds many problems for the rest of us.

Why has our own examination clashed so dramatically with the conventional wisdom?

One major reason is that we don't normally get economic analysis from our own perspective. More than half of U.S. adults in a 1976 poll agreed that economists are "pro business." Only 4% disagreed.[4]

In contrast, the analysis in Part II of this book began with the interests and needs of working people, asking how the economy affects us in our daily lives. This kind of analysis can be called **popular economics**. DUPEsters begin with the interests and problems of corporations, asking how they can increase business profits. We can call this **corporate economics.**

We saw throughout Part II that there are many fundamental conflicts between working people and corporations. So it should not be surprising that the two kinds of economics come to such conflicting conclusions about the economy. The chart on these pages summarizes the major differences between the two economic perspectives by pulling together the threads of the discussion in Part II.

That summary makes popular economics seem like a promising starting point, since it seems to correspond to so many of our own experiences. But corporate economics saturates the media. Its message keeps ringing in our ears. What about all those arguments on behalf of capitalism? Doesn't our economic system have many irreplaceable advantages? It may not be perfect, but isn't it still the best of all *possible* worlds?

When all of the rhetoric is distilled and bottled, corporate economics makes four main arguments in defense of capitalism:

1. That capitalism promotes *popular economic rule*—an economy *by* and *for* the people—because mass stock ownership and consumer power puts us in the

driver's seat.

2. That capitalism is the most *efficient* economic system possible because its market mechanism ensures production at the lowest possible cost and guarantees the best possible allocation of scarce resources.

3. That capitalism improves the *quality* of our lives because competition forces firms to provide attractive working conditions and appealing goods and services.

4. That capitalism helps promote *political democracy* (and is more consistent with democracy than any other economic system) because market exchange requires individual freedom and encourages individual initiative.

Each of these claims is crucial to the DUPEsters' defense of the system. If we want to consider challenging our capitalist economy, we must evaluate these arguments on its behalf very carefully. The next four chapters consider each of them in turn.

Five Main Differences in Economic Viewpoint

CORPORATE ECONOMICS

1. We are *all* alike in market economies because we are all producers and we are all consumers, meeting in the marketplace as buyers and sellers, *perfect equals* in the exchange of goods and services. So much for "classes."

2. Our incomes depend on our *productive contributions*. Capitalists are paid profits in return for the money they invest and the risks they take. Workers are paid wages in return for the labor they perform. Everyone earns by exactly the same rules, so where's the conflict and what's the gripe? You get what you deserve and you deserve what you get.

3. Bosses and hierarchy are *necessary* both because modern production is so complicated that we need managers to avoid chaos *and* because, let's face it, most people are a little lazy. They need to be leaned on if we're going to get any work out of them at all. Business is big because big firms can perform these necessary chores better than the small ones.

4. The great virtue of markets is that they enable us to coordinate our economic activities with millions of other people in both the most efficient and the free-est way possible. Interference with the market reduces efficiency and freedom. The market keeps us *free to choose* what we want.

5. Economic growth creates abundance and jobs for everyone, promoting liberty and equality for all. The system will continue providing this bounty as long as we let it work its wonders by its own rules. Its operations are so wondrous, in fact, that we will scarcely ever need the government to do anything.

POPULAR ECONOMICS

1. People are divided into two main classes under capitalism—*owners* who control the means of production and *working people* who must labor for someone else in order to survive. *We* work for *them*. (Chapter 2.)

2. The most important source of profits in capitalism is the *surplus labor* which employers extract from their workers. Owner's dependence on this surplus labor ensures that workers and bosses will have *conflicting interests*—workers wanting to work less for more pay and owners wanting more work for less pay. They want what we've got—our labor. (Chapter 3.)

3. Driven to stay ahead of their competitors and on top of their workers, corporations must constantly seek more and more *control over production*. This leads to hierarchies, job divisions, reduced work incentives, and larger and larger capitalist enterprises. People lose both control over their work *and* the power to influence corporate decisions as consumers. (Chapter 4.)

4. Capitalism's reliance on the *market*—with its disconnected production decisions and distribution according to power over resources—creates *insecurity*, generates enormous *waste*, encourages *competitive* relationships, and helps the *wealthy dominate the rest of us*. Free to choose that? (Chapter 5.)

5. Economic growth in capitalist economies both requires and generates increasing corporate power and continuing economic instability. It is doubtful that the economy will solve our problems on its own. It is equally doubtful that the government can effectively mop the mess the economy leaves behind. (Chapters 6, 7, 8)

9.

An Economy BY and FOR the People?

"Our society is what we make it. We can shape our institutions."
—The Gospel according to DUPE[1]

"Businesss is truly the servant of society."
—corporate executive at management conference[2]

"There's two things [that management] wants to keep: all the money and all the say-so. They don't want these poor workin' folks to have none of that."
—union organizer in North Carolina[3]

DUPE pushers constantly reassure us about the economy. The system will always respond to our needs and interests, they say, because we're running the show. Production for profit benefits us, on the one side, because we own stock and earn profits from production. Production for the market benefits us, on the other side, because we can use our money in the market to influence economic decisions. If we don't like what we're getting from the economy, we can vote for something better with our stock proxies and our dollar bills. The voice of the people prevails!

We certainly have voices and we frequently use them when we're angry or frustrated. But few of us feel that the economy is very responsive to our demands. Does capitalism really promote popular economic rule? Does it actually sustain an economy *by* and *for* the people?

HOW DO WE MEASURE POPULAR ECONOMIC RULE?

The DUPEsters claim that we rule the economy because we can make corporations change their policies and practices if we don't like what they're doing. They support that argument with three main points. The first focuses on our power as owners, and the other two on our power as consumers.

1. Corporate economics claims that we benefit from and ultimately control even the biggest corporations through our stock ownership. This is what is sometimes called *people's capitalism.* So many U.S. citizens buy stock in corporations, one hears, that corporations producing profit are actually serving us, their owners. There we are in the stockholders' meeting, calling the shots. Under "people's capitalism," we, the people, can keep them, the capitalists, on a tight rein.

2. As consumers in a *free enterprise* system, we have the power to reward those who respond to our desires. Suppose a corporation is

making a shoddy product or charging outrageous prices. Another entrepreneur can appear, start a new business, make better products or charge lower prices, and begin to steal away the offending corporation's business. The offending corporation must either change its practices or lose the market. "Free enterprise" implies that people are "free" to start enterprises if there is a need for them. As long as consumers want something, the free enterprise system ensures that we'll get it.

3. Some corporations may be so big, corporate economists admit, that new enterprises may not affect them for a very long time. Not to worry! Even these corporate titans can be held in check. In the end, no matter what their size, corporations must sell their products. If *we* don't want them, *they* can't sell them. If they can't sell them, they can't make a profit off that line of production. Always in search of profits, they will make something else that we will buy. Eventually, we get what we want. The consumer is *ruler* because the consumer demand ultimately determines what kinds of goods are produced. Corporate economists call this the power of *consumer sovereignty*.

This summary suggests some tests for DUPE claims of popular economic rule. We need to ask three specific questions:

■ Does widespread stock ownership mean that working people "own" and therefore "rule" the economy?

■ Does the ease of establishing new enterprises help ensure effective market discipline of corporations?

■ Are corporations responsive to and controlled by consumer demand?

With each of these questions, we must also examine trends affecting popular economic rule. Are we gaining or losing economic influence over time?

WHAT ABOUT PEOPLE'S CAPITALISM?

"Who owns America?...Not the rich. The corporations of America are owned by more than [twenty-five] million people. It is the savers who own America....The savers keep America alive."

—corporate magazine ad[4]

The DUPE pushers are fond of reminding us that roughly 25-30 million Americans—almost one out of every six adults—own stock in corporations on the official stock exchanges. The phone company has nearly three million stockholders. More than a million own stock in General Motors.[5] "Take a look at the owners of America's oil companies," Bob Hope begs us at the beginning of one of his long series of ads for Texaco, and the camera presents people *just like us*. Anybody can own Texaco! Doesn't this kind of broad-based stock ownership ensure an economy *of* the people? Won't this kind of people's capitalism guarantee corporate restraint? Isn't it great to be able to own a piece of the rock?

Some elementary facts raise serious doubts about this notion of people's capitalism.

■ The vast majority of U.S. households don't own any stock at all. In 1975, roughly 85% of U.S. households did *not* include corporate stock among their assets.[6] If majority rule means anything, then the vast majority of us don't have any access to corporate rule at all.

■ Among those who own stock, a tiny minority of households completely dominates stock ownership. In 1972, the wealthiest 1% of households controlled a solid majority—56.5%—of corporate stock all by itself.[7]

■ Even among the wealthy, relatively few own enough stock to secure real control. Most corporate economists agree that "20 or 30 percent of the shares" in a company means, as the DUPE primer puts it modestly, that their owners can "feel pretty sure of having a board of directors that will be easy to get along with."[8] How many people own

There's Hope for Democracy

30% of all the corporate stock in this country? About 100,000 families control that much stock just by themselves.[9] That doesn't leave much room for the rest of us.

So much for the simple view that the "people" of the United States own U.S. corporations. If ownership provides the ticket to control, working people are all in the same boat: when they passed out seats in the corporate board room, they forgot about us.

Still, some corporate economists have tried to assure us that people's capitalism is on the rise. Look how bad the old days were, they say. In the early part of the twentieth century, a couple of hundred wealthy families controlled the largest corporations. The Rockefellers and the

Mellons, the DuPonts and the Morgans—all had immense stock holdings and widespread corporate power. Those were the days of the "robber barons," the DUPEsters admit, but those days are far behind us now.

The DUPE makes three kinds of arguments to support that claim:

1) They argue that stock ownership is much more *widely dispersed* than it used to be. Take the largest 200 corporations. In 1929, for example, more than half of those corporations had fewer than 20,000 shareholders apiece. By 1974, less than 5% of the 200 largest corporations were owned by only 20,000 or fewer shareholders.[10] Doesn't that suggest a dramatic erosion of stock control by the wealthy few?

Those numbers must be taken with blocks of salt. In fact, they don't indicate much increase in *effective* popular rule of corporations at all. Many corporations now have scores of thousands of shareholders but their voices are too weak and scattered to command attention in the board rooms. In contrast, the twenty biggest shareholders control at least 10% voting strength in more than 70% of the largest U.S. corporations.[11] Company by company, several handfuls of owners swing enough weight to be able to call the shots.

2) Many corporate economists also argue that workers now control corporations through the investments of their *pension funds.* One management consultant has even suggested that the growing importance of these investments has established a kind of "pension fund socialism" in the United States.[12]

The recent growth in pension fund assets and investments is certainly dramatic. Before World War II, employees' pension funds hardly existed. By 1978, the total value of public and private employee pension funds had snowballed to $350 billion—more than the total gross national product of the United Kingdom.[13] And much of this wealth has been invested in stocks: available data suggest that pension funds and employee stock savings or profit sharing plans (ESPs) own nearly one quarter of all corporate stock outstanding.[14] Does this mean that workers are beginning to create their own modern version of "people's capitalism"—a pensioners' capitalism—in the United States?

The first problem is that workers with wealth in pension funds aren't treated like ordinary stockholders by the law. The Supreme Court ruled in 1979 that an employee's holding in a pension fund was not an "investment contract" like a title to a stock certificate. This means that workers are not covered by the anti-fraud provisions of the Federal securities laws. And this means that workers have no ultimate legal guarantee that their pension fund "holdings" in corporations will be honored, protected, or ultimately redeemed.[15] Not a promising beginning.

The second problem is that the banks or investment trust companies actually control about half of pension fund and ESP holdings.[16] The workers put up the money and the big moneylenders get the voting power and indirect influence which this money provides. Not a promising extension.

The final problem is that the stocks which workers do control are widely scattered among hundreds of companies. This means that pension funds and ESP's rarely own enough stock in any individual company to be able to wield effective control—to be able, at the most basic level, to influence corporate decisions. ESP's own 10% or more of total stock in only 16 of the largest 200 non-financial corporations, according to 1974 data, and pension funds exceed that level in only one.[17] Even in those cases, according to the most comprehensive recent study, ESP holdings "are even more reliably promanagement" than other kinds of outside share blocks, particularly because "employees are subject to more extensive management influence and persuasion than other shareholders."[18] Until workers gain a truly independent base within the company, this study concludes, ESPs "strengthen management control" rather than curb it.[19] So much for pensioners' capitalism.

Mix those problems together and they don't spell control. As an official of the American Banking Association recently concluded:"The beneficiaries of pension funds do not own American industry. When you [define] ownership as controlling—which is, as far as I'm concerned, the only real instance of ownership—then certainly [the workers] can't own industry."[20]

3. The DUPE pushers also suggest that *managers* have much more influence over corporations than their owners, that wealthy coupon-clippers are no longer a match for savvy executives in the day-to-day struggle for ultimate control of the firm. "As a result," the DUPE primer concludes, "most modern corporations are [actually] run by professional managers trained in law, engineering, business management or finance."[21]

What difference does this make? The DUPE perspective seems to suggest that managers and executives are less ruthless than the earlier capitalists who launched large corporations, that they're somehow more sensitive to the public interest than, in the DUPE primer's words, "the 'rugged individualists' who started the enterprises."[22]

There are two obvious flaws in this notion that managerial control has created, as an economist once put it, the "modern soulful corporation."[23]

First, just like owners, managers are chasing the bucks. Even in the mid-1970s, when the stock market was depressed, the typical senior executive of the largest corporations owned at least $1 million worth of his or her company's common stock.[24] In four-fifths of the largest 100 industrial corporations in 1975, top officers owned at least $1 million worth of stock.[25] At least one-fifth of the typical top officer's salary comes from stock-related compensation.[26] Managers with that kind of stake in their companies are spurred by the same profit-seeking motive as owners with large blocks of stock. The higher the level of corporate profits, the higher their dividend earnings and the more stock options they receive. The returns are irresistible.

Second, the executives of large U.S. corporations tend to come from the same backgrounds and share the same interests as people from traditionally wealthy families.[27] They attend the same elite schools, visit the same posh resorts, eat at the same privileged clubs. Even more important, they believe in the same economic system—one which puts corporate profits ahead of people's needs. Managers may control many large corporations, but only the DUPEsters would ever confuse their interests with ours.

The result, in the end, is that large corporations behave the same way whether they're controlled by inside executives or outside owners. Many economists have tried to show that managers pursue different objectives than wealthy owners. But they've failed to find the evidence. After all that effort, the record seems fairly clear. As the most recent review of those studies concludes, "In sum, the triumph of management control in many large corporations has not left them in the hands of neutral technocrats. The control groups of these organizations seem as devoted to profitable growth as are the leaders of entrepreneurial and owner-dominated companies, past and present."[28] They still want profits and power, whoever they are.

So Who's in the Driver's Seat?

If the people don't own and control U.S. corporations, who does?

The wealthy try to obscure their power as much as possible, of course, but some detailed investigations have recently provided a fairly clear portrait of corporate ownership and control in the United States. Four somewhat overlapping groups of wealthy and powerful people call the shots.[29]

Some wealthy families, like the Mellons and Hunts, still exercise *direct family control* of large corporations through their dominant stock ownership. These billionaires control roughly 30-40 of the largest 200 nonfinancial corporations.

Wealthy families or closely allied groups of families also exercise control through *banks.* The Rockefeller family now exercises much of its control, for example, through the Chase Manhattan Bank and allied financial institutions. The eight major bank groups in the U.S., almost all of them controlled by wealthy ownership interests, probably control between 40 and 60 of the largest 200 corporations.

Handfuls of top executives also control many corporations. Something like 1,000 executives manage the largest 200 corporations, earning in the hundreds of thousands of dollars per year and typically owning at least $1 million in company stock. In roughly 100-130 of the largest corporations, these handfuls of wealthy and powerful officers call the shots without significant outside ownership interference.

Lying behind these three small groups and providing them with much of their capital are the roughly 100,000 families who own the lion's share of corporate stock. They don't directly determine corporate decisions, but they enjoy the opportunity to reap many of the benefits.

All of these four groups are interested in preserving and increasing their own wealth. None of them cares much about the ownership claims of the rest of us. The "people" in "people's capitalism," in short, have about as much influence on corporate decisions as the "spectators" in "spectator sports" have on the plays called in the huddle.

As Robert Townsend, former top executive of Avis Rent-a-Car, recently concluded, "People's capitalism? Hogwash!"[30]

Fig. 9.1

Who Controls the Economy?

The largest 200 corporations are vital.

Wealthy families still exercise direct family control over 30-40 of the largest 200 companies.

Eight major bank groups control 40-60 of the largest 200.

Handfuls of **wealthy executives** control the other 100-130 of the largest 200.

Behind these controlling interests, roughly **100,000 wealthy households** own the lion's share of corporate stock.

People's Capitalism?

Source: See note #29.

WHAT ABOUT FREE ENTERPRISE?

**"The American free enterprise system allows us to organize
and operate any business we choose almost without limitation."**
                                                    —DUPE film guide[31]

When consumers don't like what corporations are producing, the
DUPE analysis suggests, some new company will appear to satisfy our
demands. And it must be fairly easy to start a new business in the
United States because there are so many of them. In 1970 there were
more than 12 million businesses—or one for every six households in
the country.[32] If we don't like what the corporations are dishing out,
why don't we start a restaurant of our own?

While it is true that people can easily start new businesses, it's not

Don't like what corporations are dishing out?
Why don't we start a restaurant of our own?

so obvious that people can start new businesses which *matter*. For this
DUPE argument about an economy *for* the people to hold water, new
enterprises would have to compete effectively with the large corporations which have the greatest influence over the products we use and
need. It's one thing to talk about new grass springing up in the garden.
It's quite another to suggest that new corporate skyscrapers can rise up
to rival the old, affecting basic decisions in the corporate board rooms.

We can examine the DUPE claim about free enterprise in three
steps: first, by looking at which businesses have the most influence
now; second, by checking out what happens to those who dare to
challenge the kings of the mountain; and third, by exploring the problems in trying to compete with the most powerful corporations.

Who's On Top?

There are three legal forms of doing business in the United States.
One can operate a *proprietorship*, a business owned by one person or
family. (The corner grocery, drug store, and barber shop are typical
examples.) Or one can operate a *partnership*, an organization owned by
two or more parties in which assets and profits are distributed by
careful legal agreements. (Law firms and doctors' offices are often run
as partnerships.) Or one can form a *corporation*, an organization which
is jointly owned by all the people who buy stocks and whose debts and
legal obligations are not the personal responsibility of the shareholders. (All giant corporations use this form.)

If we want to study economic influence, we should clearly focus on
the *corporations*. In 1973, there were 12 million proprietorships and
partnerships, representing 86% of all businesses in the United States.
Despite their numbers, however, these 12 million firms earned only
15% of all business revenues. Corporations, although they represented
only 14% of enterprises, received 85% of all business revenues.[33]

And if we want to understand which corporations matter most, we
should clearly look at the *giant corporations*.

■ There were roughly two million corporations in the United States in 1973. Of these, 98% had less than $5 million in assets. Out of those two million corporations, the 2,000 largest, each with at least $250 million in assets, alone accounted for nearly 60% of all corporate profits.[34]

■ As we saw throughout Part II of this book, control of the basic means of production is critical for economic control. In 1974, the 500 largest industrial corporations controlled more than three-quarters of all manufacturing assets.[35]

Giant corporations exercise particularly decisive influence because they control such huge shares of key industries on which everyone else depends—industries supplying the energy and basic materials which nearly every other corporation requires for its business. Data show clearly the depth of this control over key industries: in 1963, for example, two-fifths of all manufacturing output was produced in industries where the four largest firms controlled at least 50% of total sales.[36] That control gives them enormous leverage over other firms.

These (roughly) 500 giant corporations form what we can call the *core* of the economy. Their size almost boggles the mind. The *smallest* of the 500 largest industrial companies had $285 million in assets in 1980.[37] The combined sales of the five largest companies by themselves are greater than the gross national products of all but nine countries in the world.[38]

What Happens to the Challengers?

These giant corporations aren't on top because everyone else is lazy. Someone comes along with a "better idea" nearly every day. New businesses are formed continuously. Thousands of entrepreneurs take a crack at challenging the king of the mountain.

The first thing that is obvious is that most small businesses fail. In the 1960s, roughly one-twelfth of all businesses were failing every year.[39] In the early 1970s, over just seven years, almost three-fifths of all small firms (with 20 or fewer employees) folded.[40] The odds are

---

Almost 10% of small firms fail every year. Others are often swallowed up like small fish.

---

clearly against survival.

Even those who survive, like small fish in the ocean, are often swallowed. When small and medium firms begin to display some strength and competitive muscle, they are often purchased by the giant companies—both to steal their ideas and to protect against their competition. In manufacturing, for example, roughly 1% of manufacturing companies are bought up by other companies every year—meaning that a tenth of industrial firms are absorbed every decade.[41] And the giant corporations are typically the ones which do the swallowing. Five-sixths of the growth in the relative wealth of the 200 largest U.S. corporations during the postwar period was due to their purchases of other firms.[42]

The other side of the coin is equally obvious; the giant corporations remain in the driver's seat. We can look at the 100 largest industrial companies in 1929. By 1975, 93 of those 100 companies were still big enough to be part of the core economy.[43] Once they become kings of the mountain, it's very difficult to dislodge them.

Why Is It So Hard to Mount a Challenge?

It is obviously rare that the giant corporations lose ground to their small competitors. Why is it so hard for a new enterprise to challenge the core firms?

To begin with, it requires huge amounts of capital to compete in key industrial sectors. Constructing a modern steel mill or auto plant requires hundreds of millions of dollars. Few new companies can put together that kind of money.

The giant corporations also have an easier time raising what they don't already have. On the stock market, new companies don't have a track record and are less attractive to investors. (This disadvantage is getting much more severe; stock offerings by "unseasoned companies," as they're called on Wall Street, fell from more than 60% of offerings on the market in the early 1960s to only 16% in 1976.[44]) In the banking community, the banks with the big bucks like to do business with the biggest corporations. As the chair of the New York Stock Exchange admitted, "small businesses borrow from commercial banks at a far higher rate than do larger corporations."[45] Since small businesses already suffer other important disadvantages, these higher interest rates can often be the last straw.

The giant corporations work together, finally, and often help each other. Many large companies have common (or "interlocking") directors, for example, through whom they can share information and strategies. (Of the 250 largest corporations in 1975, only 15 were *not* interlocked with at least five other companies in the top 250.[46]) Many large companies, particularly the energy giants, also participate in joint ventures to pool risks and resources. One way or another, they find

**Leave It
to Booger**

ways to stick together. As the most detailed recent study concluded, giant corporations have "a huge number of supraindustry connections that bind its members together not ony by economic ties but also socially, politically, and ideologically."[47]

Are the challenges getting any easier? Is the potential influence of new enterprises growing over time, promising more and more consumer protection from the free enterprise system?

As we have already seen in Chapter 7, the evidence all points in the other direction.

■ The scale of assets required to compete with the dominant corporations has become more and more awesome. In 1919, for instance, there were only five or six firms that controlled as much as $1 billion in total assets. By 1969, controlling for inflation, there were almost 100 corporations larger than that threshold.[48]

■ The giant corporations' control over the means of production has also increased significantly. In 1947, the 100 largest manufacturing firms controlled less than 40% of all manufacturing assets. By 1968, their share had climbed to almost exactly half.[49] Over the past few years, large corporations have been going on yet another binge and this share of manufacturing assets may have increased even more.[50] Those are *not* the signs of a dissolving core.

What's our conclusion? "The American enterprise system allows us," to repeat the opening quote of this section, "to organize and operate any business we choose almost without limitation." That much comes close to the truth.

But the "American enterprise system," also makes it nearly impossible to organize a business which can *effectively compete with and change the practices of the dominant corporations.* Just as most workers are "free" to starve if they don't want to work for a boss, so are entrepreneurs "free" to start their own businesses and run the risks of irrelevance or bankruptcy. If consumers are waiting for new enterprises to improve standards of living, then consumers beware.

WHAT ABOUT CONSUMERS' SOVEREIGNTY?

"Every day, we make decisions to buy or not to buy, and these decisions directly affect our economy....To succeed, producers must continue to offer goods and services that consumers want."

—the DUPE booklet[51]

"When you vote daily in the supermarket, you get precisely what you voted for, and so does everyone else."

—the Gospel according to DUPE[52]

The final source of popular economic rule is the most important, the corporate economists insist. "While...consumers, producers and governments [all] make decisions in our economic system," the DUPE booklet argues, "the *key* role that makes everything work is played by you, in your role as a consumer."[53] If we don't like what they're selling, we don't have to buy it. Sooner or later even the largest corporations will fall to their knees. "Individual consumers," the DUPE primer concludes, "[are] the real 'bosses' of the American economy."[54]

There is obviously some truth to the argument about consumer sovereignty. Business introduces roughly 6000 new products every year. Many of them float like lead balloons. (Remember Ford's classic lemon, the Edsel?) Close to 90% of new products fail for lack of consumer interest.[55] And corporations also obviously try to cater to new product interests when they develop. Who would deny the great advances in home video recorders, recreation equipment, and power tools? And the list goes on.

Despite these examples, however, there are clear limits to consumer power. The DUPEsters often use the image of the ballot box, suggesting that consumers have as much power as citizens in a pure democracy. In fact, consumers' sovereignty is circumscribed by many economic constraints.

The first limit on consumer power is the most obvious. In any democracy, people's power is determined by the influence of their votes. *Market* elections are governed by "one dollar, one vote." If we don't have any money, we don't get any votes. When our votes are counted next to those of the wealthiest people in the economy, they don't count for much.

We feel the effects of this market bias all the time. Many households desperately need better housing, but only the most affluent 15% of households can now afford to buy a new home.[56] Some households find food so expensive that they're driven to pet food. (One study in Philadelphia found that 25% of pet food sold was consumed by people.[57]) Recent studies indicate that close to half of U.S. households cannot afford the health care they need.[58]

The general point is clear. Voting in the market is weighted by the distribution of income. There are more health spas for the wealthy than there are day care centers for the children of working people—all because the wealthy can stuff the ballot box.

There is a second, more subtle limit to consumers' power. Even those of us who have a little money to spend may not be able to get what we want in the market because we cannot influence corporate decisions about what to produce.

■ We may try to withhold our votes from some product in order to force corporations to change their quality or their prices, but the corporations can almost always outlast us if they choose. In 1973, for instance, over a quarter of all U.S. households participated in the consumer boycott to protest spiralling meat prices. The large food chains didn't lower their prices because they sold many other items during the boycott and so had enough money in reserve to weather the shift away from beef.[59]

■ Consumers are very hard to organize because people are so dispersed and shop in so many different places. Corporations can coordinate their strategies in a few board rooms, while it takes months for us to organize battles in the marketplace. Buyers and sellers are supposed to meet as equals in the market, but trying to fight corporate power through boycotts is about as promising as stepping into the ring with a young Muhammed Ali. The odds against the consumers are very steep.

■ We may desire some change in product quality but the market may not deliver it because it's not "profitable" to produce those kinds of products. Energy companies have been reluctant to develop solar energy, for example, because they feared they would not be able to monopolize that source of energy supply. (How do you meter the sun?) If companies cannot achieve centralized control over the production of a particular product, in general, they may not supply it no matter how many votes we may want to cast. (We discuss this problem in more detail in Chapters 10 and 11.)

■ The way the economy is organized also limits our power as consumers. If factories move to the suburbs, we have to buy cars to get to work. Those of us who live in the northeastern United States may prefer to stay in our own communities—enjoying traditional ties with friends and relatives—but more and more of us are finding it difficult to exercise that choice because it's getting harder to find employment in that region. We can't vote with our dollars if the basic structure of the economy stacks the deck against us.

There is one final limit to our power as consumers. The traditional DUPE argument assumes that we know what we want and then vote with our dollars to get it. But large corporations can sometimes influence or even determine what we want through advertising and manipulation of tastes. *Corporations spent more than $40 billion on advertising in 1979.*[60] They start in on us as soon as we're old enough to see and hear—the influence of television ads on children's preferences is well known. As we grow up, ads shape our tastes for cars, homes, furnishings, foods, cosmetics, clothes...nearly everything we use in our daily lives. The corporations have been clear about the usefulness of advertising since the 1920s. As one advertising pioneer put it in 1930, "advertising helps to keep the masses dissatisfied with ugly things around them. Satisfied customers are not as profitable as discontented ones." As another affirmed, "the future of business lies in its ability to manufacture customers as well as products."[61]

Despite all these barriers, are consumers becoming more and more sovereign over time?

■ As we saw in Chapter 7, inequalities in the distribution of income and wealth have not declined. This means that the market election is just as rigged as before.

■ Since corporate size and control have been increasing, the odds against consumers winning fights in the marketplace are growing steeper. And, as households are scattered more and more widely throughout suburban areas, it gets even harder for consumers to organize.

■ The growing complexity of the market systems of transportation and communication are also making it less and less likely that corporations will respond to consumer votes. Once they sink such large amounts of money into a particular product and a particular system for getting it around, it requires ever more massive withdrawals of consumer votes to convince them to change their ways.

■ As corporations grow larger, finally, their planning horizons grow longer. They want to be more and more certain about the level of demand three, five, and ten years from now. And that means they devote even more resources to shaping and manipulating consumer demand. While gross national product in the U.S. increased by 500% between 1950 and 1976, money spent on television advertising increased by almost 3800%.

By these indicators, it would be difficult to argue that our power as consumers was growing.

POPULAR ECONOMIC RULE—NOW OR EVER?

"The ones who run this country are the multinationals, the banks, the Fortune 500. It all comes together at a point. There's commonality of interest. They don't need a conspiracy. How many banks need to sit down and discuss how much they have to charge for interest rates? How many oil companies need to sit down and discuss how to distribute oil and how much to charge? No need."

—former U.S. Senator[62]

We can now review our answers to the questions about popular rule which we posed at the beginning of this chapter:

■ *Does widespread stock ownership mean that working people "own" the economy?* Most people own no stock. Among those who do own shares in corporations, a small group of wealthy families, banks, and executives maintains close and decisive control over the largest U.S. corporations.

■ *Does the ease of establishing new enterprises help ensure effective market discipline of corporations?* Giant U.S. corporations have grown to awesome size and thoroughly dominate the core of the economy. It is now close to impossible to start new enterprises which can effectively compete with those mammoth enterprises. It happens every once and a while, but there's a lot of waiting in between.

■ *Are corporations responsive to and controlled by consumer demands?*
They have to be somewhat responsive or they can't sell their wares.
(People didn't want the Edsel.) But there are very clear limits to consumer sovereignty. Unequal income distribution, large corporations, and
the broader economic structure place strict limits on the range of
choices available to us. Corporations also exercise clear influence over
our preferences among those available options through their
advertising.

■ *Are we gaining or losing popular economic influence over time?* There
is no real evidence that people are gaining more effective popular
economic rule along any of these three dimensions and there is plenty
of evidence that our control is diminishing. And, at one level, people
know it: one poll in 1976 found that 75% of U.S. adults agree that
"monopolies are growing."[63]

Why Do We Believe?

And yet, many people still believe that there is also popular economic rule in our economy? What makes us so gullible?

One obvious answer, of course, is that corporations spend lots of

---

We get to vote our stock options and consumer dollars, but large corporations and the economy largely shape what's on the ballot.

---

money trying to convince us that the system serves our interests, that
the free enterprise system puts us in the economic driver's seat. (See
"Why We Need This Book" for examples.)

But there is also another reason. There are aspects of our lives in
the U.S. economy which give credence to those myths. We *do* have lots
of choices from day to day. When we go into the supermarket, we can
choose from thousands of products. If we have savings, we can choose
among savings banks and bonds and corporate stock and our own
mattresses. If we don't like our present jobs, we are "free" to go look for
another one.

The availability of these choices indicates that we have some
influence over the economy. And when we hear or read Milton and
Rose Friedman, in the Gospel according to DUPE, telling us that we're
"free to choose," some of it sounds right.

But it's one thing to have "influence" and quite another to have
real power. We are free to choose, as long as we restrict ourselves to the
alternatives offered by the corporations. We get to vote our stock
options and consumer dollars, but, as this chapter has argued, large
corporations and the economic system largely shape what's listed on
the ballot. If the corporate structure decides to give us the shaft, all
they ask us is where we want it.

Couldn't We Just Bust the Trusts?

One of the main reasons we do *not* have popular economic rule, as
this chapter has argued, is that the largest corporations in our economy

exercise decisive control. Can't we create popular economic rule simply by breaking up those huge companies and creating competition among them? Won't that guarantee that consumers will finally be able to move to the front of the bus?

A bit of history is helpful. After 1900, when the first merger wave produced giant consolidated corporations, many people called for busting the trusts. Huge companies like Standard Oil and American Tobacco were broken into several parts. New laws like the Clayton Antitrust Act were passed to try to keep new trusts from emerging.

But the large corporations had such solid control over the government that the anti-trust movement was turned on its head. The first anti-trust laws were used against labor unions more than against trusts. Then corporations used the laws to help protect them against competition from other companies.[64] Much more recently, companies like Xerox are using the anti-trust statutes to help them gain entry into markets dominated by other giant firms like IBM. Anti-trust legislation has not prevented, in short, the continuing growth of giant corporate power.

Can't we just mobilize even more effectively and force the government to bust the trusts in *our* interests?

Although the monopolies' power should and must be challenged, breaking up the large companies won't be enough. As we saw in Part II, there are many other features of our economic system which combine to limit our control over its directions. The fact that owners of the means of production use their private control over wealth to produce for their *own profit* means that corporations, no matter how small or who controls them, will place higher priority on their private interests than on our social needs. And the growth of capitalism itself, as we saw in Chapter 6, tends to create larger and larger firms even if they start small. If we broke up the trusts without changing anything else about our economic system, economic growth would create powerful, oversized corporations all over again. And then we would have to bust them again. And then they would grow again....

Busting the trusts, in short, will not be *enough* to guarantee popular economic rule. We will have to change a lot more about our economic system to provide us the kind of power and control we might like. We explore in Part VI of this book some of the other kinds of changes which would be likely, at last, to turn the myth of popular economic control into a reality we could enjoy and defend.

"The price system works so well, so efficiently, that we are not aware of it most of the time."

—The Gospel According to Dupe[1]

"How does this company expect us to work harder and keep costs down? They get to keep all the profits and the only thing we get to keep is a lot of sore muscles."

—autoworker in New Jersey[2]

Is It Worth the Price?

We've always learned that the "free enterprise" economy is the most "efficient" system for producing and distributing the things we need. Which would you prefer, they always ask us: standing in line for hours for your ration of stale bread?...Or sharing the continual flow of delights from the capitalist cornucopia? Who would ever choose stale bread?

The proof of the pudding is in the eating. Prices of necessities have been soaring, not falling. Few of us can afford the price of a new home any more. The cost of medical care is enough to make many of us sign our own pacts with disease.

Does capitalism really promote the most efficient economy possible? Is it worth the price?

HOW DO WE MEASURE ECONOMIC EFFICIENCY?

"Competition among producers...creates a general competitive environment, which motivates our economic goal of efficiency....Our economic system encourages inventiveness. It does this through its...economic reward for enterprise."

—DUPE film guide[3]

The DUPE argument about economic efficiency is fairly easy to follow—especially since we hear it spouted all the time.

They define efficiency by looking at the relationship between what's produced and what's available to produce it. They say that a system has achieved the greatest efficiency possible if it generates more products from available resources than any other possible system. There is another way of looking at efficiency which amounts to the same thing: does a system use fewer resources to produce a certain quantity of goods and services than any other possible method of producing that output?

One way or the other, "most efficient" means the biggest bang for a buck. The DUPE pushers use three arguments to support their claims about the efficiency of capitalist economies:

1) They say that there is hardly any waste in capitalist economies

because the drive for profits and the fear of competition, like teachers' rulers, will discipline firms to use every available resource. No waste, no want.

2) Given available (and unwasted) resources, according to corporate economists, firms will also make the best use of them, producing at the lowest cost possible. Why? Every firm will try to earn the highest possible profits. They'll try to reduce their costs as much as possible because lower costs will mean higher profits. This drive to cut costs will lead, in the end, to the least expensive methods possible for producing goods and services. For corporate economists, profit is always the mother of invention.

3) People can't benefit from these innovations, of course, unless the cost-savings are passed on to consumers through lower prices. Corporate economists also argue that competition will force firms to provide at least some of these savings for consumers. If some firm tries to keep all of the savings for itself, some other firm will undersell it slightly—eventually stealing its customers. And we, the consumers, will reap the harvest of relatively lower prices.

This summary of the DUPE on efficiency points toward some tests of their arguments. We need to ask three specific questions:

■ Does competition and profit-seeking reduce waste to the barest minimum?

■ Do capitalist firms always pursue and implement available methods of organizing production which would cut their costs and increase their efficiency?

■ Do consumers alway benefit from cost reductions through at least partial price reductions?

With each of these questions, we must also examine changes over time: are capitalist economies getting more or less efficient as they develop?

IS CAPITALISM WASTEFUL?

"Each consumer...can [get what] he feels most suits his own special needs and resources....This sensitive tailoring of productive resources...is a fundamental...characteristic of our system....Unlike the political system, every person can win in an economic 'election.' "
—chairman of General Motors before Congress[4]

How could there possibly be any waste, the DUPEsters ask. If some resource were lying idle, squandering its potential productiveness through inactivity, a profit-seeking corporation would smell easy money and scoop it up, combining it with other available resources and turning out even more goods and services. Unused resources can never get any rest, according to corporate economists, because the quest for profits keeps sounding the alarm.

It should be easy to test these claims. We can simply look at both productive resources and available goods and services in the United States and check whether any of those resources are being wasted to any significant degree.

Are Resources Idle?

One important resource is land. Food prices have been rising rapidly for ten years, and many people don't get enough to eat. Is it possible that we waste available farm land which might help keep food prices down?

Some farm land has been pulled out of production for speculation, with landowners waiting for higher prices from urban sprawl. Some goes unused because high energy and interest costs make small farms more and more difficult to maintain.

The result is waste. In the late 1970s roughly 30-40 million acres of "tillable" cropland were idle. This amounted to nearly 10% of all available land currently suitable for farming. (Another 75 million acres could be converted back to agricultural production with some relatively simple conservation planning.)[5]

If we used these 30-40 million acres immediately available for farming, we could have produced in 1980 more than enough wheat, rice, corn, and peas to feed the population of the 15 largest metropolitan areas in the United States.[6]

What about factories and machines? Are there idle resources here too? During the 1970s, U.S. industrial corporations operated their businesses at an average of little more than 80% of their total capacity.[7] While some of these factories and machines were obsolete, this still means that total manufacturing production could have been at least 10-15% higher if corporations had made fuller use of factories and machines which *already existed*.

We already know the score on human resources. As Figure 1.3 showed, an accurate tally of unemployment finds roughly 14 million people in the United States who want work and can't find it—at any one time. We apparently waste nearly 13% of our labor power as well.

All these wasted resources add up. We can compute how much output—measured in terms of goods and services in the market—the economy *could* have produced if our resources were used to their fullest potential. During the last completed business cycle from 1973 to 1978, according to the government's fairly conservative methods for computing potential output, the economy produced at an average of 13% below capacity. This means that production in 1978, a year of peak prosperity during that business cycle, could still have been almost $300 billion more than it was.[8] *The economy wasted nearly one-seventh of its potential output during the mid-1970s.* Conditions have not improved since.

The economy wasted nearly 1/7 of its potential output during the mid-'70s.

What Happens to Resources We Use?

We have been counting how much of our reservoir of productive resources is left idle by the economy. We also need to consider what happens to the resources we actually use.

The answer seems fairly clear. The economy not only wastes available resources but also *destroys potential productive resources* which it might otherwise preserve or develop.

■ Much of our land and natural resources are squandered

through destructive productive practices. Heavy use of chemicals in agriculture has reduced the productivity of some agricultural land, poisoned fish, disrupted the ecology and has even begun to invade our supplies of drinking water. As one government official recently concluded, our "national treasure [of water supplies] is now seriously threatened by chemical contamination of the worst sort."[9] The economic crisis has also cut into farmers' margins so heavily that "during the last decade," according to the New York Times, "an increasing number of farmers have abandoned many of the conservation practices of the 1930s."[10] Reckless strip-mining has led to soil erosion and flooding four to five times the normal averages in rural areas, costing millions in property damage.[11]

■ Reckless operation of factories and offices exposes workers to treacherous health-and-safety hazards on the job. If workers had been able to work productively during all the millions of hours they lose each year as a result of injuries on the job, their total annual output would be at least $4.5 billion higher than it is now.[12]

■ Perhaps most important, the economy destroys potential labor power by failing to develop people's potential productive activity. Many workers never have the chance to develop their skills. Virtually all of us could be much more productive than we are if the economic system placed much higher priority on training workers and structuring jobs in such a way that we continually developed our physical and mental potential. While we wait, our skills atrophy. And if the arguments in Chapter 7 made any sense, we'll have to wait a long time.

Do We Waste What We Produce?

Despite all these wasted resources, we still manage to produce huge volumes of goods and services. Do we fully use what's available?

Our use of the food we produce is probably the most important test case. In 1970, according to a government study summarized by the New York Times, "20 percent of all the food produced in the United States was lost or wasted before it got to the people who need it." That food alone was worth roughly $30 billion—amounting to more than 2% of our total gross national product by itself. The same government study estimated that the food "wasted during production and distribution in one recent year could have fed 49 million people."[13]

How much of other products do we never consume? We don't know with any precision, since neither corporations nor the government counts unused goods and services—cars which never leave the lots and the clothes which no one grabs from the shelves.

We can make a fairly crude guess, however, at least for the purposes of illustration. Every year, business maintains inventories worth roughly one-fifth of the value of annual GNP. Studies have found that about 40% of inventories don't "move"—that is, never get used and replaced.[14] This would mean that roughly 8% of total production is never consumed.[15]

And this would mean that there was roughly $200 billion of goods and services available in 1980 which we never consumed. That amounted to nearly $3000 for every household in the United States. Where are all of those products now that we really need them?

Why Is There So Much Waste?

Many conservatives blame the government for our economic problems. Has government caused all this waste?

■ Without government farm policies, even more farmers would go bankrupt and fail and, as a result, even more farm land would lie unused. During the 1910s and 1920s, before government farm programs emerged during the Depression, for example, unstable prices made it more and more difficult for individual farm owners to survive. Despite a growth in the total number of farms, the percentage of total farm land used in "full-owner"-operated farms fell from 53% in 1910 to 38% in 1930.[16]

■ The highest rates of "capacity utilization"—indicating those periods when buildings and machines are most fully used—have come exactly during those years when the government has intervened in the economy most actively.[17]

■ We have already seen, in Chapter 7, that government spending was responsible for almost all of the growth in total employment in the U.S. during the period of prosperity after World War II. Without government stimulus and job creation, the waste of people's labor power would apparently have been even greater than it was.

Is It the Economy? We know enough by now to suspect that the capitalist economy has something to do with all this waste. But why are the DUPEsters wrong? Why don't all those profit-hungry capitalist corporations scoop up every available resource and try to turn them to their own profit?

There are three main reasons:

First, as we saw in Chapters 6 and 7, capitalism continually creates economic instability—the economy moves up and down the economic roller coaster. Individual firms would love to keep on trucking, but the economy imposes recessions and depressions sooner or later. Idle land, factories, and workers result.

Second, capitalist firms don't use all available resources even when the economy is healthy and prospering. Capitalists care only about earning the highest possible profit. They don't care about productive capacity and people's needs. If they can't earn a profit producing useful goods and services, they'll put "their capital" in the bank or speculate on the value of available commodities. In the late 1970s, for example, corporations were investing much of their available profits in buying up other companies instead of investing in new productive buildings and equipment. (See Chapter 19.) To pick another example, land is controlled by the wealthy; about 3% of the population owns 95% of private land in the United States.[18] These large owners can afford to withhold land from production if they don't think it's worth their while. As these examples suggest, there is often a conflict between private profits and social needs...and waste often results.

Third, even when private corporations use resources, they often create more waste than their output is worth. Firms are free in capitalist economies to make decisions without regard to their social impact and implications. Capitalists can and do try to reduce their own costs by leaving a mess behind for others to clean up. A mining company may grab all the strip-mined coal it can shovel, for example, and never worry about the social costs of erosion and flooding. It may cost more to clean up and preserve the land than the coal was worth. Private investment decisions may sometimes lead to social bankruptcy.

All these sources of waste point to a single conclusion: there is enormous waste in our economy and capitalism is responsible for most of it.

WHAT ABOUT COST REDUCTION?

"Along the roads at the outskirts of almost every American city are little buildings in which the future of this country is being shaped....As the successful ones grow, they will hire more and more men and women, and plow profits back into better equipment that will help them grow faster. That is the way jobs and futures...are created in America, and it will continue only as long as the opportunity for profit is not destroyed in this nation."

—corporate magazine ad[19]

The costs of production depend on how resources are used. Do capitalist firms always pursue and implement the least expensive available methods of production? Is profit-seeking the mother of cost reduction in capitalist economies?

The DUPE argument about cost reduction makes sense when we think about an individual firm. (Since that's what corporate economists habitually consider, it's no surprise that they're so fond of this defense.) It seems obvious at first glance that any individual firm would

have to take advantage of every possible savings in production costs in order to keep up with its competitors. How could it afford *not* to introduce cheaper raw materials, more productive machines, and less expensive or more skillful or more diligent workers?

When we look at capitalism as an economic system, however, we begin to see things differently. As we saw in Chapter 2, capitalist production builds upon *controlled* (rather than shared) labor and *disconnected* (rather than coordinated) production decisions among firms. Each of those characteristics builds economic inefficiency into our economic system.

Controlled Labor

During the 1960s and early 1970s, many U.S. corporations grew concerned about workers' productivity. They were spending money on workers' wages and not getting as much output from them as they expected. Many firms began to experiment with some different ways of organizing production and the tasks which workers perform. The history of two of these experiments tells an interesting story.

General Foods Corporation opened a new dog-food plant in Topeka, Kansas, in the early 1970s.[20] "GF had had problems with negative attitudes and low productivity in its Kankakee (Ill.) pet-food plant in the late 1960s," *Business Week* reports, and it hoped to improve productivity by giving workers much more responsibility in production. Management responsibilities were reduced far below normal levels. Workers were involved in job assignments, scheduling coffee breaks, hiring new employees, and determining pay raises. They worked in groups, rotating among more and less boring jobs. Workers regulated their own pace of work without supervisory interference.

The experiment led to dramatic cost reductions. Unit costs were 5% lower than they were in the other plants with comparable machines. Employee turnover declined. The plant went three years and eight months before the first incident of a worker losing time from an accident on the job. "From the standpoint of...economic results," a former GF manager concluded, "you can consider it a success."

But the company then pulled back from the experiment. "There was a stiffening of the Topeka system, more job classifications, less participation, more supervision." The system has *not* been fully used in any other new GF plants either in the United States or overseas.

Most observers seem to agree on the reasons for GF's apparent decision to undercut the new system of production. Many executives in the company began to fear that the experiment had opened a can of worms. "Economically it was a success," a former manager reports, "but it became a power struggle. It was too threatening to too many people." Managers in other plants and the company's headquarters feared that the Topeka workers would demand more and more privileges and profit-sharing, eroding the company's control over the workers' surplus and its claim on profits generated in that plant. The company also feared, to quote *Business Week* again, that "a bonus at Topeka could cause complications at other GF plants that do not happen to pay bonuses." The experiment raised too many questions and proved too unsettling. As one former Topeka plant manager explained, "They saw we had created something the company couldn't handle, so they put their boys [back] in."

The Polaroid Corporation provides a similar story.[21] During the late 1960s, it gave many of its workers much more responsibility in their work and much greater participation in firm decisions. As with the GF example, workers' productivity increased fairly dramatically. Then the experiments were cancelled. The reasons for cancellation at Polaroid were apparently the same as the reasons for retrenchment at GF. The experiment was "too successful," a company training director explained. "What were we going to do with the supervisors—the managers? We didn't need them any more. Management decided that it just didn't want operators so well-qualified. We tried twice to re-institute the program but had to give it up." "It's not because people are basically bad," the architect of the Polaroid experiments concluded, "it's that the system is so powerful."

These two cases are not isolated examples. Many corporations, searching for greater worker productivity, have toyed with systems providing greater variety in workers' tasks and greater worker participation in management decisions. No matter how the experiments were organized, changes which provided workers with more power in production than they normally enjoy all increased worker productivity.[22] Despite those results, few of the experiments have been continued or more widely applied. "The usual [corporate] fear," as one sociologist observes, "is that if employees are given an opportunity to influence decisions affecting them, they will soon want to participate in matters which should be none of their concern."[23]

Why Don't the Bosses Choose the Most "Efficient" Method?

The General Foods and Polaroid examples suggest that firms may choose *not* to pursue potential cost-reducing methods of organizing production. Why?

In order to explain why, we must first distinguish carefully among three different concepts: *productivity*, *control*, and *profitability*.

A worker's *productivity* refers to the value of the goods and services a worker produces in a single hour of labor activity. An enterprise reduces its costs the most, with available resources, means of production, and intensity of worker effort, if it chooses the method of production which requires the fewest minutes or hours for a worker to produce a certain level of output.

Controlled labor, as we saw in Chapter 2, involves some people—the bosses—having the power to dictate the labor activities of other people—their employees—without necessarily doing any directly productive work themselves. As we saw in Chapter 4, U.S. history is full of workers' continuing efforts to resist the bosses' control. The stronger their resistance has become, the more protection they have gained from over-exertion, unsafe working conditions, and arbitrary punishment.

Profitability refers to the level of profits which different methods of producing and distributing goods and services will provide to capitalist firms. Unless capitalist corporations pursue the most profitable methods available, they run the risk of falling behind their competitors and losing control of their workers.

How do these definitions help us understand why capitalist firms do not always use the cheapest, most efficient methods of production?

Profit is the first-string quarterback for capitalism; capitalists will do whatever is necessary to protect it. Efficiency, on the other hand, may be part of the team but it may sometimes never leave the bench. If capitalists are asked to choose between the most profitable and the most efficient way of doing things, they will choose profit every time.

But why is there ever a need to choose? The DUPEsters never tire of arguing that more profit is better for all of us. Why do profit and efficiency sometimes part company?

Profits Before Productivity. Because, as we noted above, efficiency depends upon worker productivity, but profit depends upon the bosses' ability to control labor. As we saw in Chapter 3, the foundation for corporate profits is the surplus value which employees produce through working extra hours beyond what's necessary to cover their

own wages. If capitalists gave up their control over production, workers would be able much more easily to resist exploitation and shrink the foundation for corporate profits to virtually nothing. The General Foods and Polaroid experiments may have discovered a more efficient method of production, but the results are no help to the capitalist. If those "more efficient" methods increase worker productivity but *also* help workers claim a higher share of surplus value, what's left for the boss?

Capitalist production is substantially less cost-reducing than it could be, in short, because it *is* capitalist production. Workers would apparently be much more productive if we had more varied jobs and more control over production decisions. But more workers' control would mean less bosses' control. And less bosses' control would mean less surplus value for them. And less surplus value would mean shrinking profits. And that's the capitalists' bottom line.

Supervision in Service of Profits. Besides forcing capitalists to ignore potential cost savings through more worker-controlled methods of production, the dependence of secure profits on boss-controlled work reduces efficiency in another obvious way.

In order to maintain their control over production, the bosses must invest millions of dollars in systems and personnel whose sole purpose is control and discipline of the workforce. More than two million people in the United States are employed directly as foremen, clerical supervisors, or labor relations experts.[24] If we controlled our own working activities, most of the money spent on all this supervisory labor could be diverted to more useful purposes. We could then produce much more with the same amount of individual effort—not only because we would be more productive, but also because those now performing supervisory work could join us on the line or in the office and do some real work for a change. One former manager remembers his stint on the upper floors:

> I thought this company had something to do with the manu- facture of paper. It turns out no. It has to do with the management of people. What finally got me was that all the managers did in life was to make it miserable for the people...Everybody else is out there busy doin' stuff. The managers are just up there figurin' out how little they can pay 'em, how to keep costs down, how to move people around from box to box...What got me finally was coming in super-early in the morning and...I didn't have anything to do.[25]

The profitability and supervisory dynamics feed each other, finally, creating a sort of vicious circle. Capitalists choose production methods which help maintain their control. Workers resist. This leads to heavy supervision. Which increases workers' resentment. Which leads to an even greater gap in worker productivity between pro- duction methods the capitalists choose and those in which workers would have substantially greater participation and control.

One observer of all those corporate experiments to improve worker productivity drew the obvious conclusions from both their successes and their elimination. "We may say that the worker regards as his worst enemy, not the machine, but the boss. Among the causes of distaste for work,...the most important is the disciplinary subordi- nation of the worker."[26]

After our discussion, we may say, in turn, that the "disciplinary subordination of the worker" is *also* one of the most important causes of capitalist *inefficiency. Profit-seeking is the parent of reduced worker product-*

ivity and increased supervisory costs, not of cost reduction. Only capitalists could be proud of those offspring.

Disconnected Production

As if that weren't enough to doubt the DUPEsters, there is still another major reason why capitalism creates inefficiencies and prevents the fullest cost reduction possible.

Capitalist economies are unplanned, as we saw in Chapter 2; individual firms make their own decisions about their own production. As they do, they must try to protect themselves as much as possible from the unpredictability and instability which disconnected production creates. These efforts cost money. In the end, disconnected production imposes many costs on our economy which would not be necessary in a system with coordinated production and greater economic predictability.

There are two main sources of these additional costs.

1) *Product Availability.* Capitalist firms will not always develop and produce resources and supplies which might reduce production costs below current levels. They will only invest in something if they are certain that they can earn a profit on their investments and control the future returns from their initial outlays. This means that they will sometimes refuse to develop possible products, even though such products would be cost-reducing, because they can't protect their profits in a world of disconnected decisions.

Solar energy seems to provide one clear example of this tendency. There is clear evidence that solar power is technically feasible and that solar power would probably be less expensive than nuclear power and relatively competitive with coal-based power.[27] Energy companies, by and large, have been studiously ignoring the development of solar power. Why?

One of the advantages of the energy sources they prefer is that oil, natural gas, coal, and uranium lie in the ground. Those who control the land under which those sources lie can effectively limit people's access to energy supplies. In contrast, the problem with solar energy is that companies would have a much more difficult time keeping themselves in the middle. Since they can't install venetian blinds in the stratosphere, they could only maintain control over solar energy if they designed and built huge centralized collection and distribution centers. Or they could insist on pricing mechanisms through which, as one energy consultant has realized, their "price for solar energy could be tied to the price of natural gas."[28] Either way, their interest in an energy source which could reduce energy costs depends on their ability to control supplies and pricing mechanisms.

Autos provide another example with which we've recently become intimately acquainted. For years, auto companies have insisted on building big cars because, as Henry Ford put it bluntly, "small cars mean small profits."[29] A former General Motors executive recently summarized his experience during these years:

When we should have been planning switches to smaller, more fuel-efficient, lighter cars in the late 1960s, in response to a growing demand in the marketplace, GM refused because "we make more money on big cars." It mattered not that customers wanted the smaller cars, or that a national balance of payments deficit was being built....Refusal to enter the small car market when the profits were better on bigger cars, despite the needs of the public and the national economy, was not an isolated case of corporate insensitivity. It was typical.[30]

2) *Controlling the Market.* With disconnected production, firms never know where and when new competition may arise. So they invest billions of dollars in methods which they hope will offer protection from market competition.

■ One of the main corporate methods of seeking market control, as we have already seen in Chapter 9, involves heavy advertising. The more they deluge us with their ads, the more likely we'll be to choose their product over another firm's. In the late 1970s, MacDonalds alone was spending more than $125 million a year on media advertising, intoning that they "do it all" for us. By 1979, the total corporate budget for advertising in the U.S. had increased to more than $40 billion a year.[31] Companies used to compete by lowering their prices. Now they often compete by raising their advertising budgets. Their advertising expenditures get built into their costs....and we pay the price. In another, more predictable economic setting, most of those costs would be unnecessary.

■ Companies also try to control the growth of their markets by designing new models and creating "instant obsolescence" for their old products. The auto companies are the most obvious example. One economic study estimated the additional costs per year of annual model changes. It concluded that we pay roughly 25% of the purchase price of a car to cover the costs of annual model changes.[32] For a typical U.S. car costing roughly $6,000 in 1980, this means that the purchase price might be as little as $4500 if the companies didn't spend so much on making their products obsolete. They would rather tempt us with new cars than reduce their costs.

■ Large firms also keep buying other companies in order to reduce the number of their competitors. Which means that they need to spend money on managers to supervise managers to supervise managers. The larger the empire, as the Romans discovered, the greater the costs of controlling it. The result is that we pay more and more of our consumer dollar to support managerial expenses.

Take the life insurance companies. They now maintain huge empires. It should be that our premiums go into a pool which supports current benefits and which, through investment, increases the size of our own savings. A recent government study has estimated, however, that fully thirty cents on every life insurance premium dollar covered company *expenses* and *profits*—of no direct benefit to us.[33]

One economist who has studied corporate management carefully reaches a fairly clear conclusion about the costs of corporate market control. "I am inclined toward the view that the unit costs of management...do tend to rise with the organization size....My own belief is that padding as high as ten percent of costs is not at all uncommon."[34]

The costs of controlled labor and disconnected production add up. We now spend twenty cents out of every dollar on the salaries of managers, supervisors and other non-production workers. How much of that could we save with better economic coordination and more workers' control?

A Comparison

This review suggests that capitalism does not reduce costs as much as it might. But it's difficult to provide very direct tests of these arguments because capitalism is the only system we have. It's hard to find examples in the United States which allow us to compare the costs of capitalist production with some other system.

One example provides at least a partial test. There are many publicly-owned utility companies in the United States which provide us with power and water. In 1973, three-quarters of residential customers

We now spend 20¢ of each dollar of consumption on the salaries of managers and supervisors.

were served by private, investor-owned utility companies and the other one-quarter were served by publicly-owned utilities or rural electrical cooperatives.

Customers of publicly-owned utilities paid much less per kilowatt hour than customers of privately-owned companies. Between 1946 and 1974, according to government statistics, public power customers consistently paid about one-third less per kilowatt hour (kwh) than customers of privately-owned companies. By 1979, despite huge increases in oil and gas prices, residential consumers of public power were still paying roughly one-third less per kwh than private-power customers.[35] The advantages remain.

Why is there such a large difference?

One of the major differences comes from the costs of private ownership itself. Private utilities are controlled by and must pay interest and dividends to private investors. Nearly two-thirds of the difference in basic rates between private and public power companies is accounted for by the interest and dividend payments which private power companies pay.

But aren't some of the investments on which the private utilities pay interest and dividends necessary? Doesn't public ownership mean inefficiency?

The numbers tell the opposite story. Public power companies are more efficient than private power companies, not less. In 1979, public power companies were able to produce electricity at 17% less per kwh produced. They also spent 19% less on administrative and management expenses (per $100 in revenue). Most impressively, these efficiency advantages of public power companies have increased over time; both their production and managerial cost advantages widened considerably between the 1960s and the late 1970s.

(None of the publicly-owned companies was worker-controlled, in any major sense, so this comparison helps reveal administrative inefficiencies but ignores other inefficiencies we might also expect to find in capitalist production itself.)

But What About Innovation?

The DUPEsters can't believe it! What about innovation, they insist! You haven't even mentioned the central strength of capitalism, its greatest achievement and most notable contribution. Capitalism promotes innovation and innovation reduces costs. How blind can you be?

The DUPEsters are the ones wearing blinders. They've seen one side of capitalism and believed it as the whole truth.

What is true about capitalism is that competition among firms often pushes one firm or another to pursue some cost-saving innovations. That has helped historically to spur some great improvements in workers' productivity.

But something else is also true about capitalism. As we saw in Chapter 6, it continually creates greater and greater control by a few corporations. And growing corporate control tends to suppress innovation, not to promote it. Here are some examples:[36]

■ Several studies have shown that the largest firms spend *less* on research and development than smaller firms.

■ The basic oxygen process is now the least expensive system for making steel. A small Austrian company invented it; the first U.S. company to adopt it was McLouth Steel, which had less than 1% of industry capacity. The biggest companies ignored it for years.

■ General Electric has always advertised that "progress is our most important product." A former vice-president of GE summarized his own experience: "I know of no original product invention, not even electric shavers or hearing aids, made by any of the giant [electrical] laboratories or corporations....The record of the giants is one of moving in, buying out, and absorbing the smaller concerns."

■ Ralph Nader and associates tell a story which seems to sum up the giant corporations' attitudes toward innovation:

> ...Jacob Rabinow designed the "automatic regulator," now a standard part of clocks and many watches. Manufacturers he approached conceded it made watches more accurate, but they refused to buy his innovation. One manufacturer explained, "You know, we advertise a *perfect* watch." When Rabinow said that of course no watch was perfect, the manufacturer replied, "It's not important what the watch is. What counts is what the customer thinks it is. They think it's perfect. Who needs an automatic regulator to make a perfect watch more perfect?"[37]

Corporations want higher profits, not lower costs. The more easily they can increase their profits without bothering to seek cost reduction, the less they'll reduce their costs. Is it worth the price?

DO WE REAP THE HARVEST IN CONSUMER SAVINGS?

"The vitality of the American economy is based on competition between producers....If...price is too high in terms of value received,....a product will not be 'competitive,' and its sales would suffer."

—the DUPE booklet[38]

It would do us little good if corporate owners were the only ones who benefited from cost savings in production. Do consumers always benefit from cost reductions through at least partial price reduction?

We have already seen in Chapter 9 that corporate giants, not the neighborhood grocer, determine most of the prices we pay. What effect does corporate pricing policy have on our purchasing power?

Price-Fixing By Any Other Name?

We rarely get to listen to conversations in the corporate board rooms about their pricing policies. But there was one dramatic example during the late 1950s of what can sometimes happen.

The Tennessee Valley Authority (TVA) wanted to buy a huge new turbo-generator. They asked for bids from the big U.S. electric companies and also from a couple of British firms. The U.S. firms all submitted nearly identical bids in the range of $20 million, $7 million over the lowest British bid. The TVA officials challenged the U.S. companies to lower their bids; if they reduced the costs to only $17 million, TVA would agree to "buy American." The companies refused. Eventually a Knoxville reporter uncovered the incident and the famous electrical company price-fixing trials began. In 1961, 29 companies were found guilty of price fixing and other steps to suppress competition. Seven billion dollars of equipment was involved. Potential consumer losses could have been as high as $2 billion.[39]

This is an unusually dramatic example of collusion. Companies don't usually have to fix their prices directly, and thus break the law, because their practice of "corporate price leadership" can have the same effect. One large firm—like U.S. Steel or General Motors—announces its prices for the next period and other companies follow its lead. The small firms rarely dare to cut their prices in order to lure customers away from the big boys. To do so would be suicidal. No welterweight has ever won the heavyweight championship. All the companies practice a kind of "gentleman's agreement" to avoid price wars and, therefore, competitive price reductions. "If you embark on that process step by step," as the president of Bethlehem Steel once explained, "you will end up without making any money at all."[40]

The results of these practices cost us money. For example, cereal manufacturers compete with each other through advertisements and cereal box gimmicks. But they never cut prices. Studies by the U.S. Federal Trade Commission have estimated that cereal prices are 15-25% higher than they need to be as a result of this coziness about prices.[41]

In the economy as a whole, the costs of this kind of price leadership are enormous. One government study compared current prices with what their levels would be if the four largest firms in any particular industry controlled no more than 40% of total sales in that industry. They estimated that "prices would fall by twenty-five percent or more."[42]

How can large corporations get away with this? Doesn't competition keep them honest, forcing them to charge the lowest possible price if they are to stay in business?

There is an easy way to test the truth of this argument. Do companies as a whole tend to lower prices when business is slack and they're losing customers? What about during recessions, when competition intensifies? Do prices respond?

They used to.[43] Even after World War II, competitive industries still tended, on average, to reduce the gap between their costs and their prices—what's called a "price mark-up"—during recessions. But firms in concentrated industries now do the opposite. They try to keep their revenues high by increasing the gap between their costs and their prices rather than reducing it. Given their coziness about price leadership, they don't worry about their "competitors" undercutting them.

During the recessions from 1948 to 1970, indeed, firms in highly concentrated industries increased their price mark-ups, on average, by more than 8%. (During periods of expansion, in contrast, their price mark-ups increased, on average, by only 3%.)[44] Their sales may have suffered some, but they cared more about their profits than their sales.

They may not be able to get away with these lazy pricing policies forever. As we have seen recently in the United States, foreign competition may eventually impinge. While we wait, however, we're the ones who pay the higher prices. Large corporations may occasionally discover ways of lowering their costs. But the larger they get, the less likely they are to pass those savings on to us. And since they're getting larger and larger all the time, it's getting less and less likely that we'll share in whatever cost reductions they achieve.

WILL IT EVER BE WORTH THE PRICE?

It's time for some basic review. We posed four questions about the DUPE on efficiency and cost-reduction at the beginning of this chapter:

■ *Is capitalism wasteful of our resources and productive potential?* Yes. There is widespread waste of resources in our economy. It appears that the capitalist economic system is responsible for most of it.

■ *Is profit-seeking the mother of maximum possible cost-reduction in capitalist economies?* No. Controlled labor and disconnected production mean that firms cannot afford to pursue some paths to potential cost reduction. They must also spend substantial sums on the tasks of controlling workers and the market which would not be necessary in another system.

■ *Does competition leave some of the harvest for us?* Less and less. Today's competition among giant corporations—through advertising and price leadership—does not result in lower prices and better products. On the contrary, prices are higher now and there is less and less pressure on corporations to pass cost-savings on to consumers.

■ *Are capitalist economies getting more or less efficient as they develop?* Continuing increases in corporate power have strengthened all the forces which apparently *reduce* efficiency in capitalist economies. It's certainly not getting any *more* worth the price than before.

Can't We Fix It Through Regulation?

Sometimes we have a quick impulse to take care of corporate corruption and inefficiency through government regulation. The drug companies spend too much money on advertising and research, driving up drug prices. So let's control drug prices. Food companies put poisonous chemicals in their foods. So let's regulate them....

As with trust-busting, which we considered at the end of Chapter 9, there are two main problems with government regulation of corporate inefficiency.

The first seems obvious. Large corporations have so much power to influence government practice that they can usually regulate the regulators. Nearly every federal and state regulatory board has distinguished itself by leaning over backwards to help the companies it is supposed to be regulating. Imagine the Nuclear Regulatory Commission, for example, trying to take a tough stand with the nuclear industry after the near meltdown at Three Mile Island. The government has neither the will nor the ways to play an effective regulatory role. As the former chairman of ITT admits, "The U.S. economy is so big...that whatever direction it's moving in, there is very little government can do to change it."[45]

The second reason, though less obvious, is much more important. Regulation treats corporate inefficiencies as aberrations, as minor wounds in an otherwise healthy body. But this chapter has suggested that the basic characteristics of capitalism create waste and inefficiency. For every excess we might successfully curb, the system would create a score of others.

When a foundation is weak, you can only patch the cracks for a while. Eventually, you have to start from scratch again, reconstructing the basic foundation and frame. If we want an "efficient" economic system, the arguments of this chapter suggest that we should work with a different blueprint. We explore some other possible blueprints in Part VI of this book.

11.

WARNING: Capitalism May Be Dangerous for Your Health

"Sometimes you couldn't see across the shop [for the asbestos dust]. Back in 1958, 1960, if you asked for a mask they say it's a crime. The superintendent told me: 'The only thing about this dust is that it's uncomfortable; it hasn't ever hurt anybody.'

"The doctors didn't expect me to last this long. I can't run; I have to walk slow....[They say] I have to be careful about shaking hands with people, because of the germs, and I can't stand smokers or smoggy days, when I have to stay inside with the air filter on....

"When I had to quit [because of my health] the company did nothing for me. They said, 'Go look for another job.'"

—former worker in asbestos factory[1]

"The point I am trying to make is that we are solving most of our problems...that conditions are getting better, not worse...and that the real danger is *not* from the free-enterprise Establishment that has made ours the most prosperous, most powerful and most charitable nation on earth. No, the danger today resides in the Disaster Lobby—those crepe-hangers who...are undermining the American system and threatening the lives and fortunes of the American people."

—former magazine publisher[2]

"Less than 7% of the 92 billion pounds of chemical waste generated each year receives proper disposal....[Since Love Canal in Niagara County, N.Y.,] the problem...seems only to be worsening."

—journalist on "Love Canal, U.S.A.," 1979[3]

Capitalism provides us a double blessing, the DUPE claims. Capitalist economies not only reduce costs and promote efficiency, they say, but capitalism also continually provides the highest possible *quality of life.*

The evidence lies all around, they tell us. Workers used to toil in sweat shops. Now they work in clean, modern, safe, and comfortable factories and offices. People used to grub for their daily living. Now, people in the United States enjoy the highest standard of living in the history of the world. America is the department store of the world.

Those arguments are obviously appealing. But we also face evidence every day of the seamy side of life under capitalism. Workers suffer and die from preventable occupational injuries and disease. Many workers nearly suffocate with boredom on their jobs. Media bulletins constantly broadcast environmental assaults—oil spills, chemical seepage, radioactivity, pollution. Our communities often reel from the effects of plant shutdowns or urban renewal.

Does capitalism really create the best possible quality of life?

HOW DO WE MEASURE THE QUALITY OF LIFE?

The DUPE argues that capitalism perpetually improves the quality of our lives. Corporations don't have any other choice. If they don't constantly offer us a better deal, they'll be forced out of the game altogether. This argument applies both to our lives as *workers* and to our lives as *consumers*.

1) Corporations usually make two responses to workers' complaints about the quality of their jobs. First, they shake hands with the velvet glove: "If workers are unhappy, they won't be productive; let's make them more productive by making them happier." Then they sock us with the iron fist: "Don't like your job? Get another one. Is work supposed to be a vacation? Why don't you see if they'll answer your complaints down at unemployment?"

Both responses have a common thread. They imply that workers will enjoy high quality working conditions because workers have leverage and choice. This argument relies on something called *workers' sovereignty*. (It is similar to the argument about consumers' sovereignty we discussed in Chapter 10.) Either workers will be able to improve their working conditions because the bosses need happy workers, or workers will be able to find another job which will prove more satisfying. If some jobs remain hopelessly unattractive, the workers will continue giving their notice. The bosses will have to improve those working conditions or do the work themselves.

2) Our lives as consumers also constantly improve, the DUPE argues, because competition keeps pushing corporations to make better and better products. If they make junk, it won't sell. If they make dazzling products, people will buy them. So we get dazzling products. In market economies, according to this argument, we exercise a kind of *consumer quality control*. (This is the quality side of the supposed savings and price reductions we discussed in Chapter 10.) As long as production for profit governs our economy, we'll always get what we want.

Those two arguments show us the questions we need to ask in order to test the DUPE claims about the quality of life:

1) Do workers effectively govern their working conditions and enjoy the best jobs possible? Does capitalism really promote *workers' sovereignty?*

2) Do consumers continually enjoy the highest quality products? Does capitalism really promote *consumer quality control?*

With each of these questions, as in Chapters 9 and 10, we must also trace changes over time: has capitalist development been improving the quality of our lives through the years?

WHAT ABOUT WORKER SOVEREIGNTY?

"People—our most valuable resource....Economic freedom allows people to use their skills and capabilities in the most efficient and productive manner. Through effective competition in the marketplace, people are guided to the work for which they are best suited."

—DUPE film guide[4]

"Kugler was down checking the pump at the dehexanization [station]. [The pumps] flashed and he was burnt to a crisp. That's all we know. When they found him, they picked him up with a shovel. A [company] safety man wanted to take him to the hospital. The company has this idea nobody dies in the plant. They want them to die on the way to the hospital."

—union steward at oil refinery[5]

"GM is the richest company in the world and our roof leaks when it rains."

—auto worker for General Motors[6]

Most working people have already learned the score about worker sovereignty. For millions of workers in the United States, work is neither safe nor satisfying. The health and safety hazards—both visible and invisible—are crippling. The boredom and routine of our jobs are stultifying. It's a wonder that most of us survive our days at the factory and office.

Health and Safety

Accidents on the job kill roughly 14,000 U.S. workers every year, as high a fatality rate as for U.S. soldiers in the worst year of the Vietnam war. Experts now believe that somewhere from 120,000 to 200,000 people in the United States die each year from job-related illnesses. This means that *one person dies from his or her work every three minutes.*[7]

Millions more endure injury and illness. According to government data, 5.3 million workers suffered injuries on the job in 1977. The same data show that 162,000 workers became ill at work during 1977.[8] Other studies report that anywhere from 400,000 to one million workers contract new cases of occupationally-related disease each year.[9] These totals imply that *roughly 36 workers suffer injury or illness on the job every minute of the working day.*[10]

Even these figures, as gruesome as they seem, probably understate the depth and seriousness of health and safety problems on the job.

One problem is that we rely on company reports for our evidence about health-and-safety problems. Even under the Occupational Safety and Health Act of 1970, which dramatically improved government monitoring of health and safety problems, employers are still solely responsible for reporting injury and illness. Workers have no right to check on the accuracy of their reporting, and the government

One person dies from his or her work every 3 minutes in the U.S.

does not have the means to do so.

And companies have some obvious motivation to under-report. Their insurance ratings and costs are pegged to their "experience"—to the relative frequency of injuries and illness. If companies can hide some of their accidents, they can help keep a lid on their insurance. One company maintains a Medical Manual, for example, which provides guidelines to its medical personnel for their treatment of health problems on the job. "It should be noted that all claims cases are adversary cases," the Manual warns, "and the comments of company physicians to employees must be guarded as to causation and as to liability for costs."[11]

This kind of under-reporting is common knowledge on the shop floor. One local official in the Steelworkers Union confirms, for example, that many accidents at his Republic Steel plant are never reported. He had an accident himself—tearing ligaments in his left arm while doing electrical work in the plant—which the company never reported. "They tried to claim it was arthritis, not an injury in the plant. I didn't lose any time, I just did work where I didn't have to lift my arm. Now every time I move it, it hurts."[12]

There are some other sources of information which are not as dependent on employers logs. They confirm that the problems are very widespread.

■ One study conducted since OSHA began in 1970 found in a survey of employees in small plants that more than 40% of injuries at work had gone unreported.[13]

■ A recent and comprehensive government survey found that one out of four U.S. workers is exposed on the job to some substance thought to be capable of causing death or disease.[14]

■ The same survey also found that only 5% of all factories and offices have active employers' plans to improve industrial hygiene and reduce employee exposure to hazardous substances.[15]

Workers are poignantly aware of the dangers. In a 1977 survey, 43% of all employees, including white-collar and professional workers, considered the health and safety problems to which they were exposed on the job as "significant" or "great."[16]

These problems obviously impose huge costs.

Workers pay the price in medical bills and in the income they lose while off work. The workmen's compensation system helps offset these losses only partially; only about one-fifth of the income losses from occupational injuries are recovered from compensation.[17]

The economy suffers as well. Workers who can't come to work or can't perform up to their potential because of occupational injury or illness obviously produce less than they would if healthy. We probably lose about $10 billion a year in output from reduced worktime caused by health-and-safety problems.[18]

Why Is Work So Unhealthy?
Corporations try to finger their employees, blaming workers for sloppy habits and carelessness on the job. These claims are mostly for effect, helping shift the spotlight away from the real job of cleaning up

Roughly 36 workers suffer injury or illness on the job every minute of the working day.

the workplace. And the corporations largely know this. In more candid moments, corporate representatives will admit that they can't possibly know how frequently workers are to blame. In Congressional testimony in 1971, for example, the former head of the National Safety Council—the main non-profit group supported by industry contributions—was asked if he could really say whether or not "unsafe acts" attributed to injured workers were actually their fault. He admitted that neither he nor anyone else in industry has any way of knowing.[19]

Companies also sometimes claim that they're doing the best they can—that some work is naturally dangerous. Mining is a common example. They suggest that miners must simply face the risks of their occupation. But mines *can* be much safer. Accident rates in coal mines in Europe are from two to four times lower than those in U.S. mines. In the mid-1960s, when complete data was available, the incidence of "black lung" among British coal miners was half that among U.S. coal miners.[20] What explains the difference? Throughout Europe, the government and trade unions have intervened much more actively to promote safer working conditions. Workers have more rights to participate in decisions about the quality of their work and to resist unsafe working conditions. Under those kinds of pressures, companies have managed both to promote greater safety *and* to continue earning a profit.

Are Companies to Blame? Many working people blame their companies for health-and-safety problems on the job. Years of experience lead to that accusation. Several examples provide a glimpse of corporate attitudes about their workers' health:

■ The first health-and-safety legislation was prompted by an expose of Union Carbide in 1935. The company was digging a tunnel in 1930-31 in Gauley Bridge, West Virginia. Regulations required that the blast area remain clear for at least half an hour after a detonation to allow the dust to settle. The company totally disregarded the rules. Workers were herded into the tunnel as soon as the blast force of the explosions had dissipated. Many workers knew that the swirling clouds of silica dust were lethal. But those who hesitated were driven by foremen wielding axe handles. A total of 476 people died and more than 1,500 were disabled. A third of the town of Gauley Bridge contracted terminal silicosis, a chronic lung disease. Half of all the people employed at the tunnel suffered from silicosis and many later died from it.[21]

This incident was so shocking that Congress passed the Walsh-Healy Act in 1936, establishing health-and-safety standards for companies under contract to the federal government. The Oil, Chemical and Atomic Workers Union recently surveyed the safety practices of companies covered by the Walsh-Healey Act and compared them to comparable companies which were not covered by the act. There were almost no differences between the two groups of companies. The overwhelming majority of the companies supposedly covered by the law operated in clear violation of it.[22]

■ In the textile industry, cotton dust is very likely to cause respiratory problems. Textile workers have known for decades about "cotton fever," or, as it's now occasionally called, "brown lung." Numerous medical studies since the early 1960s have confirmed that "byssinosis," as the disease is known in the medical literature, is a severe health problem for cotton textile workers, particularly those in the carding and spinning rooms. But the textile industry continues to deny the problem or downplay its seriousness. In 1969, for example, the American Textile Reporter suggested that a "good chaw of B.L. Dark" chewing tobacco would take care of the disease.[23]

■ Asbestos workers also suffer acute hazards from exposure to asbestos dust. As early as 1918, life insurance companies were refusing policies to asbestos workers because of their higher mortality rates. Despite this knowledge, companies have made almost no effort to protect their workers against dust exposure. In 1972, for example, a Pittsburgh Corning plant was closed for health hazards. The company vice-president objected in public, claiming that he knew of no employee who had suffered from a disease related to asbestos. But the company *did* know of surveys which showed that nearly 40% of workers with more than ten years' experience in the plant had asbestosis and that nearly everyone associated with the processing of asbestos has a much greater chance of developing cancer than the general population. About 11 million U.S. workers have been exposed to asbestos in their jobs since the early 1940s, but a recent government survey found that 90% of all full-time workers exposed to asbestos on the job worked without *any* protective equipment or engineering controls.[24]

This list of examples could run for pages. Why are corporations so indifferent to workers' health-and-safety problems? Why does our time in the capitalist factory pose such risks?

One source of the risks lies in our working materials. As we have already seen in Chapters 4 and 6, companies race to replace us with machines in order to raise their profits and increase their control. Many of these machines are often hazardous, particularly if installed without much attention to workers' safety. Since the postal service has gone partly private, for example, they have tried to speed up sorting and loading with many new machines. In the New York region, at least, one investigation found that "almost all of the safety devices on most of the conveyor belts...have been disconnected or left unrepaired because they slowed production." In 1979, a worker was caught in the conveyor belt and crushed to death. The belt is equipped with a jam relay which cuts off when the belt is clogged. It had been disconnected. "That disconnection," another worker concluded, "was the single thing most responsible for killing that kid."[25]

Companies have also been using more and more chemicals in production, particularly since the end of World War II. They regularly introduce these chemicals before scientists have been able to establish standards for safe exposure. About 3,000 new chemicals are introduced into industry every year, but exposure standards are being developed for only about 100 new chemicals a year. A 1970 survey estimated that from 6,000 to 12,000 toxic industrial chemicals were in common use, but exposure standards were listed for only 410 of them.[26]

None of this means that machines and chemicals should not be used. It simply means that companies tend to use them without much regard for the health risks they pose. Why are companies so inattentive to those risks?

It appears that companies make simple and hard-hearted calculations about costs. If it costs less to lose workers than to clean up their working conditions, companies will forget about the clean-up. A former workmen's compensation representative at Chrysler explains the practice:

> Every year the compensation reps at the various plants were instructed to compute an estimate of the Workmen's Compensation costs for that plant for the coming year and we had to turn those estimates in to the accountants for the corporation. The safety personnel at the plants did the same. They computed their costs...then it was just a question at the corporation of deciding which is cheaper, to take some injuries, take some deaths, pay some Workmen's Compensation or spend a lot of money and make it safe.[27]

Companies can get away with these practices because of two basic characteristics of capitalist economies. The first is that they are allowed to make decisions on the basis of their own costs and not the costs to the whole society. Their unsafe practices may cost the rest of us our health, medical expenses and mental anguish, but the companies are free to ignore all those consequences of occupational injury and illness. The second is that the economy does not provide employment for all those who need work. This leaves many workers unemployed—which means that companies can easily replace those who get injured or sick on the job. If spare parts were not available, companies would tend their machines much more carefully. If spare workers were much harder to find, they might take better care of us as well.

What About the Economy? It is important to remember that some of this corporate indifference stems from broader economic forces, from outside any individual factory or office. When we blame the companies, we tend to point at our own bosses. But some of the problem lies in the way the entire economic system works.

Take the period since World War II for an example of this kind of effect. When the economy was growing rapidly during the 1950s and early 1960s, there was enough extra margin from that rapid growth to finance some improvement in working conditions. Under pressure from workers and unions, companies appear to have taken some care with all those new machines and chemicals. Between the late 1940s and the early 1960s, industrial accident rates fell by more than one-third.

Then, as the economy slowed and company profits were squeezed from the mid-1960s (see Chapter 19 for details), companies began to speed up production. Industrial accidents became more and more frequent. After declining fairly steadily for 15 years, the rate of injury in manufacturing more than doubled between 1965 and 1979.[28] Work was becoming more and more hazardous. It wasn't that employers had suddenly become greedier. It was because the economy had plunged into a crisis for which workers were not responsible and because our economy usually makes us pay the price for its problems.

In the end, for all these numbers, the price is immensely personal. Workers feel the pain and humiliation in a way that scientists and economists can never turn into percentages and decimal points. One worker's story speaks for millions of others. A woman textile worker tripped on some holes in a concrete floor left uncovered by the company after some machines were moved. Her right knee began to swell. She was carried to the first-aid room, which was locked. She recalls:

> First they couldn't find the key to the first aid room—of course we have no nurse, nobody there...Then the overseer in the weave room said: "I'm sorry I can't stay here [with you] longer, my son's got a ballgame." I sat there alone for about 45 minutes or an hour.

She was finally given an aspirin. She had to leave work for several months because of the knee injury, but the company was so negligent about filing compensation forms that she had to threaten a suit before she finally drew compensation. When she was finally able to return to work, she still needed to see a doctor:

"My lips swolled, my eyes swolled, just like I was in a bed of red ants...."

> He was a company doctor, they told me I could *not* go to my own doctor. Yes, of course I resented that. [The company doctor was] about 90 years old, he should have retired 50 years ago, but he's still practicing and he's the only one they could get.

She also discovered she was allergic to fiberglass dust. "My lips swolled, my eyes swolled, just like I was in a bed of red ants." Once again, she threatened suit before the company would cover the bill for the allergy tests. When fiberglass dust got in her eye, "The eye waters and waters and waters and you can't git it out. They gave you an eye cup and told you to wash it out—be your own doctor, do it yourself." The company continues to feel secure in its callous treatment. "We have to hang on someway," the textile worker concludes. "If we don't do the work, somebody else will."[29]

Job Satisfaction

Most workers know our jobs are nothing to write home about. But many polls show that workers are "satisfied" with their jobs. Does our economy provide us with decent work, maintaining and even improving the quality of our lives?

The Gallup poll regularly asks a representative sample of workers, "Is your work satisfying?" From 80 to 90% of the workers interviewed answer "yes."[30] But that doesn't necessarily mean that most workers are actually satisfied. It may simply mean that people have given up any hope of work being any better than it is.

Some other surveys support this interpretation. One poll asked workers, "What type of work would you try to get into if you could start all over again?" Only 24% of blue-collar workers and 43% of

You Asked For It, You Got It.

white-collar workers said they would voluntarily choose their present careers.[31] Another study asked people if they would keep working if they inherited enough wealth to live comfortably without working. Although a substantial majority responded that they would continue working, only 9% said they would continue because they enjoyed the work they were presently doing.[32] One other survey asked working people what they would do "with the extra two hours" if each day lasted 26 hours. Only 1 out of 20 nonprofessional workers said they would use the extra time doing what they do on their jobs.[33]

The situation is clearly getting much worse. Recent surveys have found sharp declines in workers' satisfaction since the late 1960s. For example, the percentage of workers expressing satisfaction that "I am given a chance to do the things that I do best" declined by one quarter in just four years between 1973 and 1977.[34] The head of these surveys was stunned by the evidence of rapid deterioration. "The sky has finally fallen," he concluded. "Workers in virtually all occupational and demographic categories evidenced appreciable and unmistakable manifestations of rising discontent."[35]

Job satisfaction is not an idle concern. Researchers have repeatedly discovered that dissatisfaction and insecurity on the job are among the most important sources of health problems in the United States. "High risk" situations are among the leading causes of heart disease, for example; job dissatisfaction and insecurity have been found to rank among the most important of these "high-risk" conditions.[36] Another study found that 40% of assembly-line workers showed symptoms of mental-health problems. Dissatisfaction with their boring and repetitive low-skilled work turned out to be the most frequent occupational source of those mental health problems—far more frequent than concern about either wages or job security by themselves.[37]

Why Is Job Quality So Low?

Companies often try to avoid the issue of work quality by claiming workers don't really care about job satisfaction, that they care more about wages and job security. But surveys of workers don't support this contention. One recent survey asked workers to rank different "job characteristics in order of their importance. "Good pay" and "job security" ranked fifth and seventh on the list, lagging behind "interesting work," "enough help and equipment to get the job done," "enough information to get the job done," and "enough authority to get the job done."[38] More than two-thirds of working people in another survey agreed that "people don't work as hard as they could because they aren't given enough to say in decisions which affect their jobs."[39]

Why don't companies respond to all these concerns? Why don't they structure jobs which would give us more interesting and meaningful work?

The problem lies with issues of profitability and control which we discussed in the previous chapter. Company profits depend, in the end, on company control over workers. The more specialized and repetitive our work, the more we tend to lose sight of the big picture and the extent of the bosses' control. The more interest we are encouraged to take in our work, the more interest we might take in the bosses' profits and basic control.

Managers are reasonably clear about these risks. We saw in Chapter 10 that companies have frequently abandoned experiments providing more interesting work because they "succeeded too well." Most managers feared, as one journalist concluded, that "a sharing of power must mean a loss of control."[40] A research and training executive in General Motors agrees: "What is really involved is politics, the conscious sharing of control and power...[Workers involved in] rearranging the work area...may very well want to go on to topics of job assignment, the allocation of rewards, or even the selection of leadership."[41]

But what about the DUPE notion of *worker sovereignty* which we introduced at the beginning of this chapter? If we don't like our work, can't we simply find another less boring job. And won't this force employers to pay us *more* to keep us on the job if our work quality is low.

The numbers confirm what workers already know. We don't have much choice about our work and we don't get paid more for taking on relatively low-quality jobs. The workers who have the jobs with the *worst* working conditions earn *lower* wages—controlling for most other factors like education which influence earnings—than people in jobs with better working conditions. For example, white male jobs "under stress" earn an average of $2.21 an hour less than those who don't face stressful work. White female workers exposed to lots of hazards on the job earn $1.16 an hour less than white women not exposed to those conditions.[42] It turns out that we have to pay the boss for the privilege of working in a bad job!

In short, our quality of work is much lower than it could be because capitalists have a stake in our boredom. If we knew too much, or participated too actively in management decisions, we might start getting some funny ideas. As always, corporations will choose their profits and control over the quality of our lives on the job. One chemical worker talking about this issue in a recent class clearly expressed this dimension of our relations with our bosses:

> The dull work is creating a lot of absenteeism. Our company does the same thing all the time. We don't have to think. I'm supposed to be a mechanic and I can't make a decision. My friend's an operator. He has his job to do and he can't think. It's written down for him...This is industry's way of indoctrinating people so they don't think. We don't do any thinking. They fight us off every inch of the way so they can have more control.[43]

WHAT ABOUT CONSUMER QUALITY CONTROL?

"Garden-fresh vegetables the year 'round, your own private transportation..., machines in home and factory that do most of the former back-breaking work, better lighting to save your eyes, better sanitation and more of it to save your health, better education and more of it to save your future... Want to give them up—and go back?"

—company magazine ad, 1974[44]

"Toxic chemical waste may be the sleeping giant of the decade."

—congressman after Love Canal investigation[45]

We enjoy new and better products all the time. But we also seem to take our lives into our hands every day we get out of bed. Do we really have consumer quality control in our economy?

The catalogue of environmental horrors facing us in our homes and communities has become increasingly familiar:

■ The air around us is treacherous. Biologists estimate that smog levels in U.S. cities increased by at least 1,000% between 1946 and 1970.[45] Roughly 20 million people in the U.S., according to a government estimate, are exposed every day to noise which is permanently damaging to their hearing.[46] Factories, construction, cars, and trucks all contribute to the haze and clatter.

■ Land pollution has also spread since early in the 20th century. Strip mining has ripped apart vast stretches of landscape. Pesticides have destroyed wild life and polluted streams. Chemicals and spillage have reduced the fertility of many land areas and have begun to threaten our supplies of drinking water.[47]

■ We aren't even safe in our own homes. Many foods have harmful chemicals or cancer-causing ingredients added to them. Many drugs we take have harmful side effects and may cause cancer. X-rays and high frequency emissions from appliances like micro-wave ovens and color televisions may also cause cancer.[48]

■ Unnatural disasters seem more and more threatening. Trains and trucks carry deadly gases and radioactive waste; the risk of spillage or explosion is ever-present. Study after study has shown that nuclear reactors are not "perfectly" safe and that the chances of leakage or melt-down are not all that remote. There are still earthquakes and floods; our economy has added a whole new variety of disasters like Three Mile Island to the list of potential calamities.

■ Even some of the highly-touted products corporations provide us do not live up to their reputations. Many products are defective. Between 1966 and 1972 alone, more than 30 million cars and trucks were recalled for safety defects, for example, and the frequency of recalls has probably increased substantially since then. And we're all painfully familiar with problems of getting manufacturers of consumer products to repair their defects.

Some of the problems in this catalogue are simple nuisances. But many of them have disastrous consequences for our health and safety.

More than 90,000 people in the U.S. now die of cancer every year. Most studies conclude that between two-thirds and four-fifths of all cancers are environmentally caused and are therefore presumably preventable.[49] The major cause of the increase in cancer, according to the former chief of the environmental cancer section of the U.S. National Cancer Institute, has probably been "the relatively unrestrained industrialization of the economy and the little controlled chemicalization of our environment."[50]

Cancer isn't the only risk. Serious respiratory illnesses have also become more and more common, for example, particularly since World War II. The President's Science Advisory Committee estimates that a minimum of 18,000 people die each year from respiratory illnesses caused by hazardous working conditions and air pollution.[51] And the incidence of chronic bronchitis and emphysema has doubled every five years since 1945.[52]

Why Are the Risks So High?

Corporations have two kinds of explanations for these health hazards.

The first is their usual refrain: as Pogo put it, we have seen the enemy and it is us! Exxon recently republished a medical article, for instance, which attributed the bulk of cancer disease and death to smoking and "personal dietary habits."[53] If we would only change our habits, then we would be healthy once again.

The problem with this view is that research doesn't support it. Most studies, as we have just seen, attribute from 70 to 80% of cancer problems to environmental exposures over which individuals have no control. Better habits wouldn't protect us from those risks. The corporate argument is clearly self-serving; if they can convince us it's our fault, we won't look in their direction.

The second kind of corporate explanation points the finger at population growth and affluence. There are more of us and we consume more. Naturally there will be some costs to that growth. What do we want? Back to the caves?

The problem with this view is that it is also not supported by the evidence. One study looked carefully at the relative importance of population growth and rising consumption standards in creating several kinds of pollution between 1946 and 1970. Population increase accounted for little of that pollution and higher consumption standards —more consumption per household—for even less of it (except for more car travel per family). What accounted for the rest of the pollution? Most of it came as a result of more pollution per unit of output— more pollution per bushel of food and per ounce of detergent used and per quart of beer consumed and per car mile traveled. This increased pollution per unit of output accounted for 80 to 85% of increased pollution in the cases of food and detergent and beer—and about 40% for auto travel.[54]

In short, changes in the way goods are produced account for most of the pollution around us. Population growth and higher consumption standards are nowhere nearly as important.

Profits Before Higher Quality. As before, we now know to suspect that corporate behavior in capitalist economies may explain much of the environmental health risks which cannot be explained by bad habits or growing demand for products. If it's neither sloppy people nor more mouths, is it the corporate quest for profits?

There is certainly one apparent reason corporations may not promote the highest quality products and environment. As we saw about solar energy in Chapter 10, corporations like to control the returns from the products they make. Without that control, they risk losing their investments and missing out on the kind of profits to which they have been accustomed. If they know of a better product but doubt their ability to control it, they are likely to ignore it, sticking with what they already have.

A recent example helps illustrate this point. Scientists have recently discovered a remarkably potent and safe pesticide called diatomaceous earth, or "d.e." for short.[55] It is a fossil substance available in nearly unlimited supplies. In experimental use, it has not only controlled a wide variety of insects but also improved plant yields. Given all of our recent concern about air-spraying crops with dangerous chemicals like Malathion, it sounds like just what the plant doctor ordered.

It is not being developed commercially. There is no current prospect for commercial production. Why won't companies produce d.e.?

Government scientists developed the product. This means that private companies could not patent it and keep others out of the market. As one executive explained, "Once government has done the research, a product belongs to everybody and there's no way that a single company can get an exclusive or a patent on it. You need something to keep other people out...."Several small companies have tried to market d.e. but the effort has been dropped when larger chemical companies bought the smaller ones. As one scientist who has tried to develop d.e. reports: "It's a great story and it's never been told. You could protect all the country's crops with diatomaceous earth for 100 years and not even begin to scratch the surface of [the supplies we have available]....If anybody's going to sell diatomacious earth as an insecticide, it's going to have to be somebody who's outside the business." A large corporate executive agrees: "The chemical pesticides are...too profitable to challenge right now."

There is a product which we apparently need badly, in short, but companies won't make it because they don't think they can capture the returns. At least the insects are pleased.

As with the problem of the quality of our jobs, this boils down to the problem of corporate decision-making. In a capitalist economy, as we have already seen, corporations are free to base their decisions on their *own* costs, ignoring the costs which their activities and products create for the rest of us. When pollution spills out of their chimneys, we pay the laundry bills. When they refuse to develop safer and more effective pesticides, we pay for the poisoning of our lands and waters. When they want to leave their chemical wastes lying around, our children are deformed.

But what about consumer quality control? The DUPE argues that we'll get what we want because of our buying power—our power to buy or not to buy as we choose. Doesn't this give us enough leverage to demand better products over the long run.

The problem with this DUPE promise is that it's unrealistic. We can't demand something which doesn't exist. And many products require enormous investments before they become commercially feasible. If corporations choose to exercise their power and influence to block certain investments and encourage others, it's very difficult for us as consumers to do anything about it.

There is one dramatic example of this power from the years before World War II.[56] Up to the 1920s, most people either walked to work or relied on public transportion. During the 1920s, both the auto companies and the oil companies recognized the explosive profit potential of passenger car travel. So they set about destroying the competition.

In documented studies of the 1920s and 1930s, recent research has found that General Motors, often working with Standard Oil and Firestone Tire, first bought and then systematically dismantled electric trolley and transit systems in 44 cities across 16 states. They converted trolleys to diesel-powered bus lines. After acquiring and converting the lines, they often sold them back to local groups with a contractual stipulation which precluded the purchase of new equipment "using any fuel or means of propulsion other than gas." Since diesel buses don't last as long as electric trolleys and cost as much as 40% more, the transformation of local transit systems often left them with "higher operating costs, loss of patronage, and eventual bankruptcy."

In 1949, a Chicago Federal jury finally convicted GM, Standard Oil of California, Firestone, and others of criminal conspiracy to "replace electric transportation with gas- or diesel-powered buses to monopolize the sale of buses and related products to local transportation companies throughout the country." Despite the conviction and the fines, the damage had been done. Mass transit had been critically weakened. By the decades after World War II, the costs of repairing the damage had escalated enormously. GM and the rest of the auto-industrial complex earned the profits. And we paid the costs through higher fares, declining service, and exhaust fumes.

Corporate executives don't often take these issues very seriously, since they rarely bear the environmental consequences of their own actions. The rest of us know better. One of the best-known recent incidents involved the chemical dump at Love Canal, N.Y. A U.S. Senator from New York recently expressed his constituents' outrage over the callousness of the offending company, Occidental Petroleum:

> I hope Occidental pays every penny it owes to that community. There's no point in being restrained....It could end up costing a quarter of a billion, and if it does, Occidental Petroleum should end up paying it. To dismiss it as inconsequential verges on the unforgivable. They've taken enough out of that city, and left nothing but poison behind.[57]

One Love Canal resident telegraphed her governor: "We request a reprieve from death row. We are innocent of any crime."[58]

WILL IT EVER BE SAFER?

It is once again time to return to the questions with which we began the chapter.

■ *Do workers effectively govern working conditions and enjoy the best jobs possible?* No. Our jobs could be both safer and more interesting. But corporations dare not explore those possibilities for fear that their profits and control will be eroded.

■ *Do consumers continually enjoy the highest quality products?* No. We enjoy many new products as consumers, but we also pay enormous costs in environmental pollution and hazardous products. Corporations are aware of many of these costs, but they choose to ignore them because we pay the price and they keep the profits.

■ *Is the quality of our lives in our capitalist economy improving over time?* Yes and no. Much has improved, but much has also become dramatically worse. Health-and-safety on the job has deteriorated rapidly since the mid-1960s. Workers' job dissatisfaction is on the rise. Corporations are introducing more and more new and potentially dangerous products every year. And corporate power to pursue the paths they choose, ignoring the risks for us, is growing as giant corporations gain more and more control.

The situation is not completely without hope. But our hopes arise *despite* the economy, not *because* of it. Working people have made important strides in reducing the health risks of life in our economy in recent years. Union struggles helped win the Occupational Safety and Health Act of 1970; despite low funding and constant attacks on the agency, workers have been able to gain information and weapons of critical value in the battle to protect their own health on the job. Citizen struggles have similarly made a dent in some of the pollution surrounding us; both air and water pollution have improved since the late 1960s, thanks to much more careful government regulation of corporate and consumer waste.

And, despite corporate attacks, workers' rights to pursue these struggles have been upheld. The Supreme Court recently affirmed workers' rights to refuse certain work tasks when "a reasonable person would conclude that there was a real danger of death or serious injury..."[59] The Court decision was clear about the purpose of the law supporting this right. "The act does not wait for an employee to die or become injured....It authorizes...standards and...citations in the hope that these will act to prevent deaths or injuries from ever occurring. It would seen [inconsistent to prohibit] an employee, with no other reasonable alternative, the freedom to withdraw from a workplace environment that he reasonable believes is highly dangerous."[60]

Despite this progress, these victories are hardly secure. Recent corporate and government attacks have undercut most of our public weapons against hazards both on and off the job. Corporations have made clear that they will not lie down in their pursuit of profits and leave the driving to us. They cherish their freedom to make their own decisions and they are now fighting back vigorously against workers and citizens who have sought to improve the quality of our lives.

Their basic advantage in this battle is obvious. They control the means of production and they determine investment decisions. With that control, they can stay ahead of us in the struggle over quality— choosing to develop certain products and ignore others, installing certain machines and chemicals without enough regard for their consequences, pursuing their own profits while we watch in pain and uncertainty.

With that control, they can also blackmail us if we choose to fight back. They can threaten to take their investments elsewhere if we insist on higher standards where we live and work. They can threaten to shut down a plant if we demand our rights to better jobs. They can threaten to withdraw from a community if we move to protect our environment. They can and they do. As we saw in Chapter 1, indeed, they are sending us blackmail notes more and more frequently.

Would Workers' Management Solve the Problem?

This suggests that we might move quickly toward a system of workers' management in order to improve the quality of our lives. Workers could run the corporations and make their own decisions about what to produce and how to produce. Wouldn't they develop safer working conditions for themselves? And, as citizens, wouldn't they be more sensitive to problems of environmental pollution?

Movement toward workers' management of individual firms is clearly a step in the right direction. But it isn't enough. Suppose auto workers are running the auto companies, for example, and they are deciding whether to expand auto production or trolley production. They can't make the decision on their own. They would need to know where other plants will be located and what kinds of transit needs families will have. They would need to have access to accurate projections of future fuel resources and prices. They would need to know how much income people will earn in the future, what kinds of preferences people have about transit and what kinds of pollution the system can bear. All of that requires a mechanism for sharing information and coordinating decisions.

Without those mechanisms, workers in an individual factory can't be sure that they will serve both their own interests and those of other working people. In a more competitive environment, they may be forced to place their short-term interests above the interests of others—simply because they can't be certain what others want or will do. As we saw in Chapter 2, capitalism is a system of controlled work *and* disconnected production. We can't solve the problems this creates for the quality of our lives without *both* sharing *and* coordinating production decisions. Movement toward both is necessary. We discuss in Part VI how to take some first steps in those directions.

Miners carry casket of worker killed in mine accident.

At Least It Keeps Us Free?

"If you lose your economic freedom, I can guarantee you that you will lose your personal freedom as well."

—corporate executive, former government official[1]

"The same thing is happening in this country today. People are being used by those in control, those who have all the wealth....We got the greatest system of government in the world. But those who have it simply don't want those who don't have it to have any part of it."

—union organizer[2]

The corporate economists save one last argument for their goal-line defense: capitalism guarantees our freedom.

We are taught this lesson at an early age. We learn about the "free enterprise system." The United States is a "free country" and the leader of the "free world." The Gospel According to DUPE states the equation simply: "economic freedom is...essential...for political freedom."[3]

Much of what we learn is true. The United States has one of the longest and deepest democratic traditions in the world. The first successful democratic revolution against an imperial power took place in this country 200 years ago. Our freedoms and democratic traditions are probably our most important treasure.

But is it true that capitalism is necessary for this freedom and democracy? How much democracy do we actually have in the United States? Has our capitalist *economic* system actually promoted the *political* freedom and democratic rights we have? What is the relationship between capitalism and democracy?

Our democratic traditions are probably our most important treasure. Has capitalism helped?

WHAT IS DEMOCRACY?

Those who take the meat from the table
Preach contentment....
Those who eat their fill speak to the hungry
Of wonderful times to come....
Those who lead the country into the abyss
Call ruling too difficult
For the ordinary.

—Bertolt Brecht, German poet, 1937[4]

Democracy is more than just a system of government. It involves a way of life. When we practice democracy in our families or schools or unions or governments, we share power and problems—supporting each other, working together as equals, guarding against some people grabbing control from the rest of us.

None of this is easy. People have learned through history that certain rules are necessary to promote and ensure democracy. Three standards seem crucial for judging how much democracy we have.

1) *Democratic Process.* Individuals must have the right to determine the policies of the organization, including the rules by which it will

operate. Every member of the organization must have the *right to vote*, and all members must agree on the *rules for making decisions* as much as possible. Without the right to vote and majority or consensual rule, democracy is impossible.

2) *Democratic Rights*. People must be free to try to influence and protect themselves against the rule of the majority—even if the majority decided fairly by democratic process. This requires the *freedom of association*—the right to organize our own groups, associations, caucuses, or parties to seek influence over organizational decisions and policies. Without the freedom of association, government by the people remains a pipedream. It also requires that organizations protect *individual and minority rights* as much as possible. Without such protection, majority rule can quickly become majority tyranny. Everyone must always have at least a chance to speak out and seek to shape political decisions. Without those rights and opportunities, government *for* the people can easily turn *against* us.

3) *Democratic Power*. There is another criterion for judging democracy which is often overlooked. It is sometimes called a *substantive* standard because it concerns the real essence of democracy, what democracy actually amounts to. People must have the *power to implement their own decisions*. In a democracy, people exercise power and no one exercises their power for them.

How does this standard work? Imagine the following scenario:

Three men approach you on the street. "Your money or your life," they sweetly announce. "Wait a minute," you reply, "suppose I don't feel like parting with either of them?"

"Fairly asked," one of them responds. "Let's settle it democratically. We'll take a majority vote and you are free to express your own opinion. Isn't that what it takes to make a democracy?"

"But...!"

"Sorry, you're outvoted."

If we concerned ourselves only with *process* and with *rights*, most muggings like these would be democratic. In a democracy, people must not only be free to choose among alternatives. They must be able to determine what those alternatives shall be. They must be free to say, "No thank you, nothing today." In a democracy, people must have the *right* to say yes and the *power* to say no. If either the right or the power are missing, people cannot live together democratically.

These three criteria point to the questions we need to ask about the relationship between capitalism and democracy:

■ Does capitalism promote and protect democratic process, including the right to vote and determine organizational rules?

■ Does capitalism develop and maintain democratic rights, particularly the freedom of association and individual or minority rights?

■ Does capitalism support and preserve democratic power? Do people have the power to control their own lives in a capitalist society, shaping alternatives and remaining free to say "no" if necessary?

We began by noting that democracy is more than just a system of government. This means that we should investigate all the important spheres of our lives—on the job, off the job, both here and around the globe. Once we take this survey of different corners of our lives, we will be ready to pull together some more general answers to our questions about capitalism and democracy.

WHAT ABOUT DEMOCRACY ON THE JOB?

"So the foreman says, 'I'm giving you a direct order.'...He keeps at me and I wind up with a week off. Now I got a hot committee man who really stuck up for me, so you know what—they sent him home too....See it's just like the army— no, it's worse 'cause you're welded to the line. You just about need a pass to piss."

—autoworker[5]

Most working people spend from six to ten hours a day at work. Our time at work casts long shadows across the rest of our daily lives. So it seems appropriate to begin our investigation of capitalism and democracy by looking at political relationships on the job.

Democratic Process

Try to imagine the following: workers at Short Circuit Electric receive a memo from personnel. "We are deeply troubled," it begins, "because we have heard more and more complaints that management is dictatorial." The memo says that the company "believes in democracy just as much as you do." It announces a new day in company management:

> We hereby invite you to a series of employees' constitutional conventions. New by-laws and procedures for the operation of Short Circuit will be drafted and ratified. Each production worker and administrative employee will have equal voting power. We promise to abide by the decisions of these conventions. Let us hope that rules by the people will lead to people's rule!

Unimaginable, of course. Capitalist corporations don't operate by democratic procedures. We neither determine the rules by which decisions are made nor have the right to vote on them. We take the lack of democratic process so much for granted that we can scarcely dream of what it might be like to govern our working lives.

Even when unions represent us, democratic process is sharply circumscribed. Unions are free to bargain on certain issues. But those negotiations are settled by relative bargaining strength, not by vote. And, as we note in the section on "Democratic Power" below, most critical issues are excluded from the bargaining process altogether.

Even when management has moved in recent years to invite some additional participation by workers, these experiments always seem to stop short of real democratic process. When workers began to taste the hors-d'oeuvres, they wanted more of the meal. And when management realized that it was difficult to grant a little democratic process without leading to demands for a lot, they got cold feet. They realized, as one journalist concluded, that "sharing of power must mean a loss of control."[6] Capitalists choose control over democracy every time.

Democratic Rights

We are supposed to have freedom of association at work—the right to form our own labor unions. The Wagner Act of 1936 began with that basic assumption, addressing "the inequality of bargaining power between employees who do not possess...actual liberty of contract and employers who are organized in the corporate or other forms of ownership association."[7]

But this right was imposed on companies by the government. What about capitalism itself? Does it promote freedom of association on the job?

We know from history that capitalists fought tooth and nail against workers' rights to form unions. As we saw in Chapter 4 and shall see again in Chapter 17, millions of U.S. workers have learned that the struggle for unions often earned them tickets to the hospital, to jail, and even to the graveyard.

What about today? Even our legal rights are constrained. Unions cannot engage in secondary boycotting, which makes it extremely difficult for one group of organized workers to help another group seeking organization. Companies can freely distribute corporate propaganda against the unions while unions are not even entitled to solicit workers during their hours on the job.

Much more important, companies have begun to apply a whole host of new tactics to oppose unions and get rid of the ones which exist. Companies rely more and more on slick management consulting firms which specialize in both persuasion and intimidation of current employees. There are probably about 1,000 firms now specializing in union-busting. "Union-busting is now a major American industry," one union official concludes, "with annual sales well over $½ billion."[8] As a British magazine concluded in a survey of modern management tactics in the United States, "Employers no longer accept unions as a fact of life. They are fighting back—and winning."[9]

Does capitalism promote freedom of association on the job today? One union organizer in the south reports his recent experience:

> In Florida I ended up with five bullet holes in my car. Many colleagues have been badly beaten up by the police or company security men....I've been arrested and jailed around 25 to 30 times.[10]

"The only thing that has changed in union-busting by big business," an AFL-CIO official recently concluded, "is that they no longer use clubs and tear gas."[11] At least not always.

What about individual and minority rights? Most of us have to check our Bill of Rights at the factory gate and the office door. Almost all workers still find that they cannot freely exercise their "constitutional rights" at work. The list of activities for which we do not have protection at the workplace is very long. Here are only a few examples:

■ We can't make protests on our own behalf. Case: a company once fired an individual for saying "this is a hell of a place to work" and the courts upheld the dismissal.

■ We have very limited rights of freedom of speech. Case: a

company can legally fire an employee who discovers that the company's product is unsafe and reports the dangers to the press.

■ Buttons make less noise than speaking out, but we are only guaranteed the right to wear buttons which are not "provocative." Case: the telephone company once fired workers for wearing buttons which said "Ma Bell Is a Mother"; the courts upheld the dismissals.[12]

Are things getting better? Apparently not. A recent survey found that 64% of contracts include clauses providing for discharge or suspension of employees who talk back to supervisors or otherwise show disrespect. This was up from barely more than 50% in the previous round of contracts.[13] A *New York Times* report concludes, "Managers are seeking stronger authority to discipline employees for verbal abuse, and when such disputes come before the courts, the supervisors are winning."[14] Companies apparently take the issue seriously. "We tolerate a lot of loose talk," as one executive explained its suspension of an employee for swearing at the foreman, "but we will not put up with disrespect for supervisors."[15] Where company control

A company once fired a worker for saying, "this is a hell of a place to work." The courts upheld the dismissal.

and employee freedom of speech conflict, apparently, our rights of free expression play second fiddle.

What about our rights of privacy on the job? One researcher concluded that company surveillance is so widespread that roughly one-fifth of all employees "were being scrutinized under some sort of security or loyalty program." Another study concluded that at least one out of every five businesses in the country eavesdrops on its workers.[16] Most corporate surveillance techniques are apparently protected by the law. Once again, employers and the rest of us disagree about a critical issue. Asked in a recent poll whether a law should be passed to safeguard employee rights, two-thirds of the public said yes but only one-third of employers agreed.[17]

Democratic Power

We don't have it. Period. As we saw in Part II of this book, working people cannot dictate alternatives to our corporate bosses and we are not free to refuse to work. If we don't work, we don't eat. And we don't have the power to determine the alternatives we face on the job.

Most labor contracts reveal this lack of power in their "Management Rights" clauses. Here is a typical example:

> The right to hire; promote; discharge or discipline for cause and to maintain discipline and efficiency of employees, is the sole responsibility of the Corporation...In addition, the products to be manufactured, the location of plants, the schedules of production, the methods, processes and the means of manufacturing are solely and exclusively the responsibility of the corporation.[18]

There is virtually nothing left out. As one union official recently concluded, "I think our accepting those Management Rights clauses was the biggest mistake we ever made. It made us pawns in the companies' hands. No wonder we're in rough shape today."[19]

WHAT ABOUT DEMOCRACY OFF THE JOB?

"The country's never been so disjointed or disunited. More people have an extreme sense of insecurity. They have less power though they're making more money."
          —40-year-old professional worker[20]

"I think there's a giant conspiracy on the part of...the rich, the powerful, the manipulators, to make us all the same. Make sure that we watch a lot of television. Make sure that we all have credit cards and cars and houses....We're so afraid we'll lose 'em that we'll do anything they want us to do to keep those things."
          —professional musician[21]

We all know that the workplace is the bosses' domain. But what about our homes and communities? When we leave the factory and office, aren't we all equal and protected in the freedom and democracy of our private lives?

Democratic Process
What about majority rule? Don't we at least run our own PTAs

What if it was YOUR Vote?

and block associations and neighborhood groups?

The answer is obviously yes. But we do those things on our own. There are many ways in which capitalism affects our lives at home and in our communities about which we have no vote at all:

■ An oil company raises crude oil prices or cuts back on refining. Do democratically-controlled neighborhood groups get to "vote" for lower prices or more gas?

■ A toy manufacturer uses toxic chemicals in a new toy for children. Can the school PTA "vote" to keep the toy off the market?

We have already discussed the general point in the previous three chapters. Corporations largely determine what goods and services are available in the market. These products have an enormous impact on our living conditions. But our votes depend on our money, not our democratic rights as citizens. Most of us find it difficult to afford the ticket of admission to town hall.

Democratic Rights

Don't we at least have freedom to associate in our own groups? What about our associations promoting the interests of those who like rifles, vans, cooking, sports, music...? The list is nearly endless.

But the economy does not itself actively promote a fully democratic freedom of association. There are some kinds of associations which corporations actively oppose.

■ When southern farmers were not getting a good price for their crops in the 1880s, they created cooperative bulking stores where their crops were sold to the highest bidder. Corporate buyers refused to recognize these cooperatives and boycotted their sales.[22]

■ Many people have more recently tried to organize non-profit consumer and producer cooperatives in order to gain more control over what is available at what price. Banks typically refuse loans to many of these enterprises on the grounds that they don't use "sound business principles."[23]

Don't we at least have unalienable individual and minority rights?

Compared to many other countries, the United States protects a wide variety of formal rights to express our own opinions, to dissent, to differ from prevailing social practice. But it is difficult to credit the economy with these freedoms. Throughout the history of the United States, corporations and the wealthy have largely ignored the rights of

individual and minority groups, often opposing measures to improve them. This is essentially true today.

Our right to privacy is probably the clearest example. Private companies have little respect for that privacy. Private corporations spend millions of dollars securing information about our private lives and storing it in their computers, all so they can determine whether we're good credit risks. Sears Roebuck alone has 24 million active credit accounts. One credit-reporting company by itself prepares up to 35 million reports a year.[24] The consequences for us can be serious. One individual's case illustrates the problem. A businessman wrote a bad check when he was nineteen. Seven years later, he was denied credit because of an outdated private credit file. He had no recourse, and the privacy laws give no protection.[25]

What's the problem? We have rights, but when companies are worried about their profits, they don't mind invading our privacy to serve their needs.

Democratic Power
We lack the basic power to say "no" in capitalist economies.

■ When we rent from landlords, the landlords get to make the rules. We have the right to protest and struggle, but their property rights protect their basic prerogatives.

■ When we want to finance our homes or cars, the banks decide the rules for eligibility and repayment. We can complain if we're treated unfairly, but they have the basic right to say they're sorry.

■ When we put our savings in the local savings bank, they decide how and where it will be invested—either in our communities or outside of them. We earned the money, we saved it...and yet they get to determine how it's used.

■ When we want to insure our homes or cars or lives, the insurance companies make the rules for rates, eligibility, and cancellation. If they don't like our looks they can dismiss us as " bad risks." About our only power with the insurance companies is our right to belong to the risk category in which they place us.

All these examples contain the same lesson. The rights of property allow the wealthy to gain enormous leverage over our lives at home and in our communities. They have the power to say "no" to us, but we can rarely reply in kind.

A personal note in closing. A couple of our staff at the Institute for Labor Education and Research live in a relatively poor community in New York City called the Lower East Side. In recent years, we have discovered that, simply because we live in that neighborhood, we cannot get bank mortgages, cannot get regular liability or theft insurance for buildings or apartments in that area, cannot get cable television installed in our buildings, and cannot even get the *New York Times* delivered to our homes. At least they let us hang out on the front porch.

IS THE U.S. GOVERNMENT DEMOCRATIC?

Opinion poll: "Would you say the government is pretty much run by a few big interests looking out for themselves, or that it is run for the benefit of all the people?" Percent answering "few big interests": 73 percent.

—survey results, 1974[26]

What about the U.S. government? Is it a democracy? Is capitalism the best guarantee of a democratic system of government?

Democratic Process

We obviously have the right to vote. We obviously have a chance to help determine how decisions are made. But there are leaks in our power. Some people have a much better crack at influencing government decisions in our society than the rest of us.

■ As television has become more and more important, the cost of waging campaigns has sky-rocketed. More and more, the wealthy have big electoral advantages over the rest of us. In the previous Congress (for the 1979-1980 session), roughly a quarter of the 100 Senators were millionaires and the average Senator was worth close to $500,000. In the Senate and House campaigns of 1978, candidates spent roughly $150,000 apiece on their primary and general election campaign. In races for the House in 1978, the bigger spender won 82% of the time. In Senate races, the bigger spender won 85% of the contests.[27]

■ The wealthy are also able to spend millions to affect voting once our "representatives" are elected. We saw in "Why We Need This Book" that corporations have recently intensified their lobbying and promotion in Congress and in state and local government. There are thousands of lobbyists spending millions of dollars to buy votes and influence people. Government is becoming a bit like the marketplace.

We all have a right to vote. But it begins to appear that our votes are weighted by our dollars. The more we can afford to spend, the more influence we will eventually have on the government.

There are formal guarantees of democratic process in the United States, in short, but the politics of power and influence are eroding the real access that ordinary people have to government decisions. "You give a Congressman a list of people in his district," one business lobbyist explained, "he invariably looks down it to see whom he knows. He knows the prominent business people in his district. He can't ignore them. Anytime you give him an expression of how they feel he's going to think twice."[28] A Congressional staff member echoes the same observation: "There's the 23-year-old consumer lobbyist and the businessman who gives you $5,000. Whom are you going to listen to?"[29]

Democratic Rights

We clearly have strong individual and minority rights in the United States. We have fought for them and defended them.

Unfortunately, those rights do not apply to everyone. As long as the government thinks that you agree with our basic economic system, you're cool. If there's any evidence that you have different kinds of views, watch out.

Take the freedom of association. U.S. citizens are formally free to organize political associations in pursuit of their own interests. But it has always been extremely difficult to do so if we do not agree with the basic ways of doing business in this country.

One example comes from the beginning of this century. Hundreds of thousands of working people were drawn toward the policies of the Socialist Party of America and the Industrial Workers of the World (IWW) because they felt that capitalism was not working well. Business people called on the government to do something about these threats to "free enterprise." What to do?

The problem was that initial government investigations could find no cause for prosecution. One government investigator, after months of scrutiny, concluded that the Wobblies' written records "contain nothing in direct advocacy of anarchism, active opposition to organized government, or the destruction of property, private or public."[30]

So the government found other pretexts for harrassing the new movements out of business. New laws defined crimes like "sedition" for which nearly anyone could be prosecuted. The police used the laws to conduct mass round-ups in cities such as Chicago, Detroit, Sacramento, and Kansas City. "In one case," a historian reports, "the jury required only 55 minutes to convict a group of 96 men."[31] The government deported thousands from the country. By 1920, the backs of the socialists and Wobblies organizations had been broken.

A relic of the past? Apparently not. The FBI harrassed many protest groups during the 1960s and early 1970s—spying on Dr. Martin Luther King, informing on and eventually murdering members of the Black Panther Party, infiltrating a wide variety of progressive organizations. The scale of this surveillance and harrassment has recently emerged in a suit filed against the government by one small harmless political party called the Socialist Workers Party. Court documents have revealed that the government planted informants throughout the organization—among many other forms of harrassment. Betwee 1960 and 1976, the government spent a minimum of $700,000 in payments to informants. During the court case, the FBI admitted that it possessed roughly eight million documents about this small party alone.[32]

In 1978 a Federal Judge cited the government for contempt of court for this surveillance and intimidation. In his opinion, the judge spoke sternly about the government's action:

> The issues in this case relate to the most fundamental constitutional rights, which lie at the very foundation of our system of government—the right to engage in political organization and to speak freely on political subjects, without interference and harassment from governmental organs.[33]

The practices still haven't disappeared. The Immigration Service still maintains a list of 668 "proscribed groups," for example, with which immigrants should not associate.[34] An editorial in the *St. Louis Post-Dispatch* asked the obvious question: "The Immigration Service might well question its own attachment to the Constitution. Doesn't [it] respect the right of free association?"

Similar problems mar our individual minority rights. The government treats the wealthy and powerful with kid gloves. It treats many of the rest of us with spyglasses and prison bars.

■ People who commit ordinary street crimes are punished severely, often locked away for years. Corporate executives who embezzle funds and fix prices are rarely prosecuted; when they are, they usually escape with trivial fines.[35] In the federal fraud division, for example, officials have admitted that "our first priority was going after fraud in welfare, Medicare, and Medicaid." Get little folks! Of 130 criminal charges against corporations recently referred to prosecutors by the environmental agency, mostly involving cases of violations of federal regulations, charges were actually filed against only one corporation. When Internal Revenue investigates tax violations, it devotes only 2.5% of its total investigative time to large corporations.[36]

A Justice Department official explains, "A criminal case against a major corporation is all-out global war. Corporations use every weapon they can afford, and they can afford a lot."[37] As a result, another official explained, "It's just a lot easier for us to pick on the little guy."[38]

■ The government still spies on U.S. citizens for the simple offense of seeming suspicious. It appears that the government spent roughly $12 billion a year during the mid-1970s spying on U.S. citizens.[39] One journalist compiled evidence on the numbers of citizens who were the privileged recipients of this careful government attention:

> ...the CIA, which opened first-class mail for twenty years,

"It's just a lot easier to pick on the little guy."

—tax official

screened 28 million letters, photographed the outside of 2.7 million, and opened almost 215,000. For more than two decades,...the [National Security Agency] in Operation Shamrock received copies of literally millions of cables sent from, to, or through the United States. From 1955 to 1975, the FBI investigated 740,000 "subversive" targets....The Army kept files on some 100,000 Americans, including members of Congress and other civilians. The FBI...still maintains a network of 1,500 "domestic intelligence" informants whom it pays $7.4 million a year. The [Internal Revenue Service] had more than 465,000 Americans and organizations in its...intelligence files.[40]

Does this kind of surveillance matter? An English historian writing in 1863 issued a clear warning more than a century ago:

Men may be without restraints upon their liberty; they may pass to and fro at pleasure; but if their steps are tracked by spies and informers, their words noted down for crimination, their associates watched as conspirators—who shall say they are free? [Espionage] haunts men like an evil genius, chills their gaiety, restrains their wit, casts a shadow over their friendships, and blights their domestic health. The freedom of a country may be measured by its immunity from this baleful agency.[41]

Democratic Power

In the economy, working people do not control the means of production. What has that meant for our democratic power over the U.S. government? Do we have a government actually operating for and by the people?

One test of our democratic power over the government is to study the actual effects of government actions. Whose interests does the government serve?

Tax policies provide one obvious focus for investigation.

■ Our labor income is taxed almost twice as heavily as income from capital ownership.[42]

■ The typical working household pays almost twice as much of its income in taxes to the government as the average millionaire's household.[43]

■ Working households pay at least 10 to 15 times higher taxes as a percentage of their net wealth than the most affluent 1% of U.S. families.[44]

How do the wealthy get away with such murder? Aren't we supposed to have a progressive tax system, imposing higher tax burdens on those who can more easily afford their taxes?

One problem is that many of our taxes, including the property tax, sales tax, and social security tax, are not progressive. They hit people with lower incomes harder than people with higher incomes.

A second problem is that the government grants many special tax privileges—especially to the most affluent families. The most affluent 1% of households receives more than five times its proportionate share of these tax privileges—in relationship to income—than the average working family.[45]

What about the effects of government expenditures? Don't we at least benefit from the money which the federal, state, and local governments spend out of tax revenues?

Working people benefit directly from many government programs—particularly income transfer programs like Social Security and Medicaid which make survival a little more manageable for people who would otherwise find it almost impossible to make ends meet.

But large corporations also benefit from many government programs. More than one quarter of all direct government expenditures go toward defense, space, and international security programs—and that percentage is rapidly rising under the Reagan Administration. The immediate beneficiaries of these expenditures are the large corporations that dominate the space, defense, and foreign trade sectors of the economy. We get higher taxes and nuclear waste in our backyard.

This tally seems like a toss-up: some for us and some for them. But there is more to the effects of government activities than direct program expenditures. At least as important is whom the government helps out in special circumstances.

When large corporations have serious problems, for example, the government usually lends a hand. It has provided special loans, for example, to bail out large corporations like Lockheed and Penn Central and, most recently, Chrysler, when they've messed up their own affairs.

When working people have problems, in contrast, the government turns its head. After more than 10,000 steelworkers in Youngstown, Ohio had been abandoned by their employers in 1977-78, for example, workers organized a plan to save the steel works and help modernize the plants. The government denied their application for a special loan, arguing that their request for special consideration did not justify the expense. [46]

Who makes all these decisions? It probably comes as no surprise that corporate representatives have dominated the executive branch of government for decades. Key international decisions have been shaped by corporate executives, corporate lawyers, and investment bankers. We tend to associate business interests with the Republican party. But even under the Democrats, business interests occupy most of the key decisions. We learned in Chapter 1, for example, about the Trilateral Commission, an international organization helping shape and represent the interests of the largest multinational corporations. President Carter, Vice-President Mondale, and Carter's initial Secretaries of State, Defense and the Treasury were all members of this elite group before the Democrats were elected.[47]

In the face of all these facts, it is hard to sustain the faith that the United States enjoys a truly democratic government "for and by the people." "For and by the corporations" would probably be more accurate. As one former U.S. Senator has concluded from his experience in Washington, D.C.:

> We have a government that is ostensibly run by the people, for the people. It's not true. We have a government run by the establishment, for the establishment. If there are some droppings left over

for the people, well and good. But no more than droppings.[48]

We have many democratic rights, in short, but corporations have most of the power over our government. We need to preserve and strengthen our democratic process and rights. And we need to restore our democratic power. Capitalism is not helping us on either count.

MAKING THE WORLD SAFE FOR DEMOCRACY?

"I spent thirty-three years and four months in active service as a member of our country's most agile military force—the Marine Corps....And during that period I spent most of my time being a high-class muscle man for Big Business, for Wall Street, and for the bankers. In short, I was a racketeer for capitalism....I was rewarded with honors, medals, promotion. Looking back on it, I feel I might have given Al Capone a few hints. The best he could do was operate his racket in three city districts. We Marines operated on three continents.

—retired Marine major-general[49]

We have always learned in our schoolbooks that the United States has played a special historical mission, making the world safe for democracy. But we have also learned, in more recent years, that large corporations and the U.S. government have conspired to overturn democratically-elected governments abroad; that large corporations have bribed foreign governments; that the CIA has spent millions to disrupt free elections if it feared the results; and that agents of the U.S. government have actually sought to assassinate foreign leaders, sometimes successfully.

Does capitalism really promote democracy around the world?

The basic record seems so stark that we can summarize it much more briefly than in previous sections.

The U.S. government and U.S. corporations have never shown much regard for *democratic process* in other countries. They have consistently supported dictatorial governments in the Third World, even helping overthrow democratically-elected governments in countries like Chile. They have also intervened in elections in the advanced world if and when they feared the potential results. Over a 20-year period, for example, the CIA secretly spent $65 million to influence Italian elections simply because it feared the potential power of the Italian left.[50] When these interventions have been uncovered, U.S. officials have almost always justified them on the grounds that other people didn't know what was best for them. Former Secretary of State Henry Kissinger justified U.S. intervention to overturn the electoral results in Chile, for example, as a way of overcoming "the irresponsibility of its own people."[51]

The U.S. government and U.S. corporations have shown even less regard for the *democratic rights* of people in other countries. We now consider as allies all of the following countries: South Korea, Indonesia, Taiwan, Brazil, Argentina, Chile, and the Phillipines. Effective freedom of association is non-existent. Workers in those countries are either denied the right to form labor unions or denied the right to strike. None of those countries allows full freedom to form political parties.

The record on individual and minority rights is equally shoddy. The U.S. government has taken no effective actions to expand the rights of blacks in South Africa. We have done virtually nothing to reduce discrimination against Moslem minorities in the Philippines. And we almost totally ignore the pervasive imprisonment of individuals in many "allied" countries for nothing more than the simple expression of their political views. Figure 12.1 on this page summarizes the numbers of prisoners held for "political reasons" in various countries around the world. Our allies do not score well in this tally.[52]

What about *democratic power?* Few would argue that *the people* in most countries around the globe have real democratic power. What is striking is the role the U.S. government and U.S. corporations have frequently played in subverting people's power and installing anti-democratic regimes. A major study of U.S. foreign policy recently summarized its findings about the impact of the U.S. role abroad:

> In state after client state, from Argentina to Zaire, the installation of military juntas has brought with it a new power and role for foreign business and *corruption as a system....* The regimes that are so corruption-prone are products of U.S. initiative. They are part of a package that includes rule by a denationalized minority, repression of the majority, and corruption flowing out of the dependent status of rulers and the interests of their external sponsors.[53]

That appears to be the record. What does it tell us about the relationship *between* capitalism and democracy around the world?

Since the turn of the century, as we saw in Part II of this book, U.S. corporations have steadily pushed the government to intervene with military and political power overseas in order to support the spread of U.S. business. Capitalist corporations have consistently ignored the political rights of foreigners throughout the history of that expansion.[54]

These corporate pressures certainly continued into the period after World War II. Did modern multinationals worry about democratic rights and people's welfare in the countries they were conquering? No. The results of multinational penetration were themselves devastating. As one Brazilian official concluded about his own country, U.S. business expansion had brought "sudden wealth to a small number of people; [but] it has changed very little the lot of three-fourths of the population. In fact, the peasants and industrial workers

Capitalism and Freedom in the 3rd World?

Fig. 12.1

Does the spread of capitalism around the globe bring freedom and democracy with it?

One ingredient of freedom and democracy is the individual right to express one's political views without fear of repression or prison. Although it is extremely difficult to get accurate data on the numbers of "political prisoners" in the 3rd World, the Nobel-Prize-winning efforts of a group called Amnesty International make some rough estimates possible in many cases.

The table in the margins roughly classifies a selection of countries in the 3rd World into three groups: "Capitalist/U.S. Allies," "Socialist," and "Non-aligned." It then provides very rough estimates of the numbers of political detainees in those countries in 1977-78. The data, we repeat, are very approximate but nonetheless provide reasonable indication of the climate of freedom in these countries.

The point of the table is to provide information, not to argue the merits of one system or another. *At the least*, however, the information in the table seems to cast doubt on the DUPE promise that capitalism (or close association with the U.S.) is a guarantee of the freedom of expression for 3rd World people.

Source: See note #52

Political Prisoners in 1978

"Capitalist" / U.S. Allies

Indonesia	Extreme
Argentina	Extreme
Chile	Many
Uruguay	Many
Thailand	Many
So. Korea	Some
Philippines	Some
Brazil	Some

"Socialist"

Vietnam	Extreme
Cuba	Many
Mozambique	Some
Tanzania	Few
No. Korea	???

"Non-Aligned"

Guinea	Many
India	Many
Mexico	Some
Venezuela	Few

CODE:	
Extreme: More than 10,000	Many: 1,000– 10,000
Some: 100– 1,000	Few: Under 100

are worse off now than they were before in relation to other classes in society."[55] When democratic processes or popular movements stand in the way of multinational business prospects, the giant corporations think nothing of subverting the former in the interests of the latter. As one U.S. Congressman concluded after investigations of multinational behavior abroad, they "are in fact internationalists, concerned only with making billions of dollars, however and wherever they can."[56]

This preference for profits over democracy continues. Two recent examples seem typical:

■ There was both political turmoil and an assassination in South Korea in 1979. By mid-1980, a new strongman had been installed at the helm of the South Korean government. It had become clear that his regime would continue the repressive policies of the previous dictator. A *New York Times* survey concluded that U.S. businessmen were delighted. "I feel much more comfortable about things," one banker reported. "At least there's some direction now." Now that "political stability" was returning, another banker observed, "there is a definite appetite" for investments in South Korea.[57]

■ Argentina has become one of the most politically repressive countries in the world. Most U.S. businesses prefer it that way. "This Government has been very liberal toward foreign investment," a U.S. banker observed, "and I don't rule out the possibility that some investments will undergo critical review the day political parties return to power."[58] Translation: we'd rather have this government than the political parties. As the *New York Times* reports, the Argentine branch of the Chamber of Commerce is convinced that "publicity given to thousands of cases of people who disappeared...is part of an international campaign to weaken a Government that is doing what they believe is best for Argentina."[59] "We do [most of our] work now trying to explain Argentina in the U.S.," an American Chamber of Commerce official reports.[60] "As long as [the Government] keeps drilling for oil," another businessman says, "we'll be here."[61]

DEMOCRACY IN SPITE OF CAPITALISM?

"In some measure governability and democracy are warring concepts....At times, in the history of democratic government the pendulum has swung too far in one direction....[At present] the balance has tilted too far against governments."
—**task force report for business association**[62]

We've asked many questions and studied a fair amount of evidence. It seems obvious that capitalism does not promote democracy on its own. On and off the job, in this country and around the world, capitalism does more to subvert democracy than to sustain it.

Why is capitalism so unfriendly to democracy? How did we get the democracy we have? And what should we do to strengthen and preserve our democratic system?

Property Before People

Historically, capitalists have always been interested in protecting the rights of their property, not in advancing the political rights and power of people. When those two kinds of rights have come into conflict, the wealthy have almost always *opposed* democracy. Some examples:

■ In the early development of the U.S. political system, the wealthy lobbied strenuously to limit the vote to those white men who owned property. As late as the 1830s in Rhode Island, for example, people still needed to own land in order to be eligible for the vote.[63] Property-owners were clear about their reasons for such anti-democratic preferences. Democracy was dangerous, many felt, because the

"We are the rich; we own America. We got it, and we intend to keep it."

—industrialist, 1870s

property-less would use their votes to claim some of the riches of the wealthy. "The people...see the weakness of government," one property-owner at the time of the Constitution reported; "they feel at once their own poverty, compared with the opulent, and their own force, and they are determined to make use of the latter, in order to remedy the former."[64] "The great object of government," the statesman Daniel Webster insisted in the 1840s, "is the protection of property at home...."[65]

■ After the Civil War, industrialists used their influence over government not only to promote their own interests but to oppose and curb popular movements. They insisted on a limitation of popular rights of freedom of association—through unions, for instance— because they allowed people too much influence over government. "Industry may be republican," as a social critic observed, "[but] can never be democratic."[66] A member of the wealthy industrialist class was even more candid about their views of government:

> We are not politicians or public thinkers; we are the rich; we own America; we got it, God knows how, but we intend to keep it if we can by throwing all the tremendous weight of our support, our influence, our money, our political connection, our purchased senators, our hungry congressmen, our public-speaking demagogues, into the scale against any legislature, any political platform, any Presidential campaign that threatens the integrity of our estate.[67]

How Did We Get the Democracy We Have?

Every major advance toward full democracy in capitalist countries has been won by people struggling for their own rights and freedoms.

■ Working people won the right to vote—even if they didn't own property— more than 50 years after the Declaration of Independence and only after a sustained political struggle.

■ Women and blacks did not win the right to vote or full civil rights until the twentieth century. Movements of women and blacks fought to secure these rights.

■ Working people in the United States have had to fight for such basic rights as freedom of association at work, more equal access to high school and college education, freedom from government harrassment of labor organizations, and government regulation of support services like workmen's compensation and disability insurance.

The lessons are so simple that schoolchildren can learn them if they get the chance. A black woman who helped organize unions during the 1930s tells a story from her childhood:

> I decided I wasn't going to sing the Star Spangled Banner. I just stood there every morning and I didn't sing it....I went in to the principal and he asked me why I wasn't singing the Star Spangled Banner....Finally I told him. "Because it says 'The land of the free and the home of the brave' and this is not the land of the free. I don't know who's brave but I'm not going to sing it any more...." And I told him about coming through the park and if I could not swing in those swings in the park, and I couldn't sit in the park, and I could only walk in Shakespeare Park, then it couldn't be the land of the free. "Who's free?" He didn't say anything....This was the beginning of my realizing that you have to fight for freedom.[68]

Can't We Just Put the Good Guys in Office?

Why can't we solve our problems by putting our own people into the government? If capitalists tend to oppose real democracy, then we should just limit their power over government policies and decisions. Can't we create a government *for* the people by turning it into a government *by* the people first?

Electing people who really represent our interests would obviously be a promising start. But one of the main lessons of this book and this chapter is that it wouldn't be enough.

The essential reason it wouldn't be enough is that capitalism and democracy are fundamentally in conflict. As we saw in Part II, capitalism depends upon and requires *freedom of property*—the freedom of those who own the means of production to do what they want with them. As we have seen in this chapter, democracy depends upon and requires *democratic power*—the freedom and capacity of people to say "no" when they don't like the menu of political choices they're served.

Capitalism promotes an increasingly limited ownership of property, as we saw in Chapter 6. This means that its property imperatives represent the interests of fewer and fewer people through history. Democracy, in contrast, invites and encourages more and more people to demand full participation in its processes, rights, and power. This means that its democratic imperatives concern wider and wider circles through history.

The two tendencies bump into each other, repeatedly. Capitalists want special privileges, honoring "one dollar, one vote." People want equal privileges, respecting "one person, one vote."

And every time we gain enough influence over the government that it begins to limit the corporations' freedom of property, they threaten back by vowing to close down their plants or move overseas.

Since we depend on them economically, they can make us politically dependent. As one corporate executive put it crudely at a management conference, "We have to tell a state considering additional restrictions on business: 'The next plant doesn't go up here if that bill passes.' "[69]

That means that the fate of political democracy is tied to the fate of economic democracy. It's very difficult for us to make our government work for us without also making sure that we gain enough control over the economy to make it work for us too. Part VI of this book begins to explore some ways of making progress on both economic and political fronts. We won't be able to win either battle unless we're prepared to fight in both.

PART IV: THE REST OF US ARE...

"I worked in the leading rehab hospital in the country. The schedule was very rigid. Everybody punches time clocks when they come to work and when they leave....When I first took this job, they said I couldn't wear earrings: Only sluts wear pierced earrings. I told them to go to hell....The nurses, the doctors, the medical students, are set up on a rigid status kind of system. If you buy into this kind of system, you buy the idea that 'I'm not quite as good as the guy above me.'....That's what happens in hospitals—not because people are unfeeling or don't care, but because they feel put down."

—occupational therapist[1]

"Those who have all the wealth...simply don't want those who don't have it to have any part of it. Black and white. When it comes to money—the green—the other colors make no difference."

—middle-aged union organizer[2]

We are the more than 100 million people in the United States who work for a living. We are the more than 200 million people living in households who depend on wage-and-salary earnings to get by. "The rest of us" are working people.

And there are several respects in which we are all in the same boat. We live in an economy dominated by large corporations producing for profit, driven by the pressure to stay ahead of their competitors and to keep on top of us— racing to accumulate, ignoring our needs. We live in an economy which serves the needs of those giant corporations instead of serving ours. We would all have to begin rowing together if we wanted to make the economy work for us.

One of the main problems, of course, is that *many of us don't feel that we have very much in common with other working people.* Since we often feel as if we're all in different boats, how can we be expected to pull our oars together?

Do we have enough in common to join forces? Or do our differences make common action nearly impossible? It's time to take a careful look at the bonds uniting and the distances separating working people in the U.S. corporate economy.

Chapter 13 provides a brief overview of the similarities and differences among "**Working People in a Corporate Economy.**" It argues that many of our differences arise from different working experiences. It concludes that we need to tackle the basic economic structure which creates these differences if we want to begin achieving greater popular power.

Can't we avoid the problem by pulling ourselves up by our individual bootstraps? There has been a long and rich history of working people improving their living conditions through hard work and sacrifice. If our grandparents could do it, why can't we? Chapter 14, "**Immigrants, Old and New,**" explores the similarities and differences in immigrants' experiences when they arrive on U.S. shores.

Even if we decided that we need to unify, won't gender and racial differences keep us divided? Is it even possible to imagine that we could overcome the fighting and disunity which discrimination and divisions by race and sex have created? Chapter 15 on "**Women**" and Chapter 16 on "**Blacks and Hispanics**" examine these questions.

And doesn't the history of working people's struggles cast a long shadow across our current discussions? Haven't we fought continually and rarely won? Aren't the corporations too powerful for us? Those questions raise important issues about the effectiveness of people's struggles in the United States and the success our efforts have and haven't achieved. Chapter 17 on "**Traditions of Resistance and Struggle**" examines the history of people's fights to improve working and living conditions in the United States.

We've already learned in the first parts of this book that we need to know our opponents. We need to learn more about ourselves as well.

13.

Working People in a Corporate Economy

"I'm not a worker. I just work here."
—young employee at ping-pong-paddle factory[1]

"You become your job. I became what I did. I became a hustler....I don't think it's terribly different from somebody who works on the assembly line forty hours a week and comes home cut off, numb, dehumanized. People aren't built to switch on and off like water faucets."

—prostitute[2]

"I've learned to do the checking at the fastest speed the line can move. [Now] there are a few...new people, and they don't know the machines yet. Well, I'm not going to move the line any faster than they feel comfortable about....In the shop you work with other people; you don't want to screw your buddies."
—middle-aged checker in electronics assembly[3]

We all know that millions of people must work for a living in the United States. But the media and schools teach us so little about our working lives that we lose sight of our common bonds and the sources of our continuing differences.

Who are we? How much do we have in common? How deep are our differences? What can we learn about our lives as working people which might help us overcome the divisions among us?

WHAT DO WE HAVE IN COMMON?

Working people share many common conditions and many problems—most of which are rooted in the basic rules and structures of our economy. Most of us must work to support ourselves. When we do work, it's for many others, not for ourselves. And we usually work with many others, not by ourselves. These are the experiences which shape our common lives as working people in a corporate economy.

Working for a Living

We begin with the most basic tie that binds—working for a living. Roughly 90% of the people in the United States live in households which depend on wage-and-salary income for survival.[4] Somebody in those households must go to work in order to make ends meet.

We work because none of us can afford *not* to work. An average family of four needed about $23,000 in 1980 to live at what the government defines as a "modest-but-adequate" standard of living.[5] Suppose that a household wanted to enjoy that kind of consumption standard without having to work. Assuming it could earn an 8% return on its available assets, it would need a net worth of nearly $300,000 in income-producing assets to be able to live off its wealth.

Only about six million individuals in the United States currently control at least that much income-producing wealth.[6] These people represent no more than 5% of all households in this country. The remaining 95% need wage-and-salary incomes to be able to achieve an adequate standard of living.[7] Some choose not to work and to survive on less. But few can afford that choice.

In short, almost all of us must work for a living. When we work, moreover, we also share the experience of working by the hour, the day, the year, or the job; few of us share directly in the profits we make possible. In 1977, less than 9% of all employees worked on commission or for a share of profits. The other 91% of all employees were paid by salary, daily or hourly rates, piece rates, or by the job.[8]

In these respects, a vast majority of workers and households in the United States share a common experience. We do not have enough control over the means of production to be able to support ourselves on our own. We work for wage-and-salary income. We don't have enough basic economic power, in short, to be able to control our own economic survival.

Working for a Boss

We must not only work to survive, but we must also work for someone else to earn our daily bread. Among all wage-and-salary workers in the United States in 1977, 91.4% worked under a supervisor or boss; only 8.6% worked without direct supervision.[9]

Working for a boss, we share two fundamental experiences.

1. Because we work for someone else, we share a common insecurity—the risk of losing our jobs. If the boss hires us, he can almost always fire us as well. As we saw in Chapter 1, unemployment is not an isolated problem. Nearly 22 million workers experienced unemployment at one time or another in 1980. And the risks of unemployment are spreading more and more widely—facing engineers, teachers, and other professionals as directly as those more traditionally affected.

2. Because we work for a boss, we also share the common experience of being told by someone else what we can and cannot do as we walk through the factory gate or the office door.

■ Most of us have little influence over hours and working conditions: 88% of all wage-and-salary workers report that it would be hard to get their working days changed if they wanted to, and 82% report that it would be hard to get their hours changed if they so preferred.[10] Fewer than 12% of all wage-and-salary workers "strongly agree" that "I have a lot of say about what happens on my job."[11]

■ The boss or supervisor watches us closely: 90% of workers report that their supervisors "insist" that they "work hard" and 87% report that their supervisors "insist" that they "follow the rules."[12]

■ Rewards don't usually follow our performance: 71% of U.S.

workers agree that "my job requires that I work very hard," but barely a quarter report that they would "be offered a better job" if they did their jobs well.[13]

When we combine these common conditions, we find a population of working people who share two over-riding concerns: we all face the risks of losing our jobs, and think we should have much more influence over the jobs we do have. In a 1977 survey, working people were asked "how much say" they should have over a variety of issues. More than 90% said they should have at least some say over "how the work is done." And nearly 99% agreed that they should have at least some say over "safety equipment and practices."[14]

We almost all work for a boss who signs our paychecks and issues our orders—and we almost all think we ought to do a lot more of the bossing ourselves.

Working Together

We work for bosses but we also work together. Almost all working people share the experience of informal work groups on the job—pooling our resources, airing our gripes, depending on each other for help, relying on our mutual strength to resist the boss.

Neither companies nor the government collect data on these shared experiences. Workers probably tell the story better than the numbers anyway:

> **"The brother who worked next to me wanted to get a drink of water; I was a few pieces ahead, so I walked around the table and began running my buddy's job. When he came back he just took my place....There was one older worker who couldn't take the pace; so we put him on an easy job and rotated around him."**
>
> **— auto assembly-line worker[15]**

> **"This'll sound crazy, but I like to keep a certain rhythm-...going....You'd get a constant—like bum, bum, bum, zing: bum, bum, babum, zing....Sometimes I had it going with three people, so we'd all be doing it exactly together....It's like sometimes you notice that three friends will be walking in the street and their footsteps are all the same."**
>
> **—keypunch operator[16]**

> **"During lunch we kid around with each other. We like to have a little fun. That takes the drudgery out of knowing you gotta hit the floor again....We get along very well with the office workers. Every time I go in, I always give them a good morning and I always try to have something funny to say."**
>
> **—order filler in a shoe factory[17]**

"Life is a funny thing. We had this boss come in....He wanted to be very, very strict. We used to have meetings every Friday—about people comin' in late, people leavin' early, people abusin' lunch time....He would try to talk to one and see what they'd say about the other. But we'd been working all together for quite a while....He'd want to find out where someone was, we'd always say. "They're at the Xerox." Just anywhere. He couldn't get through."

—processing clerk in a large office[18]

"We try to have a compromise between doing things efficiently and doing things in a human way....On a good day it's beautiful to be here. We have a good time and work hard and we're laughing. It's a good day if we don't make too many mistakes and we have a good time."

—baker in a baking cooperative[19]

"At our office [we talk] mainly about how we should do things....We tried to get them to upgrade the secretaries. ...Management fought us. We've tried to have a say in policy making....Management fought us....The employees should help make policy, since they're closest to what's going on. It's probably the same as in auto plants. A lot of times workers can make better decisions about production than managers. The managers aren't there often enough to know what's going on."

—coordinator of government programs[20]

"I punch in about ten minutes to seven in the morning. I say hello to a couple of guys I like, I kid around with them. One guy says good morning to you and you say good morning. To another guy you say fuck you. The guy you say fuck you to is your friend....I say hello to everybody but my boss."

—steelworker[21]

Working Against the Tide

Because large corporations have control over the means of production, most working people share a final and fundamental experience: we have far too little influence over not only our jobs but the basic currents of our economy. We constantly feel that we're swimming against the tide. A 1975 survey revealed:[22]

■ Only 18% of U.S. adults feel that they have a "great deal of control" over their personal economic condition.

■ More than two-thirds of working people agree that they "don't work as hard as they could because they aren't given enough say in decisions which affect their jobs."

■ Roughly 60% of working people agree that "local community interests and needs are not represented in making company policy." Three quarters agree that having community representatives on company boards would do "more good than harm."

We don't run the country, in short, and we know it.

HOW DO WE DIFFER?

**"The problem...is that there are too many different kinds
and groups of people. The country's full of different people—
blacks, white and everyone else. That's why in *this* country
you won't have any big change. People are at each other's
throats...Of course, come to think of it, maybe [a big change]
could happen if everyone had the same beef."**

—Boston truckdriver[23]

We have a lot in common, but we also differ in many ways. We are
different genders, different races and ethnic groups, and different
ages. Some of us work in factories and some in offices. Some work for
companies and some for the government. Some of us are in unions and
some aren't.

These kinds of differences are commonplace. They are the first
things that come to mind when we try to think of the sources of our
divisions. But there are other important differences besides our sex
and color and age and work-collars. **There are important differences
rooted in the kinds of jobs we hold and the kind of work we do.**
As the prostitute quoted in the beginning of this chapter puts it, "you
become your job." When we "become" our jobs, we become similar to
those who hold similar jobs and different from those who work in
different kinds of situations. How many different kinds of jobs are
there, and how do they differ from each other?

We concentrate in this chapter on five main categories of jobs.
Some people work in *control* jobs, bossing the rest of us. Many working
people hold *responsible* jobs, combining some supervision with some
useful productive tasks. Many work in *routine* jobs, enjoying adequate
pay and job security with virtually no authority or challenge in their
work. Many hold *dead-end* jobs, enjoying neither authority nor decent
pay and working conditions. A final group does *unpaid housework*.

The differences among these five kinds of working situations are
crucial.

Control Work

**"I worked for Johns-Mansville for twelve years. Some-
where along the line, you lose an election, on the corporate
level. It's either him or me. It turned out it was me....As you
go on, there's always gonna be one, two, three guys'll lose
out."**

—former corporate executive[24]

**"Being a supervisor isn't an easy job. Handling discipline
when you know that if you make a mistake you may be
reversed or overruled by either your boss or the union
makes the job even more difficult....This [also] applies to
your boss, who must answer to higher executives and to the
company president, who in turn may have to answer to a
board of directors....So don't take your job as disciplinarian
lightly. It's a great responsibility and requires impartiality,**

good judgement, and courage."

—training textbook for supervisors[25]

A small group of wage-and-salary employees directly represents the corporations. They are the managers, foremen, and supervisors who run our lives at work. They are like officers in the army. They give the orders.

These control workers cannot avoid taking the corporate side on any particular issue or dispute. Their fortunes depend on their performance in the service of the authorities. And their successes are generally rewarded by movement up the corporate ladder. Managers and supervisors therefore stay on the job much longer than other well-paid employees; the average length of time which supervisory workers have spent on their present jobs is typically about one third longer than the present job experience of professional, technical or craft workers.[26]

How many people work as the bosses' lieutenants? The box on this page shows that there were almost five million control workers in 1970, nearly 7% of total wage-and-salary employment.[27] Five million employees looming over our shoulders.

Because control workers do the bosses' bidding, it is almost impossible for the rest of us to imagine uniting with this small group of wage-and-salary employees. The bosses' profits depend on our extra work, and these managers and supervisors are responsible for extracting it.

That doesn't mean, however, that control workers would be opposed to any and all changes in the economy. Many managers are dissatisfied with their work. There is some evidence that growing numbers of control workers are frustrated by the inefficiency of top-heavy bureaucratic structures in the largest corporations.[28] This suggests that many might welcome a move toward less rigid and more participatory work environments—simply to have a chance to do work which seems less arbitrary and somewhat more meaningful.

But they can't afford to take the lead. If they cross the bosses, they bear the cross. Control workers cannot act to change our economy on their own. The rest of us will have to take the lead. Some control workers may eventually join. As one former executive asked after being fired for bucking his bosses: "But what the hell is capitalism? Look what it's done to one of its greatest proponents. It's knocked me right on the head, and I'm crawling around on the street, trying to breathe."[29]

Responsible Work

"My work is everything to me...I'd rather die for my work life than for my personal life...
"I run into people who say how much they admire what I do. It's embarrassing. I don't make any judgements about my work, whether it's great or worthless. It's just what I do best."

—high school teacher[30]

"The difficulty is not in running a crane. Anyone can run it.

Fig. 13.1
Control Work in 1970

	Number (in millions)	%
Control Employment	4.7	6.8%
Total Employment	68.2	100.0

Source: See note #27

But making it do what it is supposed to do, that's the big thing. It only comes with experience....You could never learn to run a hoist or a tower crane by reading. It's experience and common sense....

"That building we put up, a medical building. Well, that granite was imported from Canada. It was really expensive. Well, I set all this granite around there. So you do this and you know you did it good. Where somebody walks by this building you can say, 'Well, I did that.' "

—heavy equipment operator in construction[31]

Many jobs provide relatively decent pay and working conditions and provide a fair amount of responsibility for the workers who fill them. We call this *responsible* work.

Responsible jobs include administrative jobs such as accountants, supervisors, and expediters; professional and technical jobs such as teachers, lawyers, health technicians, and engineers; and craft jobs such as machinists and the building trades.

All these jobs share important similarities:

■ The pay is good. In 1980, the median annual earnings of all responsible workers was roughly $18,000.[32]

■ Many responsible workers enjoy a substantial amount of job security and stability. Some, like many teachers, earn tenure. Others, like many administrators, are often able to move up well-defined job ladders. Most craft jobs provide union job protection, although construction work is often seasonal.

■ Through this security, many responsible workers are able to advance their careers and earnings fairly steadily. One study found that responsible workers' earnings increased from ten years' experience roughly three times as rapidly as those of other workers.[33]

■ Perhaps most important, responsible workers are both permitted and required to take a large amount of responsibility for the quantity and quality of their work—deciding how to solve problems, when to change tasks, how to judge the quality of their products and services....85% of responsible workers in 1977 agreed that "it is basically my responsibility to decide how my job gets done."[34]

■ This often means that many responsible workers are also responsible for others' work—supervising, conceiving, or guiding the tasks which others perform. In 1977, nearly 40% of responsible workers reported that supervising other people was a major part of their jobs.[35] It is often the rest of us for whom they assume this supervisory role.

Because many of these characteristics make their work desirable, responsible workers tend to be much more satisfied with their jobs than other workers. They are roughly half as likely as the least responsible workers, for example, to report that they would *not* choose the same job over if they had a chance to start their careers anew.[36]

In addition to all these similarities, there is one major difference among responsible workers: different groups of their jobs involve different paths of training, hiring, and promotion. Craft jobs do not require much formal education but usually require many years of good job experience; nearly 40% of craft workers in responsible jobs require at least two years to learn their jobs. Professional and technical jobs usually require at least one educational degree beyond high school, if not several; nearly 60% of white-collar workers in responsible jobs required at least a college degree for their work. To highlight these particular differences, we refer to two groups of responsible workers—those in *professional-technical* jobs and those in *craft* jobs.

The box on this page shows that this group of jobs has become very sizable. In 1970, there were almost 18 million workers in responsible jobs, roughly a quarter of total wage-and-salary employment.

It sounds very attractive to some of the rest of us, but responsible work is not always a bed of roses.

The first problem is quite simple. Although workers in responsible jobs are given some autonomy in their work, they still work for the bosses in the end. (Remember that only 8% of wage-and-salary employees report that they have *no* supervisor.) The boss still shadows the working day, prodding for greater productivity, evaluating job performance.

The second major problem flows from the first. Bosses are always trying to find ways of gaining more and more control over work—even for employees in responsible jobs. They change rules, alter job definitions, transform working requirements...all in the pursuit of more leverage and control. Many responsible workers have experienced this assault on their job tasks in recent years—teachers, lawyers, doctors, many craft workers. A systems analyst in a computing firm reflects on these recent erosions of work responsibility:

> You know that with all the things like on-line debugging, structured code, pre-compilers, and constant machine turn-around, programmer productivity has not increased. To me it's simple: the more they give us smaller and smaller pieces of the total pie, the more we feel insignificant in the corporate structure. With jobs structured this way, why should we care?[37]

Indeed, when we look at the history of many responsible jobs, we find that corporations have often shaped the nature of the work in order to gain and maintain as much control over those kinds of workers as they could.

At the end of the nineteenth century, for example, corporations destroyed the craft system in many industries. This meant that they lost their traditional supplies of skilled workers. They tried to create substitute sources of the skills they needed—establishing special vocational institutes, sponsoring engineering programs in colleges. And they have continued to search for technologies and personnel systems which would increase their control over responsible workers as much as possible. They were clear about their objectives as early as the turn of the century. As one National Association of Manufacturers official wrote, "It is plain to see that trade schools properly protected from the domination and withering blight of organized labor are the one and only remedy for the present intolerable conditions."[38] The president of

Fig. 13.2
Responsible Work in 1970

	Number (in millions)	%
Responsible Employment	17.7	25.9%
Total Employment	68.2	100.0

Source: See note #27

the major association of engineers was equally clear about the emergent trends in 1909, "[The engineer is becoming] the tool of those whose aim it is to control men and to profit by their knowledge."[39]

Routine Work

"Believe me, there is a description of every job that anyone does at GE, a *detailed* description. There's a number for [every job], a written description, and so forth. It specifies exactly what you're supposed to do in your job."

—production worker in electrical industry[40]

"When you have a call, you fill out this IBM card....You use a special pencil so it'll go through this computer and pick up the numbers....Okay, you put that in a special slot right next to the cord light. You're ready for another one. Still you've got to watch the first one....They do keep track. How many calls you take, how well you mark your tickets, how many errors you make. You're constantly being pushed."

—18-year-old phone operator[41]

Many workers have jobs in which work is finely detailed, fairly boring, and closely supervised. These jobs nonetheless pay relatively decent wages and provide some job security. We call these *routine* jobs.

Routine jobs include many assembly jobs in manufacturing; basic production work in mining and construction; standard production work in railroads, trucking and the utilities; and many clerical jobs such as secretarial, book-keeping, programming, and general clerical jobs.

■ The most important similarity among these jobs is that they pay a lean but living wage. In 1980, the median annual earnings of workers in routine jobs was $11,200.[42]

■ A second important similarity is that routine jobs almost always

Squeeze Play

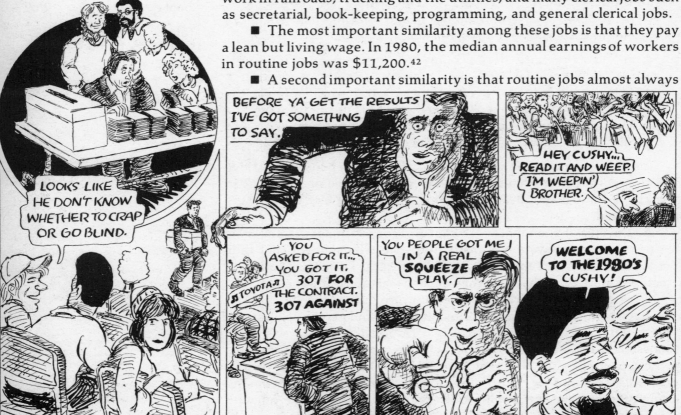

involve repetitive work at detailed tasks. Machines often enforce this job repetition. Roughly two-thirds of all routine occupations are judged by analysts to involve repetitive tasks and to experience specific supervisory instruction, and more than 60% of routine workers agree that their work is "repetitive."[43]

■ Because routine jobs involve such detailed work, they require very little experience and skill. Nearly 60% of routine jobs require less than six months to achieve *maximum* skills at that activity.[44]

■ Although routine work does not add much to people's skills, it can provide progression up a job ladder of connected routine tasks. In most unionized jobs, these steps are specified in the union contract and typically protected by seniority provisions. In non-unionized jobs, many firms provide similar job ladders (at least partly to try to prevent unionization). At non-union Polaroid, for example, there are 300 job titles in the production lines.

Because of these opportunities for job progression, routine workers stay on their jobs almost as long as responsible workers, and their earnings rise significantly over a 10-15 year period.[45]

■ Almost all routine jobs, finally, are very closely supervised. The phone company now pays one supervisor for every 6 production workers. Large non-union companies such as Polaroid keep one supervisor for every 15-20 workers.[46] And the boss has the final say: for half of all routine workers, for example, overtime is decided by the boss, not by the worker.[47]

In addition to all these important similarities; there are two important differences among routine workers.

The first is that many routine workers belong to powerful unions and many do not. Unions often add substantially to their members' earnings and job security. Although some unions have suffered an erosion of their bargaining power in recent years, many still protect their members' working conditions with some clear success. Those who do not belong to unions simply miss the chance to develop this extra power over their jobs. In 1977, 25% of routine workers belonged to unions and 75% did not.[48]

The second major difference involves the distance between the factory and the office. Factory workers, despite their job security, nonetheless face more unpleasant working conditions—facing chemicals and noise and hazardous machines which office workers seldom encounter. For example, roughly ten times as many workers in routine factory jobs report that they are exposed to health-and-safety hazards than do routine workers in clerical jobs.[49] In order to keep track of these important differences, we distinguish between routine workers in *factory* jobs and *office* jobs.

The box on this page tallies the number of routine workers in the economy in 1970. There are more routine workers than responsible workers, which should surprise few of us, and they account for more than 30% of wage-and-salary employment.

Although we have seen that routine jobs are mostly boring and subject to intensive supervisory control, many workers also find that these jobs provide a kind of blessing in disguise. Since they expect work

Fig. 13.3
Routine Work in 1970

	Number (in millions)	%
Routine Employment	21.1	31.0%
Total Employment	68.2	100.0

Source: See note #27

to be dissatisfying (see Chapter 11), many find that routine work permits them to establish a cozy kind of routine. Some even find the boredom relaxing, providing precious time for day-dreaming and casual conversation. One felter in a luggage factory explained the routine in her routine job:

> I daydream while I'm working. Your mind gets so it automatically picks out the flaws. I plan...what I'm going to have for supper and what we're gonna do for the weekend....And how to solve a grievance....You get to be automatic in what you're doing and your mind is doing something else.[50]

Dead-End Work

> "When I first worked there, I ran. They'd say, 'Copy!' and I'd run....It didn't make any difference. Then I started walking. Why the fuck should I run for them? This spring I started to shuffle. That's when the people started to complain about me....They kept telling me I should try to keep the job....I lost a year of my life working there. Was it worth it?"
>
> —former copy boy[51]

> "When I first came if you asked a question, said a single thing, the answer was always, 'Cannery workers are a dime a dozen.' Like one day [the supervisor] came over to me and he says, 'Spit it out!' Now it just happens I don't chew gum. So I says, 'Spit what out?' He says, 'Your gum.' I opened my mouth real wide. He saw I had no gum, I'm sure. But he just says 'Spit it out!' and walks away. The next day I got a pink slip."
>
> —worker in a tuna fish factory[52]

Many people are still stuck in jobs with very low wages, virtually no job security or room for advancement, and little rest from the bosses' harrassment. We call these *dead-end* jobs.

Dead-end jobs include most farm labor jobs; production work in many manufacturing firms; many sales and waiting jobs in retail stores and eating places; many temporary and low-level clerical jobs in offices; and many service jobs like attendants, personal care workers, and janitors.

■ Most of these jobs pay very low wages, much lower than in either routine or responsible work. In 1980, the median annual earnings of workers in dead-end jobs was $8,600.[53]

■ Most dead-end jobs also provide almost no job security. Firms often fail. Workers are casually fired. Unemployment rates or seasonal layoffs are often high in their industries. Workers in dead-end jobs have remained on their present jobs on average for only two-thirds the tenure of routine workers.[54]

■ This means that workers in dead-end jobs are also very likely to be unemployed workers on occasion. With so little job security and so many people looking for work, dead-end workers are especially vulnerable to spells of joblessness. Workers in dead-end jobs are considerably more likely to experience unemployment at some time during the year than workers in routine jobs.[55]

■ Not surprisingly, dead-end jobs provide virtually no room for advancement. There are few job ladders. Most dead-end workers do not receive seniority protection. Even if they stay on their jobs, they receive few rewards for their patience. Many studies have found that the earnings of workers in dead-end jobs are essentially the same no matter how many years they have toiled in the factory or office.[56]

■ Many dead-end jobs also provide virtually no benefits or other conveniences. Of workers in dead-end jobs in 1977, there were still 40% without any kind of retirement program and 55% who were not entitled to any sick leave with full pay. There were also more than 50% who said they could not decide when to take a break, and nearly 60% who must still punch in on a time clock.[57]

■ Perhaps most important, dead-end jobs provide the least workers' protection against arbitrary treatment by employers and supervisors. They are incessantly threatened with the sack. And the threats are real. Since the jobs are so easy to learn and there are so many unemployed workers at the gates, the bosses can act on nearly every whim. In 1977, 20% of dead-end workers agreed that they were "likely" to lose their present jobs, while nearly a third had been at their present jobs for only a year or less.

With all these similarities, there is one major difference among dead-end jobs. As with routine jobs, office workers face relatively less hazardous working conditions than farm workers or factory workers in dead-end jobs.[58] This leads us to distinguish between dead-end workers in the *factory* and the *office*.

The box on this page tallies workers in dead-end jobs. It turns out that these lousy jobs are the most common of the three major categories of wage-and-salary employment, accounting for 36.9 % of wage-and-salary workers in 1970.

Why So Many? We can send people to the moon but our economy cannot provide decent jobs for many people. Why are there so many dead-end jobs?

Some employers claim that they can't provide better work because available workers aren't skilled enough to perform it. There are two flaws with this argument.

First, many jobs provide decent wages and working conditions *even though they require few skills.* Most routine jobs require almost no training but still provide adequate support and security. If these jobs are good jobs despite their low skill requirements, why can't dead-end jobs provide decent employment as well?

Second, there are millions of workers in dead-end jobs with far more skills than their jobs require. In 1977, one-sixth of workers in dead-end jobs had at least some college education while half of all dead-end jobs required less than a high school degree and another 47% required no more than a high school diploma.[59]

There are three other more plausible reasons why so many jobs are dead-enders.

First, many employers simply cannot provide better work. Mil-

Fig. 13.4

Dead-End Work in 1970

	Number (in millions)	%
Dead-End Employment	24.7	36.2%
Total Employment	68.2	100.0

Source: See note #27

lions of dead-end jobs are in small firms in competitive industries—not only in manufacturing but also in stores and service jobs. These small firms cannot usually afford modern machinery and find it difficult to compete with larger firms. This makes it difficult for them to afford higher wages or improve working conditions. And they can get away with their lousy job offers because there are so many unemployed workers eager for almost any job which comes along.

The second reason for so many dead-end jobs is that many large corporations *choose* to provide dead-end work, even though they could afford otherwise, if they think they can get away with it. Many large firms have been moving to the sunbelt and overseas. In office work, many large firms maintain highly stratified job structures creating job clusters like keypunching, typing pools, and messenger work, which they deliberately isolate from better-paying and more secure jobs. As long as these jobs remain isolated, workers holding them may be less likely to demand equal pay and better working conditions.

The third reason brings us to labor unions. In many cases, labor unions have been able not only to provide better wages and security but also to upgrade basic working conditions. In other cases, they have scarcely tried.

One study compared the influence of strong and weak unions in a single industry, comparing the impact of militant union activity on longshore work on the west and east coasts. The west coast longshoremen waged militant strikes during the 1930s while the east coast union sat on its hands. The effects of the strong union action were dramatic: in 1939, the average annual earnings of the west coast longshoremen were almost twice those of the east coast workers. The west coast workers were protected by specific loading limits, had reduced their accident rates, established a grievance procedure, and worked through a hiring hall in which the dispatcher was elected by the

So What's the Story Cushy?

union. The east coast longshoremen shared none of these benefits. It is little wonder, then, that nearly half of all non-unionized workers in dead-end jobs would like to belong to a union.[60]

All three of these explanations are similar in one respect. They suggest that dead-end jobs are not the fault of individual workers. Instead, the nature of the economy—competition weakening many firms and large corporations gaining significant leverage in many areas—creates and maintains many dead-end jobs. These explanations also suggest that workers' collective action is necessary to begin the process of upgrading wages and working conditions in dead-end jobs. No wonder that so many firms have recently rushed to weaken unions and bust the ones they already have.

Unpaid Housework

"My mother always saw her job as raising children. All of a sudden her job's over. There's nothing left. She wakes up, she's fifty-two, fifty-three years old, and says: 'Who needs me any more?' "

—29-year-old vocational counsellor[61]

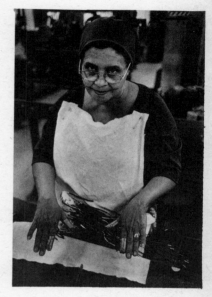

Millions of workers, mostly women, hold full-time jobs for no pay. They do most of the housework upon which we all depend. They average 40-50 hours a week on their jobs. No pay.

The government does not collect official data on this group of workers, but it is likely that there were about 33 million unpaid house-hold workers in 1970—people who held no other jobs and maintained our homes as productive contributions to the economy.

Most of us know what this work is like—particularly since so many of us try to avoid it. It is tiring and often boring. It is often unrelenting. And still no pay.

One of the most striking characteristics of unpaid housework is the isolation of those who do it. Particularly since World War II, as more and more families have moved into dispersed, single-family sub-urban homes, houseworkers are frequently by themselves, typically alone during much of the day.[62]

This means that these workers need to build alliances so we can all join together in trying to forge a better economy. And it means that their struggles for equal rights in the home are particularly exposed and especially intense. This is one group of workers in our economy which does not share the joys and frustrations of "working together." None of the quotes in that section at the beginning of this chapter were from unpaid houseworkers. Few of these workers share the experiences reflected in those commentaries.

They work nonetheless. We'll review in Chapter 15 on "Women" some of the main obstacles to improving working conditions and sharing work in the home. For the moment, it is simply important to remember that whether we do unpaid work in the home or paid work in the factory and office, we all work just as hard. As one housewife recently concluded, "That's why I can't understand this bullshit when they talk about women'll have to be forced to do the work that men do. Hell, we've been doing it all the time."[63]

Fig. 13.5
Work in the Office and Factory, 1970

	Office Work	Factory Work
Responsible Employment	35.1%	29.0%
Routine Employment	32.8	27.8
Dead-End Employment	32.1	43.1
Total	100.0	100.0

Source: See note #27

ARE THERE OTHER IMPORTANT DIFFERENCES?

We've looked at five kinds of jobs. The differences among those kinds of work seem enormous. But many of us are not used to thinking in those terms. We're used to thinking about whether a job is in an office or a factory. Or whether we work for a private firm or for the government. How do these differences compare to the ones we've already considered?

Office and Factory Work

At the beginning of the twentieth century, the distinction between blue-collar and white-collar work was critical. People who managed to land jobs in the office had much higher salaries and better working conditions. They were often training to rise to the top of their firms—working in a kind of managerial apprenticeship. White-collar workers earned roughly twice as much as the average blue-collar worker in manufacturing.[64]

This influenced many people's impressions of the desirability of jobs for many decades. Surveys have asked people to rank "desirable jobs." Studies in the 1920s, 1940s, and the early 1960s all showed the same results. People consistently ranked office jobs—even those at the lowest rungs of the office hierarchy—as more desirable than factory jobs.[65]

But the differences between factory and office work have blurred since the beginning of the century. As corporations have grown, the number of office jobs has increased rapidly. Some of those jobs still provide decent pay and working conditions. But many office jobs pay very low wages, offer little job security, and require almost no skills.

Indeed, there are essentially equal numbers of good and bad jobs in both blue-collar and white-collar work. Figure 13.5 compares the two work settings.

As the box shows, many responsible, routine, and dead-end jobs can be found in both the factory and the office. A blue-collar worker still has three chances in ten of getting a responsible job, and an office worker now has nearly one chance in three of winding up in a dead-end job.

As other data show, the differences in pay between the office and factory have narrowed. Although professional and technical workers still have a slight edge on craft workers, both operatives and laborers in blue-collar work earn more than clerical and service workers.[66]

Private and Government Work

Our jobs are mostly shaped by the efforts of corporations to reduce their costs and control our labor. Their quest for profits comes ahead of our needs as working people. Does this mean that government employees work in a kind of sanctuary, protected from the greedy capitalists?

There are some important advantages in working for the government. For one thing, unlike private corporations, the government can't move away when workers gain strength or when their wages rise. This gives government workers a certain protection from the threat of runaway shops.

For another thing, our bosses in the government are not goaded by the daily concern about their profit-and-loss sheets, constantly pushing to make up for yesterday's losses, constantly answering to their coupon-clipping owners. This can sometimes mean that our supervisors in government work may take it easy, respecting our problems and concerns.

But there are also some disadvantages in working for the government. The public sector is a kind of step-child in a capitalist economy. It only gets as much revenue to maintain its services as the private economy and its corporations allow. During the 1960s, when the economy was growing rapidly, wages and working conditions improved dramatically for many government employees. During the 1970s and early 1980s, the economy has been stagnating and corporations are pushing hard for curbs on government spending. They value their own profits more than they value many government services.

The result has been that governments are under sharp pressure to cap workers' wages and speed up their employees. For many millions of public employees, government work doesn't seem like such a sanctuary after all. The air traffic controllers have learned this lesson painfully.

These advantages and disadvantages tend to balance out. There are both good jobs and bad jobs in the government sector. And the earnings of government workers are not much different from workers' earnings in the private sector. The box on this page compares the composition of public and private work.[67]

As the box shows, there are roughly comparable numbers of responsible, routine and dead-end jobs in the private and public sectors. There is a somewhat higher percentage of responsible jobs in the public sector because of the large numbers of teachers and health workers. There is a somewhat lower percentage of dead-end jobs primarily because governments are not subject to the sharp pressures of competition which force many firms to sacrifice their workers' interests.

The differences in earnings are also slight. The major difference is that operatives, laborers, and service workers have somewhat higher annual earnings in government than in the private sector. This is primarily a result of the large numbers of very low-paid service workers in small private firms.

In general, then, workers for private firms and workers for the government are in much the same boat. The character of the economy as a whole has as much or more to do with wages and working conditions as the particular employer for whom we work. Even government workers are not immune from the pressures and insecurity which capitalist economies impose.

Fig. 13.6
Work in the Private and Public Sectors, 1970

	Private-Sector Work	Public-Sector Work
Responsible Employment	30.8%	41.3%
Routine Employment	29.9	34.0
Dead-End Employment	39.3	24.7
Total	100.0	100.0

Source: See note #27

BEATING DIVISIONS INTO UNITY?

This has been a long journey through the work of working people. We've looked at many similarities in our jobs and many differences.

We've examined a long series of facts and figures about our lives on the job. What does it tell us?

1. The first conclusion is the basic lesson of the chapter. There are, indeed, *both* similarities *and* differences among working people. The chart on this page summarizes all of the main facts about our similarities and differences. It's important to study it carefully so that we all learn more and more about who we are.

2. The second lesson seems obvious upon a moment's reflection. These differences at work spill over into the rest of our lives. Our different experiences at work are likely to generate different attitudes about our lives off the job—about politics, our communities, our family lives. Some simple examples illustrate the point:

■ Control workers are likely to side with management on many economic and political issues—because they've acquired the habit of siding with management on the job.

■ Responsible workers are bound to place high priority on issues concerning the quality of life—like ecological issues—because they have a chance to take responsibility for the quality of their working lives as well.

■ Routine workers are inclined to emphasize basic issues of economic growth and stability, since their relatively decent wages and job security depend on a rapidly growing economy.

■ Dead-end workers are likely to place a high priority on government income support programs—like public assistance and unemployment compensation—precisely because their private working experiences provide such inadequate and unreliable income support on the job.

■ Unpaid houseworkers are prone to focus on a wide variety of issues affecting family life, like abortion rights and day care benefits, because their isolation within the family enforces a focus on this major institution in their daily lives.

None of these inclinations imply that working people cannot

Fig. 13.7

Kinds of Employment In the U.S., 1970

Kind of Employment	% of Measured Employment, 1970	Approx. Median Earnings, 1980	Job Characteristics
Control Employment	6.8%	$23,000	Good pay, works directly for corporation
Responsible Employment	25.9	17,900	Decent pay, in charge of own work
Routine Employment	31.0	11,200	Good pay, reasonable job security
Dead-End Employment	36.2	8,600	Low pay, little advancement, insecure jobs
Unpaid Housework	48.2*	----	No pay, isolated, often difficult work
	148.2*		

* Unpaid housework is expressed as a % of "measured" employment in the labor force to keep numbers consistent with Figs. 13.1–13.4. The first four rows add to 100% and the unpaid housework is over and above that total.

Source: See note #27.

develop common concerns. They suggest, instead, that any program for common action among working people must pay special attention to the special needs and concerns of different groups of workers.

3. The third and final lesson is crucial. The differences in our jobs have deep roots in the character of our economic system. We've seen that many responsible jobs are being chipped away—as corporations seek more and more leverage over their most trusted employees. And we've also seen that the main differences between routine and dead-end jobs depend on the power and action of large firms and workers' organizations, not on the particular skills of the individual workers who hold those jobs.

This means that we must tackle the basic structure of the economy if we want to improve our own lives at work or reduce the divisions which weaken our power as working people. We need to reduce those divisions in order to increase our chances of challenging the corporations. And we need to challenge the corporations in order to begin changing the structures of work which underlie many of our differences. It's not easy and we can't do it by ourselves. We need to learn much more about the other differences among us and the history of our collective struggles before we can feel confident about how to proceed.

14.

Immigrants, Old and New

"All of us...are descended from immigrants."

—Franklin D. Roosevelt, 1938[1]

"You know, in the old days down here some big guy go down to the stone shed, he asked for a job, he couldn't get one, because he was Italian. Scotsmen wouldn't work with Italians. I'm talking back, fifty, sixty, seventy years ago.... You ever hear that word? Dago? Ol' Frenchmen? But now you don't hear that no more. The young people got more education."

—Italian stonecutter, immigrant to U.S. in 1901[2]

"When I started working at the hospital, I was a technical assistant—*supposedly*. Ended up to be a charwoman....They keep you in your place....They never listen to anybody, Americans, never....I do not know if it's jealousy, but West Indians have no place in America....I found so much ignorance when I came here. It was amazing."

—Trinidadian secretary, immigrant to U.S. in 1960s[3]

Working people in the United States have many common problems. Many of us have found historically that we can best solve our problems if we unite to seek common solutions.

But unity is difficult when so many hostilities and tensions divide us. We view each other uneasily across a landscape cleft by differences in color, language, religion, culture, and experience in this country. Are the canyons too wide to bridge?

Do we even need to bridge them? Can't we make it on our own? Didn't our parents, grandparents, great-grandparents (and theirs before them) manage to solve their problems through hard work and individual initiative? Why do we need to worry about overcoming our differences if we can "overcome" by ourselves?

In fact, the full history of the "American Dream" is more complicated. Not everyone who worked hard managed to climb the hillsides of individual success; the structure of the economy often placed huge boulders in their paths. And those who succeeded rarely acted entirely on their own; new immigrants to the U.S. have always found that they needed to work *together* in order to create enough space for *any* of them to succeed.

Our conclusions about individual initiative and collective action hinge, in short, on how we interpret the history of immigrants in the U.S. Who has come to this country and why? What happened once they arrived? For those who succeeded, what was the key to their success?

WAVES OF IMMIGRATION, SHIFTING ECONOMIC SANDS

"The bosom of America is open to receive not only the opulent and respectable stranger, but the oppressed and persecuted of all nations and religions...."

—George Washington, 1783[4]

"An Indian who is as bad as the white men could not live in our nation....We told them to leave us alone, and keep away from us; they followed on, and beset our paths, and they coiled themselves among us, like the snake....The white men do not scalp the head; but they do worse—they poison the heart."

—Indian chief Black Hawk upon surrender, 1832[5]

The first migrants to our country came long before Christopher Columbus or the Pilgrims. Ancestors of people we call American Indians or Native Americans probably migrated to North America from Asia more than 10,000 years ago. By the time Columbus sighted the Western World in 1492, there were apparently five "well-defined areas of Indian settlement...within the present area of the United States."[6]

The first European settlers frequently enslaved or murdered Native Americans. The well-known nineteenth-century historian Francis Parkman described some of the early explorers as "kidnappers of children and ravishers of squaws."[7] Eventually, Native Americans were forced to protect themselves either by moving westward—away from the early European settlers—or by fighting to protect their own lands, families, and ways of life. Since other Indian nations claimed and occupied lands to the west, many Indian tribes therefore had no alternative to wars of self-defense with the colonists.

This meant, from the very beginning, that the history of immi-

Workers at U.S. Steel, late 1800s.

gration was always threaded with a territorial logic. Conflict existed between the people who *already* lived in the United States and the people who came later and wanted to join them. That pattern continued long after the Native Americans had died or retreated from the paths of the European invasions. Each successive wave of immigrants to the United States found that their fortunes in the "promised land" depended *not only* on their own pluck and luck *but also* on the power and ambition of those who preceded them *and* on the structure of economic and social opportunities which greeted them on the U.S. shores. As we trace this history, we find four main waves of immigration. In each successive wave, both the characteristics of the arrivals and the character of the country they encountered changed substantially. The story of immigrants' individual initiative and collective action unfolds through these shifting tides and sands.

1. The First European Settlers

"A healthy industrious farmer is a more valuable accession to the political strength [of the United States] than a mercantile house with a large capital from a foreign country."
—a Philadelphian speaking in 1819[8]

Through the 1840s, the early settlers found an agricultural nation not yet dominated by the growth and spread of industrial capitalism. For most of them, their fortunes hinged on the space they were able to find for themselves in a huge and sprawling land.

Many of the early arrivals had little choice about their options, of course, since they were shipped to this country in slavery or servitude. By 1840, the slave population in the U.S. had climbed to 2.5 million.[9] In addition, at least half of total white immigration to the thirteen colonies before Independence arrived as "bound labor"—as indentured servants obligated to work for their masters for terms ranging from two to seven years.[10] "It was not until the 1830s," a leading labor historian concludes, "that one could confidently find an end to white servitude."[11]

From 1790 to the 1840s, most free immigrants came from northern and western Europe—from Great Britain, Germany, France, and the Low Countries. As Figure 14.1 shows, immigrants from these countries accounted for almost 80% of all immigrants between 1820 and 1840.[12]

Many who came from those countries not only arrived as free citizens but also traveled in search of freedom. Some left their homelands because of religious persecution. Others left because traditional restrictions on land ownership or craft work made it difficult (if not impossible) for them to secure economic independence. For the farmers, land was plentiful: as one manual reported in 1832, "in such a country as the United States, there is a wide field of choice, a thousand circumstances to be considered."[13] The advantages for skilled craft workers were apparently comparable. "Artisans receive better pay in America than in Europe," another guide suggested in 1830, "and can live with less exertion, and more comfort....Industrious men need never lack employment in America."[14]

Fig. 14.1

1st Wave of Immigration, 1820-1840

Area & Country	% of Total
Northwest Europe	**78.1%**
United Kingdom	13.6
Ireland	34.5
Ger., France & Low Countries	29.7
Scandinavia	0.3
So. & East. Europe	**1.2**
Americas	**7.0**
Asia	**0.1**
Other	**13.6**
Total	**100.0**

Source: See note #12

These opportunities did not create heaven on earth for everyone, however, and some of the new immigrants found grounds for complaint in their new home.

Some complained that others were trying to impede their progress to social and economic independence. During the 1820s and 1830s, for instance, many small farmers grumbled about their difficulties in getting credit from the banks to help finance their ploughing and planting. Others protested against the private wealth of the merchants in the cities, who seemed to be gaining greater power with each passing decade. One handbill in New York City complained about a judge's ruling against early trade union organization: "They have established the precedent that workingmen have no right to regulate the price of labor, or, in other words, the rich are the only judges of the wants of the poor man."[15]

Still, through the early 1840s, the vast majority of immigrants to the United States were able to achieve economic independence— working for themselves, controlling their own economic lives. Their success did not depend upon some special skills and ingenuity which they marshalled and which remained beyond the reach of later generations of immigrants. Rather, their continuing independence built upon an economic structure in the U.S. which largely supported the ambitions of small farmers and artisans. There was apparently enough economic space for most immigrants to enjoy a place in the sun.

2. Economic Refugees, Industrial Shadows

"This was goin' down six hundred years—imagine being under the [English] thumb for that length of time! But one consolation, when America opened up. It took an awful lot of needy people here and it opened a gap for them, like God done at sea."

—Irish immigrant in 1903, remembering the earliest Irish immigrations[16]

"The worst part of the whole business is this. It brutalizes a man. You can't help it. You start in to be a man, but you become more and more a machine, and pleasures are few and far between....It drags you down mentally and morally."

—immigrant steelworker, 1894[17]

After the 1840s, immigrants' experiences began to change rapidly and dramatically. Millions fled capitalism in Europe. But industrial capitalism was sweeping across the "promised land" as well. While millions came to the U.S. for their place in the sun, the huge factories and banks of the industrial cities began to cast long shadows across the immigrants' dreams. The immigrant experience would never be the same.

Political and economic events in Europe helped spur the first waves of this new stage of immigration. The spread of industry and the commercialization of agriculture drove out the poor. As a Norwegian peasant poet complained, "Farewell, thou Mother Norway, now I must leave thee!/...All too sparing were thee in providing food/ For the throng of thy laborers/ Though thou givest more than enough/ to thy well-schooled sons."[18]

Even for the million or so Irish who fled the potato famine of the mid-1840s, more basic economic conditions were the underlying cause of their distress. When the potato blight first struck in 1845, the peasants were already vulnerable from growing landlord pressures— their coffers low, living far too close to the margin. As one parish priest reported in 1847: "The people...had some little means, some resources up to the present. Those are all gone now for the purchase of food; and famine, with its invariable attendant, disease, is making fearful inroads on the unfortunate victims of both."[19]

Compared to these European conditions, the rapid growth and democratic traditions of the United States seemed attractive. Millions came. The numbers tell the bare facts of this stage of immigration. Between 1841 and 1890, 14.6 million immigrants arrived in the United States—a pace nearly eight times more rapid than the two previous decades. As Figure 14.2 shows, these vast numbers of immigrants came from essentially the same western and northern European countries as in the previous period. More than 80% came from England, Germany, Ireland, the Low Countries, France, Switzerland, and Scandinavia. Many also came from Canada and a substantial number also came, for the first time, from Asia—mostly from China.

For growing numbers of these new arrivals, unfortunately, their dreams of economic independence never materialized. Increasingly from the 1840s through the 1890s, industrial capitalism posed greater and greater obstacles to their economic ambitions.

Most important, many never escaped the huge industrial cities at which they disembarked. Many had to work in the factories while they tried to save enough to establish themselves. But wages in the factories were so low that workers had enough trouble just surviving, much less putting money aside for a farm or a trade. Surveys in the 1870s and 1880s typically found that about 40% of families earned *less* than what was necessary to enjoy basic necessities. Almost all the rest had incomes "which, in good times, clung precariously above the poverty level."[20]

As immigration continued and economic growth faltered in the 1870s and 1880s, millions in the cities felt the common press of their number and their poverty. Their pride and ambition was a meager defense against the disease and hunger which spread like epidemics in the industrial cities. "There are no places within the settled portions of their city," a public official in Boston concluded, "...where the low-paid toiler can find a home of decency and comfort."[21]

Some more-affluent citizens blamed the immigrants for their plight, of course, chiding them for their "ignorance, indolence, and immorality."[22] But growing numbers of immigrants understood that they suffered from circumstances largely beyond their control. They were caught in a powerful undertow which kept dragging them out to sea. It didn't matter how powerfully they tried to swim back to shore.

Immigrants reacted to this powerful undertow in two somewhat different ways.

Fig. 14.2
2nd Wave of Immigration, 1841-1890

Area & Country	% of Total
Northwest Europe	**81.0%**
United Kingdom	18.1
Ireland	21.9
Ger., France & Low Countries	33.8
Scandinavia	7.2
So. & East. Europe	**8.3**
Americas	**7.8**
Canada	7.0
Asia	**2.0**
Other	**0.9**
Total	**100.0**

Source: See note #12

First, many immigrants organized on their own, by ethnic group, to provide mutual support and to help their members with the problems of basic survival. Through their families, their churches and their social organizations, as one historian reports, "the immigrants turned to one another for assistance....The later arrivals profited by the mistakes and experiences of those who had come before them."[23]

This tendency was counter-balanced by the second kind of response. While many ethnic groups naturally relied on their own internal ties, immigrants were nonetheless thrown together by the labor market in which they all struggled to stay afloat. Most immigrants were increasingly likely to work in similar kinds of jobs, blending "into the scenery with amazing rapidity."[24]

These common circumstances led to many common efforts to improve their working and living conditions. During the 1880s, for example, thousands of immigrants from many different countries joined the Knights of Labor, hoping for industrial unions to improve their common lot. Many farmers, regardless of their ethnic origins, supported the Populists' political challenge against the financial elite. The preamble to the national convention of the new People's Party in 1892 broadcast this discontent clearly: "The fruits of the toil of millions are boldly stolen to build up colossal fortunes....From the same prolific womb of governmental injustice we breed two classes—paupers and millionaires."[25]

The immigrants had learned a painful lesson. The promised land did not provide a season's ticket to easy street. Economic forces dominated the individual efforts of millions of immigrants. Hundreds of thousands of immigrants began to reply with the unity and collective action which those economic forces required.

3. New Origins, Corporate Obstacles

"I am Polish man. I want to be American citizen. But my friends are Polish people. I must live with them....I stay all the time with them—at home, in the shop, anywhere."
                                        —Polish immigrant, 1913[26]

"[We've employed Swedes] only for this week. Last week, we employed Slovaks. We change about among different nationalities and languages. It prevents them from getting together. We have the thing systematized. We have a luncheon each week of the employment managers of the large firms of the Chicago district....It is wonderful to watch the effect."
                                        —personnel officer at Swift & Co., 1904[27]

After the early 1890s, the experience of immigration changed once again. Divisions among ethnic groups intensified. Large corporations loomed over those divisions like bettors at a cockfight, creating and promoting ethnic rivalry. The scars of those rivalries still remain.

This stage of immigration began with a dramatic shift in the national origins of the immigrants themselves. Until 1890, as Figures 14.1 and 14.2 showed, the vast majority of immigrants to the United States had come from western and northern Europe. After 1890, immigrants began to come from southern and eastern Europe—from Italy, Greece, Poland, Russia and other Baltic, Slavic, and Balkan nations. As Figure 14.3 shows, this shift in countries of origin is reflected in the data for immigration from 1890 to 1940: whereas only 8% of U.S. immigrants between 1840 and 1890 had come from southern and eastern Europe, 55% of immigrants between 1890 and 1940 came from those areas.

Economic conditions in those countries apparently stimulated the sudden surge of immigration after 1890. Commercial farming and speculation were spreading across agricultural land. Serfs were being freed; land prices were rising; economic insecurity was pushing people off their farms. Many fewer of this new generation of workers came from industrial and craft backgrounds than in the previous periods.

When these new migrants arrived, they confronted many of the same obstacles to economic independence which earlier migrants had faced. Industry was growing but competition among workers kept wages low. Workers crowded into the largest industrial cities and found escape from the factories difficult. One Italian worker who arrived in Massachusetts in 1904 recalled his early childhood:

> Everybody lived close. Kids died of diptheria, measles, tuberculosis. In them days, they were poor, believe me....All you could hear was women cryin' because a child died....I know whole families who were completely wiped out.[28]

Something else had changed, however, which fundamentally shaped the new immigrants' experiences. The corporate merger movement of 1898-1902 created huge new "combinations" of companies—firms with far greater assets and market power than ever before. Taking advantage of their resources, these firms began to go after their rebellious employees. One of their principal strategies was ethnic "divide-and-conquer." They hired by ethnic group and played one group against another—spreading rumours in different languages, blaming one nationality for another group's problems, using some particular group as strike-breakers. As the U.S. Immigration Commission concluded in 1911:

> In many cases the conscious policy of the employers [is] mixing the races in certain departments and divisions,...preventing concert of action on the part of the employees....[Firms] realized that by placing the recent immigrants in these positions they would break the strength of unionism for at least a generation.[29]

The combination of low wages, employment insecurity, and employers' manipulation of ethnic divisions led almost inevitably to a dramatic increase in tensions among ethnic groups after the turn of the century.

In the east, "native" U.S. workers began to demand restrictions against immigration. "I see employment furnished to foreigners every day at good pay where Americans are not wanted," a worker with generational roots in the U.S. wrote in 1912. "I have reached the limit. I have been out of work until I can stand it no longer."[30]

Fig. 14.3

3rd Wave of Immigration, 1891-1940

Area & Country	% of Total
Northwest Europe	**26.5%**
United Kingdom	6.6
Ireland	4.9
Ger., France & Low Countries	9.3
Scandinavia	5.7
So. & East. Europe	**56.3**
Poland, Other Central	18.5
Italy, Other Southern	22.5
Russia, Other Eastern	15.3
Americas	**14.0**
Canada	8.6
Asia	**2.7**
Other	**0.5**
Total	**100.0**

Source: See note #12

In the west, similar tensions fanned prejudice against Asians, particularly the Japanese. Between 1900 and 1906, movements emerged to ban all Asians from employment, to boycott oriental businesses, and to segregate Asian students in the public schools.

Once started, the tension and hatred acquired a momentum of its own. In 1913, for example, an Italian was lynched by a mob in Illinois and in 1915 a Jew was murdered by a mob in Georgia.[31] Some of the most intense "nativist" movements against immigrants spread in the midwest and south: after World War I, the Ku Klux Klan had more than five million members pledged against both blacks and other "foreign elements."

The irony, of course, was that "natives" had themselves been immigrants. All that distinguished the "new" and "old" immigrant groups was the haze of time—which blurred "native" workers' memories of their earlier arrivals. In that haze, prejudice flourished.

Its spread made virtually inevitable, among other consequences, the growth of immigration restriction legislation, culminating in the Immigration Act of 1924. This statute imposed annual immigration quotas on immigration from all European, African, and Asian nations. (The Americas were excluded.)

Immigrants responded to these manipulations, divisions, and tensions as in the previous decades.

The first response involved ethnic self-reliance. Various ethnic groups formed even stronger associations for their own support and advancement, building neighborhood associations, working through their churches, relying on family ties. Immigrants' recollecting this period remember these ties clearly:

"I was born into a self-contained Yiddish ghetto. Though we were the majority, the ghetto also housed Poles, Russians, Irish and Italians. All of us had our special places, dictated to us by our faces, our speech, our jobs, our music, dances, and books—and, of course, our religion and country of origin. Each one lived in a ghetto within a ghetto. Did we mind it? We wanted to be among our own people, our own language, our own religion...."

—a Jew in New York[32]

"With so much [discrimination] against 'em at that time they decided that they couldn't get justice anywhere, even if they were right. Certain people began to think what should we do? They organized this [Hellenic Association]. This same thing happened with all the nationalities at that time."

—a Greek in Massachusetts[33]

"[My father] knew that American public schools would take care of our English, but he had to be the watchdog to nurture our Chinese knowledge....In the midst of a foreign environment, he clung to a combination of the familiar old standards and what was permissible in the newly learned Christian ideals.

—a Chinese in San Francisco[34]

Fig. 14.4
4th Wave of Immigration, 1941-1970

Area & Country	% of Total
Northwest Europe	**29.1%**
United Kingdom & Ireland	9.5
Northern Europe	19.6
So. & East. Europe	**15.6**
Poland, USSR & Eastern	4.5
Italy, Other Southern	11.1
Americas	**44.7**
Mexico	11.9
Caribbean	9.4
Latin America	9.4
Canada	14.0
Asia	**8.8**
Other	**1.7**
Total	**100.0**

Source: See note #12

Immigrants also found, as they had earlier, that they needed to organize *across* ethnic lines in order to protect their interests and improve their lives.

In the first decade of this century, many southern and eastern European immigrants joined to support the Industrial Workers of the World (IWW), for example, which emphasized the need for industrial unions to overcome the divisions which were weakening workers' power against employers. One of the most dramatic signs of this recognition came in the famous strike of textile workers in Lawrence, Massachusetts in 1912. Employers had sought to keep the ethnic groups—particularly Italians and Poles—divided by spreading rumors in their different languages. Eventually, when the employers cut wages drastically, the workers discovered that they had to fight together. As one contemporary account of the strike reported:

> Out of the Everett Mill they rushed, these hundreds of peaceful workers, now aroused, passionate and tense....Men, women and Children—Italians, Poles, Syrians—all races, all creeds, already aroused to action....ran through the thousands of feet of floor space, shouting 'Strike! Strike!'[35]

The prejudice against newer arrivals by "native" residents and the imprisonment of many IWW and radical leaders during and after World War I set back these movements for a time. But when the Great Depression of the 1930s arrived, as we shall see in later chapters, ethnic groups discovered once again that they needed each other in order to accomplish even the most basic individual and group objectives. Once again, they found they could not go it alone.

4. American Origins, American Destinies?

"I was born in Harlem, and I live downtown. And I am a migrant, for if a migration is anything, it is a state of mind....I am very much a migrant because I am still not quite at home in America."

—second-generation Puerto Rican in New York[36]

"I see all kinds of new immigrants starting out all over again, trying to work their way into the system. They're going through new battles, yet they're old battles. They want to share in the American Dream. The stream never ends."

—former head of immigration service, 1980[37]

From 1931 through 1945, during the Great Depression and World War II, immigration slowed to a trickle. During the prosperous decades after World War II, immigration resumed its rapid pace. The strictures of the 1924 Immigration Act shaped the composition of this postwar generation of arrivals. Immigration from Europe and Asia was limited to an annual total of 150,000—with country quotas still pegged to their respective ethnic proportions of the domestic population. Because the economy was expanding rapidly, the labor market lured millions of "migrants" from several new sources outside of Europe and Asia.

Three main groups responded to the siren's call.

1. The first group involved people who were already, in one sense or another, "Americans." Millions of U.S. women left their homes and traveled into the labor market for the first time, filling the kinds of jobs which earlier generations of immigrants had cornered. Millions of U.S. blacks left southern farms and traveled to the cities in search of whatever work the urban economy could offer. And millions of Puerto Ricans took advantage of their special Commonwealth status to head north, as one of them described the trek, because "he thinks he can make a buck."[38] While these working people played an important part in the history of postwar immigration, they also share another kind of common condition—as victims of continuing discrimination. Because of that common experience, we discuss their experiences separately in the next two chapters on "Women" and "Blacks and Hispanics."

2. A second group came from outside the United States. Since the Immigration Act of 1924 permitted immigration from the Americas without specific numerical limit, there was for many years a dramatic shift in the composition of legal, measured immigration. Figure 14.4 presents the proportions of immigrants between 1941 and 1970 coming from different regions. Only 44% of immigrants now came from European countries. More than half of immigrants between 1941 and 1970 came from Mexico, the Caribbean, Latin America, and Asia— from continents which had weighed lightly in the three earlier waves of U.S. immigration.

3. The third group followed in the shadows of the second. By the time the economy was booming in the 1960s, the permits granted by the government fell far below the economy's thirst for new labor supplies. Increasingly through the 1960s and 1970s, "illegal" immigrants outnumbered their "legal" counterparts. No one knows exactly how many undocumented workers have crossed U.S. borders in recent years, but reasonable estimates suggest an annual volume of something like 800,000—at least twice the levels permitted and counted by the government.[39] If these numbers are correct, total foreign immigration to the United States in the late 1960s probably equalled or exceeded the previous record flows during the peak years from 1905 to 1914.[40] Sneaking across borders at night, swimming the boundary lakes and rivers, brandishing forged documents—millions came despite "legal restrictions." They sought, as had millions before them, a smoother economic journey than their own countries provided.

None of these three groups enjoyed easy or immediate success, facing low wages, unemployment, and crowded cities. Millions shared, in short, the fears and fates of all the earlier generations of immigrants. While they struggled to gain a foothold on the hillside of economic success, millions discovered once again that the footing was slippery and treacherous. As one Hispanic migrant concluded, "Dick and Jane were dead, man."[41]

But differences in the experiences of this last wave of immigrants are more important for our story than similarities. Postwar immigrants suffered three important handicaps which earlier generations of immigrants had not encountered. For many, these handicaps dragged like weights around their ankles.

1. *Widening Rungs on the Ladder.* One important difference grew out of the labor market structure facing the postwar immigrants. Until World War II, the economy had tended to make most jobs more and more similar. Although immigrants usually entered the factories on the bottom rungs, the distances between the rungs were growing narrower. Even the unemployed had a chance. "If a foreman was short of hands," as a personnel manager described the practice in 1922, "he went to the gate, looked over the crowd, picked out the man he wanted, and hired him."[42]

Increasingly after World War II, the distance between rungs began to grow wider. Millions of unionized and professional workers took advantage of their collective power and individual skills to bargain for greater security and better working conditions. Their jobs bestowed privileges and opportunities which workers in "dead-end" jobs—as we called them in Chapter 13—could neither enjoy nor win for themselves. Dead-end jobs remained like those jobs for which the foreman "looked over the crowd." Routine and responsible jobs began to provide their occupants with security, power and prerogatives which earlier generations would scarcely recognize.

Those who have arrived more recently are therefore more isolated when they start at the bottom. The distances are barely perceptible to the workers affected, but the impact of that gulf is eventually felt. One Puerto Rican recently described this impact on the postwar generation of his youth:

> Into an ancient neighborhood came pouring four to five times more people than it had been designed to hold. Men who came running at the promise of jobs were jobless as the war ended. They could not see the economic forces that ruled their lives....[43]

2. *Where Do You Run To?* Earlier groups of immigrants rarely "made it" in their own lives. But they were "brought up in an environment," as one child of that earlier generation puts it, "with the idea that each generation wants something better for their kids."[44]

There was room for "their kids," in part, because the economy provided plenty of jobs for new labor market entrants. Working hours were declining, which meant that available work was shared among a continually widening pool of younger and older workers.

After World War II, working hours no longer declined, which meant that potential employment was not being shared as widely as it had been in earlier decades. The numbers reveal this difference clearly.

■ Between 1902 and 1948, average hours worked in manufacturing fell from 55 hours to 40 hours a week. From 1948 to 1968, average weekly hours didn't change at all, holding steady at almost exactly 40 per week.[45]

■ This meant that postwar economic growth generated far fewer jobs than in the earlier period. Between 1948 and 1968, the economy was providing *only two jobs for every five generated by the same amount of growth during the first half of the century.*[46]

■ Younger workers felt the effects most severely. Between

1948 and 1968, the ratio of teenage unemployment rates to adult unemployment rates increased by two-thirds.[47]

Earlier generations had assumed that jobs would be available for their children, in short, and plenty of jobs were there for the taking. "That's been my whole life," as one older worker put it in the late 1960s, "trying to get enough money ahead so my boys'd get what I didn't have....There is something wonderful when you think of [their success]."[48]

More recent migrants have found it much more difficult to sustain those hopes. As a black newspaperman reflects on the postwar period,

> Well, we are north now. We are at the Promised Land. The Promised Land has less hope now than it had....The catch is I might get a good job, but the community I'm living in is going to be so overwhelmed by other people's poverty that I won't be able to enjoy it....There simply aren't enough jobs to go around.[49]

3. *Hiding Out from Immigration.* "Undocumented" workers do not have the basic political rights of U.S. citizens. Rather than fighting their disadvantages through the political arena, they must continually hide in fear of the immigration agents.

This handicap is crucial. Earlier generations of immigrants won many of their most important battles through the government—winning the right to form unions, pushing for the continuing expansion of the public school system, providing a critical electoral base for aspiring politicians.

There are probably about 8 million "undocumented" workers in the United States today.[50] Including their families, at least 12-15 million people are living in the shadows of the law, foreign-born but without legal sanction or legal rights.

This legal impotence is chilling. Undocumented workers, when

"The Promised Land has less hope than it had. There simply aren't enough jobs to go around."

—black editor, 1980

---

they dare to speak at all, describe continuing intimidation and harrassment. One undocumented worker reports his experiences:

> My wife and I have worked in many places....There are no benefits, no deductions, no union....The places, like us who work in them, don't officially exist....The possibility of being deported, and the fear of it, is for all of us the central fact. If immigration shows up at your front door, you must be ready to crawl out the back window....You can never take it for granted that your home today will be your home tomorrow.[51]

If uncovered, undocumented workers face uncertainty and occasional beatings. A journalist recounts one Jamaican's experience:

> The INS put Buckham on a plane to deport him to Jamaica. But the Jamaican authorities didn't accept his papers and they sent him back....Two days later, center guards came to deport him again.

Provided with no new documents, he balked. He still has a hole in his front teeth where guards smashed his dentures out of his mouth....After five months in the deportation center, Buckham finally managed to meet his $1000 bond. He's now awaiting an immigration trial to determine what country, if any, he belongs to.[52]

The government officials are often unsympathetic. As one INS deportation official comments: "They broke our laws. We would be more inclined to help and accommodate them as human beings if they had not already been helping themselves to a drink of our water. After all, what kind of treatment would we get in *their* countries? Have you seen 'Midnight Express'?"[53]

Reviewing the Immigrant Experience

What do we make of this long and twisting history of immigration to the United States? What lessons can we learn about those who have come and their experiences once they have arrived?

Every wave of immigrants seems to have shared five common experiences:

1. Every immigrant group faced some *new* experiences; none precisely repeated the previous group's journey.

2. Every immigrant group has always entered the U.S. economy as *outsiders*. No one ever got the red carpet treatment.

3. Every group since the 1840s has begun its stay in the United States in *poverty and insecurity.* Conditions in late nineteenth-century immigrant neighborhoods and the urban ghettos of the 1960s and 1970s were surprisingly similar.

4. These initial experiences forced immigrants to *fight* for their ambitions and livelihoods. None could wait idly for the gravy train to arrive at the station.

5. In waging those battles for survival and a better life, immigrants have always relied on both their own ethnic and racial strengths *and* on unity with other groups of working people. Isolation and divisions always hurt; connections and unity always helped.

These similarities help point to the most important differences. As each immigrant group stepped across the U.S. borders, they encountered different economic tendencies which affected their ability *both* to advance their own objectives *and* to achieve unity with others.

■ *The height of the economic hurdles confronting different groups of immigrants increased from one stage to the next.* From the first wave to the second, spreading economic insecurity raised the barriers to economic independence. After 1900, these difficulties were further compounded by the scope and effectiveness of corporate "divide-and-conquer" tactics. After World War II, the widening distances among different kinds of jobs and the more sluggish growth of employment confronted newcomers with even more serious obstacles to economic success.

■ At least partly as a result, *successive waves of immigrants encountered changing political and legal obstacles.* The first wave avoided native hostility by moving past established settlements to the frontiers. The second wave encountered more serious hostility but these suspicions often melted as immigrants and natives were quickly mixed together by their common ethnic heritage, common working conditions, and labor market experiences. For the third wave, after 1900, continuing job competition and corporate manipulations generated increasingly strident opposition to newer immigrants—eventually resulting in violence and the restrictive legislation of the 1920s. After World War II, as the decades passed, growing proportions of immigrants faced the intractable political problems of coping while remaining "undocumented" and largely invisible.

■ These differences meant that *immigrants developed different methods of struggle for their places in the U.S. sun.* The first wave accomplished much on its own. The second wave combined its efforts spontaneously, spilling out into the streets in protest. The third wave, facing much higher hurdles, formed much stronger ethnic ties and, eventually through the industrial unions, much more organized and powerful methods of uniting for common objectives. The history of the fourth wave's struggles is not yet complete. The example of the black civil rights movement suggests that isolation and weakness in the modern world also leads to organization and protest. Every other immigrant group has had to rely on similar collective movements to "make it" in the U.S.; recent struggles for civil rights and equal opportunities are following a long and honorable tradition.

WHAT ABOUT RAGS-TO-RICHES?

Q: "To what do you attribute your success?"
A: "Just hard work, that's all....You've got to have a challenge, feel inside of you that really you *could* do it without anyone else discouraging you....You have to have a dream of what you want to be. You can find it. It will take time, like everything else takes time, the sooner you dream the better."

—Greek immigrant to the U.S. in 1912[54]

Those may be the lessons of history, some may respond, but aren't conditions different and better today? Isn't there plenty of room for the modern self-improvers who dare to dream and dare to succeed?

These questions are continually fed to us by the DUPEsters. There is a notion in the United States, introduced in school and reinforced by advertising, that the race goes to the smartest and the most persistent.

This impression builds on several critical assumptions which deserve careful re-examination: 1) The economy rewards native intelligence. 2) The economy rewards schooling achievement. 3) The economy rewards hard work. 4) Family handicaps matter less and less for those who struggle to overcome them.

It turns out that each of these assumptions is only partly valid. They are just true enough so that our daily experiences provide some examples which seem to confirm them. But they are just misleading enough so that those who remain content to apply their practical lessons take terrible risks with their own futures. The modern "rags-to-riches" manual provides a shaky pole for those who want to vault to fame and fortune.

The flaws in the manual emerge if we look at each of its arguments in turn.

Riches to the Smartest?

Those who earn more appear to be smarter—they have higher IQs. But the main reason for this is that they come from more affluent families in the first place: IQ tests measure certain kinds of intelligence which affluent families encourage in their children.[55] And people from the most affluent families have huge advantages over children from the poorest families in the climb to the top of the labor market.

This means that even smart kids from poor families have little chance of "making it." A boy with average IQ from one of the most affluent families is more than *seven times* more likely to climb into the

This Bud's For You.

top fifth of the adult income distribution than a boy with the same IQ from one of the poorest families.[56]

What this suggests is that the family you come from matters much more than your test scores. Suppose an average boy from one of the poorest families could "choose" between acquiring "average intelligence" or joining a family with average affluence. The family-switching strategy would be ten times more effective as a way of "making it" than the "get smarter" strategy.[57] Don't study vocabulary, kid; trade in your parents. That's a measure of how much more important family background is than childhood intelligence in affecting our fortunes in the labor market.

Riches to the Best Achievers?

The achievement myth also suggests that some people learn more, and therefore get farther in school and the labor market than those who laze about, wasting precious opportunities. This suggests that nearly anybody could improve their economic chances if they learned more either in school or on the job.

It is true that people who earn more have stayed longer in school. The problem is that performance both in school and on the job relates only dimly to how much people have learned or how much they can "contribute" to their employers.

■ Studies of high school students with comparable intelligence and achievement scores have found that those who are rated as "creative," "aggressive," and "independent" by their fellow students *are actually penalized* in their grade point averages. Students who are judged to have characteristics like "predictability," "dependability," "punctuality," and who respond to authority are rewarded in their grade point averages. Those who "behave well" in school are much more likely to get higher grades, in short, than those who show imagination or initiative.[58]

■ Studies of workers' success on the job confirm some of these impressions. Among those with the same levels of education, according to one comprehensive survey, achievement test scores "have virtually no effect" on what kinds of jobs people get when they leave school.[59] Once on the job, people who play by the rules fare much better than those who learned a lot in school or exhibit imagination and initiative. Studies have found, for example, that "creative" and "independent" workers are penalized on the job, and that workers' "dependability" and "adherence to rules" matter much more than any other factors in determining their job success.[60]

The conclusion seems decisive. If people want to improve their economic fortunes, they will improve their chances more if they follow

the rules than if they study hard and learn more. As one recent review of the evidence concluded, "neither how well students do in school nor the quality of education they receive is the critical factor."[61] Indeed, if they show too much "creativity," "independence," or "aggressiveness," they may reduce their chances of success. Play by the rules. Don't make waves. And some of you may get ahead.

Riches to the Hardest Workers?

Maybe the reason that those who play by the rules get ahead is that they work harder? Perhaps the rags-to-riches myth at least explains the apparent rewards for diligence?

We can check this maxim by looking at people once they begin working. If hard work makes a big difference, we should find that some of those who end up on top "made it" because they worked harder during their careers and climbed over those who were resting on their laurels. But it turns out that differences among people when they *begin* working explain virtually all of their later success. Although the numbers are tricky, people's characteristics when they enter the labor force—such as their family background and schooling—probably explain close to *ten times* as much of their eventual job success as their diligence after they begin working.[62]

What about people's diligence before they enter the labor market? Don't the good jobs go to those who aim the highest when they're still in school? Studies find little evidence for that claim. The most complete recent study found that high school students'"aspirations" play a "very limited role" in influencing their eventual success.[63] And look at the kinds of "aspirations" and behavior which have even "limited" effect. Those who read more in high school do not get better jobs and actually earn *less* as adults, other things equal, than those who read less. In contrast, those who "date more" earn relatively more as adults than their less social peers.[64] The "glad-handers" are better rewarded than the "eggheads," it appears, but that doesn't seem to have much to do with working harder in school.

Easier to Make It Than Before?

These results cast serious doubt on the rags-to-riches myths. But perhaps they're biased because they look at the job success of people from earlier generations when family background mattered so much. Hasn't the spread of college brought the American Dream much closer to fulfillment for many children from less affluent families?

There is no evidence for this assurance. According to the best available studies, the handicaps of the poor haven't changed since capitalism first dominated the United States in the 1840s. Studying the first 100 years of that period, one historian found that the influence of class background on children's fortunes "was nearly identical for youths born at any time between 1840 and 1930"[65] A major study of the more recent period found that the "influence of social origins has

WE'RE GOING NOW TO A LIVE REPORT FROM DEIRDRE FRENCH WHO'S WITH CUSHY BEALE, THE PRESIDENT OF F.I.E.R.C.E. UNION LOCAL 597

MR. BEALE... DID YOU **KNOW** THIS WAS **COMING?**

DEE-DRA... THIS WAS OUTTA LEFT FIELD **WE** WERE BARGAINING IN **GOOD FAITH.** YOU KNOW... **YOU** MAKE AN OFFER- **THEY** REFUSE-YOU DISCUSS- THEY COUNTER-YOU GO **AWAY-** YOU COME BACK-YOU GO AWAY **AGAIN...**

BUT THIS... **THIS** IS SOMETHING **ELSE!**

IT SEEMS INDICATIVE OF A **TREND** IN CORPORATE-LABOR RELATIONSHIPS. LIKE IN THE **PATCO** STRIKE DEE-DRA... **WELCOME TO THE 1980's!**

remained constant since World War I."[66] Another comprehensive review of the past 140 years finds that "there is no evidence of a lessening of the economic importance of family background on life chances."[67] A child from a poor family is no more likely to turn his rags into riches today than he was before the Civil War.

So Who Does Get Ahead?

The rags-to-riches myths apparently don't reveal very much about economic success in the United States. We can see why if we take another kind of look at economic success and who gets it.

The most important influence on economic success is the job tier in which people begin and continue to work. And here, the evidence on influences seems fairly clear. People from the most affluent families acquire the kind of training at home and in school which gives them the best shot at the best jobs. People from working-class families have the kinds of experience and connections which help them find and keep routine jobs. And people from poor and recent immigrant families are most likely to get stuck in what's left—dead-end jobs.[68]

The result is that children who come from poor families must work miracles to improve their chances of competing with those from affluent families. A recent study of childrens' futures reached sober conclusions:

> In the United States, as elsewhere, it is a penalty to be born poor. It is a compounding penalty to be born to parents with little education. It is a further penalty to be born to parents who are frequently unemployed and whose employment opportunities are limited to relatively uninteresting, dead-end jobs....Together, [these penalties] produce the odds that make [an affluent child's] probable future a vista rich with possibilities and [a poor child's] future a small door into a small room.[69]

"A poor child's future is a small door into a small room."

—study of children in U.S.

CAN WE MAKE IT ON OUR OWN?

"Once a policeman asked me if I liked school and I said sometimes I did and then he said I was wasting my time there, because you don't need a lot of reading and writing to pick the crops, and if you get too much of schooling, he said, you start getting too big for your shoes, and cause a lot of trouble, and then you'll end up in jail pretty fast and never get out if you don't watch your step—never get out."

—child of migrant worker in late 1960s[70]

"When I first came here I was so excited about coming to this wonderful country that I said, 'Oh, my God, it's going to be so different'....I was like anybody else, brainwashed. But now that I have learned the language and I can communicate...I see what goes on, I say, it's not such a wonderful country, it's just a big country, that's all, where everybody's a number. You are no longer a person."

—Guatemalan immigrant in the 1960s[71]

Immigrants have always sought to improve their conditions through self-reliance. Since the 1840s when capitalism began to dominate this country, however, self-reliance has never been enough. People have always needed to join together to improve their chances for success. And the structure of the economy has always had a big influence on the ways in which they found it necessary to join together.

The lessons hold today. People's family backgrounds—characteristics over which they have no personal control—have more to do with their economic chances than their intelligence or achievement or diligence. Since people can't control their family backgrounds, there are only two alternatives for less advantaged people trying to improve their working and living conditions. One would involve their fighting directly with those from more advantaged backgrounds for the relatively few good jobs which the economy provides. The other would involve joining together to change the structure of the economy so that many more decent jobs were available for everyone. The next three chapters explore these alternatives further.

The first alternative is subtly encouraged by large corporations, who have always pitted one working group against another. One of the main ways in which working people are pitted against each other in the 1980s involves "affirmative action"—which appears to require that white men step aside so that women and minority workers can have a shot at better jobs. Chapters 15 and 16 look at the causes of inequalities by sex and race and at possible strategies for overcoming those divisions.

The second alternative involves struggles for unity and power. Many working people feel that such unity and power is difficult if not impossible. And yet, working people have won scores of important victories over the past two centuries. Chapter 17 studies that history of "resistance and struggle," trying to uncover the keys to unity and power for all working people—regardless of our race, sex, creed, nation, or how recently we happen to have arrived on these shores.

"[The company] had a lot of women that were really pushed around a lot before the assorting department was eliminated....That was management's way of keeping them from promoting....You take a corporation the size of U.S. Steel. I've learned you just really can't buck them [by yourself]. It's a lot of work....And it takes an organization, not an individual....At first when we started to organize, the men thought it was funny. But I think they're beginning to see that we mean business."

—steelworker in Indiana[1]

Women

Inequalities and conflicts between men and women pose especially difficult barriers to unity and effective action among working people. The evidence of these conflicts surrounds us: debate over the Equal Rights Amendment and abortion rights, tension over affirmative action, rapists' physical assaults on women....

Why are these divisions by sex so deep and difficult to overcome?

At one level, there is an obvious answer: women suffer severe discrimination in the economy and are angry about the inequalities they constantly confront. The issues cannot be avoided.

The evidence of these inequalities is obvious. Two comparisons tell much of the story.

■ Women workers totalled 41% of all workers in the U.S. economy in 1970. But they accounted for only 14% of all managers and supervisors. Only 45% of white men worked in routine and dead-end jobs, while 82% of all women employees worked in routine and dead-end jobs.[2]

■ Women workers earn much less than white men. And this is not because many women have less education or work part-time more frequently. Even if we compare workers of the *same age* with the *same levels of education* who worked *full-time for the entire year* in 1977, substantial inequalities in income remain. Even with this controlled a comparison, white women earned only 53% as much as white men, black women 73% as much as black men, and hispanic women 60% as much as hispanic men. No matter how we make the comparisons, the economy does not reward women's labor as highly as men's.[3]

Where do these inequalities come from? What maintains them? Why is there so much resistance to reducing them?

THE SECOND SEX AT HOME AND AT WORK?

"The male supervisor has decided advantages in technical efficiency and control of general shop conditions....The authority which the foreman represents is less open to unfavorable comparisons. The distance between the two sexes helps to maintain discipline."

—corporate handbook for foremen[4]

"A failure to fight against such open [company] discrimination will hurt all union efforts. Please don't allow the company to continue such divide and conquer tactics between women and men, Black and white. Must women lift twice as much as men in order to keep their jobs?"

—pamphlet by a caucus of women steelworkers[5]

Many of us have grown accustomed to thinking that women have "separate and unequal" tasks in the economy. Haven't they always done most of the household work? Haven't they always worked at "less important" jobs than men?

These assumptions actually come from relatively recent history. Over a much longer sweep of centuries, men and women have worked at a wide variety of tasks. Women have sometimes done heavier physical work than men...and sometimes lighter work.[6] Women have sometimes taken sole care of the children...and have sometimes shared childcare with men.[7] Women and men have frequently done household work together; and men have sometimes worked "at home" while some women worked outside the home;...and women have often stoked the home fires by themselves.[8]

Given this variety, why do we construct such casual definitions of women's work in our modern economy?

We need to trace the history of women in the U.S. economy very carefully. When did women begin to work at home by themselves? When did women's and men's work become so different? When did women's work become "less important" than men's?

The Early Years

In the eighteenth and early nineteenth centuries, most Americans (except for slaves and Native Americans) lived on family farms. On those farms, men and women shared work both inside the home and with others in the community. "Family and community," as one historian concludes, "...supported [each] other and they became in a sense indistinguishable."[9] When families shared work, as one historian reported in 1898 about the colonial families,

....it was the custom both among men and women to join forces on a smaller scale and have a little neighborly visiting by what was called 'change-work.'...Even those evil days of New England households, the annual housecleaning, were robbed of some of their dismal terrors by what was known as a 'whang,' a gathering of...neighbors to assist one another in that dire time, and thus speed and shorten the hours of misery.[10]

Even though women more often worked in the house and men in the fields, there was little to distinguish men's and women's work in those early years in terms of load or importance. Both worked long hours. Both performed physically demanding tasks. Since women shared in securing food, shelter, and clothing, it would have been difficult to label women's work as "inferior."

Women also shared in the tasks of rebellion against the British and the wealthy. A contemporary described the actions of women against a merchant who hoarded food during the Revolutionary War:

> A number of females, some say a hundred, some say more, assembled with cart and trunks, marched down to the warehouse and demanded the keys which [the merchant] refused to deliver. Upon which one of them seized him by his neck and tossed him into the cart...then opened the warehouse, hoisted out the coffee themselves, put it into the trunks and drove off.[11]

Women Into the Factories

The appearance of the first factories in the 1820s and 1830s did little to change the division of labor between men and women. In the early years, at least, men and women still shared separate but equal tasks in the home. And the first factory workers included large numbers of women as well as men. Indeed, the largest and most modern factories built during the 1820s in Lowell and Lawrence, Mass. were designed especially to attract young single girls from the surrounding farm communities.

Many families needed some extra income to buy some of the goods they didn't make themselves—like shoes and metal and salt. Older daughters of New England farming families trickled into the factories for a few years to earn spare money for their families. Mill owners had to provide decent working conditions in order to convince the daughters and their families that the work was respectable. The corporations promised, as one of their spokesmen put it, "a strict system of moral police."[12]

Mill owners also sought a profit. Competitive conditions in their industry eventually forced them to "speed-up" the pace of the looms. The "respectable" working women protested by "turning out" into the streets to protest their wages and working conditions. In Lowell, for example, they formed a Factory Girls Association in 1836 to coordinate their protests. They were "daughters of freemen," their pamphlets proclaimed. "As our fathers resisted unto blood the lordly avarice of the British..., so we their daughters never will wear the yoke which has been prepared for us."[13]

The Home as Women's Preserve

Industrial capitalism spread rapidly in the United States after the 1840s. Millions of immigrants arrived in the United States, filling the factories. Because a large proportion of arriving immigrant workers were men, a rising proportion of factory workers were men.

As men took over many factory occupations, some began to define women's work as "home work." Although women had worked in the factories as early as men had, many mid-nineteenth century journals and schoolbooks defined the home as the women's preserve. "When a woman quits her own [home],...she departs from that sphere which is assigned to her in the order of society."[14] The argument began to stick. As one organizer of women workers remarked in 1887, "if there is one cause more than another that fastens the chains on...working women it is their foolish pride, they deeming it a disgrace to have it known that they engaged in honest toil [for wages outside the home]."[15]

Why did women become convinced that their work for wages was "a disgrace?"

We obviously can't explain this development by judging that women's work inside and outside the home was unimportant. Inside the home, women performed a wide variety of important jobs like cooking and sewing and tending the children. Their work outside the home was equally essential. As a Massachusetts official noted in 1882, "the man with a family of small children to support, unless his wife works also, has a small chance of living properly."[16]

One important reason for the redefinition of women's working roles was that employers benefited from the downgrading of female labor. Throughout the second half of the nineteenth century, female wages averaged from one-third to one-half of male wages—at levels so low that not even single women could support themselves on their incomes.[17] This helped employers pit men and women workers against each other. Employers used women as strikebreakers—in the cigar industries in 1877, for example, they called the strike a "blessing in disguise" because it helped them secure "workers whose services may be depended on at low wages."[18]

Another reason for the redefinition of women's work as "house work" was that many male workers were able to uphold their position as the head of the family through this redefinition. Before the age of the factory, men held onto family dominance through their legal property ownership and their customary role as family patriarch. After the factory undercut the viability of growing numbers of family farms, many men had to leave their homes to help secure family livelihood in the labor market. Many dealt with the tensions of their reduced economic independence by claiming superiority in their working positions. As early as 1829, a journalist noted that husbands were most likely to cope successfully with their transition to industrial work if their women were kept "dependent by means of insufficient wages."[19]

A third reason is that many women preferred the home to the factory—particularly because they preferred the independence of their own working activities in the home to the bosses' control they faced in the factory. Homework was relatively varied and often provided opportunities for creativity. Factory work, by contrast, was dull and repetitive.

Whatever the balance between employers' and husbands' influences, and the preferences of the women themselves, some of the main dimensions of the changes in women's work had become clear by 1890.

■ In the 1820s and 1830s both men and women worked outside the home. By 1890, 45% of adult men worked outside the home while only 14% of women worked in non-farm jobs.[20]

■ Men and women had shared jobs around the house. By 1890, women were doing most of the household work.[21]

■ At the beginning of the century, men and women both did work which society considered to be more or less equally productive. By 1890, society had begun to consider the work which women did outside the home as less important than the work performed by men.

The result, as the century came to a close, was that women could rarely support themselves and were pushed toward growing dependence on men. One organizer of women workers described this dependence in 1869:

> Some girls in the city of Boston got out of employment last winter. They went to a firm on Winter Street, and asked for employment. They were told that they could not be given enough to support them, but if they had gentlemen friends to dress them, they would be hired.[22]

New Careers, Same Old Work

Dependent or not, women began to work outside the home in growing numbers toward the end of the nineteenth century. The total number of women working in non-farm jobs increased from 1.4 million in 1870 to 6.3 million in 1920. The percentage of women working in non-farm jobs outside the home rose from 10.3% to 18.5% over those 50 years.[23]

There were two main reasons for this increase in the number of women working for wages.

First, the continuing spread of the factory system made it more and more difficult for many families to make ends meet on the man's earnings. Some studies of family life in large cities in 1906-1920 found, for example, that as many as two-thirds of all families of wage earners failed to earn what they needed for a decent standard of living. A group of women explained their reasons for working the night shift at a cord factory in New York in 1914:

M.N.: You can't feed and clothe a lot of children on what a man makes anymore.

Y.Z.: I want to work nights so I can take care of my children in the day. Why ain't men's pay more so women wouldn't have to work?

N.M.: I would rather work days if I could leave my baby with someone. I burn up my pay envelopes, my pay is so small I am ashamed.[24]

Other women went to work for a somewhat different set of reasons. Women in more affluent families did not always need to work to support the household income. Instead, they chose to work because they felt bored and isolated playing their "women's role" at home. Many of those women were daughters and wives in non-immigrant families; the percentage of working women who came from "native" parents increased from 35% in 1890 to 44% in 1920.[25]

These developments point toward the beginning of one of the most important changes in family life in the past century—more and more *married* women worked outside the home. The percentage of working women who were married increased from 14% in 1890 to nearly 25% in 1920.[26] The seeds of women's "liberation" from the home, which blossomed after World War II, had clearly been planted during these earlier decades.

This did not mean, of course, that work in the home stopped being important. Households still produced many products themselves. In 1890, for example, Brooklyn—already the nation's fifth largest city— was still semirural, and many households still did some farming.[27] Rather than buying baked bread, most families baked their own bread at home. Many families also owned sewing machines or made their own clothes by hand. A large number of families also rented out a room or two to a boarder. In these and other ways, households saved money and earned extra cash—for the same reasons that led women to work outside the home: most households were poor and needed to struggle for subsistence however and wherever they could.

Most households continued to assume, moreover, that *women were responsible for this household work.* The work was critical to the household's survival and the women worked long hours to help support their husbands and children. If the family owned a plot of ground, the wife was expected to grow vegetables. She might also do laundry for the neighbors, or sell eggs and dairy products from the household farm animals. The women provided indispensable savings in the kitchen— working with raw ingredients rather than prepared foods, substituting their time in cooking for income the household would otherwise have to earn in the market.

Despite these obvious contributions by women in the home, the history of men's power and the limits on women's opportunities continued to impose special burdens on women both inside the home and outside in the labor market.

■ More and more women worked long hours at regular jobs. And yet, *women did just as much housework as before.*[28] This double standard began to seem more and more apparent to many women as they watched the changes in working roles. Married women who worked bore the heaviest strain. A study of night shift workers in 1914 reported:

> All the women with families did their own housework; they prepared three meals a day, including breakfast, after a night's work. They also did the washing for the family. They averaged about 4½ hours sleep a day....Some slept an hour or two in the morning and for a time in the afternoon; others slept at intervals of about an hour each during the day.[29]

But even houseworkers who *didn't* work outside the home began to pay attention to the low esteem in which their contributions were held. As one women wrote in a pamphlet in 1908:

> The average housewife...works the longest hours and gets the lowest remuneration. The average toilers' work is done when the sun is down, but the housewife's work is never done....It is true that the man has to bring home enough money to maintain the rest of the family, but this does not mean that he supports the woman, who often does a greater amount of work than he [does]. No sooner does [the man] come home, than he becomes the monarch of his small domain...very often reminding her how hard he has to slave for her.[30]

■ More and more women worked but this did not lead to an upgrading of women's wages relative to those of men. It remained true throughout this period that *employers paid much lower wages to women than to men*—even when they did comparable kinds of work. A variety of studies from 1905 to 1920 showed that "at least sixty percent of America's wage-earning women did not receive wages sufficient to maintain health, strength, ...to provide comforts, ...and to make possible some saving for sickness, unemployment, or other major emergencies." The general result, as one study concluded about this period, was "that the wages of women workers frequently bear little relationship to their...productivity."[31]

■ As much or more than ever, *women were channeled into "women's work" in the labor market.* While the number of occupations in which they worked was rapidly expanding, it remained true that they were usually segregated from men. By 1930, of the 9.8 million nonagricultural female employees, 79% worked in just five main occupational categories—as teachers, clerical workers, retail salesworkers, operatives in the textile and garment industries, and domestic and personal service workers.[32] All of these had become primarily women's jobs.

Employers were clearly responsible for much of this segregation. They found that they could more easily reduce wages and job status in many occupations if they created special classes of women's work. This apparently explains, for example, why office work became so quickly segregated into men's and women's jobs. Before 1900, men did many

"The housewife's work is never done."
—*1908 pamphlet*

clerical chores. Increasingly after 1920, many secretarial jobs were defined as "women's work." As *Fortune* magazine concluded in 1935, "women occupy the office because the male employer wants them there."[33]

Many trade unionists also contributed to this occupational segregation. Many craft unions in the American Federation of Labor pushed after 1900 for "protective legislation" which regulated the conditions under which women could work—and eventually had the effect of pushing them out of certain kinds of jobs. Trade unionists had perceived the potential benefit of such laws as soon as women began to work in greater numbers. As the secretary of the Cigar Makers Union concluded in 1879, "we cannot drive the females out of the trade but we can [at least] restrict their daily quota of labor through factory laws."[34]

Women did not passively accept the double standards imposed on them. Millions began to fight for a wide variety of economic and political rights which would improve their status and power. They fought for and finally won the right to vote in 1920. They formed their own organizations, like the Consumers Leagues and the Women's Trade Union League. They pushed for better working conditions, shorter hours, and more equal pay. And they began to make the rest of the country pay attention. A *New York Times* reporter wrote in 1913:

> In a women's suffrage demonstration today the capital saw the greatest parade of women in its history....It was an astonishing demonstration. It was estimated...that 500,000 persons watched the women march for their cause.[35]

Women fought some of their toughest battles for the right to unionize. They played a critical role in the organizing drives which added 300,000 garment workers to the union movement between 1908 and 1918. They helped lead the famous Lawrence strike in Massachusetts in 1912. To the surprise of many men, they refused to abandon some of the jobs they had gained during World War I (while many men were fighting in the war). They often fought with men workers over their right to equal union protection. (Women laundry workers refused in 1913 to support a male laundry workers' wage demand, for example, "until the demand for a higher wage was extended to every branch."[36])

Male unionists had mixed feelings about these struggles. Men sometimes criticized women workers because they had left, as an AFL paper put it, the "family circle—the divine injunction."[37] But men also discovered that women workers were powerful allies and often fought harder than men for their rights as workers. A report on a butcher workers' boycott in 1902 noted, for example, that "several of the women leaders...laughed at the fear of the men in doing damage."[38]

As women struggled, indeed, they recognized more and more that the battle for their own rights would necessarily involve the struggle for all working people. As one woman organizer described in 1912 their intentions with the suffrage, "working women must use the ballot in order to bring about conditions where all may be able to live and grow because they work. The ballot used as we mean to use it will abolish the

"Women occupy the office because the male employer wants them there."

—*Fortune magazine, 1935*

burning and crushing of [all] our bodies for the profit of a very few."[39]

Work and struggle...and still second-class citizens and workers. Many women felt the tension between their growing responsiblity and their continued subordination as they watched the movement toward "protective legislation." On the one hand, many women understood that these laws might close down some of the jobs which provided the most plentiful employment for women. On the other hand, they recogognized that they would remain second-class workers forever unless they pushed politically for equal treatment.

This tension was reflected in conflicting attitudes over the Equal Rights Amendment when it was first introduced in the 1920s. Many women trade unionists opposed the bill because, as one organizer put it, "I have always been afraid that if laws were made discriminating for women it would work a handicap upon them." Many others supported the bill because they took a longer view of the position of women. The same organizer had changed her position by 1923 and now supported the Equal Rights Amendment. "It would in time raise the entire standard," she concluded, "rather than make it hard for women."[40]

Out of the Home for Good?

"Well, I know it's not much of a job in the eyes of anyone else. Even the secretaries look down on file clerks—especially a file clerk in her forties....But to me the job is something....I never went to college, I never worked before I was married, and I don't really have the training for anything more....It makes me feel both that I'm independent and that I'm contributing something to the household."

—file clerk, 1973[41]

What began slowly at the beginning of the twentieth century mushroomed after 1940. Women worked in greater numbers. And they began more seriously to challenge their second-class status.

Female non-farm employment rose slowly between 1920 and 1940—from 7.5 million to 10.7 million. Then it took off, rising to 28.6 million in 1970 and 38.2 million in 1978—almost four times the levels in 1940. As Figure 15.1 on this page shows, female labor force participation rates rose rapidly as well, climbing from roughly 20% of adult women in the labor force in 1920 to 43% in 1970 and finally breaking

Fig. 15.1
More and More Women Join the Labor Force

The graph measures the percentage of women over 16 years old who were in the labor force—that is, either working or looking for work.

Source: See note #42

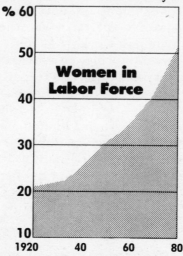

50% in 1978.[42] *More than half of all adult women now work for wage-and-salary income.*

Two important changes helped fuel this accelerating movement of women into the labor force.

1. Many more women placed rising priority on working. This led to more women working while they were married. The percentage of married women (still living with their husbands) who worked increased from 14% in 1940 to 40% in 1970 and 48% in 1978.[43]

2. The economy expanded during the post-war period in many areas which had traditionally been "women's work" like the clerical and service occupations. The total number of female clerical workers alone increased, for example, from 4.4 million in 1950 to 13.5 million in 1978.[44]

But neither of these changes yet transformed the earlier conditions of women's subordination in the home or at work.

■ It is still true that millions of women both work and still do most of the housework, that *women still do double duty in the economy.* Working women still spend an average of nearly 40 hours a week on housework.[45] When that's added to their average hours of paid work in the labor market, it becomes clear that women contribute substantially more (paid and unpaid) work to the economy than do men.[46]

■ It also remains true that *women earn much less than men,* that women still suffer the stigma of second-class workers. As we saw at the beginning of this chapter, women who work full-time year-round still earn only about 60% of what men earn. Even within the same occupations, these differences persist. Figure 15.2 on this page compares the annual earnings of white men and women within the same occupations who worked full-time year-round in 1970.[47] No matter what the occupation, the women earn only three-quarters of male earnings *at best.*

■ Despite all of the employment gains women have made in recent years, finally, it also remains true that *women are segregated into just a few kinds of jobs.* In 1970, 95% of women worked in just four areas—competitive manufacturing industries, clerical work, retail trade, and the health and education sectors.[48] All that's changed during the twentieth century, in large part, is that they now use more varied titles for the work which women primarily perform. Before they were nurses, for example, and now they're also EKG technicians and X-ray technicians....No matter what they call it, women's work largely remains women's work.

Employers still play an active role in segregating women from men in the factory and office. As recently as 1968, a supervisor's handbook argued that segregation made sense because the "role of achievers still belongs to men....Women as a rule don't seek job promotion—their emotions are secure in a limited job."[49] Employers also encourage the employment of "over-qualified" women for the same reasons they segregated office work in the 1920s. As an insurance executive explained the advantages in the late 1960s, clerical personnel

....are easily trained for their jobs; ...if they stayed on in large

Fig. 15.2
Women Earn Less— No Matter What the Job

Occupation	Women's Earnings as % of Men's, 1970
Professional & technical	79.7%
Managerial	58.1
Sales	41.4
Clerical	65.8
Craft	59.6
Operatives	60.1
Laborers	70.8
Service	59.3
Private household	70.3
Total	62.3

The earnings figures are adjusted for differences in part-time work and full-time work, so they represent differences in pay levels, not differences in hours worked.

Source: See note #47

numbers they would become wage problems—we'd have to keep raising them or end up fighting with them; they would form unions and who knows what the hell else. It's better to hire girls who are too well educated to *stay* happy with the jobs we assign them to do. That way they get out before it's too late.[50]

Working men have been lukewarm supporters of women, at best. Many large unions have made little effort to organize women workers in the postwar period. Many men still gain a sense of security from working above women and occasionally ordering them around on the job. And many men therefore pay little more than lip service to women's struggles against inequality. One woman chemical worker explained her suspicion of her union's position at recent hearings on the Equal Rights Amendment:

The officials of [our local] tell us that we should not fight for our rights because we are a minority. [But] even the predominantly women's unions are governed and controlled by men. These males running the labor unions are merely trying to monopolize better jobs for themselves....American working women have learned the lesson that the black people have learned. There is no such thing as separate but equal.[51]

And so, as in earlier decades, women have fought for their rights

"If women stayed on in large numbers, they'd form unions and who knows what else."

—insurance executive, 1960s

as they have played a more and more important role in the economy. Women played a key role in helping organize the industrial unions during the 1930s. The women's movement has increasingly involved working-class women as well as middle-class women, leading to the formation of organizations like the Coalition of Labor Union Women (CLUW). Women activists are running for union offices and helping organize women. While neither employers nor many of their male co-workers have responded to women's struggles with enthusiasm, women argue that the time has come for a complete transformation of women's roles both in the home and on the job. Nothing less will be enough. Two women organizers tell their own stories of the commitment this requires:

"The strike was one of the hardest and most important periods of my life. We had to fight the whole power structure of Charleston and of South Carolina....Just because we wanted to have a union....And if I didn't learn but one thing it was that if you are ready and willing to fight for yourself, other folks will be ready and willing to fight for you. We learned that you gotta be together. That's what a union is all about."

—hospital workers organizer[52]

"[I know] my letters [seem] depressing....Working too hard to attain an unattainable goal, trying too hard to please others...fighting for rights that society says I should have but won't let me have, accepting oppression which too often ends with a lump in my throat. All that boils down to one thing: stress...[But I'm] still in there fighting, and I'll never give up."

—organizer of university workers[53]

JUST REWARDS?

"Dammit, no! A wife's got to learn to be number two. That's just the way it is, and that's what she better learn. She's not going to work. She's going to stay home and take care of the family like a wife's supposed to do."

—a husband about his wife's working[54]

This history of women in the U.S economy provides several clear lessons about the divisions and conflicts between women and men:

■ The current pattern of inequality and division is not permanent and unchanging. It has grown out of specific historical circumstances and is constantly changing. If it has changed in the past, it can be changed in the future.

■ And yet, the special disadvantages of women—doing double duty at home and work, confronting inequalities on and off the job—have too many deep roots for us to expect them to disappear overnight. It will require real commitment and real struggle to create equality between men and women.

■ This is especially true because corporations have strong interests in maintaining divisions between men and women workers. They helped create those divisions and continue to profit from them.

■ It is even more true because many men also benefit from and therefore have a stake in maintaining the inequalities which women face at home and at work. Men are unlikely to toss away some of their privileges without at least some hesitation and grumbling.

■ Such struggles are necessary, finally, not only for women but for all of us. All of us suffer from the weakness which divisions between men and women create. When women lose, all of us lose some of the strength and power we need to advance our own needs and interests.

Many working people appreciate all of these lessons. And yet many also hesitate about (if not oppose) special efforts to promote greater equality. People offer a wide variety of reasons, many supported by corporate propaganda, for their hesitations. These reasons need to be addressed carefully and clearly, since they stand as barriers to potential unity among working people.

Too Few Skills?
Do women have poor jobs and earn low wages because they have too few skills? Would we be wasting our resources if we made special efforts to promote women to positions requiring more skills?

The answers seem clear. Women have as many skills as men. And women earn less than men *regardless* of their skill levels. Women earn on average, as we have seen, about 60% of male earnings. No matter how we try to explain that gap—by controlling for the skills women have acquired, or their years of schooling, or their vocational training—it always comes out roughly the same. As close as we can get to comparing women and men of comparable skill levels, women still earn no more than about two-thirds of what men with comparable skill levels earn.[55]

We cannot assume, in short, that women would solve their problems if they studied harder and learned more. Women need to be able to get in the same kinds of jobs as men and be paid equal wages, not to acquire more skills.

Bad Risks on the Job?

Employers often justify the lower job status of women by arguing that they'll quit to raise their families. Where will they be, employers ask, when we really need them? We'd like to help, they say, but I just can't afford the risk.

Here again, the arguments are myths which turn into self-fulfilling prophecies.

Many studies have found that the differences in work tenure between men and women are very low. Working women who have children leave their jobs for only short periods—unless, of course, their lack of maternity benefits leaves their jobs unprotected. In manufacturing, the "quit rates" for men and women are almost exactly comparable. Many studies have found that most of the differences between the job turnover of men and women are due to the characteristics of their jobs, not the basic differences between the sexes.[56] Because women are more likely to work in dead-end jobs—with low wages and few fringe benefits, working without many promotional opportunities—they are less likely to stay on a job *simply because* they would be sacrificing seniority or promotional opportunities if they left.[57]

One study has recently provided very clear evidence about this explanation of lower earnings for women. It looked at higher-level occupations in a publishing company, therefore studying jobs to which we can assume women would be committed and relatively unlikely, as with dead-end jobs, to walk away in frustration. The earnings gap between men and women within job categories was just as wide as for the economy as a whole. Was it because the women were poor risks? Married women had worked longer at the company, on average, than either men or single childless women. The biggest source of an earnings gap between the male and female employees was that the men's earnings increased much more for each year of experience on the job than did the women's earnings. The problem was that women didn't get paid as much for the time they put in, not that they put in less time. The author reached a simple final conclusion: "The company rewards men with families because they are *thought* to 'deserve' higher salaries and fails to reward women because they are *thought* not to be so deserving."[58] The inequalities are based on employers' preferences and discrimination, in short, and not on real differences between their workers.

And so, we get a vicious circle. Employers keep women out of better jobs because they claim that they're bad risks. But by far the principal reason that women have somewhat more uneven employment records than men is that *employers keep them out of better jobs*. Solution? Open better jobs to women (and provide adequate day-care facilities for those with children).

Too Lazy and Fearful?

Another common argument is that women have poor attitudes for certain kinds of work. The rap on women is that they don't take charge and can't be trusted with important responsibilities.

There is some evidence that women workers are less "competitive" and "aggressive" than men.[59] But the rap on women's attitudes points toward the wrong conclusion about these differences. They don't mean that women fail at important responsibilities. In situations where women do have professional or supervisory responsibilities without other handicaps, indeed, studies have found that women perform with complete and equivalent competence.[60] Women simply tend to perform those responsibilities with slightly different attitudes than men. One women, a skilled printer, commented on the difference in the mid-1970s:

> I've noticed quite a difference in the way men and women will teach you a job. The men are a lot more competitive. They tend either to assume you are stupid and incapable of learning, or they act as if you should already know the job and don't tell you what you need to know. The whole process is designed to show how much more than you they know and can do. I've never had that kind of problem with women.[61]

The issue, then, arises because of men's egos, not the requirements of better jobs. One of the main reasons that many women workers don't care to play those kinds of games is that they've been the butt of aggressive behavior too many times. They know what it feels like. One woman, a process clerk, commented on the pattern in a recent interview:

> They just don't want to give you anything. The personnel man, all of them, they show you why you don't deserve a promotion....Oh, we love it when the bosses go to those long meetings, those important conferences. (Laughs) We just leave in a group and go for a show....They know they better not say anything, 'cause they've done nothing when we've been gone anyhow....I'm just tired of this type of thing. I just think we ought to be human.[62]

What About Numero Uno?

Many people worry, finally, that they can't help solve the problems of women because they have enough trouble solving their own. "We'd like to help," men respond, "but why should I have to make the sacrifices?"

These feelings are obviously encouraged by employers. As we learned from our trip through the history of women in the economy, employers have always played one group against another. Men have, indeed, felt that their jobs were being threatened by women entrants into the labor market.

But haven't we also learned that we are *all* much stronger when we stop fighting with each other? Doesn't this lesson apply to questions like affirmative action as well?

Our economy has two characteristics which affect this discussion about divisions and unity. First, as we saw in Chapters 6 and 7, it does not tend to promote full employment or create jobs for everyone who needs them. Second, as we saw in Chapter 4, employers often create job titles and arbitrary divisions among jobs in order to maintain control and encourage competition for promotions.

As long as we leave the economy in its doldrums, doing nothing about full employment, then we're all understandably worried about our job prospects. And as long as we allow those job ladders to remain as they are, without any changes in job structure, affirmative action programs advancing the job prospects of women will mean that some white men have to step aside in order to allow women room at higher rungs on the ladder.

But suppose we no longer accept as given or necessary the job structures which large corporations have created. Suppose we begin moving from the hierarchies companies have created to a job structure providing *more* and *better* production jobs, both in the factory and office? Then there would be room for women to move into better jobs without affecting the job prospects of any but the few who love leaping over the rest of us in their climb toward the pinnacles of power.

These two alternative approaches obviously have substantially different implications. One approach, which leaves job structures as they are, leaves us fighting among ourselves because we don't challenge the bosses' power to keep us divided through work organization. The other approach creates at least the possibility of unity among us by challenging the corporations' control over job structures and moving toward more equal and less hierarchical organization of work. Whatever the difficulties of beginning to reshape our jobs, the advantages of the second approach seem clear—both for women and for all the rest of us who need unity to strengthen our powers of resistance and struggle.

A woman working as a coordinator of government programs describes her gradual recognition of our need to follow this latter course:

The reasons people get paid now are wrong. I think the reward system should be different...So people in a work situation wouldn't be so frightened. People are intimidated and the system works to emphasize that. They get what they want out of people by threatening them economically. It makes people apple polishers and ass kissers. I used to hear people say, "work needs to be redefined." I thought they were crazy. Now I know they're not.[63]

16.

Blacks and Hispanics

"Don't get me wrong; I'm not saying that race is not a factor—all you have to do is look at what's written on the walls in the bathroom to know it's there. But it has no effect on how people act. Our plant is one-third black, one-third white and one-third Chicano, but when it comes to the way we organize on the job, everybody works together pretty well."

—black autoworker in Michigan[1]

"According to Mom, I was born on a cotton sack out in the fields, 'cause she had no money to go to the hospital....I'd go barefoot to school. The bad thing was they used to laugh at us, the Anglo kids. They would laugh because we'd bring tortillas and frijoles to lunch....

"[Where I work now,] all kinds of people are farm workers, not just Chicanos. Filipinos started the strike. We have Puerto Ricans and Appalachians too, Arabs, some Japanese, some Chinese. At one time they used us against each other. But now they can't and they're scared, the growers.... Suffering people never dream it could be different. [Now we] grasp the idea— and this is what scares the growers."

—hispanic farm-worker in California[2]

Racial and ethnic divisions also confront U.S. working people with continuing conflicts and disunity. We argue about quotas and affirmative action, about busing and formulae for school funding, about redistricting, about immigration laws and the rights of undocumented workers.

As with divisions between men and women, these tensions along racial and ethnic lines persist in large part because many minorities in the United States still encounter discrimination and resent the inequalities to which they are persistently exposed. As long as those inequalities remain so unyielding, racial and ethnic anger and tensions will continue to smolder.

Blacks and hispanics are the two largest minority groups in the United States and they continue to face the most chronic discrimination. Taken together, blacks and hispanics now constitute roughly 18% of the U.S. population.

As with women, the inequalities affecting blacks and hispanics are unmistakable:

■ Black and hispanic workers were 14% of all workers in the U.S. economy in 1970. They nonetheless accounted for only 6% of all managers and supervisors. While only 25% of white men held dead-end jobs, 60% of black workers and 50% of hispanic workers faced the low wages and employment insecurity of dead-end jobs.[3]

■ We have already seen in Chapter 15 that black and hispanic women earn less than white men. Inequalities in earnings also plague black and hispanic men. We can compare the earnings of men of the *same age* with the *same levels of education* who worked *full-time for the entire year in 1977*. Even among this group of comparable workers with the same age, education, and work experience, black men earned only three-quarters as much as white men, while hispanic men earned less than five-sixths as much as white men. Taking black and hispanic workers together, the earnings gap among comparable minority and white males is more than 20%. Equal pay for equal work?

These inequalities cannot be ignored. Blacks and hispanics continue to face occupational segregation and earnings disadvantages. Why? What sustains this kind of discrimination? How could we overcome it?

BLACKS IN THE U.S. ECONOMY

"Because of our persistent preoccupation with race-related issues,...we have not been fair to ourselves. When people are divided against themselves on racial grounds, they have no time to demand a fair shake on taxes, utility bills, consumer protection, government services, environmental preservation, and other problems."

—former governor of Florida, 1972[4]

"When I first started working here, I saw the black guys sitting down when they finished working, so I sat down too. A white kid came up to me and said, 'Don't sit down, the boss will get on you.' I said, 'What do you mean, those guys are sitting down.' He said, 'Well, they're afraid to do anything to the blacks.' So I said, 'Shit, we should all sit down and let them be afraid of all of us.' "

—steelworker in Detroit, 1975[5]

There are now 26 million blacks living in the United States. Blacks have lived here as long as whites.[6] Despite these equal terms of residence, however, blacks and whites have faced dramatically different conditions in their U.S. experience since the beginning.

Voyages into Slavery

Blacks entered the United States in chains. Millions of slaves were imported to the Americas during the seventeenth and eighteenth centuries. By the beginning of the Civil War in 1860, there were close to four million slaves in this country and only 488,000 free blacks.[7]

The slave system imposed two massive burdens on blacks.

First, and obviously, black slaves had to work very hard for their masters. One historian summarizes their living conditions:

Most slaves lived in rude, drafty, and leaky clapboard shacks, frequently without furniture, and quite often filthy and overcrowded....For much of the year they were barefooted in tattered clothes, and in the freezing winters most slaves did not have enough clothes to keep them warm.[8]

Since slaves got nothing more from their masters if they worked harder, they naturally avoided work whenever they could. "Negro slaves felt no compulsion to extend themselves in their work unless the planter or overseer forced them....In the effort to get work out of slaves the lash was frequently used."[9] Few slaves "ever completely escaped the whip."[10]

Second, southerners invented all kinds of myths about black slaves in order to try to justify their conditions. Slave owners were constantly exposed to the conflict, as Thomas Jefferson put it, between the American ideal of "justice" and the southern practice of "avarice and oppression."[11] To provide a moral cover for this "avarice and oppression," southern plantation owners created the legend of "black Sambo"—of lazy, shiftless, shuffling good-for-nothings who needed and actually preferred their masters for comfort and care. "Racism has been common in all ages and in virtually all parts of the world," a black economist notes. "What was peculiar about racism in the South was the extremes to which this doctrine was carried and the powerful emotions behind it."[12] This racist mythology left deep scars which have marked racial relations ever since.

Both slaves and free blacks belied the myths through their own skills and actions. Many blacks—both free and slave—became accomplished craft workers, working as carpenters, blacksmiths, brickmasons, and in many other skilled occupations. More important for their own survival, blacks continually organized opposition to the slave system. Thousands of slaves escaped from the plantations through the "underground railroad" and other less organized routes. And thousands of slaves periodically rebelled, facing overpowering odds, unable to tolerate their conditions any longer. Historians have counted over 200 revolts; many others undoubtedly escaped notice. The threat was so persistent that the slave-holders mounted a massive counter-force. As one historian observes about a typical southern state, "In 1831, Virginia was an armed and garrisoned state....During a period when neither the State nor the nation faced any sort of exterior threat, we find that Virginia [maintained] a security force roughly ten percent of...its inhabitants...."[13] The causes of escape and revolt were usually obvious. A Georgia overseer reported to his plantation owner: "[Your hands] displeased me with their work and I give some of them a few lashes, Tom with the rest. On Wednesday morning, they were missing."[14]

Pre-Civil-War slave family.

Out of Slavery, Into Debt

The northern victory in the Civil War led to the immediate abolition of slavery. Blacks hoped that their new freedom would permit economic independence.

For a brief period after the Civil War, it appeared that many southern blacks would be able to get their "forty acres and a mule." But wealthy white southerners fought back. Between 1865 and 1876, whites formed their own militias, the Ku Klux Klan and other vigilante

groups intimidated free blacks, and white northerners lost their will in the battle for black equality. From 1876 through the turn of the century, white southerners reconstructed the basis for white supremacy over blacks in the south.

The key, of course, was the distribution of land. Wealthy whites retained control of the biggest and most fertile sections. In Georgia in 1880, for example, blacks comprised 40% of the population but owned only 1.6% of the land.[15]

Relying on this control of land, wealthy whites developed a new system to control blacks as tenant farmers. They needed labor to work their land, so they divided the land into small plots and offered to rent these plots to blacks in return for a sizable share of the product. They secured laws in the legislatures which made geographic movement by renters extremely difficult. And the landlords charged such high rents that their tenant farmers were never able to save enough to buy their own land somewhere else. Blacks fell into a kind of *debt slavery*, held in place by their lack of access to land, kept in place by the great wealth of the southern landlords and their combined action through the courts and legislatures. By the 1880s, it seemed to many southern blacks that little had changed. As one discontented tenant farmer explained in 1880, "We seed that the whole South—every state in the South—had got into the hands of the very men that held us slaves."[16]

Poor whites were dragged into debt bondage as well. Since poor whites had little land themselves, they had trouble raising the necessary funds for planting and marketing. When they turned to the bankers and landlords for help, they confronted the same kinds of high interest rates which poor blacks faced. Many lost their land through foreclosures. The percentage of whites who rented (rather than owned) their land increased steadily from the 1870s through the turn of the century.[17] Debt bondage was a contagious condition.

By the 1880s, many poor whites recognized that they needed to unify with poor blacks in order to improve their conditions. The Populist movement began in the south among poor white tenant farmers and spread quickly. As one of its major leaders appealed to blacks and whites in 1892:

> Now the People's Party says to these two men, "You are kept apart that you may be separately fleeced of your earnings. You are made to hate each other because upon that hatred is rested the keystone of the arch of financial despotism which enslaves you both. You are deceived and blinded that you may not see how this race antagonism perpetuates a monetary system that beggars both."[18]

Industrial workers began to reach similar conclusions. White dockworkers in New Orleans, steelworkers in Alabama, and coal miners in Alabama and West Virginia found that they needed to form industrial unions to improve their wages and working conditions. Throughout the 1890s, white workers in all these southern industries joined with blacks to fight for union recognition. Their early victories spurred both the workers involved and the cause of racial unity. As one black miner wrote in 1899, "I believe that the United Mine Workers has done more to erase the word white from the Constitution than the Fourteenth Amendment."[19] A journalist concluded about the coordinated dockworkers action, which involved a city-wide sympathy strike in support of black workers, that the unions have "done more to break the color line in New Orleans than any other thing...since emancipation of the slaves."[20]

Wealthy southerners in agriculture and industry struck back. During the 1890s, as a leading southern historian concludes, they fought with "fraud, intimidation, bribery, violence, and terror..., stirring up fears of Negro domination...., stopping at nothing."[21] "Jim Crow" laws effectively robbed blacks of the vote and the right to share equally in public life. Laws establishing segregation in education, eating, and government followed quickly. Many have blamed this reversal on racist attitudes among poor whites. But the "Jim Crow" laws were passed only *after* the Populist challenge was defeated by the wealthy.[22] As long as the poor whites and blacks worked together, they marshalled enough strength to hold back the flood of racist legislation.

Moving North—An Escape?

As late as 1900, 90% of blacks still lived in the south and 75% on southern farms.[23] Those blacks who lived in the north often enjoyed better working and living conditions than some of the more recent immigrants from Europe.[24] It was almost inevitable that some blacks would begin to move north to escape from the Jim Crow south—just as they had travelled the underground railroad to escape from slavery.

Most blacks who moved north did so after 1914, when the outbreak of World War I in Europe increased the demand for U.S.-produced supplies and material. Recruiters blanketed the south with handbills promising good jobs, high wages, and no Jim Crow. Many of the leading newspapers of the black community passed on the call, and millions left the south for northern cities.[25]

This northward migration coincided with efforts of many northern workers to organize large industrial unions. Between 1915 and 1919 a strike wave swept the industrial states in support of demands for union recognition and more control on the job. Northern industrialists responded with every weapon they could muster. As part of their counter-attack, they tried to use the northward migration of southern blacks for their own purposes, attempting to deploy them as strikebreakers wherever possible. Few of the new arrivals let themselves be used in this way. But, just as "native" workers discriminated against immigrants with increasing intensity after World War I (see Chapter 14), so did northern whites focus mounting anger on those blacks who were used as strikebreakers. Blacks arriving north often received a welcome mat of thorns.

White unionists did not rush to help. Many unions in the American Federation of Labor (AFL) excluded blacks from membership; AFL president Samuel Gompers continued to insist that the race problem was one with which "you people in the Southland will have to deal...."[26] Blacks often appealed to white unionists for support but were typically rebuffed. Employers were pitting black workers against white, but many blacks eventually focused their resentment on white workers, not the bosses. "Unwillingly we assume the role of strikebreakers," as the *Chicago Defender*, a black newspaper, editorialized in 1919. "The unions drive us to it."[27] W.E.B. DuBois, a leading black spokesman, agreed, concluding in 1913: "The net result of all this has been to convince the American Negro that his greatest enemy is not the employer who robs him, but his fellow white workingman."[28]

This history provided the background to the industrial union organizing drives of the 1930s. By the 1930s, blacks accounted for as many as 17% of laborers and operatives in meatpacking and 13% of auto workers in some plants.[29] Industrial unionists found that they could not organize successfully in many of those industries without including blacks; they had simply become too important.

The drive to organize the Ford Motor Company was a key test. Ford answered the union organizing drives with rumors about black workers and threats of strikebreaking. After several years of stand-off, the UAW finally overcame black workers' suspicions (with the help of black community leaders) and a united union beat the company.[30]

The Congress of Industrial Organizations (CIO) passed a resolution in 1938 that it "pledges itself to uncompromising opposition to any form of discrimination, whether political or economic, based on race, color, creed or nationality."[31] Armed with that resolution, the CIO helped organize scores of thousands of black workers. By 1940, more than 500,000 black workers belonged to unions.[32] Many CIO contracts contained clauses outlawing discrimination and unequal pay.

A door seemed to be opening for blacks. A black union organizer expressed this hope and determination when he responded to a white skeptic. "I love Negroes," the white worker assured him, "but I like to see 'em in their place." "Brothers, I agree with him," the organizer replied to the union meeting. "The place of black people is in the labor movement...and I'm going to see that everyone out there can be put in their place."[33]

Summa these People are Crazy!

From the Farm Into the Frying Pan

"We...had to listen to [my mother's] unending commentary on my father's 'shiftlessness.' But he had not been a lazy man. Work as he knew it, as he had always known it, had run out for him....There had been times when I went with my father in search of a job to those public places where jobs were sometimes available. The faces of the applicants were crushed, beaten; the men wore dirty, crumpled caps and the stink of poverty, black and white, hung thickly in the air....My father was not lazy."

—black writer raised in the north[34]

Many blacks in the U.S. felt a surge of hope in the 1940s. World War II opened up many jobs. The civil rights movement of those years helped secure new federal legislation which barred segregation and discrimination in many areas, including the military services and federally-funded housing. The industrial unions continued to surge, and black workers' hopes soared with them. By the end of World War II, black union membership had risen to 1.25 million, more than double its level just five years earlier.[35] Conditions seemed to be changing rapidly.

Some of the basic changes in blacks' lives came from their movement off the southern farms. Between 1940 and 1960 alone, nearly three million blacks left the south, moving north and west. By 1970, only 17% of all blacks still lived in the rural south, and many of those worked in factories. By 1970, a higher proportion of blacks lived in cities than whites.[36] Blacks had become "citified."

Two important forces fostered this continuing movement.

In the south, as we have already seen in Chapter 14, the farms themselves changed dramatically as machines replaced hand-labor. The push had begun in the Depression when cotton prices fell and agricultural production suffered. During and after World War II, herbicides and mechanization transformed both cotton and tobacco picking. As one southern black farmer remembers this period, "The plantations didn't break up, but there comest the doin' away of labor. Comest the tearin' down the sharecroppers' houses, the timber shacks. There's machinery now....and they didn't need the labor no more."[37]

The second force represented an attraction. At least momentarily, jobs in the north drew many blacks. During World War II, war-time production opened many factory jobs to blacks as it had in World War I. The boom years after the war helped keep many of those jobs open. The number of blacks working in manufacturing more than doubled between 1940 and 1950.[38] Many blacks began the northward trek with clear hopes of steady and decent employment.

For many, those hopes have been fulfilled. But for blacks as a group, inequality continues as a basic fact of life in the United States. It seems crucial to examine carefully this mix of progress for some but not for all.

The rapid movement out of the south opened up schooling for much larger numbers of blacks than before. Many took advantage of it.

As a result, blacks now stay in school nearly as long as whites. The gap between the schooling levels of the typical white and black male closed from 3.5 grades of school in 1940 to half a grade in 1970. The gap between black and white women was even smaller.[39] Between 1960 and 1976, the number of blacks enrolled in college increased by nearly 400%.[40] College and high school diplomas were helping open many doors to blacks—even before the civil rights movement of the 1960s—which had long been closed to them.

Blacks were able to move through many of those open doors in significant numbers. From the Depression through the 1970s, the jobs which blacks held changed fairly rapidly.[41]

■ In 1930, only 10% of black males and 4% of black females worked as professionals, as managers, or as clerical, sales, and craft workers. By 1970, that percentage had risen to 34% for black men and 37% for black women.

■ In 1930, by contrast, 67% of black men worked as laborers, farmers, and farm workers; that percentage dropped to 21% in 1970. In 1930, similarly, 77% of black women worked as domestics or farm workers; by 1970, only 19% of black women worked in those menial jobs.

■ By 1977, indeed, 15% of all black full-time, year-round workers held professional, technical, or managerial jobs; and 21% of black women worked at those jobs. In 1930, only 3% of both black men and

black women had achieved those occupational levels. These were clearly the ingredients of a large black upper-middle-class.

These gains were limited, however, and did not spread among all blacks. For many others, there were few jobs and continuing discrimination. While some blacks were able to make huge economic strides, many other blacks walked an economic treadmill.

The net result was that blacks as a group did not make much progress toward equality after World War II. We can look at the relationship between the incomes of black households and white households. Before World War II, blacks lived in rural poverty in the south. As they left the south and some improved their economic opportunities, we would expect that the gap between black and white incomes would close fairly rapidly. For a time, up to the early 1950s, this kind of narrowing of the inequality gap seems to have occurred. Since then, as official data show, blacks have progressed during periods of prosperity and fallen back during periods of recession and instability. In the late 1970s, blacks as a group were scarcely ahead of where they were in the 1950s. At the current rate of progress, according to a recent study, black family incomes are not likely to catch up with white family incomes, on average, *until about 2100 A.D.—if then.*[42]

Why has there been such slow progress? The problem involves some of the changes we discussed in Chapter 14 which have affected the fates of all newcomers to the U.S. economy after World War II. The number of good jobs, particularly in areas where black men have worked in the greatest numbers, has not been expanding. Widening distances have arisen between good jobs and dead-end jobs. Many blacks can find work only in jobs paying low wages and providing little employment security. For black teenagers there are virtually no jobs at

all. While there has been some room near the top for some blacks, there's been nowhere nearly enough room for most blacks to step off the treadmill.

The postwar decades opened some doors for some blacks, in short, but millions of blacks have been left out in the cold. As one black congressman concluded in 1979, "I don't blame young people for being apathetic. I don't blame them for saying, 'There is no way I can win in this system,' because they look at their fathers, who have been unemployed for the past five years..., and they say, 'If Dad can't win, I can't win.' "[43] Another successful black who migrated to the north shares similar concerns: "I have less hope now for the vast majority of black people than I did when I first came here. I don't see solutions to the problems the way I did then. There simply aren't enough jobs to go around."[44]

HISPANICS IN THE U.S. ECONOMY

"We were here for hundreds of years before the Pilgrims but were conquered and became a colonized people. We have suffered the same kinds of problems as blacks but without nearly the degree of publicity. We endured lynchings, gerrymandering, police brutality. The Jews have been discriminated against because of religion, the blacks because of race, the Slaves because of culture. But we get all of it."

—chicano activist, 1978[45]

"A lot of kids want an education to get out of here. But in order to survive, they're [hustling out on the streets]. Kids ten and eleven make more money than their old man in the factory."

—Puerto Rican teenager in N.Y., 1978[46]

Hispanics are rapidly approaching blacks in total numbers in the United States. The 1980 Census counted 15 million. If we count undocumented hispanics, there were probably close to 20 million living in the U.S. in that year.[47] These numbers include close to 14 million of Mexican origin, roughly 2 million Puerto Ricans, perhaps 700,000 Cubans, and nearly 3 million immigrants from Caribbean and other Latin American countries.[48]

There are many historic and cultural differences among these national groups, but they also share many common experiences. Long ignored, frequently hidden from view, continually expanding through immigration from the south, hispanics are becoming a force and a voice. As one chicano organizer puts it, "we're finally beginning to make some kind of impact."[49]

The First Refugees and Recruits

Mexico, Puerto Rico, and many other Latin nations were first conquered by European countries several centuries ago. Many chicanos descend from areas in the southwest which the U.S. conquered after the "Mexican War" of the 1840s. Puerto Rico itself became a U.S. colony after the Spanish-American War in 1898. Most hispanics already lived here, in short, when immigrants from Europe first arrived, but the new arrivals conveyed their greetings with guns. Relations have been tense ever since.

Around 1900, despite these initial greetings, hispanics already in the U.S. lived fairly isolated lives.

■ Puerto Rico was now a colony; its population totalled 953,000 in 1899.[50] Most Island residents lived and worked in small villages, although some worked as agricultural laborers on the large sugar and tobacco plantations.

■ In the southwest, there were probably about 100,000 descendants of the Mexican families living in the territories conquered during the "Mexican War."[51] Most of those hispanics—calling themselves *tejanos, hispanos, mexicanos,* and even *pochos*—were scattered in isolated rural areas.

...on ranches lost in the South Texas chaparral, on plantations marooned on the central Texas Black Waxy, in villages hidden in the wooded hollows of northern New Mexico's Sangre de Cristo Mountains, in mining camps, tiered up Arizona's bare and baking Gila Hills, on the big farms and orchards and vineyards fenced into California's San Joaquin and Sacramento valleys, in boxcar barracks stationed along the railroad tracks, always on the wrong side.[52]

The first substantial increases in the hispanic population in the U.S. began with migration from Mexico. The Mexican Revolution uprooted millions south of the U.S. border; roughly 800,000 Mexicans entered the U.S. between 1910 and 1920. After post-World War I tensions had slowed European immigration to a trickle, even more Mexicans crossed the borders in search of work and decent wages. During the 1920s, another 1.5 million Mexicans probably entered the U.S.[53]

Many moved into the cities, into the *barrios*, into the neighborhoods they sometimes called the *colonia*. As one immigrant during this period remembers:

> The *colonia* was like a sponge....it kept filling with newcomers who found families who took in boarders: basements, alleys, shanties, run-down rooming houses and flop joints where they could live. Crowded as it was, the *colonia* found a place for these *chicanos*, the name by which we called an unskilled worker born in Mexico and just arrived in the United States. The *chicanos* were fond of identifying themselves by saying they had just arrived from *el macizo*, by which they meant the solid Mexican homeland, the good native earth....They didn't go back. They remained, as they said of themselves, *pura raza*.[54]

Many eventually found work in the U.S., mostly on the farms of California and the southwest, some in northern factories. (Perhaps 100,000 had joined other immigrants in industry.) Whether in the fields or the factories, their wages were near the bottom of the scale. Conditions in the fields were so poor, as one worker remembers, that there "was then a regular joke about 'the Mexican breakfast': a cigarette and a piss."[55]

Many fewer Puerto Ricans had yet come to the mainland. The rapid spread of plantations and cash-crop farming in Puerto Rico had uprooted many farmers in the villages, but most moved directly into the cities and plantations of the colony for wage-work. Only about 5,000 Puerto Ricans per year left the Island during the 1920s. By 1930, there were only about 100,000 Puerto Ricans living in the United States. Most lived in New York City. Almost all of those working settled into light factories and small shops as operatives, craftworkers, and small businessmen.[56]

For most of the hispanics during this period, their weak toeholds in the U.S. economy exposed them to dirt-cheap wages. Many found jobs with relatively small farmers who themselves operated near the margin. When Mexicans demanded higher wages, farmers organized themselves to recruit more. They made widespread use of labor recruiters and contractors who brought Mexicans over the border to fill in where labor was short. "It is the same situation as where you have had a stream of water running through your ranch," one farmer explained. "If someone turns its source off you want to put up a dam to hold what you have."[57]

The net effect of these conditions was that Mexican workers were often brought into competition with other U.S. workers who needed work. In the 1920s, black and chicano farmworkers were sometimes in competition with each other—though not in the same regions—because the crops they picked were sold on national markets. A Mississippi onion farmer crowed during this period: "They tell me the Mexicans [in Texas] earn $2 a day. In the Mississippi delta we get twelve to fourteen hours out of the Negroes at this time of the year—from sun to sun, we pay $1.50."[58]

There could be such a thing as too *much* cheap labor, however. The wealthy and the government moved during the Depression to deport many Mexicans—they called it "repatriation"—because they feared that growing surpluses of unemployed chicanos would "cause trouble" and excite the "native" workers who wandered in search of work. "In an effort to break strikes [on the farms]," one historian reports, "it was not unusual for county authorities in league with employers to threaten sending into strike areas batches of Mexicans on the welfare rolls."[59] When this failed, repatriation efforts became serious. The Depression deportations probably reached close to 500,000, *perhaps as many as half of them already U.S. citizens.*[60] The *anglos* didn't make fine distinctions among hispanics, whether or not they had become citizens. As one California law enforcement official explained the attitude: "We protect our farmers....But the Mexicans are trash. They have no standard of living. We herd them like pigs."[61]

Though isolated and subject to such harrassment, hispanics during this early period frequently organized themselves to fight for better working and living conditions.

■ Puerto Rican workers had affiliated with the American Federation of Labor as early as 1901, and Puerto Rican workers in New York City continued their support of unions throughout the 1920s and 1930s.[62] Because of harrassment in their neighborhoods, New York Puerto Ricans also formed organizations like the Puerto Rican and Spanish-American League for Civic Defense and supported many hispanic political candidates.

■ In the southwest, rural farmworkers frequently sought union organization—usually to bump up against the difficulties of organizing in conditions of surplus labor. Urban workers also pursued unionization. In Los Angeles, for example, chicanos founded the *Confederacion de Uniones Obreras Mexicanas* in 1927 and rapidly built its membership during the first years of the Depression. The union pledged a "class struggle in order to effect an economic and moral betterment of [our] conditions."[63]

The Depression hit these efforts with force, however, both

because of the competition from the unemployed and because employers used the tool of deportation to hit specifically at union militants. "The Mexican on relief is being unionized," a spokesman for the L.A. Chamber of Commerce complained, "and is being used to foment strikes among the still loyal Mexican workers. The Mexican casual laborer is lost to the Californian farmer unless immediate action [against these unions] is taken."[64] Although hispanics had not yet acquired anything close to their current numbers, employers had already developed clear notions about "their place."

"Sal Si Puedes"—Get Out If You Can

"In school, Mr. Miller, goddamn him to hell forever, took a Puerto Rican boy named Luis and kept him under the teacher's desk during class periods. When Luis would moan, Miller would kick him. Between periods, Miller walked Luis around the school, keeping him in a painful armlock. Mr. Flax, the principal, laughed....To whom did you complain about a teacher—a laughing principal?"

—Puerto Rican in New York[65]

World War II pulled many hispanics out of their previous isolation. Close to 400,000 served in the U.S. Army during World War II.[66] Many others worked in war-time industries. After World War II, the pace of hispanic movement to the continental U.S. accelerated. Between 1941 and 1970, close to a million Mexicans crossed the border with documentation. Roughly 800,000 Puerto Ricans moved to the United States during those same years, joining another 650,000 from the Caribbean.[67]

From the beginning, these new hispanic populations faced ethnic suspicion and hostility. In 1943 in Los Angeles, for example, hundreds of chicanos were injured when inflamed anglo soldiers and civilians invaded local neighborhoods in search of "zoot suiters." Hispanics were denied housing, harrassed by police, taunted by other children in schools.

Despite the hostility, hispanics gradually began moving into wider reaches of the country and the economy.

■ In the 1940s, more than 90% of chicanos lived in California and the southwest and more than 90% of Puerto Ricans lived in New York. By the 1970s, significant hispanic communities had opened up much more widely throughout the country. In 1976, for example, 1.7 million hispanics lived in ten other important states outside the regions of their traditional residence: Colorado, Connecticut, Illinois, Indiana, Massachusetts, Michigan, New Jersey, Ohio, Pennsylvania, and Washington.[68]

■ They also began moving out of their traditional occupations. By 1977, only 3.4% of hispanics counted by the Census worked as farm workers, although many more worked without documentation.[69] By 1970, 12% of hispanics had been able to climb into what we called (in Chapter 13) "control" and "responsible" jobs. And 20% of hispanic households earned more than $25,000 a year in 1979.[70]

And yet, hispanics' efforts to join the mainstream of the U.S.

economy have been plagued continually by prejudice and disadvantage. Whether from Puerto Rico or Mexico, from migrant farm camps, the southwest *barrios* or New York City slums, hispanics have climbed over and through an unending series of obstacles.

One important problem has been that many hispanics still worked as contract laborers or illegal workers, only partly free to seek their own jobs at decent wages. For years, many Mexicans worked under the government's *bracero* program which permitted their entry into the U.S. as migrant farm workers and required their return when they were done. Puerto Rican workers were also frequently recruited for contract work.[71] The contractors had monstrous control:

> There was never any doubt about the contractor and his power over us. He could fire a man and his family on the spot and make them wait days for their wages. A man could be forced to quit by assigning him regularly to the thinnest pickings in the field. The worst thing one could do was to ask for fresh water on the job, regardless of the heat of the day....He usually had a pistol—to protect the payroll, so it was said.[72]

And when contract workers tried to unionize, employers brought in the *braceros*. As one union study concluded in the 1950s, "virtually every one of [our] strikes has been broken by the unrestricted use of *braceros* behind the union's picket-lines."[73]

Hispanics shared a second crippling problem with blacks leaving southern farms. Although the economy was growing rapidly during the 1950s and 1960s, it was not generating very many good jobs. (See Chapter 14.) As late arrivals, hispanics found themselves largely confined to dead-end jobs in both manufacturing and the services. And always, like shadows, stood the potential competitors—living in poverty in Mexico, Puerto Rico, and other Latin countries. Many leave for the United States despite their own preferences. "I love Mexico," one recent undocumented worker recounts. "It is very beautiful, but you can't live there. Coming to the U.S. was a question of economics."[74]

So many hispanics tread water in the stagnant tidal pools of the U.S. economy. In 1978, nearly 20% of chicano families and close to 40% of Puerto Rican families lived in poverty.[75] The chances of an hispanic household living in deficient housing are more than twice the average for the whole population.[76] As we saw at the beginning of this chapter,

hispanic workers earn incomes substantially below those of white males. And all these figures do not even count the roughly 7 million undocumented hispanic workers around the country.

Like blacks, hispanics have turned increasingly to militant struggle to try to overcome many of these disadvantages. Chicanos and Puerto Ricans have formed a wide variety of political and civil rights organizations to support their battles for equal rights and equal status. Hispanics have also turned increasingly to union organization as another way of improving their working and living conditions. Perhaps most dramatically, hispanic farmworkers have finally succeeded in bringing labor organization to the fields in which they've struggled for pennies for 50 years. A farmworkers' organizer conveys some of the importance of this emerging movement:

> **"You'd see the people on the picket lines at four in the morning, at the camp fires, heating up beans and coffee and tortillas. It gave me a sense of belonging. These were my own people and they wanted change....I just didn't know it before....Working in the fields is not in itself a degrading job....But the growers don't recognize us as persons. That's the worst thing, the way they treat you. Like we have no brains. Now we see they have no brains. They have only a wallet in their head. The more you squeeze it, the more they cry out."** [77]

JUST REWARDS?

> **"What kills me are these people that are on welfare and things like that—or like these colored people that're always squawking. Yet they don't wanta work. I go out, I work sometimes nine, ten days in a row, I got five children. That's what burns me...like this woman on the street here that collects welfare. She's a phony...and we pay for it."**
> —bricklayer in Boston [78]

As with the problems of women in the U.S. economy, this discussion of blacks and hispanics suggests several obvious lessons:

The history of inequalities is not fixed in concrete but is frequently changing. Its roots are deep and its causes fundamental. Employers constantly manipulate the differences which exist. Many whites also appear to be able to take advantage of minorities' vulnerability. And yet, time and time again, whites in struggle have discovered they needed to unify with workers of every race and ethnicity.

Most working people understand many of these lessons. And yet many hesitate to attack the basic sources of racial and ethnic discrimination and oppression. Many feel, in ways we discussed in Chapter 14, that we can each succeed on our own. Many seem to feel that blacks and hispanics have not tried hard enough—that they're somehow to blame for their own problems.

These impressions, as with those blocking unity between men and women, must be considered very carefully. We consider them in the same order as presented in Chapter 15.

Too Few Skills?

Are blacks and hispanics trapped in dead-end jobs because they have too few skills? Shouldn't they just stay in school longer?

It is true, on average, that blacks and hispanics have stayed in school for less time than whites and that they have received less skills training on the job. But there are three problems with the immediate conclusion that we can attribute minority workers' lower job status and earnings to their lower skills.

1) Only part of the earnings gap between whites and minority workers is attributable to differences in skills. At least one-third of the gap between white men and black men and probably as much of the gap between white men and hispanic men persists even when we compare people with essentially the same skills characteristics.[79]

2) The gap between the earnings of white and minority men has remained roughly constant over the past 30 years despite dramatic reductions in the schooling gap. Blacks now stay in school nearly as long as whites, for example, but their earnings remain far lower. For minorities graduating from college, education matters. For almost all the rest, there is very little return to staying in school a few years more.[80]

3) One of the main reasons that whites and minorities have different skills and different earnings levels involves differences in their family backgrounds. We saw in Chapter 14 that, among white men considered by themselves, family background makes an enormous difference in how much schooling and how many skills they acquire. The same conclusions apply for comparisons between whites and minorities. Roughly 30% of the earnings gap between black and white men, for example, is due to differences in family background.[81] In order to improve chances for future generations, we would need to begin improving the working and living conditions of minorities in the present.

Some people have also wondered about differences in intelligence. Although by the 1960s fewer than 20% of whites thought that blacks were less "intelligent" than whites,[82] some people still seem to spread the suspicion that minorities have less intelligence.

Here the evidence is clear. Blacks and whites raised in comparable settings have no differences in measured intelligence.[83] IQ tests measure certain kinds of abilities which are best encouraged in affluent families. The IQ gap between poor and affluent families is much wider than the IQ gap between average black and average white children.[84]

In short, minority workers face many obstacles on the job, only one of which is somewhat lower skills. And most of these skill handicaps are due to the relative poverty of their families, not to their lack of diligence in acquiring skills. We cannot assume that minority workers would solve their problems if they studied harder and learned more. They need access to better jobs. And minority families in this generation need much more equal incomes and job security in order to provide the basis for their children acquiring equal skills. Discrimination and poverty are the most important problems, not skill levels.

Bad Risks on the Job?

Do minority workers end up in dead-end jobs because they don't stick to their work and keep at it long enough?

The problem, once again, lies in the jobs, not the people. Many of the jobs in which minority workers are concentrated provide no inducements for steady work since they provide little opportunity for advancement. And many of their jobs expose them to exhausting physical conditions and continuing stress—making it more and more difficult for them to remain on those jobs. *When minority workers have good jobs, the data show that they stay on those jobs as long as white workers.*[85]

Create enough good jobs for minority workers, in short, and the "bad risk" rap will seem like a distant memory.

Too Lazy and Shiftless?

These myths about minorities have insidious effects. They lead to support for cutbacks in necessary government services which *both* whites and minorities desperately need. All to get back at the "chiselers and cheaters."

The myths are indeed myths. Minority workers are likely to have special problems because they're poor, not because of their racial or ethnic backgrounds. Studies have shown, for example, that the high proportion of family break-up in minority families is almost entirely due to their higher rates of poverty and unemployment, not to some special racial and ethnic traits.[86] Other studies have shown that higher rates of teenage pregnancy among minority youth are explained by their relative poverty, not by their race.[87]

Perhaps most strikingly, studies have found that teenagers of all different races and class backgrounds commit crimes in roughly equal proportions. What differs by race is that the police and courts tend to arrest blacks and hispanics and put them through the "system" in much higher numbers. White kids and middle-class kids are much more likely to be handed over to their families and their shrinks for some stern words of caution and a little slap on the wrist.[88] These differences in the way they're treated mean, of course, that black and hispanic kids get a "record" and have more trouble getting good jobs later on.

Are minorities really different? Or do they just want a decent job like everyone else? The numbers say that they're like the rest of us. And their experiences confirm the numbers. One researcher interviewed scores of unemployed teenagers in Boston:

> More than half of the youngsters...said that they had [recently] engaged in illegal activity....[They] sold marijuana frequently, and some reported that robbery, pickpocketing, burglary and breaking and entering took up most of their time the week prior....[But] *all of the teenagers wanted a full-time permanent job.*[89]

What About Numero Uno?

Aren't times hard enough? Don't we have enough on our hands watching out for ourselves? How can we also worry about uniting with blacks and hispanics?

In fact, whites and minorities have always discovered, in the end, that they need to organize together to advance any of their separate objectives. Without this unity, employers and the wealthy can play one group off against another.

A recent study provides some interesting evidence supporting this lesson.[90] It finds that the wealthy are best off when there are the greatest gaps *between* whites and minorities. The study looks at the distribution of income *among whites*. And it shows that a 10% greater gap between white incomes and black incomes—meaning greater racial inequality—is associated with the wealthiest 1% of whites earning a significantly higher share of *white* income. That greater gap is correspondingly associated with the poorest and middle-level white families earning *less* of white income.

Why is this? Why do working whites feel the pinch of greater racial inequality as well as blacks? The explanation comes from our own experiences in struggle. When we're united, we get more from the large corporations and the wealthy. When racial and ethnic divisions increase, our bargaining power suffers. When we're divided, even white workers get less—and the wealthy and powerful bank the difference.

These lessons have a long history. A white business agent of the carpenters' union in Georgia explained why his union was trying to organize black carpenters and joiners in 1902:

> We are always in competition with them. The contractors prefer them because they can get them cheap....So I say we must organize them; for if we can afford to work all day on a scaffold beside them, then we can surely afford to meet them in the hall for an hour or so....The mere fact that all of the boss builders in the South are advocating leaving the negroes out of the union is a good reason why we should organize them....Let the good work go on, and let us hope for the day when there will be equal rights for all and special privileges to none.[91]

And the history continues. As one black editor concludes in 1980:

> The city is not heaven any more....It is not a city of hope. The whites are victims, too. They have no power. Being white has not paid off for them, but it's the only thing they've got....We have to work out a strategy to give ordinary people power. We've been bullshitting ourselves. We always were every man for himself.... There must be a new way of thinking.[92]

17.

Traditions of Resistance and Struggle

"[We marched] to the public works and the workmen joined with us. Employment ceased, business was at a standstill, shirt-sleeves were rolled up, aprons on, working tools in hand were the orders of the day."

—organizer of a protest for the 10-hour day, 1835[1]

"It was like we was soldiers holding the fort. It was like war. I remember as a kid in school readin' about Davy Crockett and the last stand at the Alamo. You know, mister, that's just how I felt. Yes sir, Chevy No. 4 was my Alamo."

—participant in sit-down at GM, 1937[2]

"My husband and I were like most people. We'd sit in our backyards, have a drink and complain about the politicians...[A community group wanted to use the school building.] The aldermen were going to limit use of school buildings so you had to get an okay from the board of aldermen, the mayor's office, the school board and the building department to have a meeting. If that's not an infringement of my constitutional rights, what is? [The community group protested at the aldermen's meeting and won.] I don't think I will ever enjoy anything more in my life than that night, letting the politicians know we're not so dumb. Once any citizen recognizes that can be done, that is the turning point of their community life."

—participant in community protest, 1976[3]

Millions of working people in the United States are angry—eager and determined to redress grievances on and off the job. But many of us hesitate to press ahead, wondering if we can win, doubting our power.

And yet, in our history, working people have rallied repeatedly in spite of these hesitations—we usually haven't a choice. There is a long, rich history of successful people's resistance and struggle in the United States. This tradition of resistance and struggle has never completely solved anybody's problems; we wouldn't be in the mess we are today if it had. Nonetheless, people have won fundamental, historically irreversible victories over the past 300 years in the United States. Our lives are incomparably better today as a result of those victories.

How have earlier generations waged their struggles in similar situations? What problems generated temporary failures? How did people overcome failure and march toward (at least partial) success?

This chapter reviews the tradition of popular resistance and struggle in the United States. It aims both to remind us of the richness and power of that tradition and to draw some lessons from it—toward reducing the chances of failure and improving our chances for success. On and off the job, in our private and public lives...how have we fought for ourselves in U.S. history?

WORKERS' RESISTANCE AND STRUGGLE

"[The strike started on Wednesday.] We met the police again. This time they really took a swat at us, and they were beating the hell out of everybody in the front lines....

"This got a lot of union people mad....So we decided to hold a big meeting the following Sunday, which was Memorial Day....Everybody said we should picket; now we were going to picket.

"After the meeting was over we started to march, and I went down with the front group, right by the flag, and there we met about 650 cops lined up....I didn't like it. Don't ever think that anybody's that brave. But I was an organizer in charge of the picket line, so I walked along....And I looked up and said, 'Well, here we are. We'd like to go through. Would you escort us? We'd like to picket.'...

"They began to shoot us, club us, and gas us....I could smell the gunpowder—I'll never forget it—and then I began to see people fall. I saw a boy run by, and his foot was bleeding. Then it dawned on me. They were shooting real bullets. This was for keeps."

—participant in "Memorial Day Massacre," Chicago, 1937[4]

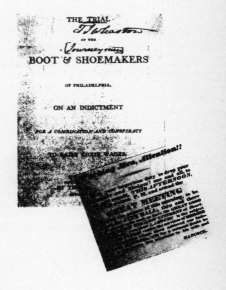

Working people have been joining together in resistance and struggle in the United States as long as they've been working here. Maine fishermen struck in 1736. Georgia carpenters struck in 1746. Indentured servants helped lead Bacon's Rebellion in Virginia in 1676. Slaves rebelled against their bondage and working conditions in New York as early as 1712 and in South Carolina as early as 1739. Many craft workers formed secret societies to pursue their common economic interests—often cloaking their intentions in what were typically called "friendly societies."[5]

These early struggles were usually brief. As we saw in Chapter 2, wage workers formed a small minority of the adult population in the 18th and early 19th centuries. From then on, the early spread of capitalism exposed hundreds of thousands of wage workers to deprivation and insecurity. A printer who arrived in New York in 1820 reflected the conditions of many: "I had barely two dollars in my pocket when I got here with my family. We lived eight days without tea, sugar, or meat—on bread and butter only with cold water. It is pinching times."[6] Sustained fights for better conditions followed close behind.

Early Lessons

As workers' unrest spread, protesters quickly learned two obvious lessons on the barriers to successful protest:

1) Employers' power to hire and fire gave them huge advantages as long as there was a surplus of potential workers within the bosses' reach. Children provided some of this surplus in early years. It was therefore common, a New Jersey newspaper reported in 1835, "to see little children...running through the snows and storms with a crust in their hands...lest by being a few minutes too late they should incur the

displeasure of their employer and get discharged."[7]

2) Public officials could not be counted on to take the side of the majority; they frequently sided with employers. Workers learned that they had to rely on their own organizations and not look to the government or outsiders to solve their problems.

These lessons suggested some clear strategies in response:[8]

■ Workers *needed to build their own organizations* and, unlike the earlier strikes by journeymen, to make them stick. Many working groups in the 1820s and 1830s formed trade alliances and political parties to support and extend their struggles. (The early unions were generally called "trades" and the phrase "trade union" originally came from connections among those trades—hence, a "union of trades" or a "trades' union.")

For example, the Philadelphia Trades' Union had 50 member societies by 1836 with a membership of 10,000. A general strike in 1835 forced the adoption of the ten-hour day throughout the city. According to the strike's leader, the "blood-sucking aristocracy...stood aghast, terror-stricken; they thought the day of retribution had come...."[9] He was right. "If such is to be the reward of turn-outs," the *New York Journal* moaned, "there will be no end to them."[10]

■ Self-organization was usually not enough. Particularly for women and children workers, successful protests required successful *public appeals and alliances.* A children's strike in Paterson, New Jersey in 1835 provides one example. The children struck for a shorter working-day. Their parents and guardians formed the "Paterson Association for the Protection of the Working Classes of Paterson." Weak within the city because of opposition to the strike, they called for help from neighboring communities. Newark workers raised money, condemning the factories as conditions "more congenial to the climate of his majesty the emperor and autocrat of all of the Russia...."[11] The children and parents held out and eventually won a reduction of up to two hours in the working day.

■ Workers also found, finally, that they had *to back their demands with clear displays of determination and force.* In 1835 in Philadelphia, for example, the strike for a ten-hour day began with a protest among Irish workers on the Schuylkill River coal wharves. As was their habit, the bosses sent immediately for scabs to break the strike. According to a Philadelphia paper, "three hundred of [the striking workers], headed by a man armed with a sword, paraded along the Canal, threatening death to those who unload or transfer the cargoes to the 75 vessels waiting in the river."[12] The scabs disappeared, the Irish workers won their demands, and the ten-hour movement spread throughout the city.

Facing a National Labor Market

For a time, despite the *New York Journal*'s fears, there was an "end to them." Working people were learning still another difficult lesson in the next several decades: just as they were beginning to achieve some success, the economy would undercut them. They might be able to out-organize and outfight employers in one set of conditions, but

"The blood-sucking aristocracy stood aghast. . . ."
—*1835 newspaper*

changing conditions in some other part of the country might blunt their swords. The force of national labor market competition was spreading.

Employers soon discovered, for example, that they could discipline new immigrant workers better than native workers. New arrivals were isolated in the factory towns, were often resented by native workers, and had trouble building the kinds of connections and alliances which protests seemed to require. By the 1850s, employers were beginning to race around Europe, searching for more immigrants to maintain the flow. Industrialists were ready to admit, as one employer put it in the late 1850s, that they could not "obtain good interest for their money, were they deprived of this constant influx of foreign labor."[13]

These developments produced two important changes in working people's approach to their resistance and struggle. The more developed these strategies, the greater the chances of successful protest.

■ Trade unions recognized the need for mechanisms for *coordinating and sustaining their struggles reaching beyond their local labor markets.* (These state and national organizations were organized on a craft-union basis.) In New York State, for example, nearly 15,000 workers enjoyed the eight-hour day earlier than workers elsewhere in the U.S. because they recognized that they would have to continue to fight—using whatever organizational muscle they could muster—to protect the gains they had formally won through the law. As many as 100,000 workers struck in New York in 1872, coordinated by a broad union coalition, to ensure that protection.[14]

■ Probably even more important, working people discovered that they could only cope with the divisions fostered by labor market competition if they *strengthened their local trade councils and district assemblies to steer and unify their protests.* Two climactic moments in the history of the U.S. labor movement both illustrate this lesson:[15]

The first occurred in 1877. The economy had experienced four bitter years of depression. As many as one million workers were unemployed. Wages had fallen by as much as 25%. The time hardly seemed ripe for successful protest. But workers could no longer tolerate their conditions. The Great Upheaval of 1877, as it was called, spread like a prairie fire.

It started with a railroad strike in Martinsburg, West Virginia. Word of the workers' success travelled the rails as quickly as the trains steamed from town to town. Thousands of railroad workers joined in protests against wage cuts. When police and troops moved to quell the strikes, workers in many other industries joined to protest the military intervention. Perhaps most dramatically, a general strike committee virtually ran St. Louis. The railroad workers kept the trains running themselves; the committee allowed the bread factories to remain open so that people could eat.

The mass movement was so successful that it could only be beaten, finally, by violent military force. The strikers had demonstrated the extraordinary power of people massing to express common grievances. The strikes spread spontaneously because working people shared a

Employers needed immigrants to obtain "good interest for their money"
—employer, 1850s

common conviction. "There was no concert of action at the start," a labor journalist reported. "It spread because the workmen of Pittsburgh felt the same oppression that was felt by the workmen of West Virginia and so with the workmen of Chicago and St. Louis."[16]

A similar prairie fire spread in May, 1886. Conditions had not improved since the 1870s; if anything, they were still worse. Once again, contagious strikes spread. The strikes were often linked by an organization called the Knights of Labor whose motto was "An injury to one is the concern of all." By 1886, the membership of the Knights of Labor had climbed from 71,000 to 730,000 in just five years.

Workers were demanding an eight-hour day. Strikes spread everywhere on May Day. A parade in Baltimore captured the contagious spirit:

> The third of May will be remembered in Baltimore as witnessing the largest and most imposing street parades of organized workingmen ever seen in this section....The streets along the road were

Wotta Pickle!

> a blaze of light, lit up by thousands of torches and lanterns carried by the men in line.[17]

As many as 200,000 workers won reductions in their working days through the protests. Although military force once again contained the rebellion, the May Day fever showed what mass strength could accomplish. As a labor paper reported on the spirit in Chicago: "It is an eight-hour boom, and we are scoring victory after victory....Men are wild with joy at the grand victory they have gained."[18]

Large Corporations Come to Dinner

Employers now realized that more than the threat of labor market competition was necessary to withstand workers' struggles. In many cases, like the 1892 Homestead Strike described in Chapter 4, they used navy vessels and called in huge numbers of state and federal troops. More and more, as well, they systematically promoted divisions among different racial and ethnic groups of workers—trying to undercut the unity which working people had demonstrated they could achieve.

Companies relied on a wide variety of tactics. They moved factories to the suburbs, scattering their workers among isolated pockets of what they called industrial "satellites." They invented job ladders to promote worker competition. They played around with different kinds of piece rates. Perhaps most important, they played different ethnic groups against each other. The U.S. Industrial Commission concluded in 1911:

> In many cases the conscious policy of the employers [is] mixing the races in certain departments and divisions,...preventing concert of action on the part of the employees....[These policies] made it possible for the employers to carry out their policy of undermining the unions' elements of strength and control in the industry.[19]

For a time, the labor movement tried to fight these employer assaults with their traditional strategies.

The craft unions continued to rely on organized and sustained drives among skilled workers. The American Federation of Labor, which had been formed in the depression of the 1880s, emerged as the leader of the skilled trades. After the economy began to grow again, in the late 1890s, the AFL unions began to grow and sustain their strength. Whenever the economy prospered, the craft unions grew

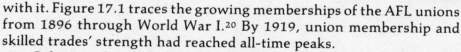
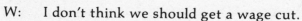

with it. Figure 17.1 traces the growing memberships of the AFL unions from 1896 through World War I.[20] By 1919, union membership and skilled trades' strength had reached all-time peaks.

Other workers, ignored by the AFL, continued to rely on mass strikes and unified organizing among all industrial workers. Most important were efforts by the Industrial Workers of the World (IWW), which had been formed in 1905 to promote unity among all workers. One of the IWW's greatest victories came at the Lawrence, Mass. strike of 1912. Many had learned the lessons about unity from earlier struggles. One native worker (W) had signed a strike petition. The foreman (F) asked him why:

W: I don't think we should get a wage cut.

F: You shouldn't have your name with these foreigners.

W: I work with them, don't I?

F: Yes, but you want to get a better position soon, don't you? Stand by the company. I'll cross off your name.

W: I'm going on strike if the others do.[21]

The problem was that these two strands of the labor movement needed each other but failed to work together. The AFL was strong as long as skilled workers were necessary in production. If and when employers eliminated their reliance on skilled workers, the craft unions went out the window. And the skilled workers' isolation from laborers and operatives left them without allies and defenses when employers undercut their base of strength.

In contrast, the mass movements needed the sustaining support of national organizations and connections to maintain their momentum. The victories at Lawrence and Paterson in 1912 and 1913 were not followed by others in subsequent years at least partly because the IWW was not able (and did not fully try) to establish a powerful national organization.

Working apart, in short, each movement missed the other's strength and corporations gained correspondingly. The years immediately following World War I demonstrated this lesson dramatically.

■ On the one hand, labor's greatest strength came through *coordinated and organized struggles among all workers.* The Seattle General Strike of 1919 provides the clearest example.[22] AFL unions joined with the IWW and with separately organized Japanese workers to manage the strike. A General Strike Committee, composed of three members elected by the rank-and-file from each striking local, administered the strike. The Strike's commissary fed 30,000 people a day. The milkmen organized a separate distribution system to transport milk while bypassing the employers at whom the strike was aimed. A trained strike militia kept peace on the streets; the U.S. General in charge of Seattle forces admitted grudgingly that he had not seen a city so quiet and orderly in his 40 years of military experience.

The General Strike provided an important message. Workers

could run their own economy peacefully and democratically if they built enough unity within their ranks. The threat of violence which finally ended the strike came from outside the movement. As one labor paper concluded, "Violence would have come in Seattle, if it had come, not from the workers, but from attempts by armed opponents of the strike to break down the authority of the strike committee over its own members."[23]

■ On the other hand, the labor movement *suffered the greatest losses when it became most divided.* After 1921, swooping like vultures sensing the labor movement's vulnerability, employers attacked with a wide variety of strategies aimed at fragmenting unions and workers. The labor movement faltered badly under this pressure. Union membership itself declined from a peak of 5 million in 1920 to 3.5 million just four years later.

Finally, after several years of Depression, the dams broke. Millions joined the mass industrial unions of the Congress of Industrial Organizations (CIO) during the mid- and late-1930s.

Learning obvious lessons from the previous retreats, workers largely based their successful organizing on two basic principles: *industrial unionism* and *political mobilization.* In applying those principles, workers developed new tactics to overcome four important obstacles to earlier struggles:

1) Divisions had continued to plague organizing efforts. Ford was the last auto company organized, as we saw in Chapter 16, at least partly because it had cultivated a special force of black workers on whom it relied for strike-breaking at crucial moments. The United Auto Workers (UAW) finally mobilized leaders in the black community to help overcome this suspicion of the unions by black workers. The outreach worked, the organizing drives succeeded, and Henry Ford was crushed. "This was the last straw," Ford's aide reported. "He was never the same after that."[24]

2) The unions had also been hurt by companies' efforts to manipulate job assignments. Rank-and-file workers insisted that unions oppose the bosses' arbitrary job power; unions increasingly demanded both grievance procedures and seniority systems as methods for grabbing back some of this power over job assignment. The victory was important, as one labor historian concludes, because it dramatically restricted "management's discretion...in making arbitrary or discriminatory choices."[25]

3) Many earlier organizing efforts had been thwarted by the government. Unions recognized that they must neutralize government support for business by establishing their rights *on the books.* Unions won several critical legislative victories during the 1930s which helped weaken employers' grip on the courts and the legislatures. Both the Wagner Act and the Norris-LaGuardia Act gave organizing a much greater legitimacy and free rein than it had formerly been granted.

4) Perhaps most important, unions discovered a way of overcoming their earlier vulnerability to strike-breakers and their isolation in scattered plants. Before, when workers struck, the bosses could import strike-breakers and workers found it difficult to attract enough sup-

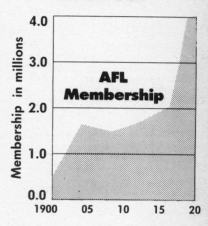

Fig. 17.1
Union Membership Takes Off

AFL Membership

The graph shows the number of members of the American Federation of Labor (in millions) from 1900 through World War I.

Source: See note #20

Diverse ethnic members, clothing workers union, early 1900s.

port to close the plant. Solution: the sit-down strike. When workers "seized" the factories, strike-breakers were useless. Employers feared to charge the plants with troops because the battle might result in damage to their machines and building. If the workers could hold the building long enough for union reinforcements and auxiliary support to arrive, they could turn their isolation on its head.

The sit-down strike was a brilliant innovation by workers after years of difficulty and weakness. Workers could feel the force of their victories. As one worker at a GM plant explained: "The inhuman high speed is *no more.* We now have a voice, and have slowed up the speed of the line. And [we] are now treated as human beings, and not as part of the machinery....It proves clearly that united we stand, divided or alone we fall."[26]

The victories of the late 1930s galvanized the labor movement through and after World War II. Figure 17.2 shows the growth in union membership from 1920 to 1950. Strikes continued to spread when necessary. Workers continued to improve their working and living conditions throughout the country. Working people appeared to be on the march.

The pace of that march slowed during the 1950s and 1960s. We shall return for a closer look in the next two chapters of this book, but one might already make a reasonable guess that the union movement began to slow because workers began to face new obstacles—like plant movement and "multi-sourcing" of firm supplies—and had not yet developed new strategies to overcome those obstacles.

One way or another, such responses will come. For if this history of workers' resistance and struggle tells us anything, it reveals a continuing historical force. As long as bosses have had control, working people have been forced to respond to their attacks and their harrassments. As one local union president recently observed:

> I feel good all around when I'm able to stand up and speak for another guy's rights. That's how I got involved in this whole stinkin' mess....[The workers] just want to be treated with dignity. That's not asking a hell of a lot.[27]

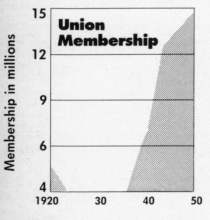

Fig. 17.2
Union Membership Soars Higher

The graph traces the growth in total labor union membership (in millions) from the end of World War I through the rapid growth during and after World War II.

Source: See note #20

COMMUNITY RESISTANCE AND STRUGGLE

"There are alternate routes—Memorial Drive, Albany Street —but they figure they're going to step on the little guy [by running that freeway through here]....It's just a kick in the teeth these people around here don't need."
          —participant in 1960s community protest against expressway[28]

"It makes me so mad. It's supposed to be the people's government and those politicians get up there and they don't do anything the people tell them to do. They do what the special interests want them to do."
          —microfilm clerk in Los Angeles, 1978[29]

We work but we also live as residents and citizens—in our homes, in our neighborhoods, in our communities, our cities, states, and country. Our lives in those spaces have never been as well protected as "castles," but most people in the United States have expected and demanded basic rights to self-determination and democracy from the beginning of our history. Those rights have often been denied. And so, people have been protesting in our communities for centuries. Most of the space and rights we currently command never fell like manna from heaven. They resulted from continuing community resistance and struggle.

The Earliest Battles

The first community protests focused on food prices and rents—the basic essentials of popular life in the colonies.

In the cities, people often grew angry over sudden changes in food prices—which were supposedly regulated by custom and habit. When food prices suddenly soared, people quickly mobilized to bring them back down to earth. In 1710, for example, about 50 Bostonians joined in a crowd to seize some ships bearing food, hoping to keep the grain in the town and prevent its export. In 1772, to pick another example, a Rhode Island crowd actually burned a British ship because its captain had been "stealing sheep, hogs, poultry, etc. from farmers around the bay, and cutting down their fruit and other trees for firewood." That was bad enough, but it came at a time of "deepest calamity," as the local governor put it, because food prices were rising steeply.[30]

In the countryside, tenants mobilized against the high rents charged by distant landlords. A historian has recently summarized these uprisings:

> The tenant riots in New Jersey in the 1740s, the New York tenant uprisings of the 1750s and 1760s in the Hudson Valley, and the rebellion in northeastern New York that led to the carving of Vermont out of New York State were all more than sporadic rioting. They were long-lasting social movements, highly organized, involving the creation of countergovernments. They were aimed at a handful of rich landlords....[31]

Factory occupants in sit-down strike, 1937.

These early protests seemed so deeply rooted, indeed, that the Founding Fathers sensed both their permanence and their necessity. "I can't describe the sighing after independence," one merchant wrote to John Adams. "It is universal."[32] "What country can preserve its liberties," Thomas Jefferson wrote in 1787, "if their rulers are not warned from time to time that their people preserve the spirit of resistance?... [It is] a medicine necessary for the sound health of government."[33]

And the country had not grown very old after its freedom from English rule before some people felt it necessary to apply that medicine. One of the first and most important rebellions was Shay's Rebellion in Massachusetts in 1785. The "sighing" after liberty had been "universal," but the new property requirements for voting were exclusive. "No one could hold state office without being quite wealthy," a historian writes, and the legislature was not issuing enough money "to make it easier for debt-ridden farmers to pay off their creditors."[34] Local farmers in western Massachusetts began holding their own conventions and courts. When offical courts tried to seize debtors' property, the farmers massed to bar the courts from meeting.

Within months, the rebellion led to armed conflict with the state militia. Bad weather and superior firepower combined to defeat the rebels. Several were hanged on the principle, as Samuel Adams put it, "that the man who dares rebel against the laws of the republic ought to suffer death."[35] But the rebels had spoken and acted clearly. One of their ranks, a farmer named Plough Jogger, explained their anger:

> I have been greatly abused, have been obliged to do more than my part in the war; been loaded with class rates, town rates, province rates, Continental rates and all rates....The great men are going to get all we have and I think it is time for us to rise and put a stop to it....[36]

Seeking a Voice in the New Nation

The United States after Independence provided a new space in the sun for many who had formerly rebelled. There was land west of the Appalachian mountains. The British were off our backs. The spirit of democracy, stirred by the triumph of a successful revolution, rustled the trees.

As the decades progressed, however, more and more people began to wonder about the *realities* of democracy.

Economic life itself became more and more uncertain as prices fluctuated and land values contracted speculative fever. People needed wealth to weather the epidemics of surging prices and speculation, of course, but the distribution of wealth became more and more unequal in the 1820s and 1830s.[37] It became increasingly apparent that, although all men had the right to vote, some men were getting much more from the government than others.

Popular protest followed quickly. Much of its venom aimed at the banks and their power. Many objected, as one popular paper put it, that the mechanic was "obliged to appear cap in hand, with an unbecoming self-abasement, before the aristocratic moneylender." They demanded changes in the banking system, as one political resolution put it, which "would prevent the man of doubtful honesty, whatever might be his wealth, from obtaining very extensive credit; and [which] would enable the honest man, however poor, to obtain as much credit as he ought."[38]

This anger produced two different streams of community protest.

■ For those who had most direct access to the political system, parties and electoral politics held real promise. In New York State, for example, the Workingmen's Party was formed in 1829. At various times over the 20 years, the party or its constituents demanded public support of education for everyone, control of the banks, and representative governments.[39] By 1846, the pressure they generated resulted in some sweeping changes in the New York State Constitution which reflected their concerns. Most offices were now elective rather than appointive. Judges were also to be elected for short terms. The law was to be rewritten and systematized so that everyone could understand it—a law for the many instead of the privileged and the palm-readers. The state was obligated to establish a general fund to support "common schools" even where communities were unable to fund them.[40] As one merchant predictably lamented after the new constitution was passed, "the tendency of universal suffrage is to jeopardize the rights of property."[41]

■ Others had less access to the levers of government. Neither black slaves nor Native Americans were yet recognized as people with legitimate political interests. A British visitor to the United States in 1832 noted the double standards by which white men ran their "democratic" government:

> They inveigh against the governments of Europe, because, as they say, they favour the powerful and oppress the weak....[But] you will see [the Americans] with one hand hoisting the cap of liberty, and the other flogging their slaves. You will see them one hour lecturing...on the [indivisible] rights of man, and the next driving from their homes the children of the soil [Native Americans], whom they have bound themselves to protect by the most solemn treaties.[42]

Given fewer and fewer places to run or escape, both blacks and Native Americans began during these early decades the long, slow struggle—still incomplete—for equal rights and equal influence on "their" government.

Women's struggles for democratic rights also began to gather steam during the 1830s and 1840s. The abolitionist crusade against slavery inevitably raised questions about women's political rights as well. If black slaves should be free and be allowed to vote, why not women? Angelina Grimké, one of the first leaders of the women's rights movement, argued in the 1830s that sex should have as little to do with political rights as race, creed, or color. "What then can woman do for the slave," she asked, "when she herself is under the feet of man and shamed into silence?"[43] The issue was most squarely joined at a convention on women's rights in 1851, when a woman named Sojourner Truth, who had been born a slave, criticized some male ministers who had been dominating the discussion:

That man over there says that woman needs to be helped into carriages and lifted over ditches....Nobody ever helps me into carriages, or over mud-puddles or gives me any best place. And ain't I a woman? I would work as much and eat as much as a man, when I could get it, and bear the lash as well. And ain't I a woman?[44]

Even poor white men felt excluded from the politics shaping their lives. Much of their anger crested during the Civil War, when poor and working people demonstrated against the draft—apparently feeling that the poor were being conscripted to fight for the wealthy. In New York City in 1863, for example, nearly 50,000 joined in marches against the draft. "The draft office was burned. For four days following, mobs of working men and lower-class citizens broke into the stores and homes of the rich...." Historians have estimated that as many as 2,000 were dead by the time police and troops finally quelled the angry mobs.[45]

Making Protest Stick

These earlier protests, while they often gained immediate concessions, did not always have lasting effect. After the Civil War, various coalitions turned more and more toward permanent organizations and political parties which would sustain their movements and support their demands with more enduring impact.

In the countryside, many farmers grew increasingly angry about rising rents and interest charges. In the early 1870s, the Grange—an organization of small farmers—spread quickly throughout the midwest. It had about 14,000 local chapters and probably close to 500,000 farmer members. According to one historian, the Grange "became a powerful political force overnight, obtaining the passage of state laws regulating railroad and grain elevators and...restricting the practices of businessmen engaged in marketing and transporting farm products."[46] The political strength of U.S. farmers stems in large part from the successes of the Grange movement during those decades.

In the cities, many joined in protests against the weight of burdensome property taxes. Henry George spoke for many in his book, *Poverty and Progress*, calling for a "single tax" on the growing wealth of landlords....The single tax movement spread widely. George himself won 31% of the mayoral vote in New York City in 1886. A labor candidate similarly won 28% of the vote in Chicago and the popular movement elected the mayor of Milwaukee. George's platform in the New York election expressed the breadth of concerns of many in these urban movements, demanding, for example:

that property qualification be abolished for members of juries;
that the police not interfere with peaceful meetings;
that contract labor be abolished in public works;
that there be equal pay for equal work for women; and
that the streetcars be owned by the municipal government.[47]

Urban and rural movements began to combine as the Depression continued through the 1880s. The Populists, as they were called,

In the 1870s, the farmers' Grange had close to 500,000 members.

emerged as the voice of people's anger against the wealthy and the power of money. With hundreds of thousands of supporters by the early 1890s, the Populists defined a sweeping agenda for social and political change in their communities. They demanded a system of price supports to help sustain farmers' incomes. They insisted on a graduated income tax so that those who could best afford taxes would pay more. They demanded *direct* election of Senators to protect against their appointment by the wealthy. They pushed for public ownership of basic services like the railroads, telephone and telegraph so that the wealthy would not profit from "natural monopolies." And they called for subsidized loans at no more than 2% of interest.[48]

The point of all these demands was clear. "We believe," the Populist party platform affirmed in 1892, "that the powers of government— in other words, of the people—should be expanded...to the end that oppression, injustice, and poverty shall eventually cease in the land."[49] And the wealthy believed them. Hearing about the 1892 convention, one wealthy woman in Indiana left quickly for Europe. "I am going to spend my money," she explained, "before those crazy people take it."[50]

It took decades for many of these reforms to come to pass. But continuing protest ultimately won direct election of Senators, suffrage for women, the right to public referenda, and government regulation of many "natural monopolies." With those victories, new concerns and objects of protest replaced the old.

Digging in for the Long Haul

People had gained many *rights of representation* through the movements of the late 19th and early 20th centuries. But communities discovered soon enough that representation was not enough. As people struggled to cope with the growing size and complexity of institutions in the 20th century, three more lessons became increasingly evident.

■ Representation was no substitute for the strength of ties and bonds in the local community. Some issues required direct action, and there was no way that the government was likely to act either quickly or responsively.

One clear example involved neighborhood actions during the Depression. Many found it difficult to pay their rents, of course, and most landlords quickly ordered eviction. Neighborhood groups would immediately rally supporters from the community. Marshalls or police would sometimes be greeted by 4,000-5,000 demonstrators surrounding the buildings. It sometimes took as many as 100-200 police to deliver an eviction notice. One estimate suggests that at least 75,000 evicted families were restored to their apartments by neighborhood movements in New York City alone.[51]

The key to successful protest was the network of community connections. People heard it through the grapevine. As one Chicago resident recalls,

A lot of 'em was put out. As soon as [the bailiffs] would leave, we would put 'em back where they came out. All we had to do was call....Look, such and such a place, there's a family sittin' out there.

> "I'm spending my money before those crazy people take it."
> —wealthy Indianan, 1892

Everybody...had one person they would call. When that one person came, he'd have fifty people with him....Take that stuff right on back up there....Put the furniture back just like you had it, so it don't look like you been out the door.[52]

■ A second lesson became more and more obvious after World War II. Government agencies were themselves growing large and everpresent. It was no longer enough for people to be able to exercise *electoral* influence. It became increasingly important for people to be able to exercise direct *administrative* influence as well. Government agencies could affect the future of entire neighborhoods. Communities discovered that they needed to organize on their own to protect their own interests.

One historian recounts one example of such efforts, tracing the struggle by a neighborhood in Boston to control the impact of airport expansion on its own community life:

> In September 1968, the residents of Maverick Street, tired of having six hundred trucks a day use their streets going to and from the airport, decided to conduct a "baby-carriage blockage." A group of women and children parked themselves on the street and physically blocked the trucks for a week. Police were called, but turned out to be in sympathy with the blockaders. Under pressure from the mayor, the Massachusetts Port Authority finally agreed to construct a new road on airport property to relieve the traffic....
>
> Direct action tactics were next applied to oppose further airport expansion. In early 1969, residents conducted a series of coordinated slowdowns and blockades on bridges and tunnels leading to the airport. "Telephone trees" linked residents in various neighborhoods....[These] direct action techniques were used to oppose a proposed runway expansion, finally forcing the governor of the state to intervene against it.[53]

■ People have also discovered, finally, that formal protection by the law often means little—that *people need to organize continually and militantly to protect and extend their rights.* The black struggle for civil

These are OUR People!

rights in the 1950s and 1960s is a recent and clear example. The 14th Amendment was supposed to guarantee equal protection under the law. Blacks in the South knew better. The government had assured black leaders that "equality" and "justice" for all was on the way. Blacks knew better. The lawyers couldn't deliver, so people marched. People sat-in at public facilities. People faced the threat of jail. And people even risked their lives—all in pursuit of their legal rights.

Few would argue today that blacks would have gained basic civil rights, including the effective right to vote in the South, without "taking it to the streets." Early in the civil rights movement, Martin Luther King, Jr. recognized this need and possibility:

> We have known humiliation, we have known abusive language, we have been plunged into the abyss of oppression. And we have decided to raise up only with the weapon of protest....If we are arrested every day, if we are exploited every day, if we are trampled over every day, don't ever let anyone pull you so low....We stand in life at midnight, we are always on the threshold of a new dawn.[54]

LEARNING THE LESSONS OF RESISTANCE AND STRUGGLE

"[Our] slogan goes 'the people shall rule.' That is what America is. That is what [we want]. Nothing more and nothing less."

—leader of southern community organization[55]

None of these recurrent movements of resistance and struggle have been easy. But people have won countless victories both large and small. It is time to summarize from this long, rich history some lessons about effective (and ineffective) struggle.

■ The first lesson, as we have seen, has been obvious from the beginning of people's struggles in the early 19th century: *we need our own organizations to support and sustain our resistance and struggle.* This was true in Philadelphia in 1835, in the CIO organizing of the 1930s, in tenant protection during the Depression, in the black civil rights movement...throughout this long history. Protest comes naturally— flowing out of the anger and resentment of dependence and insecurity. But *effective* protest needs more than just anger, and our own organizations have provided some of the support and focus we needed.

■ The second lesson has followed naturally: *successful protest requires that we bring our struggles out of the private realm into the public and political arena, building alliances and coalitions to back our demands.* Farmers and workers both discovered this lesson in the 1870s and 1880s, and so did community protesters in the 1950s and 1960s. Politics is the realm where the basic power to affect our individual lives and social relations is held and finally determined. Each time we take our protests into the realms where that power resides, we advance our chances of winning. If we hold back—limiting our protests to the shops and offices, streets and ballot boxes where we first experience our grievances—we lose the chance to win what we're seeking to change.

■ The third lesson seems obvious but is continually rediscovered: *united we stand, divided we fall.* The Populists gained strength when blacks and whites in the south worked together, but they began to fall apart when racists succeeded in turning many poor whites against poor blacks. The drive to organize Ford Motor Company, as we have seen, stalled until black workers were integrated into the organizing campaign. The protest against the Vietnam War seemed futile as long as it stayed on the campuses, but gained strength rapidly when many different interest groups joined in common protest. The wealthy have their power and use it. The rest of us have our numbers and must build unity to take advantage of that strength.

■ A final lesson will prove critical for struggles to solve our current problems: *people must base our protests on our own feelings, our own leadership, and our own analysis of the sources of our problems.* The sit-down strikes of the 1930s are a classic example. Workers built upon their own sense of outrage at employers' power and callousness. They trusted their instincts and leadership, resisting employer opposition and government hostility. And they understood that the national power and force of the large corporation required some new tactics to overcome workers' earlier disadvantages. Nothing else seemed to work, but the sit-down strikes helped break the dam.

This final lesson points the way toward our next task. The five chapters of this section have traced who we are, how we're divided, and how we can unify to build upon our strengths. This will help us join our common feelings and build our common alliances and leadership. But what are the sources of our current problems? How can we understand those problems from the perspective of working people, not from the viewpoint of the wealthy and powerful? This is where we turn next.

Women arrested for picketing in support of miners' strike, Harlan County, Kentucky, 1973.

PART V: THE MAKING OF THE CURRENT ECONOMIC CRISIS

"The Great American Dream is like a balloon. Don't inflate it too much or it will blow up."
—salesman in California[1]

"Something's got to give. The whole bottom is going to fall out soon, and I'm afraid it'll fall on us."
—housewife in New York[2]

Corporate economists are masters at finger-pointing. They blame our current economic crisis on everyone but themselves—on OPEC, on the government, on workers, on foreign competition.

Their finger-pointing sometimes prompts defensive accusations in return. Hasn't corporate rip-off caused inflation? Haven't the energy companies created the energy crisis? Haven't giant multinationals been running away with our jobs?

There is some truth in these charges against big business, as we shall see in Chapter 19. But blaming big business for the current crisis only scratches the surface of our economic problems. The real sources of the current crisis lie in the basic operations of the postwar capitalist economy.

Postwar prosperity was only possible for a while because large corporations were able to establish, through force and power, a new system enhancing their wealth and power both here and abroad. Constructing and maintaining that system involved huge costs which corporations were able to impose on others. Many in the United States and overseas eventually found those costs unbearable and began to resist their burdens. As resistance spread, the postwar system experienced growing strains and friction. Economic crisis was the eventual outcome.

This kind of interpretation suggests that we can only understand the causes of our current problems by examining the structure and inner tensions of the postwar system. This section of the book pursues that examination. Chapter 18, **"From Depression to Prosperity,"** explores the country's escape from the Depression of the 1930s and the pillars of the system which eventually made prosperity possible. Chapter 19, **"From Prosperity to Crisis,"** shows how the tensions of that system created spreading instability and, in the end, unmanageable economic crisis.

These two chapters together suggest a crucial challenge. If we want to develop adequate solutions to our current economic problems, we need to begin with an adequate analysis of its causes. The analysis presented in Chapters 18 and 19 is complex, but it is not impossibly intricate or difficult to understand. It goes beyond finger-pointing and scapegoating to questions of basic economic power and control. And those questions of power and control are the ones which will matter most as we turn in Part VI of this book to considering different solutions to our current economic problems. Improvement in our working and living conditions will depend on the quality and depth of our answers.

"People have forgotten what it was like in the lean years... when they squirted fire hoses at us....
"I can remember back to the days when we were trying to negotiate a pension plan with the vice president of Gulf Oil. And he said to us, 'Pension!?!? Don't we pay a man for every hour that he works?' Now this was only in 1946!
"There are a lot of young people that come in and say, 'oh well, why the hell should I fight the company; I've *gotten* this.' He didn't get it. He's getting the profits from it, from what other union people had to do before."

—oil worker in New Jersey[1]

"Back then everything was slower....But after the war it was easy to find a job. People were running around building families. We didn't have as much time to think about all these things."

—recently retired worker[2]

From Depression to Prosperity

The Depression was a trauma for nearly everyone who lived through it. Then there was the War. Then the postwar scramble for jobs and cars and houses and the college cap and gown. Life began to seem easier, more secure, pointed toward a decent future for us and our children and our neighbors. It seemed as if the good times would go on forever.

We should have known better. Bad times have returned and they seem likely to stay for a while. We need to understand why.

What changed after the Depression to make prosperity possible? And why was prosperity so vulnerable to the shifting tides?

ESCAPING THE DEPRESSION—WHO CALLED THE SHOTS AND WHO PAID THE PRICE?

"There is mean things happenin' in this land;
There is mean things happenin' in this land.
Oh, the rich man boasts and brags,
While the poor man goes in rags,
There is mean things happenin' in this land."

—sharecroppers chant during the 1930s[3]

"Those were terrible days, remarkable days....This terrible sense of wondering how we're going to get out of things. Then we got out. And we felt good."

—doctor active with unions during the 1930s[4]

One thing that nearly everyone remembers about the Depression is its force. It struck like a hammer between the eyes. Some numbers help recall the impact of the blow.

■ The economy had roared during the 1920s. Suddenly, after the Crash, it was only a whisper of its former self. Total production fell by almost exactly one third between 1929 and 1933 (controlling for prices).[5]

■ Workers felt the blow first and hardest. By 1933, one quarter of the work force—almost 13 million people—were unemployed.[6]

■ With production slumping and workers on the streets, households became more and more concerned with basic survival. Average spendable income per person fell by 28% from 1929 to 1933. Daily protein consumption fell by 1933 to a level 12% below its pre-Depression peak.[7]

■ Paddling desperately to stay afloat, households and businesses sped to the bank to withdraw their savings. Between 1930 and 1933, more than 9,000 banks failed because they couldn't fund the withdrawals. In 1933 alone, at the height of the panic before a bank "holiday" was declared, more than 4,000 banks—accounting for nearly one seventh of total bank deposits in the U.S.—threw in the towel.[8]

■ In the end, the Depression's impact on people's health and sanity tells the story most poignantly. Between 1931 and 1933, the suicide rate was 40% higher than ten years before.[9]

Since the economic system no longer guaranteed people their survival, many began to take matters into their own hands. Miners in Pennsylvania, laid off from idle mines, organized a "bootleg" coal operation to heat their homes and earn some extra cash. In Seattle, the Unemployed Citizens' League helped provide fishing boats to the unemployed so they could work to feed their families. One New York newspaperman described a survival technique common by 1932:

> [Thirty or forty men would enter a chain grocery store.] When the clerk tells them business is for cash only, they bid him stand aside; they don't want to harm him, but they must have things to eat. They load up and depart.[10]

Soon enough, many of these direct actions also began to reflect more *political* anger and orientation. As people came increasingly to realize that their miseries weren't just *their own* fault, they began to mobilize with much clearer collective focus and force.

The story of some textile workers in North Carolina is typical. In July, 1932, more than 1,000 workers struck to protest wage cuts. Joined by the unemployed, they succeeded in closing roughly 100 factories. One group marched into a movie theater and demanded admission, "declaring that they were out of work and entitled to entertainment." When the police broke up their marches and expelled them from the movie theater, the strikers retaliated by shutting down the town's electricity. They hoped, one worker explained, "to teach the big fellows that we hain't going to stand for no more bad treatment."[11] The state governor got the message: "This outburst...was almost spontaneous and spread like the plague," he wrote to a friend. "It only confirms my general feeling that the spirit of revolt is widespread."[12]

A union organizer recalls some parallel impressions as a high school student in the early years of union organizing in Akron:

"We hoped to teach the big fellows that we hain't going to stand for no more bad treament."
—*worker in North Carolina*

The idea of community solidarity was pretty well impressed on me at that time....It was winter, Akron's coldest winter up to that time. [The striking workers] had shanties set up along the "longest picket line in the world," built out of waste wood....When they came down the street for a collection for the striking rubber workers, they went to the pool rooms, they went to the butcher shop, they went to my grandfather's store, and they went to the whorehouse. Everybody chipped in. Everybody knew, "These are our boys. If they don't make it, we don't make it."[13]

The wealthy and powerful soon recognized the threat posed by this spreading "community solidarity." Some business executives were stubborn, refusing to give an inch—preferring, as the obstinate chairman of Republic Steel put it, to "dig potatoes than ever sign a contract with any labor organization."[14] But many important business and government officials realized that simple and stubborn opposition to people's demands wouldn't work. "We're in serious trouble," one banker remembers thinking at the time, "Something has to be done."[15]

This fear led many bankers and corporate executives to promote and cooperate with efforts to save capitalism by reforming it. A government official recalls the receptiveness of many corporate leaders to the New Deal:

The fact that people acted as they did, in violation of law and order, was itself a revolutionary act....The industrialists who had some understanding recognized this right away. [Roosevelt] could not have done what he did without the support of important elements of the wealthy class. They did not sabotage the programs. Just the opposite.[16]

So the issues were now becoming clear: U.S. capitalism had to change. How? On whose terms? At what costs?

Economic Recovery—The Struggle for Control

The easy stuff didn't work. When Roosevelt became president in 1932, he quickly offered some tranquilizers to soothe the nation's nerves. He declared a Bank Holiday. He told people they had "nothing to fear but fear itself." He served an alphabet soup of government programs to cope with the symptoms of the Depression.

But none of it made much difference. The Depression continued. The unemployment rate stayed above 14% for ten straight years (and above 20% for four of those years). One official remembers people's surprise that the New Deal programs made such a small dent. "It lasted so long and went so deep. Usually, when you get a depression—even a severe one—you get two, three years of a decline and in another two, three years, you're back where you were. But ten years?"[17]

By the mid-1930s, corporate leaders were beginning to focus on the kinds of changes they hoped would make a difference.

They concentrated first on putting their own house in order. Roosevelt echoed their concerns, emphasizing the need for industrial self-discipline and cooperation: "The responsible heads of finance and industry, instead of acting each for himself, must,...where necessary

> **"We're in serious trouble and something had to be done."**
> —banker in 1930s

sacrifice this or that private advantage...."[18] With industrial support and encouragement, the government began to establish codes of business practices, the administration of which it left to business itself. The effects were predictable. In the actual execution of these codes, one historian concludes, "the private interests of business corporations overwhelmed the public interest."[19] As the New Deal progressed, one critic acidly remarked that Roosevelt was simply "pulling petals off the daisy with representatives of big business."[20]

A second major effort planted the seeds of foreign expansion. Corporations wanted more access to foreign markets. "The future of capitalism depends," one relatively liberal government policy-maker suggested, "on increased foreign purchasing of our exports."[21] Supporting this quest for new markets, many began to argue for an expanded naval force—long before our actual entry into World War II. Traditional fears of "foreign entanglements" went out the window. "The commitment to overseas markets and raw materials was so strong among corporations and government leaders," according to one historian of the period, "that it was impossible to pass a law...effectively...maintaining [military] neutrality."[22]

Working people were also beginning to concentrate on a few major objectives for reform. They focused increasingly on three main concerns.

First, workers pushed harder than ever to organize labor unions. The National Recovery Act (NRA) of 1932, one of the first major pieces of New Deal legislation, included a clause specifically declaring the right of workers to organize trade unions. John L. Lewis took advantage of the provision while organizing coal miners who had been without union protection for years, telling them all "the President wants you to join the union."[23]

Later, in 1935, the same broad political coalition that secured passage of this section of the NRA finally forced a reluctant Congress to adopt the National Labor Relations Act (NLRA). The Wagner Act, as it is usually called after its principal Congressional sponsor, provided strong guarantees to workers of their basic right to form unions.

The data clearly show the effects of this legislation. By 1940, union membership had soared to 8.9 million, up from only 2.9 million in 1933. People felt the effects not only in their shops but also at home and

Shanty-town in Seattle during Depression, 1930s.

in their communities. A steel worker who was in high school during the successful union drive in Campbell, Ohio remembers its impact:

It was a wonder, the difference the strike made. I have never seen anything like it in America since. A whole town achieved dignity....But the big taste I got...was what I saw at our house. It just changed the whole life of the house. The family was more secure. Our parents got along better. Everything.[24]

Second, workers also demanded a new kind of security on the job from employers' arbitrary actions. During the 1920s and 1930s, when unions were particularly weak, companies had begun increasingly to move workers around, to install new processes, and to hire and fire more or less at will.[25] Workers' resentment at this authority resulted in demands for *grievance procedures* and *seniority systems*—simple mechanisms for handling complaints and for protecting workers against arbitrary hiring and firing.

By the end of the Depression, almost all the industrial unions had won some sort of grievance procedure. At least 75% of union contracts toward the end of the Depression also provided for seniority guarantees.[26] One worker recalls how many people got involved in this push for more control in the shop:

In those days there were more than twenty assistant grievers and hundreds of stewards. The grievance committee set-up could handle the affairs of the people on every shift and every turn with every group....What I'm trying to get at is the spontaneous action of people who are swept up in a movement they know is right and correct and want to do something about.[27]

Third, working people and the unemployed fought for some kind of security against the constant and widespread risks of unemployment and loss of income. These struggles finally resulted in another significant piece of Congressional legislation, the Social Security Act of 1935.

For the first time in the United States, the government accepted responsibility for ensuring benefits to retired workers and to the unemployed. The final bill was watered down, but it nonetheless represented a major breakthrough. One organizer from this period described the experience at a meeting in the early 1970s:

A Hunger March came through led by a man named Claude Lightfoot. So I got my gang ready...all those who could go to Washington getting aboard the train. The train was moving in for unemployment insurance, social security, and $6 a day with a five-day week....And if anybody here doesn't know, that's the way it was got....The old fellows here, I know they know. Everything that we gained there came through struggle.[28]

The government led the way to the first compromises on social security, arguing with the business community that it should even bear some of the costs. "The true conservative," Roosevelt argued, "seeks to protect the system of private property and free enterprise by correcting such injustices and inequalities as arise from it."[29] Increasingly by 1936-37, some employers began on their own to recognize the need for compromise.

Almost all employers initially opposed the new labor relations legislation, for instance. Once the law was passed, however, many began to trim their sails of opposition. Some changed, of course, simply because "they found reliance upon traditional belligerent tactics legally dangerous...."[30] Others began to realize that working *with* unions might actually moderate some of the problems which they had hoped to avoid by working against unions. As one small steel company executive remarked in 1937, expressing more than a little surprise, "We signed an agreement for a year, the union was formed, about half the men joined, a grievance committee was organized, the thing began to work out....It seemed to act as a sort of collective vent."[31]

Hot and Cold War Finally Paves the Way

After beginning his new presidential term in 1937, President Roosevelt charged that "a concentration of private power without equal in history is growing....Private enterprise is ceasing to be free enterprise and is becoming...a concealed cartel system...."[32] At his initiative a Temporary National Economic Commission began to investigate the effect of large monopoly corporations on the U.S. economy. Some of the president's advisors argued that it would take new programs of strategic national economic planning and public investment to permit recovery from the Depression.

As it happened, these remedies were applied. But, instead of emerging slowly as part of a popular movement to control corporate power, they were instituted quickly—as part of a crash program largely controlled by the corporations themselves—to prepare the country for war.[33]

War had broken out in Asia in 1937 and in Europe in 1939. The Japanese attacked Pearl Harbor on December 7, 1941, and the United States declared war on both Japan and Germany the next day.

The government immediately assumed significant control over the economy, marshalling huge portions of its resources for war-time production. This solved the investment problem and provided ready demand for the products of business. Through war-time planning and controls, the government achieved a coordination of business activity which most of the frightened and disorganized business community had been unable to achieve on its own.

Not surprisingly, the economy quickly showed signs of life:

■ In 1940, production was no higher than it had been 11 years before. From 1941 to 1943, output per person soared, increasing by more than 11% (in constant dollars) each of those first three years.[34]

■ People's spendable income followed close behind. Between 1940 and 1943, disposable personal income per capita (in constant dollars) grew at an average rate of almost 10% per year.[35]

■ There was work for nearly everyone. In 1940, the unemployment rate was still close to 15%; more than eight million were out of work. By 1943, there were only 670,000 out of work and the unemployment rate had dropped to just 1.2%.[36]

Much more important, World War II and the Cold War which followed provided a framework within which necessary economic reforms could unfold. The wealthy and powerful moved quickly to channel those reforms to their own advantage.

First, war-time spending and the huge military budget, which became standard practice a few years after the end of World War II (particularly with the Korean War), provided the ready-made demand for products necessary to establish a foundation for prosperity. And without that foundation, as one Senator concluded during the war, "it is impossible to see how a depression can be avoided much worse than any depression which the country has ever known."[37]

Second, both the war and the Cold War capped the triumphant emergence of the United States as the premier national power in the international economy. Corporate and government officials weren't interested in this new international role for reasons of patriotism or national pride. They wanted economic power. As early as the beginning of the war, corporations were already drooling with anticipation. The head of a corporate think tank expressed their eager mood in 1941: "America has embarked on a career of imperialism, both in world affairs and in every other aspect of her life....The path of empire takes its way, and in modern times...the scepter passes to the United States."[38]

Neither of those first two war-time effects were yet enough to establish a new reign of corporate power. A third development was essential: the militance and radical spirit of the movements which had spread during the Depression had to be stifled.

Corporations took advantage of war-time conditions to attack labor militance and worker control on the shop floor. The National War Labor Board, established at the beginning of the war, and the War Labor Disputes Act of 1943 installed machinery for government intervention in labor conflict in the plants. The War Labor Board noted the favorable corporate attitude as early as 1942. "It is in the interests of management, these companies have found, to cooperate with the unions....If union leadership is responsible and cooperative, then irresponsible and uncooperative members cannot escape discipline by getting out of the union and thus disrupt relations and hamper production."[39]

Workers often ignored the machinery, striking more and more frequently during the war to protest speed-up and defend their increased control over production. Companies and the government agencies battled back. Corporate employers fired militant workers and union leaders. The War Labor Board undercut guarantees of union security if and when any workers went on strike. These kinds of policies were "hailed by management people," *Business Week* noted, "[because they] feel that only a few examples of this kind are necessary to bring labor relations back to a level keel."[40] Seizing on these war-time precedents, as one labor economist noted, "business was resolved to 'restore efficiency'...by breaking the de facto control of production won by workers [before and] during the war."[41]

This drive for restored corporate control required an isolation and elimination of "radical" influences within unions and other progressive organizations. During the war and immediately afterwards, corporations and the government joined to harrass and even to imprison people whom they identified as "Communists" or "radicals." Organizers, activist, and radicals from this period remember how quickly the new campaigns began to have an effect.

■ Earlier we often faced red-baiting, but the creation of second-class citizenship for radicals within the unions and the signing of non-Communist affidavits were...not ordinary bad times....As I saw it, [nobody] had the moral right to pry into the political philosophy of workers....[But] I remember how...the climate changed overnight.[42]

■ After we got the union built, something happened [and our president] made an agreement with the steel trusts, it seems to me, that he would fire the Communists. And that's what happened. The union didn't open its mouth.[43]

The tide began to turn. Aided by the government, large corporations regained the initiative. Taking advantage of their enormous power, they dominated the process of recovery and reform. Still slightly stained with blood from these struggles over restructuring, capitalism finally staggered back to its feet.

PROSPERITY IN SIX (NOT SO EASY) LESSONS

"World opinion? I don't believe in world opinion. The only thing that matters is power."

—key financial adviser to president, 1963[44]

"Every day at quitting time, at the five-minute whistle for clean-up, the men would all line up waiting for the second bell to ring, like at the line in a race. When the second bell would ring, they would *run*, as fast as they could go, down the aisles to the time clocks. During the first few days I thought they were out of their minds. A week later, I was butting them out of line to get my place at the starting point too."

—union organizer in auto in the early 1950s[45]

Memories of the 1940s and 1950s faded for most working people in the United States. But those memories are important because the foundation of our recent prosperity was poured during those decades. That prosperity didn't fall from the sky. Its construction involved a complex social process—millions of daily activities and struggles. The edifice which emerged, through force and through struggle, remains a major obstacle as we search for solutions to our current problems.

We have simplified this process of prosperity-in-the-making into six (not so easy) lessons. Each of the lessons will prove invaluable as we

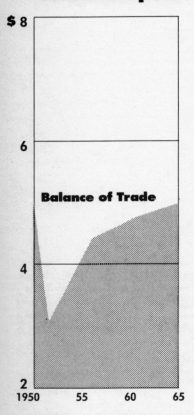

Fig. 18.1
The Trade Cushion Expands

The graph measures the net U.S. balance of trade (in constant dollars). This balance is positive if exports exceed imports and negative if imports are greater than exports.

Source: See note #50

turn, in the following chapter, to an analysis of the sources of our current crisis.

1. Pax Americana—A New King of the Mountain

"[It is doubtful] whether the American capitalist system could continue to function [unless we can organize] the economic resources of the world so as to make possible a return to the system of free enterprise in every country."
—editor of business magazine, 1940[46]

The world economy's plunge into depression had been so steep at least partly because of the international rivalry among leading capitalist countries before and after World War I.[47] The buoyant prosperity after World War II was possible, in contrast, at least partly because the United States emerged as the leading international economic power and imposed some discipline on the world capitalist system.

A leading economic historian recounts the dimensions of this sudden shift in relative economic power:

> While destruction stalked the earth and the economies of many rival nations were ruined, the U.S.A....was able vastly to increase its productive ability....At the end of the war *more than half the total manufacturing production of the world took place within the U.S.A.*[48]

The combination of growth in the U.S. and war-time destruction elsewhere made U.S. workers much more productive than their counterparts in Europe and Japan. In 1950, for example, each U.S. worker was producing about twice as much as the average worker in northwestern Europe.[49]

These effects gave U.S. corporations huge advantages. Higher worker productivity meant that they could easily sell U.S. products to other industrial countries. It also meant that they had much more money available (in profits) to invest abroad, penetrating foreign markets even further.

The graphs on these pages show the effects of this economic leverage.

In Figure 18.1, the line labelled "balance of trade" shows how many more products were exported by U.S. corporations than were brought into this country as imports from other competing nations. Controlling for inflation, this measure of U.S. corporate strength maintained a healthy surplus throughout the period, increasing by nearly 60% from 1951 to 1966.[50]

Figure 18.2 traces the rapid growth in U.S. corporate penetration abroad. The line labelled "direct foreign investment" shows the continuing increases in the value of overseas investments by U.S. corporations and the line labelled "foreign profits" shows the rapid increases in the returns on those investments. By 1965, U.S. corporate profits on overseas investments had grown to more than 2.5 times their levels in 1950.[51]

U.S. corporations did not achieve this international power on their own. From the 1930s, the U.S. government played a critical role in

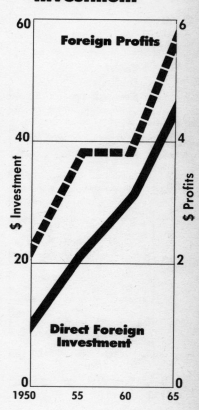

Fig. 18.2
And So Does Overseas Investment

The line marked "direct foreign investment" shows the value (in constant dollars) of overseas assets owned by U.S. corporations. The line marked "foreign profits" traces the profits earned on those investments.

Source: See note #51

promoting the growing world power of U.S. corporations and the U.S. economy.

One important step was taken toward the end of World War II. At an international conference at Bretton Woods (in New Hampshire) in 1944, the leading industrial countries agreed to a new international money system in which the U.S. dollar played a crucial role. (Countries could now use the dollar, as well as gold, as a reserve currency to help cope with balance of payments problems.) This meant that many countries were eager to get dollars. This meant, in turn, that countries were eager to trade with the U.S. and to accept its foreign aid. This preference for dollars naturally reinforced U.S. corporate power, further strengthening their pivotal position at the center of postwar international trade.

The U.S. government also promoted U.S. power through its program of aid to foreign countries. Between 1945 and 1970, it funneled a total of $134 billion in grants and credits to foreign countries.[52]

This aid was often cited as evidence of U.S. good will and generosity. In fact, from the beginning, tight strings were attached. Countries had to use their dollars to purchase products from U.S. corporations. And they usually had to adopt specific government policies which would promote free enterprise and enhance the role of U.S. corporations in those countries. Congress mandated that the Development Loan Fund be used, for example, only for the purpose of supporting the growth in recipient countries of "a competitive free enterprise system."[53] As Dean Rusk, Secretary of State in the early 1960s, explained, "U.S. foreign aid is designed to stimulate the mobilization of private capital and not to replace it."[54]

Where the velvet glove of foreign aid could not achieve these objectives, the U.S. government added the iron fist of military power. This military support took two forms.

First, the U.S. government itself maintained a huge military establishment, ostensibly necessary to "deter" the Soviet Union but in fact aimed equally at extending U.S. power over poorer countries. Figure 18.3 shows the continuing growth of military spending in the U.S. The line labelled "total defense spending" shows that military spending continued to grow rapidly (in constant dollars) from 1956 to 1964, even after the Korean War was over and before the Vietnam War intensified.[55]

The U.S. government also provided direct military aid to foreign governments whose policies it supported. Between 1945 and 1970, total U.S. military aid to foreign governments totalled $49 billion.[56]

As we saw in Chapter 12, it is hard to argue that this aid supported democracy abroad. A recent study has shown that a huge share of military assistance was channeled in the postwar period to governments which had recently experienced military coups and which had drastically reduced democratic rights.[57] A U.S. banker candidly explained the U.S. business community's preference for dictatorships: "Quick and tough decisions can be made in a relatively short time in a

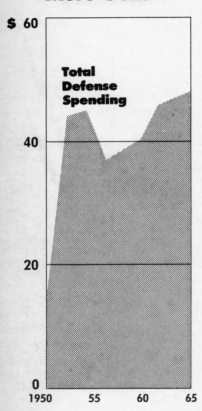

Fig. 18.3
More Guns

Total
Defense
Spending

$ 60

40

20

0

1950   55   60   65

Total defense spending measures federal government expenditures for the functions of military and civil defense (in constant dollars).

Source: See note #55

country such as Brazil compared to the difficulty there is in reaching agreement on what actions to take in a democracy."[58]

For a time, Pax Americana worked so well in the United States because everyone seemed to share its assumptions—conservatives and liberals, Republicans and Democrats, hawks and doves. The administration of John F. Kennedy, a reasonably liberal Democrat, was just as devoted to U.S. private capital and U.S. intervention overseas as the Republican administration of former general Dwight D. Eisenhower. Kennedy left no doubts about his orientation, for example, in a speech to a group of executives of large U.S. corporations toward the beginning of his administration: "Our [national] success [is] dependent upon your profits and success. Far from being natural enemies, government and business are necessary allies....We are anxious to do everything we can to make your way easier."[59]

2. Global Corporations—More Power to Them

"I have long dreamed of buying an island owned by no nation and of establishing the World Headquarters of the Dow Company on the truly neutral ground of such an island, beholden to no nation or society."

—spokesman for the Dow Chemical Co.[60]

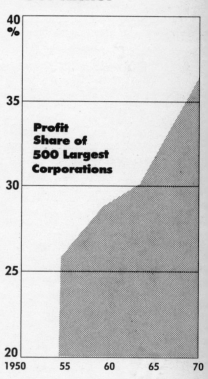

Fig. 18.4
The Rich Get Richer

Profit Share of 500 Largest Corporations

The graph measures the percentage of profits earned by all private non-financial corporations which were earned by the 500 largest industrial corporations.

Source: See note #61

Flourishing like well-nourished plants, giant U.S. corporations grew and grew during the years of postwar prosperity. They took advantage of the new opportunities afforded by U.S. international economic power. And these growing advantages concentrated resources in their hands—the investment of which helped spur rapid economic growth.

The result, as we saw in Chapter 7, was that large U.S. corporations dramatically increased their size and influence in the decades following World War II. This increased size and power gave large corporations growing advantages over their competitors. Those advantages showed up in profits. Figure 18.4 shows this growth in power. The line labelled "profits of the 500 largest industrial corporations" traces the rising share of the profits of the 500 largest industrial corporations in all profits earned by private non-financial corporations. Their share increased from barely a quarter in 1954 to 36% in 1969, an increase of nearly 40%.[61]

The very largest corporations often used these profits to buy up other companies and extend their power even further. Consider the years between 1965 and 1969, for example, at the end of this period when large corporations were cornering so much of industrial profits. During those five years, 8,213 companies were "merged or acquired." Purchases by the largest 200 corporations accounted for 57.4% of all assets involved in mergers and acquisitions—a clearly dominant role.[62]

The very largest corporations also dominated foreign activity by U.S. corporations. By 1970, the largest 50 U.S. corporations (ranked by foreign activity) captured roughly half of all profits earned abroad by U.S. corporations.[63]

What this meant, in the end, was that the largest U.S. corportions now rivaled countries as global powers. In 1971, there were about 160 nations in the world. The seven largest U.S. corporations were each larger than 120 of those countries.[64] No wonder they were getting their way. "The political boundaries of nation-states," as one leading banker boasted in the 1960s, "are too narrow and constricted to define the scope and sweep of modern business."[65]

3. Containing Labor—Building the Postwar Truce

"I never went on strike in my life, never ran a strike in my life, never ordered anyone else to run a strike in my life, never had anything to do with a picket line....In the final analysis, there is not a great difference between the things I stand for and the things that NAM [National Association of Manufacturers] leaders stand for....I believe in the free enterprise system completely."

—George Meany, head of AFL-CIO, 1956[66]

Workers' drive for union recognition and power continued through and after World War II. The first six months of 1946 witnessed, for example, what the government called "the most concentrated period of labor-management strife in the country's history."[67]

Gradually, from the 1940s through the early 1950s, this labor militance cooled. Corporations and union leadership established a kind of "truce" which lasted for nearly twenty years.

Unions were clear about the advantages to labor of the truce: they gained promises of protection for unions' right to exist—through a formalization of the check-off system for union dues, for example, and the continuation into the postwar period of the National Labor Relations Board's protection of union recognition elections.

Unions and workers paid somewhat less attention, during the process of building the truce, to corporate gains. Most corporations were able to garner four important advantages from this institutional bargain:

a. *Favorable Contracts.* Companies moved quickly to secure contract clauses forbidding strikes during the term of contract; they also demanded that union leadership help enforce those clauses. (By 1947, 90% of union contracts already pledged no strikes during the contract.[68]) They also won union agreement to compulsory arbitration of grievances. (This removed final settlement of grievances from the hands of workers and restricted their ability to strike over those grievances.) And, finally, companies demanded that contracts sanctify management's control over production. "Management's Rights" clauses soon appeared in nearly all contracts, certifying the bosses' unilateral control over most critical issues about production. (See Chapter 12 for an example and discussion of these clauses.) Management thus won back at the bargaining table much of the leverage they had begun to lose during the 1930s and 1940s.

b. *The Productivity Bargain.* Corporations also insisted that wage gains negotiated in bargaining be tied to increases in workers' productivity. Workers had to *earn* their wages and they effectively promised not to increase their share of the bosses' surplus value. Union leaders aiming at lucrative contracts, in effect, promised to help make workers more productive, while the "management rights" clauses left decision-making about production as management's exclusive preserve. General Motors pioneered this kind of "productivity bargaining" in the late 1940s. By 1950, *Fortune* magazine was already applauding the move:

> GM may have paid a billion for peace [but] it got a bargain. General Motors has regained control over one of the crucial management functions....In planning freedom alone the contract is worth 15 cents per man per hour to the corporation.[69]

c. *Control Over the Labor Process.* Corporations rapidly installed new job structures and job rules which reduced worker solidarity in the shop and office and increased companies' leverage over their performance. In the Polaroid Corporation by the early 1970s, for example, there were roughly 2,100 individual job "slots" for its 6,397 hourly workers.[70] At General Electric, as one worker explained, "There's a number [and] a description of every job that anyone does at GE, a *detailed* description....It specifies *exactly* what you're supposed to do...."[71] These job divisions and rules had the effect of further substituting the bosses' planning and control over our work for our own coordination of our daily activities on the job.

d. *More Supervision.* Companies used more and more supervisors to watch over all these rules and jobs. Companies also defined many jobs as "supervisory" simply because the National Labor Relations Act specifies that "supervisors" and "managers" may not be included in a collective bargaining unit.

The structure of supervision in the phone company, though

Fig. 18.5
More Supervisors

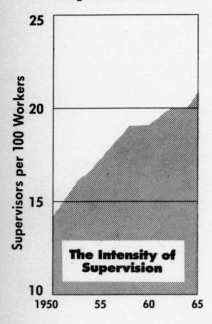

The "intensity of supervision" measures the number of supervisory employees in the private sector per 100 nonsupervisory (or production) workers.

Source: See note #73

somewhat exaggerated, is nonetheless illustrative. As one worker described the system:

> [My supervisor] is the supervisor of five women. She reports to a Manager who manages four supervisors (about twenty women) and he reports to the District Supervisor along with two other managers...[The District Supervisors] report to the Chief of the Southern Division, himself a soldier in an army of division chiefs.[72]

All this supervision added up. Figure 18.5 traces the ratio of supervisory workers to production workers throughout the private sector. Its curve measures the relative amount of supervisory and managerial time devoted to each hour of production workers' labor. As the graph shows, the intensity of supervision increased significantly between 1947 and 1969, growing by more than 70%.[73]

This truce between management and labor—based on consolidated union power *within* a structure of tighter management control—had three important consequences which helped support the growing power of the largest corporations.

■ Unions became less and less important. As Figure 18.6 shows, union membership as a percentage of the non-agricultural workforce increased steadily through the strike waves and organizing activity of the late 1940s and early 1950s. It peaked in 1954, however, and declined steadily from then through 1970.[74] The postwar truce helped spare corporations, in this respect, from the spreading nuisance of trade unions in the economy.

■ Workers were also less and less likely to strike. Figure 18.7 graphs the percentage of total (non-agricultural) working hours lost

Fig. 18.6
Fewer Union Members

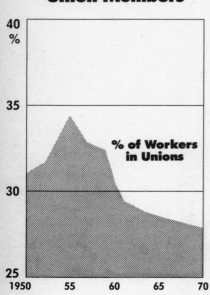

The graph measures the percentage of the non-agricultural labor force which belonged to labor unions.

Source: See note #74

Fig. 18.7
And Fewer Strikes

The graph tracing the "incidence of strikes" measures the percent of total (non-agricultural) working hours lost as a result of strikes.

Source: See note #75

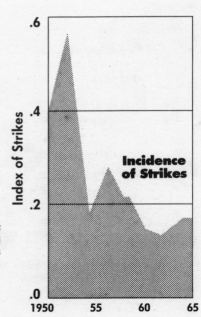

because of strikes. Relative strike activity remained high and volatile through the early 1950s, but declined fairly steadily—with the exception of the long steel strike in 1959-60—through 1966.[75]

■ This truce paid off for companies in dollars and cents. Given the new system of productivity bargaining, companies now measured the effectiveness of their peace with labor by the difference between the increase in labor productivity and the increase in workers' wages. The difference went into (or came out of) corporate surplus. The more docile workers became and the greater the leverage companies acquired over production, the more rapidly productivity rose compared to wages. Figure 18.8 graphs this "corporate output dividend," tracing the difference between the rate of increase in output per production worker hour—in worker productivity—and the rate of increase in production workers' wages. As the graph shows, this dividend rose and the truce worked increasingly to companies' benefit as the 1950s and 1960s progressed.[76]

Although some of this history has faded from workers' memories, workers active on the shop floor during this period remember some of its effects clearly:

> What makes me mad, and what makes thousands of other people in the mill mad, is that the companies became smart and understood that in order to accommodate themselves to a labor organizaton they could not oppose that labor organization....The government and the employers...learned how to adopt, co-opt, and engulf the union and make it part of the establishment. And in making it part of the establishment they took the guts, the militancy, and the fight out of the people who work for a living.[77]

4....Inequality at Home and Abroad

"[In school] they taught us a simplistic world view....There was a heavy overtone of the old British colonial atitude. Nothing about the slaves. Minority history just didn't exist. The world somehow is the garden of the white people, and everybody else kind of fits in someplace."

—Native American of the Sioux tribe[78]

There was prosperity, and then there was prosperity. The structure of the postwar period helped the strong take increasing advantage of the weak. Those with the greatest power in the U.S. economy were often able to profit from those with the least power to protect and advance their own interests.

We have already seen that large corporations were able to increase their size and relative power during the years of prosperity. They could protect their profits, in part, by continually increasing their prices. This meant that unionized workers in these large corporations had an easier time winning wage increases than most other workers simply because their employers could pass on the wage hikes to consumers. During the 1950s and 1960s, this difference affected workers' fortunes considerably.

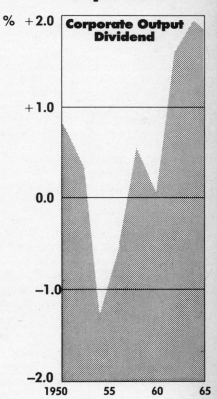

Fig. 18.8
More Surplus for the Corporations

This graph measures the difference between the annual rate of increase in production-workers' productivity and the annual rate of increase in production-workers' wages. If it is greater than 0.0, it means that corporate surplus is increasing.

Source: See note #76

Figure 18.9 traces what we call the "core workers' dividend"—the difference between the increase in workers' wages in core industries dominated by large corporations and the increase in workers' wages in other industries. Workers in core industries were able to increase their earnings advantage over other workers by more than 20% between 1947 and 1966.[79]

Similar differences in fortunes divided men from women and whites from minorities. As we saw in Chapters 15 and 16, women and minorities tended to work in jobs paying relatively lower wages. This meant that corporations that employed relatively larger proportions of women and blacks were able, other things being equal, to earn relatively higher profits. One study of manufacturing industries in 1970 found, for example, that profits were relatively higher in industries where the income gap between blacks and whites was widest.[80]

Important gaps also widened between the U.S. (and other advanced countries) and developing countries in the Third World. Three important trends reflect this spreading international inequality:

■ Third World countries were pushed to specialize in certain kinds of raw materials and speciality crops for export to the advanced world—commodities such as oil, rubber, tin, coffee, and cocoa. U.S. agribusiness also pushed increasing dependence on food imports from the U.S., helping promote policies which reduced Third World countries' own food-growing capacity.[81] The effects were dramatic. During the mid-1930s, the countries of Asia, Africa, and Latin America were *net exporters* of food—shipping abroad at least three million metric tons of grain a year *more* than they imported. By 1966, countries on

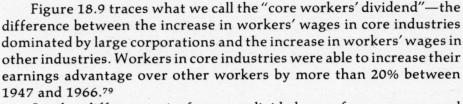

I Feel for You but I just Can't Reach You

these continents were *net importers* of grain; in 1960 alone, they bought at least 36 million metric tons of grain more than they exported.[82]

■ The advanced countries, especially U.S. corporations, also used their international power to keep the prices of Third World exports as low as possible. This resulted in a weaker and weaker Third World position in world trade. Figure 18.10 shows this trend, graphing the relative export-import trade terms between Third World countries and the advanced world from 1951 to 1968. The sharp downward slope of the line shows that the prices Third World countries were earning for products they were selling to the advanced world were not rising as rapidly as the prices for the goods they were buying from the wealthier economies.[83]

■ The result was that Third World countries were facing increasingly severe pressure on their own currencies and national reserves. By 1965, non-oil-producing Third World countries were running annual deficits in their trade balances of roughly six billion dollars a year.[84] Their only recourse was more debt to the rich countries. By the late 1960s, non-oil-producing Third World countries were borrowing more than four billion dollars a year from the wealthy of the world.[85]

Unorganized, women, and minority workers in the U.S., poor people in Third World countries around the globe—all of them paid a special price for the sake of "prosperity." By the mid-1960s, many of them were beginning to feel that weight. One Detroit organizer captured some of their anger in a documentary monologue from the late 1960s:

> He gives you little bullshit amounts of money...to cool your ass and then steals it all back with shit called interest....This man is ...Kennicott. He is Anaconda. He is United Fruit....He ain't never produced anything his whole life. Investment banker. Stockbroker. Insurance man. He don't do nothing. We see that...this little clique...is sucking and destroying the life of workers everywhere.[86]

5. The Physical Ingredients for Prosperity

"Oil, enough oil, within our certain grasp, seemed ardently necessary to greatness and independence in the twentieth century."

—**U.S. State Department adviser, 1946**[87]

It took roughly fifteen years before the raw materials that fueled postwar prosperity were available in sufficient supply. This process tells a great deal about the basis of our former prosperity and the dependencies it later created.

One of the most important ingredients, of course, was oil. Large oil companies had begun laying plans for postwar expansion in the late 1930s and during World War II. They recognized that their oil supplies in the U.S. would not provide enough for U.S. needs. They maneuvered during the War to establish special access to Latin American and Middle Eastern oil. They convinced the governments of those countries to sign pacts which provided access at very low prices. From the beginning, the giant oil companies realized that the terms of these agreements were a steal. One company lawyer wondered as early as 1947, "I can not believe that a comparatively few companies for any great length of time are going to be permitted to control world oil resources without some sort of regulation."[88]

Once they had control over resources, the companies also had to construct a system of supply—piping it from the fields to tankers, shipping it across the oceans, pumping it through refineries and into

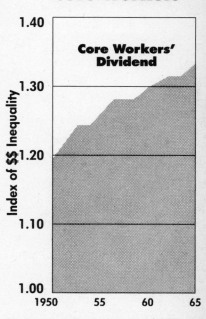

Fig. 18.9
More for Core Workers

The graph measures the ratio of earnings among workers in "core industries" to earnings among workers not in "core industries" for each year. Source: #79

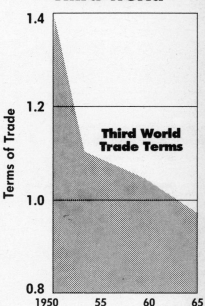

Fig. 18.10
And Less for Third World

The graph measures the ratio of the average prices which Third World countries received for their exports to the average prices received for their imports. If these terms of trade decline, it shows that poor countries are facing more and more strain in their balance of payments.   Source: See note #83

Fig. 18.11
Cheaper Energy

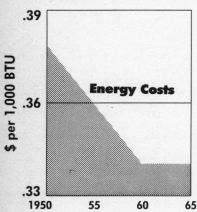

The graph measures the dollar cost (in constant dollars) per energy unit, measured in 1,000 BTUs (or British Thermal Units). Declining costs show that energy was becoming less expensive.

Source: See note #89

Fig. 18.12
More Oil

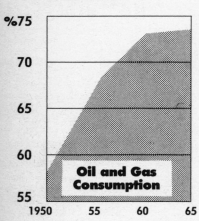

The graph measures the percentage of total energy consumption in U.S. accounted for by consumption of oil and natural gas.

Source: See note #90

the economy. This system was constructed during the 1940s and early 1950s. Costs fell continuously after it was laid in place. Figure 18.11 shows the real dollar cost per energy unit, measured in BTUs (British Thermal Units) of oil and natural gas in the United States. As the graph shows, costs dropped steadily from 1950 through the 1960s.[89] This was the dividend of U.S. corporate power during and after the war.

We all enjoyed the benefits...for a time. Figure 18.12 shows the portion of total U.S. energy consumption which was based on oil and natural gas. More and more, postwar prosperity was greased with petroleum products.[90] And we had become more and more dependent on continuing access to those supplies.

We also relied increasingly on highways and trucks for transportation. Until World War II, railroads had dominated transport in the United States. The combined business interests of the trucking, auto, highway, and oil interests, as we have already seen in Chapter 11, promoted truck transport as a substitute.

This required a physical system of highways. The U.S. Highways Trust Act provided the mechanism and funding for their construction—financed by taxes on gasoline purchases. Figure 18.13 shows the steady rise in highway construction through the 1950s—with construction peaking in 1955 just after the passage of the Highways Act. The graph also shows the number of new rails laid for railroads in the U.S. during the same period. The two lines together show clearly that highways were being built *instead* of railroads.[91] We were locked increasingly into a new mode of transport, and freight shipped by trucks (and pipelines) climbed steadily as a result.[92]

Low energy costs also paved the way for another physical ingredient of postwar prosperity—more and more reliance on machines and energy in production. Figure 18.14 traces this development. The line marked "horsepower per worker" shows the horsepower of machinery used in manufacturing for every 1,000 production worker hours. Similar trends accompanied the rising use of energy during this

Fig. 18.13
More Highways

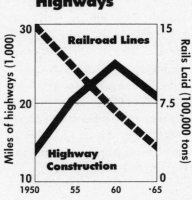

The graph measures (a) the miles of interstate highways constructed per year and (b) the level of railroad construction, measured by rails laid (in 100,000 short tons) per year.

Source: See note #91

Fig. 18.14
More Machines

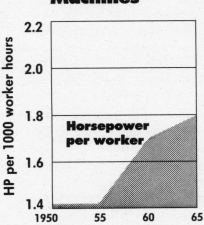

The graph measures the horsepower of machinery in industry per 1000 worker hours in industry.   Source: See #93

period. As with machinery, energy consumption (per worker) increased steadily and dramatically from the 1940s through the 1960s.[93] After a while, it began to appear that we couldn't produce any other way.

The final aspect of the physical structure of postwar prosperity involved our own consumption. More and more people lived in single-family homes—many in suburbs, many relying on private autos for transportation, many of us centering our lives more and more around the television. Figure 18.15 shows two dimensions of this change in physical life-style. The line marked "cars" shows the percentage of households in the U.S. which owned at least one automobile. The line marked "TVs" shows the percentage of households with at least one television in the home. Both lines rise rapidly during the 1950s—when the new lifestyle was being forged—and then level off after the early 1960s.[94]

Once it was in place, we took this physical structure for granted. Hadn't we always used oil? Hadn't there always been trucks and highways everywhere? Wasn't ours a paradise created by advanced production technology? Hadn't we always driven our own cars and watched our own televisions?

Until things changed, of course—until it became more and more expensive to continue organizing our physical economy in the same way. Then, many people began to realize how dependent upon that particular physical structure we had allowed ourselves to become.

6. Providing the Political and Ideological Cushion for Prosperity

"Once in a while one of my business friends speaks to me of Government planning as if it were either ridiculous or dangerous. I reply that when I was in business, planning was fundamental to successful management and I don't suppose things have changed since....The core of [the government's] whole postwar...economic program is the expansion of private trade and the encouragement of private enterprise, with such assistance as is required from the Government.
—U.S. Secretary of State after World War II[95]

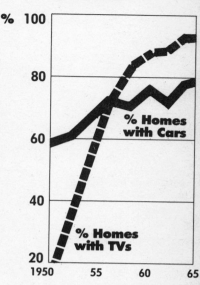

Fig. 18.15
More TVs and Cars

The lines measure the percentage of all households owning televisions and the percentage of all households owning at least one automobile. Source: See #94

Fig. 18.16
The Spreading Safety Net

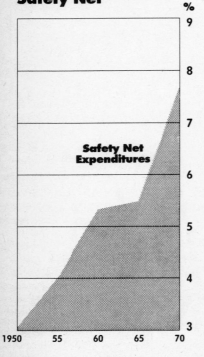

The graph shows the percentage of total national product going for expenditures on social security and public assistance.

Source: See note #100

The U.S. government played a critical role in laying the foundations for postwar prosperity. And it was joined by the institutions which influence public opinion—the media, the schools, advertising....

Direct Government Programs. Various government programs helped build prosperity in two important ways. First, they provided direct services and support to private business, particularly large corporations. Second, they also helped ease the way for U.S. capitalism by smoothing out some of its worst problems and isolating some of its worst critics.

1. The direct services to private companies were legion. The government provided much of the system of transportation and communications from which large corporations profited throughout the period. The government also built and financed many factories and machines which it turned over to private business at low rentals or even for free. (By 1967, a government study found that 1,900 companies were using federally-owned production equipment worth more than $2.5 billion.[96]) Wherever it seemed possible, the government supported technological research and development whose fruits it eventually laid on the corporate platters.

One example of this kind of support tells the more general story. The U.S. government paved the way for the development of communications satellites—now an essential part of many corporate systems of communications. The government developed the rocket technology, financed research on the satellite systems themselves, and sponsored the first trial launchings. When the system was essentially completed, however, the government immediately ceded control of this valuable public resource to a private corporation—the Communications Satellite Corporation. Four communications giants—AT&T, ITT, General Telephone, and RCA—quickly controlled 45.5% of total stock in the corporation, more than enough for working control over Comsat. Would Comsat serve the interests of these original stockholders? Its first president seemed clear enough: "Who is there first," he said a year after Comsat's formation, "has a priority."[97] And thanks to government help, the largest companies got there far ahead of anyone else.

Perhaps the most important support for corporate profits came from rising U.S. government spending for defense. The government used a system of "cost-plus" contracting, paying private companies fixed fees to supply military equipment. The companies loved the business because, once a contract was signed, they could stop worrying about their competitors.

As a result, during the fifties and sixties, large corporations began to chase the golden ring of defense contracts. By the mid-1960s, according to a detailed study, between 40% and 50% of the 500 largest corporations were "significantly involved in military production, either through their primary industry of production, through diversification into the defense sector, or through military research and development contracts."[98] This meant both that the government was subsidizing more and more large corporations, directly or indirectly, and that the private sector was becoming more and more dependent on high levels of military spending.

2. The government also played an important role in tempering some of the most disruptive effects of capital accumulation.

Responding to the trauma of the Depression, the government began much more actively to try to smooth the business cycle. This intervention seemed to work—at least for a time. Business cycles between 1946 and 1970 were more than two-thirds less severe than business cycles during a comparable period of expansion after the turn of the century. Some of the bumps in the road of the capitalist economy had been levelled.[99]

A second important change flowed from New Deal legislation to moderate the income inequalities which resulted from both growth and depression. The government played a continually expanding role in cushioning the impact of labor market insecurities.

Figure 18.16 traces this growing government effort, measuring social security and welfare expenditures as a percentage of total national product. It shows clearly the steady rise in income support, particularly during the 1960s when both the civil rights movement and mobilization among the elderly deepened the public commitment to those whom the private economy was leaving behind.[100]

This effort had clear effects. Between 1950 and 1970, the income distribution became somewhat more equal *after* government taxes and transfers—an increase in equality of roughly 6%. All of this equalization was a result of government intervention; the distribution of private-sector incomes, before government taxes and transfers, had actually become more unequal—by about 2% over those two decades.[101] If the government hadn't moved to smooth those rough edges, people would have been much angrier about private-sector inequalities by the 1960s...and they were already angry enough.

Ideological Combat. These efforts to smooth the rough edges of capitalist growth are easy to trace. Other interventions are more difficult to record. But they were nonetheless critical. They reflected a continuing and concerted effort by those in power in the United States to convince the rest of us that capitalism was good and that anything else was both sinister and self-destructive.

We have traced in earlier chapters some of the most direct

examples of political and ideological repression—the red-baiting and purges of the McCarthy period in U.S. politics, for example, and corporate efforts to curb rank-and-file militance in labor unions. These examples represent only the tip of the iceberg. Other examples are only recently beginning to surface. They tell even more important stories of what amounts to direct business brainwashing of the public—brainwashing tolerated and often supported by the government.

One of the most important examples involved the schools. Many of our impressions of society are fashioned in our early years of schooling. It turns out that those impressions were, for most of the postwar period, strongly stamped by a militant business crusade.

From about 1910 through the 1930s, many secondary school social sciences texts admitted that the U.S. was far from perfect. They talked candidly about the power of large corporations and some of the inequalities among the rest of the population. Business said, enough already! A recent study of secondary school texts concludes that "such social realism in the texts was brought to an end in the early nineteen-forties, by the nationwide attack, sponsored by the National Association of Manufacturers," on the most "liberal" of the textbooks.[102]

The effect of that attack was apparently chilling. The books were as purely boosterish in their description of the "American way of life" as a Radio Free Europe broadcast....The books went on and on about the glories of free enterprise—they were far more enthusiastic about it than about the Bill of Rights—but they never

actually explained how the American economy worked, or how it had changed over time.[103]

The books became equally ardent in their support of U.S. foreign policy and the Cold War. By 1950, most texts were writing with celebration about the United States as "a bastion of the free nations," "locked in struggle" with the Soviet Union. The change was sudden and dramatic. For example, the same text was compared in its 1942 and 1950 editions. Between editions, the recent study reports, "the country has become more prosperous; there are no more poor people or bad social conditions. Pages have been added explaining the superiority of the American democratic system to the Russian police state."[104]

By the mid-1950s, the textbooks had become weapons of McCarthyism, indulging in such paranoia that they effectively encouraged schoolchildren to believe "that an American tradition is that of police informer." One leading text concludes its final chapter with a warning about "A Citizen's Rights and Duties":

> The FBI urges Americans to report directly to its offices any suspicions they may have about Communist activity on the part of their fellow Americans. The FBI is expertly trained to sift out the truth of such reports under the laws of our free nation. When Americans handle their suspicions in this way...they are acting in line with American traditions.[105]

An organizer growing up in this period remembers the same kinds of warnings. The books "taught us," he recalls, that "we're all Americans and none of us is ever disloyal. The United States has never been on the wrong side of anything. The government has never lied to the people. The FBI is there to help you, and if you see anything suspicious, call them."[106]

With such ominous responsibilities, how could we have ever spared the time or found the peace of mind to learn about how our country really worked?

WHAT PRICE SUCCESS?

We have seen that postwar prosperity in the United States rested on six pillars:

1) U.S. domination of the world economy;

2) increasing concentration of economic power in large corporations;

3) a corporate-labor truce;

4) widening inequality at home and abroad;

5) a new system securing raw materials and providing demand for economic expansion;

6) political and ideological mechanisms providing support for private corporate power.

All these different aspects of U.S. society in the postwar period fit together, reinforcing each other. The reliance on autos worked, for example, because the relative price of oil declined. Corporations were able to move their profits abroad, in part, because the truce with labor helped provide them a productivity dividend with which they could maneuver.

This structure of interconnected parts required years of construction. It worked at least partly because it was so difficult to do anything about it once it was in place.

However imposing, the system was nonetheless laced with internal tensions, conflicts, and delicate compromises. Cracks soon appeared. In order to understand the origins and character of our present economic crisis, we need to retrace our steps all the way back to the 1950s. For it was then that fissures first became evident. As early as 1957, a leading *New York Times* columnist sensed the emergent unease:

> There is an overwhelming feeling...that somehow we have lost our way. Nobody seems to know just how or why, but everyone feels that something's wrong....An impression of haphazard greed, and a system debased and out of balance.[107]

From Prosperity to Crisis

"The sooner we suffer the pain, the sooner we will be through."

—chairman of the DuPont Corporation[1]

"You remember the American dream? Work hard, save your money, get an education, get ahead? I'm kind of discouraged in all that now. I'm surrounded by all the things I've ever wanted....

"I wanted a family and two cars and an educational background, and now I've got it all, but I don't have a job....

"I feel like I'm falling backwards. You climb up to heaven, and fall back to hell."

—unemployed autoworker, 1981[2]

Corporate economists blame our current problems on simple accidents and obvious villains like the government or OPEC. This chapter argues that the current economic crisis stems from the internal costs and tensions of the systems upon which postwar prosperity was built.

We obviously can't compare these different explanations by looking only at current symptoms like energy prices and government tax rates. Instead, if we want to weigh the usefulness of these two different analyses, we need to go back to the beginning of the postwar period.

Were there some flaws in the basic structure of postwar prosperity? If so, do we need to change that system in order to solve our current problems? Or did the postwar system work just fine, falling prey to temporary difficulty which had nothing to do with its basic operations? If so, can we solve our problems simply by tuning the postwar machine to eliminate those annoying difficulties?

We explore these questions in this chapter by reviewing the entire transition from prosperity to crisis, beginning in the 1950s. Our review suggests that the roots of the crisis lay in the foundations of prosperity.

WAS THAT THE ONE WHERE THEY INFILTRATED A *TUPPERWARE* PARTY AND FOUND THEY WERE *MOONIES*?

THAT WAS *TWO WEEKS AGO.* LAST WEEK WAS THE *SUNBELT.*

THEY HAVE *SMOG.* THEY HAVE *CRIME.* THEY EVEN HAVE *UNEMPLOYMENT!*

ALREADY?

CONT'D.

We use that analysis in a series of boxes—inserted toward the end of the chapter—to dispel the simple finger-pointing explanations of the current crisis which dominate so much of current debate.

POSTWAR PROSPERITY—A FREE LUNCH OR A COSTLY MEAL?

"I do not believe in democracy. I think it stinks. I believe in a republic operated by elected representatives who are permitted to do the job, as the board of directors should."
—lobbyist for landlords, 1949[3]

"I see America destroying itself out of fear, wasting its resources, betraying its past...."
—progressive journalist, 1948[4]

There is no question about the basic facts of prosperity during the 1950s and early 1960s. Between 1948 and 1966, controlling for inflation, the economy grew by roughly 5.5% a year—after not having grown at all during the 1930s.[5] And households' real spendable earnings increased over these years, as we have already seen in Chapter 7, by a cumulative total of 36%. For many working people in the U.S. there was an obvious temptation to believe that they had found the land of plenty. "I think the working people got too fat," an oil worker remembered recently about this period. "They got to be fat cats."[6]

The question is not about the facts of prosperity, but about its costs. Was it a free lunch—a sort of costless paradise providing tasty benefits for all? Or was it a costly meal? And if so, who picked up the tab?

We find our first clues by looking at the 1950s—at the very beginning of those years of rapid growth. Although the economy was soaring, corporations were growing a little restless.

Figure 19.1 reveals the source of their concern. The bars measure the average rate of profit for corporations in the U.S. economy during the 1950s. (As we learned in Chapter 7, it is always important in these kinds of discussions to avoid comparing years at different points in the

expansion-and-recession roller coaster. In this graph and others throughout the chapter, we control for these ups and downs by comparing years which come at the *peaks* of various short-term business cycles.) The graph shows clearly that postwar reconstruction had boosted corporate profits to very high levels in 1950 but that they began to plunge during the 1950s. By 1959, the average corporate rate of profit had fallen by nearly a quarter.[7]

   And the economy was beginning to feel the effects. Because corporations had succeeded in restoring their power after World War II, what was bad for business was bad for the economy. If corporations weren't earning high enough profits, they tended to reduce their investments. When investments lagged, the economy slowed its growth. Between 1955 and 1959, investment increased by only 1.2% per year—a third of its growth rate in the two previous business cycles. By the end of the 1950s, controlling for inflation, income per person was scarcely growing at all.[8] Where was the bounty which so many had promised? The government was certainly failing to deliver on its advertisements of the American Dream. "Eisenhower...was a massive disappointment to the pro-growth [forces]," one historian reports. "Faced with a sputtering economy, the general did little to bring about perpetual prosperity."[9]

   Why was the foundation of postwar prosperity so incomplete? Corporations often blame workers for their problems, but these charges don't work for the 1950s. Neither rising wages nor lagging worker output were squeezing corporate profits. Between 1950 and 1959, corporate revenues were growing nearly a third more rapidly than the labor costs of producing that corporate output.[10] As far as their employees were concerned, there was still plenty of room for corporate profits.

   If workers weren't the culprits, why else were corporate profits falling?

   We saw in Chapter 18 that corporate profits after World War II rested on a system of power. The U.S. dominated much of the rest of the world—relying on both economic clout and military might. And U.S. corporations regained much of their power over workers at home—deploying shiny fleets of new machines and mounting brigades of managers and supervisors.

   The problem for corporations was that all these pillars of corporate power cost money. Lots of it.

■ Between 1950 and 1959, government expenditures for defense increased, controlling for inflation, from $16 billion to $47 billion (in 1959 prices), an increase of 182%. Corporations had to pay for much of this increase through higher corporate profits taxes to the federal government.

■ Machines and supervisory employees cost plenty too. Between 1950 and 1959, corporate expenditures on depreciation and interest rose by 70% (in constant prices). Even more dramatically, corporate expenditures on the salaries of managers and supervisors, again controlling for inflation, rose by more than 75%, climbing from $25 billion in 1950 to $44 billion in 1959 (in constant 1959 prices).[11]

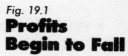

Fig. 19.1
Profits Begin to Fall

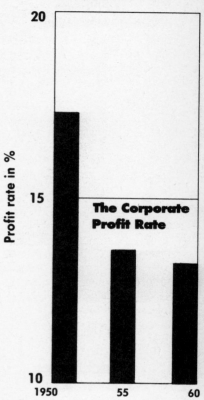

The Corporate Profit Rate

Profit rate in %

20

15

10

1950   55   60

The bars measure the rate of return for nonfinancial corporations, measured as before-tax profits divided by capital stock.
Source: See note #7

Fig. 19.2
More Dividends from Workers

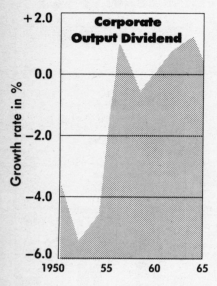

The graph measures the difference between the rate of growth in labor productivity and the rate of growth of production workers' earnings.

Source: See note #14

Fig. 19.3
... And More Tax Breaks From Government

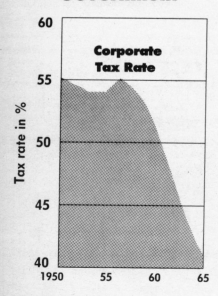

The graph measures the ratio of corporate profits taxes to total before-tax profits for the nonfinancial corporate business sector.   Source: See note #16

We can call these the *costs of systems control*—the costs of maintaining control over workers in the U.S. and other countries around the globe.[12] *These costs of system control account for all of the decline in corporate profits during the 1950s.* Corporations were finding their profits squeezed because they were spending more and more of their gross revenues on machines, supervisors, and managers. These rising costs of control were *not* paying for themselves by generating enough of an increase in workers' output or U.S. market shares around the globe.

Corporations had created a mechanical and administrative beast, in short, which was feeding on itself. There were two obvious possible solutions: corporations could cut back on their apparatus of control; or they could push the costs of control off on someone else.

Corporations have never willingly ceded control. So they chose the second alternative—they begged and pleaded for relief. And they found a friend in the new Democratic administration in 1960. Eager to consolidate its narrow margin of victory, the Kennedy administration rushed to reassure the business community and to provide it the comfort it sought. As Kennedy explained in a 1961 press conference:

> This country cannot prosper unless business prospers. This country cannot meet its obligations and tax obligations and all the rest unless business is doing well. Business will not do well and we [will not] have full employment unless they feel there is a chance to make a profit.[13]

Corporations asked for relief. And they spelled relief, *lower labor costs* and *government tax breaks*. The government pushed its labor allies to reduce wage demands and extend a helping hand to corporate profits. The government also soothed corporate fears by cutting back on their tax obligations.

The corporations had pulled out their crying towels, in effect, and the government heeded their wails and moans. The strategy worked wonders.

■ Figure 19.2 shows the effects of the strategy on labor costs. The key variable for corporations involves the *difference* between the growth in production workers' hourly output and the hourly costs of hiring those production workers. If output rises more slowly than workers' wages, profits will be squeezed and out come the crying towels. If hourly output outstrips the growth of labor costs, the corporate coffers fill and the corporate smiles spread. We call this variable the *corporate output dividend*. As figure 19.2 shows, the margin of output growth over wage growth went into the black consistently during the early 1960s, rising to its postwar peaks in 1963-64.[14]

Workers' wage shares mirrored this trend in the corporate output dividend. The more that went into profits, the lower the workers' share of total output. Production workers' wages as a portion of total national output fell by more than 10% from the early 1950s to 1964-65.[15] Corporations gained control over the rest.

■ Figure 19.3 shows the comparable effects of the strategy on corporate tax obligations. It traces the percentage of (non-financial) corporate profits paid to the federal government in corporate profits taxes. Companies had been paying an "excess profits tax" during the Korean War. The graph picks them up in 1950, before the excess profits tax was lifted. Tax obligations stayed fairly constant through the rest of the 1950s. And then the Democrats responded to the crying towels. Corporations earned "accelerated depreciation allowances" in 1961 and an "investment tax credit" in 1963—both aimed at reducing the profits squeeze and encouraging investment. As figure 19.3 shows, the share of corporate profits going to the federal government in taxes fell promptly and steadily, declining by more than one-fifth from 1961 to 1965.[16]

At last the corporations could breathe more easily. The corporate profit rate jumped back to 16%, higher than its previous peak in 1950.[17] Investment was soaring. Prosperity seemed to have arrived.

But the foundations of prosperity were costly. We can now review the distribution of those costs. We can look at changes in the composition of net national output between 1950 and 1965. We can compare the shares of output going in four different directions.[18]

(1) *Corporate profits* (after taxes);

(2) *The costs of system control*, including the costs of supervision and defense;

(3) *The support of production workers*, including both their earnings from work and their net benefits from the government;

(4) Income support for those who, for whatever reasons, became dependent on *government transfer payments* for their subsistence.

Figure 19.4 demonstrates the costs of establishing and maintaining the postwar system. The first bar shows that corporations gained obvious benefits between 1950 and 1965. Corporate profits increased as a percentage of output by 2.8 percentage points. The next bar shows what made these profits possible: the costs of system control increased by 3.6 percentage points. The last two bars show who paid the costs of the postwar system: production workers' share of total output declined by 5.7 percentage points and transfer payments declined by nearly 1 percentage point.[19]

How long would workers and others in the U.S. and overseas be willing to bear these costs of higher profits and tighter system control?

SPREADING DIFFICULTIES— CHICKENS COMING HOME TO ROOST?

"[Recent successes] strengthen the conviction that recessions can be increasingly avoided and ultimately wiped out."
—President's Council of Economic Advisors, late 1960s[20]

"The dangers [of a crash] are greater than in the 1930s....In the end the world may very well escape disaster, but there is no way it can escape change."
—*Business Week* **magazine, 1974**[21]

Around 1965 and 1966, corporations and their economists were exultant. The economy was growing rapidly. Corporate profits were booming. Everything seemed to be breaking right for the wealthy and

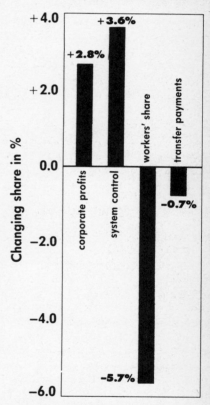

Fig. 19.4
The Key to Prosperity (for the Corporations)

Changes in distribution of output in U.S. economy, 1950-1965

Each bar measures the change in the share of total national output going to each of those four kinds of economic activities. Over this period, for example, the portion of national output going to workers declined by 5.7 percentage points.

Source: See note #19

powerful.

By 1974-75, the tears had returned to their eyes. The economy had just plunged through the sharpest recession since the Great Depression of the 1930s. Corporate profits had collapsed. What was wrong?

The clearest explanation comes from reviewing the structure of postwar prosperity itself. As we have already seen in Chapter 18, its foundations involved four relations of power and control.

(1) U.S. corporations dominated lucrative markets in Europe and Japan, keeping in check less-powerful corporations in those countries.

(2) U.S. corporations, with help from their friends in the government, profited from inexpensive resources and labor in the Third World.

(3) Building on the postwar truce with workers and unions, corporations gained growing control over their own employees.

(4) Corporations and their most-rewarded employees gained increasing advantage over less-powerful workers, particularly women and minorities, and those who were excluded from employment altogether.

In each of these four relations, important actors in the postwar system were supposed to "accept" their subordinate position—*European and Japanese companies, people in the Third World, powerful production workers in the U.S.*, and the *less-powerful in the U.S.*

It turned out that none were willing to be so cooperative and compliant. Rebellion and resistance built in each of those four quarters, and each fed upon and reinforced the others. As each of these junior partners in the system of postwar prosperity began to assert itself, economic difficulties spread. We review these sources of spreading difficulties more or less in the order of their appearance on the postwar scene.

1) Third World Rebellion

There had been flickers of rebellion in Third World countries throughout the 1950s. Iran elected a nationalist president; the CIA arranged for his overthrow. Guatemala responded in similar fashion with the election of Jacobo Arbenz, and the CIA responded similarly. Rebels became unruly in the Middle East, and the Marines landed in Lebanon in 1958. Third World governments had begun to organize coordinated political opposition, resulting in several conferences during the 1950s which expressed overt hostility toward the U.S.[22]

By the time the Kennedy administration took power in 1961, U.S. corporations and the government were on edge. They pursued a new military strategy which would prepare them better for Third World revolts; as President Kennedy argued, "the greater our variety of weapons, the more political choices we can make in any given situation."[23] And they vowed stronger action against future disrespect for U.S. authority abroad; as Kennedy proclaimed about mounting rebellion in Southeast Asia, "we cannot and will not accept any visible humiliation...."[24]

The fat hit the fire in the mid-1960s. The U.S. helped sponsor a military coup in Brazil in 1964, thwarting increasingly populist tendencies in the democratically-elected government under Joao

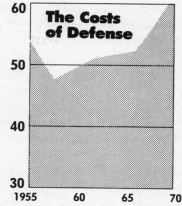

Fig. 19.5
The Defense Price Tag Climbs

The graph measures the real cost of defense spending, adjusting federal defense expenditures for inflation.

Source: See Note #27

Fig. 19.6
Race and Sex Inequalities Widen

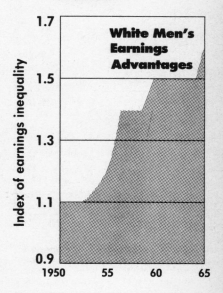

The graph measures the gap between white male earnings and the earnings of white women and black workers (weighted by their labor force shares). A value of 1.0 would be perfect equality. As the index rises, it reflects rising earnings advantages for white men, on the one hand, compared to white women and blacks, on the other.

Source: See note #28

Goulart.[25] The U.S. marines invaded the Dominican Republic in 1965, helping suppress a spreading nationalist and leftist rebellion in that Caribbean country. Most important, the U.S. escalated its involvement in Vietnam, pouring soldiers and material into that country after 1964 in a frantic effort to protect the pro-business client regime in the South against mounting insurrection.

All of these responses were expensive. And for a reason. As one U.S. journalist wrote in the early 1960s:

> Why is it that we must use top-notch elite forces...armed with the very best that advanced technology can provide to defeat Viet-Cong, Algerians, or Malay[s]..., almost none of whom can lay claim to similar expert training and....fire power? The answer is very simple. It takes all the technical proficiency our system can provide to make up for the woeful lack of popular support and political savvy of most of the regimes that the West has thus far sought to prop up.[26]

The costs of propping up these unpopular regimes grew rapidly and suddenly as a result of the U.S. decision to "fight to the finish" in Vietnam. Figure 19.5 shows the effects, tracing the government's defense expenditures (in constant dollars to control for inflation).[27] The graph shows clearly that the price tag for U.S. dominance around the world began to soar after 1964-65.

2) Rebellion of the Excluded in the U.S.

Minorities had fallen behind the majority in the U.S during the 1950s, as we have already seen in Chapter 16. So had women workers, as Chapter 15 showed. These disadvantages mounted through the early 1960s.

Figure 19.6 traces the inequities dividing U.S. workers, showing the growing advantages of white adult male workers over their female and minority counterparts.[28] As those advantages increased, it was increasingly likely that minorities and women would demand a more equitable piece of the action.

Minorities began to protest in the early 1960s. The civil rights movement in the south and intense urban demonstrations and riots in northern ghettos marked this discontent. Blacks (and hispanics, to a

Fig. 19.7

Safety Net Expenditures Increase

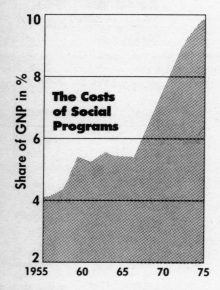

The graph measures the percentage of total output going to government social programs and to transfer payments, including social security and Medicare.

Source: See note #30

Fig. 19.8

The Trade Balance Goes Into the Red

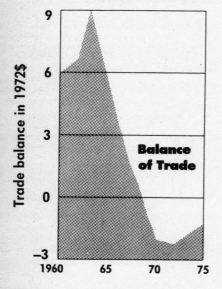

The graph traces the balance of trade (on merchandise account) in constant (1972) dollars. Negative numbers mean that imports are higher than exports.

Source: See note #31

lesser extent) pushed for voting rights, more equal job opportunities, and substantial increases in public assistance for those who could not find decent employment.

Another group acted somewhat more quietly during this period. But they eventually had an equally important effect. Older people had also been left behind by the prosperity of the 50s and early 60s. There had been a great deal of job movement. This made it more difficult for families to stay together with their parents and grandparents. Families split apart. This meant that growing numbers of older people, often living by themselves, had trouble in making their own household ends meet. By the early 1960s, 23% of households considered "poor" by the government were headed by people 65 years or over.[29]

As a result, public pressure mounted gradually from the late 1950s for expanded social security benefits and some kind of health insurance for the elderly—particularly from areas like Florida where there were large concentrations of older households. This pressure eventually resulted in the Kerr-Mills bill in 1961, through which the Congress mandated health care for the elderly on a "needs" basis, and ultimately in legislation establishing Medicare in 1965, which provided more broadly-based health care subsidies for the elderly.

Women also began to mobilize against their subordinate position. The women's movement gathered force in the mid-1960s, beginning to push for affirmative action programs and equal protection under the law. Some of their demands were increasingly translated into government programs with a price tag, like publicly-subsidized daycare programs.

These three different movements of the excluded in the U.S. came together with a common effect—they produced pressure toward expanded government programs, particularly for public assistance, social support, and care for the elderly. And this pressure came together in a short period of time: much of the legislation enabling this extended government support was passed in the mid-1960s—particularly including the Great Society programs and Medicare in 1965.

Figure 19.7 shows the effect of this combined pressure on government spending. It charts the percentage of total national income allocated for government social programs and for transfer programs, including social security and Medicare.[30] As the figure shows, there was little growth in this measure of government support for the needy until 1966, when it began to mushroom.

3) Mounting Competition from Europe and Japan

Many U.S. corporations had begun to rest on their laurels during the 1950s. Their international economic power had gained them huge shares of the markets in other advanced countries. European and Japanese companies were bound to struggle back to their feet....and to pursue cost-reducing innovations which might stagger the corporate giants on their perches. In the steel industry, for example, German and Japanese firms introduced many new techniques during the 1950s and early 1960s which U.S. steel companies blithely chose to ignore.

By the mid-1960s, these foreign corporations were beginning to challenge U.S. corporations on many blocks around the world. This meant that U.S. companies were beginning to have more trouble exporting goods. And this showed up in the U.S. balance of trade. We saw in Chapter 18 that U.S. companies were exporting more than U.S. purchasers were importing in the 1950s and early 1960s. As Figure 19.8 shows, the balance of trade began to slide downhill after 1965, turning into a negative balance—into what is called a "deficit"—after 1967.[31]

4) Growing Worker Resistance

These first three problems combined to help spark a fourth and increasingly severe rebellion—among more powerful U.S. production workers.

On the one hand, mounting international competition made it more and more difficult for U.S. corporations to adjust to their problems by raising their prices. If they did, they would simply compound their problems in world markets.

The overheated economy created close to full employment, with unemployment rates falling to their lowest levels in the postwar period. These tight labor markets helped workers improve their bargaining power and resist corporate harrassment on the job. Figure 19.9 shows the result. It extends Figure 19.2 on the *corporate output dividend*, showing the difference between annual growth in output and annual growth in production workers' wages. The dividend began wearing thin soon after its peak in 1963-64 and plunged into negative figures after 1966.[32]

Many corporate economists wanted the government to slow down the economy in order to restore discipline to the labor market.[33] The quickest path to such disciplinary action would have relied on increases in income taxes. But working people were already bearing most of the costs of rising government expenditures; corporations had already succeeded in escaping government taxes more and more effectively (recall the trends in Figure 19.3 on corporate profits taxes). The result was that production workers' total taxes (as a portion of their earnings) had increased by nearly 40% between 1965 and 1969.[34]

Given these increases in taxes already on the books and biting into workers' pay, the politicians feared a further tax increase. They let the economy blaze along its overheated paths. And worker power continued to grow.

Figure 19.10 shows the effects. Corporate profits quickly felt the pinch of both mounting international competition and growing worker power. The graph extends the earlier series on the (non-financial) corporate rate of profit. After hitting its peak in 1965, it dropped sharply through 1969—even before the recession of 1969-70 knocked it for a further loop.

Where were the corporations to turn? Their workers had gained greater bargaining power. They were more and more reluctant to raise their prices because of international competition. And there was less and less margin for them to escape further government taxation.

There was one more recourse. As we saw in Chapters 3 and 4, company profits depend not only on their workers' wages but also on

Economic Pressures Begin to Mount. . . .

Fig. 19.9
The Corporate Output Share Begins to Plunge

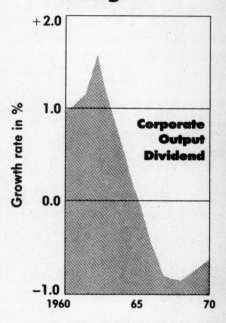

As in Fig. 19.2, the graph measures the difference between the growth of labor productivity and the growth of workers' earnings. Negative figures mean that corporate profits are being squeezed.

Source: See note #32

how hard their employees work on the job. With profits ebbing, companies devoted more and more energy to squeezing extra output from their workers—and eventually to speed-up.

General Motors was a fairly typical case. It created its General Motors Assembly Division (GMAD) in 1965, according to *Business Week*, to establish " 'get tough' tactics" in production. "The need for GMAD's belt-tightening role was underscored during the late 1960s when GM's profit margin dropped from 10 percent to 7 percent." GMAD adopted its tougher procedures, the magazine concluded, to "boost productivity."[35] In the Chevrolet Vega plant in Lordstown, Ohio, the results of its belt-tightening efforts were obvious: it increased the speed of the line from 60 cars an hour to more than 100.[36]

This kind of speed-up usually results in rising accident rates. During the late 1940s and early 1950s, when corporations and unions established the postwar labor truce, accident rates in manufacturing fell. They remained roughly constant through the early 1960s. And then speed-up struck. Figure 19.11 traces the frequency of workdays lost from accidents on the job from 1950 through 1973. As the graph shows, the industrial accident rate increased by one-third between 1965 and 1973.[37]

Workers began to feel more and more angry about these corporate assaults on their working conditions. We saw in Chapter 18 that strikes had declined after the truce of the early 1950s. But the truce began to unravel as speed-up spread. After 1966-67, the frequency of strikes increased substantially, rising by 146% from 1966 to 1970.[38] Workers also struck more frequently over working conditions. And the frequency of wildcat strikes—strikes called during the term of contract—also increased substantially during the same years, rising by 25% from the early 1960s to the end of the decade.[39]

Workers were themselves clear about their reasons for striking. They had been promised better working conditions. But they had begun to feel the pressure of speed-up and automation. For many, it became more and more important to draw the line. As one autoworker at the Chevrolet Vega plant in Lordstown explained: "People refused to do extra work. The more the company pressured them, the less work they turned out. Cars went down the line without repairs.[40]

Government to the Rescue—Whoops!

The spreading difficulties seemed more and more systemic. They weren't limited to one sector or one country. They flowed from the actions of corporations and workers, excluded U.S. citizens and Third World people, international corporations and domestic managers. The system of postwar prosperity involved an integrated set of institutions, as we saw in Chapter 18, and the frictions resulting from its inner tensions were beginning to spread throughout the system.

Why didn't the government race to the rescue of corporate profits and power? We saw in Chapters 8 and 12 that the government usually provides as much help to its friends in business as it can. Why did the government fail to grease the bearings in the late 1960s? Why did it allow the economy to smoke with overheated parts?

Fig. 19.10
...And Corporate Profits Begin to Dip

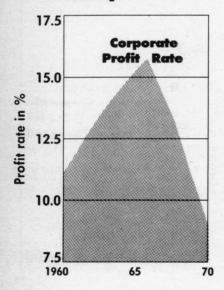

As in Fig. 19.1, the graph measures the profit rate for nonfinancial corporations—expressed as before-tax profits divided by the capital stock.

Source: See note #7

The principal answer is that the government did its best but failed. Between 1969 and 1973, the government took three major kinds of actions aimed at restoring corporate profits and the stability upon which continuing economic growth depended.

1. *"Saving the Dollar."* We have seen that there was a growing deficit in the U.S. balance of trade (see Figure 19.8). This resulted in a continuing drain of U.S. gold reserves. By the mid-1960s, foreign banks were anxious about holding dollars in their accounts; they feared that the dollar might lose its value and that their holdings of dollars would purchase less and less. So many foreign banks began to cash in their dollars for gold—all at the guaranteed exchange rate of $35 an ounce of gold.[41]

In 1971, President Nixon took two dramatic steps to address these twin problems of mounting trade deficits and draining gold reserves.

First, Nixon "freed" the dollar from gold, abruptly abandoning the long-standing promise to pay $35 for every ounce of gold. This meant that foreign banks might eventually be forced to pay much more than $35 for an ounce of precious gold from the Fort Knox reserves.

Second, he "devalued the dollar." This followed naturally from the end of the guaranteed dollar-price of gold. Now, the U.S. government would allow the exchange rates between other currencies and the U.S. dollar to sort themselves out. Many people were holding more dollars than they wanted. This meant that they wanted to sell dollars and buy other "healthy" currencies—like the German mark and the Japanese yen. And this meant, in turn, that the price of the dollar would fall *in relation to* the price of those other currencies—that the dollar would be worth relatively less in relation to those currencies than it used to be or, in other words, that it would be "devalued."

Why were these measures so important? The mounting trade deficits and declining gold reserves had been placing sharp limits on the government's freedom to maneuver in economic policy. If it tried to cut into workers' power by forcing a recession, interest rates would fall. This would result in capital leaving the country to look for higher interest rates—and in sharpening pressure on the balance of payments because of that refugee capital. The government policies aimed to reduce the pressure on the balance of payments in order to clear the space necessary for other salvage efforts.

2. *Cooling Off the Economy.* Both in 1969 and in late 1973, the government took steps clearly intended to cause a recession in the economy. As we saw in Chapter 6, recessions help restore capitalist profits by curbing workers' bargaining power. By the late 1960s, such a curb seemed to corporations more essential than ever.

How do we know that the government acted to cause recessions? We can look at short-term government spending policy. If the government suddenly puts the lid on federal spending, causing a sudden increase in the government margin of revenues over expenditures, economists interpret that action as a "deflationary" measure—a set of actions designed to cool off the economy.

There is clear evidence that the government took such steps both in 1969 and in 1973.[42] The reasons for their concern were self-evident.

Fig. 19.11

Response? Speed-up and Rising Accidents

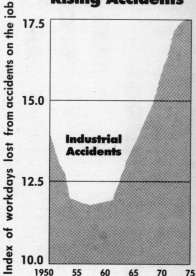

The graph measures the number of workdays lost as a result of accidents on the job (per one million worker-hours). A rise in this index of workplace accidents indicates a greater relative frequency of accidents, not simply a rise in total employment.

Source: See note #37

Fig. 19.12

The Key to Spreading Economic Difficulties

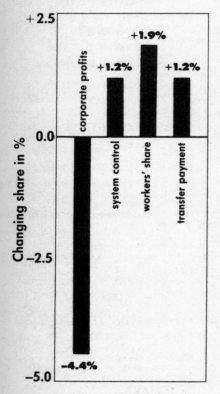

Changes in distribution of output in U.S. economy, 1965–1973

As in Fig. 19.4, each bar measures the change in the share of total national output going to each of those four kinds of economic activities. Over this period, for example, the portion of national output going to corporate profits declined by 4.4 percentage points.

Source: See note #47

Workers had been gaining too much power. Higher unemployment rates would instill some honest discipline. As one corporate executive reported during the 1970 recession, "Corporate executives I've checked with are cautiously optimistic....There is what I call a wholesome recession. We're just at the point of a sprint...." As the *Wall Street Journal* concluded in the same period, "Many manufacturing executives...[had] openly complained in recent years that too much control had passed from management to labor."[43]

3. *Putting a Lid on Wages and Prices.* The Nixon Administration also imposed wage-price controls from 1971 to 1973—an unusual and largely unexpected policy measure.

The government justified these controls as an arrow in the battle against inflation. But there was an underlying and much more important motivation: the government hoped to curb wages until labor markets became looser and, as a result, to restore profits to their former levels. It was important to control spiralling wages, as one of the program administrators reported, but profits should be free of controls because profits during this period were too "low."[44] Workers might have argued that their own wages were "too low" as well, but the wage-price control officials never asked them for their views.

For all their novelty and drama, all three of these government salvage efforts failed:

■ Corporate profits had climbed to an average of 16.3% (on equity investment) in 1965, before the spreading difficulties of 1966-73. Despite all these government rescue attempts, the corporate rate of profit had returned to only 11.1% in the business cycle peak of 1972—before the slowdown leading to the late 1973 recession.[45] The government had done its best, but corporate profits were still suffering.

■ The devaluation of the dollar had helped momentarily, but the balance of payments did not substantially recover. In 1973, after a second devaluation of the dollar, the balance of payments improved slightly, but the deficit in 1974 was as large as those in 1971 and 1972.[46]

Something was wrong! The government economists had promised steady growth. Corporations had been hoping for steady profits. In their place the economy was producing shrinking profits and periodic—but apparently necessary—recessions. Would you buy a used economy from these people? With hindsight, we can see that the problems were too deeply rooted for these government salvage efforts to be effective. The government's attempts at repair involved little more than adding some motor oil to lubricate the overheated engine. But the difficulties were coming from much more basic malfunctions, and their heat simply overwhelmed the government lubricant.

The Causes and Consequences of Spreading Difficulties

Causes. This account of the sources of spreading difficulties in the postwar economy helps us account for its causes. We can return to our earlier analysis of the composition of net national output. We had seen that profits during the period of prosperity were supported by the postwar systems of control and financed out of workers' living standards and relatively declining transfer payments (see Figure 19.4).

EARLY SYMPTOMS OF STAGFLATION

Fig. 19.13a
Productivity Growth Slows

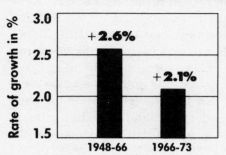

The bars measure the average annual rate of growth, in each period, of total output per production worker hour.

Source: See note #47

The bars measure the average annual rate of growth, in each period, of prices as measured by the consumer price index.

Source: See note #47

Fig. 19.13b
Prices Rise

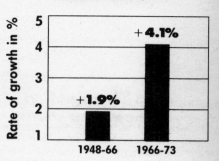

From 1965 to 1973, corporate power began to erode. U.S. workers and government clients fought back, reclaiming many of their earlier losses. Foreign competition and Third World rebellions narrowed corporate margins for maneuver. But the system of control—the defense expenditures and the costs of supervision—were not easily forsaken; the military and bureaucratic machines continued to demand their own fuel and support.

Figure 19.12 shows the results of these conflicting pressures on the postwar system.[47] The last two bars show the effects of people's rebellion: the share of workers' subsistence and of transfer payments in national output grew from 1965 to 1973 by 1.9 and 1.2 percentage points respectively. The second bar shows the stubborn costs of system control: defense and supervisory expenditures commanded yet another 1.2 percentage points of net national output.

And corporate profits suffered accordingly. Their share of national output fell, as the first bar in the graph shows, by 4.4 percentage points. Corporations were already paying the price of both the resistance to and the inflexibility of the system which made their earlier gold mines a temporary possibility.

Consequences. This spreading difficulty in the postwar economy had five different effects. The charts in Figure 19.13 show the main impacts of these effects.

■ Growth in hourly output slowed dramatically. As workers began to resist the onslaught of corporate speed-up and took advantage of tighter labor markets to support their resistance, continuing corporate investment had less and less effect. Figure 19.13a shows that the average annual rate of growth in hourly output dropped considerably from 1948-1966 to 1966-1973, falling by roughly 20%.

■ Inflation followed as a direct consequence of the slowdown in hourly output. There was less and less output available for a growing population. But neither corporations nor the government could force workers and government clients to accept a reduction in their demands for decent living conditions. Corporations were no more willing to accept a slowdown in their rate of investment, borrowing heavily to make up for declining profits. And government spending itself continued to soar. With less rapidly growing output and continuously growing demand, both banks and the government were pressured to make up the difference in expanding credit and easier money—

Fig. 19.13c
Unemployment Begins to Climb

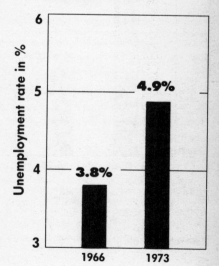

The bars measure the civilian unemployment rate for the business cycle peak year at the end of each of the two periods being compared. 1973, like 1966, is *not* a recession year.

Source: See note #47

continually increasing the amount of money available for corporations and households to use in their purchases.

The result was an increase in the rate of inflation. Figure 19.13b compares the average annual rate of price increase between 1948 and 1966 with the average rate of inflation between 1966 and 1973. The inflation rate more than doubled in the period of spreading economic difficulties.

■ Interest rates also climbed. Corporations and households were borrowing more and more to make up for slower growth in their incomes. And with inflation rising, lenders demanded higher interest rates to keep up with the increase in prices. Official data show the slow growth in the rate of interest on corporate bonds as the economy slowed down.[48]

■ Unemployment rates also moved upwards. Investment rates slowed slightly, partly reducing the employment provided by the private sector. And the government was beginning to move toward policies aimed at curbing inflation and restoring discipline to the labor market. Figure 19.13c compares unemployment rates between 1966 and 1973, when joblessness was at its lowest point in those respective business cycles. Unemployment rates had risen by 1.1 percentage points from 1966 to 1973, an increase of 29%.[49]

■ The final consequence was the one which mattered most for working people. We saw at the beginning of Chapter 1 that workers' real spendable earnings—what they have left after inflation and taxes—have taken a beating during the current crisis. Figure 19.13d shows that workers' real spendable earnings first began to feel the pinch during these early years of slowing growth. The graph compares the rate of growth in real spendable earnings between 1948 and 1966 with the rate of growth between 1966 and 1973. The rate of increase in what workers could buy with their earnings had dropped by 59%.[50]

And The Rest of Us Feel the Pinch

Fig. 19.13d
Workers' Earnings Begin to Stagnate

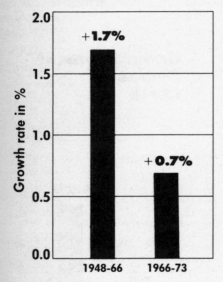

The bars measure the average annual rate of growth in the average production worker's real spendable earnings—taking into account both inflation and taxes.

Source: See note #47

CRISIS ARRIVES—FROM SPARKS TO PRAIRIE FIRES

"We should not be misled by the appearance of a light at the end of the tunnel. It is probably an oncoming train."
—U.S. corporate executive, 1975[51]

"You hear a labor leader say: 'What's good for the company is good for us, because if they make a profit, we get more wages.' That's bullshit. U.S. steel is making more profit. We're sure as hell not making more wages."
—steelworker union local leader[52]

The economy had been experiencing increasing difficulties and corporate executives had been spreading the alarms. The events of 1973-1975 convinced them that their problems were even more serious than they feared.

■ Oil prices suddenly soared as OPEC countries organized themselves and energy companies took advantage of the increases. Crude oil prices charged by oil-exporting countries nearly quadrupled in 1973. More important for the over-all state of the economy, the price which companies had to pay for basic fuel as a raw material in production increased by 68% in just two years—in 1973 and 1974.[53]

■ The recession of 1974-75 was much, much deeper than anyone expected. Production suffered its biggest decline since the start of the Great Depression in 1929-30. By 1975, the "official" unemployment rate had climbed to 8.5%—its highest level since the end of the Depression in 1940. To make matters worse, the rate of inflation actually increased substantially during the recession—the first time that had happened in the peace-time history of recorded prices in the U.S.[54]

From then on, all the problems of the late 1960s and early 1970s grew steadily worse. The economy began to seem out of control. As we saw in Chapter 1, perceptions of crisis gradually spread. Since we have already reviewed some of the more recent events of that crisis in the first chapter, we do not now need to recount its details.

Two more important tasks remain. First, we need to use our analysis of the roots and early onset of the crisis to dispel some of the simplistic explanations of our problems repeatedly echoed in the media. In a series of "De-Duping Exercises" in the boxes at the end of the chapter, we examine and "de-DUPE" the most common misplaced explanations of crisis, using the facts and insights of this chapter.

Second, we need to explore the *connections* between the early tensions of the postwar system which triggered instability in the mid-1960s and the later symptoms of crisis during the 1970s. It was not simply that the economy, once unglued, began to unravel. Much more important, the directions in which the economy unraveled after 1973-1975 grew out of and were channeled by the sources of its initial problems.

From Band-Aids to Surgery

During the late 1960s and early 1970s, as we have seen, corporations and the government responded to early instability with makeshift policies. They tried to patch up the cracks in the postwar system. They responded with short-term solutions.

Those band-aid measures did not work. Corporations began to recognize, by the mid-1970s, that some basic faults in the foundation of postwar prosperity had appeared and were widening. Corporations stopped simply adjusting to their changing circumstances. They began to address what they perceived to be the sources of their problems, seeking basic changes in the environment surrounding them. They had begun to feel, as the reporters at a corporate executives conference in 1974-75 concluded, that the "current crisis stems [from an inadequate] social organization to cope with the problems of a highly industrialized system."[55] In order to lay the basis for new solutions to their problems, they began attacking the economic forces which they felt would stand in their way.

Attacking Labor. The system of postwar prosperity had built upon, as we saw in Chapter 18, a truce between large corporations and organized labor. By the mid-1970s, corporations signalled their intentions of breaking the truce. As Douglas Fraser, president of the United Auto Workers Unions, concluded in 1978, "The leaders of industry, commerce and finance in the United States have broken and discarded

Workers Feel The Pressure

Fig. 19.14
Union Membership Continues to Drop

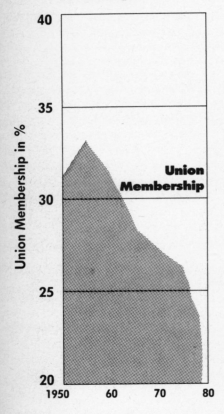

The graph measures the percentage of the total (non-agricultural) labor force which belongs to a labor union.

Source: See note #59

the fragile, unwritten compact previously existing during a past period of growth and progress....I am convinced there has been a shift on the part of the business community toward confrontation, rather than cooperation."[56]

Fraser knew what he was talking about. The evidence was all around:

■ Corporations began mobilizing massive resources against labor union power. They turned increasingly to sophisticated management consultants for help in preventing unions and ousting ones already in place. They may be spending, according to various estimates, as much as $100-500 million a year in fees to such firms alone.[57] A British magazine, *The Economist*, recently reviewed the reasons for this spending splurge:

Managers are desperate for maximum flexibility in adopting new technology to stay ahead of the game. They are also keen to save a bit on wages. So they would prefer to do without even the limited resistance of unions to change.[58]

There are two measures of the effectiveness of these corporate efforts. One is union decertification elections. Most such elections come about as a result of company pressure and manipulation. Decertification elections have soared since the early 1970s. The other measure is declining union representation. As Figure 19.14 shows, the percentage of union membership in the labor force has fallen steadily since 1954 and its decline has accelerated since the early 1970s.[59]

■ Corporations have been increasingly inclined, it appears, to speed up the pace of production. We had already seen that accident rates had begun to rise during the late 1960s. They continued to rise during the 1970s. By 1980, they had nearly doubled their levels in 1963-64 and were as high as the worst year of high-speed production during World War II.[60] (See Figure 19.15.)

■ Corporations accelerated their movement of capital resources away from regions in the United States where unions had traditionally been strong. The shift of jobs to the Sunbelt accelerated after 1971-1973.[61] So did the careful targeting of overseas investment; large corporations tended increasingly to choose countries like the Philippines and Argentina where popular power was most restricted and opportunities for profit were relatively high. The result, below the bottom line, was that the ratio of overseas profits to profits on U.S. investments increased steadily during the 1970s.[62]

This trend gave corporations dramatically greater leverage in bargaining with many unions and workers: if workers balked, companies could threaten runaways and shutdowns. Corporate pressure for "concessions" and "givebacks" grew steadily from the mid-1970s to the present—with job loss and unemployment hanging like the threat of an economic guillotine over the necks of corporate employees.

These several dimensions of attack on labor were hardly confined to the United States. Throughout the advanced capitalist countries, employers were tending more and more toward collective corporate efforts to undermine labor's bargaining and political strength. A 1976 report by the Organization for Economic Cooperation and Development (OECD)—a semi-official advisory organization for the advanced countries—summarized this trend:

> Labour unrest....was causing employers to think more than heretofore in terms of joint [employer] solidarity....In blunt terms...a stronger employers' organization and an increase in bargaining power means that high profits can be achieved....There [has been] general acceptance of the need for employers, both individually and collectively, to take a strong part....[63]

Attacking Government Regulation. Corporations took aim at many government policies and programs which either restrained business activities or strengthened popular leverage over business. Corporations became increasingly interested in reshaping their economic environment. And they didn't want Uncle Sam peering over their shoulder.

The attack on government regulation began at roughly the same time as the attack on labor—around 1974-75. Corporations mobilized their public and political resources to erode or eliminate regulations they didn't like. "We need more business involvement in the policy process," as one participant concluded at a management conference at that time. "If you don't know your senator on a first-name basis," another concluded, "you are not doing an adequate job for your share-holders."[64]

These attacks on government regulation began long before the Reagan Administration arrived in Washington in 1981. Business lobbyists had been swarming through the citadels of government since the mid-1970s. They took aim at five important targets, seeking relaxation of (1) environmental regulation; (2) health-and-safety standards; and (3) ceilings on oil and gas prices; while aiming simultaneously to block (4) labor law reform legislation; and (5) efforts to close tax loopholes benefiting corporations and the wealthy.

And these early attacks on government regulation gained effective momentum *before* the Reagan Administration came to power. Irving Kristol, often called the "guru" of the "new right" attack on government, concluded in 1979 that the business campaign against government regulation was already in high gear. The public "was very slow getting on a new learning curve" about "government overregulation of business, etc.," but "more recently....," he concluded, "there have been hopeful signs of...an increasing recognition of the need for an economic policy to spur economic growth instead of being indifferent or hostile to it."[65] The arrival of the Reagan Administration and its "supply-siders" helped nail the lid tight, but earlier corporate assaults had built the coffin and lain the government corpse inside.

Early critics of these business attacks worried about the corporate disregard for popular power and government support for the less fortunate. Corporations were concerned about other issues. The onset of crisis had flowed, as we have already seen, from popular challenges to corporate power both at home and abroad. Corporations were now conscious of the need to repel those challenges and re-establish their

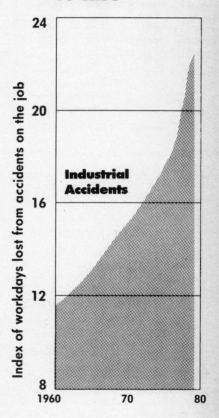

Fig. 19.15
Accidents Continue to Rise

Industrial Accidents

Index of workdays lost from accidents on the job

As in Fig. 19.11, the graph measures the number of workdays lost as a result of accidents on the job (per million worker-hours).

Source: See note #60.

Fig. 19.16
Corporations Turn toward Paper Investments

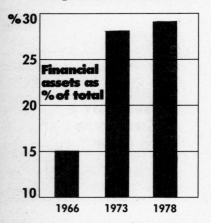

The bars measure the percentage of total corporate funds applied to investments which "increase financial assets"—for example, for mergers and speculation. As this increases, real investments in plant and equipment decline.

Source: See note #67

Fig. 19.17
With High Unemployment, Strikes Are Down

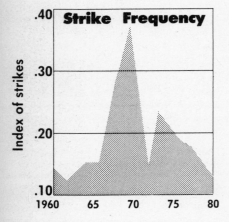

The graph measures the frequency of strikes in the private non-agricultural work force (adjusted for total levels of employment).

Source: See note #74

control. If it became necessary to sacrifice democratic values in the process, so be it. A major business study of the current political crisis, sponsored by the international corporate advisory group called the Trilateral Commission, concluded in 1975:

> Al Smith once remarked that 'the only cure for the evils of democracy is more democracy.' Our analysis suggests that applying that cure at the present time could well be adding fuel to the flames. Instead, some of the problems of governance in the United States today stem from an excess of democracy....Needed, instead, is a greater degree of moderation of democracy.[66]

Putting Growth on the Backburner. While corporations sought this restoration of their power over the economic environment, they put economic growth on the backburner. They took two kinds of actions which tended to shift the economy's gears into neutral.

■ When corporations are interested in expanding and deepening their economic ties to a particular region or country, they make long-term investments in real *physical* buildings and machines; that's the only way they'll be able to expand their production and their profits over the long run. (Stable profits lie, as we saw in Chapter 3, in production, not exchange.) But when corporations fear that a particular economic environment is not hospitable—when they are seeking structural changes in the economic landscape—they tend to reduce their physical investments and shift money into *paper* investments— buying up other companies, speculating in currencies and commodities, shifting their money from one paper asset to another.

This shift toward paper investments involves a kind of waiting game—holding out on real investment until corporations feel that conditions are more favorable. And that is the game companies began playing after 1970. Figure 19.16 shows the trend clearly. The three bars compare the percentage of investable funds available to corporations which they were using to "increase their financial assets"—by investing in paper rather than real wealth—over the three main phases of the postwar period. By 1966, they were investing an average of only about 15% of available funds in "increases in financial assets." From 1973-1978, that portion had nearly doubled.[67]

This points to a clear "capital strike" by corporations. If U.S. corporations were still investing in physical capital at the same rates as they did in earlier periods, *they would have poured an additional $100 billion into the real productive capacity of the U.S. economy.*[68] Instead, they were siphoning that money into their bank accounts. While their accounts ballooned, their capital was out on strike against the "real" economy.

■ Corporations also sought government policies to douse the economy in a cold bath. Workers had gained too much power during the years of low unemployment in the mid-1960s, they concluded. In order to restore profits, workers needed the discipline of higher unemployment. As *Fortune* magazine argued in 1976, "Unemployment must remain at much higher levels than conventional political rhetoric demands....It would be better to err on the side of conservatism, and stop nudging down the unemployment rate...."[69]

And, not surprisingly, governments were essentially willing to honor these corporate preferences. Throughout the advanced economies, after 1977-78, governments pursued policies of budgetary restraint, keeping their feet on the brakes, holding down the rate of growth. "Throughout the industrial world," as one business journal reported in 1979, "central banks and governments have come to believe that slow is beautiful."[70] A report by an international economic organization was clear about the sources of steadily higher unemployment rates:

> The world economy has been stumbling along for most of the decade in a vain effort to recapture the earlier confidence and progress....The present unemployment is not due to a failure of aggregate demand but to a...view...[which] rests on the belief that inflation can only be fought by unemployment.[71]

Suppressed Resistance and Anger

"You start bitchin' about the air, and people say you want to shut the mill town down....That's how successful the [corporations] have been. There's economic blackmail today."
—local steelworker official[72]

Popular responses to these corporate attacks have been two-sided.

On the one side, many people feel the threat of blackmail—fearing that they will lose their jobs if they resist, worrying about their bank accounts as they feel the squeeze, anticipating the moving vans to the Sunbelt if they protest occupational hazards. Three symptoms of this intimidation are evident:

■ Many workers and unions have responded to corporate demands for concessions and givebacks—feeling that they have little choice. There are no statistics kept on these aspects of bargaining, so no one knows how many concessions labor has reluctantly granted. One recent survey in the *New York Times* concluded that they have been widespread:

> Concessions are occurring not only in the automobile and trucking industries but also in steel, rubber, the airlines, rail transportation and other industries. Experts expect concessions to bring a transfer of millions of dollars from employees to employers, a situation that has not occurred since labor-management contract bargaining became a formalized institution in the 1930s and 1940s.[73]

■ Strike activity had been rising, as we saw, through the late 1960s. As unemployment rates began to creep upward after 1973, however, strikes seemed more and more dangerous. Figure 19.17 traces the frequency of workdays lost from strikes through 1980. It shows a rise in the late 1960s and early 1970s—and then the low rates after the sharp recession of 1974-75.[74]

■ Many people have accepted the necessity of sharp cutbacks in government spending for social programs—even though they think those programs are necessary. In one poll in 1979, 70% of adults

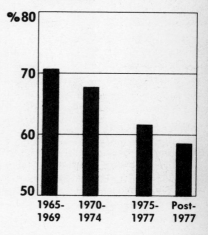

Fig. 19.18
Job Satisfaction Down

The bars measure the percentage of workers who respond that they like the kind of work they do "very much" or "a good deal."

Source: See note #76

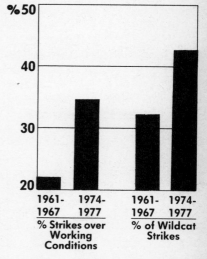

Fig. 19.19
Job Action, Wildcat Strikes Rise

The bars measure (1) the percentage of all strikes which focused on issues about working conditions; and (2) the percentage of all strikes which were during the term of contract (or wildcat strikes).

Source: See note #77

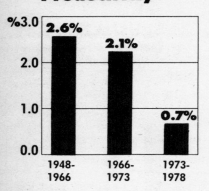

Fig. 19.20a
Productivity

The bars measure the average annual rate of increase in hourly output of production workers for each of the periods   Source: See note #79

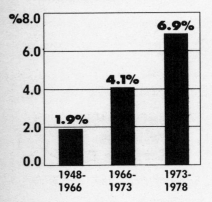

Fig. 19.20b
Inflation

The bars measure the average annual rate of increase in the consumer price index for each of the periods indicated.

Source: See note #79

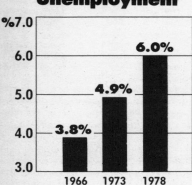

Fig. 19.20c
Unemployment

The bars measure the unemployment rate in the end year of each of the periods compared in other graphs of Figure 19.20.   Source: See note #79

surveyed agreed that government social programs should be reduced in order to fight inflation.[75] There seemed to be no other choice.

On the other hand, many people are becoming more and more frustrated.

■ Workers' job dissatisfaction has been rising sharply. Figure 19.18 shows one index of worker dissatisfaction, measuring the percentage of workers who feel that "I am not happy with my job." After falling through in the mid-1960s, this measure of subterranean discontent has increased rapidly.[76]

■ Workers are more and more likely to engage in new and unauthorized kinds of protests. Figure 19.19 shows the rise in these forms of resistance: the percentage of strikes which are "wildcats," or during the term of contract, has increased. So has the percentage of strikes over working conditions. And so has the percentage of contract settlements rejected by union membership.[77]

Symptoms of Crisis

The foundations of postwar prosperity continue to crumble. Corporations have gone on the attack. People feel a muted but spreading anger. Where once there was stability within a structure of power, there is now increasing instability among the ruins of that structure. Evidence of this spreading instability and crisis lies all around us.

Figures 19.20a-e continue the earlier graphs on the main symptoms of crisis. From the first to the second to the third periods of the postwar era, as these figures show, there has been a steady and continuing deterioration:[78]

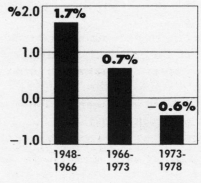

Fig. 19.20d
Workers' Earnings Buy Less

The bars measure the rate of increase in the average production worker's real spendable earnings (controlling for inflation and taxes) for each of the periods indicated.

Source: See note #79

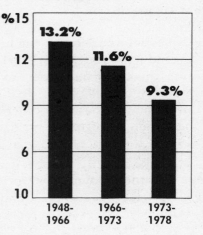

Fig. 19.20e
And Corporate Profits Plunge

The bars measure the average rate of profit (on invested capital) for the nonfinancial corporate sector for each of the periods indicated.

Source: See note #79

Three additional dimensions of crisis have become more and more important. Both reflect the spread of crisis throughout the world economy and the international economic instability which has resulted.

■ As we saw in Chapter 18, the dollar had been the grease for postwar prosperity throughout the capitalist world. As world conditions began to deteriorate and the strength of the U.S. economy eroded, however, bankers and governments grew more and more concerned about the strength of the dollar. No other single currency was an obvious substitute. So more and more people began to buy gold. This produced a rapid increase in the price of gold and, once its price had reached nearly astronomic proportions, rapid fluctuations in its price.

■ When crisis deepens, the least powerful typically suffer the worst. Many Third World countries have been caught by declining world demand for their exports and a weakened internal capacity to protect themselves from the international crisis. This has led to more and more Third World borrowing just to keep their domestic economies afloat. By the beginning of the 1980s, Third World countries owed roughly $400 billion to First World banks and international funds. Few believe they can possibly repay those loans. The risk of default is a storm cloud over international finance. As one banker put it in 1980: "The Third World has overborrowed. Any default might have a domino effect [which could produce] a catastrophe."[79]

■ When economies slump, they often resort to what is called "protectionism"—trying to protect their own economies by erecting walls against goods from other competing countries. As crisis has spread, so has the threat of protectionism. Tariff barriers rise. Special trade quotas proliferate. "Beggar thy neighbor" in order to save oneself. When negotiations convene to halt the process, no one dares take the first step. As one economic minister reported about a 1979 trade conference, "We couldn't even find agreement on describing [the problem]."[80]

De-Duping Exercise #1

What About OPEC?

Many like to blame our problems, particularly inflation, on OPEC—that is, on the sharp increases in energy prices which resulted in 1973-74 and again in 1978-79 from the coordinated actions of most oil-producing countries. Is OPEC to blame?

The first problem with blaming OPEC is that almost all of our problems had already begun long before 1973—during the period from 1966 to 1973 reviewed in this chapter in "Spreading Difficulties...."

The second problem is that energy price increases themselves account for a very small portion of our problems *even after 1973*. One study by a leading economist found that energy price hikes in 1973-74 accounted for only 10% of the rise in the rate of inflation in later years in all the advanced countries. Their impact on U.S. inflation was even smaller because of our relatively lighter dependence on OPEC oil supplies.

• Source: See note #83

De-Duping Exercise #2

What About Big Government?

Many conservatives blame our problems on government taxation and regulation. Is big government the source of our current crisis?

* Countries where the government has played a much more substantial role during the postwar period, like Austria, the Netherlands, and Sweden, have grown more rapidly than the U.S. *and* have weathered the current crisis much more effectively. Even in Japan, the government plays a much more active role in subsidizing business and allocating capital.

* What about government taxes? The rate of business taxation on corporations in the U.S. has *fallen* during the same period when the economy has deteriorated since the mid-1960s. So how can we blame our problems on government taxes? The economy fell apart precisely at the same time that the government tax load on business lightened.

* What about government regulation of business? First, many of the regulations which corporations hate most, like health-and-safety and environmental regulation, began to take some effect in the mid-1970s, many years after our economic problems had become serious. Second, there was a very mixed pattern of regulation in the 1970s. In many industries, regulation grew lighter, not heavier. Productivity growth declined in as many industries where regulation was lightened as in those where regulation became tighter. Problems developed, in short, no matter what the trend in regulation.

Source: See note #84

THE NEED FOR RESTRUCTURING

What About Workers' Wages?

Corporations have been pinning some of the blame on workers' wages, in effect, because they've been pulling out their crying towels and demanding wage-and-benefit concessions and givebacks.

The problem with this charge is that it's way off the mark. What companies care about in this regard is called *unit labor costs*—how much a given unit of output (per worker hour) costs in terms of workers' wages and benefits.

Unit labor costs rose *more slowly* during the 1960s and 1970s than in any other advanced country—including both Europe and Japan. This means that U.S. companies were gaining relative advantages, in terms of labor costs, over corporations in those countries. If they couldn't take advantage of those gains, it wasn't workers' fault.

Source: See note #85

"You'll see the economic, social, and political system changing. The system we now have operates solely on the basis of greed. It works fairly well when there's enough, so that even the greedy are satiated. But when we run out,... there'll be a change.

"Maybe the Indians knew it all along. They smelled it way back. Know what they say? Custer had it coming."

—former U.S. Senator[81]

This chapter has argued that crisis resulted from the internal erosion of the postwar system of prosperity. That system was based on U.S. corporate domination of the domestic and international economy. It was threaded with relationships of power—of some groups gaining advantage from others. The disadvantaged eventually fought back, forging new and eventually irrepressible challenges to the wealthy and powerful who had earned the greatest profits from prosperity—while it lasted. With those challenges to the structure of power and domination, difficulties spread and growth slowed. Once growth slowed, the powerful went on the attack, seeking new ways of restoring their power. And crisis spread.

This argument has a simple, fundamental implication. A new period of prosperity will not be possible until a new system of economic relationships is constructed. It is hardly likely to resemble the postwar system—simply because many have learned important lessons from the collapse of that system. This suggests that a *new structure of economic relationships must be forged if we are to escape from crisis.* **We are entering a period of economic restructuring.**[82]

The problem, then, is not whether or not to change. *The economy is changing whether we like it or not.* The critical issue is now clear. *How should the economy change? If restructuring is necessary in any case, whose interests should it serve?*

Part VI of this book, **"Welcome to the 1980s,"** begins with these central questions. It reviews the logic of the *corporate response*, demonstrating both the fallacies and the underlying greed of the business plan for restructuring. It then suggests the outlines of a *popular alternative*.

What About Corporate Rip-Offs and Military Waste?

Some of us blame monopoly power and military waste for our current problems. But this finger-pointing is too simple.

* The corporate rip-off argument suggests, for example, that rising inflation has resulted from growing concentration of corporate power. As corporations have gained greater monopoly leverage over prices, it suggests, they have been able to push more of their costs onto us.

But the facts contradict this suggestion. Concentration of corporate power increased during the 1950s and early 1960s, when prices did not rise rapidly. In the late 1960s and 1970s, corporate concentration did *not* increase. Indeed, one major study has found that U.S. corporations have faced growing competition during the 1960s and 1970s. Inflation must have come from some other source. There is clearly too much corporate power, as Chapter 20 makes clear, but the sources of inflation run deeper than simple monopoly pricing.

* Military spending is clearly wasteful. But it is hard to blame all our problems on the defense industry. If they were to blame, we would find that military spending has risen, as a percentage of GNP, during the late 1960s and 1970s when our problems developed. But the opposite happened; resources going to the defense industry declined in relative terms. There is far too much waste in military spending, to be sure, but we need a more complete explanation of our problems than a focus on military spending can provide.

Source: See note #86

PART VI: WELCOME TO THE 1980S

"Whenever I get worried about the economy, I go up to the top of the mountain to see the Great Exalted Economists....'Blessed Guru, what is the answer?'
" 'The only solution is to bite the bullet....But while biting the bullet, we should not throw the baby out with the bath water. We must hold our hand firmly on the rudder until the storm blows over, keeping all options open even if it means tightening our belts....'
" 'I knew you would have the answer, Exalted One,' I said

with tears in my eyes....
"He turned to go into his cave to broil his steak. The last words he said to me were, 'Then again, I could be wrong.' "

—Art Buchwald, 1978[1]

"I see changes coming. I hear guys talking of things today you didn't hear fifteen years ago. I hear guys talkin' about inflation and blaming the boss and profits for that crap....I'm not talkin' about radicals. I'm talking about guys who've been doin' their trick for twenty years in the mill."

—steelworker[2]

2.16 pm, Roll-Call

We have seen that our present problems result from the collapse of the postwar system of prosperity. Solving our problems will therefore require establishing a new structure of economic relationships to replace the old. What kind of structure? How do we get there?

Chapter 20, **"Economic Recovery: We Don't Have to Say We're Sorry,"** reviews two alternative approaches to economic restructuring—the *corporate strategy* and a *popular alternative*. It shows that the dominant business strategies, clearly reflected in Reaganomics, build on faulty logic. They are not likely to work because they do not address the real problems of the economy. Once the cloak of their misleading analysis is lifted, the greed upon which they rest is bared for all to see.

What could a popular and democratic alternative look like? Chapter 20 reviews the conclusions of Part V on "The Making of the Current Economic Crisis" and sum-marizes its implications for policy. Based on that review, it suggests the outline of an alternative economic program for the 1980s which could *both* solve the real and fundamental problems we face *and* foster popular and democratic values.

The problem, of course, is that the wealthy and powerful will oppose such a program.

This suggests two further questions. Why must we keep facing these periodic economic crises? And why should the few have such wealth and power? Chapter 21 faces the next and obvious issue: **"There Must Be a Better Way?"** As we move out of our present crisis, can we point toward a brighter economic future? If capitalism creates such problems, can't we replace it with something healthier for children and other living things?

None of this will be easy. Chapter 22 concludes this guide with the most obvious and urgent question of all: **"How Do We Begin?"**

"It is inevitable that the U.S. economy will grow more slowly....Some people will obviously have to do with less.... Yet it will be a hard pill for many Americans to swallow—the idea of doing with less so that big business can have more. It will be particularly hard to swallow because it is quite obvious that...[big business is] in large measure the cause of...what ails the... Economy."

—*Business Week* magazine, 1974[1]

"I still feel we're a healthy country, a healthy people....The city neighborhoods can be self-reliant. You can have a neighborhood that can get together and rebuild....We're gonna have to start talking about big changes.... What [people] want here is a community....I don't think it has to have a label. It's just the way a lot of Americans have worked together, cooperatively."

—community organizer[2]

Economic Recovery....We Don't Have to Say We're Sorry

This chapter compares two alternative economic programs for the 1980s—a corporate program and a popular alternative. The corporate program builds upon misleading analyses and economic greed. The popular alternative, working from the analysis of preceding chapters, points in some promising directions. Will we be "free to choose"?

WHO'S BITING THE BULLET?

"It comes down to—who's gonna be the survivor. It will test the strength of a lot of people....You cannot stand still. You grow or die."

—chief executive of multinational corporation[3]

We have heard the logic of the corporate program so many times that we can almost recite it in our sleep. The arrival of "Reaganomics" has made that logic more apparent than ever.

Figure 20.1 on the following page presents the logic of that corporate program in the form of a series of obvious steps: (a) Working people should make short-term sacrifices. (b) This will result in higher profits and more for the wealthy. (c) More profits and savings will produce more investment. (d) More investment will restore productivity and generate more rapid economic growth. (e) More rapid growth will reward us for our patience and sacrifice, providing future compensation through rising wages, more jobs, and improving working and living conditions.

Fig. 20.1

The Logic of the Corporate Program

Fig. 20.2

Q: Who Gains from Reaganomics?

By early 1982, the Reagan Administration had proposed and gained many cuts in social programs and changes in tax policy. A study recently estimated who gains and who loses from those proposals. The following table presents some estimates of the net gains (or losses) in 1983 from the combination of benefit cuts and tax breaks in the Reagan budget proposals.

Household Income Class	Net $$ Gains from Reagan Program
Less than $10,000	– **240**
$10,000–20,000	+ **220**
More than $80,000	+**15,130**

A plus (+) indicates that tax breaks more than offset cuts in social programs for a household of that income class, while a minus (-) indicates that cuts in social programs amount to more than the benefits from tax breaks.

Source: See note #52

A:They Do.

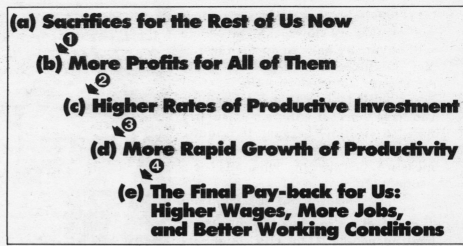

(a) Sacrifices for the Rest of Us Now
①
(b) More Profits for All of Them
②
(c) Higher Rates of Productive Investment
③
(d) More Rapid Growth of Productivity
④
(e) The Final Pay-back for Us: Higher Wages, More Jobs, and Better Working Conditions

It sounds irresistible—which helps explain why so many people have subscribed to the corporate program despite the initial sacrifices it requires. But will it work? Are its premises valid? Does it build from an accurate analysis of the sources of our current crisis?

The easiest way to examine the promise of the corporate program is to examine each of the links in its logic. If we examine the premises of the corporate program step by step, is it true that immediate sacrifices will lead to future rewards for the vast majority of working people in the United States?

1. From Popular Sacrifices to Higher Profits and More for the Wealthy?

The first step seems plausible. Less for us is likely to mean more for them.

And, as it has been turning out in recent years, it does. Both in the private and the public arenas, the corporate assaults on labor and the government, supported by the recent conservative offensive, are clearly resulting in a redistribution of income and power from working people to the wealthy.

The Private Sector. We saw at the end of Chapter 19 that corporations have been waging an increasingly aggressive campaign against labor. It finally began to bear fruit in the late 1970s. According to official government statistics, that campaign has resulted in a recent reduction in the share of total revenues going to production workers. During the business cycle from 1974 to 1978, production workers garnered an average of 49% of total business revenues. During the more recent business cycle of 1979-1980, the share of revenues going to production workers dropped to 47%, a decline of more than 4%.[4] The difference, as we saw in Part II, has gone to the corporations.

The Public Sector. Beginning in the last years of the Carter Administration and progressing by leaps and bounds in the years of Reagan, the government has been dismantling social programs and offering relief to the wealthy. Many have catalogued the effects of these recent changes in government policy, so it is not necessary to provide chapter and verse. Two conclusions seem most important:

■ On the tax side, the government has been serving relief to the wealthy and powerful on a procession of silver platters.

■ On the program side, the government has pushed through many changes in public policy which strengthen corporate power and undermine popular defenses. In one direction, to pick only a few examples, the government has deregulated oil and gas prices, relaxed anti-trust policy, and cut back on regulation of environmental and health-and-safety standards: all these are changes which will enhance the power of the largest corporations. In the other direction, the government has cut back on eligibility for welfare and food stamps, reduced student loans, virtually eliminated government jobs programs, and nearly obliterated special programs providing tailored assistance to those with particular social and economic disadvantages.

One recent study estimated the effects of these changes during the first year of the Reagan Administration. Figure 20.2 summarizes its conclusions. On balance, government benefits for working people are declining substantially while government benefits for the wealthy are ballooning.[5]

It seems clear, in short, that *the corporate program will increase corporate profits.*

2. Will Higher Profits Promote More Rapid Investment?

The hucksters for the corporate program promise that corporations will diligently devote every dollar of tax breaks and worker concessions to productive investment. Since we have no control over what they do with their money, we must trust in their promises. Are they for real?

If we give back a dollar from our wages and salaries, as we saw in Chapter 3, this increases corporate *surplus* by an equivalent dollar. Let us call this a **giveback dollar.** What happens to our giveback dollars?

We can trace their likely destinations by charting what corporations did with their surplus (over production workers' compensation) in 1980. Figure 20.3 on this page provides the data we need. It shows that the largest portion of the surplus went to management salaries. Much of it also reverted to the government. Substantial shares also flowed to dividends, interest payments, and overseas investment.

Only 25 cents of every surplus dollar went to investment. And 6 of those cents went toward investments to "increase financial assets"- money spent on mergers and speculation. That left only 19 cents for investment in the U.S. in *real plant and equipment*—in the machines and factories which they are promising will help make us more productive.[6]

We may give them back a dollar, it appears, but the law of averages tells us that *less than 20 cents will go into productive domestic investment.* Even pawn shops provide better deals.

If anything, as we have learned from Chapter 19, this deal is likely to get worse in the

Fig. 20.3

The Giveback Dollar

Suppose we give a dollar of our wages or benefits "back" to the corporations. What do they do with it?

These figures represent the composition of total corporate surplus in 1980—the distribution of all money in net national product above production workers' compensation. If that is how corporations spend their gross surplus now, there is no particular reason to assume that they will spend a giveback dollar any differently.

Source: See note #6

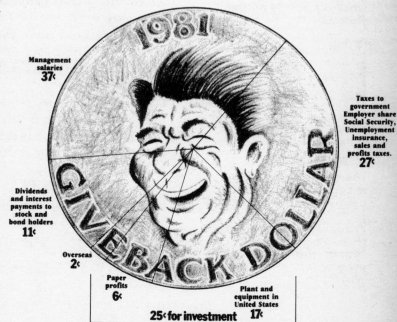

Management salaries 37¢

Taxes to government Employer share Social Security, Unemployment insurance, sales and profits taxes. 27¢

Dividends and interest payments to stock and bond holders 11¢

Overseas 2¢

Paper profits 6¢

Plant and equipment in United States 17¢

25¢ for investment

Fig. 20.4

Has Slower Investment Caused Stagnating Productivity?

The corporate analysis says that stagnant investment has caused stagnant productivity.

If this were true, there should be a close relationship between trends in the two variables.

Let's look at the facts:

Over the postwar period, machines per worker *increased* at faster and faster rates.

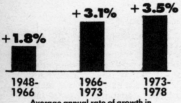

+1.8%   +3.1%   +3.5%

| 1948-1966 | 1966-1973 | 1973-1978 |

Average annual rate of growth in capital-labor ratio in manufacturing

BUT...
over the same period, growth in production worker's hourly output *slowed*.

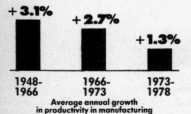

+3.1%   +2.7%   +1.3%

| 1948-1966 | 1966-1973 | 1973-1978 |

Average annual growth in productivity in manufacturing

CONCLUSION...
There was an expansion in capital per worker but a slowdown in productivity.

Productivity apparently slowed for some other reason than stagnant investment.

Source: See note #7

coming years. Since the mid-1970s, corporations have grown more and more insecure about the investment environment. The proportion of their funds going into "financial" investments has been rising. We hear about major new merger bids nearly every month. Corporations are unlikely to devote substantially greater proportions of their capital to productive domestic investment until they feel confident that they have crushed the sources of popular power which, as we saw in chapter 19, began to erode their profits after the mid-1960s. And that effort, if we pay any attention to the history traced in Chapter 17, is likely to provoke a powerful popular reaction.

3. Will More Rapid Investment Increase Productivity Growth?

Not to worry, they tell us. Any amount of increased investment will spur the economy, promoting more rapid growth in productivity. As long as investment increases, there will be more for all of us.

This promise depends on a particular proposition—the DUPE claim that *productivity growth has slowed because investment has slowed.* Corporate representatives constantly repeat the diagnosis.

Rarely have so many people been so wrong about such an important issue. There is surprisingly little evidence to support this proposition about investment and productivity.

The key measure of the relationship between investment and productivity is an indicator called the *capital-labor ratio.* This is a measure of how large a stock of factories, offices, and machines are used by production workers. The more rapid the growth in the capital-labor ratio, the more rapid the *potential* growth in workers' productivity.

If an investment slowdown had been the source of the productivity slowdown in the late 1960s and 1970s, then we would expect to find parallel slowdowns in both hourly output and the capital-labor ratio. Workers could not increase their output as rapidly as before, this would suggest, because available capital was not increasing as rapidly as in earlier years.

Figure 20.4 reviews these data for the manufacturing sector—where the link between hourly output and available capital should probably be the tightest. The data confound the corporate explanation! Hourly output slowed from each period to the next, but the capital-labor ratio increased over those same years. Productivity growth fell by half, while growth in the capital-labor ratio doubled.[7]

This conclusion is surprising only to the DUPEsters and those who get their economic information solely from DUPE sources. Even establishment economists, many of whom would love to find evidence supporting the DUPE position, admit that there is remarkably little evidence for the investment explanation of the productivity slowdown. One of the most careful conventional studies finds that only 12% of the drop in productivity growth from the period of postwar prosperity to the 1970s can be explained by slower growth in the capital-labor ratio.[8]

And yet, despite this lack of supporting evidence, the DUPEsters keep singing their continuing refrains about the need for more investment. If we join in the choruses, we may not solve our productivity problems but at least we'll fill the corporate coffers.

4. Will Rapid Economic Growth Reward Our Patience with Future Gains?

Even if the corporate program succeeds in reviving the economy at least to some degree, it may do us little good.

a) *Jobs.* It is more and more likely that corporate investments will flow toward technologies which *eliminate* jobs. We have already seen the first platoons in a new army of robots and other computerized wizards. These technological innovations are likely to affect, as one expert on automation concludes, "virtually every production activity in society from the office to the machine shop."[9]

b) *Wages and Benefits.* Employment will expand in some areas. Since 1973, the most rapidly expanding employment sectors have been concentrated in the retail trades and services, particularly in eating and drinking places, business services, and health services. What are these jobs like?[10]

We have compiled some data on these "new" jobs, comparing them with the "old" jobs which, on an average basis, they are now replacing. Figures 20.5a-c compare the earnings, benefits, and average unionization of "new" and "old" jobs.[11] If those are the jobs which will "reward" our patience in the future, it's hard to argue that we'll be "better off" than those holding "old" jobs have been.

c) *Working Conditions.* As corporations have pushed toward speed-up since the mid-1960s, according to data presented in Chapter 19, workers have paid the price in soaring accident rates. On-the-job exposure to dangerous chemicals has also spread.

The corporate game plan provides us little hope that these trends will be reversed. Corporations have intensified their attack on agencies like the Occupational Safety and Health Administration which seek to improve job safety. Corporations have also continued their warfare against unions, reducing workers' access to the principal instrument with which they can seek protection against workplace hazards. And the rapid push toward robotization in many industries, as currently promoted, will have the ultimate effect of subjecting us to a more and more regulated work pace—one of the most persistent causes of accidents on the job and the probable cause, as one expert concludes, of "a deteriorated quality of working life."[12]

They've asked us to make sacrifices in the short run. If we wait patiently, our rewards will come. The evidence suggests we may be waiting till hell freezes over.

So What's the Story?

"It [was] kind of hard to sell 'trickle down,' so the supply-side formula was the only way to get a tax policy that was really 'trickle down.' I mean, [our tax cut proposals were] always a Trojan horse to bring down the top [tax] rate....
"Whenever there are great strains or changes in the economic system, it tends to generate crackpot theories...."

—Reagan administration budget director, 1981[13]

Fig. 20.5a

LOW PAYING JOBS	
Average weekly earnings, November 1980	
New Jobs	
Eating & Drinking	$97.50
Business Services	$202.70
Health Services	$194.18
Old Jobs	
Motor Vehicles	$441.83
Primary Metals	$481.60
Communications	$378.39

Fig. 20.5b

FEWER BENEFITS		
% of plant workers covered (1974-1976)		
New Jobs	Retail	Services
Pension Plan	69%	48%
Pd. holidays (9 days +)	22%	19%
Old Jobs	Mgf.	Trans., Comm., Util.
Pension Plan	86%	84%
Pd. holidays (9 days +)	72%	81%

Fig. 20.5c

NON-UNION JOBS	
% of workers in unions (1976)	
New Jobs	
Retail/Wholesale	8.4%
Services	14.0%
Old Jobs	
Transportation/Equipment	85.0%
Primary Metals	85.0%
Telegraph/Telephone	49.0%

Source: See note #11

We have reviewed the logic of the corporate program, exploring the links in the chain of logic outlined in Figure 20.1. The program's promise is not impressive:

■ The most plausible link in the program is the one which directly assaults our working and living conditions. In the short run, *we make concessions and sacrifices in order to increases corporate profits and power.*

■ The next link is doubtful. Some of those higher profits will lead to greater investment, but huge proportions will also flow into dividends, management salaries, overseas investment, and financial or paper investments. *The portion of the giveback dollar financing productive investment is low and declining. Only further deterioration in our wages and power on the job will persuade corporations to commit more of their profits to productive revitalization.*

■ The third link is even more doubtful. There is remarkably little evidence that the productivity slowdown has resulted from an investment slowdown. Some other problems have apparently caused the bulk of the stagnation in growth of hourly output. Until we identify those problems, we have little reason to feel confident that rising investment would restore productivity growth. We might get more machines *and* a continuing decline in the rate of growth in worker's hourly output *at the same time. Increased investment might accomplish many things, like putting us out of owrk, but restored economic growth may not be one of those accomplishments.*

■ The final link is probably the least likely of all. If economic growth is restored, it will be concentrated in jobs which offer relatively low wages, sparse benefits, weak bargaining power, and indecent working conditions. *Even if the corporate game plan succeeded in recharging the U.S. economy, it is likely to do much more for corporate profits and power than for our working and living conditions.*

If their program is so unlikely to solve our problems, why do they push it? Why don't they look for a more promising plan?

The answer should be evident by now. The corporate program for restructuring the U.S. economy aims at restoring corporate profits and power. That is the abiding concern of the giant corporations who run our economy. Capitalists pursue profits, not employment. They seek power, not better working and living conditions. If their program puts *their* priorities over *ours*, it should only surprise those who still believe in the DUPE. It's time for the rest of us to develop and promote a popular alternative. A steelworkers union official concludes:

> You hear a labor leader say: "What's good for the company is good for us, because if they make a profit, we get more wages." That's bullshit. U.S. Steel is making more profit. We're sure as hell not making more wages. There are two hundred thousand less steelworkers today than there were twenty years ago.... Labor has been buffaloed. Now they're getting wise....[14]

PEOPLE ARE PART OF THE SOLUTION, NOT THE PROBLEM

"When we own land and we're working it for ourselves, we're gonna save everything that we can. We're not about to waste anything or lose anythng....Before we divided the money, we saw there was a problem. We had to have the right amount for each family....So we said: 'We're gonna divide these rows between us all.' It worked out fine. There were no fights about who's doing more work, who's getting paid more money. When you sit down with a group of people and discuss how you're gonna do things, things will work out fine."

—member of family farming cooperative[15]

"I place my faith in the working stiff, regardless of his hangups. He's still the most reliable guy on the street when push comes to shove."

—steelworker[16]

The corporate program won't solve our current economic problems. Is there a popular alternative? Is there a popular program which can get the economy moving again *and* which can improve our working and living conditions?

There are two steps in constructing the foundation of a popular alternative.

1. *We must consolidate our own analysis of the sources of our current economic problems.* It will do us little good to construct a program which does not address the causes of those problems. We studied the emergence of those problems carefully in Chapters 18 and 19. What fundamental conclusions should we draw from that analysis?

2. *We must use that analysis of our current problems to outline the blueprint of a popular economic program.* Once we begin to agree on basic principles, we can set to work on the details of the blueprint. But the

**Solidarity Day
Washington, D.C.
September 19, 1981**

basic principles must come first. And they must clearly address the problems plaguing all our houses. What fundamental principles should we apply as the basis for a popular economic program?

If We're Not the Problem, Are They?

We saw in Chapter 19 that one cannot blame our current economic problems on simple scapegoats like government spending, workers' wages, or OPEC pirates. We argued instead that our economic crisis resulted from the internal erosion of the system which made postwar prosperity possible. What caused that erosion?

Looking back over the analysis of Chapter 19, it appears that there were four principal sources of the collapse of the postwar system. Each of these resulted from the ways in which large corporations established and applied their economic might: 1) Corporations developed and abused **too much supervisory control in production.** 2) Corporations erected and nearly strangled us with a **top-heavy corporate bureaucracy.** 3) Less and less subject to market or popular discipline, corporations generated **spreading waste of resources and products.** 4) Underneath all these problems, problems emerged as more and more people found it necessary to rebel against **corporate domination in the domestic and world economy.**

We review and clarify each of these conclusions in turn.

1. Too Much Corporate Control over Production? We saw in Chapter 18 that corporations took advantage of the postwar truce with labor to restore and consolidate their control over production. The ratio of supervisory to non-supervisory labor in the economy rose by almost 75% between 1948 and 1966. More and more of them watched us more and more intensively.

All this supervisory control worked as long as workers were getting something in return. Those rewards encouraged productive worker effort and cooperation.

As economic problems developed after the mid-1960s, however, workers' incentives declined and corporations turned the supervisory apparatus more and more against their employees—much as southern sheriffs turned fire hoses against civil rights demonstrators protesting inequality. As the 60s turned into the 70s, the assaults spread and worker resistance intensified.

The critical result is that worker effort has declined steadily from the mid-1960s to the present. As cooperation has turned to confrontation, workers' inclination to maintain their hourly output has gradually dissolved. The structure of corporate control over production has created a powerful counter-reaction. All the king's horses and all the king's men haven't been able to put that structure (or worker effort) back together again.

2. Too Much Corporate Bureaucracy? In addition to intensive supervision of production itself, corporations developed a top-heavy corporate bureaucracy—aimed at controlling supplies and markets all around the world. The corporate towers grew taller and taller.

As long as no one challenged the corporations, the basic problems of huge bureaucracies were veiled. Once the challenges arrived, however, the corporate bureaucracy, like the Roman Empire, proved sluggish and unresponsive. Rather than trimming their sails in order to move with the winds of change, the giant corporations simply sought to squelch the competition and suppress the rebellions. The damage done to our basic economic operations by these responses—whether measured by the failures of the auto companies to innovate or the loss of technological leadership in many other sectors—has only begun to be felt.

The DUPEsters hate to acknowledge corporate inefficiency in public, of course, but many of their advisors and consultants have begun to criticize the corporate bureaucracies in a stream of private condemnations. "Resistance to change remains endemic in corporate America," a report by *Business Week* magazine concludes. An influential study in the *Harvard Business Review* echoed this conclusion: "There is prime evidence of a broad managerial failure—a failure of both vision and leadership—that over time has eroded both the inclination and the capacity of U.S. companies to innovate."[17]

3. Too Much Corporate Waste? We saw throughout Chapters 10 and 11 that corporations make decisions to increase their profits, not necessarily to reduce waste or inefficiency. Increasingly through the 1970s, this tendency haunted the U.S. economy:

■ Corporations locked us into an inflexible energy system and have since encouraged development of even more wasteful systems— like nuclear power and synthetic fuels—in order to maintain their tight control over energy supplies and production.

■ Corporations have pushed the government to apply the economic brakes—resulting in rising unemployment and wasted productive capacity—in order to frighten workers, erode workers' resistance, and ultimately to increase corporate profits from production.

■ Corporations have used more and more of their assets for investments in financial assets, as we saw in Figure 19.16, and have therefore withheld available resources from potentially productive investment. Why? Because they preferred to pursue short-term profits instead of longer-term economic improvements. As long as

**Solidarity Day
Washington, D.C.
September 19, 1981**

they didn't like the terms available in the productive economy, they chose increasingly to pick up their marbles and pull out of the game.

The result was more and more waste of available resources and products. As long as corporations can score below the bottom line, they don't care. They don't have to wait on line at the employment office.

4. Too Much Corporate Power? These first three problems reflect the vulnerability and inflexibility of the postwar corporate system *once initial problems develop*. Why did those problems develop in the first place?

The postwar system was founded upon U.S. corporate domination of the domestic and world economies. That domination involved and depended upon the subordination of many others. People do not accept their subordination for long, particularly if it has been recently imposed. The Vietnamese didn't, the Europeans and Japanese wouldn't, and women, minorities, and the elderly in the U.S. similarly refused. In another system and another context, workers in Poland have taken parallel steps toward rebellion.

As always—with the Romans and the Nazis as much as with giant corporations—the costs of suppressing or coopting rebellion run very high. Those costs can become cancerous. And once the cancers spread, they are often difficult to remove.

Large U.S. corporations tried to run the world economy for a while. They couldn't make their power stick. And we have all wound up paying the price.

How Does This Explain Stagflation?

This analysis of the sources of our current crisis leads directly to an explanation of the main symptoms of stagflation—productivity slow-down, inflation, and rising unemployment.

a) *Understanding the Productivity Slowdown*. The growth of workers' hourly output, as we saw in Chapter 19, first began to slow between 1966 and 1973.

■ The major cause of this initial slowdown was the system of *corporate control over production*: corporations began pushing workers harder and workers began to resist, with declining worker effort as a result.

■ After the mid-1970s, the second and third sources of our problems joined the first: *too much corporate bureaucracy* led to defensive and sluggish company responses, reducing the rate of innovation; and *too much corporate waste*—within our system of *disconnected* decisions— led to rising financial speculation (reducing the rate of investment lower than it needed to be) and pushing the economy toward lower and lower utilization of its resources. Recent studies of the underlying data confirm this set of conclusions from the history of Chapter 19.

b) *Understanding Inflation*. This analysis provides the two clues necessary for unraveling the mystery of soaring inflation.

■ First, the *slowdown in productivity* itself creates inflationary pressures: if the growth in output is slowing, other things equal, people are likely to line up for the relatively fewer goods and services available; this growing demand pressure is likely to create upward pressure on prices. (A glance back at Figures 19.12a and b and 19.20a and b shows that increases in the rate of inflation mirrored the slowdown in productivity growth in both the first and second stages of the evolution of crisis in the 1960s and 1970s.

■ Second, the *lack of planning* in the economy makes it especially difficult to adjust to this underlying slowdown in productivity. If everyone were willing to reduce the growth in their demand by amounts proportional to the productivity slowdown, the inflation would not need to follow. But there is no planning process to ensure this result. Even worse, we see corporations grabbing everything they can for themselves and we are forced to protect our own living standards in return.

Given corporate power to pursue its own interests, it is hard to imagine that inflation would *not* be the natural consequence of slower growth in hourly output.

c) *Understanding Higher Unemployment.* Higher rates of joblessness followed directly from the causes of the productivity slowdown and galloping inflation. More people needed to work in the 1970s because slower output growth and rising prices were cutting into household earnings. But corporations could not tolerate pressure on the government to provide jobs for those who needed them. Quite to the contrary, corporations wanted what one capitalist quoted in Chapter 19 called "wholesome" recessions in order to undercut workers' bargaining power and to force consumers to restrict their demand for the relatively fewer goods and services available. Given *too much corporate power*, the corporations had it their way.

If They're Not the Solution, Are We?

These four problems lie at the roots of our current economic problems. If we must restructure the U.S. economy anyway, it seems obvious that we should pursue paths of restructuring which will address those four problems at their roots. Can We?

1. *Too Much Corporate Control over Production?* **Try Workplace Democracy.** We have argued that intensive corporate supervision of

**Solidarity Day
Washington, D.C.
September 19, 1981**

production began to backfire in the late 1960s and 1970s. Workers began to resist corporate control of the workplace; worker effort began to wane.

The basic sources of this problem should now be clear. If there is an essentially undemocratic system of control in production—as we have had throughout the history of the capitalist economy in the United States—it is likely that workers will rebel from time to time. Employers may be unable to provide enough rewards to establish strong work incentives. Or the foremen and supervisors may overplay their strong hands.

The shortest route to a solution lies through progress toward greater workplace democracy. If workers can play a central role in determining the conditions and character of work, we are likely to feel strong connections to the production process. With those connections we may be able both to improve our working conditions and to restore our work incentives. We reviewed several examples in Chapter 10 which suggest that much greater worker participation in and control over production decisions will increase workers' hourly output *because* it increases worker incentives and, therefore, worker effort.

This principle is not pie-in-the-sky prophecy for the future. There are concrete steps we can take toward greater workplace democracy which would simply follow directions already pioneered in Europe and Japan.

■ We could adopt legislation, following a Swedish example, which would guarantee workers' rights to negotiate (in collective bargaining) about anything related to production. (This could simply be an amendment to the National Labor Relations Act.) Current "Management Rights" clauses in most contracts now make this difficult.

■ Unions—and even non-unionized workers—could form worker committees to negotiate about the organization of production. Tax credits could be granted to workers on such committees in order to provide incentives for workers to get involved in this kind of process.

■ Following the Japanese example, unions could demand life-time employment security so that workers would feel they had a stake in their own enterprises. Conservatives in the U.S. have always argued that job security reduces worker incentives. In Japan, it has the opposite effect.

2. *Too Much Corporate Bureaucracy?* **Try Community Enterprises.**

The problem with giant corporations is that they are too large. The problem with nationalized government enterprises is that they face too little competition. And the problem with tiny profit-making businesses is that they go out of business the minute they become unprofitable—which happens frequently.

The solution seems to lie in what growing numbers of people in the U.S. call *community enterprises*. A community enterprise can be defined as a "firm" engaged in production or distribution, controlled democratically by a group of workers or community residents, in which the community has placed its hopes and economic interests through investment, technical, and planning support.

Because these enterprises would be controlled democratically, it is relatively unlikely that they would develop top-heavy bureaucracies. And because they would be supported through investment, technical, and planning assistance from the government, it is unlikely that they would be as inefficient and uncompetitive as many small businesses.

The readings suggested at the end of the chapter provide concrete details about how community enterprises could gain access to the capital, technical skills, and product markets they would need. The opportunities are evident and the possibilities widespread. If these possibilities are pursued intelligently, as a report from a recent conference supported by more than 500 union and community groups concluded:

> ....we can at once expand the productive capacity of the nation and include in that increased prosperity those persons long denied access to the economic mainstream. Here is the opportunity to develop new industries; to create jobs; to harness entrepreneurial talent and the wasted productive capacity of involuntarily unemployed people; [and] to develop businesses and viable economies in depressed urban and rural areas and in communities hard-hit by plant shutdowns.[18]

Will more power and profits for the giant corporations support those objectives?

3. *Too Much Corporate Waste?* **Try Democratic Planning.** During the 1970s, as we saw in Chapter 10, the U.S. economy wasted roughly one-seventh of its potential output—through unemployment, and through wasted factories, machines, and offices.

a) *Full Employment.* The first solution is straightforward. We need public policies committed to maintaining our economy at full employment—dedicated to providing a regular job at decent wages to everyone who wants and needs one. This was the conclusion which many drew after the despair of the Depression of the 1930s. Forceful economic planning can easily achieve full employment. Why has it taken us so long to sustain that commitment?

**Solidarity Day
Washington, D.C.
September 19, 1981**

Corporations have feared full employment because it reduces employer leverage over their workers. They have frequently sought "wholesome" recessions. If we are prepared to put our needs above those of profits, if we are ready to pursue real workplace democracy, then this reason for fearing full employment should cease to haunt us.

b) *Price Controls.* The second fear about full employment policies has involved concern about inflation.

There have been places and times when full employment and stable prices have come together—in the U.S. during World War II, in many European countries during the postwar period. The combination is not impossible.

The key, as with full employment, is a public commitment to stable prices and a ceiling on private-sector price increases. As long as the government provides subsidies and assistance to companies whose costs increase for reasons outside their control—as with OPEC energy price hikes—there is no reason for unusual cost increases to squeeze enterprise profits.

If price controls are manageable in a variety of forms—again, see the references at the end of the chapter for details—then why are companies and economists so scornful? In general, companies oppose price controls because they fervently hope for situations in which, like energy companies over the past several years, they could earn windfall profits through unregulated price increases.

For their sakes, they consistently oppose price controls. For our sakes—in order to facilitate the transition to full employment *and* to reduce our vulnerability to sudden price increases—a popular program must include a program of price controls.

c) *A Needs Inventory.* Another source of waste in our capitalist economy, as we saw in Part III, is that profit-making corporations do not always (or even typically) produce what we need most.

A program of democratic planning can directly address this problem through a needs inventory of the U.S. population, conducting periodic and systematic surveys of households to determine what they most want and need and what the private system of production and distribution is providing least adequately. These surveys would be easy to administer, since the government already surveys us on a regular basis, and they would help nudge our giant economy in the directions we directly desire. The price system in the private sector, as we have seen throughout, is a poor substitute.

4. *Too Much Corporate Power?* **Try Democratic Capital Controls.** Corporations gain their ultimate power through their control of the means of production. We hesitate to challenge them on other issues for fear that they'll pack their bags and machines and move away. This suggests that democratic capital controls must provide the kind of foundation for a popular economic program which corporate control over the means of production provides for corporate power. Without such controls, the popular orchestra will never finish the overture.

a) *Democratic Allocation of Savings.* It's not that we don't have plenty of savings we could use for investment.

There are three main funds into which working households pour their savings: pension funds (both private and public); savings bank deposits; and insurance reserves. These three pools of working households' savings could provide us enormous economic leverage if we chose to use them.

Consider the numbers for 1979:

■ Corporate stock equity assets were worth $906.9 billion; this was a measure of the market value of their owned means of production.

■ Pension fund reserves totalled $622.1 billion. Working households' shares of savings bank deposits and insurance reserves totalled another $915.1 billion. Together, working households' total fund of savings amounted to $1,537.2 billion—two-thirds greater than corporate equity.[19]

If we controlled the investment of those funds in the ways that corporations control their own assets, we could withstand their blackmail threats of capital strike. And we could channel our own savings into projects and enterprises which, in our collective judgment, would best serve our own needs. It would not be all that difficult:

■ Unions could make their own decisions about their own pension fund investments, setting priorities to serve members' needs.

■ Community investment boards could allocate savings deposits and insurance company assets, allocating them according to community priorities.

In either case, members and resident priorities could easily be determined through surveys or elections.

b) *Plant Closing Legislation.* These steps would help provide greater independence through use of our own savings. What about the leverage which corporations retain through use of their assets?

Many European countries provide for plant closing legislation. These laws establish minimum notification, such as two-year warning periods, if firms are planning to close their plants; and a system providing for company compensation to the community if the consequences of dislocation are severe. In West Germany, for example:

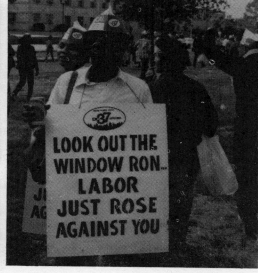

Solidarity Day
Washington, D.C.
September 19, 1981

....any relocation or transfer of work must be approved by the government and submitted to a works council elected by employees. If they do not agree to the proposed shifts, binding mediation occurs. No plant may close without a permit from the state exchange, which can reject the proposed action when substantial unemployment exists in the areas affected.[20]

Such legislation can dramatically reduce corporate leverage and, therefore, increase our democratic control over capital.

c) *A New International Economic Order.* Suppose we gain greater democratic control over the allocation of capital in the United States. Won't we still be vulnerable to the manipulations of multinationals and powerful suppliers like OPEC which lie outside our domestic political jurisdiction?

This is much less of a problem for the U.S. than it is for other countries in the world because foreign trade plays a relatively small role in our economy. Still, the role it plays can be crucial, as we saw in the 1970s. We must pursue two different strategies.

■ First, we must move toward greater domestic self-sufficiency wherever possible. The economic policies of the last 20 years have encouraged corporations to export our jobs and to import necessities. Our emphasis must be the opposite. We need to require U.S. corporations to invest in the United States, providing U.S. workers with jobs and U.S. consumers with greater domestic self-sufficiency. And we need to make productive investments in order to reduce the costs of domestically-produced necessities to the point at which our domestic costs are at least as low as those for the imports on which we have been dependent. Through such investments, we can *both* increase our control over our economic welfare *and* avoid the costs of lower standards of living.

■ Second, we must work to create a new international economic order based on the same economic principles that we are following domestically. As we saw in Chapters 18 and 19, the prosperity of the U.S. after World War II was purchased at the expense of the rest of the world. As long as we live in a world in which the strong prey on the weak, the rich gain at the expense of the poor, the haves take from the have-nots..., our own economic welfare will always be threatened by

Fig. 20.6

FROM PROBLEMS TO SOLUTIONS—
THE OUTLINE OF A POPULAR ALTERNATIVE

Sources of Our Problems   Possible Solutions to Those Problems

1. Too Much Control over Production? ... Try Workplace Democracy

2. Too Much Corporate Bureaucracy? ... Try Community Enterprises

3. Too Much Corporate Waste? ... Try Democratic Planning

4. Too Much Corporate Power? ... Try Democratic Capital Controls

the political instability—from rebellions or even World War III—which such conditions of domination are always likely to breed.

FROM PRINCIPLES TO PROGRESS?

We have suggested some basic principles for the blueprint of a popular economic program. Each of these principles aims to solve one of the four fundamental sources of our current economic problems. Figure 20.6 reviews these connections, tracing the links between the sources of our current problems and the pillars of a popular alternative to the corporate program.

Once we understand these principles, how do we put such a program into action? Three steps are necessary:

1. *We must translate principles into detailed program planks.* We at our Institute are not the proper authors of this translation. These planks should come from all the different popular organizations which constitute the backbone of progressive movements in the United States. The references listed at the end of the chapter provide some suggestions, but the real debate and drafting must take place in our workplaces and communities, through all the connections we have with each other. The blueprint outlined in this chapter can help guide those discussions, but the details must come from those who hold the key to its success—working people in the United States. If we are to

become the solution to our economic problems, we must draft that solution ourselves.

2. *We must prepare for dismissal by the DUPEsters.* The blueprint for a popular program makes sense, drawing upon a careful and promising analysis of the sources of our current crisis. But the DUPE will dismiss our program as unrealistic, if not "unAmerican." We must prepare ourselves for these arguments. This involves a final review of the principles by which economies operate and the reasons for DUPE opposition to the kinds of policies suggested in this chapter. We provide one approach to this final review in the next chapter, **"There Must Be a Better Way?"**

3. *We need to begin mobilizing support for the popular alternative.* Corporations will not step aside for our program; they will fight it with money and muscle. We shall need to muster all of our numbers and energy to promote our own interests through our own program. None of it will be easy, but, as Chapter 17 recounted, people have organized and won before in the United States. Chapter 22 closes the book with a final summary of principles for popular mobilization. After that review in **"How Do We Begin?"** the basis for a popular program to cure what's wrong with the U.S. economy will have been fully outlined.

For Further Reading—

Because of the scope of this book, we have not been able to provide great detail on the analysis and program ideas in this chapter.

For further development of all the arguments in this chapter, see Samuel Bowles, David M. Gordon, and Thomas E. Weisskopf, **Free Lunch: A Democratic Alternative to the Economics of Greed,** *forthcoming 1982.*

"I'd like to have a lot of money, but when I see people that are very poor, it's unsettling to me, I just think: if I had a lot of money, I couldn't really enjoy it when all these people are like this. I would like to see a time when nobody—it sounds like a kind of Communist state (laughs)—but where nobody was without. That would be nice to see, you know?"

—clerk in a Cleveland bookstore[1]

"We have got to invest in ourselves. If the community's gonna change, neighborhood's gonna change, society's gonna change, the world's gonna change, it's by individuals. Not by big bureaucracy, not by Exxons, not by all that....If we take the time to educate people, they will have the tools to act with....If he has tools, he understands: This is your street, this is your house, whether you're a tenant or whether you own, this is your community....We've got a motto. It's all written up: 'Your house is part of this block. This block is part of this city. This city is part of this state. This state is part of the United States of America. You're involved all the way.' "

—community organizer in Chicago[2]

There Must Be a Better Way?

The blueprint outlined in Chapter 20 suggests some principles for pulling ourselves out of the current economic crisis. But capitalists will oppose our efforts. Even if we succeed in achieving large parts of our program, there will still be lots of capitalists to kick around. And the features of capitalism which helped bring us this economic crisis, as we saw in Chapter 6, will be likely to bring us another some time in the future. Capitalism does not breed economic peace and security.

Do we need these recurring headaches? Shouldn't we begin exloring other ways of organizing the economy? *There must be a better way.*

IF IT DOESN'T WORK, REPLACE IT!

"I been to other countries. I ain't giving up on this one. I don't buy 'love it or leave it.' You can love it and stay here and try to do somethin' about what's wrong with it."

—activist in support organization for prisoners[3]

When a machine is fundamentally flawed, we scrap it and look for another one. Economies are no different. If we have concluded through this review that capitalism is fundamentally flawed, why not trade it in for something better?

How do we figure out what might work better? How do we determine how else we might be able to organize our economy?

The quickest route to answering those questions simply requires that we get back to basics. In Chapter 2, we reviewed the basic tasks of an economy and the different ways in which those tasks can be organized. As presented in Figure 2.2, that introduction suggested that there are *two* basically different ways of organizing each economic tasks. If we conclude that capitalism does not serve our needs, then we should check out the *other* way of fulfilling each of our principal economic requirements.

Figure 21.1 combines the lessons of Chapter 2 into a guide for this final review. In the first column of the chart, it lists the features of capitalism. In the second column, it lists the opposite way of organizing each of those separate tasks. The dots moving from the capitalist system toward the alternative symbolically raise the basic questions: is it possible to organize the economy differently—and will those different economic methods be an improvement over what we now have? *Is there a better way?*

Let's turn to each of those six transitions in Figure 21.1. *Is there a better way?*

1) From Private Property to Common Property?

We have been taught to shudder at the thought of any infringement of our private property rights. But, if we have learned the lessons of this book properly, we should also have learned to shudder at the costs of continuing corporate control over the means of production. Is there a way to wiggle off the horns of this dilemma?

Fig. 21.1

IS THERE A BETTER WAY?

FROM CAPITALISM ...	TO SYSTEM X?
1. From Private Property ...	to Common Property?
2a. From Controlled Labor ...	to Shared Labor?
2b. From Disconnected Production ...	to Coordinated Production?
3a. From Exploitation ...	to Mutuality?
3b. From Distribution by Power ...	to Distribution by Need?
3c. From Commodity Exchange ...	to Exchange through Social Relationships?

The key is the distinction between all *wealth* and the *means of production* which we reviewed in Chapter 2. There are many different kinds of wealth—personal savings, private homes, machines....But only some of that wealth can be used to produce the goods and services we need. It is that wealth which we call the means of production. And it is that wealth which is crucial for establishing control over our own economic destinies.

Let's explore this distinction just one step further:

If we control our own personal property, like our homes or apartments, then we don't affect other people's economic fortunes (provided that everyone has enough personal property to survive). But if one of us controls the factories and machines upon which we rely for our homes and autos, then we all become dependent on the single owner.

Why should private individuals gain such powerful influence? Not because they have built the factories with their own hands, of course. Nor because they have earned some special merit badges for which factory ownership is their just reward. The answer in capitalist economies is that there is a closed circle: given private property rights, individuals lay claim to some of the means of production. That control leads to more and more control. Private control breeds more private control.

If we don't like the costs and consequences, we will simply have to break out of the closed circle, denying 1% of our population the right to control the rest of our economic lives through their private control over the means of production. If we do, we could call that a system of *common property*.

■ Such a system would involve shared popular control over the means of production, *not* other forms of personal wealth and property. We already have limited instances of such popular control over the means of production, as with schools and highways.

■ As the examples of schools and highways suggest, such a system of common property need not involve a single all-powerful central government controlling everything we need. Communities could "own" the factories and offices and machines they have built or need, bringing people in each separate community closer to the basic decision-making about their use and allocation.

The crucial feature of a system of common property should be that the people who built or rely on the means of production have the most direct possible control over their use—through factory councils, office associations, or community boards, through unions or local governments. This would ensure, on the one hand, that a few individuals do not gain control over the rest of us and, on the other hand, that crucial decisions are influenced, as much as possible, by those most immediately affected.

There is no fixed rule for achieving this kind of common property system. Some energy production would probably have to be controlled over a fairly broad geographic area, while some food processing plants could be "owned" and controlled by fairly local groups. More important than the details is the basic principle: *if we all depend on the use of the basic means of production in a democratic society, then we should all control them.*

2a) From Controlled Labor to Shared Labor?

We saw in Chapter 4 that capitalists seized control of the production process in order to establish a stable foundation for their profits. We saw in Chapters 10 and 11 that production could be better organized if workers had greater participation in and more control over decisions affecting the organization of production.

It appears that everyone (but the capitalists) would be better off if there were shared labor in production—if the people who do the work also made decisions about how to do it. Workers would benefit because their working conditions would undoubtedly improve. And consumers would benefit because the costs of production would probably decline as a result of greater worker effort and productivity.

Why not? Some people worry that modern production may be too complicated for workers to be able to control it. But workers already understand production conditions better than those outside the work, and workers can easily learn about the implications of one or another kind of technology. What they don't know, they can learn quickly. The myths of complexity are typically created by those who would like to retain their own power and control. "If the boss had his way," as one steelworker recently put it, "you'd never find libraries and books. They're too dangerous."[4]

2b) From Disconnected to Coordinated Production?

We pay the costs every day of disconnected decisions. Can't we coordinate our economic efforts? Can't we at least plan ahead a little?

There are many different ways to coordinate economic decision-making. A central information agency can circulate information on what consumers need and what kinds of goods and services producers are planning to generate. (Modern computer technology makes this kind of information gathering and sharing much easier than it used to be.) Local and state governments can provide incentives and subsidies to different enterprises to try to ensure that enough of certain basic necessities are available. Local communities can directly build and equip factories to produce necessities not otherwise available.

The principle seems simple. Instead of praying that the market will deliver what we need—which, as we have seen, it often doesn't—we can develop planning systems to help ensure that we get what we need.

The DUPEsters warn of inefficiency. But we have learned that their treasured "market system" hardly scores well by that standard. (See Chapters 10 and 11.) There is not yet common agreement on the best combination of planning techniques to apply in advanced economies; see the reference at the end of Chapter 20 for some discussion of various alternatives.

What does seem clear, however, is that disconnected production decisions serve the interests only of those who profit from shortages or windfall price increases. The more we coordinate the production of what we need, in the end, the greater the economic security and independence we can achieve.

3a) From Exploitation to Mutuality?

DUPEsters don't defend exploitation. They simply deny it takes place. Once one admits its existence, there is no evident justification for it. If people live in a mutually-dependent society, they should mutually earn and share its products. No one who is capable of productive work should live off the labor of others. Period.

This principle is obviously a two-edged sword. On one side, it would mean that those who are so wealthy that they live off their capital income without raising a finger would have to contribute productively to our economic livelihood in the future. On the other side, it also obviously implies that a society must provide opportunities for *everyone* to engage in productive work. If we don't organize employment opportunities for everyone, we can hardly require that everyone must work before they can gain access to at least a share of total product.

This two-edged sword helps illustrate the interconnections among the different methods outlined in Figure 21.1. We can't move effectively toward mutuality until we move effectively toward coordinated planning systems which fully utilize our resources and provide productive roles for everyone. If an end to exploitation requires attention to

those interconnections, the extra effort will be more than repaid.

3b) From Distribution by Power Over Resources to Distribution by Need?

In economic systems over which people have had the most direct control, there has usually been a heavy reliance on distribution *according to need*. This is often true of our own households, for example: we provide extra food and clothing for teens while they're growing and we take special care of the health needs of the elderly and disabled.

The dominance of distribution by *power over resources* typically operates in economies where there is already a system of exploitation. Those in the driver's seat choose distributional rules which favor those with the most resource control—themselves. Suppose mutuality replaced exploitation as the basic rule for access to a share of total product. It would then be much easier to explore the possibility of distribution according to need.

Why should we explore it? Simple human concerns seem most important here. People with special needs are usually unable to ignore or dispense with those needs—children can't immediately become adults; the elderly can't suddenly recapture their youth; the handicapped cannot usually eliminate their disadvantages overnight. When special needs are unavoidable, we often feel that we should undeniably devote special resources to fill those needs. Hurricane victims have special needs, and so, quite often, do victims of equally unavoidable economic fates.

But won't people work less diligently if they can't capture the returns to their work through both greater power over resources *and* economic product?

The truth, as we saw in Chapter 2, is that economic self-interest is not the only instinct by which we live. People often act selfishly in capitalist economies because there is so little outlet for more cooperative instincts.

At the same time, most of us have had experiences in which we have acted on cooperative impulses and seen them in others. We share within our households. We help out (without promise of reward) in times of emergency. And many of us work at our jobs at least in part because we love the work and the services it provides, not because our salaries increase as a result of our greater effort. (This is most likely among those in reponsible jobs, as defined in Chapter 13, and less likely among others.)

A much less competitive economy—in which we were guaranteed a more secure existence, in which we had the chance to do the work we cared about, in which we realized the opportunity to help others as part of our daily lives—would encourage our less competitive instincts. As we begin to move away from other features of capitalist economies, we would undoubtedly begin to move away from one of the central features of those economic systems—their emphasis on selfish, self-interested, competitive behavior by individuals.

We should move in these directions cautiously, in a spirit of exploration. We all recognize the common sense of paying greater attention to distribution according to need. We shall simply need to pay careful attention to the impact and implications of such an emphasis. It seems worth the effort. The price of refusing that effort, if we can judge by our recent economic experiences, is likely to remain very high.

3c) From Commodity Exchange to Exchange through Social Relationships?

Money is a convenience. For that reason, it seems likely that we shall always choose to remain reliant on money as a means of exchange to some degree.

But money in a capitalist economy is also the main motivation for all productive work. If we don't have it, we are denied a basic economic legitimacy. Greed thus comes to dominate need, and the more we rely on money, the more it colors all the rest of our social relationships. (See Chapter 5 for an exploration of this theme.)

The basic question involves priorities. Should money dominate the ways we relate to each other? Or should the ways we would like to relate to each other dominate the influence of money over our lives?

It seems likely that most people would choose need before greed

I Could Get Behind That

HELLUVA WEEKEND FOR THE OLD POLE-SKI.
I HAVEN'T HAD SO MUCH FUN SINCE I BURNED MY 'NAM MEDALS IN FRONT OF THE WHITE HOUSE IN '69.
GOTTA HAND IT TO ROSIE AND DUPE. THEY PUT IT **TOGETHER. THREE BUSSES** FULL OF EX CIRCUIT JERKS.

and social relationships before the market *if we could.*

Can we escape the dictatorship of the dollar?

Imagine a more democratically-controlled economy in which everyone able to work had a productive job. There are two obvious ways in which decisions could be made about what to produce and how much to produce on a basis other than greed and in a way that brings people together rather than driving them apart.

One way is by the "needs inventory" we mentioned earlier. Cooperatively-owned or democratically-managed firms could be provided with incentives to produce those goods and services the needs inventory identified as undersupplied by profit-making corporations. The goal would be to make available to the whole population all the necessities of life at a price everyone could afford. Basic necessities like health care and housing could even be provided without requiring money for their purchases, just as education and access to highways are provided now.

A second way to escape the dictatorship of the dollar could be through a process of decentralized planning in which groups of workers as well as individuals exchange the products of their labor with one another directly rather than indirectly through the market. This is not an impossible dream. In many parts of the country in the last few years, trade exchanges or barter clubs have sprung up which bring together people with particular needs and the people with the skills or the products to meet that need. No one knows exactly how many such exchanges there are, nor how many exchanges occur in this way. Because the exchanges take place outside the normal cash economy, they are not taxable by the IRS, and those who engage in them are reluctant to spill the beans.

But one thing is clear: the system works. One of the largest trading services organizes exchanges worth the equivalent of more than $200 million annually, and its subscribers include roughly 100 companies, including such household names as Kaiser Aluminum.[5] The same technology can be harnessed to provide everyone with access to goods and services outside the cash market. Indeed, it provides a way of conducting a needs inventory and planning what to produce, how much to produce, and for whom to produce it, all at the same time. At this level, money simply gets in the way of more human relationships.

Can We Bake Half a Loaf?

This discussion is only an *introduction* to the possibilities of alternative economic systems. We shall have to learn about many of the issues raised in this discussion by practice, testing different methods of moving away from these features of the capitalist system through experimentation and debate.

That suggests a complex process of change and transformation. Are there some short-cuts? Can we take the changes one at a time?

Some of the discussion in the previous section should suggest the answer. The movements depicted in Figure 21.1 are all connected to each other. It is hard to imagine coordinated production without movement toward common ownership of the means of production. It is

I BETCHA **90%** OF THOSE PEOPLE WOULDA LIKED TO KICK MY ASS IN '69.
WELCOME TO THE 1980'S. SOLIDARITY-FOR-FUCKING-**EVER!**
I WONDER WHAT WE'RE GONNA **DO** WITH IT?
START A LABOR PARTY? I COULD GET BEHIND **THAT.**
SOMEBODY BETTER HAVE SOME IDEAS ABOUT HOW TO START IT.
I SURE AS HELL DON'T.

Clerical . . . the Wave of the Future

IF MY EX COULD'VE SEEN ME THIS WEEKEND, HE'D HAVE PISSED.

THAT WIMP!

*I DON'T **BELIEVE** ALL THE WOMEN THERE. IT WAS FANTASTIC. BLACK ONES. MARRIED ONES. SPANISH ONES. LESBIANS. WOW... I THINK THOSE WERE THE FIRST LESBIANS I EVER MET. I THINK. MAYBE NOT. HOW WOULD I KNOW?*

I DON'T THINK I HEARD ONE SPEECH, WE WERE SO FAR BACK.

*BIG DEAL, SPEECHES! THE **REAL** ACTION WAS ON THE FIELD.*

*SO MANY DIFFERENT **OFFICE** WORKERS. WE WERE **THERE**. CLERICAL LOOKS LIKE THE WAVE OF THE FUTURE.*

hard to imagine shared labor without an effective end to exploitation. It is hard to imagine distribution according to need without establishing a stronger foundation for social relationships as a partial means of exchange.

It seems likely, in short, that we shall need to pursue all these directions of change more or less at the same time. We can't bake half a loaf. We need to change capitalism as a system, not piece by piece or part by part.

At first blush, that makes the task seem more difficult. Upon further consideration, however, it may make the project much easier. If we can all agree that the changes make sense, we can all struggle toward a common objective. If we moved on a piece-by-piece basis, we might end up wasting time and energy debating which dimension of change deserved the highest priority.

Can we agree? We need to study the logic of change reflected in Figure 21.1 very carefully. And we need to debate the merits of an alternative to capitalism.

And we also need a name for this alternative.

WHAT'S IN A NAME?

> "I hear guys saying about how horseshit medicine is in this country, and goddamn it, it's about time we had national health. Call it what you want, call it socialism, damn it, so be it."
>
> —local union official[6]

For the moment, let's call the system operating by the principles outlined in the right-hand column of Figure 21.1 *System X.*

It involves common property, shared labor, coordinated production, mutuality, distribution by need, and social relationships as a principal means of exchange. We have considered it piece by piece as an alternative to capitalism. What do we call it?

Suddenly some of us may grow queasy. Is it socialism? Is it communism? Are we "better dead than red?"

The DUPEsters smile a lot but they also play for keeps. They are quick to label any opposition as "radical" or "left" or "foreign"—or even as "socialist." People who took part in the struggles for unions in the 1930s remember that tactic well.

But what's in a name? Millions of people around the world who have fought for greater control over their economic lives have marched under the banner of "socialism." (A majority of French voters recently elected a "socialist" as President.) Many in the United States feel more comfortable using terms like "economic democracy." The Populists fought for many of the features of System X in the late nineteenth century, using simple terms like "industrial freedom" and the "people's party," striving ultimately for what they called a "cooperative commonwealth." Throughout these movements, people have fought for common goals under uncommon and varying names.

What matters most is that we agree on what we want, not what we call it. That is why we have placed such emphasis in Chapter 2 and again in this chapter on what it takes to structure an economy. If the features of System X make more sense than the opposite poles in Figure 21.1, that is what we should seek. And that is what we should debate.

As we pursue that debate, and as we eventually choose a name with more meaning than System X, we should remember two final lessons:

■ We should decide what we want on our own terms, not because of what has happened or failed to happen in other countries. Many are haunted by the bugaboo of the Soviet Union, which calls itself a "socialist" country. But if we look clearly, we can see that the Soviet Union does not closely resemble the characteristics of System X: its labor is more controlled than shared, for example, and the ruling government elites have such tight control over resources that it would be hard to tout its distributive system as one which features mutuality. There is little doubt that DUPEsters will wave the example of the Soviet Union in our faces as we discuss alternatives to capitalism. So what? As long as we are clear about what we want, we can recognize that we neither want nor need either the Soviet system or our present capitalist system. Let them wave.

■ We should remember the warning on page 35 of Chapter 2. We are discussing features of the *economy*, not characteristics of our *political system*. We are discussing alternatives to *capitalism*, not alternatives to *democracy*. Our democratic traditions are our greatest strength in the United States. Our economic mission is to bolster those traditions, not to undermine them. As we have seen throughout this book, we have achieved our democratic rights and freedoms in the United States *in spite of* capitalism, not because of it. (See Chapters 12 and 17.)

All of the features of System X are compatible with democratic politics. All of them, indeed, would help increase our democratic control over our economic lives. As we dare to challenge the capitalists, we should fly with the democratic winds, not shy before rhetoric about big government and loss of freedom. Ordinary people in the United States are not currently doubting the advisability of democracy; it is those with power—as we saw in Chapter 1—who are worrying about the conflicts between democracy and their ability to govern. Democracy is not the problem; it's part of the solution.

In the end, we should define our objectives by our own instincts and our own sense of justice and decency. There is a long tradition in the United States of doing just that.

The story of Eugene Debs is a telling example. Debs eventually became a socialist candidate for president, winning close to one million votes in 1912, roughly 6% of the total. But Debs did not begin as a socialist. He began as a strong trade unionist, struggling for simple protection against the insecurity and powerlessness which the capitalist economy imposed. "It seems to me that if it were not for resistance to degrading conditions," Debs argued in 1894, "the tendency of our

THAT BLACK WOMAN FROM PHILLY... SHE SAID I OUGHT TO BE AN ORGANIZER. SHE SAID I WAS A NATURAL.
FIRST, I BETTER **GET** IN A UNION. ACTUALLY I THINK I BETTER GET A **JOB.** EVERYBODY'S GOTTA START **SOMEPLACE.**

whole civilization would be downward; after a while we would reach a point where there would be no resistance, and slavery would come."[5]

But he soon realized that one needed an alternative to capitalism in order to fight it properly. This led him to stand for socialism—the name he chose to attach to System X—as a constructive alternative. His logic was simple. And it bears repeating in the 1980s:

> The issue is Socialism versus Capitalism. I am for Socialism because I am for humanity. We have been cursed with the reign of gold long enough. Money constitutes no proper basis for civilization. The time has come to regenerate society.[6]

Jack London, the novelist, echoed Debs. He thought that the arguments for something like System X were obvious. As one of London's characters pronounced in a 1906 novel,

> Let us not destroy those wonderful machines that produce efficiently and cheaply. Let us control them. Let us profit by their efficiency and cheapness. Let us run them for ourselves. That, gentlemen, is socialism.[7]

We could call it socialism. We could call it economic democracy. We could call it System X. The point is to understand what we want and why. And then to use our popular and democratic power to get it.

Rather Fight than Switch

POWER TO THE PEOPLE, RIGHT ON! HUH. MUST BE **10 YEARS** SINCE I SAID THAT. WHAT A SHOW!

THAT JIVE DONKEY REAGAN DIDN'T EVEN HAVE THE GUTS TO SHOW HIS WRINKLY OLD FACE.

SURE WOULD BE NICE TO GO TO WORK T'MORRA SEEING ALL THOSE PEOPLE READY TO RAISE **HELL**.

ON THE OTHER HAND, MOST OF 'EM PROBABLY WOULDN'T HAVE **GONE** IF THEY HADN'T BEEN LAID-OFF.

I'M GLAD WE TOOK THE KIDS. THEY BETTER REMEMBER IT. THEY SAW MORE BROTHERS AND SISTERS FROM ALL OVER THE COUNTRY THAN THEY WILL SEE IN HEARTLAND IN THEIR WHOLE **LIVES**!

GOOD THING WILLOW'S STILL WORKING. I THINK IT'S GONNA BE A LONG HAUL HERE.

LOT OF PEOPLE LEAVING. WHERE THEY GOING? THE SUNBELT? I DON'T NEED NO SUN-TAN. BESIDES... WE'D HAVE TO FIND **TWO** JOBS THERE. HERE WE ONLY GOTTA FIND ONE WHICH ALREADY IS NO PICNIC.

ANYWAY, I'D RATHER DUKE IT OUT IN HEARTLAND THAN START OVER IN HOUSTON.

'If there's ever gonna be change in America, it's gonna be because every community in America's ready for it and—boom! There's gonna be a big tidal wave, and it's just gonna crash down on Washington, and the people are finally gonna be heard."

—community organizer[1]

"The only thing that makes me sad is that this change didn't come about until I was old. I wish I was thirty, thirty-five years old right now, where I knew I'd have many more years. I'm the sort of person that will not sit back in a rocking chair when I get older and just feel sorry for myself. There always has to be something to do. There always is if you want to do it."

—elderly rural organizer[2]

How Do We Begin?

We are ready to conclude. We have reviewed how our economy works. We have confronted the DUPE claims about capitalism. We have reviewed our strengths and the divisions among us. We have studied the sources of our current crisis and the contours of a popular program to resolve it. How do we begin to pursue that program?

Many of us have the feeling that we can't win. But, as Chapter 17 showed, we have often won in the past. There are millions of us and few of them. We live in a democracy where each of us is supposed to have an equal voice in our futures. If we can agree on a common popular alternative to the corporate program, why can't we get it?

We are divided, of course, and many of us have forgotten how to fight for what we want and need. But our past successes can remind us of the keys to effective mobilization.

How do we begin? We begin with what we know and where we're strong.

TOWARD SOME PRINCIPLES OF POPULAR MOBILIZATION

"We shall march with the utmost dispatch,....on the first proper notice...with [our] whole force if required...to the relief of those that shall, are, or may be in danger...."
—agreement of colonial militia during War of Independence[3]

"First of all, you have to want to do it—you have to realize that it's important. Then, you just make a point of trying to get to know people in different parts of the plant—like you would anyway, but a little more deliberately. Then when a situation arises where there's some kind of action to take, you make a point of spreading the word about it to the people

The Hippies of the 80's?

I'M SO EXHAUSTED I CAN'T SLEEP. MAYBE I'M STILL EXCITED.

I'VE NEVER SEEN SO MANY PEOPLE IN ONE PLACE.

LIKE THE SIXTIES WITHOUT THE HIPPIES.

ARE WE THE HIPPIES NOW? WORKING PEOPLE ARE THE HIPPIES OF THE 1980'S?

SO NOW WE'RE GOING HOME. WHAT A LETDOWN. NO JOB-NO MONEY... NO GUYS.

you know, so that those channels get built up in a kind of organized way."

—**mechanic in a truck-building factory**[4]

We're in a difficult political and economic situation. As we fight harder to protect our working and living conditions, corporate pressures, if anything, will intensify. We have to understand the situation in which we're fighting in order to take maximum advantage of our potential strength. If each of us goes a separate way on separate days, the corporations are bound to swamp us with their money, power, and propaganda. If we follow some common rules for resistance, however, the unity of our numbers, intelligence, and commitment can begin to turn the tide.

The lessons of this book and the characteristics of the current economic crisis point toward seven important guides for our resistance to corporate attacks.

1. Don't Believe Everything You're Told

The corporations are waging a public relations campaign to convince us that their cause is just and that their needs are greater than ours. Remember the corporate executive quoted at the beginning of this book: "Don't quote me, but we're propagandizing, we're selling." Through their own public relations machinery, through their allies in the media and the government, the corporations are peddling a common line.

They tell us that we're all in the current mess together and that we all have to sacrifice together. They tell us that we've all been too greedy and need to tighten our belts. They tell us that we need to solve our problems on our own, relying on our individual initiative and ambition. Above all, they tell us that protecting and increasing corporate profits is the key to our economic survival. Their ads feed us this line nearly every day.

We've learned in this book that there are two important reasons for skepticism about the corporate line. First, we've learned that it's *never* true, as an ad recently published by Chase Bank puts it, that "profits...should be celebrated, not condemned; encouraged, not assailed."[5] Business profits come out of our labor and our pocketbooks; the more that goes to them, the worse our working and living conditions. Second, we've also seen that corporations are waging an unusually vigorous attack on our working and living conditions during the current economic crisis. They're speaking softly, as we saw in Chapters 1 and 19, while they're carrying a monstrous stick.

This means that we must all practice some simple rules-of-thumb. Don't believe what corporations tell us is in our own best interests. Treat the media with skepticism. Take government officials and politicians with a healthy dose of salt. As much as we possibly can, we have to develop our own sources of information and analysis. As the worker quoted at the beginning of this section put it, "you make a point of spreading the word...to the people you know, so that those channels get built up in a kind of organized way."

2. Let Capitalism Stand Trial, Not Its Victims

Corporations and the government tell us that we must make sacrifices if we're to lick stagflation and climb out of the economic muck. They suggest that we can play a role in forging solutions to our present problems.

But the analyses of this book have taught us that their logic is fundamentally flawed. The basic operations of the capitalist economy have caused our current crisis, not ordinary working people. Those who control the means of production in capitalism—the giant corporations who control the core of the economy—have largely shaped the policies and practices which got us into this mess in the first place. The economy and the giant corporations should stand trial, not the rest of us. As long as the economy and the corporations deny us basic control over our economic lives, then we should refuse to take responsibility for finding "solutions" to our problems on their terms and on their turf.

This suggests a second obvious rule. We must organize ourselves to try to protect our own working and living conditions. We should not be deterred from those efforts if they tell us that our policies will make their lives difficult or that our struggles will create economic instability and conflict. Their policies have already made our lives intolerable. And their economy has itself created instability and conflict.

We are innocent of direct responsiblity for the current economic crisis. If they can't solve their own problems without us, so much the worse for them. Their economy is on trial. We should place the blame where it belongs. We're not the problem; we're the solution.

3. Let the Wealthy Make Sacrifices, Not the Rest of Us

No matter how we fight to protect our working and living conditions, it will take us quite a while to put the economy back together again. Many of us will remain jobless. Millions of working households will continue to have trouble making ends meet. The economy and the current crisis are imposing harsh sacrifices, and those burdens must be borne for many years to come.

The corporations suggest a "democratic" rule for the distribution of those burdens. They suggest that we all have a stake in our economy and that we should therefore all share in the sacrifices. They suggest a kind of perfect equality in the penalty box: equal sacrifice per capita. One person, one burden.

We've learned in this book that their argument is completely out of order. Capitalist economies don't distribute power on the principle of equal power and responsibility per capita. Capitalism weights our power with respect to our control over the means of production and our personal wealth. One dollar, one vote. The giant corporations who control the means of production are able to shape the basic economic decisions which affect our lives. And the wealthy who "own" the means of production are able to reap the benefits of those economic decisions.

That leads to the third rule. Those who sing the song should pay the piper. Those who make the decisions should take responsibility for

SPEAKING OF GUYS...
I WONDER IF I'LL EVER
SEE THAT STEELWORKER
FROM PITTSBURGH AGAIN?
WAS HE EVER CUTE!
LAYING AROUND ON THE
MALL, SHARIN' A JOINT,
TALKIN' ABOUT RUNAWAY
SHOPS. A REAL MODERN
ROMANCE.
    WELCOME TO THE 1980's.
GOTTA THINK OF
SOMETHING TO CHEER
ME UP......

their effects. Those who get the benefits should also pay the costs. Since large corporations and the wealthy share the power and win the rewards of our economic system, they should also share the sacrifices which that economic system has demanded. Capitalism distributes shares of social product, as we saw in Chapter 2, according to power over resources. We should also insist that the *costs* of capitalism must be distributed according to power over resources. Them that's got should get the bad news as well as the good news. When they ask us to sacrifice for the sake of their economic system, we should ignore their demands.

4. One for All and All for One
Capitalism creates and manipulates many divisions among the people it rules. The system itself creates many different kinds of competition along many different dimensions. And corporations have learned that they can prosper whenever we are fighting among ourselves.

Working people have also learned a critical lesson through the history of struggles to protect and improve working and living conditions. If we fight together, the odds of victory improve. If we overcome our divisions and build upon our common interests and strengths, we stand a better chance of translating our numbers into the power they potentially contain.

This points toward the fourth—and perhaps the most important—rule. Wherever we fight and however we organize ourselves, we must always make a special effort to build unity among all working people. We share a common condition—we work and live in an economy over which we have little control and which compromises our needs and interests. The corporations are quick to take advantage of our divisions whenever they recur. We must be quick to overcome those divisions and build a common purpose and a common fighting strength. Divisions have been our Achilles heel. Unity can help provide the muscle we need.

Although this rule for resistance is obviously critical, it is also especially difficult to practice. As we saw in Chapters 13-16, many of our divisions are rooted in our jobs, our personal histories, and our personal characteristics. The system plays upon those basic differences. Many of us have acquired the habit of paying more attention to our differences than our similarities. The DUPE addicts us to thinking of our problems in isolation, to competing with other groups of working people. Uniting to protect our working and living conditions will be as hard as going cold turkey. Fortunately, we have no other choice.

5. Learning to Do It Our Way
Capitalism and the corporations foster another bad habit. They build structures and organizations which leave decision-making and responsibility in their hands. They encourage us to "leave it to the experts." By "experts," of course, they mean the professionals and technicians who support corporate interests and defend them with slick talk and fancy numbers.

As we increase our resistance to corporate attacks, we must also increase our resistance to corporate methods. All of us must learn to

Gotta Lotta Work to Do

YOU OLD DUPER, YOU. IT'S TIME TO CHANGE YOUR MONIKER.

I'LL NEVER BE DUPE DAGAIN AGAIN.

WHEN THEY MAKE THE MOVIE OF MY LIFE, IT AINT GONNA BE NO ARCHIE BUNKER STORY, NO-SIR-EE!

I'LL BE PLAYED BY... JOHN WAYNE.

NAHHH... THE DUKE IS DEAD.

HOLD IT. THE DUKE... DUKE DAGAIN. SOUNDS GOOD. I LIKE IT.

THAT AINT A BAD NAME FOR A MILITANT TRADE UNIONIST LIKE MYSELF.

IT'S TAKEN 28 YEARS TO RECOGNIZE MY REAL LEADERSHIP POTENTIAL.

contribute not only action but thought. All of us must learn to share the responsibility for leading ourselves, for mapping out the strategies we pursue. If we leave the thinking to someone else, how can we be sure that they're thinking in our interest? Abraham Lincoln was right when he stressed that democracy must always be not only *for* the people but also *of* and *by* the people. The more we get involved in charting programs to protect our working and living conditions, the more certainty we can feel that those programs will actually serve our needs.

So the fifth rule is also fairly obvious. We must always couple our struggles against the corporations with a struggle for democracy within our own organizations. And that democracy must go beyond formal votes of approval and disapproval. All of us must learn to do it our way by learning to think for ourselves and judge for ourselves.

This doesn't mean that we don't need or shouldn't have leaders who play a special role in coordinating our efforts. It does mean that we can never leave it only to our own leaders, much less their experts. We choose and respect our own leaders if they can help articulate and defend our interests. We must always be involved enough so that we can be sure they continue to deserve that respect. One steelworker, who has worked actively in his union, captured this relationship between our leaders and the rest of us when he talked about democracy in his union:

> I think we need more leaders, not less of them. Like this guy Bob where I work. Everybody listens to Bob. When there's a question about what to do, people go with him. He knows the situation; he's a fighter....They know they can trust him....Of course, you have to have a strong rank and file to serve as a check on the leaders. I wouldn't want to be in a leadership position myself without that.[6]

6. Forging Our Own Organizations for Our Own Needs

We can't get anywhere without our own fighting instruments, our own organizations to promote our needs and concerns.

We need strong unions aimed at the right issues. Few would provide a blanket defense of labor unions in the U.S.; they have ignored certain key issues and have played patsy on others. But we need unions to fight for our needs at work and against the giant corporations who run our lives on the job. We can't abandon unions; we need to make them stronger. We can't forsake unions; we need to organize them where they don't exist. If we don't like our unions now, we can change them. If we want stronger unions, we can forge them. If we don't have unions to protect us, we can form them.

Without strong unions, in short, we'll be fighting with pillows. *With* strong unions promoting a popular program, we can apply some of the muscle we need.

We'll also need strong political parties promoting our interests. Here, the principle is somewhat different. In the case of labor unions, we need *one* union to bargain with *one* employer. This means that we need to strengthen the unions already in place, and form strong unions where there are none, rather than creating alternative, competing

I ... I MEAN **WE** GOT A LOTTA **WORK** TO DO. WE GOTTA REVERSE DECLINING MEMBERSHIP. NO MORE SCAPEGOATING THE JAPS. WE GOTTA SOLVE OUR PROBLEMS ON OUR **OWN**. DID I SAY JAPS? DAM! SOME HABITS ARE HARD TO BREAK. GUESS I GOTTA WORK ON THAT TOO. INTERNATIONAL SOLIDARITY! THAT'S THE TICKET. PRETTY GOOD SLOGAN. HMMM. HOW ABOUT "DEMOCRACY IS A PICNIC IN EVERY BACK YARD." OR ..."DEMOCRACY IS NEVER HAVING TO TELL THE BOSS YOU'RE SORRY.

unions.

In the case of political parties, there is only one government and many different interests seek to shape its policies. If one party refuses to serve our interests, we should consider forming another one. This book is not the place to take a position on either the Republican or Democratic parties—much less smaller parties in their orbit. The basic principle is more immediate. If existing political parties consistently refuse to serve our interests, we should consider alternatives.

How do we choose? Suppose we begin to agree on the principles of Chapters 20 and 21—on the need for a popular economic program and a future alternative to capitalism. We should then move toward a political instrument for all those who agree with those principles. None

Who Gets to Decide What's America?

YIPES!

TOMORROW MORNING I HAFTA DO SHOW'N'TELL FOR MISSING CLASSES ON FRIDAY.

MR. THOMAS, **HE** SHOULDA BEEN THERE.

I THINK I'LL SHOW ALL THE TEE-SHIRTS I GOT.

I WONDER WHICH WAS MY FAVORITE? I KINDA LIKE **BONZO** ECONOMICS.

MAYBE I SHOULD BRING THE PICKET SIGNS I GOT WHEN WE WERE CLEANING UP.

SUPPLY-SIDE, MY BACKSIDE! THAT WAS A NEAT ONE.

BOY, IT WAS FAR-OUT WHEN WE MARCHED WITH OUR BANNERS THAT SAID **1500 CIRCUIT-JERKS: OUT OF WORK-OUT OF PATIENCE.**

I THINK IT'S WEIRD... GETTING CHEERED FOR BEING OUT OF WORK.

"I tell people there's a tremendous possibility in this country to stop wars, the battles, the struggles, the fights between people....I don't think it's an impossible dream."

—union organizer[7]

"I would rather let the damn matter go to a strike than have an artificial settlement. Again, it's my faith in the people. If the policemen have a legitimate grievance, the public will back 'em. If they do not, damn it, the public won't back 'em. That's the way I was brought up in the labor movement, right? You take it to the streets. That's where I came from— the streets. And I'm proud of it....You can get a hell of an education out there."

—city-government official in Detroit[8]

"You know what kind of dream I'd like to see? The way I'd love to see America? I'd jus' love to see it that all folks could shake hands an' be brothers and forget they're different. Me and you jus' shake hands and be brothers. I live happy, treat you nice, and you treat me nice, and you forget I'm black and I forget you white. And just live."

—75-year-old black rural organizer[9]

"For a long time, we lived with *shikataganai*—'it can't be helped.' Until many of us said, 'What the hell do you mean, it can't be helped? No more of this silence, hell, no!'"

—Japanese-American in Seattle[10]

of that process will be easy, but at least we'll know what we're fighting for and why we refuse to support the existing parties. Is it any easier to put up with the current choices before us?

7. Speaking with Our Own Voice

There are many who would speak for us. There are many who speak with glib and forked tongues. We are the majority. We are the 90% who must work to survive. We have many experiences and interests in common. We should listen to our own voices. And speak with them. We end this book where it began—with the voices and concerns of working people in the United States:

> "You don't need an army, you don't need ten thousand people, you need a few people determined to win....I just don't believe poor people is just gonna sit still and take it. A man can't run scared. If he does, he might as well end it right now."
>
> —storekeeper in Kentucky[11]

> "I want to live a long time. I want to see the world really turn about-face and people get together. 'Cause it doesn't have to be like it is now."
>
> —retired farmer in Missouri[12]

> "Down in the country, we used to have to ring the bell if there was trouble or we'd ring it for dinner. You used to pull this rope. Sometime, especially if it was cold, you'd keep pullin' and keep pullin' the bell. You'd thing you'd never hear a sound. Maybe by the time your hands got raw almost, you'd hear a little tinklin' of the bell. That's just the way I visualize the community. We all keep pullin' at the rope and our hands are gettin' raw, but you do hear a little tinklin.' It does give you some hope that after a while the bell is gonna ring. We gotta do it, we must do it. We have no other choice. As my father said: 'If you're the only one doin' it, the only one left in the world to do it, you must do it.' We gotta keep pullin'. And I believe the bell will ring."
>
> —community organizer in Chicago[13]

THEY SHOULDA HAD SOME BETTER MUSIC LIKE AT **NO NUKES**. I WISHED I COULDA SEEN BRUCE **SPRINGSTEEN**.

I HOPE WE DON'T HAFTA MOVE LIKE KENNY AND LARRY. I **HATE** THE DALLAS COWBOYS! WHO SAYS THEY'RE AMERICA'S TEAM? WHAT ABOUT THE **STEELERS?**

I SHOULD ASK MR. THOMAS ABOUT THAT. **WHO** GETS TO **DECIDE** WHAT'S AMERICA?

I THOUGHT THIS WAS A **DEMOCRACY**. I THOUGHT WE GOT TO DECIDE FOR **OURSELVES**.

MR. THOMAS SAYS WE GET TO DECIDE WHAT KIND OF **JOBS** WE WANT.

HE NEVER SAID HOW MANY WOULD BE **LEFT** WHEN WE GROW UP.

Footnotes

We have used several sources repeatedly as reference material for this book. In order to save space in these footnotes, we have referred to these sources by the following set of initials:

HSUS: U.S. Bureau of the Census, *Historical Statistics of the United States, Colonial Times to 1970, Bicentennial Edition* (Washington D.C.: U.S. Government Printing Office, 1975), Parts 1 and 2.

SAUS: U.S. Bureau of the Census, *Statistical Abstract of the United States, 1980* (Washington D.C.: U.S. Government Printing Office, 1981).

ERP: Economic Report of the President, 1981 (Washington D.C.: U.S. Government Printing Office, 1981).

ETRP: Employment and Training Report of the President, 1981 (Washington D.C.: U.S. Government Printing Office, 1981).

ADLF: Studs Terkel, *American Dreams Lost and Found* (New York: Pantheon, 1981).

We have also frequently referred to the four sources for the Dominant (Unofficial) Perspective on the Economy which we originally cited in "How to Use This Book." Again, for the purposes of saving space, we refer to them here as:

The DUPE booklet: The American Economic System—and your part in it. (N.Y.: Advertising Council, 1976).

The DUPE film guide: Teachers' companion film guides for "American Enterprise," "made possible by Phillips Petroleum." The film and guides are available from Playback Associates, 708 Third Ave., New York, N.Y. 10017.

The DUPE Primer: "The ABC's of How Our Economy Works," *U.S. News and World Report,* May 1, 1978, pp. 41-64.

The Gospel According to DUPE: Milton and Rose Friedman, *Free to Choose: A Personal Statement* (N.Y.: Harcourt Brace Jovanovich, 1980).

Back Cover

Top Left: Quoted in *New York Times,* February 25, 1979, p. 31.

Top Right: *ADLF,* p. 210.

Lower Left: Quoted in *New York Times,* February 6, 1982, p. 10.

Lower Right: *ADLF,* p. 225.

Front Page

1. Quoted in R.R. Palmer, *The Age of the Democratic Revolution* (Princeton: Princeton Univ. Press, 1959), Vol. 1, p. 174.
2. Tom Paine, "Common Sense," in Howard Fast, *The Selected Works of Tom Paine and Citizen Tom Paine* (N.Y.: Modern Library, 1945), p. 31.
3. Quoted in Howard Zinn, *A People's History of the United States* (N.Y.: Harper Colophon Books, 1980), p. 94.
4. *Business Week,* October 12, 1974.
5. Quoted in *ADLF,* p. 236.

Why We Need This Book

1. N.Y. Stock Exchange, "America's Economic Challenge—Public Expectations," A Survey by Garth-Friedmand-Morris, Inc., 1981, Questions one and three.
2. *Ibid.* Question four.
3. The data are based on Internal Revenue Service, *Statistics of Income—1978, Individual Income Tax Returns* (Washington D.C.: U.S. Government Printing Office, 1980), Preliminary Report, Tables 1 and 4. Earned income includes wage-and-salary income, business and professional income, and pensions. Unearned income includes all other sources. The 1978 income levels dividing the classes were inflated to approximate 1980 levels by the Consumer Price Index, in the case of the division between affluent and wealthy families,

and by the trend in average production worker's weekly earnings, for the cutoff between working and affluent households. See chapter 1, text and note #6 for justification of this distinction in treatment of the two different income levels.
4. First results from poll conducted by Peter D. Hart and Associates in July 1975, summarized in Jeremy Rifkin, *Own Your Own Job* (N.Y.: Bantam Books, 1977), p. 141. Harris poll results reported in Leonard Silk and David Vogel, *Ethics and Profits: The Crisis of Confidence in American Business* (N.Y.: Simon and Schuster, 1976), p. 21.
5. Quoted in *Harper's Weekly,* September 12, 1975, p. 9.
6. Quoted in *ibid.,* p. 9.
7. Quoted in Silk and Vogel, *op. cit.,* p. 118.
8. Quoted in *ibid.,* p. 126.
9. Quoted in *ibid.,* p. 69.
10. From an ad in *Business Week,* February 16, 1976, p. 30.
11. Quoted in Silk and Vogel, *op. cit.,* p. 179.
12. Quoted in *Harper's Weekly,* September 12, 1975, p. 9.
13. Quoted in Dom Bonafede, "The Bull Market in Business/Economics Reporting," *Washington Journalism Review,* July-August, 1980, p. 27.
14. Paul H. Weaver, "Corporations are Defending Themselves with the Wrong Weapon," *Fortune,* June 1977, p. 186.
15. *Ibid.*
16. Facts in the paragraph on the insert page come from Weaver, *op. cit., Fortune,* June, 1977, unless otherwise cited.
17. Reported in "A Status Report on the Advertising Council's Public Service Campaign on the American Economic System," printed by the Advertising Council, 1977; and in *Economic Communicator,* July, 1977, p. 1. (The latter is a newsletter published by the Ad Council to provide information on its campaign.)
18. *Dollars and Sense,* (N.Y.: Advertising Council, 1978.)
19. Quoted in *Economic Communicator,* July, 1977, p. 3.
20. From a Phillips ad in *Business Week,* February 16, 1976, p. 31. The figure on the cost of the films comes from the *New York Times,* April 20, 1976.
21. From an ad by Playback Associates, *New York Times,* January 7, 1979, "National Economic Survey," p. 33, with data updated by distributors.
22. Quoted in Irwin Ross, "Public Relations Isn't Kid Glove Stuff at Mobil," *Fortune,* September, 1976, p. 202.
23. Quoted in Weaver, *op. cit., Fortune,* June 1977, p. 192.
24. See *New York Times,* March 7, 1976, Business Section, p. 3; and Walter Guzzardi, Jr., "Business is Learning How to Win in Washington," *Fortune,* March 27, 1978, p. 53. Quote from *New York Times,* April 17, 1978, p. D7.
25. Quoted in Weaver, *op. cit., Fortune,* June 1977, p. 197. (Emphasis in the original.)
26. Money figure comes from *New York Times,* March 7, 1976, Business and Finance Section, p. 3. Quote comes from *Time,* August 7, 1978, p. 17.
27. Quoted in *Wall Street Journal,* May 10, 1978, p. 1.
28. Karen W. Arenson, "Outlook for Economics in Schools is Bullish," *New York Times,* November 11, 1979, Education Section, p. 30.
29. Quoted in *ibid.,* Education Section, p. 30.
30. Quoted in *Wall Street Journal,* May 10, 1978, p. 1.
31. Myron Emanuel et al., *Corporate Economic Education Programs: An Evaluation and Appraisal* (N.Y.: Financial Executives Research Foundation, 1979), p. 11.
32. Estimate based on *ibid.,* p. 353. Survey results inflated to 1980 by the Consumer Price Index and inflated to aggregate estimate by reports in *ibid.*

on percentage of large corporations responding to their survey and likely to have programs.
33. *Ibid.,* p. 14.
34. *Ibid.* p. 362.
35. Facts and quote from *Time,* August 7, 1978, pp. 15, 17.
36. *Ibid.* p. 17.
37. *New York Times,* May 14, 1978, p. D1; *National Journal,* August 9, 1980, p. 1305; and S. M. Lipset, *Party Coalitions in the 1980s* (San Francisco Institute for Contemporary Studies, 1981).
38. *New York Times* April 17, 1978, p. D7.
39. William Greider, "The Education of David Stockman," *Atlantic Monthly,* December 1981, p. 38.
40. *Ibid.,* p. 47.
41. Weaver, *op. cit., Fortune,* June 1977, p. 192.
42. Quoted in *Time,* August, 7, 1978, p. 17.
43. Quoted in Silk and Vogel, *op. cit.,* p. 67.
44. Letter of resignation from the Labor-Management Advisory Committee, July 19, 1978, by Douglas Fraser, President of the United Auto Workers, p. 1. (Emphasis added.)

How To Use This Book

1. *The DUPE booklet* was "prepared in the public interest by the Advertising Council and the U.S. Department of Commerce in cooperation with the U.S. Department of Labor." Single copies of the booklet are available without charge by writing "Economics," Pueblo, Colorado, 81009. For further information about the booklet and the Ad Council's campaign, you can write The Advertising Council, 825 Third Avenue, New York, N.Y. 10022.
2. The film series is called "American Enterprise." It was "made possible by Phillips Petroleum Company." The five films are "Land," "People," "Innovation," "Organization," and "Government." The films, the teacher's guides, and a newsletter for teachers are available through Playback Associates, 708 Third Ave., New York, N.Y. 10017.
3. Reprints of *The DUPE Primer* are available (for a charge) by writing Subscriber Service, U.S. News and World Report, 2300 N Street, N.W., Washington D.C. 20037.
4. Milton and Rose Friedman, *Free To Choose: A Personal Statement* (N.Y.: Harcourt Brace Jovanovich, 1980).

Chapter 1

1. *ADLF,* p. 135.
2. *ADLF,* p. 142.
3. Quoted in *U.S. News & World Report,* May 8, 1978, p. 19.
4. Quoted in *New York Times,* February 25, 1979, p. 31.
5. Price changes are measured by the consumer price index and are available from *ERP.* Tax burdens can be computed from Appendix Tables C-13 and C-15 of *ETRP* by comparing the total weekly earnings with the total spendable earnings series; the difference is the average tax burden. Data for real spendable earnings come from *ETRP,* Table C-15 and are available on an up-dated basis in Table 20 of any issue of the *Monthly Labor Review.*
6. These data are based on Table 14 of "Money Income of Families and Persons in the United States," *Current Population Reports,* Series P-60, No. 129, November 1981. They are derived by measuring rates of change in the income limits of the respective fifths in the income distribution reported in that table.
7. Data in the text and the box come from "Family Budgets," *Monthly Labor Review,* August 1981, p. 56. Detailed data on the items in the budget come from U.S. Bureau of Labor Statistics, "City

Worker's Family Budget, Autumn 1966," *Bulletin* 1570-1, 1977.

8. The percentage of working households earning less than this standard is derived in the following way: the budget standard for 1967 for families of different sizes was taken from Jean C. Brackett, "New BLS Budgets Provide Yardsticks for Measuring Family Living Costs," *Monthly Labor Review*, April 1969, p. 16. These standards (by family size) were adjusted to 1977 levels from data in U.S. Department of Labor, *News Release*, 79-305, April 29, 1979. These varying standards by family size were then laid over the income distribution by family size available from the annual volumes of the *Current Population Reports*, Series P-60, on "Money Income of Families and Persons...." In 1977, 34.6 million households earned below this standard by family size. This amounted to 51.9% of working households (who were themselves estimated to be 90% of all households by virtue of the calculations reported in note #3 of "Why We Need...."). Data on savings by household income distribution come from U.S. Bureau of Labor Statistics, "Consumer Expenditure Survey Series: Interview Survey, 1972-73," *Report* 455-4, 1977. Families below $10,000 are taken to have no net savings because their average annual savings are no greater than the rate of inflation on the average market value of their assets. There were therefore 34 million households with no savings.

9. *New York Times*, October 29, 1974, p. 39.

10. Quoted in T. Riddell *et al.*, *Economics: A Tool for Understanding Society* (Reading, Mass.: Addison-Wesley, 1979), p. 221.

11. Poverty standard and data from *SAUS*, Table Nos. 770 and 773.

12. See Mollie Orshansky, "Counting the Poor," *Social Security Bulletin*, January 1965, p. 12; and Orshansky, "Children of the Poor: New Dimensions," *Proceedings*, National Conference on Social Welfare, Atlantic, N.J., 1966, p. 8.

13. Polls and data on income reported in Lee Rainwater, *What Money Buys* (N.Y.: Basic Books, 1974), p. 53ff.

14. *The DUPE booklet*, p. 14.

15. Quoted in Harry Maurer, *Not Working: An Oral History of the Unemployed* (N.Y.: Holt, Rinehart and Winston, 1979), p. 19.

16. Quoted in *New York Times*, January 2, 1978, p. 1.

17. Quoted in Maurer, *op. cit.*, p. 24.

18. Quoted in flyer advertising "Job Strategies for Urban Youth," published by Work in America Institute, Inc., 700 White Plains Rd., Scarsdale, N.Y. 10583.

19. *ETRP*, Table A-1.

20. *ETRP*, Table B-19, adjusted to 1980 totals by assuming that the ratio of total annual to average monthly unemployment was the same in 1980 as it was in 1979.

21. *ETRP*, Table A-15. This is a better measure than the narrower measure of "discouraged workers" used by the government because it does not exclude people who may no longer say they "want a job."

22. *ETRP*, Table A-26.

23. *ETRP*, Table B-17.

24. The box sums unemployment, discouraged workers, and involuntary part-time for unemployment at one time. For unemployment during the year, it assumes that half of discouraged workers had left the labor force, on average, at some point during the year; and assumes, conservatively, that only two times the average involuntary part-time workers (rather than the average of three times for total unemployment) experienced involuntary part-time status at some time during the year.

25. Data from *Current Population Reports*, Series P-

60, No. 129, *op.cit.*, Table 12.

26. Samuel Bowles and Herbert Gintis, *Schooling in Capitalist America* (N.Y.: Basic Books, 1976), p. 121.

27. Data on differential unemployment rates from *ETRP*, Tables A-30, A-32.

28. Quoted in *New York Times*, July 20, 1980.

29. Studs Terkel, *Working People* (N.Y.: Avon Books, 1975), pp. 224, 226.

30. *Ibid.*, p. 57.

31. *Ibid.*, p. 402.

32. These numbers are summarized in Jeanne M. Stellman and Susan M. Daum, *Work Is Dangerous to Your Health* (N.Y.: Vintage Books, 1973), p. 3; and Nicholas A. Ashford, *Crisis in the Workplace: Occupational Disease and Injury* (Cambridge, Mass.: MIT Press, 1976), pp. 8-12. The quote comes from Stellman and Daum, *op. cit.*, p. 3.

33. *New York Times*, October 3, 1977, p. 1.

34. *Ibid.*, p. 22.

35. Harold Luft, *Poverty and Health* (Boston: Ballinger, 1978).

36. *Ibid.*

37. Quote from "Your Job or Your Life?," slide show by Institute for Labor Education and Research, 1980.

38. See *Work in America* (Cambridge, Mass.: MIT Press, 1973), pp. 81ff.

39. Reported in *New York Post*, August 10, 1977, p. 59.

40. Based on *Quality of Employment Survey, 1977* (Ann Arbor: University of Michigan Press, 1979). Quote from *World of Work Report*, February 1979 (Work in America Institute), p. 9.

41. Terkel, *Working*, *op. cit.*, p. 222.

42. *Ibid.*, p. 263.

43. *Ibid.*, p. 655.

44. Quoted in Michael Brown, *Laying Waste: The Poisoning of America by Toxic Chemicals* (N.Y.: Pantheon Books, 1980), p. 143.

45. Frances Moore Lappe and Joseph Collins, *Food First: Beyond the Myth of Scarcity* (N.Y.: Ballantine Books, 1978), rev. ed., p. 326.

46. For these and other conclusions, see David M. Gordon, ed., *Problems in Political Economy* (Lexington, Mass.: D.C. Heath, 1977), 2nd ed., Chapter 7.

47. For auto accidents, see *SAUS*, Table 116.

48. See John G. Fuller, *We Almost Lost Detroit* (New York: Readers Digest Press, 1975).

49. Quoted in *U.S. News & World Report*, May 8, 1978, p. 23.

50. Quoted in *New York Post*, January 23, 1978, p. 29.

51. Quoted in *New York Times*, October 18, 1979, p. A1.

52. Quoted in *New York Times*, March 14, 1980, p. D2.

53. Quoted in Andre Gunder Frank, "Mainstream Economists as Astrologers," in URPE, *U.S. Capitalism in Crisis* (N.Y.: Union for Radical Political Economics), p. 9.

54. *Fortune*, July 1974.

55. New York Times, *National Economic Survey*, January 1976.

56. Quoted in *New York Post*, January 23, 1978, p. 29.

57. *Business Week*, October 12, 1974.

58. *Warner and Swasey Company, 1776-1976: What has really changed?* (Cleveland: Warner and Swasey Co., 1976).

59. Quoted in Leonard Silk and David Vogel, *Ethics and Profits: The Crisis of Confidence in American Business* (N.Y.: Simon & Schuster, 1976), p. 70.

60. Based on summaries of Fortune 500 Corporations in *Fortune*, May 8, 1978 and May 5, 1980.

61. Based on summaries of surveys in *Business Week*, first issue of May, 1977-81.

62. See Holly Sklar, ed., *Trilateralism* (Boston: South End Press, 1980).

63. Quotes extracted from Samuel Bowles, "The

Trilateral Commission: Have Capitalism and Democracy Come to a Parting of the Ways?" in URPE, *U.S. Capitalism in Crisis*, *op. cit.*, p. 263.

64. Quoted in Silk and Vogel, *op. cit.*, pp. 78, 189, 189, 75, and 75 respectively.

65. *Ibid.*, pp. 76, 43.

66. Quoted in *New York Times Career Section*, October 12, 1980, p. 14.

67. Quoted in *New York Times*, March 12, 1980, p. D4.

68. Quoted in *New York Times*, August 5, 1980.

69. Quoted in *New York Times*, October 19, 1980, p. 24.

70. Backgrounds of public representatives reported in *New York Times*, June 29, 1977, p. II,2.

71. Quoted in *New York Times*, September 15, 1980, p. B10.

72. Quoted in Silk and Vogel, *op. cit.*, p. 71.

73. *Ibid.*, p. 75.

74. Quoted in Emma Rothschild, *Paradise Lost: The Decline of the Auto-Industrial Age* (N.Y.: Vintage Books, 1974), p. 72.

75. N.Y. Stock Exchange, "America's Economic Challenge—Public Expectations," A Survey by Garth-Friedmand-Morris, Inc., 1981, Questions 5, 6, and 12.

76. Quoted in *Fortune*, October 8, 1979, p. 88.

Introduction to Part II

1. Quoted in David M. Gordon, "Recession is Capitalism as Usual," *N.Y. Sunday Magazine*, April 27, 1975.

2. *ADLF*, p. 417.

3. *Ibid.*, p. 459.

4. Quoted in Jeremy Brecher and Tim Costello, *Common Sense for Hard Times* (Boston: South End Press, 1979), p. 223.

Chapter 2

1. Quoted in Richard Sennett and Jonathan Cobb, *The Hidden Injuries of Class* (N.Y.: Knopf, 1972), p. 96.

2. Quoted in Studs Terkel, *Working* (N.Y.: Avon Books, 1975), pp. 340-1, 342, 343.

3. Quoted in *Harper's Weekly*, September 12, 1975, p. 9.

4. *The Gospel According to DUPE*, p. 1.

5. Warner and Swazey Company, *1776-1976: What has really changed?* (Cleveland: Warner and Swasey Company, 1976), pp. 83, 87.

6. Quoted in Terkel, *op. cit.*, p. 53.

7. Quoted in *ibid.*, p. 360.

8. Quoted in Sennett and Cobb, *op cit.*, p. 28.

9. *The DUPE booklet*, p. 15.

10. These numbers come from U.S. Bureau of the Census, *1970 Census of Population*, "Earnings by Occupation and Education," Vol. PC(2)-8B (Washington, D.C.: U.S. Government Printing Office, January 1973).

11. Cited in *Work in America* (Cambridge, Mass.: MIT Press, 1973), p. 64.

12. Janet Hooks, "The Contribution of Household Production to the National Income," Unpublished Ph.D. dissertation, University of Illinois, 1960, provides careful estimates of the value of unpaid housekeeping services up to 1950. Between 1920 and 1950, her estimates show that they remained roughly constant at around 20 percent of national income; it is therefore unlikely that they have dropped much below one-sixth of national income since then. In 1980, national income was $2,120.5 billion. *ERP*, Table B-18. It seems reasonable to estimate that current unpaid household services would be valued at at least $350 billion, or 16.5 percent.

13. This includes proprietors' income, dividends, rent, and interest—a total of $473.2 billion in 1980. *ERP*, Table B-20.

14. U.S. Internal Revenue Service, *Statistics of Income—1978, Individual Tax Returns*, (Washington

D.C.: U.S. Government Printing Office, 1980), Table 4.

15. The figure on the share of wage-and-salary income received by women and minority males is approximate, because available data do not provide exactly the right breakdown for minority males, but it is undoubtedly close to the correct figure; we have taken the average of the two extremes. The maximum estimate of minority male income comes from the income received by all Black and Hispanic males over 14 receiving income, whether employed or not; and the minimum comes from the income of all Black and Hispanic males working full-time year-round. The former totalled $74.8 billion in 1978 while the latter totalled $54.5 billion the same year. We have taken the average of these two numbers, or $64.65 billion, as our estimate. The estimate for females is direct, based on data for all females with earnings during 1978; the total was $254 billion. The same data report total income of all those with earnings in 1978 as $1017.2 billion. The share of female and minority male earnings in that year was therefore 31.2%.

For 1980, we took 31.2% of total wage-and-salary disbursements (plus other labor income) or $461.9 billion; $350 billion as the estimate of unpaid household work (see note 12 above); and $473.2 billion as the sum of property income (see note 13 above). These three sources of income total $1285.1 billion. For the denominator, we summed total personal income, $2160.5 billion, and the estimate for unpaid household income not reported in the official national income accounts, $350 billion, for a total of $2510.5 billion. The share of these three sources of income in total personal income is therefore 51.2%. Sources: For female and minority male earnings, U.S. Bureau of the Census, "Money Income of Families & Persons in the United States: 1978," *Current Population Reports*, Series P-60, No. 123, Tables K,L. For all data on personal income, *ERP*, Table B-20. (Note: The sources on female and minority male earnings report median, not mean, earnings, but we used the same source for both the numerator and the denominator in our estimate of the female and minority male *share*, so this problem is unlikely to effect our estimate very substantially.)

16. *The DUPE booklet, op. cit.*, p. 2.

17. Alice Hanson Jones, *American Colonial Wealth: Documents and Methods* (N.Y.: Arno Press, 1977), Vol. III, p. 1942.

18. For analyses of the effort devoted to labor-management on the slave plantations, see Eugene Genovese, *Roll, Jordan, Roll* (N.Y.: Pantheon Books, 1974).

19. This estimate of surplus labor time appropriated by feudal masters is based on George Duby, *Rural Economy and Country Life in the Medieval West* (Columbia, S.C.: University of South Carolina Press, 1968).

20. There was, of course, another economy around 1800—the urban (and commercial) economy. We have excluded this economy from our discussion because the structure of this economy was determined largely by its relations with another external economic influence—the British capitalist economy—and because only about 4% of the total U.S. population lived in the major port cities manifesting a different economic structure. On population estimates, see *HSUS*, Series A57, 63-5.

21. *HSUS*, Series A119-134.

22. This summary of the characteristics of the slave economy is based on Eugene Genovese, *The Political Economy of Slavery* (N.Y.: Vintage, 1967) and *Roll, Jordan, Roll* (N.Y.: Vintage 1976).

23. Quoted in Edward Kirkland, *A History of American Economic Life* (N.Y.: Appleton-Century-Crofts, 1969), p. 117.

24. This summary of the early U.S. family economy is based on Nancy Cott, *The Bonds of Womanhood* (New Haven: Yale University Press, 1976) and Michael Merrill, "Cash is Good to Eat," *Radical History Review* III: 4 (Fall 1976), pp. 42-71.

25. Rolla M. Tryon, *Household Manufactures in the United States, 1640-1860* (Chicago: University of Chicago Press, 1917), p. 125.

26. *HSUS*, Series K110, and *SAUS*, Table 1200.

27. Data for the table on wealth are based on the following sources: For 1774, wealth distributions for New England and Middle Colonies from Jones, *American Colonial Wealth, op. cit.*, pp. 2106, 2107, weighted by number of free wealth-holders in those groups of colonies, p. 1789. For 1870, Lee Soltow, *Men and Wealth in the United States* (New Haven: Yale University Press, 1975), p. 99. For 1962, Dorothy Projector and Gertrude Weiss, *Survey of Financial Characteristics of Consumers, 1962* (Washington D.C.: Federal Reserve Board, 1966), p. 285, with numbers interpolated on logarithmic scale.

28. Data for chart on wage-and-salary workers from following sources: For 1780, based on Jackson Main, *The Social Structure of Revolutionary America* (Princeton: Princeton University Press, 1965), pp. 270-271. For 1880 and 1970, Michael Reich, "The Development of the Wage-Labor Force," in R.C. Edwards *et al.*, eds., *The Capitalist System* (Englewood Cliffs, N.J.: Prentice-Hall, 1978), 2nd ed., p. 180.

29. Data for chart on household production: for 1810, U.S. Census Office, *Twelfth Census of the United States, 1900* (Washington, D.C.: U.S. Census Office, 1902), "Manufactures, Part I, pp. 1i-1ii, for 1810; and for 1860, household production figure from Rolla M. Tryon, *Household Manufacturers in the United States, 1640-1860* (Chicago: University of Chicago Press, 1917) p. 308, and figure for total manufacturing from Carroll D. Wright, *The Industrial Evolution of the United States* (N.Y.: Flood and Vincent, 1895), p. 138. (The two series are consistent, since the figures for household manufactures from the Twelfth Census and from Tryon overlap for 1840 and are exactly the same figure. The Twelfth Census figure for 1810 is different from Tryon's because of re-estimation of Census manuscripts.)

30. *SAUS*, Table 790.

31. Two different sources provide convergent estimates. On the share of the wealthy, James D. Smith and Stephen D. Franklin, "The Concentration of Personal Wealth, 1922-1969," *American Economic Review*, May 1974, p. 163, provide a "best estimate" that the wealthiest 0.5% controlled 25% of total personal wealth in 1969. Dorothy Projector and Gertrude Weiss, *Survey of Financial Characteristics of Consumers, op. cit.*, estimate that the top 0.3% of households control 21.7% of total personal wealth and that the top 17.4% of households controlled 74.2% of wealth. The figures for the wealthiest 0.5% and the poorest 90% are based on logarithmic interpolations of these data.

32. In 1972, according to the best available estimates, the wealthiest 0.5% of households owned 49.2% of all corporate stock. *SAUS*, Table 786. Since these estimates are based on a method which Smith and Franklin, *op. cit.*, conclude must surely underestimate the wealth of the wealthiest it seems very likely that the stock share of the top 0.5% of the households is substantially over 50%.

33. Opinion Research Corporation results reported in ad by Cyprus Mine Corporation, *Wall Street Journal*, 1976.

34. Reported in Leonard Silk and David Vogel, *Ethics and Profits: The Crisis of Confidence in American Business* (N.Y.: Simon and Schuster, 1976), p. 21.

35. Cyprus Corporation advertisement, *Wall Street Journal*, 1976.

36. Pamphlet published by Mobil Oil Corporation, "Toward a Healthier Economic Climate,"

1976, p. 4.

Chapter 3

1. Quoted in Lee Rainwater, *What Money Buys: Inequality and the Social Meanings of Income* (N.Y.: Basic Books, 1974), p. 175.

2. *ADLF*, p. 182.

3. Quoted in Studs Terkel, *Working* (N.Y.: Avon Books, 1975), pp. 714, 716, 720, 721.

4. Quoted from newspaper ad by Allied Chemical Corporation, "Profits Are for People," 1976.

5. Cited in Jeremy Rifkin, *Own Your Own Job* (N.Y.: Bantam Books, 1977), p. 137. For this poll result, the figures for "working people" are a weighted average of the responses of those earning $15,000 or less.

6. Quoted in Jeremy Brecher and Tim Costello, *Common Sense for Hard Times* (N.Y.: Two Continents, 1976), p. 106.

7. Cited in Rifkin, *op. cit.*, p. 138; and *U.S. News and World Report*, "1976 Study of American Opinion," (Washington D.C.: U.S. News and World Report, 1976), p. 15.

8. Based on extrapolation of R.C. Edwards *et al.*, eds., *The Capitalist System* (Englewood Cliffs, N.J.: Prentice-Hall, 1978), 2nd ed., Figure 4-C.

9. From transcript of a class for oil and chemical workers, winter 1974-75, New Brunswick, New Jersey.

10. This figure is based on the following calculations. One study has shown recently that the only firms which seem to benefit from monopoly power are large firms (with assets greater than $100 million) in what economists call "core industries" (industries in which considerable industrial concentration has taken place). For these firms, the average profit rate from 1858-1971 was 10.8% (on assets), compared to an (unweighted) average profit rate for all other manufacturing firms of 8.33%. This suggests that 2.47 percentage points, or .229, of core large firms' profits can be attributed to their differential monopoly power. [Figures from Richard C. Edwards, *Contested Terrain: The Transformation of the Workplace in the Twentieth Century* (N.Y.: Basic Books, 1979), p. 83.] Suppose we then take all corporations with assets greater than $100 million. Their share of total (non-financial) corporate profits in 1970 was 64.9%, or $33.62 billion in 1970. If we assume that .229 of those profits can be attributed to their differential monopoly power, then $7.70 billion in corporate profits in 1970 could be attributed to that power. All corporate profits totalled $69.2 billion in 1970. So, $7.70 billion constituted 11.1% of total corporate profits. This number is certainly an over-estimate of the amount attributable to "differential monopoly pricing power" in at least two respects. First, as Edwards points out, only large firms in "core industries" benefit from monopoly power; we hve attributed the differential to all firms over $100 million. Second, our estimate ascribes all of the difference in profit rates to "pricing power"; some of it may be due to efficiencies of scale which larger firms in these industries realize. There is only one potential under-estimate in our figure: we have ascribed differential power only to non-financial corporations; if we also assumed that financial corporations could earn higher rates of return as a result of their size and power, then the maximum estimate would rise to 14.9%. (Figures on corporate profits and share of firms with assets greater than $100 million come from *HSUS*, Series V151, V182-196, and V108-140.

11. Pamphlet published by Mobil Oil, "Toward a Healthier Economic Climate," 1976, p. 2. (Emphasis added.)

12. *The DUPE primer*, p. 47.

13. Figures from *Fortune*, May 4, 1981, pp. 324-5.

14. Quoted in Nancy Seifer, *Nobody Speaks for Me!*

(N.Y.: Simon and Schuster, 1976), pp. 227-8.

15. From transcript of a class for oil and chemical workers, winter 1974-75, New Brunswick, New Jersey.

16. Figures for General Motors from the 1979 GM Annual Report.

17. *DUPE film guide*, "People," p. 8.

18. Textron Corporation, "How Private Enterprise Works at Textron," (Providence, R.I.: Textron Corp., no date), p. 1.

19. *The DUPE booklet*, p. 5.

20. *DUPE film guide*, "Organization," pp. 7, 10.

21. *Forbes*, February 15, 1975, p. 48.

22. *DUPE film guide*, "Organization," p. 7; and *ibid.*, p. 7; and *The DUPE booklet*, p. 8.

23. *DUPE film guide*, "Innovation," p. 7.

24. From film, "Controlling Interest," quoted in *Seven Days*, June 16, 1978, p. 29; and from "International Industry and Labor Film Project," by the Educational TV and Film Center (1747 Connecticut Ave., N.W., Washington, D.C. 20009), p. 69.

25. Quoted in E.P. Thompson, "Time, Work Discipline, and Industrial Capitalism," *Past and Present*, December 1967, p. 86.

26. Cited in Norman Ware, *The Industrial Worker, 1840-1860*, (Chicago: Quadrangle Books, 1964), p. 130n; and in David Brody, *Steelworkers: the Non-Union Era* (Cambridge, MA: Harvard University Press, 1960), pp. 37-8.

27. See, for instance, Hannah Josephson, *The Golden Threads: New England Mill Girls and Magnates* (N.Y.: Duell, Sloan and Pearce, 1949).

28. See, for instance, John R. Commons, *Races and Immigrants in America* (N.Y.: Macmillan, 1924), 2nd ed.

29. Stanley B. Mathewson, *Restriction in Output among Unorganized Workers* (N.Y.: Viking, 1931), p. 146.

30. Quoted in Stanley Aronowitz, *False Promises* (N.Y.: McGraw-Hill, 1974), p. 22.

31. Emma Rothschild, *Paradise Lost: The Decline of the Auto-Industrial Age* (N.Y.: Vintage, 1974), p. 109.

32. Quoted in Aronowitz, *False Promises, op. cit.*, p. 42.

33. Quoted in Sumner H. Slichter, *Union Policies and Industrial Management* (Washington, D.C.: The Brookings Institution, 1941), p. 207.

34. Cited in W. Jess Lauch and Edgar Sydenstricker, *Conditions of Labor in American Industries* (N.Y.: Funk & Wagnalls, 1917), p. 198.

35. Quoted in Mathewson, *op. cit.*, p. 118.

36. Quoted in Leonard Silk and David Vogel, *Ethics and Profits: The Crisis of Confidence in American Business* (N.Y.: Simon and Schuster, 1976), p. 70.

37. Quoted in Nick Kotz, "Oilcan Eddie Takes on the Old Guard," *N.Y. Times Sunday Magazine*, December 14, 1976, p. 33.

38. Poll results cited in Rifkin, *Own Your Own Job, op. cit.*, p. 136. The results figures represent a weighted average of results for white collar, skilled blue-collar, and unskilled blue collar.

Chapter 4

1. Quoted in Barbara Garson, *All the Livelong Day: The Meaning and Demeaning of Work* (London: Penguin, 1975), p. 6.

2. Quoted in Studs Terkel, *Working* (N.Y.: Avon Books, 1974), pp. 261, 262, 263.

3. Lester R. Bittel, *What Every Supervisor Should Know* (N.Y.: McGraw-Hill, 1974), 3rd ed., p. 209.

4. Quoted in George Katsiaficas, "The Meaning of May 1968," *Monthly Review*, May 1978, p. 18.

5. *The DUPE booklet*, p. 5.

6. *DUPE film guide*, "Organization," p. 6.

7. Quoted in Emma Rothschild, *Paradise Lost: The Decline of the Auto-Industrial Age* (N.Y.: Vintage Books, 1974), p. 151.

8. Quoted in *ibid.*, p. 118.

9. Quoted in *ibid.*, p. 34.

10. Quoted in Frederic C. Lane, *Venetian Ships and*

Shipbuilders of the Renaissance (Westport, Ct.: Greenwood Press, 1975), pp. 207-8.

11. *Ibid.*, p. 211.

12. Stevenson W. Fletcher, *Pennsylvania Agriculture and Country Life, 1640-1840* (Harrisburg, Pa.: Harrisburg Historical and Museum Commission, 1950). p. 119.

13. *Ibid.*, p. 439.

14. *Ibid.*, pp. 439-444.

15. Quoted in Herbert G. Gutman, "The Workers' Search for Power," in H. Wayne Morgan, ed., *The Gilded Age* (Syracuse: Syracuse University Press, 1970), rev. ed., p. 53.

16. Quoted in David F. Noble, *America by Design: Science, Technology, and the Rise of Corporate Capitalism* (N.Y.: Knopf, 1977), p. 263.

17. Quoted in Reinhard Bendix, *Work and Authority in Industry* (Berkeley, Ca.: University of California Press, 1974), p. 59.

18. Quoted in E. P. Thompson, "Time, Work Discipline, and Industrial Capitalism," *Past and Present*, December 1967, p. 81.

19. Oscar Handlin, "Boston's Immigrants: The Economic Adjustment," in Paul Kramer and Frederick Holborn, eds., *The City in American Life* (N.Y.: Putnam's, 1970), p. 94.

20. David Wells, *Recent Economic Changes* (N.Y.: Appleton, 1895), p. 34.

21. Quoted in Robert Ozanne, *A Century of Labor-Management Relations at McCormick and International Harvester* (Madison, Wis.: University of Wisconsin Press, 1967), p. 20.

22. *Ibid.*, p. 20.

23. *Ibid.*, p. 27.

24. Quoted in Loren Baritz, *The Servants of Power* (Westport, Ct.: Greenwood Press, 1974), pp. 97-8.

25. Quoted in Harry Braverman, *Labor and Monopoly Capital* (N.Y.: Monthly Review Press, 1974), p. 102.

26. Quoted in *ibid.*, p. 101.

27. Quoted in *ibid.*, p. 120.

28. Quoted in Rothschild, *Paradise Lost, op. cit.*, p. 109.

29. See, for instance, Stanley B. Mathewson, *Restriction of Output Among Unorganized Workers* (N.Y.: Viking Press, 1931).

30. Quoted in Daivd Montgomery, "The 'New Unionism' and The Transformation of Workers' Consciousness in America, 1909-22," *Journal of Social History*, Fall 1974, p. 518.

31. Quoted in Jeremy Brecher and Tim Costello, *Common Sense for Hard Times* (N.Y.: Two Continents Press, 1976), p. 51.

32. See H. Millis and R. Montgomery, *Organized Labor* (N.Y.: McGraw-Hill, 1945), p. 118.

33. See David M. Gordon *et al.*, *Segmented Work, Divided Workers* (N.Y.: Cambridge University Press, 1982), Ch. 4.

34. David Brody, *The Steel Workers in America: The Non-Union Era* (Cambridge, Ma.: Harvard University Press, 1960).

35. William Henry Leffingwell, *Office Management: Principles and Practice* (Chicago: A. W. Shaw, 1925), p. 61.

36. From transcript of a class for oil and chemical workers, winter 1974-1975, New Brunswick, N.J.

37. Quoted in Braverman, *Labor and Monopoly Capital, op. cit.*, p. 202.

38. Quoted in Rothschild, *Paradise Lost, op. cit.*, p. 107.

39. Quoted in Philip Kraft, *Programmers and Managers: The Routinization of Computer Programming in the United States* (N.Y.: Springer-Verlag, 1977), p. 62.

40. Quoted in Braverman, *Labor and Monopoly Capital, op. cit.*, p. 339.

41. Quoted in *ibid.*, p. 336.

42. Sumner Slichter, *The Turnover of Factory Labor* (N.Y.: Appleton, 1919), p. 436.

43. Richard Lester, *As Unions Mature* (Princeton: Princeton University Press, 1958), pp. 40, 39.

44. Based on occupational data in *ETRP*, Tables A-22, C-6.

45. Quoted in Brecher and Costello, *Common Sense for Hard Times, op. cit.*, p. 43.

46. Quoted in *ibid.*, p. 46.

47. Quoted in Richard C. Edwards, *Contested Terrain: The Transformation of the Workplace in the Twentieth Century* (N.Y.: Basic Books, 1979), p. 60.

48. Quoted in Rothschild, *Paradise Lost, op. cit.*, p. 119.

49. Quoted in Norman Ware, *The Industrial Worker, 1840-1860* (Chicago: Quadrangle, 1964), pp. 229, 230.

50. Quoted in *ibid.*, p. 236.

51. Quoted in *ibid.*, p. xvi.

52. Quoted in Katherine Stone, "The Origins of Job Structures in the Steel Industry," in R.C. Edwards *et al.*, eds., *Labor Market Segmentation* (Lexington, Ma.: Lexington Books, 1975), p. 32.

53. Quoted in Jeremy Brecher, *Strike!* (S.F.: Straight Arrow Press, 1972), p. 54.

54. Quoted in Philip S. Foner, *History of the Labor Movement in the United States* (N.Y.: International Publishers, 1975), Vol. II, 2nd ed., pp. 211-12.

55. Quoted in *ibid.*, Vol. II, p. 212.

56. Quoted in *ibid.*, Vol. II, p. 218.

57. Quoted in Brecher, *Strike!, op. cit.*, p. 110.

58. Quoted in Edwards, *Contested Terrain, op. cit.*, p. 63.

59. Mathewson, *Restriction of Output..., op. cit.*, p. 68.

60. See Brecher, *Strike!, op. cit.*, pp. 180-81.

61. Irving Bernstein, *Turbulent Years: A History of the American Worker, 1933-1941* (Boston: Houghton-Mifflin, 1971), p. 526.

62. *Ibid.*, pp. 527-28.

63. *Ibid.*, p. 500.

64. Quoted in *ibid.*, p. 501.

65. Quoted in Terkel, *Working, op. cit.*, pp. 1-2.

Chapter 5

1. Quoted in Richard Edwards, *Contested Terrain, The Transformation of the Workplace in the Twentieth Century* (N.Y.: Basic Books, 1979), p. 8.

2. Quoted in Richard Sennett and Jonathan Cobb, *The Hidden Injuries of Class* (N.Y.: Knopf, 1972), p. 168.

3. Quoted in Jeremy Brecher and Tim Costello, *Common Sense for Hard Times* (N.Y.: Two Continents, 1976), p. 119.

4. See Emma Rothschild, *Paradise Lost* (N.Y.: Vintage Books, 1974), Ch. 8.

5. Based on independent research, including information from Hershey Co., by the Institute for Labor Education and Research.

6. *The DUPE booklet*, p. 9.

7. *The Gospel according to Dupe*, p. 15.

8. Quoted in Leonard Silk and David Vogel, *Ethics and Profits: The Crisis of Confidence in American Business* (N.Y.: Simon and Schuster, 1976), p. 176.

9. John Steinbeck, *The Grapes of Wrath* (N.Y.: Viking Press, 1939), p. 477.

10. *Wall Street Journal*, July 15, 1974.

11. Quoted in Lillian Breslow Rubin, *Worlds of Pain: Life in the Working-Class Family* (N.Y.: Basic Books, 1976), p. 158.

12. Quoted in *ibid.*, p. 200.

13. From transcript of a course for oil and chemical workers, New Brunswick, N.J., 1975.

14. Quoted in Lee Rainwater, *What Money Buys: Inequality and the Social Meanings of Income* (N.Y.: Basic Books, 1974), p. 84.

15. Quoted in *ibid.*, p. 81.

16. Quoted in *ibid.*, p. 83.

17. Fernand Braudel, *Capitalism and Material Life, 1400-1800* (N.Y.: Harper Colophon Books, 1975), p. 85.

18. *Ibid.*, p. 86.

19. Quoted in Rolla M. Tryon, *Household Manufactures in the United States, 1640-1860* (Chicago: Univ. of Chicago Press, 1917), p. 156.

20. Quoted in Stuart Ewen, *Captains of Consciousness: Advertising and the Social Roots of the Consumer Culture* (N.Y.: McGraw-Hill, 1977), p. 26.

21. Norman Ware, *The Industrial Worker, 1840-1860* (Chicago: Quadrangle Books, 1964), pp. 39-40.

22. *Ibid.*, p. 40.

23. *Ibid.*, p. 46.

24. Quoted in *ibid.*, p. 45.

25. Quoted in Braudel, *Capitalism and Material Life, op. cit.*, p. 328.

26. Quoted in Michael Merrill, "Cash Is Good to Eat: Self-Sufficiency and Exchange in the Rural Economy of the United States," *Radical History Review*, Winter 1977, p. 57.

27. Quoted in David Montgomery, *Beyond Equality: Labor and the Radical Republicans, 1862-1872* (N.Y.: Vintage Books, 1967), p. 443.

28. Quoted in Howard Zinn, *A People's History of the United States* (N.Y.: Harper Colophon Books, 1980), p. 282.

29. Ernest Mandel, *Late Capitalism* (London: New Left Books, 1975), p. 57.

30. *Ibid.*, p. 57.

31. Quoted in Ewen, *Captains of Consciousness..., op. cit.*, p. 26.

32. Quoted in *ibid.*, p. 22.

32. Quoted in *ibid.*, p. 22.

33. Quoted in *ibid.*, p. 118.

34. Quoted in Rothschild, *Paradise Lost, op. cit.*, p. 44.

35. F. Fisher, Z. Griliches, and C. Kaysen, "The Costs of Automobile Changes Since 1949," *Journal of Political Economy*, October 1962.

36. Quoted in Rothschild, *Paradise Lost, op. cit.*, p. 81.

37. *The Gospel according to DUPE*, p. 14.

38. *The DUPE primer*, p. 44.

39. Merrill, "Cash Is Good to Eat...," *op. cit.*, p. 55.

40. Anwar Shaikh, "The Transformation from Marx to Sraffa (Prelude to a Critique of the Neo-Ricardians)," New School for Social Research, March 1980, pp. 40-41.

41. John Kenneth Galbraith, *The Age of Uncertainty* (Boston: Houghton Mifflin, 1977), p. 181.

Chapter 6

1. Quoted in Studs Terkel, *Working* (N.Y.: Avon Books, 1974), p. 4.

2. Quoted in Leonard Silk and David Vogel, *Ethics and Profits: The Crisis of Confidence in American Business* (N.Y.: Simon and Schuster, 1976), p. 139.

3. In Sigmund Diamond, ed., *The Nation Transformed: The Creation of an Industrial Society* (N.Y.: Braziller, 1968), p. 62.

4. Quoted in Louise Kapp Howe, *Pink Collar Workers* (N.Y.: Putnam, 1977), pp. 149, 150.

5. Michael Goodwin, "Stompin' in the Delta," *Village Voice*, April 17, 1978, p. 60.

6. See Henry Ford, *My Life and Work* (N.Y.: Arno, 1973).

7. Quoted in Francesca Maltese, "Notes for a Study of the Auto Industry," in Richard Edwards, et. al., eds., *Labor Market Segmentation* (Lexington, Ma.: Lexington Books, 1975), p. 88.

8. H. Feldman, *The Regularizaton of Employment* (N.Y.: Harper, 1925), p. 62.

9. *Ibid.* p. 239.

10. See F. M. Lappe and Joseph Collins, *Food First: Beyond the Myth of Scarcity* (N.Y.: Ballantine Books, 1978), Chs. 21-23.

11. Quoted in Richard J. Barnet and Ronald E. Muller, *Global Reach: The Power of the Multinational Corporations* (N.Y.: Simon and Schuster, 1974), p. 21.

12. Quoted in Lee Rainwater, *What Money Buys: Inequality and the Social Meaning of Income* (N.Y.: Basic Books, 1974), p. 85.

13. Quoted in Silk and Vogel, *Ethics and Profits... op. cit.*, p. 129.

Chapter 7

1. From Warner and Swasey Company, *1776-1976: What Has Really Changed?* (Cleveland: Warner and Swasey Co., 1976), p. 87.

2. Quoted in Lee Rainwater, *What Money Buys: Inequality and the Social Meanings of Income* (N.Y.: Basic Books, 1974), p. 84.

3. *The Dupe booklet*, p. 19.

4. *The Dupe film guide*, "People," p. 8.

5. See Howard Zinn, *A People's History of the United States* (N.Y.: Harper Colophon Books, 1980), pp. 28ff.

6. *Ibid.*, pp. 30ff.

7. Daniel P. Mannix, *Black Cargoes* (N.Y.: Viking, 1962), p. 157.

8. *Ibid.*, p. 161.

9. E.P. Thompson, *The Making of the English Working Class* (N.Y.: Vintage, 1966), p. 318.

10. *Ibid.*, pp. 318ff.

11. Quoted in *ibid.*, p. 329.

12. Quoted in Maurice Dobb, *Studies in the Development of Capitalism* (N.Y.: International Publishers, 1963), p. 208.

13. Karl Polanyi, *The Great Transformation* (N.Y.: Holt, Rinehart and Winston, 1944), p. 160.

14. See Zinn, *A People's History..., op. cit.*, pp. 32ff.

15. Thompson, *The Making of the English Working Class, op. cit.*, p. 203.

16. See Dobb, *Studies in the Development of Capitalism, op. cit.*

17. Based on *HSUS*, Series C89.

18. See Oscar Handlin, *Boston's Immigrants* (N.Y.: Atheneum, 1974), Ch. II.

19. *Ibid.*, pp. 48ff.

20. *Ibid.*, Ch. II.

21. David Montgomery, "Labor in the Industrial Era," in U.S. Department of Labor, *The American Worker* (Washington, D.C.: U.S. Government Printing Office, 1976), p. 110.

22. *Ibid.*, p. 110-111.

23. *Ibid.*, p. 111.

24. Zinn, *A People's History..., op. cit.*, Ch. 11.

25. Quoted in Montgomery, "Labor in the Industrial Era," *op. cit.*, p. 118.

26. See, for instance, Allan Spear, *Black Chicago* (Chicago: University of Chicago Press, 1967), Ch. 7.

27. *ADLF*, p. 193.

28. Claude Brown, *Manchild in the Promised Land* (N.Y.: Macmillan, 1965), pp. 7-8.

29. Based on business failure rate, *ERP*, Table B-91.

30. The official history of U.S. armed involvement has been prepared by the U.S. Department of Defense and is printed as "Use of U.S. Armed Forces in Foreign Countries" in U.S. Congress, *Congressional Record*, 91st Congress, 1st Session, Vol. 115, Part 13, June 23, 1969, pp. 16840-16843. The list included in Figure 7.1 includes 29 of the full list of 62 separately catalogued uses of U.S. forces overseas between 1900 and 1965.

31. Quoted in Leonard Silk and David Vogel, *Ethics & Profits: The Crisis of Confidence in American Business* (N.Y.: Simon and Schuster, 1976), p. 129.

32. *The Dupe booklet*, pp. 14, 13, 3, 1.

33. From transcript of class with oil and chemical workers, New Brunswick, N.J., 1975.

34. Estimates on total employment and total population from *ETRP*, Table A-1. Estimates on private-sector employment derived by subtracting from total employment an estimate of public and private employment resulting from "Government Purchases of Goods and Services," *ETRP*, Table G-5. These data are available only back to 1963, so that the estimate for 1948 assumes a constant multiplier of government-generated employment to government purchases of goods and services (in constant dollars) between 1948 and 1963. If government purchases actually generated fewer

jobs per dollar of government purchases over time, which is not particularly likely—since productivity does not advance much in the government sector—then employment generated by the government would have been higher in 1948 and, therefore, the estimate of private-sector employment somewhat lower. At the most, however, there is only a spread of about 2.5 million jobs between the lower and upper bounds of possible estimates for 1948 (with the upper bound established by backcasting a straight-line fall in the job multiplier on the basis of its slight decline from 1963 to 1966). At the most, then, private-sector employment might have increased by four million instead of only 1.5 million, still only 13.3% of the total increase in the adult population.

35. The dates for the expansion and contraction periods of the business cycle are based on Arthur Burns and Wesley C. Mitchell, *Measuring Business Cycles* (N.Y.: National Bureau of Economic Research, 1946), p. 78; and Center for International Business Cycle Research, "Growth Cyle Chronologies, 13 Countries," unpublished data, Rutgers University, 1981.

36. Barbara Garson, *All the Livelong Day* (N.Y.: Penguin, 1977), p. 90.

37. Studs Terkel, *Working* (N.Y.: Avon Books, 1974), p. 680.

38. Michael Reich, "The Development of the Wage-Labor Force," in R. Edwards *et al.*, eds. *The Capitalist System* (Englewood Cliffs, N.J.: Prentice-Hall, 1978) 2nd ed., p. 180.

39. See Michael R. Cooper *et al.*, "Early Warning Signals: Growing Discontent Among Managers," *Business*, January-February 1980, for data on declining work satisfaction among hourly employees.

40. Based on data for supervisory and nonsupervisory employees, corrected for business cycle fluctuations, in *ETRP*, Table C-8.

41. *SAUS*, Table 953.

42. Richard Edwards, *Contested Terrain: The Transformation of the Workplace in the Twentieth Century* (N.Y.: Basic Books, 1975), Appendix Table A-7.

43. *HSUS*, Series D927.

44. Edwards, *Contested Terrain, op. cit.*, p. 85.

45. *HSUS*, Series T444.

46. *The Dupe primer*, p. 46.

47. Quoted in Rainwater, *What Money Buys, op. cit.*, p. 168.

48. See James D. Smith and Stephen D. Franklin, "The Concentration of Personal Wealth, 1922-1969," *American Economic Review*, May 1974.

49. David M. Gordon *et al.*, *Segmented Work, Divided Workers: The Historical Transformation of Labor in the United States* (N.Y.: Cambridge University Press, 1982), Table 5.6.

50. U.S. Bureau of the Census, "Money Income of Families and Persons in the United States: 1978," *Current Population Reports*, Series P-60, No. 118, March 1979, Table 10.

51. *Ibid.*, Table 53.

52. *Loc. cit.* For useful discussion of these trends, examining their real meaning and implications, see Michael Reich, *Racial Inequality: A Political-Economic Analysis* (Princeton: Princeton University Press, 1981), Ch. 2.

53. Based on data reported in Samuel Bowles and Herbert Gintis, *Schooling in Capitalist America* (N.Y.: Basic Books, 1976), Ch. 5; and also on private communication from authors.

54. Quoted in Rainwater, *What Money Buys, op. cit.*, p. 86.

55. Quoted in *ibid.*, p. 89.

56. Quoted in *ibid.*, p. 92.

57. U.S. Bureau of the Census, "Money Income....1978," *op. cit.*, Table 9.

58. Median incomes adjusted for increase in consumer price index, *ERP*, Table B-50.

59. Incomes adjusted for the average taxes paid

by a household headed by the average production worker, with three dependents, from *ETRP*, Table C-15.

60. Based on data reported in Rainwater, *What Money Buys, op. cit.*, p. 53.

61. Surveys reported in *ibid.*, p. 53.

62. *HSUS*, Series G849-856.

63. *The Dupe booklet*, p. 16.

64. These data are based on the composition of gross national product, reported in *ERP*, Tables B-11 and B-12. Data on workers' hourly earnings from *ERP*, Table B-38. The decomposition of total employee conpensation between producton and supervisory workers' compensation is based on the supervisory workers' share of total employment, *ETRP*, Table C-8, and production workers' hourly earnings and average weekly hours, *ERP*, Table B-38.

Chapter 8

1. Ad published by Mobil Oil, 1977.

2. See Jeremy Rifkin, *Own Your Own Job* (N.Y.: Bantam Books, 1975), p. 140.

3. Quoted in Leonard Silk and David Vogel, *Ethics & Profits: The Crisis of Confidence of American Business* (N.Y.: Simon and Schuster, 1976), p. 139.

4. See Art Preis, *Labor's Giant Step* (N.Y.: Pathfinder Press, 1972), pp. 298ff.

5. Quoted in Silk and Vogel, *Ethics & Profits, op. cit.*, p. 66.

6. *ADLF*, p. 341.

7. This argument is obviously premised on the assumption that a dollar of capital invested by the government (in non-defense projects) will have a higher employment/capital ratio than private-sector investments. For discussion of some of the evidence for and implications of this argument, see Barry Bluestone and Bennett Harrison, *Capital Mobility and Economic Dislocation* (Washington, D.C.: The Progressive Alliance, 1980).

8. See, for example, Walter W. Heller, *New Dimensions of Political Economy* (N.Y.: Norton, 1967).

9. Quoted in David M. Gordon, "Capital vs. Labor: The Current Crisis in the Sphere of Production," in *Radical Perspectives on the Economic Crisis* (N.Y.: Union for Radical Political Economics, 1975), p. 33.

10. Quoted in *Wall Street Journal*, November 18, 1974, p. 1.

11. All three quotes from Silk and Vogel, *Ethics & Profits, op. cit.*, p. 64.

12. Quoted in David M. Gordon, ed., *Problems in Political Economy* (Lexington, Ma.: D.C.Heath, 1971), p. 227.

13. Robert D. Plotnick and Felicity Skidmore, *Progress Against Poverty: A Review of the 1964-1974 Decade* (N.Y.: Academic Press, 1975), p. 175.

14. Quoted in Jeremy Brecher and Timothy Costello, *Common Sense for Hard Times* (Boston: South End Press, 1979), p. 100.

Introduction to Part III

1. Lester R. Bittel, *What Every Supervisor Should Know* (N.Y.: McGraw-Hill, 1974), 3rd ed., p. 655.

2. *ADLF*, p. 409.

Chapter 9

1. *The Gospel According to DUPE*, p. 37.

2. Quoted in Silk and Vogel, *Ethics and Profits...*, *op. cit.*, p. 21.

3. *ADLF*, p. 210.

4. Warner and Swasey Company, *1776-1976: What has really changed?* (Cleveland: Warner and Swasey Company, 1976), p. 38.

5. *The DUPE Primer*, p. 49.

6. This number is based on the inverse of the number cited in note #5. If roughly 27.5 million adults own stock, this constitutes, on average, roughly 20.5% of households. (There were 1.9 adults per household in the U.S. in 1975. See

SAUS, Tables 34, 64.)

7. *SAUS*, Table 786.

8. *The DUPE Primer*, p. 50.

9. Maurice Zeitlin, "Who Owns America? The Same Old Gang," *The Progressive*, June 1978, p. 15.

10. Edward Herman, *Corporate Control, Corporate Power* (N.Y.: Cambridge Univ. Press, 1981), p. 11.

11. *Ibid.* p. 102.

12. See, for instance, Peter F. Drucker, *The Unseen Revolution: How Pension Fund Socialism Came to America*, (N.Y.: Harper and Row, 1976).

13. Herman, *Corporate Control, Corporate Power, op. cit.*, p. 102.

14. *Ibid.* p. 138; and Jeremy Rifkin and Randy Barber, *The North Will Rise Again: Pensions, Politics, and Power in the 1980s*, (Boston: Beacon Press, 1978), p. 89.

15. *New York Times*, January 17, 1979, p. D-1.

16. Rifkin and Barber, *The North Will Rise Again, op. cit.*, p. 114.

17. Herman, *Corporate Control, Corporate Power, op. cit.*, Table 4-8.

18. *Ibid.* pp. 151, 152.

19. *Ibid.* p. 144.

20. Quoted in Rifkin and Barber, *op. cit.*, pp. 127-128.

21. *The DUPE Primer*, p. 50.

22. *Loc. Cit.*

23. See, for a classic statement, Carl Kaysen, "The Social Significance of the Modern Corporation," *American Economic Review*, May 1957.

24. See both Herman, *Corporate Control, Corporate Power, op. cit.*, p. 91; and Wilbur G. Lewellen, *The Ownership Income of Management* (N.Y.: National Bureau of Economic Research, 1971), p. 11.

25. Herman, *Corporate Control, Corporate Power, op. cit.*, Table 3-4.

26. *Ibid.* p. 95.

27. See, for example, G. William Domhoff, *The Higher Circles: The Governing Class in America* (N.Y.: Vintage, 1971).

28. Herman, *Corporate Control, Corporate Power, op. cit.*, pp. 112-13.

29. This summary is based on the complementary (though slightly differing) estimates presented in David Kotz, *Financial Control in America* (Berkeley: Univ. of California Press, 1978); and Herman, *Corporate Control, Corporate Power, op. cit.*

30. Quoted in the film, "Rip-off at the Top," available from the Institute for Labor Education and Research.

31. *The DUPE film guide*, "Organization," p. 7.

32. *SAUS*, Table 926.

33. U.S. Chamber of Commerce, *The Years of Change* (Washington, D.C.: U.S. Chamber of Commerce, 1976) p. 50.

34. *Ibid.* p. 52.

35. *Ibid.*

36. Based on data reported in John M. Blair, *Economic Concentration* (N.Y.: Harcourt Brace Jovanovich, 1972), Ch. 1.

37. See *Fortune*, May 4, 1981.

38. See table in Holly Sklar, ed., *Trilateralism* (Boston: South End Press, 1980), p. 10.

39. Gus Tyler, "The Other Economy," *The New Leader*, May 8, 1978, p. 7.

40. Data reported in David M. Gordon, *The Working Poor* (Washington D.C.: Council of State Planning Agencies, 1980), p. 55.

41. Based on Blair, *Economic Concentration, op. cit.*, p. 275, and *HSUS*, Series P-1.

42. Blair, *op. cit.*, p. 307.

43. Herman, *Corporate Control, Corporate Power, op. cit.*, p. 69.

44. Tyler, "The Other Economy," *op. cit.*, p. 8.

45. *Loc. cit.*

46. Herman, *Corporate Control, Corporate Power,*

op. cit., Table 6-5.

47. *Ibid.* p. 217.

48. Richard Edwards, *Contested Terrain: The Transformation of the Worplace in the Twentieth Century* (N.Y.: Basic Books, 1979), p. 84.

49. Herman, *Corporate Control, Corporate Power, op. cit.*, p. 192.

50. See a series of articles in *Business Week* in 1978 and 1979.

51. *The DUPE Booklet*, p.4.

52. *The Gospel According to DUPE*, pp. 65-6.

53. *The DUPE Booklet*, p. 3.

54. *The DUPE Primer*, p. 44.

55. *Ibid.* p. 45.

56. This estimate is based on a variety of reports in the daily press and magazines from 1978 through 1980.

57. Reported in the *New York Post*, June 6,1977.

58. See a series of articles on the U.S. health care system, *New York Times*, March 1982.

59. Jeremy Brecher and Tim Costello, *Common Sense for Hard Times*, (Boston: South End Press, 1979), p. 111.

60. *The DUPE Primer*, p. 46.

61. Stuart Ewen, *Captains of Consciousness* (N.Y.: McGraw Hill, 1976), pp.39, 34.

62. *ADLF*, p. 341.

63. *U.S. News and World Report*, "1976 Study of American Opinion," (Washington D.C.: U.S. News and World Report, 1976), p. 5.

64. See Gabriel Kolko, *The Triumph of Conservatism* (N.Y.: Free Press, 1963).

Chapter 10

1. *The Gospel According to DUPE*, p. 14.

2. Quoted from workshop on economics with autoworkers in New Jersey, 1980.

3. *The DUPE Film Guide*, "Organization," p. 7; and "Innovations," p. 7.

4. Quoted in Silk and Vogel, *Ethics and Profits op. cit.*, p. 91.

5. Based on Peter Meyer, "Land Rush," *Harper's*, January 1979, p. 54.

6. *Ibid.*, p. 54.

7. *ERP*, Table B-86.

8. This is based on earlier calculations by the President's Council of Economic Advisers of "potential GNP" before revisions in 1976 and 1978. These revisions were based on artificial assumptions about changes in the character of the labor force which seem to us to be unwarranted.

9. *New York Times*, August 13, 1981, p. B-6.

10. *New York Times*, October 27, 1980, p. D-4.

11. *New York Times*, August 27, 1977.

12. Estimate based on David M. Gordon, "Unions in a Vise," *New York Times*, July 19, 1979.

13. *New York Times*, July 10, 1979, p. C-10.

14. *SAUS, Table, 942; and* Moses Abramowitz, *Inventories and Business Cycles* (N.Y.: National Bureau of Economic Research, 1950).

15. This estimate is based on the facts in the previous sentence: 20% times 40% equals 8%.

16. *HSUS*, Series K109-153.

17. This is supported by comparing rates of capacity utilization, in *ERP*, Table, B-86, with data on the government's "full employment budget surplus"—the level of government surplus or deficit controlling for the business cycle—available from the President's Council of Economic Advisers.

18. Meyer, "Land Rush," *op. cit.*, p. 49.

19. Warner and Swasey Company, *1776-1976: What has really changed?* (Cleveland: Warner and Swasey Company, 1976), p. 80.

20. Based on *Business Week*, March 28, 1977, pp. 78-82.

21. Based on Richard Edwards, *Contested Terrain: The Transormation of the Workplae in the Twentieth Century* (N.Y.: Basic Books, 1979), p. 156; and David Jenkins, *Job Power* (Baltimore: Penguin

Books, 1974), pp. 314-15.

22. For a summary of these studies see Paul Blumberg, *Industrial Democracy: The Sociology of Participation* (N.Y.: Schocken Books, 1973), pp. 124-28.

23. Jenkins, *op. cit.* p. 291.

24. Based on *SAUS*, Table 697.

25. *ADLF*, p. 376.

26. Blumberg, *Industrial Democracy, op. cit.*, p. 270.

27. See "The Costs of Nuclear Power," *Dollars and Sense*, April 1978, p. 12; and *New York Times*, April 11, 1978.

28. Quoted in Ray Reece, *The Sun Betrayed* (Boston: South End Press, 1979), p. 155.

29. Barry Commoner, *The Poverty of Power* (N.Y.: Knopf, 1976), Chapters 7 & 8.

30. John Z. De Lorean, "A Look Inside G.M." in Mark Green and Robert Massie, Jr., eds., *The Big Business Reader* (N.Y.: The Pilgrim Press, 1980), p. 39.

31. Figures on MacDonalds from *Nutrition Action*, June 1979, p. 10. Aggregate data from *SAUS*, Table 1016.

32. F. Fisher, Z. Griliches, and C Kaysen, "The Costs of Automobile Changes Since 1949," *Journal of Political Economy*, October 1962.

33. *New York Times*, July 11, 1979.

34. Ralph Nader et. al., *Taming of the Giant Corporation* (N.Y.: W.W. Norton, 1976), pp. 218-19.

35. Data and comparisons from "Public Systems Provide Consumers Lower Cost Power," *Public Power*, July-August 1976, pp. 18-20; and "Public Power Costs Less," *Public Power*, May-June 1981, pp. 14-16.

36. For the general point, see John Blair, *Economic Concentration* (N.Y.: Harcourt Brace Jovanovich, 1972), Chapters 9-10. Quote from former GE executive from Nader et al., *op. cit.* p. 221.

37. *Ibid.* p. 222.

38. *The DUPE Booklet*, p. 20.

39. See Blair, *Economic Concentration, op. cit.*, p. 576ff.

40. *Ibid.* p. 504.

41. See studies reported in Blair, *Economic Concentration, op. cit.*, Ch. 18.

42. Quoted in Mark Green, *Winning Back America* (N.Y.: Bantam Books, 1982), p. 29.

43. See Jeffrey Sachs, "The Changing Cyclical Behavior of Wages and Prices: 1890-1976," *American Economic Review*, March 1980.

44. See Howard Wachtel and Peter Adelsheim, "How Recession Feeds Inflation: Price Mark-Ups in a Concentrated Economy," *Challenge*, Sept.-Oct. 1977.

45. Edward Herman, *Corporate Control, Corporate Power*, (N.Y.: Cambidge University Press, 1981), p. 408, note #134.

Chapter Eleven

1. Quoted in Daniel M. Berman, *Death on the Job* (N.Y.: Monthly Review Press, 1978), pp. 2-3.

2. Quoted in Barry Commoner, *The Closing Circle* (N.Y.: Knopf, 1972), p. 9.

3. *The DUPE Film Guide*, "People," p. 8.

4. Quoted in Rachel Scott, *Muscle and Blood* (N.Y.: Dutton, 1974), p. 113.

5. Quoted in Emma Rothschild, *Paradise Lost* (N.Y.: Vintage, 1974), p. 119.

6. Figures presented and justified in Les Boden and David Wegman, "Increasing OSHA's Clout: Sixty Million New Inspectors," *Working Papers*, May-June 1978.

7. This figure is based on the midpoint of the estimated 120,000-200,000 per year, from *Ibid.*

8. For these data, see the annual series of reports by the U.S. Bureau of Statistics, *Occupational Injuries and Illnesses*. The data cited in the text come from *Ibid.* 1977, Report 561.

9. See Nicholas Ashford, *Crisis in the Work-place* (Cambridge: MIT Press, 1976), p. 93.

10. This is derived by summing injuries (equal to 5.3 million) plus the mid-point of the disease estimate (equal to 700,000) and dividing that by the total number of minutes in the year.

11. Quoted in Berman, *Death on the Job, op. cit.*, p. 108.

12. Quoted in Scott, *Muscle and Blood, op. cit.* p. 57.

13. Berman, *Death on the Job, op. cit.*, p. 44.

14. Cited in *New York Times*, October 3, 1977, p. 1.

15. *Ibid.* p. 22.

16. Survey cited in Boden and Wegman, "Increasing OSHA's Clout....," *op. cit.*

17. Berman, *Death on the Job op. cit.* p. 71.

18. These numbers are based on an estimate of the current average output per hour of production workers multiplied times the total number of hours lost per year as a result of injuries and illness on the job.

19. U.S. Senate Committee on Labor, *Hearings on Occupational Safety and Health Act, 91st Congress, 1st Session, 1971.* Vol. 113, p. 384.

20. See National Coal Board, *Annual Report, 1967-68*, Figure 1.

21. Joseph A. Page and Mary-Win O'Brien, *Bitter Wages* (N.Y.: Grossman, 1973), pp. 59-60.

22. Hearings on Occupational Safety and Health Act, *op. cit.* Vol. 114, p. 1009.

23. U.S. House Committee on Education and Labor, *Hearings on Occupational Safety and Health Act, 91st Congress, 1st Session, 1971*, Vol. 106, pp. 886-87.

24. See Paul Brodeur, *Expendable Americans* (N.Y.: Viking, 1974); and *New York Times*, July 15, 1979.

25. David Neustadt, "Did Mike McDermott Die in Vain?" *Village Voice*, January 7, 1980, pp. 11-12.

26. Cited in Jeanne M. Stellman and Susan M. Daum, *Work Is Dangerous to Your Health* (N.Y.: Vintage Books, 1973), pp. xiv-xv.

27. Quoted in Berman, *Death on the Job, op. cit.* p. 104.

28. Accident rate data based on data transformations of official government data. Method reported in Michele I. Naples and David M. Gordon, "Creating a Continuous Accident Rate Series," Institute for Labor Education and Research, December 1981.

29. Glora Emerson, "Sucking Dust," *Village Voice*, July 16, 1979, pp. 11ff.

30. These are Gallup Poll results reported in *Work in America* (Cambridge: MIT Press, 1973), p. 14.

31. *Ibid.* p. 15.

32. *Ibid.* p. 9.

33. *Ibid.* p. 16.

34. Work in America Institute, *World of Work Report*, February 1979, p. 14.

35. Graham Staines, "Is Worker Dissatisfaction Rising?" *Challenge*, May-June 1979.

36. Cited in *Work in America, op. cit.* pp. 79-81.

37. Arthur Kornhauser, *Mental Health of the Industrial Worker* (N.Y.: Wiley, 1965).

38. *Work in America, op. cit.* p. 13.

39. Reported in Jeremy Rifkin, *Own Your Own Job* (N.Y.: Bantam, 1977), p. 137.

40. Quoted in David Jenkins, *Job Power, op. cit.* p. 325.

41. Quoted in Rothschild, *Paradise Lost, op. cit.* p. 163.

42. Lester C. Thurow and Robert E.B. Lucas, *The American Distribution of Income: A Structural Problem.* Study for the Joint Economic Committee. (Washington, D.C.: U.S. Government Printing Office, 1972), Appendix Tables.

43. Transcript of a class for oil and chemical workers, New Brunswick, N.J., 1975.

44. Warner and Swasey Company, *1776-1976: What Has Really Changed?* (Cleveland: Warner and Swasey, 1976), p. 87.

45. Quoted in Michael H. Brown, "Love Canal, U.S.A.," *New York Times Magazine*, January 21, 1979, p. 23.

46. Based on Commoner, *The Closing Circle, op. cit.* p. 167; and *New York Times*, June 30, 1980.

47. See *New York Times*, August 13, 1981, p. B-6.

48. Rothschild, *Paradise Lost, op. cit.* p. 8.

49. See Ashford, *Crisis in the Workplace, op. cit.* p. 94.

50. Quoted in Irving Sax, *Industrial Pollution* (N.Y.: Van Nostrand Reinhold, 1974), p. 118.

51. Ashford, *Crisis in the Workplace, op. cit.* pp. 94-96.

52. *Loc. cit.*

53. Reported in *The Medical Bulletin*, Summer 1976, p. 40.

54.

55. Based on William Tucker, "The Good Earth Pesticide," *New Times*, August 21, 1978.

56. Based on Bradford Snell, "American Ground Transport," Report to the U.S. Senate Subcommittee on Antitrust and Monopoly of the Judiciary Committee, 1974.

57. Quoted in Michael H. Brown, *Laying Waste* (N.Y.: Pantheon, 1980), p. 96.

58. Quoted in Brown, "Love Canal, U.S.A.," *op. cit.* p. 44.

59. *New York Times*, February 27, 1980.

60. *Ibid.*

Chapter 12

1. Quoted in Leonard Silk and David Vogel, *Ethics and Profits: The Crisis of Confidence in American Business* (N.Y.: Simon and Schuster, 1976), p. 167.

2. *ADLF*, p. 205.

3. *The Gospel According to DUPE*, p. 2.

4. Bertolt Brecht, "Those Who Take Meat From the Table," in Brecht, *Selected Poems*, (N.Y.: Grove Press, 1959), Translated by H.R. Hays.

5. Quoted in Andrew Levison, *The Working Class Majority* (N.Y.: Penguin, 1974), pp. 71-72.

6. Quoted in David Jenkins, *Job Power* (Baltimore: Penguin, 1973), p. 325.

7. Quoted in Staughton Lynd, *Labor Law for the Rank and Filer* (San Pedro, Ca.: Singlejack Books, 1978).

8. Robert Georgine, "The Modern Art of Union Busting," in Mark Green and Robert Massie Jr., eds., *Big Business Reader* (N.Y.: The Pilgrim Press, 1980), p. 91.

9. *The Economist*, November 17, 1979, p. 39.

10. *Ibid.* p. 46.

11. *Fortune*, July 31, 1978, p. 82.

12. All the examples are drawn from Lynd, *Labor Law...*, *op. cit.*

13. *New York Times*, July, 1, 1979, p. F-3.

14. *Ibid.*

15. *Ibid.*

16. Ralph Nader, et. al., *Taming the Giant Corporation* (N.Y.: W.W. Norton, 1976), p. 158.

17. *New York Times*, July 2, 1979, p. B-10.

18. Agreement between General Motors and the United Automobile Workers, November 22, 1976, Paragraph 8, p. 13.

19. Interview with official of the United Autoworkers, November 1980, Institute for Labor Education and Research.

20. Quoted in Lee Rainwater, *What Money Buys: Inequality and the Social Meanings of Income* (N.Y.: Basic Books, 1974), p. 68.

21. *ADLF*, p. 43.

22. See Lawrence Goodwin, *Democratic Promise: The Populist Movement in America* (N.Y.: Oxford Univ. Press, 1976).

23. See Frances Moore Lappe and Joseph Collins, *Food First: Beyond the Myth of Scarcity* (N.Y.: Ballantine Books, 1978), rev. ed.

24. *Business Week*, April 4, 1977, p. 104.
25. *Ibid.* p. 104.
26. Cited in D. Yankelovitch and B. Lefkowitz, "The Public Debate on Growth," unpublished paper, May 1979.
27. Facts cited in *New York Times*, Dec. 27, 1978 and January 18, 1979, p. A-19.
28. The Consumers' Union, "The Rise of Business Lobbying," in Green and Massie, *Big Business Reader, op. cit.* p. 260.
29. *Ibid.* p. 263.
30. Alan Wolfe, *The Seamy Side of Democracy: Repression in America* (N.Y.: Longman, 1978) 2nd ed., p. 24.
31. *Ibid.* p. 24; and William Appleman Williams, *Americans in a Changing World* (N.Y.: Harper and Row, 1978), p. 47.
32. From material supplied by the Political Rights Defense Fund, P.O. Box 649, Cooper Station, New York, N.Y., 10003. See in particular "What the FBI Spies Did in Social Workers Party v. Attorney General."
33. Judge Thomas P. Grisea, *Opinion*, United States District Court, Southern District of New York, 73 Civ. 3160, June 30, 1978.
34. *New York Times*, October 27, 1980; and *St. Louis Post Dispatch*, October 28, 1980.
35. Jeffrey Reiman, *The Rich Get Richer and the Poor Get Prison: Ideology, Class, and Criminal Justice* (N.Y.: Wiley, 1979), pp. 95ff.
36. *New York Times*, July 15, 1979, p. 29.
37. *Ibid.*
38. *Ibid.*
39. David Wise, *The American Police State: The Government Against the People* (N.Y.: Vintage, 1978), p. 399.
40. *Ibid.* pp. 399-400.
41. Quoted in Wolfe, *Seamy Side of Democracy, op. cit.* p. 93.
42. Joseph A. Pechman, "The Distribution of Federal and State Income Taxes by Income Classes," *Journal of Finance*, May 1972.
43. Union for Radical Political Economics, *Taxes for the Rich and the Rest* (N.Y.: URPE, 1979), p. 14. Pamphlet available from URPE, 41 Union Sq. West, Room 901, N.Y., N.Y., 10003.
44. *Ibid.* p. 16.
45. *Ibid.* p. 9.
46. See David Moberg, "Shuttered Factories, Shattered Communities," *In These Times*, June 27, 1979.
47. See Holly Sklar, ed., *Trilateralism* (Boston: South End Press, 1980).
48. *ADLF*, p. 340.
49. Quoted in Arthur MacEwan, "Capitalist Expansion and the Sources of Imperialism," in Edwards, et. al., eds., *The Capitalist System* (Englewood Cliffs, N.J.: Prentice Hall, 1978), 2nd. ed., p. 486.
50. Wolfe, *Seamy Side of Democracy, op. cit.* p. x.
51. *Ibid.* p. xi.
52. Data based on reports from Amnesty International, particularly *Report 1978* and *1980* (London: Amnesty International Publications).
53. Noam Chomsky and Edward S. Herman, *The Washington Connection and Third World Fascism* (Boston: South End Press, 1979), pp. 25-26.
54. For a general survey, see William Appleman Williams, *Empire as a Way of Life* (N.Y.: Oxford University Press, 1980); and Richard Barnet and Ronald Muller, *Global Reach* (N.Y.: Simon and Schuster, 1975).
55. Quoted in Williams, *Americans in a Changing World, op. cit.*, p. 372.
56. Quoted in Jack Anderson, "Profits Before People," *Washington Post*, September 18, 1974.
57. *New York Times*, September 22, 1980, pp. D-1, D-7.
58. *New York Times*, December 7, 1979, p. A-8.
59. *Ibid.*
60. *Ibid.*

61. *Ibid.*
62. Quoted in Alan Wolfe, *The Limits of Legitimacy: Political Contradictions of Contemporary Capitalism* (N.Y.: The Free Press, 1977), p. 329.
63. See Howard Zinn, *A People's History of the United States* (N.Y.: Harper Colophon Books, 1980), pp 209ff.
64. Quoted in *Ibid.* pp. 94-95.
65. Quoted in *Ibid.* p. 215.
66. Quoted in Wolfe, *The Limits of Legitimacy, op. cit.* p. 57.
67. *Ibid.* p. 67.
68. Quoted in Alice and Staughton Lynd, *Rank and File: Personal Histories of Working-Class Organizers* (Boston: Beacon Press, 1973), pp. 114, 115, 116.

Introduction to Part IV

1. Studs Terkel, *Working* (N.Y.: Avon Books, 1974), pp. 643, 646, 642, 643.
2. *ADLF*, p. 205.

Chapter 13

1. Quoted in Barbara Garson, *All the Livelong Day* (NY.: Penguin, 1977), p. 3.
2. Studs Terkel, *Working* (N.Y.: Avon, 1974), p. 102.
3. Quoted in Richard Sennett and Jonathan Cobb, *Hidden Injuries of Class* (N.Y.: Knopf, 1972), pp. 99, 100.
4. See "Who Are the Rest of Us" in "Why We Need This Book" for documentation of this estimate.
5. See Chapter One.
6. See Lester C. Thurow, *Generating Inequality* (N.Y.: Basic Books, 1975).
7. Wealth data adjusted for average number of people in wealthy households, *SAUS*, Tables 787, 788.
8. Many of the conclusions reported in this chapter are based on separate tabulations prepared by John Evansohn of the Institute for Labor Education and Research from the data files for the 1977 Quality of Work Survey by the Institute for Social Research, University of Michigan. These tabulations will hereafter be cited as *QWS*. Where supporting data are also published in the tabulation of that survey, *Quality of Worklife, 1977* (Ann Arbor: Institute for Social Research, 1979), we refer to those as *QWS** with the page reference.
9. *QWS**, p. 175.
10. *Ibid.* pp. 81, 85.
11. *Ibid.* pp. 194-95.
12. *Ibid.* p. 177.
13. *Ibid.* pp. 241, 244.
14. *Ibid.* p. 178.
15. Quoted in Jeremy Brecher and Tim Costello, *Common Sense for Hard Times* (N.Y.: Two Continents, 1975), p. 68.
16. Quoted in Garson, *All the Livelong Day, op. cit.* pp. 155, 156.
17. Terkel, *Working, op. cit.* pp. 359. 360.
18. *Ibid.* p. 458.
19. *Ibid.* p. 612.
20. *Ibid.* p. 453.
21. *Ibid.* p. 5.
22. Poll results based on Jeremy Rifkin, *op. cit.* pp. 128, 130, 136, 137, 138, 141.
23. Quoted in Brecher and Costello, *Common Sense..., op. cit.* p. 152.
24. *ADLF*, p. 74.
25. Lester R. Bittel, *What Every Supervisor Should Know* (N.Y.: McGraw-Hill, 1974), 3rd ed., pp. 286, 288.
26. See David M. Gordon, "Segmentation by the Numbers," unpublished paper, New School for Social Research, 1982.
27. This box and the subsequent summaries in the following sections are based on method and

tabulations reported in *Ibid.* See also David M. Gordon, *The Working Poor* (Washington D.C.: Council of State Planning Agencies, 1980).
28. See Work in America Institute, *World of Work Report*, February 1979.
29. Terkel, *Working, op. cit.* pp. 639, 640, 642.
30. *Ibid.* pp. 49, 50, 52.
31. *QWS*.
32. Reported in Richard Edwards, *Contested Terrain: The Transformation of the Workplace in the Twentieth Century* (N.Y.: Basic Books, 1979), p. 175.
33. *QWS**, pp. 30, 203.
34. *Ibid.* p. 194.
35. *Ibid.* p. 178.
36. *Work in America, op. cit.* p. 16.
37. Joan Greenbaum, *In the Name of Efficiency* (Philadelphia: Temple University Press, 1979), p. 151.
38. Quoted in Samuel Bowles and Herbert Gintis, *Schooling in Capitalist America* (N.Y.: Basic Books, 1975), p. 193.
39. Quoted in David Noble, *America By Design* (N.Y.: Knopf, 1977), p. 44.
40. Quoted in Edwards, *Contested Terrain, op. cit.* p. 138.
41. Terkel, *Working, op. cit.* pp. 67-68.
42. *QWS*.
43. Gordon, "Segmentation by the Numbers," *op. cit.*
44. *Ibid.*
45. Cited in Edwards, *Contested Terrain, op. cit.* pp. 172, 176. Aggregate conclusion based on *QWS*.
46. Edwards, *op. cit.* pp. 132ff.
47. *QWS*.
48. *Ibid.*
49. *QWS**, pp. 104, 114.
50. Terkel, *Working, op. cit.* p. 387.
51. *Ibid.* pp. 576, 577, 578.
52. Quoted in Garson, *All the Livelong Day, op. cit.* pp. 37, 38-39.
53. *QWS*.
54. See studies reported in Edwards, *Contested Terrain, op. cit.* p. 169; and *QWS*.
55. See summaries in Edwards, *Ibid.* pp. 167ff.
56. See, for instance, reports in *Ibid.* p. 170.
57. *QWS**, pp. 58, 87, and *QWS*.
58. *QWS*.
59. *Ibid.*
60. Lawrence W. Kahn, "Unions and Labor Market Segmentation," unpublished doctoral dissertation, University of California at Berkeley, 1975, especially pp. 112, 113.
61. *ADLF*, p. 422.
62. See Eli Zaretsky, "Capitalism, the Family, and Personal Life: Part 2," *Socialist Revolution*, No. 15, May-June 1973,
63. *ADLF*, p. 119.
64. See Michael Reich, "Evolution of the Wage-Labor Force," in Edwards et. al., eds., *The Capitalist System* (Englewood Cliffs, N.J.: Prentice Hall, 1978), 2nd edition, p. 185.
65. See summaries in Sennett and Cobb, *Hidden Injuries of Class, op. cit.*; and Peter Blau and Otis Dudley Duncan, *The American Occupational Structure* (N.Y.: Wiley, 1967).
66. Based on tabulations reported in Gordon, "Segmentation by the Numbers," *op. cit.*
67. *Ibid.*

Chapter 14

1. Quoted in Thomas C. Wheeler, ed., *The Immigrant Experience: The Anguish of Becoming American* (N.Y.: Penguin, 1971), p. 2.
2. June Namias, *First Generation: In the Words of Twentieth-Century American Immigrants* (Boston: Beacon Press, 1978), p. 43.
3. *Ibid.*, pp. 194, 195.
4. Quoted in J. Joseph Huthmacher, *A Nation of*

Newcomers: Ethnic Minority Groups in American History (N.Y.: Dell, 1967), p. 108.

5. Quoted in Howard Zinn, *A People's History of the United States* (N.Y.: Harper Colophon Books, 1980), pp. 129-130.

6. Kathleen Wright, *The Other Americans: Minorities in American History* (Greenwich, Ct.: Fawcett, 1969), p. 14.

7. Cited in *ibid.*, p. 17.

8. Oscar Handlin, ed., *Immigration as a Factor in American History* (Englewood Cliffs, N.J.: Prentice-Hall, 1959), p. 8.

9. *HSUS*, Series A119.

10. Richard B. Morris, *Government and Labor in Early America* (N.Y.: Harper Torchbooks, 1965), pp. 315-316.

11. Richard B. Morris, "The Emergence of American Labor," in U.S. Department of Labor, *The American Worker* (Washington, D.C.: U.S. Government Printing Office, 1976), p. 31.

12. These and the subsequent data for Figures 14.2-14.4 come from summations of country totals in *HSUS*, Series C89-119. No data are available in that series for years before 1820.

13. Handlin, *Immigration as a Factor...*, *op. cit.*, p. 47.

14. *Ibid.*, p. 48.

15. Quoted in Zinn, *A People's History of the United States*, *op cit.*, p. 218.

16. Namias, *First Generation*, *op. cit.*, pp. 15-16.

17. Quoted in U.S. Department of Labor, *The American Worker*, *op. cit.*, p. 196.

18. Quoted in Wheeler, *The Immigrant Experience*, *op. cit.*, p. 55.

19. Handlin, *Immigration as a Factor...*, *op. cit.*, p. 21.

20. Data and conclusion from David Montgomery, "Labor in the Industrial Era," in the U.S. Department of Labor, *The American Worker*, *op. cit.*, pp. 117-118.

21. Quoted in David Montgomery, *Beyond Inequality: Labor and the Radical Republicans, 1862-1872* (N.Y.: Knopf, 1967), p. 41.

22. Characterizations from Montgomery, "Labor in the Industrial Era," *op. cit.*, p. 114.

23. Handlin, *Immigration as a Factor...*, *op. cit.*, p. 76.

24. Montgomery, *Beyond Inequality*, *op. cit.*, p. 36.

25. Zinn, *A People's History of the United States*, *op. cit.*, p. 282.

26. Handlin, *Immigration as a Factor...*, *op. cit.*, p. 164.

27. Quoted in John R. Commons et al., *History of Labor in the United States* (N.Y.: Macmillan, 1935), Vol. III, p. xxv.

28. Namias, *First Generation*, *op. cit.*, p. 34.

29. U.S. Immigration Commission, *Abstracts of Reports*, (Washington, D.C.: U.S. Government Printing Office, 1911), Vol. I, pp. 531, 538.

30. John Higham, *Strangers in the Land: Patterns of American Nativism, 1860-1925* (N.Y.: Atheneum, 1973), p. 183.

31. *Ibid.*, pp. 184-186.

32. Wheeler, *The Immigrant Experience*, *op. cit.*, p. 152.

33. Namias, *First Generation*, *op. cit.*, p. 30.

34. Wheeler, *The Immigrant Experience*, *op. cit.*, p. 111.

ler, *The Immigrant Experience*, *op. cit.*, p. 152.

33. Namias, *First Generation*, *op. cit.*, p. 30.

34. Wheeler, *The Immigrant Experience*, *op. cit.*, p. 111.

35. From Joyce L. Kornbluh, ed., *Rebel Voices: An I.W.W. Anthology* (Ann Arbor: University of Michigan Press, 1968), p.170.

36. Wheeler, *The Immigrant Experience*, *op. cit.*, pp. 104, 105.

37. *ADLF*, p. 10.

38. Wheeler, *The Immigrant Experience*, *op. cit.*, p. 104.

39. See Michael Piore, *Birds of Passage* (New York: Cambridge University Press, 1979).

40. This figure is based on comparisons between the sum of average official immigration during the 1960s and estimated undocumented immigra-

tion, on the one hand, and average official immigration at the turn of the century, on the other. For figures on official immigration, see *HSUS*, Series C89.

41. Wheeler, *The Immigrant Experience*, *op. cit.*, p. 93.

42. Quoted in Daniel Nelson, *Managers and Workers: Origins of the New Factory System in the United States, 1880-1920* (Madison: University of Wisconsin Press, 1975), p. 79.

43. Wheeler, *The Immigrant Experience*, *op. cit.*, pp. 92, 94.

44. From transcript of a class with oil and chemical workers, New Brunswick, N.J., 1975.

45. For data at beginning of century, see Ethel B. Jones, "New Estimates of Hours of Work Per Week and Hourly Earnings, 1900-1957," *Review of Economics and Statistics*, November 1963, p. 375. For subsequent data on hours, 1932 to 1970, see *HSUS*, Series D803.

46. Data comparisons of trends in employment and output based on *HSUS*, Series F3 and D5; and *ETRP*, Table A-1.

47. *ETRP*, Tables A-3, A-19.

48. Quoted in Richard Sennett and Jonathan Cobb, *Hidden Injuries of Class* (N.Y.: Knopf, 1972), pp. 132-33.

49. *ADLF*, p. 87.

50. For range of estimates, see *New York Times*, June 1, 1981.

51. Miguel C., "...And, on Shaky Grounds," *New York Times*, November 11, 1978, p. 23.

52. Julia Preston, "Stalking the Shadow People," *Village Voice*, October 15, 1979.

53. *Ibid.*

54. Namias, *First Generation*, *op. cit.*, p. 29.

55. For example, a boy from one of the 10% most affluent families is almost nine times more likely to rank in the top fifth on IQ scores than a boy from one of the 10% poorest families. See Samuel Bowles and Herbert Gintis, *Schooling in Capitalist America* (N.Y.: Basic Books, 1976), p. 119.

56. *Ibid.*, Table 4-3, p. 121.

57. Based on data in *ibid.*, Figure 4-2.

58. *Ibid.*, pp. 13ff.

59. Christopher Jencks et al., *Who Gets Ahead? The Determinants of Economic Success in America* (N.Y.: Basic Books, 1979), p. 219.

60. Richard C. Edwards, "Individual Traits and Organizational Incentives: What Makes a 'Good' Worker?" *Journal of Human Resources*, Winter 1976.

61. Richard H. de Lone, *Small Futures* (N.Y.: Harcourt Brace Jovanovich, 1979), p. 100.

62. Based on data in Jencks et al., *Who Gets Ahead?*, *op. cit.*, p. 303.

63. *Ibid.*, p. 77.

64. *Ibid.*, p. 157.

65. Quoted in de Lone, *Small Futures*, *op. cit.*, pp.14-15.

66. Quoted in *ibid.*, p. 15.

67. Bowles and Gintis, *Schooling in Capitalist America*, *op. cit.*, p. 88.

68. See David M. Gordon, *The Working Poor* (Washington, D.C.: Council of State Planning Agencies, 1979).

69. Quoted in de Lone, *Small Futures*, *op. cit.*, p. 19.

70. Namias, *First Generation*, *op. cit.*, p. 201.

71. *Ibid.*, p. 184.

Chapter 15

1. Nancy Seifer, *Nobody Speaks for Me! Self-Portraits of American Workng Class Women* (N.Y.: Simon & Schuster, 1976), pp. 279, 289, 278.

2. Based on data reported in David M. Gordon, "Segmentation by the Numbers," unpublished paper, New School for Social Research, 1982.

3. U.S. Bureau of the Census, "Money Income in 1977 of Families and Persons in the United States," *Current Population Reports*, Series P-60, No. 118, March 1979, Table 48.

4. Carl Hegel, ed., *The Foreman's Handbook* (N.Y.:

McGraw-Hill, 1967), 4th ed., p. 264.

5. Seifer, *Nobody Speaks for Me!*, *op. cit.*, p. 435.

6. Nancy Chodorow, "Mothering, Male Dominance, and Capitalism," in Zillah R. Eisenstein, *Capitalist Patriarchy and the Case for Socialist Feminism* (N.Y.: Monthly Review Press, 1979), especially pp. 84-90 and notes.

7. *Ibid.*

8. . *Ibid.*

9. Quoted in Alice Kessler-Harris, "Stratifying by Sex: Understanding the History of Working Women," in R. Edwards et al., eds., *Labor Market Segmentation* (Lexington, Ma.: Lexington Books, 1975), p. 219.

10. From R. Baxandall et al., eds., *America's Working Women: A Documentary History, 1600 to the Present* (N.Y.: Vintage, 1976), p. 15.

11. Philip S. Foner, *Women and the American Labor Movement—From Colonial Times to the Eve of World War I* (N.Y.: The Free Press, 1979), p. 15.

12. *Ibid.*, p. 22.

13. *Ibid.*, p. 35.

14. Quoted in Kessler-Harris, "Stratifying by Sex...," *op. cit.*, p. 223.

15. Quoted in *ibid.*, p. 223.

16. Quoted in John A. Garraty, *The New Commonwealth, 1877-1890* (N.Y.: Harper Torchbooks, 1968), pp. 129-130.

17. Kessler-Harris, "Stratifying by Sex...," *op. cit.*, p. 223.

18. In Baxandall et al., *America's Working Women*, *op. cit.*, p. 91.

19. Quoted in Kessler-Harris, "Stratifying by Sex...," *op. cit.*, p. 225.

20. *HSUS*, Series D11, D17.

21. See Kessler-Harris, "Stratifying by Sex...," *op. cit.*, pp. 224-225.

22. In Baxandall et al., *America's Working Women*, *op. cit.*, p. 108.

23. *HSUS*, Series D11, D17.

24. In Baxandall et al., *America's Working Women*, *op. cit.*, p. 160.

25. In Kessler-Harris, "Stratifying by Sex...," *op. cit.*, p. 229.

26. HSUS, Series D55.

27. See Robert W. Smuts, *Women and Work in America* (N.Y.: Cambridge Univ. Press, 1959), pp. 12ff.

28. See Heidi Hartmann, "Capitalism and Women's Work in the Home, 1900-1930," unpublished doctoral dissertation, Yale Univ., 1974.

29. In Baxandall et al., *America's Working Women*, *op. cit.*, p. 160.

30. In *ibid.*, p. 211.

31. See Harry A. Millis and Royal E. Montgomery, *The Economics of Labor* (N.Y.: McGraw-Hill, 1938), Vol. I, pp. 408-409, 415.

32. *HSUS*, Series D182-232; and David M. Gordon et al., *Segmented Work, Divided Workers: The Historical Transformation of Labor in the United States* (N.Y.: Cambridge Univ. Press, 1982), p. 151.

33. Quoted in Margery Davies, "Women's Place Is at the Typewriter: The Feminization of the Clerical Labor Force," in R. Edwards et al., *Labor Market Segmentation*, *op. cit.*, p. 293.

34. Quoted in Kessler-Harris, "Stratifying by Sex...," *op. cit.*, p. 228.

35. Quoted in Howard Zinn, *A People's History of the United States* (N.Y.: Harper Colophon Books, 1980), p. 337.

36. In Baxandall et al., *America's Working Women*, *op. cit.*, p. 172. For general reference, see Foner, *Women and the American Labor Movement*, *op. cit.*, Chs. 25-27.

37. In Baxandall et al., *America's Working Women*, *op. cit.*, p. 168.

38. In *ibid.*, p. 185.

39. In *ibid.*, p. 218.

40. In Kessler-Harris, "Stratifying by Sex...," *op. cit.*, p. 231.

41. In Baxandall *et al.*, *America's Working Women*, *op. cit.*, p. 387.

42. Employment data from *ETRP*, Table A-1. Participation rates from *HSUS*, Series D11, D17.

43. *HSUS*, Series D11, D17.

44. *HSUS*, Series D51-55, *ETRP*, Table B-2.

45. *HSUS*, Series D220; *ETRP*, Table A-6.

46. This is based on the sum of women's household work plus average annual hours in the labor force. It is a comparison based on hours alone and does not make presuppositions about the relative output per hour of male and female workers.

47. Data reported in National Research Council, National Academy of Sciences, *Women, Work, and Wages: Equal Pay for Jobs of Equal Value* (Washington, D.C.: National Academy Press, 1981), Table 8.

48. Gordon *et al.*, *Segmented Work, Divided Workers*, *op. cit.*, p. 206.

49. Quoted in Jeremy Brecher and Timothy Costello, *Common Sense for Hard Times* (N.Y.: Two Continents, 1975), p. 183.

50. Quoted in *ibid.*, p. 184.

51. In Baxandall *et al.*, *America's Working Women*, *op. cit.*, p. 380.

52. In *ibid.*, p. 361.

53. In *ibid.*, p. 374.

54. Quoted in Lillian Breslow Rubin, *Worlds of Pain: Life in the Working-Class Family* (N.Y.: Harper Colophon Books, 1976), p. 183.

55. See National Research Council, *Women, Work, and Wages*, *op. cit.*, Ch. 2; and Cynthia B. Lloyd and Beth T. Niemi, *The Economics of Sex Differentials* (N.Y.: Columbia Univ. Press, 1979), Ch. 5.

56. See summaries in Mary Stevenson, "Women's Wages and Job Segregation," in R. Edwards *et al.*, *Labor Market Segmentation*, *op. cit.*, p. 244.

57. See *ibid.*, and *Work in America*, *op. cit.*, p. 59.

58. Paul Osterman, "Sex Discrimination in Professional Employment," *Industrial and Labor Relations Review*, July 1979.

59. See Caroline Bird, *Born Female* (N.Y.: Pocket Books, 1969).

60. See Stevenson, "Women's Wages and Job Segregation," *op. cit.*; and Harold Wilensky, "Women's Work: Economic Growth, Ideology, Structure," *Industrial Relations*, May 1968.

61. Quoted in Brecher and Costello, *Common Sense for Hard, Times*, *op. cit.*, p. 186.

62. Studs Terkel, *Working* (N.Y.: Avon Books, 1974), pp. 459, 461-462.

63. *Ibid.*, p. 456.

Chapter 16

1. Quoted in Jeremy Brecher and Timothy Costello, *Common Sense for Hard Times* (N.Y.: Two Continents, 1975), p. 174.

2. Studs Terkel, *Working* (N.Y.: Avon Books, 1974), pp. 31, 32, 37-38.

3. Based on data from David M. Gordon, "Segmentation by the Numbers," unpublished paper, New School for Social Research, 1982.

4. Quoted in Michael Reich, *Racial Inequality: A Political-Economic Analysis* (Princeton, N.J.: Princeton Univ. Press, 1981), p. 10.

5. Quoted in Brecher and Costello, *Common Sense for Hard Times*, *op. cit.*, p. 175.

6. Population data from *World Almanac and Book of Facts, 1982* (N.Y.: Newspaper Enterprise Assoc., Inc., 1981). Blacks have lived in the U.S. as long as whites in the simple sense that some of the first European settlers brought black slaves with them. Black slaves were imported at least as early as 1619. See Howard Zinn, *A People's History of the United States* (N.Y.: Harper Colophon Books, 1980), Ch. 2.

7. *HSUS*, Series A119.

8. August Meier and Elliot Rudwick, *From Plantation to Ghetto* (N.Y.: Hill and Wang, 1970), rev. ed., p. 64.

9. John Hope Franklin, *From Slavery to Freedom: A History of Negro Americans* (N.Y.: Knopf, 1974), 4th ed., p. 144.

10. Meier and Rudwick, *From Plantation to Ghetto*, *op. cit.*, p. 66.

11. Quoted in Thomas Sowell, *Race and Economics* (N.Y.: McKay, 1975), p. 20.

12. *Ibid.*, p. 20.

13. Quoted in Zinn, *A People's History of the United States*, *op. cit.*, p. 170.

14. Quoted in *ibid.*, pp. 171-172.

15. Reich, *Racial Inequality*, *op. cit.*, p. 226.

16. Quoted in Zinn, *A People's History of the United States*, *op. cit.*, p. 204.

17. Reich, *Racial Inequality*, *op. cit.*, p. 232.

18. Quoted in *ibid.*, p. 234.

19. Quoted in *ibid.*, p. 240.

20. Quoted in *ibid.*, p. 243.

21. Quoted in *ibid.*, p. 235.

22. See summary and references in *ibid.*, pp. 237-238.

23. *Ibid.*, p. 63.

24. See David M. Gordon *et al.*, *Segmented Work, Divided Workers: The Historical Transformation of Labor in the United States* (N.Y.: Cambridge Univ. Press, 1982), pp. 152-153.

25. *Loc. cit.*

26. Quoted in Zinn, *A People's History of the United States*, *op. cit.*, p. 321.

27. Quoted in William M. Tuttle, Jr., "Labor Conflict and Racial Violence in Chicago, 1894-1919," *Labor History*, Summer 1969, p. 427.

28. Quoted in Zinn, *A People's History of the United States*, *op. cit.*, p. 321.

29. Reich, *Racial Inequality*, *op. cit.*, p. 257.

30. See, for instance, Irving Bernstein, *Turbulent Years* (Boston: Houghton Mifflin, 1971), pp. 744-745.

31. Reich, *Racial Inequality*, *op. cit.*, pp. 257-258.

32. *Ibid.*, p. 258.

33. William Appleman Williams, *Americans in a Changing World* (N.Y.: Harper & Row, 1978), p. 277.

34. In Thomas C. Wheeler, ed., *The Immigrant Experience: The Anguish of Becoming American* (N.Y.: Penguin, 1971), p. 140.

35. Reich, *Racial Inequality*, *op. cit.*, p. 258.

36. *Ibid.*, pp. 62-65.

37. *ADLF*, p. 193.

38. Reich, *Racial Inequality*, *op. cit.*, p. 51.

39. *Ibid.*, pp. 65-69.

40. *SAUS*, Table 274.

41. U.S. Bureau of the Census, "Money Income in 1977 of Families and Persons in the United States," *Current Population Reports*, Series P-60, No. 118, March 1979, Table 53.

42. See Reich, *Racial Inequality*, *op. cit.*, pp. 31-45.

43. *New York Times*, March 10, 1979.

44. *ADLF*, p. 87.

45. *U.S. News & World Report*, May 22, 1978, p. 61.

46. *Time*, October 16, 1978, p. 58.

47. *Ibid.*, p. 48; and *World Almanac and Book of Facts*, *op. cit.*

48. *Time*, October 16, 1978.

49. *U.S. News & World Report*, May 22, 1978, p. 61. Since writing this chapter, we have come across two additional and very valuable references on hispanics upon which we were not able to draw for this chapter but which seem exceptionally useful: Leobardo F. Estrada *et al.*, "Chicanos in the United States: A History of Exploitation and Resistance"; and Frank Bonilla and Ricardo Campos, "A Wealth of Poor: Puerto Ricans in the New Economic Order," in *Daedalus*, Spring 1981.

50. History Task Force, Centro de Estudios Puertorriquenos, *Labor Migration Under Capitalism: The Puerto Rican Experience* (N.Y.: Monthly Review Press, 1979), p. 121.

51. John Womack, Jr., "The Chicanos," *New York Review of Books*, August 31, 1972, p. 445.

52. *Loc. cit.*

53. *Loc. cit.*

54. Ernesto Galarza, *Barrio Boy* (Notre Dame, Ind.: Univ. of Notre Dame Press, 1971), p. 200.

55. Womack, Jr., "The Chicanos," *op. ct.*, p. 446.

56. History Task Force, *Labor Migration Under Capitalism*, *op. cit.*, pp. 147-148.

57. Paul S. Taylor, "Mexican Labor in the United States: Dimmit County, Winter Garden District, South Texas," in H. Gutman and G. Kenley, ed., *Many Pasts: Readings in American Social History, 1865-The Present* (Englewood Cliffs, N.J.: Prentice-Hall, 1973), Vol. II, p. 336.

58. *Ibid.*, p. 333.

59. John Helmer, *Drugs and Minority Oppression* (N.Y.: Seabury, 1975), p. 73.

60. *Ibid.*, p. 74; and Womack, Jr., "The Chicanos," *op. cit.*, p. 446.

61. *Ibid.*, p. 447.

62. History Task Force, *Labor Migration Under Capitalism*, *op. cit.*, pp. 101, 146, 149.

63. Helmer, *Drugs and Minority Oppression*, *op. cit.*, p. 72.

64. *Ibid.*, p. 73.

65. Wheeler, *The Immigrant Experience*, *op. cit.*, p. 102.

66. Womack, "The Chicanos," *op. cit.*, p. 447.

67. *HSUS*, Series C112; and History Task Force, *Labor Migration Under Capitalism*, *op. cit.*, Table 7.1.

68. *Time*, October 16, 1978, p. 51.

69. U.S. Bureau of the Census, "Population Profile of the United States: 1977," *Current Population Reports*, Series P-20, No. 324, April 1978, p. 55.

70. Employment data based on David M. Gordon, "Segmentation by the Numbers," unpublished paper, New School for Social Research, 1982. Income data from U.S. Bureau of the Census, "Money Income in 1978 of Families and Persons in the United States," *Current Population Reports*, Series P-60, No. 129, November 1981, Table 12.

71. History Task Force, *Labor Migration Under Capitalism*, *op. cit.*, Chs. 5, 8.

72. Galarza, *Barrio Boy*, *op. cit.*, p. 263.

73. Kathleen Wright, *The Other Americans: Minorities in American History* (Greenwich, Ct.: Fawcett, 1971), p. 237.

74. *Time*, October 16, 1978, p. 61.

75. U.S. Bureau of the Census, "Persons of Spanish Origin in the United States: March 1978 (Advance Report)," *Current Population Reports*, Series P-20, No. 328, August 1978, Table 10.

76. U.S. Department of Housing and Urban Development, "How Well Are We Housed? 1. Hispanics" (Washington, D.C.: U.S. Government Printing Office, 1978).

77. Terkel, *Working*, *op. cit.*, pp. 37, 38.

78. Quoted in Richard Sennett and Jonathan Cobb, *Hidden Injuries of Class* (N.Y.: Knopf, 1972), p. 135.

79. See Stanley Masters, *Black-White Income Differentials* (N.Y.: Academic Press, 1975), Ch. 5.

80. Christopher Jencks, *Who Gets Ahead? The Determinants of Economic Success in America* (N.Y.: Basic Books, 1979), p. 199.

81. Averages from *ibid.*, p. 206.

82. Reich, *Racial Inequality*, *op. cit.*, Ch. 2, for summary on changes in attitudes.

83. Richard H. de Lone, *Small Futures* (N.Y.: Harcourt Brace Jovanovich, 1979), pp. 124-125.

84. *Ibid.*, p. 124.

85. See Gordon, "Segmentation by the Numbers," *op. cit.*

86. de Lone, *Small Futures*, *op. cit.*, p. 129.

87. *Loc. cit.*

88. For one review of research supporting this conclusion, see Barry Krisberg and James Austin, *The Children of Ishmael: Critical Perspectives on Juvenile Justice* (Palo Alto, Ca.: Mayfield, 1978), pp. 87-105.

89. *New York Times*, November 10, 1979, emphasis added.

90. See Reich, *Racial Inequality*, *op. cit.*, Ch. 4.

91. Quoted in Brecher and Costello, *Common Sense for Hard Times, op. cit.*, p. 172.
92. *ADLF*, p. 92.

Chapter 17

1. Philip Foner, *History of the Labor Movement in the United States* (N.Y.: International Publishers, 1947), Vol. I, p. 117.
2. Quoted in Harry C. Boyte, *The Backyard Revolution: Understanding the New Citizen Movement* (Philadelphia: Temple Univ. Press, 1980), p. 32.
4. Quoted in U.S. Department of Labor, *The American Worker, op. cit.*, p. 245.
5. See *ibid.*, pp. 20ff.; and Foner *History of the Labor Movement..., Vol. I, op. cit.*, Chs. 1-3.
6. Quoted in David Montgomery, "The Working Classes in New Industrial Cities in the U.S., 1800-1840," *Labor History*, Fall 1968, p. 362.
7. Quoted in Foner, *History of the Labor Movement..., op. cit.*, p. 101.
8. For general history, see *ibid.*, Vol. I, Chs. 7-8.
9. Quoted in *ibid.*, p. 117.
10. Quoted in *ibid.*, p. 118.
11. Quoted in *ibid.*, p. 111.
12. Quoted in *ibid.*, p. 116.
13. Quoted in Oscar Handlin, "Boston's Immigrants: The Economic Adjustment," in P. Kramer and F. Holborn, eds., *The City in American Life* (N.Y.: Putnam, 1970), p. 91.
14. David Montgomery, *Beyond Equality: Labor and the Radical Republicans* (N.Y.: Knopf, 1967), pp. 323-324.
15. These accounts are based on Jeremy Brecher, *Strike! The True History of Mass Insurgency from 1877 to the Present* (San Francisco: Straight Arrow Books, 1972), Chs. 1-2.
16. Quoted in *ibid.*, p. 21.
17. Quoted in *ibid.*, p. 43.
18. Quoted in *ibid.*, p. 45.
19. U.S. Industrial Commission, *Abstracts of Reports* (Washington, D.C.: U.S. Government Printing Office, 1911), Vol. I, pp. 531, 538.
20. *HSUS*, Series D 942.
21. Joyce L Kornbluh, ed., *Rebel Voices: An I.W.W. Anthology* (Ann Arbor: Univ. of Michigan Press, 1968), p. 177.
22. See Brecher, *Strike!, op. cit.*, pp. 104ff.
23. Quoted in *ibid.*, p. 114.
24. Quoted in Irving Bernstein, *Turbulent Years* (Boston: Houghton Mifflin, 1971), p. 746. Conclusion on bargaining victories is from *ibid.*, p. 775.
25. Quoted in Brecher, *Strike!, op. cit.*, p. 203, emphasis in original.
26. Studs Terkel, *Working* (N.Y.: Avon, 1974), pp. 260, 265.
27. Quoted in Andrew Levison, *The Working-Class Majority* (N.Y.: Penguin, 1974), p. 118.
28. Quoted in Boyte, *The Backyard Revolution, op. cit.*, prepublication manuscript, Ch. 1, p. 18.
29. Pauline Maier, "Popular Uprisings and Civil Authority in Eighteenth-Century America," in B.W. Cooke et al., eds., *Past Imperfect: Alternative Essays in American History* (N.Y.: Knopf, 1973), Vol. I, p. 43.
30. Quoted in *ibid.*, p. 48.
31. Howard Zinn, *A People's History of the United States* (N.Y.: Harper Colophon Books, 1980), p. 62.
32. Quoted in Page Smith, *A New Age Now Begins: A People's History of the American Revolution* (N.Y.: McGraw-Hill, 1976), Vol. I, p. 684.
33. Quoted in Zinn, *A People's History of the United States, op. cit.*, p. 94.
34. *Ibid.*, pp. 90-91.
35. Quoted in *ibid.*, p. 94.
36. Quoted in *ibid.*, p. 91.
37. See J.G. Williamson and P.H. Lindert, *American Inequality* (N.Y.: Academic Press, 1980).
38. Quoted in Walter Hugins, *Jacksonian Democracy and the Working Class* (Palo Alto, Ca.: Stanford Univ. Press, 1960), pp. 194, 197.

39. *Ibid., passim.*
40. *Ibid.*, p. 217.
41. Quoted in *ibid.*, p. 218
42. Quoted in Blanche Weisen Cook, "In Pursuit of Property: The Dispossession of the American Indian," in Cook *et al., Past Imperfect, op. cit.*, Vol. I, p. 202.
43. Quoted in Aileen S. Kraditor, "The Woman Question," in *ibid.*, Vol. I, p. 258.
44. Quoted in Zinn, *A People's History of the United States, op. cit.*, p. 122.
45. Sam Bass Warner, Jr., *The Urban Wilderness* (N.Y.: Harper & Row, 1972), pp. 80-81.
46. John Garraty, *The New Commonwealth, 1877-1890* (N.Y.: Harper Torchbooks, 1968), p. 52.
47. Summarized in Zinn, *A People's History of the United States, op. cit.*, p. 267.
48. Summarized in Eric Goldman, "From the Bottom Up," in Cook *et al., Past Imperfect, op. cit.*, Vol. II, pp. 60-63.
49. Quoted in *ibid.*, p. 62.
50. Quoted in *ibid.*, p. 63.
51. Frances Fox Piven and Richard Cloward, *Poor People's Movements* (N.Y.: Pantheon, 1979), p. 54.
52. Quoted in Zinn, *A People's History of the United States, op. cit.*, p. 384.
53. Quoted in Jeremy Brecher and Timothy Costello, *Common Sense for Hard Times* (N.Y.: Two Continents, 1975), p. 140.
54. Quoted in Zinn, *A People's History of the United States, op. cit.*, p. 443.
55. Quoted in Harry C. Boyte, *The Backyard Revolution, op. cit.*, prepublication manuscript, Ch. 1, p. 28.

Introduction to Part V

1. Quoted in *Newsweek*, May 29, 1978, p. 69.
2. Quoted in the *New York Times*, June 5, 1978, p. D-4.

Chapter 18

1. Transcripts from class for oil and chemical workers, New Brunswick, N.J., 1975.
2. Quoted in Lee Rainwater, *What Money Buys: Inequality and the Social Meanings of Income* (N.Y.: Basic Books, 1974), p. 81.
3. Quoted in William Appleman Williams, *Americans in a Changing World* (N.Y.: Harper & Row, 1978), p. 385.
4. Studs Terkel, *Hard Times: An Oral History of the Great Depression* (N.Y.: Pocket Books, 1970), p. 176.
5. *HSUS*, Series F4.
6. *HSUS*, Series D25-26.
7. *HSUS*, Series F26, G856.
8. *HSUS*, Series X741, X748, and X689.
9. *HSUS*, Series B166.
10. Quoted in Jeremy Brecher, *Strike! The True History of Mass Insurgency from 1877 to the Present* (San Francisco: Straight Arrow Books, 1972), p. 144. For general histories of these efforts, see Brecher, *ibid.*, Ch. 5; and Frances Fox Piven and Richard Cloward, *Poor People's Movements* (N.Y.: Pantheon, 1979), Ch. 2.
11. Irving Bernstein, *The Lean Years: A History of the American Worker, 1920-1933* (Boston: Houghton Mifflin, 1960), p. 421.
12. *Ibid.*, pp. 421-422.
13. Alice and Staughton Lynd, *Rank and File: Personal Histories of Working-Class Organizers* (Boston: Beacon, 1973), p. 155.
14. Quoted in Williams, *Americans in a Changing World, op. cit.*, p. 284.
15. Terkel, *Hard Times, op. cit.*, p. 317.
16. *Ibid.*, p. 310.
17. *Ibid.*, p. 310.
18. Quoted in Alan Wolfe, *The Limits of Legitimacy: Political Contradictions of Contemporary Capitalism* (N.Y.: The Free Press, 1977), p. 129.
19. Quoted in *ibid.*, p. 130.
20. Quoted in Williams, *Americans in a Changing World, op. cit.*, p. 291.

21. Quoted in *ibid.*, p. 311.
22. Quoted in *ibid.*, p. 301.
23. *HSUS*, Series D927, D940.
24. Lynds, *Rank and File, op. cit.*, pp. 268-269.
25. See David M. Gordon *et al., Segmented Work, Divided Workers: The Historical Transformation of Labor in the United States* (N.Y.: Cambridge Univ. Press, 1982), Ch. 5.
26. On grievance procedures, see Irving Bernstein, *The Turbulent Years: A History of the American Worker, 1933-1941* (Boston: Houghton Mifflin, 1971), pp. 775-776. On seniority systems, see Sumner Slichter, *Union Policies and Industrial Management* (Washington, D.C.: Brookings Institution, 1941), pp. 105-107.
27. Lynds, *Rank and File, op. cit.*, pp. 108-109.
28. *Ibid.*, pp. 101-102.
29. Quoted in Williams, *Americans in a Changing World, op. cit.*, p. 263.
30. Bernstein, *Turbulent Years, op. cit.*, p. 790.
31. Brecher, *Strike!, op. cit.*, p. 213.
32. Franklin D. Roosevelt, *Rendezvous with Destiny: Addresses and Opinions* (N.Y.: Dryden, 1944), ed. by J.B.S. Hardman, pp. 113, 116.
33. On war-time preparations, see Williams, *Americans in a Changing World, op. cit.*, pp. 305ff.
34. *HSUS*, Series F4.
35. *HSUS*, Series F26.
36. *HSUS*, Series D85-86.
37. Quoted in Williams, *Americans in a Changing World, op. cit.*, p. 340.
38. Quoted in *ibid.*, p. 314.
39. Brecher, *Strike!, op. cit.*, p. 223.
40. Quoted in *ibid.*, p. 226.
41. Quoted in *ibid.*, p. 227.
42. Lynds, *Rank and File, op. cit.*, pp. 144-145.
43. *Ibid.*, p. 104.
44. Quoted in Wolfe, *Limits of Legitimacy, op. cit.*, p. 176.
45. Lynds, *Rank and File, op. cit.*, p. 190.
46. Quoted in Williams, *Americans in a Changing World, op. cit.*, p. 339.
47. See Charles P. Kindelberger, *World Depression, 1929-1939* (Berkeley, Ca.: Univ. of California Press, 1974), Ch. 1.
48. William Ashworth, *A Short History of the International Economy Since 1850* (London: Longmans, Green, 1962), 2nd. ed., p. 259, emphasis added.
49. Edward P. Denison, *Why Growth Rates Differ* (Washington, D.C.: Brookings Institution, 1967), p. 23.
50. Data for figure from *HSUS*, Series U15, deflated by GNP deflator from *HSUS*, Series F5.
51. Data for figure from *HSUS*, Series U29, deflated by GNP deflator.
52. *HSUS*, Series U75.
53. Quoted in Williams, *Americans in a Changing World, op. cit.*, pp. 374-375.
54. Quoted in Wolfe, *Limits of Legitimacy, op. cit.*, p. 214.
55. Data for figure from *HSUS*, Series Y616, deflated by GNP deflator.
56. *HSUS*, Series U78.
57. See Noam Chomsky and Edward S. Herman, *The Washington Connection and Third World Fascism* (Boston: South End Press, 1979), *The Political Economy of Human Rights*, Vol. I.
58. Quoted in *ibid.*, Vol. I, p. 53.
59. Quoted in Wolfe, *Limits of Legitimacy, op. cit.*, p. 214.
60. Quoted in Richard Barnet and Ronald Muller, *Global Reach* (N.Y.: Simon & Schuster, 1974), p. 16.
61. Based on data reported in Edwards *et al., The Capitalist System, op. cit.*, p. 132.
62. See *Ibid.*, p. 129.
63. *Ibid.*, p. 481.
64. See Holly Sklar ed., *Trilateralism* (Boston: South End Press, 1980), Table 1.
65. Edwards *et al., The Capitalist System, op. cit.*, p. 479.

66. Quoted in Williams, *Americans in a Changing World, op. cit.*, p. 401.

67. Quoted in Brecher, *Strike!, op. cit.*, p. 228.

68. *Ibid.*, p. 230.

69. Quoted in William Serrin, *The Company and the Union* (N.Y.: Vintage Books, 1974), p. 170.

70. Richard Edwards, *Contested Terrain: Transformation of the Workplace in the Twentieth Century* (N.Y.: Basic Books, 1979), p. 134.

71. Quoted in *ibid.*, p. 138.

72. Quoted in *ibid.*, p. 137.

73. Based on a business-cycle adjustment of data reported in *ETRP*, Table C-8.

74. Union membership from *HSUS*, Series D927, 935; labor force data from *ETRP*, Table A-1.

75. *ETRP*, Table G-8.

76. This series is a three-year moving average of the difference in the (logarithmic) rates of growth of real output per production worker hour and real production worker's compensation. For underlying data, see *ERP*, Table B-38.

77. Quoted in Lynds, *Rank and File, op. cit.*, pp. 109, 110.

78. *ADLF*, p. 49.

79. Based on data reported in Gordon *et al.*, *Segmented Work, Divided Workers, op. cit.*, Figure 5.1a.

80. Michael Reich, *Racial Inequality: A Political-Economic Analysis* (Princeton: Princeton University Press, 1981), pp. 300-303.

81. See, for example, Frances Moore Lappe and Joseph Collins, *Food First: Beyond the Myth of Scarcity* (N.Y.: Ballantine books, 1978), rev. ed., Part III.

82. W.W. Rostow, *The World Economy: History and Prospect* (Austin, TX: Univ. of Texas Press, 1978), Fig. III-55, pp. 248-249.

84. *ERP*, Table B-105.

85. Howard Wachtel, *The New Gnomes: Multinational Banks in the Third World* (Washington, D.C.: The Transnational Institute, 1977), Appendix Table A, p. 45.

86. Quoted in Dan Georgakas and Marvin Surkin, *Detroit: I Do Mind Dying* (N.Y.: St. Martin's, 1975), p. 140.

87. Quoted in Michael B. Stoff, *Oil, War, and American Security* (New Haven: Yale Univ. Press, 1980), p. 1.

88. Quoted in *ibid.*, pp. 197-198.

89. Based on *SAUS*, Table 1033, and underlying data reported in source for that table.

90. *Ibid.*, Table 1028.

91. *HSUS*, Series Q65, Q391.

92. This figure includes freight shipped by both motor vehicles and pipelines, the two main components of the postwar trade system. See *HSUS*, Series Q16-20.

93. *HSUS*, Series S6, P6.

94. *HSUS*, Series Q175 and A288 for cars; Series R105 for televisions.

95. Quoted in Lloyd C. Gardner, "The New Deal, New Frontiers, and the Cold War," in David Horowitz, ed., *Corporations and the Cold War* (N.Y.: Monthly Review Press, 1969), p. 127.

96. Cited in Albert Szymanski, *The Capitalist State and the Politics of Class* (Cambridge, Ma.: Winthrop, 1978), p. 202.

97. Both figures and quote from Joseph D. Phillips, "The Economic Effects of the Cold War," in Horowitz, ed., *Corporations and the Cold War, op. cit.*, pp. 195, 196.

98. Charles E. Nathanson, "The Militarization of the American Economy," in Horowitz, *ibid.*, p. 231.

99. See Jeffrey Sachs, "The Changing Cyclical Behavior of Wages and Prices," *American Economic Review*, March 1980.

100. *ERP*, Tables B-74 and B-76.

101. Cited in Samuel Bowles and Herbert Gintis, "The Crisis of Liberal Democratic Capitalism," *Politics and Society*, Winter 1982, Table 3.

102. For a general discussion, see Frances Fitz-gerald, *America Revised* (Boston: Little, Brown, 1979), pp. 108ff.

103. *Ibid.*, pp. 108-109.

104. *Ibid.*, pp. 117-118.

105. Quoted in *ibid.*, p. 121.

106. *ADLF*, p. 49.

107. Quoted in Williams, *Americans in a Changing World, op. cit.*, p. 411.

Chapter 19

1. Quoted in *New York Times*, October 13, 1979, p. 31.

2. Quoted in *New York Times*, November 23, 1981.

3. Quoted in Alan Wolfe, *America's Impasse: The Rise and Fall of the Politics of Growth* (N.Y.: Pantheon, 1981), p. 83.

4. Quoted in *ibid.*, p. 19.

5. Based on data for Gross National Product in 1972 prices; see *ERP*, Table B-2.

6. Transcript from a class with oil and chemical workers, New Brunswick, N.J., 1975.

7. Data on profits for private nonfinancial corporations from national income accounts, adjusted for periodic changes in definitions, supplied to ILER by Thomas E. Weisskopf. The data report profit rates for the quarter in the business cycle at which the profit rates themselves peaked.

8. See *ERP*, Table B-2. and the data on profit rates cited in note #7.

9. Wolfe, *America's Impasse, op. cit.*, p. 26.

10. This is based on a comparison of rates of growth for corporate output and unit labor costs. See *ERP*, Tables B-38 and B-39.

11. Data on military spending: *HSUS*, Series Y615. Data on depreciation and interest payments, *ERP*, Table B-11. Data on compensation of supervisory workers: total compensation from *ERP*, Table B-11. Share of supervisory workers out of total compensation based on their employment share, from *ETRP*, Table B-38, and series on hours worked per year, based on average weekly hours, *ERP*, Table B-36.

12. The costs of systems control include the costs of supervisory control, as measured by method in note #11., and the total costs of defense spending and international security, reported in *HSUS*, Series Y614 -616. These numbers are then expressed as share of total gross national product. The increase in their share was exactly equal to the decrease in the share of corporate profits between 1950 and 1959.

13. Quoted in Wolfe, *America's Impasse, op. cit.*, p. 67.

14. For definition and sources of this series, see Chapter 18, note #76.

15. Based on calculations reported and sourced in note #12 above.

16. *ERP*, Table B-11.

17. See data sources reported in note #7 above.

18. This comparison divides gross national product into four components: after-tax profits in the private business sector; costs of system control, as defined in note #12 above; total production worker compensation; and total (federal, state, and local) transfer payments. In computing shares going to producton worker and supervisory compensation, we have included their net benefits from government expenditures (other than transfer payments). These net benefits are calculated by assuming personal and social security tax payments in proportion to income—see Joseph A. Pechman and Benjamin A. Okner, *Who Bears the Tax Burden?* (Washinton, D.C.: Brookings Institution, 1974), Chs. 2, 5, for a justification of this provisional assumption—and benefits from government (non-defense) expenditures on an equal per capita basis.

19. All data necessary for these computations, in addition to those reported in note #12 above, are contained in *ERP*, Table B-12 and, for tax payments out of personal income, Table B-8.

20. Quoted in Wolfe, *America's Impasse, op. cit.*, p. 69.

21. *Business Week*, October 12, 1974.

22. For some of this history, see William A. Williams, *Americans in a Changing World* (N.Y.: Harper and Row, 1978), Ch. 19.

23. Quoted in Wolfe, *America's Impasse, op. cit.*, p. 125.

24. Quoted in *ibid.*, p. 126.

25. For some detail on the history of the Brazil case, see Noam Chomsky and Edward S. Herman, *The Washington Connection and Third World Fascism* (Boston: South End Press, 1979), *The Political Economy of Human Rights*, Vol. I.

26. Quoted in *ibid.*, p. 104.

27. *HSUS*, Series Y615.

28. This is based on a separate series computed by David M. Gordon of the ILER. It is a sum of the ratios of median white male earnings (for full-time, year-round workers) to the median earnings of (full-time, year-round) female and black male workers, with the ratios weighted by the respective shares of women and black males in the labor force. Underlying data based on Bureau of Census "Money Income of Families and Persons in the United States, 1978," *Current Population Reports*, Series P-60, No. 123, June 1980, Table 65.

29. Data reported in David M. Gordon, ed., *Problems in Political Economy: An Urban Perspective* (Lexington, Ma.: D.C. Heath, 1971), 1st ed., "Trends in Poverty," Table 3.

30. Based on sum of transfer payments by federal government, *ERP*, Table B-74, and state and local governments, Table B-76, as share of GNP, Table B-1.

31. *ERP*, Table B-99.

32. See Chapter 18, note #76.

33. See Andre Gunder Frank, *Crisis: In the World Economy* (N.Y.: Holmes and Meier, 1980), pp. 34-72.

34. These figures are based on the tax share in the series for real spendable earnings for the average production worker with three dependents, as reported in *ETRP*, Table C-15.

35. Quoted in Stanley Aronowitz, *False Promises* (N.Y.: McGraw-Hill, 1974), p. 22.

36. *Ibid.*, pp. 22-23.

37. The data on accident rates are from the U.S. Bureau of Labor Statistics. Statistical work has been necessary to splice the series up to 1970 with the years following changes in reporting practices in 1970-1971. For methods used and final data, see Michele I. Naples and David M. Gordon, "The Industrial Accident Rate: Creating a Continuous Series," Technical Note, Institute for Labor Education and Research, December 1981.

38. *ETRP*, Table G-8.

39. Data compilations reported in Michele I. Naples, "Industrial Conflict and Its Implications for Productivity Growth," *American Economic Review*, May 1981, Table 1.

40. Quoted in Aronowitz, *False Promises, op. cit.*, p. 42.

41. For much of this history, see Fred Block, *The Origins of International Economic Disorder* (Berkeley: University of California Press, 1977).

42. The most rigorous basis for such a conclusion is to look at figures for the "high employment budget surplus," a measure of fiscal restrictiveness controlling for the effects of the business cycle on the federal budget surplus (or deficit). Though unpublished, these data are available from the U.S. President's Council of Economic Advisers. They show sharp increases in the high employment budget surplus just before the 1969 and 1973 recessions began.

43. Quoted in *New York Times Magazine*, December 20, 1970, p. 50.

44. See Arnold Weber, *In Pursuit of Price Stability:*

The Wage-Price Freeze of 1971 (Washington, D.C.: The Brookings Institution, 1973), p. 38.

45. See data sourced in note #7 above.

46. *ERP*, Table B-99.

47. The data for Figure 19.12 are based on the same sources and methods as reported in notes #18-19 above. Data for Figures 19.13a-d are based on data on productivity growth in the private business sector, corrected for changes in definition, supplied by Thomas E. Weisskopf; *ERP*, Table B-50; *ETRP*, Table A-1; and *ETRP*, Table C-15.

48. The conclusions here are important, as we shall see in De-Duping Exercise #1, because they show that the first stages of the increase in inflation preceded increases in oil prices as a result of OPEC actions in 1973-1974.

49. See, for example, data on corporate bonds, *ERP*, Table B-65.

50. Both here and in Figure 19.20d below, it is important to note that this is a better measure of the impact of crisis on people, from the popular economic perspective, than average income per household or per capita. The series on earnings reports how much we earn, in terms of purchasing power, *for each hour of labor we apply*. The latter series does not take into account increased labor effort.

51. Quoted in Leonard Silk and David Vogel, *Ethics & Profits: The Crisis of Confidence in American Business* (N.Y.: Simon and Schuster, 1976), p. 71.

52. *ADLF*, p. 240.

53. *ERP*, Table B-56.

54. *ETRP*, Table A-1; and *HSUS*, Series E52, E40, and E23.

55. Silk and Vogel, *Ethics & Profits, op. cit.*, p. 21.

56. Douglas Fraser, Letter to Labor-Manageent Group, 1978, reproduced and circulated by United Auto Workers.

57. Estimates based on Robert Georgine, "The Modern Art of Union Busting," in M. Green and R. Massie, Jr., eds., *The Big Business Reader* (N.Y.: Pilgrim Press, 1980); and "America: Union Busters Are Back," *The Economist*, November 17-23, 1979.

58. *The Economist*, November 17-23, 1979, p. 40.

59. *SAUS*, Table 715, and sources of underlying data reported in that table.

60. Naples and Gordon, "The Industrial Accident Rate...," op. cit.

61. See Barry Bluestone and Bennett Harrison, *Capital Mobility and Economic Dislocation* (Washington, D.C.: The Progressive Alliance, 1980).

62. Data reported in Arthur MacEwan, "International Economic Crisis and the Limits of Macropolicy," unpublished paper, Univeristy of Massachusetts at Boston, 1980.

63. Quoted in Frank, *Crisis: In the World Economy, op. cit.*, p. 158.

64. Both quotes from Silk and Vogel, *Ethics & Profits, op. cit.*, p. 65.

65. *Wall Street Journal*, November 26, 1979.

66. Quoted in Frank, *Crisis: In the World Economy, op. cit.*, p. 158.

67. Based on *ERP*, Table B-87.

68. Based on *ibid*. The difference between the "increase in financial assets share" for 1966 and for the average of 1973 and 1978—i.e., 13.5%—was applied against the sum of total uses of corporate funds from 1974 to 1978 to arrive at the $100 billion figure.

69. Quoted in Frank, *Crisis: In the World Economy, op. cit.*, p. 124.

70. Quoted in *ibid.*, p. 129.

71. Quoted in *ibid.*, p. 132.

72. *ADLF*, p. 239.

73. *New York Times*, January 7, 1982, p. A-1.

74. *ETRP*, Table G-8.

75. *New York Times*, November 8, 1979, p. A-16.

76. Data from Opinion Research Corporation, reported in Michael R. Cooper *et al.*, "Early Warning Signals: Growing Discontent Among Managers," *Business*, January-February 1980.

77. Naples, "Industrial Conflict...," op. cit., Table 1.

78. The data reported in Figures 19.20a-e draw on the same sources reported in notes #47 and #7 above.

79. Quoted in *Wall Street Journal*, January 29, 1981.

80. Quoted in Frank, *Crisis: In the World Economy, op. cit.*, p. 304.

81. *ADLF*, p. 341.

82. This argument is developed in full detail in both Wolfe, *America's Impasse, op. cit.*; and Samuel Bowles, David M. Gordon, and Thomas E. Weisskopf, *Free Lunch: A Democratic Alternative to the Economics of Greed*, forthcoming 1982.

83. See *ibid.*, Ch. 3 for details.

84. *Loc. cit.*

85. *Loc. cit.*

86. *Loc. cit.*

Introduction to Part VI

1. Quoted in Andre Gunder Frank, *Crisis: In the World Economy* (N.Y.: Holmes and Meier, 1980), p. 85.

2. *ADLF*, p. 241.

Chapter 20

1. *Business Week*, October 12, 1974.

2. *ADLF*, p. 377.

3. *Ibid.*, p. 15.

4. Based on series for production workers' compensation share of total gross national product, based on methods and sources reported in Chapter 19, note #11.

5. Reported in *New York Times*, February 28, 1982, p. A-1.

6. Based on *ERP*, Table B-12.

7. Based on data on growth in productivity and the capital-labor ratio for manufacturing, corrected for data revisions, supplied by Thomas E. Weisskopf.

8. See W.D. Nordhaus, "Policy Responses to the Productivity Slowdown," in Federal Reserve Bank of Boston, *The Decline in Productivity Growth* (Boston: Federal Reserve Bank, 1980).

9. Harley Shaiken, "A Robot Is After Your Job," *New York Times*, September 3, 1980.

10. Data compiled by Institute for Labor Education and Research for special issue of *The Grapevine*, April 1981.

11. *Ibid.*

12. Shaiken, "A Robot Is After Your Job," op. cit.

13. Quoted in William Greider, "The Education of David Stockman," *The Atlantic Monthly*, December 1981, pp. 47, 46, 54.

14. *ADLF*, p. 240.

15. *ADLF*, p. 156.

16. *ADLF*, p. 242.

17. The Business Week Team, *The Reindustrialization of America* (N.Y.: McGraw-Hill, 1982), p. 59; and Robert H. Hayes and William J. Abernathy, "Managing Our Way to Economic Decline," *Harvard Business Review*, July-August 1980, p. 69.

18. "Foreword" to Robert Friedman and William Schweke, eds., *Expanding the Opportunity to Produce: Revitalizing the American Economy through New Enterprise Development* (Washington, D.C.: The Corporation for Enterprise Development, 1981), p. xii.

19. Based on data in *SAUS*, Tables 862 and 863, with allocation of savings bank deposits and life insurance reserves to working households on the basis of their total share of personal wealth—see Figure 2.3. This is undoubtedly an underestimate of working households' share of these two forms of savings, since wealthier households are much more likely to own corporate stock and various kinds of tax-exempt bonds. It is likely, therefore, that the stock of assets owned by working households is larger than the number reported in the text.

20. Martin Carnoy and Derek Shearer, *Economic Democracy* (White Plains, N.Y.: M.E. Sharpe, 1980), p. 266.

Chapter 21

1. *ADLF*, p. 312.

2. *ADLF*, p. 274, 276.

3. *ADLF*, p. 225.

4. *ADLF*, p. 239.

5. Both quotes from Debs quoted in Howard Zinn, *A People's History of the United States* (N.Y.: Harper Colophon Books, 1980), p. 275.

6. Quoted in *ibid.*, p. 315.

Chapter 22

1. *ADLF*, p. 461.

2. *ADLF*, pp. 160-61.

3. Quoted in Jeremy Brecher and Timothy Costello, *Common Sense for Hard Times* (Boston: South End Press, 1979), p. 205.

4. Quoted in *ibid.*, p. 216.

5. Advertisement printed by Chase Bank, 1976.

6. Quoted in Brecher and Costello, *Common Sense for Hard Times, op. cit.*, p. 220.

7. *ADLF*, p. 211.

8. *ADLF*, p. 366.

9. *ADLF*, p. 200.

10. *ADLF*, p. 171.

11. *ADLF*, p. 189.

12. *ADLF*, p. 302.

13. *ADLF*, pp. 276-77.